Children with Disabilities

Children with
Disabilities

■ *A Medical Primer* ■

THIRD
EDITION

by

Mark L. Batshaw, M.D.
Physician-in-Chief
Children's Seashore House
Chief, Division of Child Development
   and Rehabilitation Medicine
The Children's Hospital of Philadelphia
W.T. Grant Professor of Pediatrics
Professor of Neurology
University of Pennsylvania School of Medicine
Philadelphia, Pennsylvania

and

Yvonne M. Perret, M.A., M.S.W., L.C.S.W.
Director
Day Treatment Program
Walter P. Carter Center
Baltimore, Maryland

·P·A·U·L·H·
BROOKES
PUBLISHING C◦

Baltimore • London • Toronto • Sydney

Paul H. Brookes Publishing Co.
Post Office Box 10624
Baltimore, Maryland 21285-0624

Typeset by Brushwood Graphics, Inc., Baltimore, Maryland.
Manufactured in the United States of America by
Rose Printing Company, Inc., Tallahassee, Florida.

Second printing, July 1993.

Library of Congress Cataloging-in-Publication Data

Batshaw, Mark L., 1945–
   Children with disabilities : a medical primer / by Mark L. Batshaw and
Yvonne M. Perret. — 3rd ed.
     p.   cm.
   Rev. ed. of: Children with handicaps, 2nd ed. © 1986.
   Includes bibliographical references and index.
   ISBN 1-55766-102-2
   1. Child development deviations. 2. Child development deviations—
Etiology. 3. Developmentally disabled children—Care. 4. Handicapped
children—Care. 5. Handicapped.   I. Perret, Yvonne M., 1946–
II. Batshaw, Mark L., 1945–   Children with handicaps.   III. Title.
   [DNLM: 1. Birth Injuries. 2. Child Development Disorders.
3. Rehabilitation—in infancy & childhood.   WS 368 8334c]
RJ135.B38 1992
618.92—dc20
DNLM/DLC
for Library of Congress   91-43243
                                            CIP

(British Library Cataloguing-in-Publication data are available
from the British Library.)

Contents

Approaches to Intervention
Mary: An Adolescent with Mental Retardation and
   Depression
Summary

      with Lisa Kurtz

Causes of Cerebral Palsy
Types of Cerebral Palsy
Early Diagnosis of Cerebral Palsy
Primitive Reflexes
Automatic Movement Reactions
Walking
Disabilities Associated with Cerebral Palsy
Treatment and Intervention
Case Studies of Children with Cerebral Palsy
Prognosis
Summary

      Edward B. Charney

Incidence and Causes of Neural Tube Defects
Prenatal Diagnosis
Neurological Deficits
Disabilities Associated with Neural Tube Defects
Psychosocial Issues
Multidisciplinary Management
Brian: A Child with Myelomeningocele
Prognosis
Summary

What Is a Seizure?
Occurrence of Seizures
Types of Seizures
Epileptic Syndromes
Self-Limited and Epileptic-Like Disorders
Diagnosing Epilepsy
Treatment of Seizure Disorders
What To Do in the Event of a Seizure
Multidisciplinary Management
Case Studies of Children with Epilepsy
Prognosis
Summary

      Linda J. Michaud and Ann-Christine Duhaime

Incidence of Head Injuries
Causes of Traumatic Brain Injury

About the Authors

Mark Levitt Batshaw, M.D., is the Physician-in-Chief of Children's Seashore House, a regional children's hospital for specialized care and rehabilitation. He is also Chief of the Division of Child Development and Rehabilitation at The Children's Hospital of Philadelphia and the W.T. Grant Professor of Pediatrics and Professor of Neurology at The University of Pennsylvania School of Medicine in Philadelphia.

Dr. Batshaw's experience includes almost 20 years of treating children with developmental disabilities. While on the faculty at Johns Hopkins University, Dr. Batshaw was the recipient of the Alexander Schaffer Teaching Award in Pediatrics. A course he taught, "Medical and Physical Aspects of the Disabled Child," led him to co-author *Children with Disabilities: A Medical Primer*.

Recognized as an international authority on inborn errors of metabolism, Dr. Batshaw has published more than 70 articles in such highly respected journals as *The New England Journal of Medicine, Science, Lancet*, and the *Journal of Pediatrics* and is also author of *Your Child Has a Disability: A Complete Sourcebook of Daily and Medical Care*.

A Joseph P. Kennedy, Jr. Scholar and recipient of major grants from the National Foundation March of Dimes and the National Institutes of Health (NIH), Dr. Batshaw is currently director of the NIH-funded Mental Retardation Research Center at The University of Pennsylvania. He is also a member of the Mental Retardation Study Section at the National Institutes of Child Health and Human Development. Dr. Batshaw is a Fellow of the American Academy of Pediatrics and the Royal College of Physicians and Surgeons (Canada), as well as a member of the American Pediatric Society, the Society of Pediatric Research, the Society for Inherited Metabolic Disorders, and the Society for Developmental Pediatrics.

Dr. Batshaw lives in Philadelphia with his wife, who is a social worker, and their three children.

Yvonne Marie Perret, M.A., M.S.W., L.C.S.W., is the Director of the Day Treatment Program, an intensive, adult psychiatric treatment program, at the Walter P. Carter Center, a state mental health and mental retardation center, in Baltimore, Maryland.

Prior to her work at the Walter P. Carter Center, Ms. Perret was a developmental research associate at The Kennedy Institute for Handicapped Children, where she coordinated a project on premature infants. Since 1968, her social work and family work has included counseling families and their children and persons with chronic physical illnesses, parent–adolescent counseling, work in child welfare, and, more recently, in mental health, primarily with adults. Ms. Perret also served as staff director of the Project on Women in Midlife Development at Cornell University and as developmental editor for *Human Development*, by Karen Freiberg (Duxbury Press, 1979).

Most recently, Ms. Perret has been appointed Adjunct Clinical Assistant Professor at the University of Maryland School of Social Work, and she has published in *Hospital and Community Psychiatry*.

In addition to her social work experience, Ms. Perret has a master's degree in journalism from the Newhouse School at Syracuse University. She has several years' experience as a writer and editor and has published articles on law, the environment, health care, and public policy.

Acknowledgments

A book such as *Children with Disabilities: A Medical Primer* is best understood with illustrations that help to explain medical concepts. A medical illustrator is indispensable in this effort, and two of the best, Elaine Kasmer and Lynn Reynolds, have contributed to this endeavor. They were given the ideas that needed illustration and produced the more than 100 beautiful images that fill this book. I gratefully acknowledge their important contribution. Elaine Kasmer contributed the following figures: 1.1, 1.2, 1.4, 1.7, 2.1, 2.2, 2.3, 2.4, 2.5, 2.6, 3.2, 3.3, 4.1, 4.2, 4.3, 4.4, 5.1, 5.2, 6.1, 6.2, 6.4, 6.5, 6.6, 7.3, 7.5, 11.2, 12.1, 12.3, 13.1, 13.2, 13.3, 14.1, 14.2, 14.3, 14.4, 14.5, 14.6, 14.7, 14.8, 14.9, 14.10, 14.11, 15.1, 15.2B, 15.4, 15.5, 15.6, 15.7, 17.1, 17.2, 17.4, 17.5, 17.6, 17.8, 17.10, 17.11, 17.14, 18.1, 18.2, 18.3, 18.4A, 19.1, 21.1, 21.2, 24.2, 24.3, 24.4, 24.5, 24.6, 24.7, 24.11, 24.12, 24.13, 25.2, 25.6, 26.2, 26.3, 26.4, 26.5, 26.6, 26.7, and 26.9. Lynn Reynolds contributed the following figures: 1.5, 1.6, 3.5, 3.6, 3.7, 6.3, 7.6, 8.1, 8.2, 8.3, 9.1, 9.2, 9.4, 10.3, 10.4, 12.2, 12.4, 12.6, 15.2A, 16.2, 16.3, 16.4, 17.9, 17.15, 18.4B, 18.5, 18.6, 18.8, 18.10, 23.1, 24.1, 24.9, 24.10, 25.1, 25.3, 25.4, 25.5, 25.8, 26.11, and 29.1.

I also acknowledge my assistant, Margaret Rose, who helped to copyedit the manuscript, obtained consents, revised the resource section, and kept me and my colleagues on schedule throughout the production of this third edition. She is a wonderful person, who is irreplaceable. I also thank my production editor at Brookes Publishing, Kathy Boyd, who enhanced the book by her careful and expert editing and advice.

I greatly appreciate the work of my collaborators, who in writing their chapters presented their areas of expertise clearly and in an easy-to-read style: Charles J. Conlon, Susan Levy, Sharon Pilmer, Peggy Monahan Eicher, Bruce Shapiro, Ken Bleile, Robin Gallico, Mary Ellen Lewis, Marianne Mercugliano, Mark Reber, Lisa Kurtz, Ed Charney, Linda Michaud, Tina Duhaime, Symme Trachtenberg, and Carolyn Bay.

Finally, many friends and colleagues at Children's Seashore House, The Children's Hospital of Philadelphia, and elsewhere reviewed and edited the manuscript for content and accuracy. I would like to acknowledge their efforts: Lisa Bain, Shelly Beaser, Judy Bernbaum, Robert Clancy, John Dormans, Jane Davies, Deborah Driscoll, Adadot Hayes, Mark Helpin, Connie Lindenbaum, Noel Matkin, Trish Middaugh, Sheryl Menacker, and Richard Rutstein.

MLB

Preface

The first edition of *Children with Handicaps: A Medical Primer* was published in 1981. It was written to be used as a college textbook and as a reference for students and professionals who were studying or already working with children with developmental disabilities—special educators, physical therapists, occupational therapists, speech-language pathologists, psychologists, child life specialists, social workers, and nurses. We learned that these professionals did read the book, but so did many others. Many parents found the book beneficial to them, saying that it answered many questions they had about caring for their children and the possible causes of their children's disabilities. In addition, other professionals, such as developmental disabilities lawyers and other health care workers, used the book.

Continuing in the tradition of the first and second editions, this third edition has a similar purpose—to answer the question "Why this child?" As before, this version begins with discussion of what happens before, during, or after birth to cause a child to have a developmental disability, but adds new information discovered through medical and scientific advancements since 1986, when the second edition was published. The chapters that follow about the individual developmental disabilities have been updated with information on new medical, rehabilitative, and educational interventions. Five new chapters have been added (New Threats to Development: Alcohol, Cocaine, and AIDS; The Technology-Assisted Child; Dual Diagnosis: Psychiatric Disorders and Mental Retardation; Neural Tube Defects: Spina Bifida and Myelomeningocele; and Traumatic Brain Injury).

A number of organizational changes have occurred in the third edition as well, starting with the book's title and authorship. The title has been changed to *Children with Disabilities: A Medical Primer* to reflect our increasing understanding that while children are born with disabilities, they only become handicapped if society or opportunity relegates them to that role. It is the function of this book to help to prevent "children with disabilities" from becoming "children with handicaps." My co-author on the first two editions, Yvonne Perret, has moved on to other challenges. Her name is retained on this edition as her work remains an integral part of this edition. A third change is the increased number of chapters authored or co-authored by other professionals in the field of developmental disabilities; these authors share their expertise on particular issues or subspecialties.

The opening chapters of the book address the concepts underlying developmental disabilities: genetics, embryology, and fetal development, the birth process, prematurity, and early child development. The technology-assisted child is the subject of a complete chapter to acknowledge recent scientific advances. The roles of alcohol, cocaine, and AIDS in child development as well as the impact of inborn errors of metabolism are thoroughly reviewed. The book next examines the various organ systems—how they work and what can go wrong. Nutritional, feeding, and dental problems are also addressed. Full chapters provide comprehensive descriptions of various developmental disabilities: mental retardation, visual deficits, hearing impairments, speech and language disorders, learning disabilities, attention deficit hyperactivity disorder, autism, dual diagnosis, cerebral palsy, neural tube defects, seizure disorders, and traumatic brain injury. Case studies are included to illustrate each of these conditions. The final chapters concentrate on the ethical and emotional issues that are common to most families of children with disabilities and professionals who work with them. The book closes with updated appendices, including a glossary of medical terms, a description of various syndromes and inborn errors of metabolism, and a list of resources for children with disabilities, their families, and professionals.

Mark L. Batshaw

For the Reader

Throughout this book, the terms that are defined in the glossary (Appendix A) are indicated in **bold type** the first time that they appear.

The reference lists at the end of each chapter contain more references than those actually cited in the text. These additional references might be useful for anyone interested in doing further reading on a particular topic.

The case histories that are included in this book are based on actual or synthesized cases. The names used in these cases are fictitious.

To my son Andrew, a bright and courageous individual with ADHD,
and to my wife, Karen, his caring mother and effective teacher

```
                          Why me?

                          Why me?

          Why do I have to do so much more work than others?

                    Why am I so forgetful?

                    Why am I so hyperactive?

                    And why can't I spell?

                      Why me, O'why me?
```

I remember when I almost failed first grade because I couldn't read. I would cry hour after hour because my mother would try to make me read. Now I love to read. I couldn't write in cursive but my mother helped me and now I can. I don't have as bad a learning disability as others. At lest I can go to a normal school. I am trying as hard as I can (I just hope it is enough). My worst nightmare is to go to a special school because I don't want to be treated differently.

I am getting to like working. I guess since my dad is so successful and has a leaning disability, it helps make me not want to give up. Many people say that I am smart, but sometime I doubt it. I am very good at math, but sometimes I read a number like 169 as 196, so that messes things up. I also hear things incorrectly, for instants entrepreneur as horse manure (that really happened). I guess the reason why a lot of people don't like me is because I say the wrong answer a lot of times.

I had to take medication, but then I got off of the medication and did well. Then in 7th grade I wasn't doing well but I didn't tell my parents because I though they would just scream at me. My dad talked to the guidance counselor and found out. It wasn't till a week ago that I started on the medication again; I have been doing fine since than. As I have been getting more organized, I have had more free time. I guess I feel good when I succeed in things that take hard work.

This is my true story...Andrew Batshaw, 1989

Andrew Batshaw

To my brother, Edmund J. Perret II,
who faced AIDS
with courage, dignity, and inspiration

Children with Disabilities

Chapter 1

Understanding
Your Chromosomes

Upon completion of this chapter, the reader will:
— know the components of the cell and their functions
— be familiar with the various stages of mitosis and meiosis
— understand the differences between mitosis and meiosis
— be able to explain nondisjunction, translocation, and deletion

---

A child is born, and the preceding 9 months have witnessed a marvelous process. So complex and numerous are the steps involved from the fertilization of an egg to the birth of an infant that the chances for errors in that process seem limitless. The surprise, then, is not that so many children are born with birth defects, but that so few are. Tracing the path of human development, beginning with the fertilized egg, quickly points out the opportunities for mistakes to occur.

As an introduction to the discussion in the chapters that follow, this chapter describes the human cell, explains what chromosomes are, reviews the processes of **mitosis** and **meiosis,** and provides some illustrations of the errors that can occur in these processes. As you progress through this book, bear in mind that the purpose here is to focus on the abnormalities that can occur in human development; most infants are never troubled by these disabilities.

THE CELL

The cell is divided into two compartments: a central, enclosed core, the nucleus, and an outer, gelatinous area, the cytoplasm (Figure 1.1). The nucleus contains the chromosomes, structures that consist of the genetic code for our physical and biochemical traits. The cell can divide into daughter cells containing this same genetic information (Gore, 1976). The cytoplasm, under the direction of the nucleus, generates products that release energy, dispose of wastes, and are needed for the growth of the organism. The nucleus, then, provides the blueprint for an individual's eventual development, and the cytoplasm provides the products needed to complete the task.

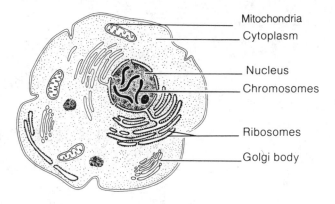

Figure 1.1. An idealized cell. The chromosomes direct the creation of a product on the ribosome. The product is then packaged in the Golgi body and released from the cell.

CHROMOSOMES

Each organism has a fixed number of chromosomes. In humans, 46 chromosomes direct the cell's activities. Except for the **germ cells** (the egg and sperm), every cell contains 23 pairs of complementary chromosomes. In each pair, one chromosome comes from the mother, and one comes from the father, thus accounting for the total of 46 chromosomes in each cell. This number is called the *diploid* number. Each germ cell contains 23 chromosomes, or half the diploid number; this number is termed the *haploid* number.

Except for the **sex chromosomes** (X and Y), the chromosomes in each pair resemble each other. The X and Y chromosomes look quite different from each other. The X chromosome is about twice as large as the Y chromosome and has a different shape (see Figure 1.3 on page 4). It is these chromosomes that determine the sex of the fetus. The remaining 22 pairs of chromosomes, called **autosomes,** define the other features of the individual.

Most types of cells divide, but not all cells divide at the same rate. Skin cells, for instance, divide rapidly and resurface the area of an abrasion in just a few days. However, the nerve cells in an adult brain do not appear to divide at all. It takes a sperm cell but a few hours to divide, while division of an egg takes years. The ability of cells to continue to divide is a major factor in the continued proper functioning of the organism. For example, the inability of nerve cells in adults to reproduce limits recovery after a stroke or other brain injury.

CELL DIVISION

The formation of a human being takes about 266 days. It is accomplished primarily through two kinds of cell division: mitosis and meiosis. There are two major differences between these kinds of cell division. In mitosis, or nonreductive division, two daughter cells are created from one parent cell, and each of the offspring cells contains 46 chromosomes. Meiosis, or reductive division, however, involves the formation of four daughter cells from one parent cell. (In the case of the egg, three of these daughter cells eventually disintegrate; only one daughter cell survives as a mature egg.) Each of the offspring cells in meiosis contains 23 chromosomes. Although mitosis occurs in all cells except red blood cells, meiosis takes place only in the germ cells.

Mitosis

Mitosis occurs in four steps: *prophase, metaphase, anaphase,* and *telophase* (Figure 1.2). Most cells undergo mitosis throughout their lives. Between the periods of mitosis is a resting phase called *interphase.* During this phase the cell grows, and the chromosomes resemble a ball of loose yarn. During *prophase,* cell division begins. The chromosomes thicken and shorten and begin to look like separate strands. In the next stage, *metaphase*, the chromosomes become double-stranded; each strand of the chromosome is a **chromatid**, and each chromatid contains the same genetic information as the chromosome. It is during this stage that one chromosome can be easily differentiated from another.

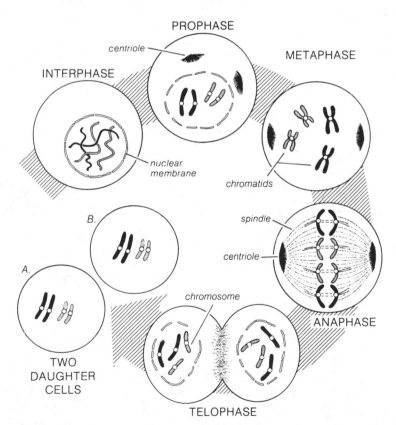

Figure 1.2.   Mitosis. This process produces two daughter cells, each containing a diploid number (46) of chromosomes.

If division is arrested at prophase or metaphase, the chromosomes appear under a microscope as large bodies that can be counted and divided into groups according to size, shape, and **banding pattern**, a process called **karyotyping** (Emery & Mueller, 1988). As an illustration, Figure 1.3 shows the karyotype of a child who has Down syndrome. Some of the child's white blood cells were obtained, and a chemical was added to start cell division. Days later, another chemical was inserted to arrest the

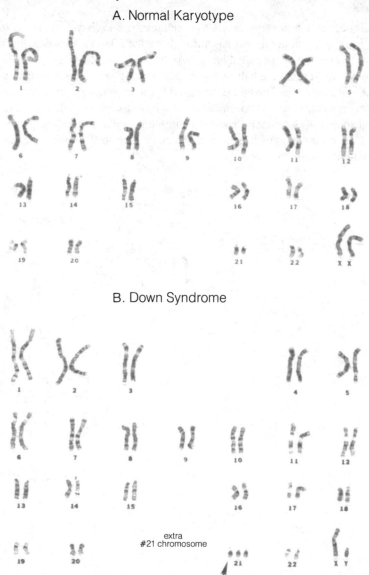

A. Normal Karyotype

B. Down Syndrome

extra #21 chromosome

Figure 1.3.   Illustration of two chromosomal patterns: A) a normal female (46, XX), and B) a boy with Down syndrome (47, XY). Note that the child with Down syndrome has 47 chromosomes; the extra one is a #21. (Courtesy of Dr. Beverly Emanuel, Children's Hospital of Philadelphia.)

division in prophase. The cell nucleus was then photographed under a microscope, and a print was made. The chromosomes were cut out, matched in pairs, and put into seven groups according to size, shape, and banding pattern. In this case, the last group had an extra #21 chromosome as well as an X and a Y chromosome, which is the karyotype of a male who has Down syndrome. In Figure 1.3, this karyotype is contrasted with the karyotype of an unaffected girl.

In the next stage, *anaphase*, the chromatids align in the center of the cell and become attached to tiny spindles. These spindles pull the chromatids toward the **centrioles**, or poles, in the two daughter cells (see Figure 1.2). Following mitosis, each daughter cell has 46 chromosomes. If, for some reason, a pair of chromatids did not split during anaphase, one daughter cell would contain 47 chromosomes and one would have 45. If no split occurred in any of the pairs of chromatids, one daughter cell would have 92, and the other would have none. Often, when cells divide unequally, or undergo **nondisjunction**, they do not survive (Nora & Fraser, 1989). During *telophase*, the division is completed, and the two daughter cells separate from each other.

Meiosis

Since meiosis is a much more complicated process than mitosis, it is more often associated with abnormalities. Unlike mitosis, meiosis involves two cell divisions instead of one; each division has stages of prophase, metaphase, anaphase, and telophase. As previously mentioned, chromosomes come in pairs. Thus, there are two #1 chromosomes, two #2 chromosomes, and so on. In prophase of the first meiotic division, the chromosomes thicken and shorten just as they do in mitosis. The same is true for the stage of metaphase, where each chromosome doubles and becomes two chromatids. It is in anaphase that a major difference between mitosis and meiosis exists. In mitosis, one of each of the doubled chromatids moves toward one daughter cell, and the other moves toward the second daughter cell. In anaphase of the first meiotic division, however, both chromatids of one #1 chromosome move toward one daughter cell, and both chromatids of the other #1 chromosome move toward the other daughter cell (Figure 1.4). At the end of the first meiotic division, each of the two daughter cells contains 23 double-stranded chromatids instead of 46 single-stranded chromosomes as in mitosis.

In the second meiotic division, the 23 double-stranded chromatids align in the center of each daughter cell and undergo a mitotic division; that is, the doubled chromatids separate. Thus, the two daughter cells that formed after the first meiotic division split into two more cells; each of these cells contains 23 chromosomes. The end result is four daughter cells that have 23 chromosomes each. As stated earlier, meiosis occurs only in the germ cells. During fertilization, the 23 chromosomes from each of the two germ cells, the sperm and the egg, combine. The resulting embryo emerges with the *diploid* number (46) of chromosomes.

WHAT CAN GO WRONG?

A number of events that subsequently affect a child's development can occur during cell division. One of these, *nondisjunction,* happens more often during meiosis than

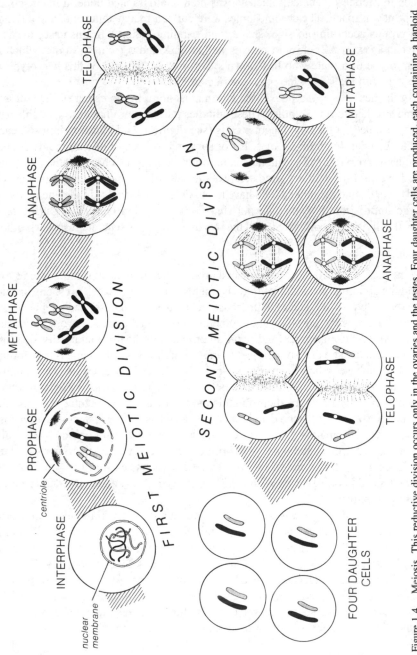

Figure 1.4. Meiosis. This reductive division occurs only in the ovaries and the testes. Four daughter cells are produced, each containing a haploid number (23) of chromosomes.

during mitosis. Nondisjunction can cause Down syndrome, as occurs in the case illustrated in Figure 1.3. (Another cause of Down syndrome, **translocation,** is discussed later in this chapter.) When nondisjunction occurs during the first meiotic division, both #21 chromosomes end up in one cell. Instead of both cells having 23 chromosomes, one cell has 24 chromosomes, and the other has 22. This imbalance takes place far more often in the formation of an egg than in the formation of a sperm. The loss of a #21 chromosome makes it difficult for the egg containing 22 chromosomes to survive. However, the egg with 24 chromosomes can survive and, if a sperm containing 23 chromosomes then fertilizes it, the result is a child with 47 chromosomes who has Down syndrome, or trisomy 21—three #21 chromosomes (Cunningham, 1990). Approximately 85% of individuals with trisomy 21 acquire it as a result of nondisjunction of the egg, and 15% from nondisjunction of the sperm (Dagna-Bricarelli, Pierluigi, Grasso, et al., 1990). Of the Down syndrome cases, 3% come from translocation.

The one disorder associated with survival despite the loss of a complete chromosome is **Turner syndrome**. In this case, nondisjunction affects the X chromosome rather than one of the autosomes. The child is born with 45 instead of 46 chromosomes; she has a single X chromosome, but no second X or Y chromosome. All children with Turner syndrome are female because the Y chromosome, responsible for the development of male sexual organs, is absent. These children are very short and have webbed necks, shield-shaped chests, widely spaced nipples, and nonfunctional ovaries (Figure 1.5). Unlike children with Down syndrome, most of these children have normal intelligence. However, they do tend to have visual-perceptual problems that lead to learning disabilities (Bender, Puck, Salbenblatt, et al., 1984).

The reason a child with an X chromosome **deletion** can survive, whereas the deletion of an autosome would be fatal, is probably because females have two X chromosomes while males have only one. In effect, the male's chromosomal structure is similar to that of a female with Turner syndrome except that the male has a Y chromosome and the Turner syndrome female does not. At present, the Y chromosome is known to be responsible only for directing the development of male sexual organs.

Besides nondisjunction, other abnormalities in cell division can also lead to birth defects. Two examples are deletion and translocation. During mitosis and meiosis, the chromosomes are close together for extended time periods. They may touch, stick to each other for a while, and then separate. When they separate, a segment of a chromosome may be pulled off and lost (deletion) or may attach itself to another chromosome (translocation). The **cri-du-chat** ("cat cry") **syndrome** is an example of a disorder resulting from a deletion. In this syndrome, the top portion of a #5 chromosome is lost (Figure 1.6). These children look unusual with microcephaly, widely spaced eyes, and small chins, and have high-pitched cries (Wilkins, Brown, Nance, et al., 1983). They have severe retardation and resemble each other, just as children with Down syndrome share similar physical characteristics.

Translocation involves the transfer of a portion of one chromosome to a completely different chromosome (Figure 1.7). For example, a part of the #21 chromosome might attach itself to the #14 chromosome. If this occurs during meiosis, one

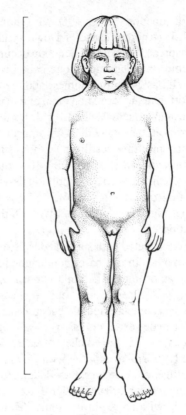

4 feet

Figure 1.5.   Girls with Turner syndrome have only one X chromosome. They are short in stature and have webbed necks, shield-shaped chests with widely spaced nipples, and nonfunctional ovaries.

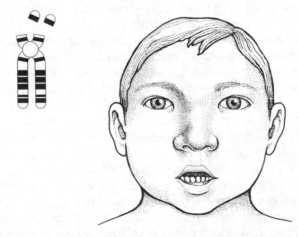

Figure 1.6.   Children with cri-du-chat syndrome have an unusual facial appearance with microcephaly, a round face, widely spaced eyes, epicanthal folds, and low-set ears. The chromosomal abnormality is a partial deletion of the short arm of the #5 chromosome.

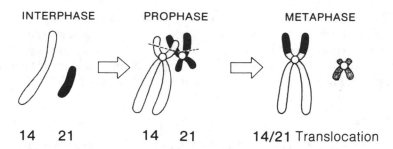

INTERPHASE   PROPHASE   METAPHASE

14   21   14   21   14/21 Translocation

Figure 1.7.   Translocation. During prophase of meiosis in a parent, there may be a transfer of a portion of one chromosome to another. In this figure, the long arm of #21 is translocated to chromosome #14, and the residual fragments are lost. The resulting translocated chromosome #14/21 places the parent at risk for having additional children with Down syndrome.

cell will then have 23 chromosomes with one #21 and one #14/21 translocated chromosome. Fertilization of the egg or sperm containing the #14/21 translocated chromosome will result in a child with 46 chromosomes, including two #21 chromosomes and one #14/21 chromosome. This child, too, will have Down syndrome because of the partial trisomy 21 caused by the translocation.

With all of these potential problems in cell division, one wonders why more children are not born with chromosomal abnormalities. The answer is that most fetuses with chromosomal abnormalities do not survive. Over 50% of the fetuses that are miscarried prior to 12 weeks gestation are found to have chromosomal abnormalities (Figure 1.8). As the fetus continues to develop, the frequency of both chromosomal abnormalities and spontaneous abortion, or miscarriage, decreases.

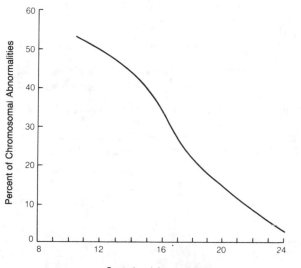

Gestational Age in Weeks

Figure 1.8.   Incidence of chromosomal abnormalities among fetuses spontaneously aborted during the first two trimesters of pregnancy. (From Creasy, M.R., Crolla, J.A., & Alberman, E.D. [1976]. *Human Genetics, 31*, Figure 3, p. 188; reprinted by permission.)

While the closeness of the chromosomes during meiosis may result in disorders, it also allows for the mutual transfer of genetic information. This transfer, or **crossing over,** is what enables us to be similar to, but not exactly like, our **siblings**. The only sibling relationship in which crossing over does not occur is in identical twins where division of the twins occurs after fertilization of the egg (Smith, 1974).

SUMMARY

Each human cell contains a full complement of genetic information entwined in 46 chromosomes. This genetic code not only determines our physical appearance and biochemical makeup, but it is also the legacy we pass on to our children. The unequal division of the reproductive cells may have significant consequences, such as Down syndrome or cri-du-chat syndrome. It is comforting to realize that, despite these potential problems and still other problems occurring during the development of the embryo and fetus, the vast majority of infants are born with no significant birth defects.

REFERENCES

Bender, B., Puck, M., Salbenblatt, J., et al., (1984). Cognitive development of unselected girls with complete and partial X monosomy. *Pediatrics, 73*, 175–182.

Creasy, M.R., Crolla, J.A., & Alberman, E.D. (1976). A cytogenetic study of human spontaneous abortions using banding techniques. *Human Genetics, 31*, 177–196.

Cunningham, C. (1988). *Down syndrome: An introduction for parents.* Cambridge, MA: Brookline Books.

Dagna-Bricarelli, F., Pierluigi, M., Grasso, M., et al. (1990). Origin of extra chromosome 21 in 343 families: Cytogenic and molecular approaches. *American Journal of Medical Genetics, 7*(Suppl.), 129–132.

Emery, A.E., & Mueller, R.F. (1988). *Elements of medical genetics* (7th ed.). New York: Churchill Livingstone.

Gore, R. (1976). The awesome worlds within a cell. *National Geographic, 150*, 354–395.

Nora, J.J., & Fraser, F.C. (1989). *Medical genetics: Principles and practice* (3rd ed.). Philadelphia: Lea & Febiger.

Smith, D.W., & Wilson, A.C. (1973). *The child with Down's syndrome.* Philadelphia: W.B. Saunders.

Wilkins, L.E., Brown, J.A., Nance, W.E., et al. (1983). Clinical heterogeneity in 80 home-reared children with cri-du-chat syndrome. *Journal of Pediatrics, 102*, 528–533.

Chapter 2

Heredity
A Toss of the Dice

Upon completion of this chapter, the reader will:
— know the differences and similarities between autosomal recessive, autosomal dominant, and sex-linked disorders
— be able to describe some of the major chromosomal abnormalities
— understand the ways in which environment and heredity contribute to the development of certain disorders
— be aware of the part genes play in some hereditary disorders

---

Whether we have brown or blue eyes is determined by genes carried on our parents' chromosomes. However, our height and weight are affected both by these genes and by our environment before and after birth. In a similar manner, genes and their interaction with environmental factors may lead to certain birth defects. **Phenylketonuria** and Tay-Sachs disease, for example, result from single-gene mutations within a chromosome. Cleft palate is a product of the interaction of environment and heredity, while the absence of a finger may happen spontaneously. This chapter describes the ways in which genetically determined birth defects are passed on from one generation to another.

THE GENETIC PRINCIPLES OF MENDEL

Gregor Mendel (1822–1884), an Austrian monk who enjoyed gardening, pioneered our understanding of genetics. He was the first to recognize the existence of genetic traits (i.e., characteristics in organisms that show variability). While cultivating pea plants, he noted two different appearing types of plants—yellow and green plants. When he bred two plants with different appearances or traits (i.e., yellow × green), the **hybrid** offspring all were green rather than mixed in color. Mendel, therefore, thought of the green trait as being dominant. He named the other trait (the yellow color), which did not appear in the hybrid offspring but sometimes appeared in subsequent generations, recessive. Later, it was determined that many birth defects are also inherited as **autosomal recessive** or **autosomal dominant** disorders. As mentioned in the introduction to this chapter, genes determine these traits in human beings.

Genes

Each chromosome consists of hundreds of genes; genes are responsible for the production of specific products—for example, hormones, enzymes, and blood type. The chromosome contains **deoxyribonucleic acid (DNA)** and looks like a double **helix,** a ladder-like structure composed of "steps" of four **nucleotides:** cytosine (C), adenine (A), thymine (T), and guanine (G) (Figure 2.1). Pairs of nucleotides link to form each step: adenine joins with thymine, and cytosine with guanine. The sides of the ladder are composed of sugar and phosphate molecules.

When a certain product is needed, the particular gene directing its production unzips so that a series of half steps are exposed. For example, if the complete step read AT, GC, GC, TA, AT, the half step would be AGGTA (see Figure 2.1). This half ladder then transcribes, or rewrites, the complementary message onto a single-stranded nucleic acid, called *messenger* **ribonucleic acid** (mRNA). A new nucleotide, uracil, is substituted for thymine so that the complementary message then reads UCCAU. This strand of mRNA then detaches from the DNA, and the double-stranded DNA zips back together. Next, the mRNA moves out of the nucleus into the cytoplasm. There it attaches to a **ribosome** (see Figure 1.1), a unit similar in function to a videocassette recorder. The ribosome reads out or translates this RNA strand in triplet groups—for example, GCU, CUA, UAG. Each triplet codes for a specific amino acid. As these triplets are read out, another type of RNA, called *transfer* RNA (tRNA), carries the requested amino acids to the ribosome. Other triplets code for the termination of production when all of the correct amino acids are in place, at which time they form a whole protein.

Once the protein is complete, it is either used by the cytoplasm or secreted. When the protein is secreted, it is transferred to the Golgi bodies (see Figure 1.1). These bodies package the protein in a form that can be released through the cell membrane and carried throughout the body.

Abnormalities in this process may result from a defective gene and can cause

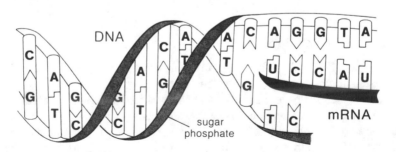

Figure 2.1. Four nucleotides form the genetic code: G = guanine, C = cytosine, A = adenine, T = thymine. On the mRNA molecule, U (uracil) substitutes for thymine. The DNA unzips to transcribe its message to the mRNA.

genetically inherited disease. An illustration of this is the production of hemoglobin, the pigment in blood. In people who have sickle cell anemia, one nucleotide is substituted for another, thymine for adenine, in the gene that directs the production of hemoglobin. As a consequence, the triplet code is misread, and the resulting hemoglobin is defective. This error causes the formation of sickle-shaped red blood cells. These cells are fragile and have shortened life spans, resulting in **anemia.**

Such a substitution is called a **mutation.** A mutation can occur by chance or as the result of external factors such as radiation, viruses, or drugs. Usually the substitution affects all the cells in the body, including the germ cells (the sperm or egg). As a result, the mutation becomes part of the person's genetic code and is passed on from one generation to another.

Geneticists generally believe that everyone carries at least four mutations, which they can pass on to their offspring. Some of these mutations are helpful and are part of the process of natural evolution. Others are harmful and predispose one to various diseases, including diabetes and cancer. Most have no observable effect and do not pose a serious threat to the well-being of our children.

Autosomal Recessive Disorders

Tay-Sachs disease is an example of an autosomal recessive disorder. It is a progressive nervous system disease caused by the absence of the enzyme hexosaminidase A that normally converts a toxic nerve cell product into a nontoxic substance. In Tay-Sachs disease, this toxic product is not broken down, and it accumulates in the brain, leading to brain damage and death.

The origin of the mutation leading to Tay-Sachs disease has been traced to Jewish families living in eastern Europe in the early 1800s. Prior to this time, Tay-Sachs disease did not exist. The original mutation occurred by chance. However, once the abnormality appeared, it was passed on from one generation to another.

A child with Tay-Sachs disease initially develops normally. At about 6 months of age, the child's health begins to deteriorate. He or she can no longer sit or babble and soon becomes blind and has severe mental retardation. Death usually occurs by 5 years of age.

Since all children with Tay-Sachs disease die, it may seem puzzling that the disease continues to be passed on from one generation to another. The reason is that Tay-Sachs disease is caused by a recessive gene. The following illustration explains this concept.

Let us assume that there are two forms of the gene for hexosaminidase A. These alternate forms of the gene, called **alleles,** are the normal gene, symbolized by an "H," and the rare, disease-carrying allele, symbolized by "h" (Figure 2.2). After fertilization, the embryo will have two genes that could carry the Tay-Sachs disorder, one passed on from the father and one from the mother. The following combinations could occur: hh, hH, Hh, HH. Since this is a recessive disorder, two abnormal or "h" genes are needed to produce a diseased child. So, for the combinations just mentioned, "hh" would be a child with Tay-Sachs disease, hH or Hh would be a child without the disease who is a carrier of it, and HH would be a healthy noncarrier.

Autosomal Recessive Disorders

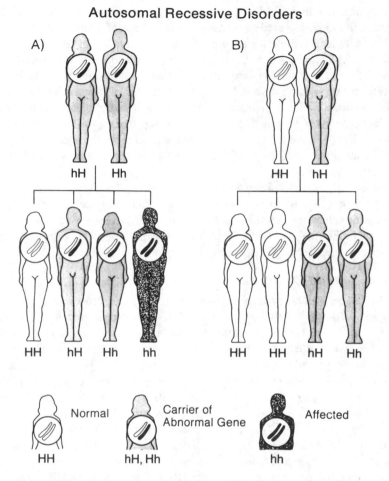

Figure 2.2. Inheritance of autosomal recessive disorders: A) Two carriers mate, resulting, on average, in 25% normal children, 50% carriers, and 25% affected children. B) A carrier and a noncarrier mate, resulting in 50% normal children and 50% carriers. No children are affected.

Therefore, it is the carriers of the abnormal gene who pass on the disease from one generation to the next. If two carriers were to mate (hH × Hh), the following combinations could occur by chance: ¼HH, ¼hH, ¼Hh, ¼hh (Figure 2.2 A). According to the law of probability, one-fourth of the children would be normal (HH), one-half would be carriers (hH or Hh), and one-fourth would have Tay-Sachs disease (hh). If a carrier had a child with a noncarrier (hH × HH), half of the children would be carriers (hH, Hh), and half would be normal noncarriers (HH). None of these children would have Tay-Sachs disease (Figure 2.2 B). Siblings of affected children are most unlikely to have affected children because they will probably marry noncarrier (HH) individuals.

Remember that the 25% risk of having an affected child when two carriers mate is a *statistical* risk. This does not mean that if a family has one affected child, the next three will be unaffected. Each new pregnancy carries the same 25% risk; the parents could have three affected children in a row or 10 normal ones.

It is important to reemphasize, however, that recessive disorders can occur only if two carriers mate. A carrier mating with a noncarrier will always produce non-affected children. Since it is unlikely for a carrier of one disease to meet another carrier of the same unusual disease, these types of disorders are quite rare, ranging from 1 in 2,000 to 1 in 200,000 (McKusick, 1990). However, when intermarriage occurs, the incidence of these disorders increases markedly because the cousin of a carrier is much more likely to be a carrier than is someone in the general population. This probably underlies the biblical proscription about marrying one's immediate relatives (Adams & Neel, 1967) (Figure 2.3).

Besides understanding the incidence of autosomal recessive disorders, it is important to keep in mind some other characteristics of these disorders. First, the mutation causing an autosomal recessive disorder often results in an enzyme deficiency of some kind. These enzyme deficiencies generally lead to biochemical abnormalities involving either the insufficiency of a needed product or the buildup of toxic materials (see Chapter 10); **mental retardation** or early death may result. Second, these disorders affect males and females equally. And third, a history of the disease in past generations rarely exists, unless blood relatives have married (consanguinity).

Autosomal Dominant Disorders

Autosomal dominant disorders are markedly different from autosomal recessive disorders in mechanism, incidence, and clinical characteristics. The most significant difference is that an individual has the disease when he or she has a single abnormal gene. Therefore, a person with the **genotype,** Aa, is affected. This makes the risk of

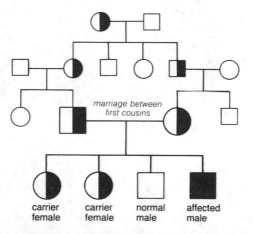

Figure 2.3. A family tree illustrating the effect of consanguinity (in this case, a marriage between first cousins) on the risk of inheriting an autosomal recessive disorder. If one parent is a carrier, the chance of the other parent being a carrier is usually less than 1 in 300. However, when first cousins marry, the chance of the other parent being a carrier rises to 1 in 8. The risk, then, of having an affected child increases almost 40-fold.

autosomal dominant diseases greater than that of autosomal recessive disorders in affected families.

To better understand this, consider the disorder of **achondroplasia,** a form of short-limbed dwarfism. Suppose "A" represents a normal gene, and "a" indicates the abnormal gene for achondroplasia. If a person with achondroplasia, Aa, mates with a normal individual, AA, half of the children, statistically speaking, will have the disorder (Aa), and half will not (AA): Aa × AA → ½Aa + ½AA(Figure 2.4 A). The nonaffected children will not have the trait at all and, therefore, cannot pass it on to their children. However, if two affected parents (Aa × Aa) mate, a double dose of the disorder is likely to hit some of the children. This double dose is usually fatal. Thus,

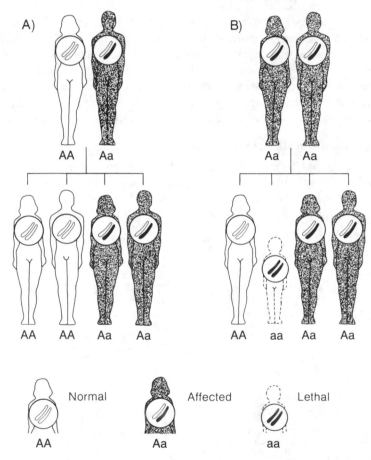

Figure 2.4.   Inheritance of autosomal dominant disorders: A) An affected person marries a normal person. Statistically, 50% of the children will be affected and 50% will be unaffected. B) If two affected people marry, 25% of the children will be unaffected, 50% will be affected, and 25% will have an often fatal double dose of the abnormal gene.

half of the affected parents' children, statistically speaking, would have achondro-plasia (Aa), one-fourth would be normal (AA), and one-fourth would have a severe form of dwarfism (aa) that leads to early death (Figure 2.4B).

As with autosomal recessive disorders, males and females are equally affected. Unlike autosomal recessive disorders, these disorders usually involve structural (physical) rather than enzymatic abnormalities. **Neurofibromatosis** (the Elephant Man disease) is an example. A family history of the disease, in which a sibling or parent is affected, is usual. However, many individuals who have the disorder will represent new mutations and will have no family history of the abnormality. Unlike autosomal recessive disorders, intermarriage is not a factor.

X-Linked Disorders

The two previous forms of heredity described by Mendel involved genes located on the 22 pairs of autosomes, or nonsex, chromosomes. The third form of genetic abnor-mality is called *sex-linked* or **X-linked recessive** because it involves genes located on the X, or female, sex chromosome. For this type of disorder, females are carriers, and males are affected. Muscular dystrophy, hemophilia, **fragile X syndrome,** and color blindness are examples of sex-linked disorders. A brief discussion of some of these X-linked disorders follows.

Boys with Duchenne muscular dystrophy usually develop normally until 6–9 years of age. Then, muscle weakness becomes evident, progresses, and forces the child to require a wheelchair by adolescence. Since the disease affects all muscles, eventually the heart muscle and the diaphragmatic muscles needed for circulation and breathing are impaired. Muscular dystrophy is usually fatal because of these compli-cations (see Chapter 15).

Hemophilia is another serious disease in which one of the blood-clotting factors is missing. As a result, a minor injury or accident can lead to uncontrolled bleeding. Injecting a concentrate of the missing clotting factor is needed to stop the bleeding. Therefore, children with hemophilia are frequently hospitalized and have a number of chronic disabilities.

Besides causing physical disabilities, X-linked disorders also contribute to intel-lectual impairment. Approximately 25% of the intellectual deficits in males are at-tributed to X-linked syndromes as well as about 10% of the learning disabilities in females (Uchida, Freeman, Jamro, et al., 1983). The most common of these is frag-ile X syndrome, which is described more fully in Chapter 16.

Fortunately, not all sex-linked disorders are associated with mental retardation or are life-threatening. For example, color blindness is also inherited in this way. The characteristic shared by these disorders is the way they are passed from one genera-tion to another, from unaffected mother to affected son.

Since women have two X chromosomes, the carrier mother has one chromo-some that bears the mutation (X^a) and one normal (X) chromosome. She is usually clinically normal but can pass the abnormality on to her children. The male child has one X chromosome and one Y chromosome; he is either normal (XY) or affected (X^aY). Suppose a woman who carries the gene for muscular dystrophy (X^aX) has a child with a normal male (XY). Half of their sons (statistically speaking) would have muscular dystrophy (X^aY), and half would be normal (XY). Also, half of their daughters would be carriers for muscular dystrophy (X^aX), and half would be normal (XX) (Figure 2.5 A). A family tree usually would reveal that maternal uncles as well as male siblings have the disease.

If a woman who is a carrier of hemophilia has a child with a hemophiliac mate (an extremely rare occurrence except in intermarriage), half of their children (statistically speaking) would have this disorder. Half of their sons would have hemophilia (X^aY), and half would be normal (XY). Half of their daughters would also have the

Sex-Linked Disorders

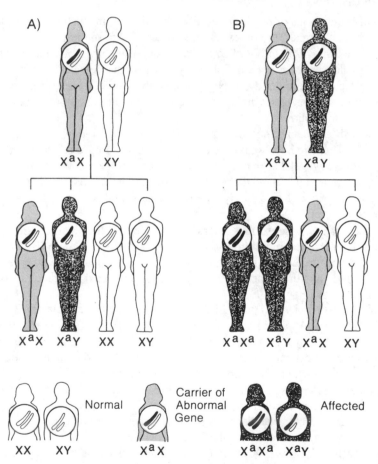

Figure 2.5.   Inheritance of sex-linked disorders: A) A carrier woman mates with a normal man. Of the male children, statistically speaking, 50% will be affected and 50% will be normal. Of the female children, 50% will be carriers and 50% will be normal. B) A carrier woman mates with an affected man. Of the male children, 50% will be normal and 50% will be affected. Of the female children, 50% will be affected and 50% will be carriers.

Table 2.1.   Incidence of Mendelian disorders per 1,000 live births

Type of disorder	Number
Autosomal dominant	7.0
Autosomal recessive	2.5
X-linked	0.4
Total	9.9

Source: Ash et al. (1977).

disease (X^aX^a), and half would be carriers of hemophilia(X^aX) (Figure 2.5B). This is one way in which a female child could manifest a sex-linked disorder. Another way that a female can show signs of a sex-linked trait is if she is a carrier and inactivates her normal X chromosome. This is uncommon; it occurs in less than 10% of women carriers of X-linked traits. However, because of this possibility, in a large family with the fragile X syndrome, some women may also have retardation, but to a lesser degree than the men (Uchida et al., 1983). Thus, sex-linked disorders primarily manifest themselves in males but are passed on from carrier females. Consanguinity is not a factor.

Over 2,000 diseases are now known to be transmitted as Mendelian traits (McKusick, 1990). Approximately 1% of the population has a Mendelian disorder (Table 2.1). Fortunately, some of these disorders can now be treated (see Chapter 10), and others can be diagnosed prenatally (see Chapter 3).

CHROMOSOMAL MALFORMATIONS

Although a single-gene mutation causes Mendelian diseases, other disorders involve the loss or addition of an entire chromosome, including hundreds of genes. These syndromes may affect either autosomes or sex chromosomes.

Autosomal chromosomal abnormalities usually lead to mental retardation and are characterized by a number of unusual physical findings. For example, in Down syndrome, the head is small, and the eyes are slanted. **Congenital** heart defects and gastrointestinal malformations are common (see Chapter 16 for further discussion of Down syndrome). Other trisomy or extra chromosome syndromes (e.g., involving chromosomes #13 or #18) produce more severe abnormalities; many do not live beyond infancy.

In the general population, the incidence of chromosomal aberrations of autosomes is about 4 in 1,000 live births or 0.4%. However, in children with mental retardation and multiple malformations, the incidence rises to between 8% and 14% (Nielsen, Hansen, Sillesen, et al., 1981). Thus, many parents of children with severe retardation and multiple congenital malformations have a chromosome analysis (karyotype) performed to help in making a diagnosis and in providing genetic counseling.

Characteristically, the physical and intellectual problems caused by sex-chromosome abnormalities are less severe than those of autosomal chromosome syndromes. These syndromes also tend to occur more frequently than the autosomal ones. As with autosomal chromosome disorders, the sex-chromosome disorders usually result from nondisjunction.

The most common sex-chromosome disorders are 45 X, 47 XXY, and 47 XYY syndromes (Stewart, Netley, & Park, 1982). The most frequent is 45 X, or Turner syndrome, described in Chapter 1.

Another common sex-chromosome abnormality is Klinefelter syndrome (47 XXY) (Ratcliff, Bancroft, Axworthy, et al., 1982). As in Turner syndrome, the sexual organs develop abnormally in this disorder. The child is male, but because testosterone (the male sex hormone) is inadequately produced, he neither develops secondary sexual characteristics nor forms sperm. He appears as a tall, slender man with breast development and small genitalia. His IQ is generally close to normal. Thus, the extra X chromosome seems to interfere with the development of normal "maleness."

However, the XYY syndrome seems to have a very different effect (Hook, 1973). These men tend to be tall, have normal sexual development, but have lower intelligence. When a number of tall, male prisoners were found to have an extra Y chromosome, the media had a field day, calling it the "criminal chromosome." There was speculation that this extra chromosome predisposed these men to aggressiveness and criminal behavior. This has not been proven to be so (Pitcher, 1982).

Other sex-chromosome abnormalities exist: 47 XXX, 48 XXXY, 48 XXYY, and 49 XXXYY syndromes. Those disorders having all X chromosomes appear in females. The presence of a single Y chromosome, even with a number of X chromosomes, results in a male. Abnormal physical, sexual, and mental development characterizes all of these syndromes. Compared to Turner, Klinefelter, and XYY syndromes (with a combined incidence of 1 in 300), these other disorders are extremely rare (Jones, 1988).

Finally, one chromosomal aberration, **mosaicism,** may involve either autosomal or sex chromosomes. Nondisjunction in the egg or sperm before or during fertilization causes the previously described syndromes. If nondisjunction happens after fertilization, mosaicism results. Suppose nondisjunction takes place shortly after fertilization when four cells are dividing to form eight cells in the **morula.** If one of the four cells divides unevenly, this would lead to 47 chromosomes in one daughter cell, 45 in another, and 46 in the remaining six cells (Figure 2.6). The cell containing 45 chromosomes will die. If the 47-chromosome cell contains a third #21 chromosome, all subsequent daughter cells of this cell will also have 47 chromosomes (trisomy 21). The end result will be a child who will have about 67% normal cells and 33% trisomic cells. The child will look as if he or she has Down syndrome. However, the physical abnormalities are less obvious, and the mental retardation is less severe (Fishler, Koch, & Donnell, 1976). Mosaicism is rare and accounts for fewer than 4% of all children with Down syndrome.

HEREDITARY–ENVIRONMENTAL INTERACTIONS

Some traits result not solely from Mendelian or chromosomal effects but rather from the interaction of heredity and environment. Weight and intelligence are traits inher-

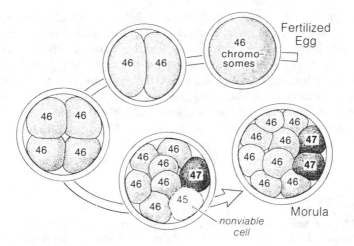

Figure 2.6. Mosaicism. Here nondisjunction occurs after fertilization. This results in a few cells with an additional or missing chromosome; the rest are normal. The cells with 45 chromosomes generally die, while those with 46 or 47 chromosomes survive and multiply. The child is a mosaic with some normal and some abnormal cells. If the abnormal cell contains an extra #21 chromosome, the child will look as though he or she has Down syndrome but will be less severely affected.

ited in this manner. Furthermore, in disorders such as cancer and hypertension, heredity and environment both play a role. Examples of birth defects that come from the interaction of heredity and environment include spina bifida, cleft palate (Shields, Bixler, & Fogh-Anderson, 1981), and pyloric stenosis.

Several factors contribute to the total effect; no one factor is sufficient to produce the particular abnormality. Consider the predominantly male disorder of pyloric stenosis, a malformation of the stomach muscle that leads to a block in the passage of food from the stomach to the small intestine. For this abnormality to occur, it is thought that an intrauterine viral infection, male gender, and genetic factors must all be present. A viral infection alone, for example, will not produce the defect. Thus, although pyloric stenosis is uncommon in the general population (1 in 250 births), it carries a recurrence risk of 1 in 20 in a family with a previously affected child (Buyse, 1990).

Similarly, bright parents have a greater chance of having bright children, and obese parents more often have obese children. However, since a number of factors are interacting, including the environment inside and outside of the uterus, two people of average intelligence can still produce a very bright child. It is just less likely than if both parents are very bright themselves.

SUMMARY

The incidence of Mendelian and chromosomal disorders is rare. Yet, it remains important for couples to be aware of any increased risk of these disorders in their families to permit the possibility of prenatal diagnosis. Although the ability to detect these disorders is imperfect and the understanding of genes and chromosomes is incomplete, progress continues. One example is the recent detection of a new type of inheritance pattern related to gene mutations and deletions in mitochondria. Mitochondria (see Figure 1.1) are organelles in the cytoplasm of cells that produce energy. They have their own genes, which come from the mother's eggs and are different from nuclear genes, half of which come from the sperm and half come from the egg. As a result, virtually all children born to mothers carrying a mitochondrial gene defect have some form of mitochondrial disease. So far, mitochondrial inheritance has been linked to Leber amaurosis, acquired deafness, disorders associated with muscle weakness, and encephalopathies (Harding, 1991). Ten years ago, knowledge such as this and many of the techniques used in prenatal diagnosis were not thought possible.

REFERENCES

Adams, M.S., & Neel, J.V. (1967). Children of incest. *Pediatrics, 40,* 55–62.
Ash, P., Vennart, J., & Carter, C.O. (1977). The incidence of hereditary disease in man. *Lancet, 1,* 849–851.
Buyse, M.L. (1990). *Birth defects encyclopedia.* Dover, MA: Center for Birth Defects Information Services.
Fishler, K., Koch, R., & Donnell, G.N. (1976). Comparison of mental development in individuals with mosaic and trisomy 21 Down's syndrome. *Pediatrics, 38,* 744–748.
Harding, A.E. (1991). Neurological disease and mitochondrial genes. *Trends in Neurosciences, 14,* 279–284.
Hook, E.B. (1973). Behavioral implications of the human XYY genotype. *Science, 179,* 139–150.
Jones, K.L. (1988). *Smith's recognizable patterns of human malformation: Genetic, embryologic, and clinical aspects* (4th ed.). Philadelphia: W.B. Saunders.
McKusick, V.A. (1990). *Mendelian inheritance in man: Catalogs of autosomal dominant, autosomal recessive, and X-linked phenotypes* (9th ed.). Baltimore: Johns Hopkins University Press.
Nielsen, J., Hansen, K.B., Sillesen, I., et al. (1981). Chromosome abnormality in newborn children: Physical aspects. *Human Genetics, 59,* 194–200.
Pitcher, D.R. (1982). Chromosomes and violence. *Practitioner, 226,* 497–501.
Ratcliff, S.G., Bancroft, J., Axworthy, D., et al. (1982). Klinefelter's syndrome in adolescence. *Archives of Disease in Childhood, 57,* 6–12.
Shields, E.D., Bixler, D., & Fogh-Anderson, P. (1981). Cleft palate: A genetic and epidemiological investigation. *Clinical Genetics, 20,* 13–24.
Smith, C. (1971). Recurrence risks for multifactorial inheritance. *American Journal of Human Genetics, 23,* 578–588.
Stewart, D.A., Netley, C.T., & Park, E. (1982). Summary of clinical findings of children with 47,XXY, 47,XYY, and 47,XXX karyotypes. *Birth Defects, 18,* 1–5.
Uchida, I.A., Freeman, V.C., Jamro, H., et al. (1983). Additional evidence for fragile-X activity in heterozygous carriers. *American Journal of Human Genetics, 35,* 861–868.

Chapter 3

Birth Defects, Prenatal Diagnosis, and Fetal Therapy

Upon completion of this chapter, the reader will:
—know the risks and benefits of amniocentesis and chorionic villus sampling
—be familiar with the prenatal diagnostic procedures of ultrasonography and DNA analysis
—be aware of certain screening tests used to diagnose diseases prenatally
—be informed about those instances in which fetal therapy is possible

---

Anne, in the fourth month of her second pregnancy, is undergoing amniocentesis. Her first child was born with **spina bifida**. By using the prenatal diagnostic technique of amniocentesis, her physician should be able to determine if the child Anne is now carrying has the same condition. In a few days, Anne learns that this child, a boy, does not have spina bifida or any of the many diagnosable chromosomal abnormalities revealed by amniocentesis. Many of her fears are allayed.

Amniocentesis, along with sonography, and some blood screening tests, are the major prenatal diagnostic tools used to identify serious medical problems in fetuses. This chapter examines these techniques and discusses the risks and benefits associated with them. The more recently implemented diagnostic methods of **chorionic villus sampling** and DNA study are also considered. The chapter concludes with the mention of a few instances where fetal therapy is possible.

It should first be noted that the majority of all pregnancies neither require nor benefit from prenatal diagnosis procedures. In deciding whether a pregnant woman should undergo a prenatal diagnostic test, the obstetrician may refer the family to a genetic clinic for counseling. Here a geneticist or genetic counselor will determine whether the couple's child is predisposed to a specific disease and whether this disease is prenatally diagnosable. Prenatal diagnostic testing is performed to detect a suspected disease; it does not ensure a healthy baby, only one who does not have the disease the test detects. As prenatal diagnostic tests are not without risk, they should be performed only when there is a specific risk and potential benefit.

PRENATAL DIAGNOSIS

Hundreds of genetic disorders are diagnosable by analyzing **amniotic fluid** and fetal cells. The most common reason for prenatal testing is advanced maternal age. As a woman ages, the risk of nondisjunction (discussed in Chapter 1) and resultant trisomy 21 (or Down syndrome) increases (Figure 3.1). In women 45 years old, the incidence is about 1 in 32 compared to 1 in 2,000 for women between 20 and 25 years old. In women 35 years old, the risk of trisomy 21 (1 in 400) as well as the possibility of other chromosomal abnormalities is considered significant enough to warrant prenatal diagnosis (Hook & Fabia, 1978).

For women younger than 35 who have already had one child with trisomy 21, the recurrence risk increases to 1 in 100. For these women, prenatal diagnosis is suggested in future pregnancies. Some cases of Down syndrome, about 3%, are caused by a chromosomal translocation (discussed in Chapter 1) rather than by trisomy 21 (Wright, Day, Muller, et al., 1967). In the case of a translocation, one parent may be a carrier, and the recurrence risk may be as high as 1 in 10, warranting prenatal diagnosis for future pregnancies. As a result of these concerns, the majority of prenatal diagnoses are performed on women concerned about Down syndrome.

In addition to checking for Down syndrome or other chromosomal abnormalities, prenatal diagnosis can be used to diagnose spina bifida (a malformation in which there is an opening in the spine) and many inherited inborn errors of metabolism. To diagnose spina bifida in a mother who has had a previously affected child, the con-

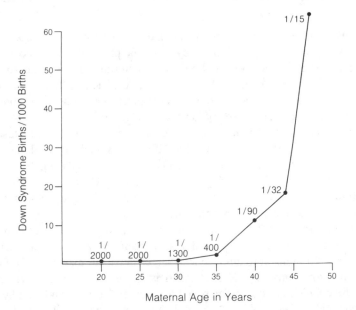

Figure 3.1.   Incidence of trisomy 21 in mothers of various ages. The risk increases markedly after 35 years of age (Hook & Fabia, 1978).

centration of a specific compound, **alpha-fetoprotein (AFP),** is measured in maternal serum and amniotic fluid. Affected fetuses have high levels of this particular protein (Hogge, Thiagarajah, Ferguson, Schnatterly, & Harbert, 1989). What seems to happen is this: AFP is plentiful in the spinal fluid. With an open spine, the AFP leaks into the amniotic fluid and then can be measured (see Chapter 25).

When testing for inborn errors of metabolism (see Chapter 10) such as Tay-Sachs disease, the fetal cells are studied for the presence of a defective enzyme. In the case of Tay-Sachs, the enzyme is hexosaminidase A. If the enzyme level is very low or zero, the fetus is diagnosed as having the disease.

Amniocentesis

The first technique developed for prenatal diagnosis was amniocentesis (Roberts, Dunn, Weiner, et al., 1983). The procedure, which is fairly simple, is usually performed between 14 and 17 weeks gestation, in the second trimester, when about 8 ounces of amniotic fluid surround the fetus. Amniocentesis involves inserting a needle through the mother's abdomen into the amniotic sac and withdrawing less than 1 ounce of this fluid. Ultrasound monitoring is done simultaneously to enable the obstetrician to do the procedure without puncturing a fetal part.

Once the amniotic fluid containing the fetal cells is removed, the cells are separated and put into a culture medium (Figure 3.2). To diagnose spina bifida, the fluid is tested for levels of AFP and acetylcholinesterase, and the results are available in a few days (Wald, Cuckle, & Nanchahal, 1989). To diagnose biochemical or chromosomal disorders, the amniotic cells are grown in a culture medium for about 2 weeks. After a sufficient number of cells have grown, a karyotype is assembled to determine the gender and to analyze the chromosomes, and a specific enzyme analysis is performed, or the DNA of the cell is studied if the family history indicates this is necessary.

Amniocentesis is performed as an outpatient procedure, and the risks to the fetus and mother are quite low. The risk of miscarriage following the procedure is about 0.5%. The risk to the mother of bleeding or infection is even lower. There is also a very small risk of fetal **morbidity** (i.e., infants born prematurely, with a scar where the needle may have touched a body part, or chronic leakage of amniotic fluid that increased the chances of an unexpanded lung or an orthopedic deformity). These problems point to the presence of some finite risk with this test. However, when used correctly, amniocentesis is an extremely useful procedure that can allay many fears and provide prospective parents with much-needed information (Canadian Collaborative CVS-Amniocentesis Clinical Trial Group, 1989).

Chorionic Villus Sampling

A newer method that is fast supplanting amniocentesis as the most commonly used form of prenatal diagnosis is chorionic villus sampling (Blakemore, 1988; Wapner & Jackson, 1988). This procedure is performed during the first trimester (8–10 weeks gestation) before the mother is noticeably pregnant and before she feels any movements from the fetus. The main advantage of this method is that a decision to termi-

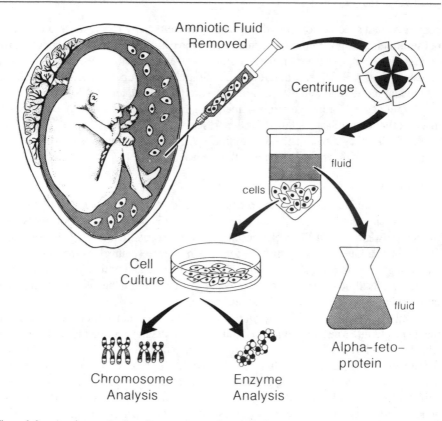

Figure 3.2. Amniocentesis. Less than one ounce of amniotic fluid is removed at 14–17 weeks gestation. It is spun in a centrifuge to separate the fluid from the fetal cells. The fluid is used immediately to test for alpha-fetoprotein. The cells are grown for 2 weeks, and then a chromosome, enzyme, or DNA analysis can be performed. Results are usually available about 3 weeks later.

nate a pregnancy is emotionally easier and medically safer for women at this stage of pregnancy. Also, the uncertainty of whether the fetus is affected lasts for a much shorter period of time. This technique can be used as a substitute for amniocentesis in virtually all situations except spina bifida detection, in which case amniotic fluid, rather than cells, is needed.

This diagnostic procedure is illustrated in Figure 3.3. A tube is inserted through the vagina into the uterus, and a minute amount of chorionic (placental) tissue is removed by suction. More recently, a transabdominal approach that is technically very similar to amniocentesis has also been used. The difference is that in chorionic villus sampling a small amount of the developing **placenta** is removed rather than amniotic fluid. Because the fetal cells of the **chorion** are rapidly dividing, they can be analyzed directly under a microscope, without waiting 2–3 weeks for them to grow, as is done with the cells removed in amniocentesis. Results may be available in a matter of days. Thus, this technique appears to be a good solution for many women

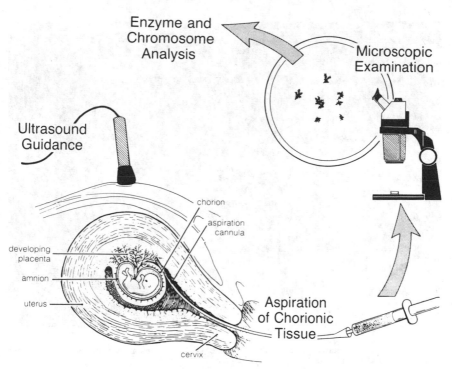

Figure 3.3. Chorionic villus sampling. A hollow instrument is inserted through the vagina into the uterus, guided by ultrasound. A small amount of chorionic tissue is suctioned. The tissue is then examined under a microscope to make sure it is sufficient. Chromosome, enzyme, or DNA analysis can be performed without first growing the cells. Results are available in about a week.

who are concerned about the possibility of having a child with abnormalities but feel that amniocentesis is available too late in pregnancy. Chorionic villus sampling appears to be slightly less safe for the fetus than amniocentesis, with a 1% greater risk of miscarriage following the procedure (Goldberg, Porter, & Golbus, 1990; Wade & Young, 1989) and possibly an increased risk for limb deformities (Burton, Schulz, & Burd, 1992). Morbidity rates for the pregnant woman are similar to those for amniocentesis.

Ultrasound

Ultrasonography (Figure 3.4) utilizes sound waves to produce an image of the fetus. The sound waves bounce off structures with different densities, allowing visualization of the individual fetal body parts as well as fetal movement. Structures as small as the lip and external genitalia can be studied. Ultrasound aids in the diagnosis of spina bifida, **anencephaly, microcephaly, hydrocephalus,** heart defects, and limb abnormalities, and in gender determination. In spina bifida, the abnormally shaped vertebral bodies can be seen and serve to confirm the diagnosis in a woman with high alpha-fetoprotein levels. In hydrocephalus, the enlarging brain **ventricles** can be fol-

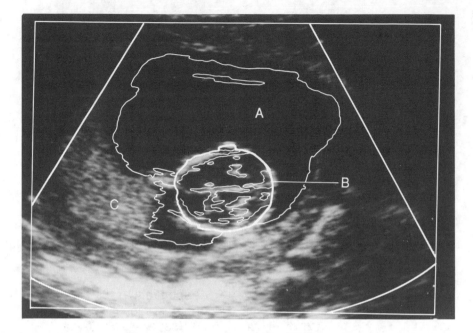

Figure 3.4.   Ultrasound showing the fetal head at 20 weeks. The following are indicated: A) the amniotic sac, B) the head of the fetus, and C) the placenta.

lowed over time. In microcephaly, the decreased growth rate of the skull can similarly be monitored. In Down syndrome, there are increased skin folds in the neck region.

In addition, sonography permits a physician to compare the gestational age of the fetus with its body size to make sure the fetus is growing normally. Fetal movement and breathing also may be assessed to determine fetal well-being (see the section on Biophysical Profile in Chapter 5). Fetal sex also can be determined with good accuracy by looking for the presence of a penis after 25 weeks gestation and, in some cases, it can be determined as early as 16 weeks (Watson, 1990). Finally, the structure of the heart can be studied with fetal **echocardiography** to detect congenital heart disease (Sanders, Chin, Parness, et al., 1985). Ultrasound can be augmented by **magnetic resonance imaging (MRI)** (see Chapter 22) in cases where fetal anomalies have been identified and a clearer picture is required (Mattison & Angtuaco, 1988). Studies have shown ultrasonography to be safe for both mother and fetus (Filkins & Russo, 1990).

DNA Studies

There are over 2,000 diseases that are inherited as Mendelian traits (discussed in Chapter 2). The revolution in molecular biology has led to the development of new techniques that permit the prenatal diagnosis of diseases for which the gene defect is known and for some disorders in which no specific chromosomal or enzymatic abnormality has yet been identified (Antonarakis, 1989; Boehm, 1988). Once the location of a gene that codes for a specific disorder has been identified, special techniques can be employed to determine if there is a mutation at that point on the chromosome in the fetus. To perform this test, amniocentesis or chorionic villus sampling is used to collect fetal cells. The DNA from these cells is then cut into small fragments using the appropriate restriction enzymes. Next, the size of these DNA fragments is measured and compared with patterns in cells from normal individuals.

For those diseases in which the specific gene defect is unknown, closely linked **restriction fragment length polymorphism (RFLP)** may predict disease with sufficient accuracy to be useful. However, diagnosis is most accurate when a mutation itself is studied, rather than a linked DNA polymorphism some distance from the mutation. Examples of diseases for which the gene defect has been recently identified include PKU, muscular dystrophy and **cystic fibrosis** (Hodgson & Bobrow, 1989; Niermeijer, Halley, Kleijer, et al., 1989). Figure 3.5 shows the use of DNA testing in a family that already has had one child with PKU (see Chapter 10). The mother is now pregnant with her fourth child. Testing of chorionic villus samples reveals that her fetus also is affected.

CARRIER DETECTION

Methods complementary to prenatal diagnosis include carrier detection with blood screening tests. Carrier detection has been used to diagnose two autosomal recessive disorders, Tay-Sachs disease and sickle cell anemia. In the past, prenatal diagnosis could only be performed after a family already had at least one affected child. Now, a blood test can identify carriers of these diseases before they have a child with the disorder. If a couple is screened and both are found to be carriers—meaning they have a 25% risk of having an affected child—the woman can undergo prenatal diagnosis and choose to terminate her pregnancy if she is found to be carrying an affected child. This can enable a **heterozygote,** or carrier, couple to have a series of normal children without ever bearing an affected child.

One of the reasons Tay-Sachs screening has been successful is because it can be limited to a relatively small number of persons, the Ashkenazic Jewish population (Clarke, Skomorowski, & Zuker, 1989). The chance of a Jewish couple bearing a child affected with Tay-Sachs disease is about 1 in 2,500. Among non-Jewish couples, the incidence is about 1 in 360,000. The screening program has proven to be extremely successful in identifying couples at risk and providing them with appropriate prenatal diagnosis. As a result, very few babies are now being born with this fatal disease.

Unlike screening for Tay-Sachs, screening for sickle cell anemia has had a checkered history. Part of the reason is that parents are less likely to consider therapeutic abortions for children who will be chronically but not terminally ill. As there is no cure, and abortion may not be an acceptable option, screening to identify carriers

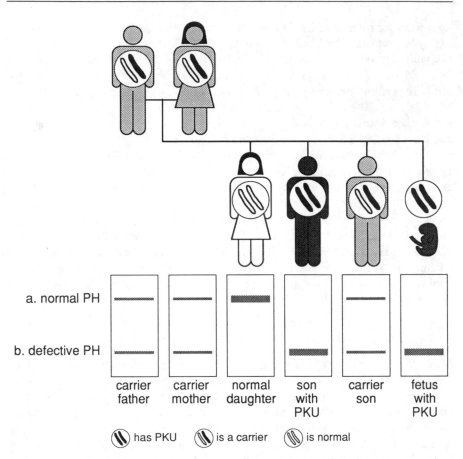

Figure 3.5. DNA analysis of a family at risk for phenylketonuria (PKU). The top figure illustrates the members of the family. One of their sons has already been diagnosed as having PKU. They have two other children who are unaffected. As this is an autosomal recessively inherited disorder, both parents must be carriers (i.e., each has one normal and one defective gene for phenylalanine hydroxylase [PH], the enzyme deficient in PKU). The mother is now pregnant with her fourth child and has undergone chorionic villus sampling to determine whether her fetus is also affected. The other members of the family were also tested using blood specimens. The bottom figure shows the results of this testing. A procedure was done in which the DNA containing the gene for PH was broken into segments of different lengths depending on whether the enzyme was normal or defective. The segments appear as bands on a special gel. In this case, the upper band (a) is associated with the gene for the normal PH while the (b) band is associated with the defective PH gene. As expected both the father and mother were shown to be carriers, each with one normal PH (a) band and one defective PH (b) band. Their daughter was shown to be normal with a double (a) band. Their first son is known to have PKU; as expected he had a double defective PH (b) band. Their next son was found to be a carrier like his parents with one (a) band and one (b) band. Finally, the fetus was found to be affected, with two (b) bands. This infant will be treated from birth with a low-phenylalanine diet.

becomes less useful. Also, insufficient genetic counseling has led some carriers to believe they have the disease, sometimes causing serious emotional consequences. More extensive and better genetic counseling has recently improved this approach to screening.

SERUM ALPHA-FETOPROTEIN IN SPINA BIFIDA AND DOWN SYNDROME

Besides carrier detection tests, another form of screening provided to most pregnant women is the maternal serum alpha-fetoprotein (AFP) test, performed at 14–18 weeks gestation (Figure 3.6). This detects a proportion of pregnant women who are carrying fetuses with spina bifida or Down syndrome (Burton, 1988). A pregnant woman with a high blood level of AFP has an increased risk of carrying a child with spina bifida or anencephaly (see Chapter 25), while a woman with a low blood level of AFP has an increased risk of carrying a child with Down syndrome (see Chapter 16). Once a woman has been identified as having an elevated or low AFP level, she is offered both ultrasound and amniocentesis to make a definitive diagnosis (Nadel, Green, Holmes, et al., 1990).

The blood AFP test is only a screening procedure. For every 10 women identified as having an abnormality, only 1 will actually be carrying an affected fetus. Other causes of elevated serum AFP, including twin pregnancies, fetal death, and incorrect gestational age, make this screening procedure less effective. Also, this test does not identify about 20% of women who are carrying fetuses with spina bifida and 80% of women who are carrying fetuses with Down syndrome (Ashwood, Cheng, & Luthy, 1987).

FETAL THERAPY

The ultimate goal of prenatal diagnosis is to identify affected fetuses and treat them before birth so that severe disabilities are prevented (Chervenak, Isaacson, & Mahoney, 1986). So far, this approach has been successful in only a few instances. One of these involves the inborn error of metabolism, **methylmalonic aciduria**, which is responsive to vitamin B_{12} therapy (see Chapter 10). Here, a mother, who had previously delivered one affected child, was found to be carrying a second child with the same disorder. The mother received weekly intravenous injections of vitamin B_{12} from 25 weeks gestation, and the child continued to receive this therapy after birth (Ampola, Mahoney, Nakamura, et al., 1974). This child has done well.

Unfortunately, most inborn errors of metabolism are not vitamin responsive and cannot be treated in this fashion. However, advances in enzyme and gene replacement therapy promise improved treatment in the future. The fetus is particularly suited to this approach as it is immunologically tolerant and therefore less likely to reject a foreign enzyme or gene (see Chapter 10). Ultimately, we may be able to treat the preimplantation (1–2 week old) embryo, obtained through *in vitro* fertilization (Edwards & Hollands, 1988).

Another approach to fetal therapy is the surgical treatment of hydrocephalus and bladder obstruction. These abnormalities can be detected by ultrasound. Hydrocephalus involves an enlargement of the ventricles in the brain, caused by a blockage of the normal flow of fluid from the head into the spine. Some cases of hydrocephalus exist during fetal development and can be diagnosed at around 25 weeks gestation because of increasing head size. Attempts have been made to correct this abnormality before the child's birth. A shunt is implanted into the ventricle in the fetus's head,

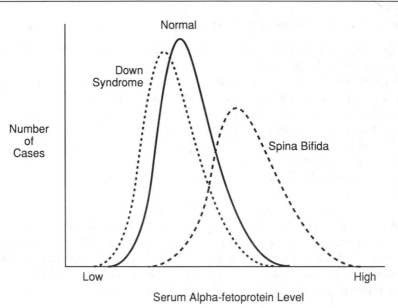

Figure 3.6. Distribution of serum alpha-fetoprotein (AFP) levels in blood from women in the second trimester of pregnancy who are carrying: a fetus with Down syndrome, a normal fetus, and a fetus with an open neural tube defect (spina bifida). In general, women carrying a fetus with Down syndrome have lower AFP levels than normal, and women carrying children with neural tube defects have higher than normal levels.

permitting drainage of cerebrospinal fluid through a one-way valve into the amniotic sac. This releases the increased pressure and prevents further enlargement of the head. The baby is then delivered at term by cesarean section. Unfortunately, the results have not been very encouraging, probably because the cause of the hydrocephalus was pre-existing abnormal brain development that cannot be corrected. A 10% mortality rate is associated with hydrocephalus, and over 50% of survivors have been found to have severe neurological disabilities (Johnson & Elias, 1988).

Surgical treatment of obstructions of the urinary tract has been more successful than treatment of hydrocephalus. Left untreated, these malformations lead to the damming of urine and subsequent bladder enlargement. This, in turn, results in backflow of urine into the kidneys, damaging them. The decreased production of urine, the primary constituent of amniotic fluid, also leads to deformation of the lungs that are normally buffered by the surrounding fluid. In fetal therapy, a shunt is placed to decompress and drain the fetal bladder (Figure 3.7). There is a 41% survival rate with this procedure, which is a significant improvement over the almost universally fatal kidney and lung failure that results if this obstruction is not treated (Manning, Harrison, Rodeck, et al., 1986).

SUMMARY

Currently, the various methods of prenatal diagnosis can identify many inherited disorders. Additional progress will come as more disorders are not only diagnosed but

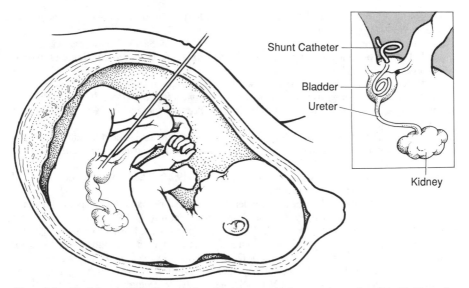

Figure 3.7. Fetal therapy. This fetus was found by ultrasound to have an obstruction of the bladder outlet. Swelling of the entire urinary tract can be seen in the large illustration that was done at the time of the surgical procedure at 20 weeks gestation. The insert shows the results of the placement of the catheter, shunting the urine from the fetal bladder into the amniotic fluid. One week after the shunt placement, the urinary tract has been effectively decompressed so that it looks nearly normal.

also become amenable to treatment before birth. Although prenatal diagnosis leads some parents to choose to abort an affected fetus, it helps others to have more children. While prenatal diagnosis can tell prospective parents about a specific abnormality, it does not ensure anyone a well-born child. Unfortunately, many causes of developmental disabilities are still not diagnosable prenatally.

REFERENCES

Ampola, M.G., Mahoney, M.J., Nakamura, E., et al. (1974). In utero treatment of methylmalonic acidemia (MMA-EMIA) with vitamin B_{12}. *Pediatric Research, 8,* 387.

Antonarakis, S.E. (1989). Diagnosis of genetic disorders at the DNA level. *New England Journal of Medicine, 320*(3), 153–163.

Ashwood, E.R., Cheng, E., & Luthy, D.A. (1987). Maternal serum alpha-fetoprotein and fetal trisomy-21 in women 35 years and older: Implications for alpha-fetoprotein screening programs. *American Journal of Medical Genetics, 26,* 531–539.

Blakemore, K.J. (1988). Prenatal diagnosis by chorionic villus sampling. *Obstetrics and Gynecology Clinics of North America, 15*(2), 179–213.

Boehm, C.D. (1988). Prenatal diagnosis and carrier detection by DNA analysis. *Progress in Medical Genetics, 7,* 143–179.

Burton, B.K. (1988). Elevated maternal serum alpha-fetoprotein (MSAFP): Interpretation and follow-up. *Clinical Obstetrics and Gynecology, 31*(2), 293–305.

Burton, B.K., Schulz, C.J., & Burd, L.I. (1992). Limb anomalies associated with chorionic villus sampling. *Obstetrics and Gynecology, 79,* 726–730.

Canadian Collaborative CVS-Amniocentesis Clinical Trial Group. (1989). Multicentre randomised clinical trial of chorion villus sampling and amniocentesis. (First report). *Lancet, 1,* 1–6.

Chervenak, F.A., Isaacson, G., & Mahoney, M.J. (1986). Advances in the diagnosis of fetal defects. *New England Journal of Medicine, 315,* 305–307.

Clarke, J.T., Skomorowski, M.A., & Zuker, S. (1989). Tay-Sachs disease carrier screening: Follow-up of a case-finding approach. *American Journal of Medical Genetics, 34*(4), 601–605.

Edwards, R.G., & Hollands, P. (1988). New advances in human embryology: Implications of the preimplantation diagnosis of genetic disease. *Human Reproduction, 3*(4), 549–556.

Filkins, K., & Russo, J.F. (Eds.). (1990). *Human prenatal diagnosis.* New York: Marcel Dekker.

Goldberg, J.D., Porter, A.E., & Golbus, M.S. (1990). Current assessment of fetal losses as a direct consequence of chorionic villus sampling. *American Journal of Medical Genetics, 35*(2), 174–177.

Harrison, M.R., Golbus, M.S., & Filly, R.A. (Eds.). (1990). *The unborn patient: Prenatal diagnosis and treatment.* Philadelphia: W.B. Saunders.

Hodgson, S.V., & Bobrow, M. (1989). Carrier detection and prenatal diagnosis in Duchenne and Becker muscular dystrophy. *British Medical Bulletin, 45*(3), 719–744.

Hogge, W.A., Thiagarajah, S., Ferguson, J.E., Schnatterly, P.T., & Harbert, G.M., Jr. (1989). The role of ultrasonography and amniocentesis in the evaluation of pregnancies at risk for neural tube defects. *American Journal of Obstetrics and Gynecology, 161*(3), 520–523.

Hook, E.B., & Fabia, J.J. (1978). Frequency of Down syndrome in live births by single-year maternal age interval: Results of a Massachusetts study. *Teratology, 17,* 223–228.

Johnson, J.M., & Elias, S. (1988). Prenatal treatment: Medical and gene therapy in the fetus. *Clinical Obstetrics and Gynecology, 31*(2), 390–407.

Manning, F.A., Harrison, M.R., Rodeck, C., & members of the International Fetal Medicine and Surgery Society. (1986). Catheter shunts for fetal hydronephrosis and hydrocephalus. *New England Journal of Medicine, 315*(5), 336–340.

Mattison, D.R., & Angtuaco, T. (1988). Magnetic resonance imaging in prenatal diagnosis. *Clinical Obstetrics and Gynecology, 31*(2), 353–389.

Nadel, A.S., Green, J.K., Holmes, L.B., et al. (1990). Absence of need for amniocentesis in patients with elevated levels of maternal serum alpha-fetoprotein and normal ultrasonographic examinations. *New England Journal of Medicine, 323*(9), 557–561.

Niermeijer, M.F., Halley, D.J., Kleijer, W.J., et al. (1989). Prenatal diagnosis and genetic counseling of cystic fibrosis. *Acta Paediatrica Scandinavica Supplement, 363,* 20–24.

Roberts, N.S., Dunn, L.K., Weiner, S., et al. (1983). Midtrimester amniocentesis: Indications, technique, risks and potential for prenatal diagnosis. *The Journal of Reproductive Medicine, 28,* 167–188.

Sanders, S.P., Chin, A.J., Parness, I.A., et al. (1985). Prenatal diagnosis of congenital heart defects in thoracoabdominally conjoined twins. *The New England Journal of Medicine, 313,* 370–374.

Wade, R.V., & Young, S.R. (1989). Analysis of fetal loss after transcervical chorionic villus sampling—A review of 719 patients. *American Journal of Obstetrics and Gynecology, 161*(3), 515–518.

Wald, N., Cuckle, H., & Nanchahal, K. (1989). Amniotic fluid acetylcholinesterase measurement in the prenatal diagnosis of open neural tube defects. Second report of the Collaborative Acetylcholinesterase Study. *Prenatal Diagnosis, 9*(12), 813–829.

Wapner, R.J., & Jackson, L. (1988). Chorionic villus sampling. *Clinical Obstetrics and Gynecology, 31*(2), 328–344.

Watson, W.J. (1990). Early second trimester fetal sex determination with ultrasound. *Journal of Reproductive Medicine, 35*(3), 247–249.

Wright, S.W., Day, R.W., Muller, H., et al. (1967). The frequency of trisomy and translocation in Down's syndrome. *Journal of Pediatrics, 70,* 420–424.

Chapter 4

Growth Before Birth

Upon completion of this chapter, the reader will:
—understand the fertilization and implantation process
—be aware of the various stages of prenatal development
—be able to discuss the effects of maternal nutrition on fetal development
—know the various causes of malformations, including the different major teratogens
—be able to identify some of the causes of deformities
—be acquainted with some of the methods available to prevent birth defects

---

Many factors, both environmental and genetic, influence the formation of a human
being from fertilization to birth. In terms of environmental factors, maternal health
and nutrition greatly influence fetal growth. Radiation, drugs, infections, and other
factors influence the fetal environment and can contribute to the development of malformations. Genetically transmitted disorders can have equally devastating results.
This chapter outlines prenatal development and describes how these factors can lead
to the birth of a child with developmental disabilities. This is further discussed in
Chapter 8, which is concerned with new environmental causes of disability: alcohol,
cocaine, and **acquired immunodeficiency syndrome (AIDS).**

FERTILIZATION

An infant girl is born with 2 million oocytes, or immature ova. Over her lifetime, only
about 500 of these will mature into fully developed eggs; by 45–55 years of age, all
the remaining oocytes will have disappeared.

During a woman's reproductive years, one mature ovum typically ripens each
month, is pushed from the ovary, and drops into the fallopian tube (Figure 4.1). Fertilization occurs about one-third of the way down the fallopian tube. If fertilization
does not occur, the **menses** wash away the egg and the lining of the uterine wall. The
cycle repeats itself unless conception takes place.

Unlike females, who are born with all the reproductive cells they will ever
possess, males continue to produce sperm throughout their lives. With ejaculation

during intercourse, hundreds of millions of sperm swim through the vagina to the cervix. Most of them die enroute. Midway through the woman's menstrual cycle, the **mucosal** secretions of the vagina and cervix are thinned and easier to penetrate. If intercourse occurs at this time, the sperm have a better chance of reaching the egg and fertilizing it. Once the sperm have pushed through the cervix and into the uterus, a few thousand of them find their way to the correct fallopian tube. The journey is difficult as they are swimming against the current created by the fallopian tube's **cilia,** the tiny, hairlike protrusions that help push the ova downward.

After the few hundred surviving sperm reach the egg, they poke and push at the egg's outer layer until one breaks through (see Figure 4.1). Why one sperm succeeds where another has failed is unclear. What is known is that once one sperm fertilizes the egg, another sperm cannot penetrate it. The rest of the sperm die within 24 hours.

Once inside the egg, the sperm nucleus quickly detaches from its **flagellum** and edges toward the ovum's nucleus. The two nuclei join, restoring to the fertilized egg the diploid number of 46 chromosomes (see Figure 4.1). Because the egg always contains an X chromosome, if the sperm nucleus also contains an X chromosome, a female (XX) will result. If the sperm carries a Y chromosome, a male (XY) will be produced. Thus, it is the sperm that determines the sex of the fetus.

On the rare occasion when two eggs instead of one are released simultaneously from the ovary and are both fertilized within a few days of each other, fraternal twins result. Although the twins share the same environment at the same time, they are as genetically distinct as any two siblings. Identical twins, however, result from a single fertilized egg that divides by chance into two separate organisms. They share the same environment and the same genetic inheritance. Yet, even they may differ because of external influences during pregnancy. For example, one may be better nourished and larger at birth than the other. The incidence of fraternal twins is 1 in 90 while the incidence of identical twins is 1 in 200 (Strandskov, 1945).

EMBRYOGENESIS

After fertilization, the egg quickly begins to divide, first into two, then four, then eight cells. At this stage, the group of multiplying cells is called the *morula*. By 5 days after conception, the cluster of cells, or **blastocyst,** contains more than 50 cells. While all the cells start out as primitive, unspecialized units, they soon develop into three distinct layers: the ectoderm, the mesoderm, and the endoderm. The ectoderm evolves into skin, the spinal cord, and teeth. The mesoderm becomes blood vessels, muscles, and bone, and the endoderm develops into the digestive system, lungs, and urinary tract (Oppenheimer & Lefevre, 1989).

Seven days after conception, the *embryo,* appearing as a hollow cluster of cells, reaches the uterus. Only about half of all fertilized eggs survive to this point. When one does survive, it attaches itself to the wall of the uterus, beginning a process called **implantation** (see Figure 4.1). To ensure this process, the embryo produces a hormone, **chorionic gonadotrophin,** that prevents the mother from menstruating and sweeping away the microscopic embryo. The spongy layers of the uterine wall, rich

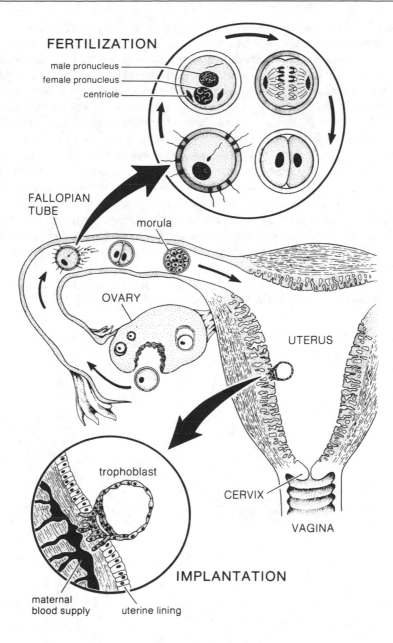

Figure 4.1. Fertilization and implantation. The ovum or egg is dropped from the ovary into the fallopian tube where it is fertilized by a sperm. The fertilized egg regains its diploid number of chromosomes and starts dividing as it travels toward the uterus. It reaches the uterus after 7 days, and implantation of the embryo then takes place.

in blood supply, allow the embryo to push its minute roots, or **villi,** alongside the maternal blood vessels that will feed it.

By the third week, a primitive placenta has formed, providing an improved means of supplying nutrition. Now oval-shaped, the embryo is beginning to round up at one end to form the brain (Figure 4.2). The pattern of development is from head to tail, or **cephalocaudal.** Surrounding the embryo is a layer that will form the amniotic sac. Fluid will gradually fill this sac to protect the embryo and keep it from drying out.

At the fourth week, the embryo is less than half a centimeter long. Yet, its central nervous system is starting to develop, with the **neural tube** folding over to form the spinal cord (see Figure 4.2). The facial structure is also taking shape; six **pharyngeal** arches will join in the center to form lips, palate, and **mandible,** or jaw.

The next week, the heart begins to form. It begins as a U-shaped tube. Seven days later, after undergoing an incredible series of changes, it will be beating about 60 times a minute. Other organs are also experiencing swift changes. During this week, the limb buds become evident (see Figure 4.2). In only 35 days, the embryo has grown from one cell to more than 10,000.

Soon, the embryo begins to take on a more human form. During the second month, the internal body organs start to function. The system of blood vessels ex-

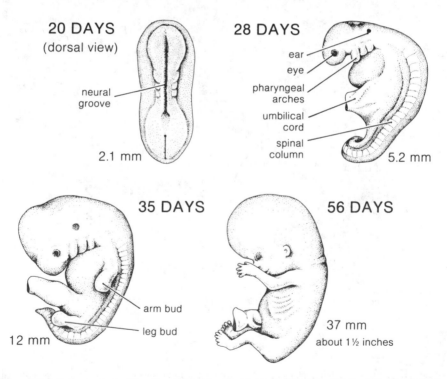

Figure 4.2.   Embryogenesis. The changes that take place in the embryo from 3 to 8 weeks after fertilization are enormous. All systems are formed, and the embryo takes on a human fetal appearance. Length increases 20-fold during this time.

pands. The brain grows rapidly. Optic swellings at the side of the **forebrain** become eyes and move toward the center of the face. Eyebrows and the **retina** are evident. The primitive sexual organs are beginning to undergo meiotic division and produce primitive eggs and sperm. The embryo is now about 1½ inches long.

During this period of development, the changes are so precise and predictable that physicians can tell when certain congenital (birth) defects took place. For example, they know that if a child is born with a cleft palate, the defect occurred between days 35 and 37 of gestation, when the **palatal** arches normally close.

FETAL DEVELOPMENT

By the end of these 2 months, the embryo has become a *fetus* (see Figure 4.2). The next 7 months of fetal development are devoted to the refining and enlarging of the organs and body parts that formed during embryogenesis. In the third month, the fetus, although weighing only about an ounce, is active, kicking, and turning. The amniotic fluid, being produced in greater quantities now, measures approximately 8 ounces. This fluid is constantly recirculated, being swallowed by the fetus and then excreted as urine. During the fourth month, the fetus, weighing about 6 ounces and measuring about 10 inches in length, kicks with authority. This is when the mother usually begins to feel movement, called **quickening.** The heartbeat is also audible.

As growth continues, the placenta assumes more and more importance to the fetus. It acts as a barrier against the penetration of harmful substances and as a remover of waste materials, as well as a source of nutrition from the maternal circulation. It functions as lungs, kidneys, intestine, and liver for the fetus. Hormones produced by the placenta aid in the continuation of the pregnancy and, later, in the production of maternal milk.

Over the fifth and sixth months, refinement of development and growth continue. Fingernails form, and the skin becomes thicker. Muscle control improves, and movements become more purposeful. The fetus startles at loud noises, stretches, and moves about. By the end of the sixth month, the baby weighs about 2 pounds and is roughly 14 inches long. Most infants born at this time or later survive.

The final 3 months are mainly taken up with weight and height gain. The baby's weight usually increases to around 7 pounds. Length increases from 14 to 19 inches. The baby is so large now that he or she assumes a single position, usually head down, awaiting the termination of the pregnancy. Total reliance on the mother's body for food and protection soon ends.

MATERNAL NUTRITION

During development, the fetus gets all its nutrition from the mother. Adequate supplies of carbohydrates, protein, fat, vitamins, minerals, and water are needed for growth and metabolic maintenance as well as for the differentiation of new organ systems. The fetus, like a parasite, absorbs the nutrition it needs from the mother.

The effect of maternal malnutrition on the fetus depends on when it occurs during pregnancy. Severe malnutrition very early in pregnancy is associated with an increased risk of miscarriage as well as an increased incidence of spina bifida, hydrocephalus, and prematurity (Brent, 1986). However, if the mother is malnourished later in pregnancy, the main effect on the fetus is low birth weight. One study of such malnutrition provides an illustration. In Holland, in 1944, the Dutch organized a transportation strike against the occupying German forces. This limited the shipment of food from the countryside to the cities. Starvation was rampant. Pregnant women were placed on rations that provided only half their nutritional requirements during the latter part of pregnancy. Yet, although their infants were small in size, they were otherwise well (Smith, 1947). The proportion of stillbirths, newborn deaths, and congenital malformations was no higher than usual. Twenty years later, follow-up studies showed the intellectual functioning of these children to be within normal limits (Stein & Susser, 1975). Thus, they were relatively resistant to the effects of maternal malnutrition. (This problem is discussed further in Chapter 11.)

MALFORMATIONS

Congenital malformations are defined as physical abnormalities of prenatal origin that are present at birth and that interfere with the child's normal development (Buyse, 1990; Vinken, Bruyn, Klawans, et al., 1987). Overall, they occur in approximately 3% of all births. These defects can result from genetic problems as well as from maternal infections, drugs, and other environmental **teratogens.** Approximately 25% of malformations can be attributed to genetic causes and 10% to environmental causes, but the remaining 65% are currently of unknown origin (Beckman & Brent, 1986).

Genetic Abnormalities

The two most common types of genetic problems are chromosomal abnormalities and single-gene defects, called *inborn errors.*

The defect in a chromosomal abnormality resides in an incomplete or incorrect message directing the development of the embryo. Chromosomal abnormalities are caused by three mechanisms: nondisjunction, deletion, and translocation (see Chapter 1). Approximately 1 in 500 newborns has such an abnormality. At least one disorder has been associated with each of the 23 pairs of chromosomes (Creasy, Crolla, & Alberman, 1976). Most of the affected children have mental retardation, are short in stature, and are unusual in appearance. Some have extra or lost fingers or toes; others have congenital heart defects.

Abnormalities resulting from single-gene defects can be equally devastating. As noted in Chapter 2, a mistake in decoding the DNA message of a single gene may lead to the production of a malfunctioning or defective enzyme and a resultant inborn error of metabolism. One example of this phenomenon is phenylketonuria (PKU). In this disorder, an enzyme necessary for the breakdown of the amino acid, phenylalanine, is not produced. Without this enzyme, phenylalanine accumulates and leads to mental retardation. Fortunately, PKU in children can now be treated effectively, and the children may have normal intellectual functioning (see Chapter 10). What was unanticipated is that normally intelligent women who were treated for PKU as children are now producing children with mental retardation. Although adults can tolerate high levels of phenylalanine, this substance is extremely toxic to the fetal brain. Preliminary results suggest that placing the woman with PKU back on a low phenylalanine diet prior to or early in pregnancy decreases the risk of mental retardation in her children (Levy, 1988).

Teratogens

A teratogen is any agent that causes a defect in the fetus. Teratogens include radiation, drugs, infections, and chronic illnesses (Brent & Beckman, 1990). The susceptibility of the fetus to a teratogen depends both on the degree and timing of the exposure. Genetic abnormalities may appear as early as the stage of the fertilized egg, manifesting themselves as malformations of the fetus or as deficient production of a specific enzyme. Exposure to environmental toxins in the first days after conception generally has an all or none effect; the embryo either dies or survives unaffected. The formation of the major body organs occurs between days 18 and 60 after conception so the fetus is at particular risk to develop malformations during this time. (An example is the effect of the drug thalidomide, discussed later in this chapter.) Environmental influences at a later date do not affect organ formation but rather the size of the fetus, producing microcephaly or a low birth weight infant.

The magnitude of the malformation is also affected by the amount of the teratogen the fetus encounters. The greater the dose, the more severe the anomaly; there is also a threshold effect below which a toxin may not be a teratogen (see the discussion of Radiation below). Finally, there is individual variation. Some fetuses will be more susceptible to teratogen-related malformations because of their individual genetic makeup (see the discussion of Anticonvulsants in this chapter).

Radiation   Radiation was the first agent shown to cause birth defects, initially in animals and later in survivors of Hiroshima and Nagasaki. Research studies found a direct relationship between the distance a pregnant woman was from the focal point of the atomic bomb explosion in Hiroshima and the amount of damage her child experienced. Women who survived the explosion and were within a half-mile of it had miscarriages. Women who were about 1¼ miles out had a very high incidence of children with microcephaly (Wood, Johnson, & Omori, 1967). Beyond 2 miles, the children were born healthy but were shown to have a high incidence of leukemia later in life (Miller, 1968).

Malformations also have been seen in fetuses of women receiving large doses of medical radiation. Dekaban (1968) reported on 22 infants exposed to an average of 250 **rads** of medical radiation between the third and 20th weeks of gestation. The mothers were being treated with radiation for tumors or diseases of the abdominal and pelvic regions. The fetuses exhibited one or more of the following abnormalities: growth retardation, mental retardation, microcephaly, eye malformations (e.g., small eyes, cataracts, retinal pigmentary abnormalities), genital malformations, and skeletal malformations.

The effect of radiation on the fetus depends not only on the amount but also on the time in gestation when exposure occurs. For the first weeks after conception, the embryo is insensitive to the teratogenic and growth-retarding effects of radiation, but is very sensitive to the lethal effects. This embryo would either die or be born healthy. During the second to third month of pregnancy the embryo is very sensitive to the growth-retarding, teratogenic, and lethal effects of irradiation. During the fourth to fifth months of pregnancy, the fetus has diminished sensitivity to the teratogenic effects but retains central nervous system sensitivity; microcephaly and eye abnormalities often occur in children exposed to radiation during those months.

Researchers are not certain how much radiation is safe for an expectant woman. However, exposure to less than 5 rads has not been observed to cause congenital malformations or growth retardation. Thus, these studies suggest that medically prescribed diagnostic X rays are safe for pregnant women and that there is no medical justification for terminating a pregnancy in women exposed to 5 rads or less. However, if another diagnostic study can provide the same information as X rays, it should be used. For example, the measurement of fetal size can and should be done using ultrasound rather than X rays.

Ultrasound and Microwave   Ultrasound and microwave energy forms have characteristics much different from X rays. They do not produce tissue **ionization** that is thought to underlie the hazards of radiation exposure. Ultrasound has been shown to be safe for the fetus (Beckman & Brent, 1986). Exposure to microwave ovens, radar, shortwave, radio waves, and emissions from computer screens also appears to be safe for the fetus (Moore, Jeng, Kaczmarek, et al., 1990).

Medication   Medications are another cause of fetal malformation. Although only a few medications are highly teratogenic, a larger number may carry some increased risk of malformation. Most teratogenic effects are noted at birth but, in a few instances, the problems appear only in later childhood. Because of the uncertainty over the effects of a number of medications, most doctors advise pregnant women to refrain, if possible, from taking any medication. Drugs about which teratogenic effects are known include thalidomide, anticonvulsants, anticancer drugs, sex hormones, acne medications, antibiotics, alcohol, drugs of abuse, and tobacco. The effects of alcohol and cocaine are discussed at length in Chapter 8.

Thalidomide   The use of thalidomide for nausea during the first trimester of pregnancy was a common practice in Europe in the late 1950s. The drug was never released in the United States because the Food and Drug Administration has stricter regulations about testing for teratogenic effects. However, after the drug was released in Europe, it apparently had few obvious side effects and it sold well to expectant mothers. A few years later, in 1961, a number of case reports appeared in the European literature about a previously rarely reported fetal malformation, **phocomelia.** Affected children had shortened or missing arms and legs. An **epidemiological** study revealed that all the women with affected children had received thalidomide during their first trimester (Taussig, 1962). In addition, a relationship existed between the day of ingestion of the drug and the type of malformation. Taken between 21–35 days after conception, thalidomide resulted in babies born with shortened or missing arms. When expectant mothers took thalidomide between 23–30 days gestation, the children had shortened or missing legs and arms. After the 35th day, no defects occurred (Figure 4.3). Apparently, thalidomide prevented the normal formation of arm and leg buds between days 21–35 (Newman, 1985). However, if the limb buds had already formed, no defects took place.

Anticonvulsants Most, if not all, drugs used to treat seizure disorders are now thought to be potential teratogens (Holmes, 1988). It had been known for some time that infants born to mothers with seizure disorders had a high incidence of cleft lip and palate (Barry & Danks, 1974). Initially, research focused on the seizures themselves being responsible for fetal malformations. Perhaps, researchers considered, the lack of oxygen or vigorous contractions during tonic-clonic seizures were the cause. However, subsequent research, focusing on the anticonvulsant phenytoin (Dilantin), found that about 10% of the children born to mothers receiving this medication had an unusual facial appearance, cleft lip and palate, congenital heart disease, microcephaly, and abnormalities of the nails and fingers. Children born to mothers with seizure disorders who were not receiving medication did not have these malformations (Van Dyke, Hodge, Heide, et al., 1988).

As studies of other anticonvulsants were performed, each of those drugs was shown to have teratogenic effects. Similar to phenytoin, carbamazepine (Tegretol) has been shown to cause **craniofacial** defects, fingernail abnormalities, and developmental delay in 10%–20% of children (Jones, Lacro, Johnson, & Adams, 1989).

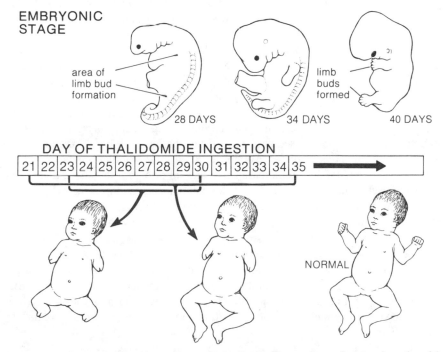

Figure 4.3.   Effects of thalidomide at various gestational ages. Phocomelia resulted from ingestion of the drug thalidomide between 21 and 35 days after conception. The extent of the malformation depended on when the ingestion occurred.

Diazepam (valium) and its derivatives have been associated with growth retardation and central nervous system abnormalities similar to fetal alcohol syndrome (Laegreid, Olegard, Conradi, et al., 1990). Phenobarbital and Primidone have been associated with fetal growth retardation and decreased head circumference (Daval, DeVasconcelos, & Lartaud, 1988). Trimethadione causes developmental delay and abnormalities of the face, ears, teeth, and cardiovascular system (Beckman & Brent, 1986). Finally, valproic acid (Depakene) has been associated with an increased incidence of spina bifida, craniofacial, and digital abnormalities (DiLiberti, Farndon, Dennis, et al., 1984; Jager-Roman, Deichl, Jakob, et al., 1986).

These malformations do not occur in all children born to women receiving anticonvulsants. Only about 10%–20% of children are affected, and the effects appear to be related to the dosages. Studies are being conducted to determine whether there are enzymes in the amniotic fluid that might indicate an increased risk in a particular pregnancy (Buehler, Delimont, Von Waes, et al., 1990). Furthermore, ultrasound studies of the fetus may reveal malformations, giving the prospective parents time to consider termination of the pregnancy if fetal malformations are evident.

Ideally, to avoid malformations, the ingestion of the antiepileptic medication is stopped before conception. This is possible in women who have been seizure-free for 2 years or more (see Chapter 26). Unfortunately, discontinuing the use of all anticonvulsants puts a woman at risk for seizures that may harm her or her fetus. For women who have frequent convulsions, the anticonvulsant dosage should be kept in the low therapeutic range, especially during the first trimester when the most harm to the fetus would occur.

Chemotherapeutic Agents Anticancer drugs are harmful to embryos for different reasons than are antiepileptic drugs. Since cancer cells grow more rapidly than normal cells, the function of anticancer drugs is to injure or kill these rapidly dividing cells within the tumor. However, in a pregnant woman, the most rapidly dividing cells are those within the developing embryo. As the anticancer drugs can cross the placenta, a high incidence of malformations and miscarriages takes place. In the case of methotrexate, a commonly used anticancer drug, there is a high risk of spina bifida and hydrocephalus (Jick, Holmes, Hunter, et al., 1981). Another anticancer agent, cyclophosphamide, carries an increased risk of fetal growth retardation, and digital and cardiovascular malformations. Other chemotherapeutic agents are also thought to lead to fetal malformations. As a result, therapeutic abortion is often suggested if anticancer therapy is needed during the first trimester of pregnancy.

Sex Hormones In the past, estrogen and progesterone (female sex hormones) were used to prevent miscarriages in mothers who had a history of recurrent miscarriages. A number of malformations followed. The use of progesterone led to enlarged sexual glands in male and female infants. Even more sinister was the effect of DES, an estrogen used primarily in the early 1950s. Many females born to women who took DES during their pregnancies developed vaginal tumors or cancer some 20 years later (Herbst, 1981).

Acne Medication Studies have found that isotretinoin (Accutane), a vitamin-A product used to treat severe acne, results in craniofacial malformations (Rosa, 1983).

Therefore, this medication should not be used either on the skin or orally during early pregnancy.

An antibiotic used to treat acne, called *tetracycline,* also can affect the fetus. Tetracycline leads to the staining of the teeth. Although both primary and permanent teeth do not emerge until much later, they are formed before birth. The defect results from the mixing of the tetracycline with calcium when the teeth are being formed. These stained teeth are at high risk for developing cavities because of defects in the **dentin.** Since many other safe antibiotics are available, pregnant women can easily avoid taking tetracycline.

Tobacco and Marijuana The main effect of smoking on the fetus seems to be low birth weight. A woman who smokes two packs a day, for example, will have an infant weighing about 1 pound less than that of a nonsmoker (Van den Eeden, Karagas, Daling, et al., 1990). No fetal malformations have been associated with smoking but there may be an increased risk of infant morbidity.

Marijuana's impact on the fetus appears to be similar to that of tobacco. It impairs fetal oxygenation by reducing blood flow to the placenta. This leads to decreased fetal growth. There is no evidence for fetal malformation (Van Dyke & Fox, 1990; Zuckerman, Frank, Hingson, et al., 1989).

Although the previously mentioned drugs have been linked to problems in prenatal development, a number of drugs, so far, appear to be harmless. These include aspirin (Slonc, Siskind, Heinonen, et al., 1976), penicillin, **acetaminophen** (Tylenol), and Benadryl, an **antihistamine** (Jick et al., 1981). Also, studies have not found an association between caffeine consumption and birth defects (Linn, Schoenbaum, Monson, et al., 1982).

Infections Besides drugs, intrauterine infections can lead to fetal malformations. Unfortunately, while the placenta acts as a barrier to some harmful substances, it does not prevent the passing of drugs or infectious organisms from the mother to the embryo. A group of infections called TORCH infections all cause similar malformations. These include **toxoplasmosis, syphilis, rubella, cytomegalovirus (CMV), and herpesvirus.**

Rubella, or German measles, illustrates this problem. Before 1969, when a vaccine was developed, rubella epidemics occurred about every 8 years. The disease itself was innocuous. The women would develop a salmon-colored rash and a low-grade fever, both of which went away in a few days. Serious complications in adults rarely followed. Unfortunately, the harm was relegated to the embryo (Table 4.1). Scores of infants were born with blindness, deafness, microcephaly, mental retardation, **cerebral palsy**, and congenital heart defects (Miller, Cradock-Watson, & Pollock, 1982). The virus could be grown from the infants' urine or body tissues for up to 2 years after birth. This placed susceptible women who were health care workers at risk for contracting rubella.

As with thalidomide, the time of the infection is crucial. If the rubella infection occurred within a month before conception, the mother has a 42% risk of having an

Table 4.1.   Pregnancy outcomes of mothers who had congenital rubella

	Age of infection	Percentage of affected infants
Preconception	0–28 days before conception	43
First trimester	0–12 weeks after conception	51
Second trimester	13–26 weeks after conception	23
Third trimester		0

Source: Miller, Cradock-Watson, and Pollock (1982); Sever, Hardy, Nelson, et al. (1969).

affected fetus. Between conception and 12 weeks, 52% of the fetuses developed a full-blown congenital rubella syndrome. Infection after 26 weeks usually resulted in a normal infant (Sever, Larsen, & Grossman, 1988).

Since the development of the rubella vaccine, very few new cases of congenital rubella have occurred. This vaccine is given to all children between ages 1 and 2 years; immunity lasts throughout life. Women who have not received the vaccine should be tested for immunity. If they are not immune, they should receive the rubella vaccine before they try to become pregnant. After they are vaccinated, women should avoid becoming pregnant for 2 months (Preblud, Stetler, Frank, et al., 1981).

If a woman is not immune and contracts rubella during the first trimester of her pregnancy, she may be able to have an affected fetus diagnosed by amniocentesis (Daffos, Forestier, Grangeot-Keros, et al., 1984). At 18–20 weeks of gestation, the amniotic fluid can be tested for the presence of IgM, an **immunoglobulin** that the fetus produces to fight the rubella virus. If this substance is present in the fluid, the fetus is presumed to have been infected. The mother could then decide whether to terminate her pregnancy. As long as this antibody is not present in the fluid, even if the mother has the virus, the fetus is probably unharmed. Overall, in the United States, fewer than 100 children are born with congenital rubella each year (Miller et al., 1982).

The story for the other TORCH infections is similar to that of rubella. In adults, cytomegaloviral infection might masquerade as a flu or **mononucleosis**-like illness. As many as 30%–60% of pregnant women have **antibodies** against this type of infection, indicating recent exposure. Between 2 and 20 per 1,000 live-born infants have sustained intrauterine infections from CMV, and 10% of these children have hearing loss or neurological deficits (Conboy, Pass, Stagno, et al., 1987; Stagno, Pass, Cloud, et al., 1986). This compares with 0.1–0.5 per 1,000 for herpes, 0.5–1.0 per 1,000 for toxoplasmosis, and 0.2–0.5 per 1,000 for nonepidemic rubella (Sever et al., 1988).

Because CMV infections are so widespread, they may represent a significant cause of microcephaly and mental retardation. When a CMV infection occurs late in pregnancy, the primary effect is on hearing; there is a 14% risk of hearing impairment

(Williamson, Percy, Yow, et al., 1990). Postnatal infections are not associated with any developmental disabilities (Conboy, Pass, Stagno, et al., 1986). The incidence of these infections among pregnant women is so high that scientists are now working to develope a vaccine that they hope will be as effective as the rubella vaccine.

Herpesvirus is the other known viral cause of malformation. Fortunately, the risk of *in utero* transmission of herpesvirus from a vaginal herpes infection is, as noted above, extremely low (Nahmias, Keyserling, & Kerrick, 1983). The clinical findings in newborn infants with congenital herpesvirus infection include growth delay, skin **vesicles** and scarring and retinal **lesions**, and microcephaly or brain atrophy. Although antiviral therapy is available and should be used on these neonates, there is no evidence that it improves their developmental outcome (Hutto, Arvin, Jacobs, Steele, et al., 1987).

Toxoplasmosis is another rare cause of birth defects. However, when it occurs, it carries with it considerable disability, including microcephaly or hydrocephalus, cataracts, blindness, deafness, and mental retardation (Sever, Ellenberg, Ley, et al., 1988). Forty percent of children born to infected mothers will be affected. Recently, a treatment has been developed for this bacteria-like organism. The antibiotic spiramycin has been demonstrated to improve outcome if given to the mother after the infection has been documented (Hohlfeld, Daffos, Thulliez, et al., 1989). Damage can be assessed by performing an ultrasound test to detect calcified areas in the brain, resulting from the infection (Sever et al., 1988). Cerebral calcifications can be seen in other TORCH diseases as well. Knowing whether this severe brain damage has occurred may be helpful in the mother's decision to continue the pregnancy.

In addition to the TORCH infections, the virus **varicella,** which causes chickenpox, has also been associated with fetal malformations. Although chickenpox is common and extremely contagious, the abnormalities it causes are both less severe and less common. The fetus may have limb, facial, skeletal, or neurological abnormalities (Alkalay, Pomerance, & Romoin, 1987; Paryani & Arvin, 1986).

Other congenital infections result in an increased risk of miscarriage but have not been shown to result in fetal malformations. These include **parvovirus, entero-virus, influenza,** mononucleosis, and **malaria.**

Chronic Illness The most common chronic maternal illnesses associated with an increased risk of birth defects are diabetes and thyroid disease. Fetuses of insulin-dependent, diabetic mothers have a 10% risk of malformations of the spine, cardiovascular system, and legs (Becerra, Khoury, Cordero, et al., 1990). However, one recent study has shown that effective control of diabetes from before conception can reduce the risk of malformation to 1% (Kitzmiller, Gavin, Gin, et al., 1991).

Thyroid disease itself does not injure the fetus, but its treatment may. Women who have **hyperthyroidism,** caused by Graves disease, are often treated with radioactive iodine, and those with **hypothyroidism,** caused by endemic **goiter,** will receive iodine supplements. Iodine crosses the placenta and can interfere with normal thyroid gland formation in the fetus. The fetus would then be born with hypothyroidism. If this is not detected early, **cretinism,** with growth delay and mental retardation, will result (Becks & Burrow, 1991). Treatment of an affected infant involves supplements of the thyroid hormone.

DEFORMATIONS

So far, this chapter has focused on malformations or birth defects that occur during the first trimester of pregnancy. Deformations, however, refer to fetal abnormalities produced by uterine constraints during the third trimester. Unlike malformations, deformations are often reversible and are not usually genetically inherited.

A number of deformities result from the fetus simply not having enough room to move in the amniotic sac. For example, if the fetus does not have normal kidney function, very little amniotic fluid (most of which is composed of fetal urine) will be produced. Without the buffering effect of the amniotic fluid, deformities of the chest wall or long bones can take place (Figure 4.4).

With **twinning,** crowding is more likely, and deformities are common. The human uterus was intended to carry one fetus. It may not be able to expand to the point of allowing free movement and kicking of two fetuses. The consequence might be a twisted or deformed foot (club foot) or a misshapen head that has been caught in one position.

Certain deformities such as bowed legs will correct themselves when the child learns to walk. Orthopedic surgery or the placing of a cast can correct other bony deformities. Thus, deformities are isolated defects usually unassociated with developmental disabilities.

SUMMARY

A multitude of malformations and deformations exist that can create longstanding problems for a child. Of these, deformations are easier to correct. Treatment of malformations is rather limited, and prevention seems to be the key.

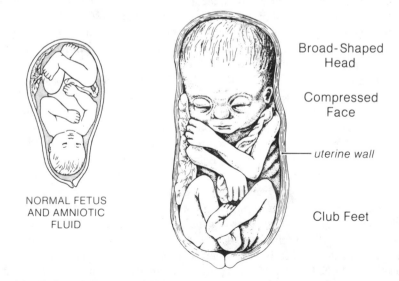

Figure 4.4.   Deformations. During the third trimester, insufficient amniotic fluid or a lack of fetal movement caused by inadequate room within the uterus may lead to bony deformities, including club foot.

The best protection against the teratogenic effects of drugs and radiation is the limitation or avoidance of all but essential medications, absence of substance abuse, abstinence from alcohol and smoking, and the avoidance of excessive radiation exposure especially during the early months of pregnancy.

To prevent congenital rubella infection, women may be tested for past rubella infection by checking their antibody level. If unprotected, nonpregnant women can be vaccinated to immunize themselves against a future rubella infection.

Even though treatment is limited for many of these conditions, it is important to realize that 20 years ago most of the reasons for these birth defects were unknown, and prenatal diagnosis was unavailable.

REFERENCES

Alkalay, A.L., Pomerance, J.J., & Romoin, D.L. (1987). Fetal varicella syndrome. *Journal of Pediatrics, 111,* 320–323.

Barry, J.E., & Danks, D.M. (1974). Anticonvulsants and congenital abnormalities. (Letter). *Lancet, 2,* 48–49.

Becerra, J.E., Khoury, M.J., Cordero, J.F., et al. (1990). Diabetes mellitus during pregnancy and the risks for specific birth defects: A population-based case-control study. *Pediatrics, 85,* 1–9.

Beckman, A.A., & Brent, R.L. (1986). Mechanism of known environmental teratogens: Drugs and chemicals. *Clinics in Perinatology, 13,* 649–687.

Becks, G.P., & Burrow, G.N. (1991). Thyroid disease and pregnancy. *Medical Clinics of North America, 75,* 121–150.

Brent, R.L. (1986). Evaluating the alleged teratogenicity of environmental agents. *Clinics in Perinatology, 13,* 609–613.

Brent, R.L., & Beckman, D.A. (1990). Environmental teratogens. *Bulletin of the New York Academy of Medicine, 66,* 123–163.

Buehler, B.A., Delimont, D., Van Waes, M., et al. (1990). Prenatal prediction of risk of the fetal hydration syndrome. *New England Journal of Medicine, 322,* 1567–1572.

Buyse, M.L. (1990). *Birth defects encyclopedia.* Dover, MA: Center for Birth Defects Information Services.

Conboy, T.J., Pass, R.F., Stagno, S., et al. (1986). Intellectual development in school-aged children with asymptomatic congenital cytomegalovirus infection. *Pediatrics, 77,* 801–806.

Conboy, T.J., Pass, R.F., Stagno, S., et al. (1987). Early clinical manifestations and intellectual outcome in children with symptomatic congenital CMV infection. *Journal of Pediatrics, 111,* 343–348.

Creasy, M.R., Crolla, J.A., & Alberman, E.D. (1976). A cytogenetic study of human spontaneous abortions using banding techniques. *Human Genetics, 31,* 177–196.

Daffos, F., Forestier, F., Grangeot-Keros, L., et al. (1984). Prenatal diagnosis of congenital rubella. *Lancet, 2,* 1–4.

Daval, J.L., DeVasconcelos, A.P., & Lartaud, I. (1988). Morphological and neurochemical effects of diazepam and phenobarbital on selective culture of neurons from fetal rat brain. *Journal of Neurochemistry, 50,* 665–672.

Dekaban, A.S. (1968). Abnormalities in children exposed to x-radiation during various stages of gestation: Tentative timetable of radiation injury to the human fetus. *Journal of Nuclear Medicine, 9,* 471–477.

DiLiberti, J.H., Farndon, P.A., Dennis, N.R., et al. (1984). The fetal valproate syndrome. *American Journal of Medical Genetics, 19,* 473–481.

Herbst, A.L. (1981). Clear cell adenocarcinoma and the current status of DES-exposed females. *Cancer, 48,* 484–488.

Hohlfeld, P., Daffos, F., Thulliez, P., et al. (1989). Fetal toxoplasmosis: Outcome of pregnancy and infant follow-up after *in utero* treatment. *Journal of Pediatrics, 115*, 765–769.

Holmes, L.B. (1988). Teratogenic effects of anticonvulsant drugs. *Journal of Pediatrics, 112*, 576–581.

Hutto, C., Arvin, A., Jacobs, R., Steele, R., et al. (1987). Intrauterine herpes simplex virus infections. *Journal of Pediatrics, 110*, 97–101.

Jager-Roman E., Deichl, A., Jakob, S., et al. (1986). Fetal growth, major malformations and minor anomalies in infants born to women receiving valproic acid. *Journal of Pediatrics, 108*, 997–1004.

Jick, H., Holmes, L.B., Hunter, J.R., et al. (1981). First-trimester drug use and congenital disorders. *Journal of the American Medical Association, 246*, 343–346.

Jones, K.L., Lacro, R.V., Johnson, K.A., & Adams, J. (1989). Pattern of malformations in the children of women treated with carbamazepine during pregnancy. *New England Journal of Medicine, 320*, 1661–1666.

Kitzmiller, J.L., Gavin, L.A., Gin, G.D., et al. (1991). Preconception care of diabetes. Glycemic control prevents congenital anomalies. *Journal of the American Medical Association, 265*, 731–736.

Laegreid, L., Olegard, R., Conradi, N., et al. (1990). Congenital malformations and maternal consumption of benzodiazepines: A case control study. *Developmental Medicine and Child Neurology, 32*, 432–441.

Levy, H.L. (1988). Maternal phenylketonuria. *Progress in Clinical and Biological Research, 281*, 227–242.

Linn, S., Schoenbaum, S.C., Monson, R.R., et al. (1982). No association between coffee consumption and adverse outcomes of pregnancy. *New England Journal of Medicine, 306*, 141–145.

Miller, E., Cradock-Watson, J.E., & Pollock, T.M. (1982). Consequences of confirmed maternal rubella at successive stages of pregnancy. *Lancet, 2*, 781–784.

Miller, R.W. (1968). Effects of ionizing radiation from the atomic bomb on Japanese children. *Pediatrics, 41*, 257–270.

Moore, R.M., Jr., Jeng, L.L., Kaczmarek, R.G., et al. (1990). Use of diagnostic ultrasound, x-ray examination, and electronic fetal monitoring in perinatal medicine. *Journal of Perinatology, 10*, 361–365.

Myrianthopoulos, N.C. (1985). *Malformations in children from 1 to 7 years.* New York: Liss.

Nahmias, A.J., Keyserling, H.L., & Kerrick, G.M. (1983). Neonatal herpes simplex virus infection. In J.S. Remington & J.O. Klein, (Eds.), *Diseases of the fetus and newborn infant* (pp. 636–678). Philadelphia: W.B. Saunders.

Newman C.G. (1985). Teratogen update: Clinical aspects of thalidomide embryopathy—A continuing preoccupation. *Teratology, 32*, 133–44.

Oppenheimer, S. B., & Lefevre, G., Jr. (1989). *Introduction to embryonic development* (3rd ed.). Newton, MA: Allyn & Bacon.

Paryani, S.G., & Arvin, A.M. (1986). Intrauterine infection with varicella—zoster virus after maternal varicella. *New England Journal of Medicine, 314*, 1542–1542.

Preblud, S.R., Stetler, H.C., Frank, J.A., Jr., et al. (1981). Fetal risk associated with rubella vaccine. *Journal of the American Medical Association, 246*, 1413–1417.

Rosa, F.W. (1983). Teratogenicity of isotretinoin. *Lancet, 2*, 513.

Sever, J.L., Ellenberg, J.H., Ley, A.C., et al. (1988). Toxoplasmosis: Maternal and pediatric findings in 23,000 pregnancies. *Pediatrics, 82*, 181–192.

Sever, J.L., Hardy, J.B., Nelson, K.B., et al. (1969). Rubella in the collaborative perinatal research study. *American Journal of Diseases of Children, 118*, 123–132.

Sever, J.L., Larsen, J.W., Jr., & Grossman, J.H., III. (1988). *Handbook of perinatal infections* (2nd ed.). Boston: Little, Brown.

Slone, D., Siskind, V., Heinonen, O.P., et al. (1976). Aspirin and congenital malformations. *Lancet, 1*, 1373–1375.

Smith, C.A. (1947). Effects of maternal undernutrition upon the newborn infant in Holland (1944–1945). *Journal of Pediatrics, 30*, 229–243.

Stagno, S., Pass, R.F., Cloud, G., et al. (1986). Primary cytomegalovirus infection in pregnancy: Incidence, transmission to fetus and clinical outcome. *Journal of the American Medical Association, 256*, 1904–1908.

Stein, Z., & Susser, M. (1975). The Dutch famine, 1944–1945, and the reproductive process. I. Effects or six indices at birth. *Pediatric Research, 9*, 70–76.

Strandskov, H.H. (1945). Plural birth frequencies in the total, the "white," and "colored" U.S. population. *American Journal of Physical Anthropology, 3*, 49–57.

Taussig, H.B. (1962). Thalidomide—A lesson in remote effects of drugs. *American Journal of Diseases of Children, 104*, 111–113.

Van den Eeden, S.K., Karagas, M.R., Daling, J.R., et al. (1990). A case-control study of maternal smoking and congenital malformations. *Paediatric and Perinatal Epidemiology, 4*, 147–155.

Van Dyke, D.C., & Fox, A.A. (1990). Fetal drug exposure and its possible implications for learning in the preschool and school-age population. *Journal of Learning Disabilities, 23*, 160–163.

Van Dyke, D.C., Hodge, S.E., Heide, F., et al. (1988). Family studies in fetal phenytoin exposure. *Journal of Pediatrics, 113*, 301–306.

Vinken, P.J., Bruyn, G.W., & Klawans, H.C. (Eds.). (1987). *Malformations*. New York: Elsevier Science Publishing Co.

Williamson, W.D., Percy, A.K., Yow, M.D., et al. (1990). Asymptomatic congenital cytomegalovirus infection. Audiologic, neuroradiologic, and neurodevelopmental abnormalities during the first year. *American Journal of Diseases of Children, 144*, 1365–1368.

Wood, J.W., Johnson, K.G., & Omori, Y. (1967). *In utero* exposure to the Hiroshima atomic bomb. An evaluation of head size and mental retardation: Twenty years later. *Pediatrics, 39*, 385–392.

Zuckerman, B., Frank, D.A., Hingson, R., et al. (1989). Effects of maternal marijuana and cocaine use on fetal growth. *New England Journal of Medicine, 320*, 762–768.

Chapter 5

Having a Baby
The Birth Process

Upon completion of this chapter, the reader will:
—be able to identify and characterize the maternal factors that cause problems during the later stages of pregnancy
—know the stages of labor
—be aware of the infant factors that cause problems during labor and delivery
—know the antenatal fetal monitoring measures used in high-risk pregnancies

---

Approximately 266 days after conception, a complex series of events leads to the birth of an infant. By an as yet unidentified mechanism, the mother's immune system tolerates the fetus and allows it to remain inside her and grow. Then, when it is time for the child to be born, another directive tells the mother's body to reject the fetus, and labor begins.

Whatever triggers the process, about 85% of women deliver within 7 days on either side of their due date (called the **estimated date of confinement [EDC]**). This date is calculated by counting back 3 months from the first day of the last menstrual period and adding 7 days. For example, a pregnant woman whose last period began on March 8 would be due around December 15. About this date, she would begin the early stages of labor.

LABOR

The first stage of labor starts with fairly mild contractions, which may be confused with the **Braxton-Hicks** contractions that occur throughout pregnancy. Within hours, however, the contractions become stronger, last longer, and are more frequent. This prolonged stage, often lasting from 12 to 30 hours, allows time for the baby's head to get molded into position for delivery.

To understand this better, it is important to go back a bit in fetal development. By the sixth month, in about 90% of the cases, the baby has settled head first into the mother's pelvis. It is unlikely the baby will shift further. This is called the **vertex**

presentation. At this time, the mother's bony pelvic girdle is closed, making it difficult for the fetus to proceed further down the birth canal. The extended period of time during the first stage of labor allows for the gradual molding of the baby's head to fit the birth canal, the spreading of the pelvic bones, and the opening of the cervix.

During the second stage, the baby's head pushes through the birth canal and appears at the vaginal opening. The cervix becomes fully dilated during this stage, which usually lasts about an hour.

The third stage, lasting about 10–15 minutes, ends with the complete expulsion, or birth, of the newborn (Cunningham, McDonald, & Grant, 1989). The infant's nose and mouth are immediately suctioned and, in 9 out of 10 cases, the mother is presented with a ruddy-cheeked, screaming, healthy baby. But what of the remaining 10%?

HIGH-RISK PREGNANCIES

Problems occurring with either the mother or the infant can affect the late stages of pregnancy as well as labor and delivery. Perinatal mortality and morbidity are attributable in two-thirds of the cases to problems in late pregnancy and in one-third of the cases to problems with labor and delivery (Table 5.1).

Maternal Factors

Women who are socially disadvantaged, abuse drugs, or have chronic illnesses are more likely to have high-risk pregnancies. Also at increased risk are teenagers and women over 35. The reasons for the increased risk to the fetus vary. Disadvantaged, teenage, and substance-abusing women may have received little prenatal care and their nutrition may have been inadequate during pregnancy. The combination of these factors increase the mother's chances of going into premature labor and of producing an infant who is small for gestational age (Zuckerman, Walker, Frank, et al., 1984). Teenage mothers and mothers over 35 years of age also have a greater likelihood of developing **toxemia** and of having placental insufficiency (Hansen, 1986).

During the third trimester, acute illness predisposes the mother and fetus to infection and resultant premature delivery. Infants of women with chronic illnesses, such as diabetes, hypertension, heart disease, and thyroid disease, have an increased likelihood of premature birth and intrauterine growth retardation. Finally, women

Table 5.1.   Number of perinatal deaths per 1,000 births in the United States by cause

Cause	Death rate
Congenital anomalies	2.0
Infections	0.2
Intrauterine hypoxia	0.2
Birth trauma	0.06
Other identifiable perinatal conditions	1.6

Source: Wegman (1990).

with obstetrical complications, such as an incompetent cervix, uterine fibroids, or a previous **placenta previa,** tend to have troubles during the later stages of pregnancy or during labor and delivery. Discussions of each of these factors follow:

Chronic Maternal Illness Probably the most worrisome chronic illness is diabetes. Uncontrolled diabetes leads to a high incidence of **preeclampsia** and prematurity. Furthermore, assessment of gestational age can be difficult because the fetuses of mothers with diabetes tend to be large for dates. This occurs because the fetal pancreas has overproduced insulin to supply both the mother and the infant during pregnancy. This excessive insulin secretion is also associated with a high incidence of **hypoglycemia** or a low blood sugar level, in the first week of life. If untreated, hypoglycemia can lead to brain damage. Recently, it has been shown that scrupulous control of the mother's glucose level during pregnancy markedly decreases the risks of prematurity, hypoglycemia, and malformations (Centers for Disease Control, 1990).

Acute Maternal Illness Chapter 4 described some of the effects of maternal infections on the developing embryo. At the time of labor and delivery, a maternal infection presents different problems. Bacterial or viral infections can no longer cause malformations, but they can be transmitted from the mother to the relatively immune-deficient newborn, sometimes with fatal results.

An example of this is the herpesvirus infection of the vagina (Baker, 1990; Landy & Grossman, 1989). Vaginal herpes is characterized by blisters and oozing lesions in the vagina. Although not all infants born vaginally to mothers with herpes are infected, many are. Obstetricians deliver babies of mothers with vaginal herpes by cesarean section so the babies are less likely to contract the virus. If herpes does develop, the child usually cannot fight it, and the virus spreads throughout the body. A disseminated herpes infection causes death in about 60% of affected infants (Kibrick, 1980). Of the survivors, half will have significant neurological defects. The use of the antiviral drug, Acyclovir, has improved the prognosis to some degree.

Maternally derived AIDS has a more insidious effect. It results in death during early childhood (Braddick, Kreiss, Embree, et al., 1990; Hutto, Parks, Lai, et al., 1991). AIDS is discussed in Chapter 8. While viral infections are usually contracted during delivery, bacterial infections more commonly develop shortly after birth and are discussed in Chapter 6.

Substance Abuse Illicit drug use is associated with a high incidence of infectious diseases that also affect the fetus, including hepatitis, AIDS, and other sexually transmitted diseases. In addition, women with these diseases tend to have inadequate prenatal care, which places their fetuses at further risk. The drugs most commonly abused are alcohol, heroin, and crack cocaine; many women use more than one drug, each having its own pattern of adverse consequences for the fetus.

As noted in Chapter 8, infants with fetal alcohol syndrome may experience intrauterine growth retardation, microcephaly, and multiple malformations. Affected fetuses are at high risk for premature delivery and perinatal complications. Heroin is not associated with fetal malformations, but the fetus may experience withdrawal symptoms if the drug is withheld from a dependent mother. These symptoms include irritability, tremulousness, and feeding and sleep disturbances. The infants also stand a risk of intrauterine growth retardation. The principal effect of cocaine use is constriction of blood vessels and decreased uterine and placental blood flow, resulting in an increased incidence of spontaneous abortions, prematurity, **abruptio placenta,** intrauterine growth retardation, and fetal distress in delivery (Rosenak, Diamant, Yaffe, et al., 1990).

Preeclampsia and Pregnancy-Induced Hypertension Pregnant women often experience high blood pressure, or hypertension, after 20 weeks gestation. When hypertension is combined with **edema** (i.e., the accumulation of fluid in tissue), and/or protein in the urine, it is called *toxemia of pregnancy* or *preeclampsia*. This syndrome is experienced more often by teenage and older women, about 10% of whom are affected. Bedrest is often helpful in stabilizing the blood pressure, but the problem will not resolve until after delivery. Thus, careful surveillance of the mother and fetus is essential. If symptoms worsen, the physician may induce labor or perform a cesarean section. Preeclampsia carries a significant risk of prematurity and intrauterine growth retardation (Gilstrap, 1990).

Symptoms of severe preeclampsia are headache, decreased urinary output, visual disturbances, abdominal pain, markedly elevated blood pressure, and liver dysfunction. Severe preeclampsia progresses to eclampsia with the development of **tonic-clonic** seizures. The treatment of eclampsia is rapid delivery of the baby either by induction of labor or by cesarean section. The seizures are treated with magnesium sulfate. Fortunately, eclampsia is rare, though when it occurs it is life-threatening to both mother and child (Hernandez & Cunningham, 1990). However, once the child is delivered, the symptoms abate.

Uteroplacental Insufficiency Intrauterine growth retardation is associated with a number of conditions, including substance abuse, chronic maternal illness, and preeclampsia. Each relates to uteroplacental insufficiency, the inadequate exchange of nutritive and/or respiratory products from the mother to the fetus. This problem does not develop overnight, but worsens gradually throughout the second and third trimesters. It results in a fetus that is small in size for gestational age. These babies are more likely to be born prematurely, have developmental disabilities, or be stillborn. Detection relies on the antenatal fetal monitoring techniques discussed later in the chapter. The treatment often entails early delivery.

Placenta Previa and Abruptio Placenta Normally, the placenta is attached about two-thirds of the way to the top of the uterus. In placenta previa, the placenta is implanted low in the uterus and lies over the cervical opening (Figure 5.1). The more extensive the overlay, the greater is the risk of bleeding as the cervix opens in late pregnancy. If the amount of bleeding is extensive, it may imperil fetal circulation (Lavery, 1990).

While the incidence of placenta previa is low, occurring in 1 in 200 pregnancies, the fetal mortality rate is high, 15% (Naeye & Tafari, 1983). Placenta previa is more common in women over 35 and in women who have had multiple previous pregnancies or cesarean sections. Women who have had a placenta previa once have about a 6% chance of recurrence during subsequent pregnancies. The cause of placenta pre-

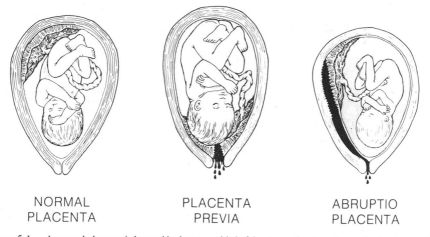

NORMAL PLACENTA   PLACENTA PREVIA   ABRUPTIO PLACENTA

Figure 5.1.   A normal placenta is located in the upper third of the uterus. In placenta previa, the placenta is abnormally placed so that it lies over the cervical opening. During labor, as the cervix dilates, the placenta tears and bleeding occurs. In abruptio, a normally placed placenta becomes partially separated from the uterine wall in the second or third trimester, and bleeding results.

via is unclear. It has been hypothesized that placenta previa develops as a result of defective uterine blood supply due to uterine inflammation or **atrophy.** Under these conditions, the placenta must branch out to get adequate nutrition and thus may extend its "roots" over the cervical opening.

Women with placenta previa are advised to get plenty of bedrest so that they can carry the fetus as long as possible. A cesarean section is frequently performed when it is determined the fetus is mature enough to survive outside the uterus. If the baby were born vaginally, the opening of the cervix during labor might burst the overlying blood vessels and lead to severe blood loss.

While placenta previa is a condition involving the abnormal placement of the placenta in the uterus, abruptio placenta involves the precipitous detachment of a normally placed placenta (see Figure 5.1). This happens during the second or third trimester. Abruptio placenta occurs in about 1 in 100 pregnancies, and the fetal mortality rate is close to 30% (Lowe & Cunningham, 1990). This condition is commonly associated with hypertension, a short umbilical cord, and physical **trauma,** such as a car accident. Unlike placenta previa, maternal age does not seem to be a factor, although multiple previous pregnancies do increase the risk.

Symptoms of an abruption include abdominal pain, profuse vaginal bleeding, decreased fetal heart sounds, and a tightly contracted uterus. If there is fetal distress, the baby will die unless removed immediately by cesarean section. The mother also may go into shock due to a loss of blood.

Premature Rupture of Membranes   If the amniotic membrane ruptures before term, it is called *premature rupture of membranes.* This can have a number of adverse consequences for the mother and child. First, it can precipitate preterm labor and delivery. Second, it may lead to infection, requiring early delivery. Finally, if delivery is delayed by weeks following the rupture, fetal deformities may result from the loss of amniotic fluid that normally buffers the fetus (Veille, 1988).

If premature delivery is unavoidable, the obstetrician may administer a steroid medication to the mother in an attempt to increase fetal lung maturity and decrease the risk of respiratory distress syndrome. However, this approach remains very controversial. If the mother becomes feverish, the baby will need to be delivered rapidly, and both mother and child will require intravenous antibiotics to treat the infection, which is called **chorioamnionitis** (Nordenvall & Sandstedt, 1990).

Dystocia   Besides the problems of infection, toxemia, and placental placement, structural abnormalities of the uterus or pelvis, called **dystocia,** may cause prolonged labor with detrimental effects on the fetus (Stewart, Dulber, Arnill, et al., 1990).

The most common bony abnormality is *cephalopelvic disproportion* (CPD), meaning the maternal pelvis is too small to allow passage of the baby's head. This leads to labor that does not progress normally and places the infant at risk for **sepsis** and intracranial hemorrhage. By measuring the pelvic region in relation to the size and position of the baby, the obstetrician is usually able to determine if CPD exists. If in doubt, an obstetrician may permit a short "trial of labor" before deciding to proceed with a vaginal delivery or a cesarean section. The use of forceps during deliveries is now less frequent than in the past.

While CPD will interfere with the normal passage of the child through the birth canal, an *incompetent cervix* will have the opposite effect, causing the uterus to dilate in the second trimester resulting in premature delivery or miscarriage (Willson, Carrington, & Ledger, 1987). To allow the woman to carry her child to term, an incompetent cervix may be closed temporarily with an operation called **cervical cerclage** (Cardwell, 1988).

Uterine Dysfunction   Even if the pelvis is wide enough to accommodate the baby's head, the progression of labor to its successful conclusion relies on the normal frequency and intensity of uterine contractions. If the uterus contracts too forcefully, it can have at least three consequences: it can interfere with fetal circulation, leading to **hypoxic** brain damage, it can result in a precipitous delivery with the risk of intracranial hemorrhage, or it can lead to an abruptio placenta. Conversely, if contractions are too weak or infrequent, labor will not progress. Thus, in high-risk pregnancies the strength and frequency of uterine contractions are closely monitored. This is particularly true in twinning, breech presentations, and women with fibroid tumors of the uterus. If abnormalities are found, medication may be used to either increase or decrease the strength of contractions. If the problem persists, a cesarean section will be performed.

During active labor, uterine contractions are considered weak if they do not result in progressive cervical dilation during a given 2-hour period or if there are fewer than three 45-second contractions per 10 minutes. Treatment for weak or infrequent contractions involves the use of an intravenous drip of *oxytocin* (Blakemore & Petrie, 1988). This medication increases contraction of the smooth muscles of the uterine wall. It is quite safe for both mother and child and is in common use. During oxytocin therapy, fetal heart rate is closely monitored. If there is significant slowing, it suggests that fetal circulation and oxygenation are being compromised and a cesarean section is necessary. If the heart rate is stable and labor progresses, a vaginal delivery is usually possible.

The use of medication to decrease excessively forceful contractions or to abort preterm labor is more controversial. The use of so-called **tocolytic agents** (most commonly terbutaline [Brethine] and ritodrine [Yutopar]) is primarily to stop labor occurring before 35 weeks (Besinger & Niebyl, 1990). Some studies support their use and others call into question their value. Thus, obstetricians will have different practices in this regard.

Infant Factors

The most common infant factors adversely affecting the late stages of pregnancy, labor, and delivery are breech presentation, birth defects, prematurity and postmaturity, multiple pregnancies, and prolapsed umbilical cord.

Breech Delivery In a breech delivery, the baby is born backside first instead of head first. Only 3% of children present in this manner (Creasy & Resnik, 1989). Breech presentation is most often related to prematurity, abnormal placement of the placenta, or weakness and decreased movement of the fetus. The problem with breech presentation is that the baby's head is the widest part of the body. When a baby is delivered head first, or in the vertex position, the head is gradually molded during labor to fit the narrow pelvic opening. In a breech birth, the backside comes through without difficulty, but the baby's head may get stuck. A prolonged labor with decreased oxygen supply may result (Croughan-Minihane, Petitti, Gordis, et al., 1990). As a result, most breech babies are delivered by cesarean section (Gimovsky & Petrie, 1989).

Birth Defects Certain intrinsic abnormalities in the fetus may lead to problems with labor and delivery. For example, an infant who has **osteogenesis imperfecta,** a birth defect causing brittle bones, may sustain multiple fractures or even die of a skull fracture during the birth process. Another example is the child with congenital hydrocephalus where the enlarged head may make vaginal delivery difficult or impossible.

A number of other defects can lead to the death of an infant, even without an abnormal labor. Five percent of stillborn infants have been found to have a major chromosomal abnormality (Valdes-Dapena & Arey, 1970). These infants may have malformations of the heart, lungs, and brain that are incompatible with survival.

Prematurity and Postmaturity Prematurity carries with it the risk of a precipitous and breech delivery, while postmature deliveries (i.e., after 44 weeks gestation) increase the risk of impaired placental blood and oxygen supply to the baby (Clark, 1989). In prematurity, the labor may be stopped by using tocolytic agents. Both premature and postmature fetuses are usually delivered by cesarean section. (Prematurity is discussed in more detail in Chapter 7.)

Multiple Pregnancies Human beings, as is true of other two-breasted mammals, are designed to produce a single offspring from a pregnancy. When a woman is carrying more than one fetus, the uterine space is crowded, and problems often develop.

Twins account for about 1% of all births. The major complications associated with twins are prematurity, toxemia, and difficult deliveries (Jones, Sbarra, & Cetrula, 1990). About 25% of the time, the second twin is lying in a breech position at the time of delivery (Cunningham et al., 1989) (Figure 5.2). The first twin generally gets out rapidly and without incident. The second twin, however, must wait a turn and then come out backward without proper molding of the head. This increases the risk of a brain injury to about three times normal. In order to avoid this problem, the obstetrician may attempt to turn the second twin so that it is vertex, or a cesarean section may be performed.

Prolapsed Umbilical Cord Besides the already-mentioned problems associated with multiple pregnancies, the likelihood of a prolapsed umbilical cord is also higher in twins and breech presentations than in single pregnancies and vertex presentations. A prolapse happens when the umbilical cord is below the fetus and precedes the fetus down the birth canal. This can result in a blockage of the flow of blood through the cord to the child and may lead to brain damage. Prolapsed cord is considered to be a surgical emergency and requires an immediate cesarean section.

ANTENATAL FETAL ASSESSMENT

As described in this chapter, the process of late pregnancy, labor, and delivery seems extremely risky and unpredictable. However, it is important to remember that this chapter has concentrated on 10% of the deliveries; the remaining 90% proceed

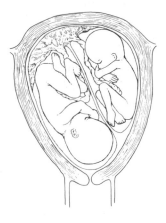

TWIN
PREGNANCY

Figure 5.2.   Twin pregnancy. The second twin to be born is often smaller than the first and is in a breech position.

smoothly. Furthermore, a number of antenatal monitoring measures now exist that have significantly reduced the risk of stillbirth and perinatal brain injury in high-risk pregnancies. These procedures that determine fetal well-being include ultrasound, fetal movement monitoring, biophysical profile, stress tests, doppler blood flow measures, fetal scalp monitoring, and amniocentesis. Multiple tests are often used as no single one gives a comprehensive view of fetal function.

Apart from the mother's recording of fetal activity, monitoring procedures are not part of normal prenatal care. They are used for high-risk pregnancies including postmaturity, hypertension, diabetes, intrauterine growth retardation, and previous stillbirths. These procedures are only useful after 26 weeks gestation, the point of fetal viability, because their purpose is to identify a fetus who would benefit from being delivered early.

A significant risk of incorrect results accompanies these tests, so many unnecessary cesarean sections may have been performed as a consequence of fetal monitoring. Yet, most fetuses with uteroplacental compromise should be identifiable by these measures, and many children have been well-born rather than stillborn or brain damaged as a consequence of antenatal monitoring.

Ultrasound

Ultrasound has taken the place of X rays in monitoring fetal development, both because the sound waves do not appear to be hazardous to the infant and the images obtained are more precise (Treacy, Smith, & Rayburn, 1990). Ultrasound may be used, for example, to visualize two skulls in a twin pregnancy (Figure 5.3). Ultrasound is also used to identify the amount of amniotic fluid, placental placement, fetal head size, growth, movement, and breathing, and to diagnose congenital anomalies.

Monitoring Fetal Movements

Movement is a marker for the well-being of a fetus. Fetal movement patterns change over time. Limb movements can be detected by ultrasound as early as the seventh week of gestation, and by the tenth week, fetal movements have assumed specific patterns often described as twitching, swimming, and jumping. As the fetus matures, the movements become more complex and coordinated. By 16 weeks, they are perceived by the mother, and at 20 weeks, the movements become forceful, frequent, and easily recognizable (Rayburn, 1990). From that point, pregnant women can discern between one-third and two-thirds of gross fetal movements.

Fetal movements vary with the time of day, especially in the third trimester. There are few movements in the morning and many in the evening, especially between 9 P.M.–1 A.M. Drugs have varying effects on fetal activity. The nicotine from smoking reduces fetal movements, but caffeine from coffee does not seem to have an effect. Sedatives, narcotics, and certain other drugs can decrease fetal activity. Malformed fetuses usually have normal fetal activity and twins tend to have twice the normal activity. Maternal illness can also affect fetal movements.

Fetal movements can be monitored subjectively by the mother or objectively using real-time ultrasound. One maternal scoring system involves counting to 10 movements. Fetal inactivity is defined as fewer than 10 movements per hour for 2

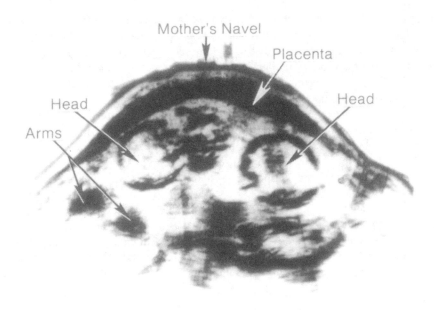

Figure 5.3.   Ultrasound of a pregnant woman carrying twins. This is a cross-section view through the maternal abdomen. The two fetal heads and the placenta lie just under the uterine wall. Fetal arms are also defined. (Courtesy of Dr. Roger Sanders, The Johns Hopkins Hospital, Baltimore.)

consecutive hours (Moore & Piacquadio, 1989). Real-time ultrasound involves the placement of an ultrasound transducer over the mother's abdomen and continuously recording fetal movement for 5–30 minutes on a video monitor. Using this approach, the fetus has been found to be active between 10%–20% of the time. Fetal activity ranges from a mean of 86 movements per 12 hours at 24 weeks, to 132 per 12 hours at 32 weeks, to 107 per 12 hours at term. This late decline relates to the increase in size of the fetus who now has less room to move. Despite this decrease, the baby should have movement visible on ultrasound at least once an hour.

Nonstress Test

Fetal body movement is normally accompanied by heart acceleration. This observation is incorporated in the nonstress test (Devoe, 1990). One can either wait for movement to occur in order to measure changes in fetal heart rate or precipitate movement by applying a vibratory acoustic stimulus, such as an artificial larynx, to the mother's abdomen (Shaw & Paul, 1990). Fetal heart rate is monitored using a transducer that continually transmits and receives an ultrasound signal. A change in the frequency of the transmitted signal occurs when it strikes a moving object, such as the fetal heart. This is called the *doppler effect*. It is perceived by the transducer and translated into an electronic signal from which the fetal heart rate can be determined (Jackson, Forouzan, & Cohen, 1991). The normal baseline heart rate is 120–160 beats per minute.

A reactive test involves an acceleration of at least 15 beats per minute. A nonreactive test involves movement without a change in heart rate. Nonreactive tests have been associated with fetuses who are growth retarded, **acidotic,** or are destined to be still-born. However, there is a high incidence of false positive results so the nonstress test can only be used as a screening procedure, not as a diagnostic test.

Biophysical Profile

In those fetuses who have a nonreactive nonstress test, a biophysical profile and/or contraction stress test (see below) will be performed. The biophysical profile is much more specific than the nonstress test. It has five elements and a 10-point scale (Manning, 1990), and takes 30 minutes to perform. The first element involves using real-time ultrasound to monitor fetal breathing. (Perhaps surprisingly, the fetus breathes a few times each half hour.) The second part of the profile involves identifying at least three gross fetal movements during the half hour. The third measure detects acceleration of the heart beat, which occurs together with movement (see the Nonstress Test). The fourth measure is muscle tone, denoted by active limb extension and flexion. Finally, the volume of amniotic fluid is assessed; decreased volume is seen in postmature babies and sometimes in those with cord compression. Two points are given for each measure so that a perfect score is 10 (Table 5.2). Scores of 6 or less have been correlated with fetal distress. If this occurs the test is either prolonged to 120 minutes or repeated in 24 hours. A repeated low score would lead the obstetrician to consider delivering the baby early either by inducing labor or by performing a cesarean section. In high-risk pregnancies, even with a normal score, the profile is usually repeated weekly during the third trimester.

Contraction Stress Test

Uterine contractions cause pressure increases in both the amniotic cavity and the uterine wall. This results in brief periods of oxygen deprivation to the fetus. A healthy fetus tolerates this without difficulty. However, a compromised fetus will have a characteristic decrease in fetal heart rate. This is the basis of the contraction stress test. An intravenous infusion of oxytocin is given after a typical fetal heart rate has been established. Following this challenge at least three contractions lasting 40 seconds or more should occur within 10 minutes. The test is considered abnormal if half of the contractions are associated with a *late deceleration* of fetal heart rate (Pircon & Freeman, 1990). Late deceleration is defined as a significant decrease in fetal heart rate beginning at or after the peak of the uterine contraction and returning to normal after the contraction has ended (Figure 5.4). This test may identify placental deterioration earlier than the nonstress test. It is not generally used before 36 weeks gestation for fear of starting preterm labor; with placenta previa, for fear of causing bleeding; in multiple gestations; following ruptured membranes; or with a preceding cesarean section.

Doppler Blood Flow Analysis

Another use of ultrasound employs the doppler effect to measure the movement of red blood cells through vessels (Arias & Retto, 1988). This is important as it can provide

Table 5.2. Biophysical profile scoring: technique and interpretation

Biophysical variable	Normal (score = 2)	Abnormal (score = 0)
Fetal breathing movements (FBM)	At least one episode of FBM of at least 30 seconds duration in a 30-minute observation	Absent FBM or no episode of > 30 seconds in 30 minutes
Gross body movements	At least three discrete body/limb movements in 30 minutes (episodes of active continuous movement considered as single movement)	Two or fewer episodes of body limb/movements in 30 minutes
Fetal tone	At least one episode of active extension with return to flexion of fetal limb(s) or trunk. Opening and closing of hand considered normal tone	Either slow extension with return to partial flexion or movement of limb in full extension. No fetal movement
Reactive fetal heart rate (FHR)	At least two episodes of fetal acceleration of > 15 beats/minute and of at least 15 seconds duration associated with fetal movement in 30 minutes	Less than two episodes of acceleration of FHR or acceleration of > 15 beats/minute in 30 minutes
Qualitative amniotic fluid volume	At least one pocket of amniotic fluid (AF) that measures at least 1 cm in two perpendicular planes	Either no AF pockets or a pocket > 1 cm in two perpendicular planes

From Manning, F.A. (1990). The fetal biophysical profile score: Current status. *Obstetrics and Gynecology Clinics of North America, 17,* 152; Copyright © 1990 by W.B. Saunders; reprinted by permission.

a direct measure of placental function. With placental insufficiency, flow through the umbilical artery is markedly decreased (Maulik, Yarlagadda, & Downing, 1990). During labor, a sudden decrease in umbilical artery blood flow signals cord compression and the need for emergency delivery. Finally, absence of cerebral blood flow has been used to confirm fetal death.

Amniotic Fluid Assessment

A relationship exists between fetal health and maturity and the amount and content of amniotic fluid. For example, **oligohydramnios** (i.e., too little amniotic fluid) can result from abnormalities in the fetal kidneys that normally produce most of the fluid. The decreased buffering capacity associated with oligohydramnios can lead to fetal deformities ranging from club foot to skull abnormalities and compressed lungs. Decreased amniotic fluid volume also occurs in infants who are either postmature or have intrauterine growth retardation. Here, decreasing amounts of amniotic fluid have been correlated with fetal death. Finally, with premature rupture of membranes,

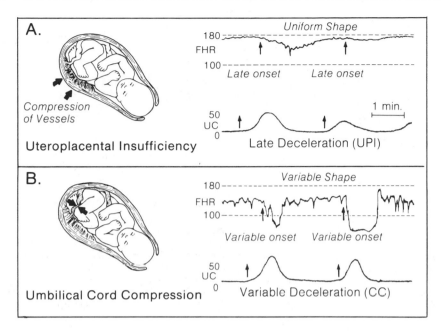

Figure 5.4. Fetal monitoring. A)Late heart deceleration occurs if the placental blood vessels are abnormally pressed together during the end of the uterine contraction. B)Variable deceleration of the heart. This abnormal finding of early, mid, and late deceleration suggests compression and obstruction of the umbilical cord circulation during labor. (UC, uterine contraction; FHR, fetal heat rate, beat/minute.) (Redrawn with permission from: Hon, E. [1968]. *An atlas of fetal heart rate patterns.* New Haven, CT: Harty.)

decreased amniotic fluid volume has been associated with a high incidence of infection. The assessment of amniotic fluid volume is part of the biophysical profile.

Besides measuring its volume, the amniotic fluid can also be sampled to assess its cellular and biochemical constitution (Smith, 1990). In terms of cellular content, the presence of white blood cells and the culturing of bacteria from amniotic fluid following premature rupture of membranes confirms chorioamnionitis and the requirement of early delivery.

Regarding biochemical constitution, fetal lung maturity is assessed either by measuring the ratio of two chemicals present in amniotic fluid, lecithin (L) and sphingomyelin (S) or by detecting phosphatidylglycerol (PG) in the fluid (Amenta & Silverman, 1983). Lecithin is necessary to produce **surfactant,** which keeps the newborn infant's lungs expanded and functioning properly. Researchers have found that the ratio of concentration of lecithin and sphingomyelin (called the *L/S ratio*) changes as the infant approaches maturity. During this time, more lecithin is produced to synthesize surfactant, but the sphingomyelin level remains unchanged. As a result, the L/S ratio increases to greater than 2:1. Lower ratios indicate immature lungs and a greater risk for respiratory distress syndrome or RDS (Figure 5.5).

More recently, the measurement of phosphatidylglycerol has proven helpful in predicting the risk of RDS especially in infants of mothers with diabetes, those with **Rh sensitization,** and those with sepsis. Its presence suggests that the child will not

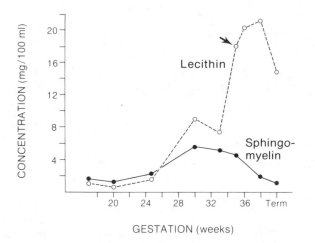

Figure 5.5.   Concentration of lecithin (L) and sphingomyelin (S) in the amniotic fluid. Note that at 34–35 weeks, the L/S ratio is more than 2:1, indicating that adequate surfactant is being produced. Respiratory distress syndrome (RDS) is less likely to develop after this stage, and a safe delivery is possible. (From Gluck, L., Kulovich, M.V., Borer, R.C., et al.[1971]. Diagnosis of the respiratory distress syndrome by amniocentesis. *American Journal of Obstetrics and Gynecology, 109,* 440; reprinted by permission.)

develop RDS. A kit for measuring "foam stability" of amniotic fluid is available as well. Amniotic fluid and ethanol are combined and shaken; the presence of a foam layer indicates the presence of surfactant and suggests a low risk of RDS. The measurement of fibronectin in vaginal secretions has been proposed as an even more straightforward predictor of prematurity because it does not require amniotic fluid (Lockwood, Senyei, Dische, et al., 1991).

Monitoring Uterine Contractions and Fetal Heart Rate

Amniocentesis and ultrasound are tools used prior to the onset of labor. Once labor begins, uterine contractions and fetal heart rate can be monitored.

With each uterine contraction, physiological changes occur in the fetus. The contractions begin in the cervix and move upward, eventually reaching the **fundus uteri,** or top of the uterus. Significant decreases in fetal heart rate during contractions suggest a number of problems that place the fetus at risk. For example, in abruptio placenta, there is deceleration of the fetal heart rate (usually below 100 beats per minute) after the peak of the contraction has occurred. With a prolapsed or compressed cord, the decline in the heart rate is profound and occurs at various times during the contractions. By recognizing these problems early, an obstetrician can regulate the labor or perform a cesarean section.

Fetal Scalp Monitoring

When a woman is in the first or second stage of labor, the infant's head descends in the birth canal. At this time, fetal scalp monitoring can be done. This involves placing a scalp electrode and/or measuring *blood pH*. The scalp electrode can directly monitor fetal heart rate. Blood pH, a marker for acidity due to hypoxia, is measured by obtaining a drop of fetal scalp blood using a lancet and then measuring the pH. If the infant's blood is acidotic, delivery must be hastened by forceps or cesarean section.

CESAREAN SECTION

The cesarean operation involves making an incision through the abdominal and uterine wall and extracting the baby. This procedure can be done with the mother awake under **epidural anesthesia,** and the baby can be removed within minutes. The cesarean section has been mentioned throughout this chapter as a means of saving the child when problems arise. However, it is a surgical procedure with some risks to both infant and mother. Therefore, it should be used only when indicated for medical reasons and not just for convenience (Myers & Gleicher, 1988). Overall, it is about twice as risky as vaginal delivery. The greatest risk to the fetus is premature delivery as a result of incorrect assessment of gestational age. Infants delivered by cesarean section are also more likely to have "wet lungs" and transient respiratory distress. This is because the infant does not undergo the first stage of labor during which the uterine contractions and passage through the birth canal squeeze most of the fluid from the fetal lungs. For the mother, problems related to cesarean section include the risk of anesthesia, infection, and bleeding (Miller, 1988).

OUTCOME

With all the potential complications in late pregnancy, labor, and delivery, it may seem surprising that over 90% of children are born without incident. Yet, this is in fact the case.

More importantly, virtually each year the newborn mortality rate decreases. In 1989, the overall stillborn rate in the United States was 9.7 per 1,000 births, the lowest ever recorded (Wegman, 1990). Perinatal mortality in high-risk pregnancies has also been reduced fourfold in the past 10 years (Creasy & Resnik, 1989). Improved survival has been attributable to many factors including selective abortion of defective fetuses, better prenatal care, improved fetal monitoring, and refined neonatal intensive care (David & Siegel, 1983). Lest we rest on our laurels, however, improvement is possible as demonstrated by 22 other nations that have lower stillbirth rates than the United States. Furthermore, the incidence of newborn deaths in certain populations in this country rivals that of developing countries. Thus, there is still much to be accomplished to improve the health of mothers and fetuses.

SUMMARY

The period of late pregnancy, labor, and delivery is a critical one for the normal development of the infant. Complications can result from such divergent sources as toxemia, cephalopelvic disproportion, and placenta previa or from the existence of twins, hydrocephalus, or congenital malformations. All these complications may lead to premature delivery, intrauterine growth retardation, or inadequate circulation of blood and oxygen during delivery. The impact of such complications can be severe and long-lasting. While new antenatal fetal monitoring techniques aid in decreasing the risk of birth injuries, additional public health measures, including improved prenatal care of teenage and disadvantaged women, are needed to ensure the health of pregnant women and their infants.

REFERENCES

Amenta, J.S., & Silverman, J.A. (1983). Amniotic fluid lecithin, phosphatidylglycerol, L/S ratio, and foam stability test in predicting respiratory distress in the newborn. *American Journal of Clinical Pathology, 79*, 52–64.

Arias, F., & Retto, H. (1988). The use of doppler waveform analysis in the evaluation of the high-risk fetus. *Obstetrics and Gynecological Clinics of North America, 15*, 265–281.

Baker, D.A. (1990). Herpes and pregnancy: New management. *Clinical Obstetrics and Gynecology, 33*, 253–257.

Besinger, R.E., & Niebyl, J.R. (1990). The safety and efficacy of tocolytic agents for the treatment of preterm labor. *Obstetrics and Gynecology Survey, 45*, 415–440.

Blakemore, K.J., & Petrie, R.H. (1988). Oxytocin for the induction of labor. *Obstetrics and Gynecological Clinics of North America, 15*, 339–353.

Braddick, M.R., Kreiss, J.K., Embree, J.B., et al. (1990). Impact of maternal HIV infection on obstetrical and early neonatal outcome. *AIDS, 4*, 1001–1005.

Cardwell, M.S. (1988). Cervical cerclage: A ten-year review in a large hospital. *Southern Medical Journal, 81*, 15–19.

Centers for Disease Control. (1990). Perinatal mortality and congenital malformations in infants born to women with insulin-dependent diabetes mellitus—United States, Canada, and Europe, 1940–1988. *Journal of the American Medical Association, 264*, 437–441.

Clark, S.L. (1989). Intrapartum management of the postdate patient. *Clinical Obstetrics and Gynecology, 32*, 278–284.

Creasy, R.K., & Resnik, R. (1989). *Maternal–fetal medicine: Principles and practice* (2nd ed.). Philadelphia: W.B. Saunders.

Croughan-Minihane, M.S., Petitti, D.B., Gordis, L., et al. (1990). Morbidity among breech infants according to method of delivery. *Obstetrics and Gynecology, 75*, 821–825.

Cunningham, F.G., MacDonald, P.C., & Gant, N.F. (1989). *Williams obstetrics* (18th ed.). Norwalk, CT: Appleton & Lange.

David, R.J., & Siegel E. (1983). Decline in neonatal mortality, 1968–1977: Better babies or better care? *Pediatrics, 71*, 531–540.

Devoe, L.D. (1990). The nonstress test. *Obstetrics and Gynecology Clinics of North America, 17*, 111–128.

Gilstrap, L.C., III. (1990). Pathophysiology of preeclampsia. *Seminars in Perinatology, 14*, 147–151.

Gimovsky, M.L., & Petrie, R.H. (1989). The intrapartum management of the breech presentation. *Clinics in Perinatology, 16*, 975–986.

Gluck, L., Kulovich, M.V., Borer, R.C., et al. (1971). Diagnosis of the respiratory distress syndrome by amniocentesis. *American Journal of Obstetrics and Gynecology, 109*, 440–445.

Hansen, J.P. (1986). Older maternal age and pregnancy outcome: A review of the literature. *Obstetrical and Gynecological Survey, 41*, 726–742.

Hon, E. (1968). *An atlas of fetal heart rate patterns*. New Haven, CT: Harty.

Hernandez, C., & Cunningham, F.G. (1990). Eclampsia. *Clinical Obstetrics and Gynecology, 33*, 460–466.

Hutto, C., Parks, W.P., Lai, S.H., et al. (1991). A hospital-based prospective study of perinatal infection with human immunodeficiency virus type 1. *Journal of Pediatrics, 118*, 347–353.

Jackson, G.M., Forouzan, I., & Cohen, A.W. (1991). Fetal well-being: Nonimaging assessment and the biophysical profile. *Seminars in Roentgenology, 26*, 21–31.

Jones, J.M., Sbarra, A.J., & Cetrulo, C.L. (1990). Antepartum management of twin gestation. *Clincal Obstetrics and Gynecology, 33*, 32–41.

Kibrick, S. (1980). Herpes simplex infection at term. What to do with mother, newborn, and nursery personnel. *Journal of the American Medical Association, 243*, 157–160.

Landy, H.J., & Grossman, J.H., III. (1989). Herpes simplex virus. *Obstetrics and Gynecology Clinics of North America, 16*, 495–515.

Lavery, J.P. (1990). Placenta previa. *Clinical Obstetrics and Gynecology, 33*, 414–421.

Lockwood, C.J., Senyei, A.E., Dische, M.R., et al. (1991). Fetal fibronectin in cervical and vaginal secretions as a predictor of preterm delivery. *New England Journal of Medicine, 325*, 669–674.

Lowe, T.W., & Cunningham, F.G. (1990). Placental abruption. *Clinical Obstetrics and Gynecology, 33*, 406–413.

Manning, F.A. (1990). The fetal biophysical profile score: Current status. *Obstetrics and Gynecology Clinics of North America, 17*, 147–162.

Maulik, D., Yarlagadda, P., & Downing, G. (1990). Doppler velocimetry in obstetrics. *Obstetrics and Gynecology Clinics of North America, 17*, 163–186.

Miller, J.M., Jr. (1988). Maternal and neonatal morbidity and mortality in cesarean section. *Obstetrics and Gynecology Clinics of North America, 15*, 629–638.

Moore, T.R., & Piacquadio, K. (1989). A prospective evaluation of fetal movement screening can reduce the incidence of antepartum fetal death. *American Journal of Obstetrics and Gynecology, 160*, 1075–1080.

Mycrs, S.A., & Gleicher, N. (1988). A successful program to lower cesarean-section rates. *New England Journal of Medicine, 319*, 1511–1516.

Naeye, R.L., & Tafari, N. (1983). *Risk factors in pregnancy and diseases of the fetus and newborn.* Baltimore: Williams & Wilkins.

Nilsson, L. (1989). *A child is born.* New York: Dell Books.

Nordenvall, M., & Sandstedt, B. (1990). Chorioamnionitis in relation to gestational outcome in a Swedish population. *European Journal of Obstetrics, Gynecology, and Reproductive Biology, 36*, 59–67.

Pircon, R.A., & Freeman, R.K. (1990). The contraction stress test. *Obstetrics and Gynecology Clinics of North America, 17*, 129–146.

Rayburn, W.F. (1990) Fetal body movement monitoring. *Obstetrics and Gynecology Clinics of North America, 17*, 95–109.

Rosenak, D., Diamant, Y.Z., Yaffe, H., et al. (1990). Cocaine: Maternal use during pregnancy and its effect on the mother, the fetus, and the infant. *Obstetrical and Gynecological Survey, 45*, 348–359.

Shaw, K.J., & Paul, R.H. (1990). Fetal response to external stimuli. *Obstetrics and Gynecology Clinics of North America, 17*, 235–248.

Smith, C.V. (1990). Amniotic fluid assessment. *Obstetrics and Gynecology Clinics of North America, 17*, 187–200.

Stewart, P.J., Dulber, C., Arnill, A.C., et al. (1990). Diagnosis of dystocia and management with cesarean section among primiparous women in Ottawa-Carleton. *Canadian Medical Association Journal, 142*, 459–463.

Treacy, B., Smith, C., & Rayburn W. (1990). Ultrasound in labor and delivery. *Obstetrics and Gynecology Survey, 45*, 213–219.

Valdes-Dapena, M.A., & Arey, J.B. (1970). The causes of neonatal mortality: An analysis of 501 autopsies on newborn infants. *Journal of Pediatrics, 77*, 366–375.

Veille, J.C. (1988). Management of preterm premature rupture of membranes. *Clinics in Perinatology, 15,* 851–862.

Wegman, M.E. (1990). Annual summary of vital statistics—1989. *Pediatrics, 86,* 835–847.

Willson, J.R., Carrington, E.R., & Ledger, W.J. (1987). *Obstetrics and gynecology* (8th ed.). St. Louis: C.V. Mosby Co.

Zuckerman, B.S., Walker, D.K., Frank, D.A., et al. (1984). Adolescent pregnancy: Biobehavioral determinants of outcome. *Journal of Pediatrics, 105,* 857–863.

Chapter 6

The First
Weeks of Life

Upon completion of this chapter, the reader will:
—understand the significance of the Apgar score
—know the physiological changes that take place immediately after birth
—comprehend the reasons infections may be devastating to a newborn
—be able to enumerate the basic components of the body's immune system
—be aware of the various kinds of intracranial hemorrhages newborns experience
 and the significance of each
—know why jaundice occurs
—understand the cause of and problems associated with Rh incompatibility
—be familiar with the reason hypoglycemia occurs and its possible consequences
 for a newborn
—understand the significance of seizures in the first week of life

---

Jessica has given the last push, and Michael's torso emerges from the birth canal. Life outside the womb has begun. On examination at 1 minute, the obstetrician notes that Michael has a heart rate of 120 beats per minute and good respiratory effort. He has some flexion of his extremities, but no active movement. His cry is vigorous. While his body is pink, his arms and legs are blue. The **Apgar score** at 1 minute is 8 (Table 6.1). The baby is fine. At 5 minutes, Michael has made more progress. He is moving about, and his entire body has become pink. The 5-minute Apgar score is 10. Jessica, relieved and pleased, smiles contentedly.

Maria, however, is having difficulty delivering her son, David. She has just undergone an emergency cesarean section because of an abruptio placenta. She has lost a great deal of blood and needed several blood transfusions. David is delivered quickly but, at 1 minute of age, he is limp and blue with no heartbeat or respiratory effort. The Apgar score is 0. Immediately, a tube is placed down David's trachea (windpipe), and he is artificially ventilated. Another tube is inserted into one of the blood vessels in his umbilical cord, and the heart is stimulated with intravenous **glucose** and **adrenalin.** After a few minutes, David is somewhat pink, his heart rate is 80, and spontaneous breathing has tentatively started. He has begun to move his

Table 6.1. The Apgar scoring system

	Points			Score			
				1 minute		5 minutes	
	0	1	2	Michael	David	Michael	David
Heart rate	Absent	<100	>100	2	0	2	1
Respiratory effort	Absent	Slow, irregular	Normal respiration; crying	2	0	2	1
Muscle tone	Limp	Some flexion	Active motion	1	0	2	1
Gag reflex	No response	Grimace	Sneeze; cough	2	0	2	1
Color	Blue all over; pale	Blue extremities	Pink all over	1	0	2	1
			Totals	8	0	10	5

extremities. The 5-minute Apgar score is 5 (see Table 6.1). The doctors breathe a tentative sigh of relief, knowing that the results of their efforts will not be known completely for many months. Years ago, David would have been stillborn.

APGAR SCORE

Michael and David have both survived. However, their risk of having a developmental disability is different. Their Apgar scores reflect this difference. This scale, developed by Dr. Virginia Apgar, measures the effect of various complications of labor and delivery on the newborn infant. There are five measures comprising the Apgar score: heart rate, respiratory effort, muscle tone, gag reflex, and body color (see Table 6.1). The newborn is given a score of 0, 1, or 2 depending on the baby's condition. Therefore, the total score is between 0 and 10 and is taken at 1 minute, 5 minutes, and sometimes 10 minutes after birth. A low Apgar score generally indicates that the child is more likely to have a developmental disability. One study reported that of 99 children who had 5-minute Apgar scores below 4, 12% (four times normal) later developed multiple disabilities including cerebral palsy, mental retardation, and seizures. Twenty-seven percent of children who were later diagnosed as having cerebral palsy were found retrospectively to have 5-minute Apgar scores below 6 (Nelson, 1989). Fifty percent of infants who had Apgar scores below 4 at 15 minutes developed disabilities (Jain, Ferre, Vidyasagar, et al., 1991). Thus, a low Apgar score beyond 5 minutes carries an increased statistical risk for disability, but the majority of children with low Apgar scores will still develop normally. Although the predictive value of the Apgar score is limited, it is safe to say that David is more likely to have developmental problems than Michael and will need close follow-up.

PHYSIOLOGICAL CHANGES AT BIRTH

As the Apgar score illustrates, many changes take place in the first few moments after birth. The most important ones involve the respiratory and circulatory systems. Other changes include the infant's ability to regulate temperature and to absorb nutrients.

For the infant, the first breath is the most difficult because the lungs are collapsed and waterlogged. An extremely strong force must be exerted to open the air pockets, or **alveoli**, to permit the adequate exchange of oxygen. The first cry increases the pressure enough to open the alveoli. The alveoli remain open even when air is expelled because of the action of a chemical discussed in Chapter 5, called *surfactant*. It is a lack of surfactant that places premature infants at risk for developing respiratory distress syndrome (see Chapter 7).

Equally important are the changes in the circulatory system. During fetal life, a number of vital organs are bypassed because the placenta takes care of **oxygenation** and **detoxification.** At birth, these bypasses must cease so the infant can function independently from the mother. The three most important bypasses are the *foramen ovale,* the *ductus arteriosus,* and the *ductus venosus.* The first two take blood around the unexpanded lungs, while the third transports blood around the fetal liver.

To understand how the first two bypasses work, it is important to know something about the normal flow of the postnatal circulation. The heart has four chambers: the right and left **atria,** or upper chambers, and the right and left ventricles, or lower chambers. Normally, the blood brought to the heart by the vena cava, one of the body's main veins, flows from the right atrium to the right ventricle. It is then carried by the **pulmonary** artery to the lungs, where it is oxygenated. The pulmonary veins later return the blood to the left atrium. The oxygenated blood then passes to the left ventricle and out to the body via the **aorta,** the body's primary artery, thus completing the cycle (Figure 6.1).

In the fetus, an opening called the *foramen ovale* permits much of the blood to flow directly from the right to the left atrium, bypassing the right ventricle and the lungs (see Figure 6.1). The blood that does not pass through the foramen ovale flows to the right ventricle and pulmonary artery. However, it is then short-circuited from entering the collapsed lungs by the ductus arteriosus. This bypass diverts the blood flow from the pulmonary artery into the aorta. Again, the lungs are bypassed.

With the first breath, a series of muscle contractions closes the ductus arteriosus. In addition, a flap folds over and covers the foramen ovale as the pulmonary artery allows more blood to flow through the lungs. The closure of these two bypasses must

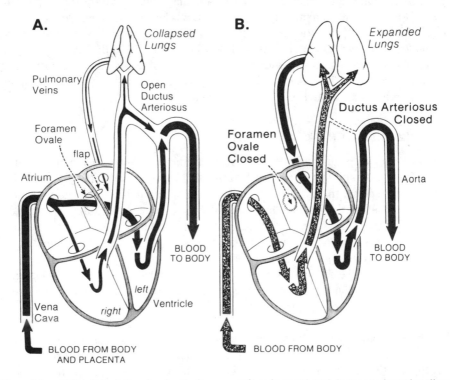

Figure 6.1. A) Fetal circulation showing the foramen ovale and patent (open) ductus arteriosus that allow the blood flow to bypass the unexpanded lungs. B) Adult circulation. The fetal bypasses close off with expansion of the lungs.

take place for proper oxygenation of the blood to occur. Usually, these bypasses have shut down by the time the infant is a few days old, and the adult circulatory pattern has been established. This often occurs more slowly in the premature infant and can lead to respiratory and circulatory problems (see discussion in Chapter 7). In a small number of children, a persistent fetal circulation may be life-threatening and may require extra corporeal membrane oxygenation (ECMO) to survive.

The third bypass involves the umbilical circulation. Normally, the liver serves as a processor of wastes in our bodies. In the fetus, however, the umbilical vessels bypass the liver, and the placenta acts as the purifier of toxic products. A small channel, the ductus venosus, accomplishes this detour around the liver (Figure 6.2). After birth, it closes along with the umbilical vein and two umbilical arteries. Venous blood then passes through the liver and is cleansed on its way back to the heart.

In addition to the closing of these three bypasses, the baby must begin to establish temperature regulation. This is very difficult because the newborn has a large surface area and little fatty tissue to protect him- or herself against temperature loss. This explains the necessity of incubators or of warm swaddling of the newborn.

A final change is the need for nourishment. Since the placental circulation is no longer available to provide nutrition, the infant must obtain it independently. The newborn must develop a strong suck and **rooting** response to seek and obtain nourishment either from the mother's breast or the bottle. This, too, is less well developed in the preterm infant. Alternate means of feeding (e.g., by nasogastric tube) are often necessary until their suck and swallow responses are better developed (see Chapter 12).

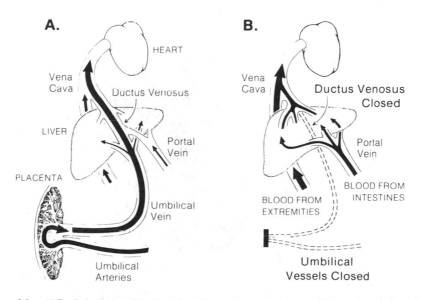

Figure 6.2. A) Fetal circulation. The blood from the umbilical vein bypasses the liver through the ductus venosus. B) Adult circulation. The umbilical vein ceases to function and the ductus venosus closes. Now blood from the body passes through the liver where it is cleansed.

CAUSES OF ILLNESS AND DEATH IN NEWBORNS

After an infant is born, the incidence of severe illness occurring during the first month of life is about 1 in 100, and the incidence of death 1 in 1,000 (Dollfus, Patetta, Siegel, et al., 1990) (Figure 6.3). Severe illnesses include **asphyxia, intracranial** hemorrhage, infection, **jaundice,** hypoglycemia, and congenital anomalies (e.g., heart disease, anencephaly). The clinical presentation of these disorders may be similar because newborns have relatively few ways of indicating severe illness. They stop feeding, have breathing difficulties, become irritable, lethargic, and floppy. This may progress to seizures, coma, and death. Early and appropriate treatment may help to avoid severe developmental disabilities in the infant.

Hypoxic-Ischemic Encephalopathy (Asphyxia)

The most evident problem immediately following birth is a combination of asphyxia (i.e., lack of oxygen) and **ischemia** (i.e., lack of circulation). An affected infant has a very low Apgar score and needs resuscitation. The causes of hypoxic-ischemic encephalopathy include placenta previa, abruptio, prolapsed cord, cephalopelvic disproportion (CPD), and prolonged labor (Brann, 1986). Fortunately, even in cases of severe hypoxia-ischemia, prognosis is generally good as long as the condition's duration is short. Treatment involves getting air into the lungs, supporting the heart, and correcting metabolic acidosis. Some experimental evidence exists to suggest that decreasing metabolism using phenobarbital and blocking **excitotoxic receptors** using dextromethorphan may also hold some benefit (Chemtob, Laudignon, & Aranda, 1987; Vannucci, 1990). Even better is prevention by fetal monitoring and early delivery when the fetus appears to be in trouble (see Chapter 5).

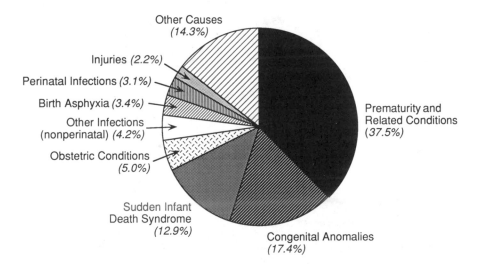

Figure 6.3.   Causes of death during the first month of life. In the United States, the neonatal mortality rate is about 1 in 1,000. (From Dollfus, C., Patetta, M., Siegel, E., et al. [1990]. Infant mortality:A practical approach to the analysis of the leading causes of death and risk factors. *Pediatrics, 86,* 176; Copyright © 1990 by Pediatrics; reprinted by permission.)

Prolonged hypoxia-ischemia is associated with seizures and coma; over half of these infants die (Shaywitz, 1987). But surprisingly, only about one-quarter of survivors of prolonged hypoxia-ischemia are severely damaged (Vannucci, 1990). Overall, only about 10% of all cases of cerebral palsy can be attributed to birth asphyxia (Nelson, 1989). Even this may be an overestimation as it includes children who have an underlying genetic abnormality that predisposes them to asphyxia. For example, 10%–30% of children with fragile X syndrome or **Prader-Willi syndrome** have perinatal asphyxia.

Hypoxic-ischemic damage can be visualized on ultrasound, **computed tomography (CT)** scan, or MRI, where there may be signs of cysts and loss of brain tissue in certain regions. The specific pattern of abnormalities have different terms associated with them. **Watershed infarcts** result from a generalized reduction in cerebral blood flow in the full-term infant. Damage occurs in the border regions between two major blood vessels, areas that are least well supplied with oxygen and nutrients. **Spastic quadriplegia** and mental retardation result in severe cases, but subtle damage may affect the association regions of the brain, leading to learning disabilities.

In premature infants, generalized ischemia leads to a different pattern called **periventricular leukomalacia (PVL).** In these infants, the brain region that surrounds the ventricles is at risk. This area controls movement of the lower limbs. Damage leads to spastic diplegia, the most common form of cerebral palsy in premature infants (see Chapter 24). Focal **necrosis** occurs when a cerebral blood vessel is blocked. **Hemiplegia** usually results. Finally, diffuse brain damage can occur because of prolonged lack of oxygen. Mental retardation, seizures, and spastic quadriplegia are common. In addition, lack of oxygen to the basal ganglia of the brain can cause **status marmoratus** and choreoathetoid cerebral palsy (Hill & Volpe, 1989).

Intracranial Hemorrhage

Hypoxia-ischemia can cause brain damage not only by directly injuring cortical tissue, but also by disrupting blood vessels. This is most common in premature infants whose developmentally immature capillary blood vessels are particularly sensitive to lack of oxygen or altered blood pressure. The result is that almost 50% of premature infants have some hemorrhaging from these capillary beds surrounding the ventricles (Allan & Volpe, 1986). The support for these capillary vessels improves by the ninth month, making this complication less common in full-term infants.

Intracranial hemorrhage can also result from direct trauma and tearing of a blood vessel. This may occur during a difficult delivery. The types of hemorrhages range from minor and inconsequential extracranial bleeds, called **cephalohematoma,** to intracranial hemorrhages, called **subarachnoid, subdural,** and **periventricular-intraventricular** hemorrhages.

After birth, many babies have a large swelling on the back of the head, a cephalohematoma (Figure 6.4). This collection of blood under the outer layer of the skull results from trauma to the blood vessels in the scalp during delivery. The incidence is 2.5%, and the prognosis is excellent (Thacker, Lim, & Drew, 1987). No treatment is necessary and the swelling usually disappears within a few weeks.

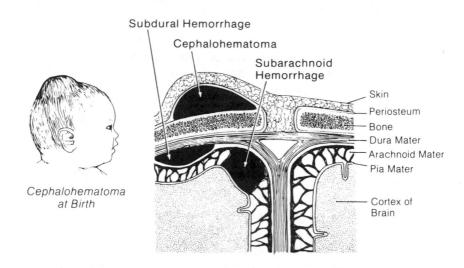

Figure 6.4. Types of hemorrhages in the newborn. Cephalohematoma is frequent, and the child with this problem has a good prognosis. Subdural and subarachnoid hemorrhages carry more guarded prognoses.

The prognosis is more variable following intracranial hemorrhages. Here there is bleeding from blood vessels surrounding or located within the brain itself. If the bleeding occurs from blood vessels beneath the outer covering of the brain, the *dura mater,* it is called a subdural hematoma. If the blood vessels below the middle layer, or *arachnoid mater,* bleed, it is called a subarachnoid hemorrhage (see Figure 6.4). If the capillary vessels surrounding the ventricles of the brain bleed, it is called a periventricular-intraventricular hemorrhage (Volpe, 1986).

Subdural hemorrhages are rare and tend to occur in full-term infants who have experienced a traumatic delivery, resulting from cephalopelvic disproportion, for example. Delivering those infants by cesarean section prevents this complication. If subdural bleeding does occur, it may cause seizures and coma. Neurosurgery may be necessary to remove the blood.

Subarachnoid hemorrhages may result from trauma or asphyxia. They are generally less severe than subdural hemorrhages and are most common in premature infants. Unlike the subdural hemorrhage, which is arterial and under pressure, the subarachnoid hemorrhage is of venous blood. Sometimes these bleeds are without symptoms, or the child may experience seizures. The outcome is generally good after traumatic injury but more uncertain if there has been asphyxia.

As noted previously, periventricular-intraventricular hemorrhages are also most frequent in premature infants, especially those with respiratory distress syndrome (Allan & Volpe, 1986). The risk of bleeding increases as gestational age decreases. Bleeding starts in the capillary vessels surrounding the ventricles (the germinal matrix) but there is usually leakage into the ventricle and sometimes bleeding spreads to the surrounding brain tissue. If the bleeding is severe, the blood count, or **hematocrit,** may drop, the soft spot of the head may bulge, the head circumference may increase, and seizures may develop. Confirmation of a hemorrhage is usually made using a CT scan (Figure 6.5) or ultrasound (Figure 6.6). The physician can see blood in the ventricles and the surrounding brain tissue.

Until recently there was no specific treatment for periventricular hemorrhage. Now there is some evidence that prophylactic use of vitamin E reduces the risk and severity of periventricular hemorrhage in premature infants (Fish, Cohen, Franzek, et al., 1990). Studies also suggest the potential value of phenobarbital and mechanical ventilation in decreasing the extent of injury.

The prognosis of periventricular-intraventricular hemorrhages correlates with the extensiveness of the bleeding. Small bleeds are common in premature infants and generally have little effect on their prognosis. However, larger hemorrhages that involve brain tissue and enlargement of the ventricles may cause hydrocephalus or **porencephalic cysts.** If the blood clots, it can obstruct the flow of the cerebrospinal fluid, causing hydrocephalus. If the blood destroys tissues it can cause a porencephalic cyst, which is a cavity in the brain substance that communicates with the ventricle. It is associated with abnormal muscle tone on the side opposite the lesion and carries an increased risk of cerebral palsy (Krishnamoorthy, Kuban, Leviton, et al., 1990).

NORMAL

INTRAVENTRICULAR
HEMORRHAGE

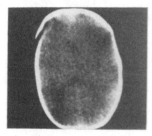
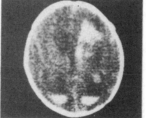

*bleeding outside
ventricles*

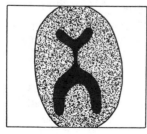
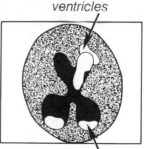

*bleeding into
ventricles*

Figure 6.5.   Intraventricular hemorrhage as shown on a CT scan. (Courtesy of Dr. Roger Sanders, Department of Radiology, The Johns Hopkins Hospital, Baltimore.)

NORMAL ULTRASOUND   INTRAVENTRICULAR HEMORRHAGE

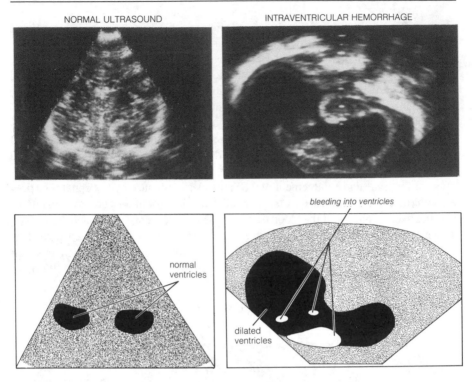

Figure 6.6. Intraventricular hemorrhage as shown on an ultrasound. (Courtesy of Dr. Roger Sanders, Department of Radiology, The Johns Hopkins Hospital, Baltimore.)

Infections

In an infant who develops symptoms of lethargy, poor feeding, and temperature instability, the pediatrician's first concern is the possibility of *sepsis,* or a generalized bacterial infection, sometimes called *blood poisoning.* Occurring in about 1 in 500 newborns, and in a higher proportion of premature infants, such infections are diagnosed by taking a blood sample and culturing it for bacteria (Ferrieri, 1990). Factors predisposing an infant to sepsis include maternal infection, prolonged rupture of membranes, and chorioamnionitis. Before antibiotics were available, more than 90% of newborn infants with sepsis died; now mortality ranges from less than 10%–50%, depending on the organism and how soon it is detected and treated (Ferrieri, 1990). Although treatment has improved, the frequency of such infections has increased because an increased number of very low birth weight infants are surviving, and these children are more susceptible to infection than are full-term children (Remington & Klein, 1983).

In newborn infants, the bacteria causing these infections are different from the bacteria that cause sepsis in older children and adults (Harris & Polin, 1983). Some of the bacteria that attack newborns are the same ones that harmlessly exist as part of the vaginal, skin, or gastrointestinal **flora** of the mother. The problem for newborns is that they lack the fully developed defense or immune system that is present in older children and adults. This system includes the skin, mucous secretions, B and T **lymphocytes, phagocytes,** and the complement system.

The Immune System　　The first line of defense against infection is the skin. It provides a protective covering and prevents the entrance of bacteria or viruses into the bloodstream. The infant's skin covering, though thinner than an older person's, is adequate. However, if this covering is removed, such as by trauma or burns, the likelihood of sepsis greatly increases.

The next wall of defense is the mucous secretions. Saliva and the secretions of the **trachea** prevent bacteria from stagnating and growing in the inviting warmth and moistness of the body. Also, these secretions contain antibodies that attack the bacteria before they can reach the bloodstream. Children with cystic fibrosis, a disease associated with a deficiency in these secretions, have an increased risk of severe respiratory infections. The secretions in the newborn are adequate, but do not contain sufficient antibodies to protect against certain respiratory infections.

B and T cells are involved in another step in immunity. In response to bacterial infections, B cells (a type of lymphocyte, or white blood cell) produce the major antibody groups, immunoglobulins G, A, and M. These antibodies attach themselves to bacteria to form complexes that can be engulfed by phagocytes, bacteria-swallowing white cells. Newborns do not produce enough of these antibodies until about 6 months of age. Before then, they must rely on the immunoglobulins transmitted from the mother during fetal life and the small amounts of immunoglobulin A contained in breast milk.

The products of B cells are principally bacteria fighters, whereas T cells combat viral infections. The newborn also lacks T cells so that viral infections, such as herpes, can cause life-threatening illness. Increasing amounts of T cells are produced after the first few months of life, so the risk to the baby diminishes over time. It is damage to the T cell by the HIV virus that leads to the clinical manifestation of AIDS.

The final armament in the body's defense mechanism is the complement system. This consists of a cascade of components produced in the body that, among other things, attracts the phagocytes to the area of infection. They act like a ZIP code, directing the immune responses of the body. Both these chemicals and phagocytes are inadequate in the newborn.

Bacterial Infections　　Since the newborn is deficient in so much of the body's immune system, it is understandable that infection in the neonate can be dangerous. Infections can be contracted through the placenta (congenital rubella), the maternal vagina (herpes), or the amniotic fluid during a difficult delivery (beta streptococcus or *strep*), or infections can be transmitted from other infants or hospital staff in the nursery (staphylococcus). Because of the ease with which newborns are infected, infants whose mothers have had infections or premature rupture of their amniotic membranes are carefully observed for signs of infection.

Early diagnosis and treatment of infection is essential, for, if untreated, it can spread rapidly throughout the infant's body. If an infant has symptoms suggestive of sepsis, the pediatrician will obtain blood cultures and start treatment with intravenous antibiotics. At present, the most common cause of sepsis is the bacteria Beta hemolytic streptococcus and the second most common organism is *E. coli* (Faxelius, Breme, Kvist-Christensen, et al., 1988). If the culture grows bacteria, antibiotics specific for the offending organism will be continued for a period of 1–3 weeks depending on the severity of the infection.

With appropriate treatment, clinical improvement generally occurs within 2–3 days. Most infants with bacterial infections of the body will recover without significant complications. However, if the infection spreads to the coverings of the brain, causing **meningitis,** the mortality rate rises to 20%–40% and about half of the survivors are left with severe neurological deficits (Feigin, 1983).

Although the classic approach to treating bacterial infections involves the use of antibiotics, two new treatment and preventive methods are being tested to improve outcome. The treatment entails giving **hyperimmune serum** that contains antibodies against a specific organism, most commonly Beta streptococcus (Ferrieri, 1990). This enhances the infant's ability to fight the infection. The preventive approach is to immunize the mother and child prenatally against the organism, thereby preventing the infection. Because of the frequency of Beta streptococcus infections, this is the first vaccine being developed (Baker, Rench, Edwards, et al., 1988). It is administered during the third trimester.

Viral Infections   Antibiotics only destroy bacteria; they have no effect in fighting viruses. Thus, different approaches must be used to treat severe viral infections. Herpes is the most common viral infection of the newborn, occurring in about 1 in 2,000 births (Whitley, 1988). It most often results from contact with infected genital secretions during delivery. The infection may either be limited to the skin and mucous membranes or become **systemic,** spreading to other body organs including the brain. If the infection is contracted *in utero,* symptoms will be present at birth (Brown, Vontver, & Benedetti, 1987). If it results from contamination during birth, symptoms develop by 1–2 weeks of life. Symptoms mimic sepsis but also may include a rash.

Two intravenous drugs have proven equally effective in treating systemic herpes: Acyclovir and Vidarabine. They interfere with viral replication and thereby limit the spread of herpesvirus. Without therapy, the mortality rate of systemic herpes is about 90%. With therapy, when the infection is localized to the skin, eye, and mouth, survival is universal and developmental outcome good, although retinal damage can occur. If the infection spreads to the brain, there is a 14% mortality rate, and two-thirds of survivors sustain severe disabilities including microcephaly, porencephalic cysts, blindness, mental retardation, and/or cerebral palsy. If the infection is disseminated throughout the body, over half the infants die, and about half of the survivors have developmental disabilities (Whitley, Arvin, Prober, et al., 1991).

Hyperbilirubinemia

The yellow discoloration of the body and eyes, due to an accumulation of bilirubin (**hyperbilirubinemia**), is called jaundice or *icterus*. It results from the following course of events: When red blood cells die, normally after a life span of about 120 days, the hemoglobin, or oxygen-carrying blood protein, is broken down into a number of components. One of these is bilirubin. The circulatory system then carries the bilirubin to the liver. There it is metabolized and neutralized in a process called *conjugation*. Bilirubin can accumulate when too many red blood cells break down or when there is a blockage in conjugation (Vohr, 1990).

While jaundice is a sign of severe liver disease in the adult, it may be quite innocuous in a newborn infant. Usually, jaundice in infants is due to the immaturity of the enzyme system necessary for conjugation of bilirubin. The infant becomes yellow-tinged at 2–3 days of age and ordinarily returns to a normal color by 1 week of age without therapy. The bilirubin level is usually below 10–15 **milligrams** (mg) per 100 **milliliters** (ml) in a full-term infant. This is called *physiological* jaundice. If jaundice persists, placement of the baby under special fluorescent lights, that aid in conjugation, leads to a drop in the bilirubin level (Ennever, 1986). The only side effects of fluorescent light treatment are diarrhea, dehydration, and occasionally a rash.

A modest elevation in the bilirubin level has little effect on the developing infant. However, a marked increase may pose a serious threat to the child. The most severe cause of hyperbilirubinemia is Rh incompatibility, in which a massive breakdown of red blood cells leads to jaundice (Connolly & Volpe, 1990). The Rh factor is a minor blood group attached to the four major blood types: A, B, AB, and O. Thus, a person may be ORh − or ORh +, ARh −, or ARh +, and so on.

Incompatibility of the Rh blood groups between mother and father may have disastrous consequences for the fetus. For this to happen, the mother must be Rh − and the father and the fetus must be Rh +. Problems develop in the following way: While the fetal and maternal circulatory systems are separate, an occasional fetal blood cell gets into the maternal circulation. The mother's immune system recognizes the baby's red cells as being foreign and forms antibodies that cross the placenta to the fetus and begin to destroy the fetus's red blood cells. This may cause the fetus to become severely anemic.

In the past, many infants died *in utero* and those who survived had brain damage and cerebral palsy, a high-frequency hearing loss, paralysis of the upward gaze, and discoloration of the teeth. This clinical syndrome is called **kernicterus.**

Over the years, treatment of Rh incompatibility changed from a palliative approach to a preventive one. Initially, in the 1950s, intrauterine blood transfusions were given to save these children. Around the 26th week of gestation, a needle was inserted through the uterus into the fetal abdominal cavity, and a transfusion of red blood cells was then given. The red blood cells were absorbed into the fetal circulation and improved the anemia. Several transfusions were required, and they were not without risk to the fetus (Liley, 1965). Once born, the babies needed repeated blood transfusions to lower the bilirubin level.

More recently, the effort has been directed toward prevention. A drug, Rho-GAM, has made this possible. RhoGAM is a gamma globulin (antibody) injection given to Rh − women after delivery or miscarriage of all Rh + infants. It works by blocking the formation of antibodies in the mother's circulation. Subsequent Rh +

infants will then be born without this anemia. This treatment has resulted in the virtual disappearance of kernicterus and a marked decrease in the need for exchange transfusions.

Hyperbilirubinemia is more of a problem for the premature than the full-term infant. Kernicterus can occur at lower levels of bilirubin than in the full-term infant (Van de Bor, Van Zeben-van der, Verloove-Vanhorick, et al., 1989). There is some evidence that phenobarbital may be useful in protecting premature infants from developing kernicterus (Valaes & Harvey-Wilkes, 1990). Phenobarbital stimulates the maturation of the enzymes that normally conjugate bilirubin in the liver. It appears to be most effective if given to the mother at least 10 days prior to delivery.

Incompatibility of the major blood groups may also result in jaundice, but this is usually a far less severe problem than Rh incompatibility and generally resolves with treatment under fluorescent lights. Bilirubin levels of up to 20 milligram per 100 milliliters do not appear to be dangerous to full-term babies unless they have Rh incompatibility (Polin, 1990).

The long-term effects of hyperbilirubinemia (above 20) in full-term infants are unclear (Bryla, 1991; Newman & Maisels, 1990; Scheidt, Graubard, Nelson, et al., 1991). There may be some delay in motor development and modest hearing impairment. New approaches to measuring damage include the use of **auditory brain stem response (ABR)** and **cry analysis.** The ABR will define subtle damage to the **brain stem** that accompanies bilirubin damage, and a shrill cry is associated with damage to the cranial nerves.

Hypoglycemia

At birth, infants are suddenly faced with the need to supply their own energy requirements for maintenance of body temperature, muscle activity, and other metabolic needs. This can only be accomplished if the infant receives sufficient oxygen and nutrients. Hypoglycemia results when too much glucose is used or not enough is produced. The infant appears lethargic, jittery, and may have intermittent breathing (**apnea**), temperature instability, and/or seizures (Ogata, 1986). If the condition is recognized early and sugar is given intravenously, neurological problems rarely result. However, if hypoglycemia is prolonged, it may lead to permanent brain damage.

Hypoglycemia most commonly occurs following asphyxia, in infants of mothers with diabetes, premature infants, and small-for-dates infants (Sann, 1990). The mechanism of the hypoglycemia varies. In asphyxia, the infant is forced to use *anaerobic* (without air) *metabolism* to produce energy. This is a very wasteful form of metabolism that rapidly depletes stored sugar. Since the ability to produce sugar is impaired in the newborn, the blood glucose level drops significantly. In the infant of a mother with diabetes, the fetal pancreas overproduces insulin to compensate for the mother's lack of insulin production. Insulin takes care of two functions: 1) lowering of blood sugar, and 2) laying down of fatty tissue. Because of the overproduction of insulin, infants of mothers with diabetes appear obese and have enlarged body organs as a result of an increase in fat content. This is further complicated because they are often born prematurely. After birth, the **islet cells** of the pancreas continue to overproduce insulin. This results in a precipitous fall in the blood sugar level that is often difficult to control. The insulin production falls off within a week or two, and the infant should do well if provided supplemental glucose during this time.

Hypoglycemia can also occur in premature, small-for-dates infants, and ill full-term infants. Premature infants have decreased quantities of *glycogen,* the storage form of glucose. Small-for-dates infants have adequate glycogen but decreased ability to metabolize it to glucose. Full-term infants have adequate glycogen stores and can utilize them to produce glucose. However, they also can become hypoglycemic under circumstances of increased metabolic need related to illness. These illnesses include sepsis, congenital heart disease, brain hemorrhage, and drug withdrawal. If the hypoglycemia is treated promptly, the primary determinant of prognosis is the condition predisposing to hypoglycemia rather than the degree of hypoglycemia itself.

In addition, mineral imbalances may lead to symptoms that simulate hypoglycemia. Most common are deficiencies in calcium and magnesium (Salle, Delvin, Glorieux, et al., 1990). These tend to occur in low birth weight infants and often accompany hypoxic-ischemic encephalopathy. As with hypoglycemia, if these disorders are diagnosed early, they can usually be corrected with an intravenous feeding of the deficient mineral.

Inborn Errors of Metabolism

A number of congenital enzyme deficiencies occur with episodes of vomiting, lethargy, and coma in the first week of life. Unlike asphyxia, these children have a normal birth history and normal Apgar scores. They generally look well for the first 24–48 hours of life and then develop severe symptoms over the next few days. If the disorder is unrecognized, most of these children will die in the first weeks of life. If diagnosis is delayed and the child remains in a coma for many days, he or she may survive but is likely to have severe disabilities. Thus, early identification is essential.

Examples of these rare disorders include **maple syrup urine disease,** the **congenital hyperammonemias,** and **organic acidemias.** Prior to birth the mother's placenta removes toxins that are produced as a result of these enzyme deficiencies. However, after birth the toxins accumulate, usually derived from the protein in the formula or breast milk that the child ingests. Treatment of metabolic coma involves **dialysis** during which the blood is cleansed (as during renal dialysis). Low protein or special diets combined with medical therapy specific to the enzyme deficiency are then started and must be continued throughout childhood. Advances in treatment modalities have significantly improved the prognosis of these children (see further discussion in Chapter 10).

Drug Addiction

A problem of increasing concern is drug withdrawal during the first week of life. The pattern varies depending on the abused drug, the size of the dose, the duration of the maternal drug use, and when the narcotic was last taken by the mother. Withdrawal from barbiturates often leads to seizures on the second or third day of life. Heroin and methadone withdrawal generally leads to a persistent and high-pitched cry, hyperactivity, sneezing, vomiting, respiratory distress, and diarrhea on days 4–7. Symptoms of methadone withdrawal can continue for 3–6 weeks. Treatment with barbiturates helps to lessen opiate withdrawal. Symptoms of alcohol and cocaine withdrawal are discussed in Chapter 8.

Neonatal Seizures

Seizures are not very unusual in newborns, and they have an appearance that is quite different from those occurring in an older child. While generalized tonic-clonic seizures are the most common form observed in older children, seizures in the newborn tend to be subtle and focal. Newborn seizures have been divided into five types based on their appearance and cause: *subtle, multifocal clonic, focal clonic, tonic,* and *myoclonic* (Volpe, 1989).

Subtle seizures have manifestations that may be overlooked. They may consist of only jerking of the eyes, drooling, sucking motions, tonic posturing of a limb, and apnea. There may be some unusual movements of the arms resembling swimming and of the legs simulating peddling. These seizures are most common in premature infants. In *multifocal clonic* seizures, one limb will shake with progression to a second limb. This type of seizure is most common in full-term infants who have sustained asphyxia. A third form is termed *focal clonic* as it involves one limb; it is common with hypoglycemia and **hypocalcemia.** The fourth type, the *tonic* seizure, appears as extensions of all extremities and occurs in premature infants with intracerebral hemorrhages. Finally, *myoclonic* seizures involve episodes of multiple jerks of upper and/or lower limbs and are commonly linked to sepsis or brain malformations. Each of these seizure types has a specific EEG pattern.

Neonatal seizures are not generalized because the newborn's immature cortex has a sparse network of neurons (Figure 6.7). Since the extent of the seizure relies on the recruitment of nearby cells, the fewer cells surrounding the abnormal area, the more localized the seizure. As a result of the focal nature, respiration is rarely impaired but feeding may be affected.

Seizures occur in the newborn period most commonly as a result of asphyxia, brain malformations, hypocalcemia, sepsis, hypoglycemia, or intracerebral hemorrhage (Volpe, 1989). Some evidence indicates that neonatal seizures themselves may cause deleterious effects on the developing brain. However, the prognosis depends most on the precipitant of the seizure. The two causes of seizures associated with the best prognosis are hypocalcemia and hypoglycemia. Infants who have seizures related to asphyxia, intracerebral hemorrhages, brain malformations, or sepsis have poorer outcomes.

Treatment with anticonvulsants, most commonly phenytoin and phenobarbital, is usually effective in controlling seizures. In some instances, the seizures never return; anticonvulsant therapy can be stopped during the neonatal period. In about 30% of cases, the seizures are a harbinger of a seizure disorder and a severe disabling

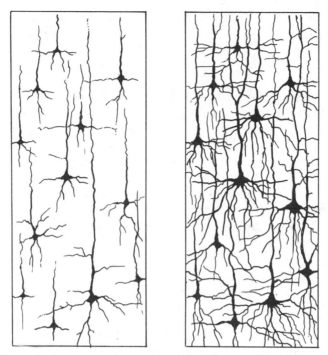

Figure 6.7. Progressive development of neurons during fetal life and the first year of life. On the left is a section of brain from a newborn infant. The right is from a 6-year-old child. Because of the few interconnections, the newborn rarely has a full-fledged generalized tonic-clonic seizure; it may well involve only one or two limbs. By 1 year, the increased interconnections lead to a typical tonic-clonic seizure in a susceptible child. (From Batshaw, M.L. [1991]. *Your child has a disability: A complete sourcebook of daily and medical care*. Boston: Little, Brown; reprinted by permission.)

condition (Volpe, 1989). Here, antiepileptic therapy may need to be continued for years. Seizures are discussed more fully in Chapter 26.

Congenital Anomalies

Developmental anomalies of the brain and other body organs are the other cause of developmental disabilities and death in the newborn period. Various types of genetic and chromosomal abnormalities that affect fetal development were discussed in Chapter 4. In addition, there are structural abnormalities of the brain, the causes of which are unclear. These include **lissencephaly, holoprosencephaly,** anencephaly, and microcephaly. The brains are too small, malformed, or missing elements. Some of these congenital defects are incompatible with survival and result in spontaneous abortions or stillbirths. With others, the infants are live-born but are more susceptible to problems in the newborn period, including intracranial hemorrhage, jaundice, hypoglycemia, and infection. These children are at increased risk for developmental disabilities both as a result of the underlying congenital anomaly and the perinatal problems. In most of these cases, treatment has little effect and the outcome is uniformly bleak.

OUTCOME

The prognosis for the disorders described in this chapter is quite variable. Children with subarachnoid hemorrhage have a 90% chance of developing normally, while those with severe intraventricular hemorrhages have less than a 10% chance for normality. Virtually no child with a developmental brain anomaly is unimpaired. Results are divided for children with hypoxic-ischemic encephalopathy and hypoglycemia with 50% doing well and 50% poorly (Volpe, 1986). Outcome of sepsis ranges from 20% to 50% based on the infecting organism (Faxelius, Breme, Kvist-Christensen, et al., 1988). Prognosis in some disorders is improved by early diagnosis, and in others by prevention. In some disorders no effective treatment is available yet.

SUMMARY

The first month of life is a critical period in the infant's development. Many metabolic and physical changes take place to enable the child to cope with the new environment outside the protection of the womb. Because these changes are so momentous and rapid, many abnormalities may occur. Some—for example, hypoglycemia—are readily correctable if identified early. Others, such as asphyxia, can best be handled preventively, with fetal monitoring and early delivery. Still others, such as some birth defects, cannot be treated. For those infants with brain damage, the extent of their deficits may not be known for several months. Overall, more than 99% of all newborns survive the first month of life, and the vast majority will grow up to be normal.

REFERENCES

Allan, W.C., & Volpe, J.J. (1986). Periventricular-intraventricular hemorrhage. *Pediatric Clinics of North America, 36,* 47–63.

Baker, C.J., Rench, M.A., Edwards, M.S., et al. (1988). Immunization of pregnant women with a polysaccharide vaccine of group B streptococcus. *New England Journal of Medicine, 319,* 1180–1185.

Batshaw, M.L. (1991). *Your child has a disability: A complete sourcebook of daily and medical care.* Boston: Little, Brown.

Brann, A.W., Jr. (1986). Hypoxic ischemic encephalopathy. *Pediatric Clinics of North America, 33,* 451–464.

Brown, Z.A., Vontver, L.A., & Benedetti, J. (1987). Effects on infants of a first episode of genital herpes during pregnancy. *New England Journal of Medicine, 317,* 1246–1251.

Bryla, D.A. (1991). Intelligence at six years in relation to neonatal bilirubin levels—Follow-up of the National Institute for Child and Human Development clinical trial of phototherapy. *Pediatrics, 87,* 797–805.

Chemtob, S., Laudignon, N., & Aranda, J.V. (1987). Drug therapy in hypoxic-ischemic cerebral insults and intraventricular hemorrhage of the newborn. *Clinics in Perinatology, 14,* 817–842.

Connolly, A.M., & Volpe, J.J. (1990). Clinical features of bilirubin encephalopathy. *Clinics in Perinatology, 17,* 371–379.

Dollfus, C., Patetta, M., Siegel, E., et al. (1990). Infant mortality: A practical approach to the analysis of the leading causes of death and risk factors. *Pediatrics, 86,* 176–183.

Ennever, J.F. (1986). Phototherapy in a new light. *Pediatric Clinics of North America, 33,* 603–620.

Faxelius, G., Breme, K., Kvist-Christensen, K., et al. (1988). Neonatal septicemia due to group B streptococci—Perinatal risk factors and outcome of subsequent pregnancies. *Journal of Perinatal Medicine, 16,* 423–430.

Feigin, R.D. (1983). Neonatal meningitis: Problems and prospects. *Hospital Practice, 18,* 175–179.

Ferrieri, P. (1990). Neonatal susceptibility and immunity to major bacterial pathogens. *Reviews of Infectious Diseases, 12,* 394–400.

Fish, W.H., Cohen, M., Franzek, D., et al. (1990). Effect of intramuscular vitamin E on mortality and intracranial hemorrhage in neonates of 1000 grams or less. *Pediatrics, 85,* 578–584.

Harris, M.C., & Polin, R.A. (1983). Neonatal septicemia. *Pediatric Clinics of North America, 30,* 243–258.

Hill, A., & Volpe, J.J. (1989). Perinatal asphyxia: Clinical aspects. *Clinics in Perinatology, 16,* 435–457.

Jain, L., Ferre, C., Vidyasagar, D., et al. (1991). Cardiopulmonary resuscitation of apparently stillborn infants: Survival and long-term outcome. *Journal of Pediatrics, 118,* 778–782.

Krishnamoorthy, K.S., Kuban, K.C., Leviton, A., et al.(1990). Periventricular-intraventricular hemorrhage, sonographic localization, phenobarbital, and motor abnormalities in low birth weight infants. *Pediatrics, 85,* 1027–1033.

Liley, A.W. (1965). The use of amniocentesis and fetal transfusion in newborn infants. *Pediatrics, 35,* 836–847.

Nelson, K.B. (1989). Relationship of intrapartum and delivery room events to long-term neurologic outcome. *Clinics in Perinatology, 16,* 995–1007.

Newman, T.B., & Maisels, M.J. (1990). Does hyperbilirubinemia damage the brain of healthy full-term infants? *Clinics in Perinatology, 17,* 331–358.

Ogata, E.S. (1986). Carbohydrate metabolism in the fetus and neonate and altered neonatal glucoregulation. *Pediatric Clinics of North America, 33,* 25–45.

Polin, R.A. (1990). Management of neonatal hyperbilirubinemia: Rational use of phototherapy. *Biology of the Neonate, 58*(Suppl. 1), 32–43.

Remington, J.S., & Klein, J.O. (1983). *Infectious diseases of the fetus and newborn infant* (2nd ed.). Philadelphia: W.B. Saunders.

Salle, B.L., Delvin, E., Glorieux, F., et al. (1990). Human neonatal hypocalcemia. *Biology of the Neonate, 58*(Suppl. 1), 22–31.

Sann, L. (1990). Neonatal hypoglycemia. *Biology of the Neonate, 58*(Suppl. 1), 16–21.

Scheidt, P.C., Graubard, B.I., Nelson, K.B., et al. (1991). Intelligence at six years in relation to neonatal bilirubin levels: Follow-up of the National Institute of Child Health and Human Development clinical trial of phototherapy. *Pediatrics, 87,* 797–805.

Shaywitz, B.A. (1987). The sequelae of hypoxic-ischemic encephalopathy. *Seminars in Perinatology, 11,* 180–190.

Thacker, K.E., Lim, T., & Drew, J.H. (1987). Cephalhaematoma: A 10-year review. *Australian and New Zealand Journal of Obstetrics and Gynaecology, 27,* 210–212.

Valaes, T.N., & Harvey-Wilkes, K. (1990). Pharmacologic approaches to the prevention and treatment of neonatal hyperbilirubinemia. *Clinics in Perinatology, 17,* 245–273.

Van de Bor, M., Van Zeben-van der Aa, T.M., Verloove-Vanhorick, S.P., et al. (1989). Hyperbilirubinemia in premature infants and neurodevelopmental outcome at 2 years of age: Results of a national collaborative survey. *Pediatrics, 83,* 915–920.

Vannucci, R.C. (1990). Current and potentially new management strategies for perinatal hypoxic-ischemic encephalopathy. *Pediatrics, 85,* 961–968.

Vohr, B.R. (1990). New approaches to assessing the risks of hyperbilirubinemia. *Clinics in Perinatology, 17,* 293–306.

Volpe, J.J. (1986). *Neurology of the newborn* (2nd ed.). Philadelphia: W.B. Saunders.

Volpe, J.J. (1989). Neonatal seizures: Current concepts and revised classification. *Pediatrics, 84,* 422–428.

Whitley, R.J. (1988). Neonatal herpes symplex virus infections. *Clinics in Perinatology, 15,* 903–916.

Whitley, R., Arvin, A., Prober, C., et al. (1991). A controlled trial comparing vidarabine with acyclovir in neonatal herpes simplex virus infection. *New England Journal of Medicine, 324,* 444–449.

Chapter 7

Born Too Soon,
Born Too Small

Upon completion of this chapter, the reader will:
—know the difference between the premature infant and the small for gestational age infant
—recognize some of the causes of prematurity
—be able to identify some of the distinguishing physical characteristics of the premature infant
—understand the complications and illnesses associated with prematurity
—be aware of the methods used to care for the premature and the small for gestational age infant
—know the results of outcome studies and the value of early intervention programs

---

Infants born too soon or too small are at risk for a number of problems during the newborn period. It is these problems that can place them at increased risk for developmental disabilities. Premature infants have more difficulty than full-term infants in adapting to the postnatal environment because their body organs are less mature. Small for gestational age (SGA) infants may have biochemical alterations and restricted growth potential. This chapter addresses the problems of low birth weight infants and discusses some new forms of medical management that have improved their prognosis.

DEFINITIONS

A *premature infant* is defined as a child born at or before the 36th week of gestation, 1 month before the estimated date of confinement. A small for gestational age infant refers to a newborn whose weight is below the 10th percentile for the gestational age. SGA babies may have been born at term or they may have been premature. For example, a baby born at 35 weeks gestation who weighs 5 pounds, or 2,250 grams, would be considered premature but appropriate in size for the gestational age; this weight falls at the 25th percentile for this age. However, if this infant were born at term weighing the same 5 pounds, he or she would be considered small for gestational age. At 40 weeks gestational age, the 10th percentile for weight is 5½ pounds, or 2,500 grams (Figure 7.1). SGA babies are sometimes also called *dysmature* or small-for-dates.

Although both premature and SGA infants have higher rates of illness and death as newborns than full-term infants, the problems for these two groups are somewhat different. The complications of prematurity will be the primary focus of this chapter, as this is the larger group.

CAUSES OF PREMATURITY

A number of maternal factors increase the likelihood of a premature delivery. Premature deliveries account for less than 5% of all births. Less than 1% will be very low birth weight infants, weighing less than 1,500 grams or about 3.5 pounds (Avery, 1987). However, this latter group accounts for 84% of all deaths in the newborn period and most of the morbidity (Klaus & Fanaroff, 1986). Although less than 5% of all pregnancies occur in adolescents, they account for 20% of all premature births (Goldberg & Craig, 1983). Why this happens is not completely clear, but physicians presume the immature uterus of the adolescent is more susceptible to early contractions than that of a woman in her early 20s. Poor nutrition, inadequate prenatal care, and toxemia also play a role. Women who have had many previous pregnancies, whose

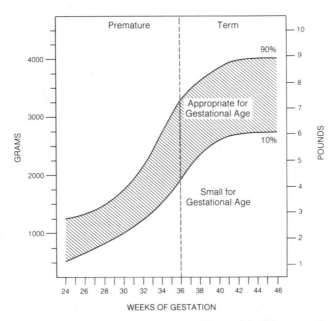

Figure 7.1. Newborn weight chart by gestational age. The shaded area between the 10th and 90th percentiles represents infants who are appropriate for gestational age. Weight below the 10th percentile makes an infant small for gestational age. Prematurity is defined as an infant born before 36 weeks gestation. (From Lubchenco, L.O. [1976]. *The high risk infant.* Philadelphia: W.B. Saunders Co.; reprinted by permission.)

cervical muscles are weak, who abuse drugs, or who are carrying twins also run a greater risk of delivering prematurely. In addition, women who develop infections during the third trimester, who have premature rupture of membranes, or who have chronic illnesses such as diabetes are more likely to deliver prematurely (Usher, 1987). Finally, certain congenital malformations or injuries to the fetus may lead to a premature birth. Although these are the most commonly cited causes of prematurity, the precipitating cause for most prematurely born infants is unknown.

PHYSICAL AND DEVELOPMENTAL CHARACTERISTICS OF PREMATURE INFANTS

Several physical and neurodevelopmental characteristics distinguish the premature infant from the full-term infant. Dubowitz, Dubowitz, and Goldberg (1970) developed a scoring system that takes into account these findings and enables physicians to confirm the mother's dates or to arrive at the gestational age when the mother's dates are unknown. Ballard, Khoury, Wedig, et al. (1991) have updated this system (Figure 7.2).

The main characteristics that distinguish a premature infant are the presence of body hair, a reddish skin color, and the absence of skin creases, ear cartilage, and breast buds (Constantine, Kraemer, Kendall-Tackett, et al., 1987). Premature infants have fine hair, or *lanugo,* over the entire body; this is lost by 38 weeks gestation. Also, the very premature infant lacks skin creases on the soles of the feet; these develop after 32 weeks. Skin color is ruddier because the blood vessels are closer to the surface, and the skin appears translucent. Finally, breast buds and cartilage in the ear lobe do not appear until around the 34th week of gestation (Figure 7.3).

Besides physical characteristics, differences in neurological development are also evident in the premature infant. In the third trimester, neurological maturation principally involves an increase in muscle tone and changes in reflex activity and joint mobility (Amiel-Tison, 1968). Before 28 weeks gestation, the infant is very floppy. After that time, tone gradually improves, starting with the legs and moving up to the arms by 32 weeks. Thus, while the premature infant lies in an extended, rag-doll position, the full-term infant rests in a semi-flexed position. Associated with increased tone is reduced flexibility of the joints. Premature babies are "double-jointed," while full-term infants are not. Finally, certain primitive reflexes such as the asymmetric tonic neck reflex (see Figure 24.3) do not appear until 30–32 weeks gestation (Capute, Accardo, Vining, et al., 1978) so that small premature infants may not have well-developed primitive reflexes at birth.

COMPLICATIONS OF PREMATURITY

In addition to having distinctive physical and neurological features, premature infants face a greater risk of complications in the newborn period compared to full-term infants. Among these problems are *respiratory distress syndrome, patent ductus arteriosus, apnea, intracerebral hemorrhage, retinopathy of prematurity,* and *biochemical abnormalities.*

Neuromuscular Maturity

	-1	0	1	2	3	4	5
Posture							
Square Window (wrist)	>90°	90°	60°	45°	30°	0°	
Arm Recoil		180°	140°-180°	110°-140°	90-110°	<90°	
Popliteal Angle	180°	160°	140°	120°	100°	90°	<90°
Scarf Sign							
Heel to Ear							

Physical Maturity

Skin	sticky friable transparent	gelatinous red, translucent	smooth pink, visible veins	superficial peeling &/or rash. few veins	cracking pale areas rare veins	parchment deep cracking no vessels	leathery cracked wrinkled
Lanugo	none	sparse	abundant	thinning	bald areas	mostly bald	
Plantar Surface	heel-toe 40-50mm: -1 <40 mm: -2	>50mm no crease	faint red marks	anterior transverse crease only	creases ant. 2/3	creases over entire sole	
Breast	imperceptible	barely perceptible	flat areola no bud	stippled areola 1-2mm bud	raised areola 3-4mm bud	full areola 5-10mm bud	
Eye/Ear	lids fused loosely:-1 tightly:-2	lids open pinna flat stays folded	sl. curved pinna; soft; slow recoil	well-curved pinna; soft but ready recoil	formed &firm instant recoil	thick cartilage ear stiff	
Genitals male	scrotum flat, smooth	scrotum empty faint rugae	testes in upper canal rare rugae	testes descending few rugae	testes down good rugae	testes pendulous deep rugae	
Genitals female	clitoris prominent labia flat	prominent clitoris small labia minora	prominent clitoris enlarging minora	majora & minora equally prominent	majora large minora small	majora cover clitoris & minora	

Maturity Rating

score	weeks
-10	20
-5	22
0	24
5	26
10	28
15	30
20	32
25	34
30	36
35	38
40	40
45	42
50	44

Figure 7.2. Scoring system to assess newborn infants. The score for each of the neuromuscular and physical signs is added together to obtain a score called the total maturity score. Gestational age is determined from this score. (From Ballard, Khoury, Wedig, et al. [1991]. New Ballard Score, expanded to include extremely premature infants. *Journal of Pediatrics, 119,* 418; reprinted by permission.)

Respiratory Distress Syndrome

Approximately 20% of all premature infants develop respiratory distress syndrome (RDS) during their first or second day of life. The degree of prematurity affects the incidence of this disorder. For example, less than 10% of the babies born between 34 and 36 weeks develop RDS, while over 60% of babies born at 32 weeks gestation or less do (Usher, 1987).

Typically, the infant's breathing pattern appears normal at birth, but he or she begins to have grunting respirations within hours. The baby starts using the abdominal muscles to help with breathing, but the lungs don't expand properly. The cause of this problem is as follows: Normally, the first breaths of a newborn open the alveoli, or air pockets, of the lungs. The alveoli are coated with surfactant, a chemical that normally prevents them from closing. However, most premature babies do not produce

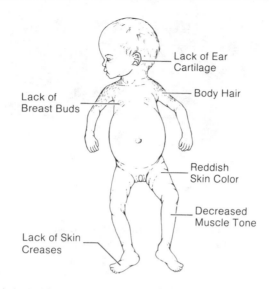

Lack of Ear Cartilage

Lack of Breast Buds

Body Hair

Reddish Skin Color

Decreased Muscle Tone

Lack of Skin Creases

Figure 7.3. Typical physical features of a premature infant.

enough surfactant to keep the alveoli open, so they collapse after each breath. The more premature the infant, the less surfactant is produced and the greater the risk of respiratory distress syndrome.

A chest X ray of the child with respiratory distress syndrome has a "ground glass" appearance. The collapsed alveoli are dense and look white on the X ray. This contrasts with normal lung expansion where the chest is filled with air that is translucent and appears black on the X ray (Figure 7.4).

Treatment of RDS involves keeping the airways open and providing adequate oxygen. In mildly affected infants this can be accomplished using supplemental oxygen alone or in combination with continuous positive airway pressure (CPAP). Here a mixture of oxygen and air is provided under pressure through short two-pronged tubes placed in the nose. More severely affected children require **intubation** (i.e., placing a tube down the airway) and a mixture of oxygen and air provided by **ventilator** under positive end expiration pressure (PEEP). The concept of PEEP is similar to CPAP, but there is more direct access to the lungs and better control of respiratory efforts. With these approaches to treatment, the survival rate has increased from 50% in 1970 to over 90% at present (Usher, 1987).

This improvement in survival is principally attributable to maintaining a constant pressure to the alveoli, keeping them open at all times, and promoting an effective exchange of oxygen and carbon dioxide. Before the use of PEEP and CPAP, enough oxygen was supplied to the lungs by ventilators, but because the alveoli remained collapsed, the exchange of oxygen between the alveoli and the pulmonary blood vessels was inadequate (Figure 7.5). Since the blood was not sufficiently oxygenated, the possibility of damage to the brain and other organs that became depleted of oxygen remained. There are now various adaptations of PEEP using jet ventilators and other devices that have further enhanced gas exchange.

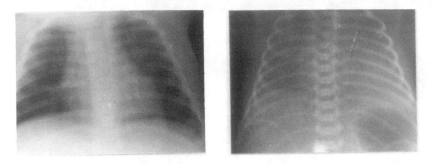

Figure 7.4. Chest X rays of a normal newborn (left) and of a premature infant with respiratory distress syndrome (RDS) (right).

Another advance that holds great promise for the treatment of RDS is surfactant replacement. If premature infants do not produce sufficient surfactant to keep their alveoli open, an obvious solution is to supply the deficient surfactant. Synthetic as well as human and cow surfactant is now available and can be administered as a spray directly into the lungs. It has been found that if a single dose of surfactant is given within 6 hours of the development of RDS, the illness will be significantly less severe (Dunn, Shennan, Zayack, et al., 1991). In these cases, less oxygen is required and artificial ventilation is needed for a shorter period of time. The risk of chronic lung disease is also decreased.

Another approach to stimulating surfactant production is to treat the mother prophylactically with the steroid medication Dexamethasone for 24–36 hours before the delivery of a premature infant (Crowley, Chalmers, & Keirse, 1990; Yeh, Torre, Rastogi, et al., 1990). During this time, labor can be slowed or stopped using tocolytic agents (see Chapter 5). Dexamethasone stimulates the fetus to produce surfactant,

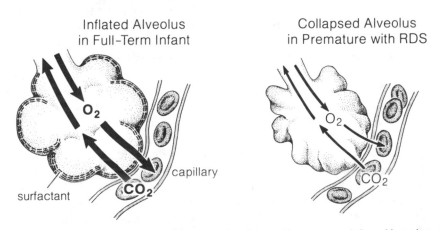

Figure 7.5. Schematic drawing of alveoli in a normal newborn and in a premature infant with respiratory distress syndrome (RDS). Note that the inflated alveolus is kept open by surfactant. Oxygen moves from the alveolus to the red blood cells in the pulmonary capillary. Carbon dioxide moves in the opposite direction. This exchange is much less efficient when the alveolus is collapsed. The result is hypoxia.

and premature infants treated this way appear to be less likely to develop respiratory distress syndrome.

The prognosis for infants who develop respiratory distress syndrome is clearly improved with these new therapies. The proportion of infants who survive without either severe intracranial hemorrhage or bronchopulmonary dysplasia is 65% in surfactant-treated infants versus 26% in untreated children (Fujiwara, Konishi, Chida, et al., 1990; Long, Corbet, Cotton, et al., 1991).

In terms of future intellectual development, the outcome for children with RDS is reassuring. Although the prognosis varies with the gestational age and weight of the infant, the risk for severe developmental delay is less than 15%. This is only slightly greater than for premature infants who do not experience RDS (Piekkala, Kero, Sillanpaa, et al., 1987).

Bronchopulmonary Dysplasia

With proper treatment, most children with respiratory distress syndrome can be weaned off oxygen or the ventilator within 2–3 weeks. However, a percentage of premature infants who have this disorder will develop a chronic lung disease termed **bronchopulmonary dysplasia (BPD)** (Shennan, Dunn, Ohlsson, et al., 1988). This disorder can result as a consequence of **barotrauma** from high inflating pressures, infection, **meconium aspiration,** or asphyxia. The walls of the immature lungs thicken, making the exchange of oxygen and carbon dioxide more difficult. The mucous lining of the lungs is also reduced as is the airway diameter. The result is an infant who has to work much harder than normal to obtain sufficient oxygen to survive. He or she may require months or even years of oxygen therapy and artificial ventilation as well as the use of bronchodilators and **diuretics** to help keep the airways open and the lungs "dry" (Meisels, Plunkett, Roloff, et al., 1986) (see Chapter 9). Even with this treatment, tolerance for exercise is limited. It is likely that this complication will become less frequent with the use of surfactant replacement therapy.

Patent Ductus Arteriosus

The **vascular** changes that occur in the first days after birth were discussed in Chapter 6. One of these changes is the closure of the ductus arteriosus, which connects the pulmonary artery and the aorta during fetal life (see Figure 6.1). However, in about 30% of premature infants, this closure does not take place. Normally, the constriction of muscle fibers that leads to closure is stimulated by oxygen intake following birth. In the premature infant with RDS, the oxygen level in the blood simply does not become high enough to stimulate muscle contraction (Gersony, 1986). Thus, besides poor ventilation, the infant must cope with a patent, or open, ductus arteriosus, leading to heart failure in about half of affected infants (Usher, 1987). If symptoms of failure develop, treatment involves the use of the medication **indomethacin,** which stimulates contraction of the muscular walls of the ductus, closing it in most cases (Peckham, Miettinen, & Ellison, 1984). If closure still does not occur, a surgical procedure must be done to close the ductus.

Apnea and Bradycardia

Another problem for the premature infant is the immaturity of the central nervous system, which controls respiratory effort. Not only does the premature infant have difficulty moving air into the lungs, but he or she often ceases to breathe for periods of 20 seconds or more. This is called *apnea*. **Bradycardia,** a fall in heart rate, often accompanies the breathing lapse. (Marchal, Bairam, & Vert, 1987). The more premature the infant, the more serious is this problem. Overall, about 10% of premature infants have apneic episodes, but over 40% of very low birth weight infants (less than 1,500 grams) have episodes of apnea and bradycardia (Usher, 1987). To treat this abnormality, a drug, theophylline (related to **caffeine**), is used to stimulate respiration. Rocker beds that also activate breathing may be used for infants who do not respond to drug therapy (Korner, Guilleminault, Van den Hoed, et al., 1978).

Persistent apnea may be a bad prognostic sign. It may indicate that the child has sustained some brain damage, or it may be a precursor of **sudden infant death syndrome (SIDS).** Twenty percent of all cases of SIDS occur in premature infants (Goyco & Beckerman, 1990). In this disorder, a previously healthy child is found lifeless in the crib, usually during the first 5 months of life. Unfortunately, no preventive treatment exists. Those premature infants who have persistent apneic/bradycardiac episodes and/or bronchopulmonary dysplasia are sent home attached to cardiorespiratory (CR) monitors that sound alarms if the babies stop breathing (Spitzer & Fox, 1986). The parents are trained to give cardiopulmonary resuscitation (CPR). This has helped parents to intervene during episodes of respiratory arrest and to improve their child's chances for survival.

Intracerebral Hemorrhage

Premature babies have a fragile network of blood vessels that supply the brain. These vessels are particularly sensitive to changes in oxygen and pressure, such as those that occur with respiratory distress syndrome and its treatment. Decreased cerebral blood flow and increased intracranial pressure may lead to hypoxic-ischemic damage (see Chapter 6). The area at greatest risk is the zone bordering the ventricles in the center of the brain (Figure 7.6). Damage to this region results in destruction of the white matter surrounding the ventricles, an abnormality termed *periventricular leukomalacia (PVL)*. This damage is visualized on ultrasound as **echodensities** or cysts in the area surrounding the ventricles (Bozynski, Nelson, Gernaze, et al., 1988). This region contains the nerve tracts that control leg movement, and damage is associated with a high incidence of spastic diplegia (Graziani, Pasto, Stanley, et al., 1986). This is the most common form of cerebral palsy in premature infants.

Most premature infants have some degree of intraventricular hemorrhage. When it is limited, it does not seem to adversely affect outcome. However, if it is severe and combined with periventricular leukomalacia, the outcome is not good. The majority of these children have severe mental retardation and spastic quadriplegia (Ford, Steichen, Steichen Asch, et al., 1989). The damage can be further complicated by blockage of blood flow to the ventricles, resulting in hydrocephalus. If this develops, the child may be treated with certain drugs, furosemide (Lasix) and acetazolamide

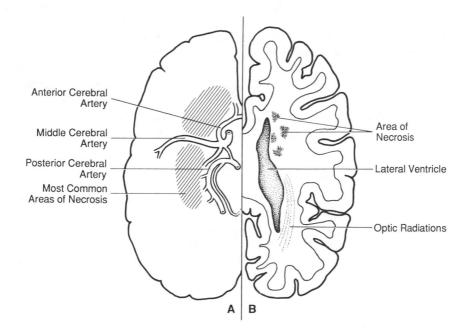

Anterior Cerebral Artery

Middle Cerebral Artery

Posterior Cerebral Artery

Most Common Areas of Necrosis

Area of Necrosis

Lateral Ventricle

Optic Radiations

A | B

Figure 7.6. Periventricular leukomalacia. A) The blood vessel supply to the brain, and B) the brain structures. The area of the white matter surrounding the lateral ventricle (particularly the top part) is especially susceptible to hypoxic-ischemic damage because it is not well supplied by blood vessels. It lies in a watershed area between the anterior, middle, and posterior cerebral arteries. In premature infants, poor oxygenation and decreased blood flow associated with respiratory distress syndrome may lead to necrosis of this brain tissue, a condition termed *periventricular leukomalacia*. When the posterior portion is affected, the optic radiations may be damaged resulting in cortical blindness.

(Diamox), to decrease production of cerebrospinal fluid. If this is not effective, a ventriculo-peritoneal shunt will be placed surgically to drain the blocked fluid.

Approximately half of very low birth weight infants have evidence of periventricular or intraventricular hemorrhage revealed by ultrasound. Fortunately, only about 18% will have the most severe hemorrhages that are associated with poor prognoses (Volpe, 1989).

No clearly effective treatment for intracerebral hemorrhage currently exists although some studies have suggested that vitamin E may make the tissue more resistent to hypoxic-ischemic damage (Fish, Cohen, Franzek, et al., 1990). Thus, this medication is often given prophylactically to infants at high risk for periventricular leukomalacia. Another approach to treatment has been the use of muscle-paralyzing drugs during artificial ventilation to avoid the marked variability of intracranial pressure that results from the infant fighting the respirator. This variable pressure has been implicated in precipitating hemorrhage (Volpe, 1989).

Necrotizing Enterocolitis

The gastrointestinal system may also be affected in premature infants. A disorder called **necrotizing enterocolitis (NEC)** develops during the first 2 weeks of life in about 2%–5% of very low birth weight infants. This is a life-threatening condition with a 20% mortality rate (Kosloske & Musemeche, 1989). Abdominal distension, lethargy, and vomiting are early signs. This may progress to gastrointestinal bleeding or bowel wall perforation. Abdominal X rays will show air in the bowel wall of the ileum or colon. NEC is thought to arise from the interaction of three factors: ischemic injury to the intestinal wall, bacteria, and early formula feedings (Kliegman, 1990). Normal intestinal bacteria acting on milk-based formula produces hydrogen gas that causes distension and ultimate rupture of an intestinal wall already weakened by lack of blood flow.

Medical management involves providing nasogastric suction to decompress the bowel, antibiotics, and intravenous fluids. Despite this therapy, about half of the infants will require surgery to remove the diseased section of bowel. In about 10% of cases, surgery will lead to a "short gut syndrome." Because the remaining bowel length is insufficient, diarrhea and poor nutrition often result. If this occurs, the child may require prolonged intravenous **hyperalimentation** using a high-caloric solution. Some evidence suggests that provision of an oral immunoglobulin mixture of IgA and IgG may decrease the risk of NEC in premature infants (Eibl, Wolf, Furnkranz, et al., 1990).

Retinopathy of Prematurity

Premature infants have also been found to be at risk for retinopathy of prematurity (ROP), previously referred to as *retrolental fibroplasia,* an eye problem that can lead to detachment of the retina and blindness. Initially, this problem was ascribed solely to excessive concentrations of oxygen used to treat respiratory distress syndrome. The reduction of the use of high concentration oxygen in treating RDS has decreased the prevalence and severity of ROP, but it has not eliminated it. Thus, in addition to oxygen, other influences must lead to this condition. Until more is known, the most effective approach is to have infants' eyes checked repeatedly by an **ophthalmologist** during the first months of life. Retinal tears can be treated with **cryotherapy** or laser therapy to prevent a retinal detachment. ROP is discussed in more detail in Chapter 17.

Biochemical Abnormalities

In addition to problems unique to premature babies, these infants are also more susceptible to the same problems experienced by full-term infants during the newborn period, including jaundice, hypoglycemia, and **hypothermia.** For example, bilirubin levels tend to rise more quickly in preterm infants because their bilirubin metabolizing system in the liver is less mature than in the full-term infant. As a result, treatment for an elevation in bilirubin is begun earlier in premature infants (van der Bor, van Zeben van der Aa, Verloove-Vanhorick, et al., 1989). Hypoglycemia is also more common because premature infants have smaller reserves of glucose than their full-term counterparts. Thus, symptoms of hypoglycemia, including lethargy, vomiting, and seizures, may occur. These symptoms are avoided by providing early feedings, administering intravenous glucose, and monitoring blood glucose levels. Finally, loss of heat, caused by inadequate insulation with fatty tissues, places the premature baby at risk for hypothermia; this is why incubators are used to warm the infants.

SMALL FOR GESTATIONAL AGE INFANTS

The SGA infant is one who is small in size for his or her gestational age. At birth, the SGA infant is not only small; he or she appears malnourished. This intrauterine growth retardation may result either from fetal abnormalities or from maternal problems. Problems in the fetus account for only a minority of cases. About 5%–10% of infants who are SGA have chromosomal or other congenital defects. An additional 10% experience negative environmental influences, such as intrauterine infections, and teratogenic effects from drugs and smoking (Teberg, Walther, & Pena, 1988).

Most of the remaining affected fetuses do not grow normally *in utero* because of inadequate supply lines for nutrition and/or oxygen. This most commonly results from mothers having obstetrical complications or chronic diseases that affect the maternal-placental circulation. In addition, women who come from lower socio-economic environments more often have infants who are small for gestational age, possibly as a result of inadequate nutritional intake during late pregnancy (Avery, 1987). Also, this condition is more common in twins and in infants of women over 40 or under 20 years of age, probably as a result of preeclampsia (see Chapter 5).

Small for gestational age infants (be they full-term or premature) have many of the same complications as premature infants. However, they tend to be spared one problem: they rarely get respiratory distress syndrome. It seems that the prenatal stresses that interfere with normal intrauterine growth stimulate the production of surfactant. One speculation has been that steroid production is increased.

Like premature infants, SGA babies experience hypothermia, hypocalcemia, and hypoglycemia. However, unlike premature infants, who by 2 years of age usually have achieved normal height and weight, SGA infants tend to remain short and under-weight throughout their lives. Also, the incidence of developmental disabilities is higher in this group of infants compared to babies whose weight is appropriate for their gestational age (Teberg et al., 1988). Full-term SGA babies are more likely to have learning disabilities (see Chapter 20), behavior problems, and attention deficit hyperactivity disorder (see Chapter 21). Premature SGA babies are at an increased risk for mental retardation and cerebral palsy, compared to appropriate for gestational age premature babies (Allen, 1984).

MEDICAL CARE OF THE LOW BIRTH WEIGHT INFANT

The best treatment for the low birth weight infant is prevention. Health officials hope that their efforts in the areas of improved education and nutrition for adolescent mothers will lead to fewer premature deliveries (Goldberg & Craig, 1983). Improved control of chronic illnesses in pregnant women should also decrease this number. Even when premature delivery seems imminent, it can often be delayed for days or even weeks using tocolytic agents to stop labor (Musci, Abbasi, Otis, et al., 1988).

For women who are at risk of having low birth weight infants, it is best to deliver the child at a hospital that has a newborn intensive care unit (NICU), even if this requires moving a woman in labor. The outcome for premature infants born at hospitals with newborn intensive care units is much better than for infants transported after birth from outlying hospitals (Usher, 1987). It is suspected that the transport itself may be an important risk factor. About half of premature infants are delivered by cesarean section, both to protect the fragile baby from the trauma of labor and to permit a controlled delivery in a hospital with a newborn intensive care unit (Malloy, Rhoads, Schramm, et al., 1989).

Once born, these infants are immediately placed under a heater to stabilize body temperature, and their respirations and heart rate are monitored. If body temperature is not controlled, the child will develop apnea, hypoglycemia, and acidosis, all of which can be life-threatening. About half of the very low birth weight infants require some respiratory support in the delivery room. This involves either giving oxygen, or intubating the baby and providing mechanical ventilation (Usher, 1987).

Most very low birth weight infants are unable to feed from a nipple. Their suck response is either decreased or absent, and their swallowing mechanism is underdeveloped. Thus, for the first few weeks of life these infants need to receive sustenance through special formula given by **nasogastric feeding-tubes.** The formula is high-caloric and contains trace elements, such as zinc and copper, and increased amounts of amino acids, such as arginine, taurine, and cystine, that are especially needed by the premature infant. This formula is also less likely to precipitate necrotizing enterocolitis. If the gastrointestinal tract is too immature to tolerate formula, intravenous hyperalimentation may be used. Over time the infant will be able to accept oral formulas. However, the feeding may be lengthy and difficult and need to be repeated at 2–3 hour intervals throughout the day and night.

As metabolic disorders are more likely to occur in the premature infant, blood samples are taken to test for glucose, calcium, bilirubin, **acid-base balance,** and **electrolyte** levels. Intravenous fluids are given to compensate for any biochemical imbalances. The most common abnormality is hyperbilirubinemia. Bilirubin levels rise to an average of 9–11 milligrams per deciliter (normal levels are less than 2 milligrams per deciliter) in three-quarters of low birth weight infants (van der Bor et al., 1989). Treatment involves placing the baby under special fluorescent lights. In rare instances in which the bilirubin level rises rapidly, the infant may require exchange blood transfusions.

Another problem is sepsis, occurring in about 17% of premature infants (Teplin, Burchinal, Johnson-Martin, et al., 1991). If signs of a generalized infection develop, such as lethargy and poor feeding, blood cultures are obtained and intravenous antibiotics are started. Fortunately, only about 2% of these children develop meningitis, with its associated poor outcome (Volpe, 1986).

ROSA: A PREMATURE INFANT

Rosa was the 32-week product of a 14-year-old adolescent. Her mother had received no prenatal care and arrived at the emergency room in labor, with her membranes already ruptured. Upset and screaming, she was taken to the labor room. Over the next 24 hours, her cervix dilated no further. A decision was made to deliver the baby by cesarean section. This went well, and Rosa weighed 1,800 grams at birth, an appropriate weight for her gestational age. She breathed spontaneously and was active; her 5-minute Apgar score was 8.

Within 4 hours, however, problems arose. Rosa began to breathe rapidly, and her chest X ray showed evidence of RDS. She was intubated and placed on a ventilator. The next day, her bilirubin level began to rise. She was treated with fluorescent lights, and the bilirubin level stabilized and gradually began to fall.

Because she was too weak to suck properly, Rosa was fed with a nasogastric tube. When she was 5 days old, an X ray showed that the RDS was resolving. The tube in her throat was removed on the seventh day. Then, other problems developed— apnea and bradycardia. Every 5 or 10 minutes, Rosa would cease breathing for about 20 seconds, her heart rate would fall, and the shrill alarm of the respiratory monitor would ring. Touching her with a finger usually made her gulp a breath of air, and she would begin to breathe again and her heart rate would increase. She was placed on theophylline and, within a few days, the episodes of apnea and bradycardia became less frequent.

Rosa was then transferred out of the intensive care unit and went home at 6 weeks of age, weighing 2,200 grams. At the time of her discharge, she followed objects visually, was alert to the sound of a bell, and appeared to be an active, healthy premature baby. Rosa's mother had received training on how to care for her and to use the cardiorespiratory monitor. Although very young, she was quite competent and loving. Rosa was entered in a home-based early intervention program; her prognosis is good.

SURVIVAL AND OUTCOME

Over the past 30 years, progress in *neonatology* (i.e., the care of newborns) has been phenomenal. The first improvement came in the care of infants weighing 1,500–2,500 grams (3.5–5.5 pounds). In these infants, it was found that immediate transfer to a newborn intensive care unit with support of respiration, maintenance of adequate nutrition, and rapid treatment of complications resulted in a markedly improved outcome. However, these children have twice the normal incidence of learning and behavior problems (McCormick, Gortmaker, & Sobol, 1990; Veen, Ens-Dokkum, Schreuder, et al., 1991).

Marked changes have also occurred in the prognosis of very low birth weight premature infants who weigh less than 1,500 grams. In 1960, more than 70% of these infants and 90% of those weighing less than 1,000 grams died during the newborn period. Of those who survived, almost one-fourth had severe mental retardation and cerebral palsy; half were moderately affected. Less than 10% of these infants turned out to be "normal" (Budetti, Barrand, McManus, et al., 1981) (Table 7.1).

At present, 90% of infants weighing 1,000–1,500 grams survive. Two-thirds of the infants weighing 750–1,000 grams survive, and one-third of infants weighing 500–750 grams survive (Hack, Horbar, Malloy, et al., 1991; Grogaard, Lindstrom, Parker, et al., 1990). Among these "micro-premies," survival by weeks is as follows: 23 weeks, 23%; 24 weeks 34%; 25 weeks, 54%; 29 weeks, 90% (Phelps, 1988). When assessed at 8 years, the overall incidence of severe disability in these very low birth weight infants is about 18% compared to 3% in the normal population (Victorian Infant Collaborative Study Group, 1991). Nine percent of these children have cerebral

Table 7.1.   Outcome at 8 years of age in infants with birth weight less than 1,000 grams

Disability	Percent affected
Cerebral palsy	9
Mental retardation	7
Visual impairment	12
Hearing loss	6
Seizure disorder	2

Source: Victorian Infant Collaborative Study Group (1991).

palsy, 12% impaired vision, 6% hearing impairment, and 7% mental retardation (see Table 7.1). A number of these children have multiple disabilities.

Among those who have escaped severe disability, twice the normal incidence of borderline normal intelligence (19% versus 9% with IQs of 70–85) and three times the incidence of learning disabilities and attention problems (45% versus 15%) exists (Klein, Hack, Breslau, et al., 1989). In general, the risk of cognitive deficits increases as birth weight decreases. It also increases with socioeconomic disadvantage. For those premature infants with normal intelligence, the prevalence of failing a grade in school is 23% versus 3% in full-term infants (Saigal, Szatmari, Rosenbaum, et al., 1990). Overall about 61% of these infants have some disability, versus 23% in the normal population (Teplin et al., 1991).

One indicator of poorer prognosis is microcephaly. Children with subnormal head size (below the 3rd percentile) at 8 months of age do more poorly in school than age-matched premature children with normal head circumference (Hack, Breslau, Weissman, et al., 1991). Microcephaly was found in 10% of very low birth weight infants, three times the normal incidence. These children scored lower on IQ tests (mean scores of 84 versus 98) and had decreased language and visual-motor skills. Academic performance in reading, math, and spelling were lower than the control group.

The incidence of cerebral palsy among premature infants is somewhat controversial. It is clear that the most common form of cerebral palsy is spastic diplegia. What is less clear is whether many of these children "grow out" of this motor abnormality. It has been suggested that one-quarter to one-half of premature infants who have evidence of spastic diplegia as infants have little evidence of this by school age (Nelson & Ellenberg, 1982). Yet, on closer inspection, the deficits, though markedly less obvious, are not completely gone. Teplin and colleagues (1991) found residual motor abnormalities, such as alterations in tone, reflexes, immaturities of speech patterns, poor balance, and strabismus, in 50% of very low birth weight infants at 6 years of age.

Different neonatal complications have been associated with different prognoses. Complications compatible with a good developmental outcome include respiratory distress syndrome, hyperbilirubinemia, hypoglycemia, and hypocalcemia. Those associated with a poorer prognosis include periventricular leukomalacia, sepsis, prolonged requirement for ventilation, and apnea. Environmental factors are also important. If the infants were transported from an outlying hospital or born to mothers of low socioeconomic status, they are likely to have poorer prognoses (Calame, Fawer, Claeys, et al., 1986). Infants who were both premature and small for gestational age fared the worst.

How well does developmental testing of premature babies in infancy predict outcome at school age? One problem is that of age correction. Should the tester give the infant credit for the prematurity and, if so, how much and for how long? The classic approach has been to completely correct for prematurity until the child reaches 2 years of age, by which time he or she is presumed to have "caught up." Thus, a 9-month-old who was born at 32 weeks would be expected to function as a 7-month-old, and when this child becomes 20 months old, he or she would be considered as an 18-month-old child. Using this approach, it has been found that in the second year, complete correction leads to an overestimation of the child's eventual IQ. Most investigators now feel that it is more accurate to completely correct only until 12 months of age, and then either to half correct or stop correcting between 1 and 2 years (Den Ouden, Rijken, Brand, et al., 1991). The general consensus is that correction should not be continued past 2 years.

Comparing 2-year assessments to 8-year follow-up, about one-quarter of these infants have their abilities overestimated and about 10% underestimated (Victorian Infant Collaborative Study Group, 1991). Comparing 5-year and 8-year assessments, the correlation (81%) was much improved. The most common causes of overestimation were missed vision and hearing deficits, while underestimation was often due to improved motor skills.

CARE IN THE HOME

Usually, a premature baby's condition stabilizes within 2–3 weeks. By then, adequate nutrition is possible and weight gain begins. The respiratory distress syndrome subsides, and the child no longer needs assisted ventilation. The jaundice abates. The baby starts maintaining a normal temperature, and biochemical levels become normal. The child is then transferred from the intensive care unit to an intermediate care unit, to feed and to grow. The baby is discharged when he or she is able to feed from a nipple, maintain temperature outside the isolette, and continue to grow well. Usually, the baby weighs between 1,800 and 2,500 grams (4–5.5 pounds) when ready for discharge from the hospital. The usual hospital stay for a 1,000–1,500 gram baby is 2–3 months (Usher, 1987).

Once the child comes home and the excitement of the new arrival subsides, the difficulty of caring for this very needy infant becomes rapidly apparent. This places major stresses on any family and is a particular challenge to the unmarried adolescent. Premature infants tend to be irritable, crying much of the time. They also have poor sleep-wake cycles such that they sleep for short periods of time throughout the day and night, leading to sleep deprivation in the parents. Their sucking pattern is immature, and they need to be fed frequently. Furthermore, their formulas may be nonstandard, difficult to find, and expensive. The infant may also have gastroesophageal reflux such that he or she will vomit after most feedings. Not only is this unpleasant to clean up, but it may give the parents the impression that they are not doing a good job. They may feel incapable of keeping adequate food in their baby to permit normal growth. There may also be medications to give for respiratory problems or to control reflux. Parents may have difficulty getting the child to take the medications without vomiting and worry that the baby will get sick because of inadequate medication. They may accidentally overmedicate the child by trying to compensate for lost medication from vomiting.

The prolonged hospitalization also may have interfered with normal maternal–infant bonding; the mother may actually be afraid of her baby, worried that she may do something wrong and the baby will be injured or die. This is more frequently the case if the child has experienced apneic episodes and is sent home on a cardiorespiratory monitor. The parents will have been taught the use of this monitor as well as cardiopulmonary resuscitation, but this may just increase their anxiety level, espewith the invariable false alarms that occur.

Because of all these stressors, it is important to provide an adequate support system to the family. These resources range from a visiting nurse to supervise the administration of medications and attachment of the monitor, to a social worker who arranges for financial resources and provides emotional support to the family. Physicians should encourage parents to enroll their infants in early intervention programs that will provide for support and training of parent and child.

EARLY INTERVENTION PROGRAMS

One recent study suggests that early intervention programs can have a beneficial effect on neurodevelopmental outcome of premature infants, especially those from disadvantaged backgrounds who have mild disabilities (Infant Health and Development Program, 1990). The program starts at discharge from the hospital and continues until 36 months corrected age. The intervention strategy incorporates home visits, attendance at a child development center, and parent group meetings. At the child development center, the child receives multidisciplinary therapy with a 1:3–1:4 ratio of teacher to infant.

At 36-month follow-up, the treatment group had mean IQ scores that were significantly higher than the control group. Despite this improvement, 18% of the infants with birth weight of 1,500–2,000 grams had IQ scores below 70 and 50% had IQ scores below 85. Furthermore, in the under 1,500 gram group, children with IQ scores of less than 70 did not demonstrate significant benefit from early intervention.

In sum, early intervention shows promise, but it may not be equally effective for all children. Once these children reach grade school those with normal intelligence and without cerebral palsy still may need speech therapy, occupational therapy, reading tutors, behavior management approaches, and treatment of emotional problems relating to school failure (Ross, Lipper, & Auld, 1990). If they do not receive this therapy, it is likely that the benefits will be lost.

SUMMARY

For premature infants, different complications lead to different prognoses. Complications consistent with a good developmental prognosis include RDS, hyperbilirubinemia, hypoglycemia, and hypocalcemia. Those associated with a poorer prognosis include severe intracerebral hemorrhage, sepsis, and periodic apnea and bradycardia. Even though an increased risk of developmental disabilities exists with these complications, many of these children still do well. With improved prenatal care and an increased number of neonatal intensive care units, the prognosis for low birth weight infants should continue to improve.

REFERENCES

Allen, M.C. (1984). Developmental outcome and followup of the small for gestational age infant. *Seminars in Perinatology, 8,* 123–156.

Amiel-Tison, C. (1968). Neurological evaluation of the maturity of newborn infants. *Archives of Disease in Childhood, 43,* 89–93.

Avery, G.B. (1987). *Neonatology, pathophysiology, and management of the newborn.* Philadelphia: J.B. Lippincott.

Ballard, J.L., Khoury, J.C., Wedig, K., et al. (1991). New Ballard score, expanded to include extremely premature infants. *Journal of Pediatrics, 119,* 417–423.

Bernbaum, J.C., & Hoffman-Williamson, M. (1991). *Primary care of the preterm infant.* St. Louis: CV Mosby/Yearbook.

Block, R.W., Saltzman, S., & Block, S.A. (1981). Teenage pregnancy. *Advances in Pediatrics, 28,* 75–98.

Bozynski, M.E., Nelson, M.N., Genaze, D., et al. (1988). Cranial ultrasonography and the prediction of cerebral palsy in infants weighing less than or equal to 1,200 grams at birth. *Developmental Medicine and Child Neurology, 30,* 342–348.

Breslau, N., Klein, N., & Allen, L. (1988). Very low birth weight: Behavioral sequelae at nine years of age. *Journal of the American Academy of Child and Adolescent Psychiatry, 27,* 605–612.

Budetti, P., Barrand, N., McManus, P., et al. (1981). *The costs and effectiveness of neonatal intensive care.* Washington, DC: Office of Technology Assessment, U.S.Government Printing Office.

Calame, A., Fawer, C.L., Claeys, V., et al. (1986). Neurodevelopmental outcome and school performance of very low birth weight infants at 8 ycars of age. *European Journal of Pediatrics, 145,* 461–465.

Capute, A.J., Accardo, P.J., Vining, E.P.G., et al. (1978). *Primitive reflex profile.* Baltimore: University Park Press.

Constantine, N.A., Kraemer, H.C., Kendall-Tackett, K.A., et al. (1987). Use of physical and neurologic observations in assessment of gestational age in low-birth-weight infants. *Journal of Pediatrics, 110,* 921–928.

Crowley, P., Chalmers, I., & Keirse, M.J. (1990). The effects of corticosteroid administration before preterm delivery: An overview of the evidence from controlled trials. *British Journal of Obstetrics and Gynaecology, 97,* 11–25.

Den Ouden, L., Rijken, M., Brand, R., et al. (1991). Is it correct to correct? Developmental milestones in 555 "normal" preterm infants compared with term infants. *Journal of Pediatrics, 118,* 399–404.

Dubowitz, L.M., Dubowitz, V., & Goldberg, C. (1970). Clinical assessment of gestational age in the newborn infant. *Journal of Pediatrics, 77,* 1–10.

Dunn, M.S., Shennan, A.T., Zayack, D., et al. (1991). Bovine surfactant replacement therapy in neonates of less than 30 weeks' gestation: A randomized controlled trial of prophylaxis versus treatment. *Pediatrics, 87,* 377–386.

Eibl, M.M., Wolf, H.M., Furnkranz, H., et al. (1990). Prophylaxis of necrotizing enterocolitis by oral IgA-IgG: Review of a clinical study in low birth weight infants and discussion of the pathogenic role of infection. *Journal of Clinical Immunology, 10,* 72S–77S.

Fish, W.H., Cohen, M., Franzek, D., et al. (1990). Effect of intramuscular vitamin E on mortality and intracranial hemorrhage in neonates of 1000 grams or less. *Pediatrics, 85,* 578–584.

Ford, L.M., Steichen, J., Steichen Asch, P.A., et al. (1989). Neurologic status and intracranial hemorrhage in very-low-birth-weight premature infants. Outcome at 1 year and 5 years. *American Journal of Diseases of Children, 143,* 1186–1190.

Fujiwara, T., Konishi, M., Chida, S., et al. (1990). Surfactant replacement therapy with a single postventilatory dose of a reconstituted bovine surfactant in preterm neonates with respiratory distress syndrome: Final analysis of a multicenter, double-blind, randomized trial and comparison with similar trials. The Surfactant-TA Group. *Pediatrics, 86,* 753–764.

Gersony, W.M. (1986). Patent ductus arteriosus in the neonate. *Pediatric Clinics of North America, 33,* 545–560.

Goldberg, G.L., & Craig, C.J. (1983). Obstetric complications in adolescent pregnancies. *South African Medical Journal, 64,* 863–864.

Goyco, P.G., & Beckerman, R.C. (1990). Sudden infant death syndrome. *Current Problems in Pediatrics, 20,* 297–346.

Graziani, L.J., Pasto, M., Stanley, C., et al. (1986). Neonatal neurosonography correlation of cerebral palsy in preterm infants. *Pediatrics, 78,* 88–95.

Grogaard, J.B., Lindstrom, D.P., Parker, R.A., et al. (1990). Increased survival rate in very low birth weight infants (1500 grams or less): No association with increased incidence of handicaps. *Journal of Pediatrics, 117,* 139–146.

Hack, M., Breslau, N., Weissman, B., et al. (1991). Effect of very low birth weight and subnormal head size on cognitive abilities at school age. *New England Journal of Medicine, 325,* 231–237.

Hack, M., Horbar, J.D., Malloy, M.H., et al. (1991). Very low birth weight outcomes of the National Institute of Child Health and Human Development neonatal network. *Pediatrics, 87,* 587–597.

Infant Health and Development Program. (1990). Enhancing the outcomes of low-birth-weight, premature infants: A multisite, randomized trial. *Journal of the American Medical Association, 263,* 3035–3042.

Klaus, M.H., & Fanaroff, A.A. (1986). *Care of the high-risk neonate* (3rd ed.). Philadelphia: W.B. Saunders.

Klein, N.K., Hack, M., & Breslau, N. (1989). Children who were very low birth weight: Development and academic achievement at nine years of age. *Journal of Developmental and Behavioral Pediatrics, 10,* 32–37.

Kliegman, R.M. (1990). Models of the pathogenesis of necrotizing enterocolitis. *Journal of Pediatrics, 117,* S2–S5.

Korner, A.F., Guilleminault, C., Van den Hoed, J., et al. (1978). Reduction of sleep apnea and bradycardia in preterm infants on oscillating water beds: A controlled polygraphic study. *Pediatrics, 61,* 528–533.

Kosloske, A.M., & Musemeche, C.A. (1989). Necrotizing enterocolitis of the neonate. *Clinics in Perinatology, 16,* 97–111.

Long, W., Corbet, A., Cotton, R., et al. (1991). A controlled trial of synthetic surfactant in infants weighing 1250 grams or more with respiratory distress syndrome. *New England Journal of Medicine, 325,* 1696–1703.

Lubchenco, L.O. (1976). *The high risk infant.* Philadelphia: W.B.Saunders.

Malloy, M.H., Rhoads, G.G., Schramm, W., et al. (1989). Increasing cesarean section rates in very low-birth weight infants. Effect on outcome. *Journal of the American Medical Association, 262,* 1475–1478.

Marchal, F., Bairam, A., & Vert, P. (1987). Neonatal apnea and apneic syndromes. *Clinics in Perinatology, 14,* 509–529.

McCormick, M.C., Gortmaker, S.L., & Sobol, A.M. (1990). Very low birth weight children: Behavior problems and school difficulty in a national sample. *Journal of Pediatrics, 117,* 687–693.

Meisels, S.J., Plunkett, J.W., Roloff, D.W., et al. (1986). Growth and development of preterm infants with respiratory distress syndrome and bronchopulmonary dysplasia. *Pediatrics, 77,* 345–352.

Musci, M.N., Jr., Abbasi, S., Otis, C., et al. (1988). Prolonged fetal ritodrine exposure and immediate neonatal outcome. *Journal of Perinatology, 8,* 27–32.

Nelson, K.B., & Ellenberg, J.H. (1982). Children who outgrew cerebral palsy. *Pediatrics, 69,* 529–536.

Peckham, G.J., Miettinen, O.S., Ellison, R.C., et al. (1984). Clinical course to 1 year of age in premature infants with patent ductus arteriosus: Results of a multicenter randomized trial of indomethacin. *Journal of Pediatrics, 105,* 285–291.

Phelps, D.L. (1988). The role of vitamin E therapy in high-risk neonates. *Clinics in Perinatology, 15,* 955–963.

Piekkala, P., Kero, P., Sillanpaa, M., et al. (1987). Growth and development of infants surviving respiratory distress syndrome: A 2-year follow-up. *Pediatrics, 79,* 529–537.

Rosetti, L. (1986). *High-risk infants: Identification, assessment and intervention.* San Diego, CA: College-Hill Press.

Ross, G., Lipper, E.G., & Auld, P. (1990). Social competence and behavior problems in premature children at school age. *Pediatrics, 86,* 391–397.

Saigal, S., Szatmari, P., Rosenbaum, P., et al. (1990). Intellectual and functional status at school entry of children who weighed 1000 grams or less at birth: A regional perspective of births in the 1980s. *Journal of Pediatrics, 116,* 409–416.

Shennan, A.T., Dunn, M.S., Ohlsson, A., et al. (1988). Abnormal pulmonary outcomes in premature infants: Predictions from oxygen requirement in the neonatal period. *Pediatrics, 82,* 527–532.

Spitzer, A.R., & Fox, W.W. (1986). Infant apnea. *Pediatric Clinics of North America, 33,* 561–581.

Taeusch, H., & Yogman, M.W. (1987). *Follow-up management of the high-risk infant.* New York: Churchill Livingstone.

Teberg, A.J., Walther, F.J., & Pena, I.C. (1988). Mortality, morbidity, and outcome of the small-for-gestational age infant. *Seminars in Perinatology, 12,* 84–94.

Teplin, S.W., Burchinal, M., Johnson-Martin, N., et al. (1991). Neurodevelopmental, health, and growth status at age 6 years of children with birth weights less than 1001 grams. *Journal of Pediatrics, 118,* 768–777.

Usher, R. (1987). Extreme prematurity. In G.B. Avery (Ed.), *Neonatology* (3rd. ed.) (pp. 264–298). Philadelphia: J.B. Lippincott.

van de Bor, M., van Zeben van der Aa, T.M., Verloove-Vanhorick, S.P., et al. (1989). Hyperbilirubinemia in preterm infants and neurodevelopmental outcome at 2 years of age: Results of a national collaborative survery. *Pediatrics, 83,* 915–920.

Veen, S., Ens-Dokkum, M.H., Schreuder, A.M., et al. (1991). Impairments, disabilities and handicaps of very preterm and very-low-birth-weight infants of five years of age. *Lancet, 338,* 33–36.

Victorian Infant Collaborative Study Group. (1991). Eight-year outcome in infants with birth weight of 500 to 999 grams: Continuing regional study of 1979 and 1980 births. *Journal of Pediatrics, 118,* 761–767.

Volpe, J.J. (1986). *Neurology of the newborn: Pathophysiology and management of the newborn* (2nd ed.). Philadelphia: W.B. Saunders.

Volpe, J.J. (1989). Intraventricular hemorrhage and brain injury in the premature infant: Diagnosis, prognosis and prevention. *Clinics in Perinatology, 16,* 387–411.

Yeh, T.F., Torre, J.A., Rastogi, A., et al. (1990). Early postnatal dexamethasone therapy in premature infants with severe respiratory distress syndrome: A double-blind, controlled study. *Journal of Pediatrics, 117,* 273–282.

Chapter 8

New Threats to Development
Alcohol, Cocaine, and AIDS

Charles J. Conlon

Upon completion of this chapter, the reader will:

—understand the impact and demographics of alcohol and cocaine use

—be able to describe the effects of prenatal exposure to alcohol and cocaine

—be aware of the neurodevelopmental alterations and long-term outcomes associated with *in utero* alcohol and cocaine exposure

—understand the biology, immunology, mode of transmission, and presentations of pediatric HIV disease

—understand the neurodevelopmental and neurological problems and outcomes of AIDS in childhood

---

Thus far, the principal focus of this book has been the genetic risks to the fetus and child. However, equally important are environmental risks, the greatest of which is poverty. In developing countries, this most commonly manifests in children as malnutrition (see Chapter 11). In the United States, where malnutrition is fortunately uncommon, the risks to the impoverished child include prematurity (see Chapter 7), substance abuse, child abuse, lead poisoning (see Chapter 11), and AIDS. The prevalence of these problems is increasing yearly, and their adverse effects on the development of the child are also growing. Learning and behavior problems are increased markedly in this population, as is the incidence of mental retardation. This chapter focuses on three of the newest environmental risks to the poor: alcohol, cocaine, and HIV infection.

Charles J. Conlon, M.D., is a developmental pediatrician in the Department of Pediatrics at the National Naval Medical Center and Assistant Professor of Pediatrics at the Uniformed Services University of Health Sciences in Bethesda, Maryland.

These three risks are linked not only by poverty but also by polydrug use. The individual who abuses one substance is likely to be a heavy user of others. Thus, alcohol abuse and cocaine abuse often occur together and may be associated with the use of nicotine, marijuana, heroin, and phencyclidine (PCP). HIV infection is strongly linked with intravenous drug use.

Polydrug use also makes it difficult to differentiate the specific syndromes associated with each substance. The child may have been affected by alcohol *and* cocaine. Other confounding effects on the fetus may be undernutrition of the mother, the presence of hepatitis or sexually transmitted diseases, and inadequate prenatal care. As a result, the following discussions must be read with the understanding that these are shared effects. Overall, affected children tend to be small for dates at birth, have microcephaly, and have cognitive deficits. There seems to be a continuum of effects; increasing severity of intake or polydrug use is associated with increased symptoms in the child.

FETAL ALCOHOL SYNDROME

Though seemingly a modern problem, maternal alcohol ingestion can be considered one of the oldest known causes of developmental disabilities (Abel, 1984). The Bible contains a proscription against alcohol consumption during pregnancy in reference to the conception of Samson: "Behold now, thou art barren, and barest not; but thou shalt conceive, and bear a son. Now therefore beware, I pray thee, and drink not wine nor strong drink" (Judges 13:3–4). Furthermore, Aristotle appears to have associated alcohol and fetal abnormalities in his tract "Problemata" (Hett, 1936). Yet, if the linkage was once known, it was not widely appreciated until the 1973 article by Jones, Smith, Ulleland, and colleagues that set forth the group of physical findings that defined **fetal alcohol syndrome** (FAS). It is presently the leading known cause of mental retardation, surpassing Down syndrome, spina bifida, and fragile X syndrome.

Features of Fetal Alcohol Syndrome

Children with FAS are generally born at term but are small for gestational age. During early childhood, they remain thin and short, but by late adolescence they may have attained normal height and weight. Characteristic physical features can help to identify those children with full-blown FAS: the head circumference is small (microcephalic), the eyes are widely spaced with narrow eyelids, and **strabismus** is often present. The nose is short and upturned, the ears large and low-set, and the groove in the midline of the lip (philtrum) shortened. The jaw is underdeveloped and there is **malocclusion** of the teeth; the fingers are shortened. There is also an increased incidence of congenital heart defects and hip dislocation (Graham, Hanson, Darby, et al., 1988) (Figure 8.1).

During the first 2 years of life, developmental delays, particularly in the area of language, become evident. The average IQ of children with FAS is in the range of 60–70 (Streissguth, Barr, Sampson, et al., 1986). In addition, many children with FAS display stereotypical behaviors associated with autism and behavior problems typical

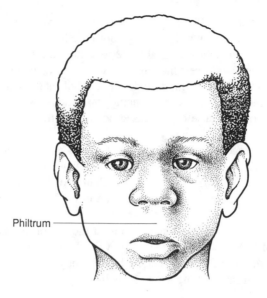

Figure 8.1.   Facial appearance of a child with fetal alcohol syndrome. These children tend to have microcephaly, widely spaced eyes with narrow eyelids, a short, upturned nose, large philtrums, large low-set ears, and underdeveloped jaws with malocclusion.

of attention deficit hyperactivity disorder (see Chapter 21) that include hyperactivity, impulsivity, and inattentiveness. The incidence of seizures is also increased.

Full-blown FAS represents one end of a continuum of alcohol-induced disabilities (Mills & Graubard, 1987). Children who have the intellectual and behavioral deficits typical of FAS but do not have the physical abnormalities are said to have fetal alcohol effects (FAE) (Day, Richardson, Robles, et al., 1990).

Prevalence of Alcohol Abuse and Fetal Alcohol Syndrome

The average amount of alcohol consumed per person varies from one country to another. As expected, the incidence of FAS parallels the degree of alcohol use. France, second in alcohol intake in the world, with a per capita average of 4 drinks (i.e., a drink is one-half ounce of alcohol) per day, was the first country to report FAS. Portugal ranks first, and the United States is 15th in alcohol consumption. In the United States, approximately 35% of adults abstain from drinking, 55% drink fewer than three alcoholic drinks a week, and 10% consume an average of 1 ounce or more of alcohol a day (American Psychiatric Association, 1987). Approximately 3% of women of childbearing age are considered to be either problem drinkers or alcoholics (Abel & Sokol, 1987). Alcohol intake tends to decrease somewhat during pregnancy, but the incidence of binge drinking (i.e., short periods of massive alcohol consumption) remains constant or increases. Compared to men, women have a lower incidence of alcoholism but are at greater risk to become intoxicated as they have decreased activity of alcohol dehydrogenase, the enzyme that detoxifies alcohol (Freeza, di-

Padova, Pozzato, et al., 1990). As a result, women accumulate alcohol more rapidly than men, and smaller amounts can damage both mother and fetus.

The overall incidence of FAS is about 2 in 1,000, and the incidence of FAE is thought to be at least 2–3 times this number. These are actually minimal estimates because it is possible that even mild/moderate alcohol intake may affect the developing fetus. The incidence also varies among populations. Native Americans are at particular genetic risk because of decreased activity of the dehydrogenase enzyme (Abel, 1984).

FAS and FAE together account for about 5% of all congenital anomalies and 10%–20% of all cases of mild mental retardation (Olegard, Sabel, Aronsson, et al., 1979). Chronic alcoholics have a 30%–50% chance of bearing a child with FAS. Once a woman has had one child with FAS, she has a 75% risk of having a second child with FAS (Abel & Sokol, 1987). The risk of bearing a child with FAS also appears to increase with maternal age, although the reason for this is unclear. Although the risk of FAS decreases with lower levels of ingestion, no safe level of alcohol intake is known. The Surgeon General has recently advised that women should abstain completely from drinking alcohol during pregnancy.

Effect of Alcohol on the Fetus

Alcohol consumed by the mother can affect the fetus because it is a small molecule that rapidly crosses the placental membrane. As a result, when the mother drinks, so does the fetus. Alcohol and its metabolite, acetaldehyde, decrease protein synthesis, impair cellular growth and migration, decrease production of neurotransmitters, and inhibit myelination of nerves (Pietrantoni & Knuppel, 1991). These effects explain the growth retardation, abnormal physical appearance, and behavioral, emotional, and cognitive problems of children with FAS.

If alcohol abuse (defined as an intake of more than 8 ounces of distilled liquor per day) occurs during the first trimester of pregnancy, the physical signs of fetal alcohol syndrome are likely to be present, and there is a 2- to 4-fold increased risk of miscarriage (Streissguth, Landesman-Dwyer, Martin, et al., 1980). If it occurs in the second trimester, growth and intellectual development are affected but there are no physical malformations. If abuse occurs in the third trimester, intelligence alone is affected. In mothers who have been imbibing in the days immediately preceding birth, the amniotic fluid will smell of alcohol, and the newborn infant may have a withdrawal syndrome marked by jitteriness, irritability, and hyperactivity. Fortunately, the withdrawal is not as frequent, severe, or long-lasting as withdrawal from heroin (see Chapter 6).

Outcome of Fetal Alcohol Syndrome

Treatment of children with fetal alcohol syndrome is directed at achieving an appropriate home and school placement and maximizing cognitive and psychosocial potential. Fewer than 10% of these children grow up in their parents' homes. Approximately two-thirds of mothers of children with FAS die from alcohol-related causes (e.g., cirrhosis, car accident, suicide, overdose) during the early years of the child's life (Abel & Sokol, 1987). Many children with FAS are removed from their parents' homes because of neglect or abuse. For children who remain at home, 86% of the mothers are cited for neglect and 52% for child abuse (Streissguth, Aase, Clarren, et al., 1991).

As a result of these problems, many of these children require foster home or adoptive placement. Unfortunately, these children are not easily placed because their extreme hyperactive and noncompliant behavior, combined with poor intellectual and language skills, makes them difficult to raise. Behavior problems are a significant issue in over 60% of the children. Adoption may be further complicated by the preponderance of ethnic minorities among these children (Abel, 1984).

The academic needs of children with FAS are a function of both their intellectual limitations and attention deficit hyperactivity symptoms. They may need to be placed in special education programs and seem to have particular problems with math (Becker, Warr-Leeper, & Leeper, 1990). Small, self-contained classes that use a behavior management approach seem to work best.

The disorder has been identified long enough to allow an assessment at adulthood, and the preliminary results are not encouraging (Spohr & Steinhauser, 1987; Streissguth, Aase, Clarren, et al., 1991). Few persons with FAS are living independently, and antisocial behavior is quite frequent. The incidence of alcohol abuse is increased in these individuals. This may be a consequence of many factors. Alcohol abuse may be more socially acceptable in cultures in which these children live, the children may have poor judgment and difficulty seeing cause and effect relationships because of their cognitive deficits, and there may be a genetic predisposition to alcohol abuse (Blume, Noble, Sheridan, et al., 1990).

In children with FAE, usually the offspring of problem drinkers, the deficits are more subtle but still present. There is often normal intelligence, but a decrease in IQ relative to genetic potential, and impaired academic achievement related to attentional and memory problems (Streissguth et al., 1991).

Prevention of Fetal Alcohol Syndrome

Like the other disorders described in this chapter, fetal alcohol syndrome is preventable. Much recent effort has been directed at educating teenagers about the problems of alcoholism and the risks of fetal alcohol syndrome. It is too soon to see the effectiveness of this approach. Placing signs in bars warning about fetal alcohol syndrome and teaching alcoholic women to decrease their intake during pregnancy has shown varying, though mostly unsatisfactory, results.

Billy: A Child with FAS

Billy is the fourth child born to Mary, a 36-year-old Native American woman living on a Navaho reservation. Mary is an alcoholic and has produced two other children with fetal alcohol syndrome. Born at term, Billy weighed only 4 pounds. He was found to have the typical features of FAS—small head, widely spaced eyes, upturned nose, large ears, and a small chin. He was also found to have a ventricular septal heart defect.

Billy did not stay with his mother long because she continued to go on alcoholic binges and was eventually hospitalized for cirrhosis of the liver, from which she died 2 years later. Billy was placed in a series of foster homes. Hyperactivity and irritability made Billy difficult to manage. When tested for school entry, he was found to have mild mental retardation. Now 7 years of age, Billy attends a self-contained special education class and still has behavior problems.

COCAINE

Cocaine is both one of the most powerfully addictive and most commonly used drugs of abuse. Its significance is expected to increase further because of the increased use of crack cocaine, which is easily available and cheap. Because most users are of childbearing age, it is not surprising that the increase in parental use has translated into an increased prevalence of "crack" babies. More than 100,000 babies born in the United States annually are believed to have been exposed to cocaine or other drugs of abuse prenatally. This represents a 2- to 10-fold increase in the past 10 years (Singer, Garber, & Kliegman, 1991; Schutzman, Frankenfield-Chernicoff, Clatterbaugh, 1991).

History of Cocaine

Cocaine is derived from the leaves of the coca plant. These leaves were chewed by the Incas in South America for thousands of years. It was considered a "heavenly plant," and chewing of the leaves was restricted to the highest socioeconomic strata of the culture (Rosenak, Diamant, Yaffe, et al., 1990). Coca leaves were brought to Europe in the 16th century by Spanish explorers of the New World. However, until the late 19th century, these leaves were only used in limited amounts to permit strenuous work. In the mid 1800s, cocaine was first extracted from coca leaves. In 1884, Sigmund Freud wrote a classic article on the use of cocaine as a local anesthetic and stimulant. He used cocaine extensively himself and became addicted to it (Freud, 1974) as did, in literature, Sherlock Holmes (Myer, 1974).

For a time, coca was a constituent of the patent medicine and pick-me-up Coca Cola. Coca is no longer used in this product. The first epidemic of addiction to cocaine was recorded in the early part of the 20th century. It is presently the most abused drug as a result of the availability of inexpensive and accessible "crack" (Abelson & Miller, 1985).

Clinical Effects and Metabolism of Cocaine

Cocaine is a potent, short-acting, central nervous system stimulant that heightens the body's natural response to pleasure, creating feelings of euphoria. Cocaine (methylbenzoylecgonine) is the principal alkaloid derived from the leaves of the coca shrub. It is available in two forms: a cocaine hydrochloride salt (the usual street preparation) and a purified alkaloidal base known as "crack" cocaine. Cocaine hydrochloride is soluble in water and is therefore readily absorbed through mucous membranes by **insufflation** (i.e., snorting) and is equally suitable for intravenous use

(Farrar & Kearns, 1989). Conversely, crack is almost insoluble in water. It vaporizes at low temperatures, and smoking is the preferred route of administration (Farrar & Kearns, 1989). Crack, also called "rock," is more than 70% pure cocaine. It is called "crack" because of the popping sound it makes when heated and "rock" because of its appearance. Other street names for cocaine include "snow," "coke," "gold dust," and "lady."

Cocaine affects brain chemistry principally by increasing levels of three neurotransmitters: norepinephrine, dopamine, and serotonin. Acute increases in norepinephrine result in constriction of blood vessels leading to rapid heart rate and elevated blood pressure. Norepinephrine is also the likely source of the euphoria experienced following cocaine intake. Alterations in serotonin levels decrease appetite and the need for sleep (Tarr & Macklin, 1987). Dopamine stimulation results in hyperactivity and sexual excitement.

The most commonly used urine screen for cocaine in adults employs the **enzyme-multiplied immunoassay technique (EMIT)** that can detect the major breakdown product of cocaine for up to 3 days after use. Tests to identify cocaine exposure in the newborn by hair or meconium analyses are currently being developed and should permit documentation of maternal drug use for up to 3–4 months prior to delivery (Farrar & Kearns, 1989).

Cocaine Addiction

Approximately 10%–15% of women of lower socioeconomic status use cocaine by smoking or intravenous administration during their pregnancies (Chasnoff, Landress, & Barrett, 1990; Frank, Zuckerman, Amaro, et al., 1988). Both methods of administration are highly and rapidly addictive. An initial intense euphoria begins 5–10 minutes after administration and lasts about 45 minutes. During this state, cocaine enhances energy, self-esteem, and the pleasure experienced in most types of activities. It also decreases anxiety and social inhibitions. However, these feelings are shortlived and followed by a prolonged period of anxiety, exhaustion, and depression. This biphasic effect results in a compulsion to re-experience the "high." Users are unable to predict or control the extent to which they will use the drug.

An acute overdose of cocaine can lead to sweating, tremors, cardiac arrhythmias, and seizures. Chronic use may induce severe weight loss, depression, sexual impotence, psychosis, and/or stroke. Other complications relate to the route of administration. Swallowing the drug may lead to intestinal obstruction, sniffing it may result in perforation of the nasal septum, and smoking it may cause lung damage. Cocaine users are also likely to use other drugs, particularly alcohol, marijuana, opiates, barbiturates, and diazepam. Finally, the sharing of syringes for intravenous administration increases the risk of viral hepatitis and HIV infection.

Effects of Cocaine on the Fetus

Approximately 10% of fetuses exposed to repeated cocaine use during the first trimester of pregnancy will have malformations. Although it has been presumed that this exposure is entirely of maternal origin, a recent study suggests that sperm may act as a vector to transport cocaine into the egg (Yazigi, Odem, & Polakoski, 1991). The pattern of malformation includes defects in the heart, gastrointestinal tract, genitourinary tract, skeletal system, and/or brain (Bingol, Fuchs, Diaz, et al., 1987; Chasnoff, Griffith, MacGregor, et al., 1989; Dominguez, Vilacaro, Slopsis, et al., 1991; Hoyme, Jones, Dixon, et al., 1990). Mouse fetuses exposed to cocaine develop similar malformations (Finnell, Toloyan, Van Waes, et al., 1990; Mahalik, Gautieri, & Mann, 1984). These birth defects are probably the result of cocaine's effect as a potent **vasoconstrictor**, leading to decreased blood supply during the period of organ formation (Moore, Sorg, Miller, et al., 1986; Woods, Plessinger, Clark, et al., 1987).

Vasoconstriction also occurs in the placenta, limiting the amount of cocaine that reaches the fetus (Woods et al., 1987). Unfortunately, this constriction, combined with hypertension and rapid heart rate, also limits oxygen transfer to the fetus, leading to an increased incidence of placental abruptions, miscarriages, premature deliveries, and stillbirths (Chasnoff, Lewis, & Squires, 1987; Levy & Koren, 1990). Among cocaine-addicted women, the rate of spontaneous abortion is 38%, abruptions 17%, and stillbirths 8% (Chasnoff, Burns, Schnoll, & Burns, 1985; Singer 1991).

Infants exposed to cocaine *in utero* may show excessive movement and elevated heart rate (Hume, O'Donnell, Stranger, et al., 1989; Roland & Volpe, 1989). At birth, approximately 20% of cocaine-exposed infants have decreased weight, length, and head circumference compared to drug-free infants of the same gestational age (Oro & Dixon, 1987; Zuckerman, Frank, Hingson, et al., 1989). This intrauterine growth retardation has been attributed to decreased oxygen transport, as well as to other maternal conditions including poor nutrition, infection, and multiple drug use (Chasnoff, Burns, & Burns, 1987).

Vascular constriction also increases the risk of intrauterine brain hemorrhage. Small areas of bleeding in the basal ganglia and frontal lobes have been found in about one-third of cocaine-exposed neonates (Dixon & Bejar, 1989). The long-term significance of these small hemorrhages is uncertain, but they clearly place the infant at increased risk for developmental and behavior problems. In rare instances, infants have experienced strokes, especially when mothers used cocaine within 48–72 hours of delivery (Chasnoff, Bussey, Savich, et al., 1986).

Effects of Cocaine on the Newborn

Cocaine undergoes detoxification in the liver. Metabolism is much slower in the fetus and newborn than in older children or adults. As a result, cocaine will accumulate in the blood and brain of the fetus and newborn at much higher levels than in the drug-abusing mother. This may lead to malformations in the fetus and clinical symptoms of withdrawal in the newborn (Oro & Dixon, 1987).

Withdrawal symptoms in the cocaine-exposed newborn include irritability, restlessness, lethargy, poor feeding, abnormal sleep pattern, tremors, increased muscle tone, vomiting, and a high-pitched cry (Doberczak, Shanzer, Senie, & Kandall, 1988; Finnegan, 1985; Hadeed & Siegel, 1989). These babies often make abrupt changes in state between sleep and crying, and are easily overloaded by environmental stimuli

(Chasnoff et al., 1985). EEGs show a pattern of excessive sharp wave activity, suggesting brain irritability (Dixon, Bresnahan, & Zuckerman, 1990). The onset of symptoms is usually within 24–48 hours of birth and withdrawal lasts 2–3 days.

The newborn may also show toxic symptoms if directly exposed to cocaine, either from contaminated breast milk, rubbing cocaine to shrink swollen gums, or inhalation (Bateman & Heagarty, 1989; Daya, Burton, Schleiss, & DiLiberti, 1988). Toxic symptoms include vomiting, diarrhea, irritability, and seizures, while physical findings involve dilated pupils, increased heart rate, increased blood pressure, and irregular breathing (Chaney, Franke, & Wadlington, 1988; Chasnoff et al., 1987).

Effects of Cocaine on the Infant

Most infants born to cocaine-abusing women demonstrate abnormalities in behavioral state, attention, muscle tone, reflexes, and movement that may persist for many months after birth (Table 8.1). These infants tend to shut out the environment by either sleeping or crying. Those who do become alert seem capable of only fleeting attention before showing signs of distress, such as rapid respiration and disorganized motor activity. Prolonged behavioral alterations of this type can interfere with the normal bonding of the mother and child and place an already fragile mother at risk for neglecting or abusing this difficult and unresponsive infant (Dixon et al., 1990).

In addition to these behavior problems, the cocaine-exposed infant exhibits abnormalities in muscle tone, primitive reflexes, and movement (Schneider & Chasnoff, 1987). The infant feels stiff because of increased muscle tone. Tremors of the hand and arm may be evident when the infant reaches for an object. Increased tone may interfere with voluntary flexion of the legs at the hips and knees and limit the use of the lower body for exploration. If these findings persist and are associated with enhanced primitive reflex activity (see Chapter 24), sitting and walking may be significantly delayed (Chasnoff, 1988). Even when these neuromotor signs are transient,

Table 8.1. Increased risk of problems prior to and following birth of "crack" babies

Prenatal effects	
Birth defects	Miscarriages
Intrauterine growth retardation	Prematurity
Intrauterine brain hemorrhage	Stillbirths
Microcephaly	
Newborn effects	
Withdrawal symptoms	Increased muscle tone
Overstimulation	Necrotizing enterocolitis
Effects in infancy	
Neurobehavioral abnormalities	Poor feeding and sleep pattern
Effects in childhood	
Learning disabilities	Behavior problems
Attention deficit hyperactivity disorder	

they are often markers for the future development of attention deficit hyperactivity disorder, learning disabilities, or behavior problems (VanDyke & Fox, 1990). There has been controversy about a possible increased risk of sudden infant death syndrome (SIDS) in "crack" babies, but this association has not been proven (Bauchner, Zuckerman, McClain, et al., 1988).

Effects of Cocaine on the Family

Cocaine use affects nearly all aspects of family life. There is often a history of family violence, psychopathology, child abuse, and neglect, as well as poor nutrition, poor health care, and limited education. The result is that many cocaine-exposed newborn infants are abandoned in the hospital. Those who are discharged with their biological parents are "at-risk" for abuse and neglect. Both New York City and Washington, D.C., have documented that more than half of all reported child abuse and neglect cases are cocaine-related (Chasnoff, 1988).

In the late 1980s and early 1990s, the number of cocaine-exposed children requiring foster care escalated so rapidly that many child welfare agencies became overwhelmed. Placement for cocaine-exposed infants is made even more difficult by the developmental and behavioral effects of this drug. The irritable, stiff, and difficult to calm infant may undergo frequent changes in placement as a result of foster parent "burnout." This disruption puts such children at further risk for developmental and behavior problems.

Treatment of the Cocaine-Exposed Child

Since most substance-abusing mothers have few resources or support systems, a team approach to caring for the whole family and its many needs is essential. One notable pilot project is the Women and Infants Clinic at Boston City Hospital. This multi-disciplinary service offers substance abuse counseling, family planning services, parenting classes for the mother, and developmental/behavioral assessments and pediatric care for the child.

Those caring for the cocaine-exposed infant must consider the infant's need for a quiet, nurturing environment. This can be achieved by swaddling, rocking, and providing a pacifier. Since these babies are easily overstimulated, using only one sensory modality at a time is most effective. For example, if the caregiver is singing to the infant, the lights should be kept low and the neonate swaddled in the crib. In addition, these infants may need frequent "time-outs" from stimulation. The combination of excessive crying, poor attention, and abnormal visual responsiveness usually improves by 1 month of age, but can persist for up to 6 months (Chasnoff et al., 1989).

Many cocaine-exposed preschoolers qualify for early intervention programs (PL 99-457, the Education of the Handicapped Act Amendments of 1986) because they are at increased risk for developmental disabilities. One example of a successful preschool program for cocaine-exposed babies is the Salvin Program in Los Angeles. This program strives to create a home and school partnership by providing home visits, maintaining frequent phone contacts, and encouraging parents or guardians to visit and perform volunteer work at the school. In order to provide stability, each child has the same teacher for 2 years and the same support team for at least 1 year. Class size is restricted to eight pupils, seat assignments and time schedules are fixed, over-stimulation is minimized, and hands-on activities with frequent positive reinforcement are emphasized. The long-term effects of this intervention are still unclear, but the short-term benefits have been encouraging in terms of gains in language acquisition and socialization skills (Dixon et al., 1990).

Prognosis of the Child Prenatally Exposed to Illicit Drugs

Children who are prenatally exposed to drugs are both biologically and environmentally at risk for developmental disabilities. In one follow-up study of over 200 cocaine-exposed infants, evaluation at 2 years of age showed catch-up growth in weight and height, but subnormal growth in head circumference (Chasnoff, 1990). Psychometric testing indicated intelligence within the normal range. However, 30%–40% of the infants showed some neurodevelopmental abnormalities, most commonly in language (Chasnoff, 1990). As preschoolers, these children displayed behavior problems, including short attention span, easy distractibility, impulsivity, and frustration intolerance. Some children did not manifest abnormalities until school age when they were found to have poor organizational skills and learning disabilities, most prominently in reading and mathematics.

Prevention of Drug Exposure

The development and behavior risks imposed by maternal use of cocaine are preventable. Prevention requires education of school-age children and their parents, teachers, and health care professionals (American Academy of Pediatrics, Committee on Substance Abuse, 1990). Health care providers should advocate for improved social support, health care, and drug treatment for cocaine-using women and their children. The prospect of parenthood may help induce some women to stop taking drugs. Furthermore, drug treatment should be emphasized at the time of childbirth.

Tommy: A Baby Prenatally Exposed to Cocaine

Tommy was born at term to a 24-year-old who was a crack cocaine user up to the time of delivery. Tommy only weighed 4½ pounds and his head circumference was small. In the first days of life, he was irritable and ate poorly. He often regurgitated formula, cried inconsolably, and did not like to be held. He did best when swaddled in a blanket and rocked. Even then he slept fitfully. The nurses were concerned that his mother would have difficulty coping with him, but this became a moot point as she abandoned him on his third day of life.

Since discharge from the hospital, Tommy has been placed in a number of foster homes. His development has been somewhat slow, but intelligence tests place him in the normal range. He is now 4 years of age and is in a preschool program. He shows signs of ADHD and his pediatrician is considering a trial on stimulant medication (to help with problems of attention and hyperactivity). It is likely that other behavior and learning problems will become evident after Tommy enters school.

PEDIATRIC HIV INFECTION AND AIDS

Intravenous drug use by a pregnant woman puts her child at risk not only for the health, behavior, and learning problems discussed earlier, but it also may expose the baby to the human immunodeficiency virus (HIV), the causative agent of acquired immunodeficiency syndrome (AIDS). AIDS can devastate a family with severe infections and progressive motor and cognitive deficits, and it ultimately can kill both mother and child. Yet, the development of the drug zidovudine (AZT) and other therapeutic medical approaches offer hope that this currently fatal disease may soon enter the category of "chronic illness," where it will join other illnesses once considered universally fatal, such as cystic fibrosis and leukemia.

Incidence of AIDS

The first cases of AIDS in adults were reported in 1981, and AIDS in children was discovered 1 year later. In the succeeding 8 years, 2,789 cases of childhood AIDS were reported in the United States (Centers for Disease Control, 1991). Approximately half of these children have died. However, these numbers represent only the tip of the iceberg. It is believed that for every child diagnosed with AIDS, at least 10 others are infected with the HIV virus (Gwinn, Pappaioanou, George, et al., 1991).

For many years, in the United States, AIDS was largely confined to homosexuals, hemophiliacs, and Haitians. Since 1988, however, the greatest increase in disease rate is seen among women and their children, and it is likely to become one of the leading causes of death and diagnosable developmental disability in children. It has become a disease of the inner city poor, with African Americans representing 58% of children with the virus and Latinos another 26%. It is one of the top two causes of death in children age 1–4 years in these groups (Chu, Buehler, Oxtoby, et al., 1991). Half of the mothers of these children have histories of intravenous drug abuse or are sexual partners with drug-abusing men. However, 40% of African American women report no identifiable risk factor. Of children with AIDS, 75% live in large cities on the East Coast (i.e., New York, Newark, Miami) or in Puerto Rico.

The Biological Basis of HIV

The human immunodeficiency virus was first identified in 1983. The virus can be cultured from blood, semen, and breast milk. The virus rarely can be isolated from other body fluids, such as tears and saliva, and thus, these are not thought to represent significant sources for transmission (Fauci, 1988).

HIV has three principal characteristics: 1) it attacks cells in many body organs; 2) it targets the helper T_4 lymphocyte, or CD_4 cell, that coordinates the immune response; and 3) it can lie dormant for years (Fauci, 1988) (Figure 8.2). The biology of the virus explains the characteristics of the disease. AIDS manifests as an immune deficiency disease with recurrent, life-threatening bacterial and viral infections (Wade, 1991). It can affect the brain, leading to progressive neurological damage. The virus also may rest quietly in a person's cells for months or years until some as yet undefined activating event triggers the onset of the disease (Gallo & Streicher, 1987).

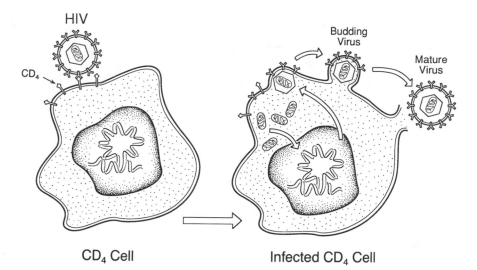

HIV

CD₄

CD₄ Cell

Budding Virus

Mature Virus

Infected CD₄ Cell

Figure 8.2.   Destruction of T₄ (CD₄) cells by HIV. The CD₄ lymphocyte is critical to immune defense and its destruction is the major cause of the progressive immunodeficiency disorder that is the hallmark of HIV infection. One mechanism of destruction involves the HIV virus entering and replicating in the CD₄ cell, and then budding from and damaging the cell membrane.

Transmission of HIV

Over 80% of infected children have acquired HIV from their mothers. The remainder have contracted the virus from contaminated blood products or, as adolescents, from sexual partners or intravenous drug use. A mother with HIV carries about a 30% risk of passing HIV to her child (Hutto, Parks, Lai, et al., 1991). There are three possible modes of mother-to-child transmission (Figure 8.3). First, HIV can cross the placenta and thereby infect the fetus. Second, transmission may occur at birth, as a result of exposure to the mother's vaginal secretions and blood (Caldwell & Rogers, 1991). Unfortunately, delivery by cesarean section does not appear to protect the child from contracting the virus (European Collaborative Study, 1988). Third, a much smaller number of children contract HIV from being breast-fed (Van de Perre, Simonon, & Msellati, 1991). As a result, even in developed countries, it is recommended that women who have the virus consider not breast-feeding their infants (World Health Organization, 1987).

Until 1985, the most common method of transmission to children between the ages of 1 and 12 was through contaminated blood products. This was a particular threat to children with **hemophilia**. However, since then, the nation's blood supply has been screened for HIV antibody, thereby greatly reducing the risk of exposure through contaminated blood and blood products. The risk is currently believed to be approximately 1 in 40,000 (Caldwell & Rogers, 1991).

In adolescents and adults, the virus most commonly enters the host after being deposited on mucous membranes during sexual intercourse (especially during anal

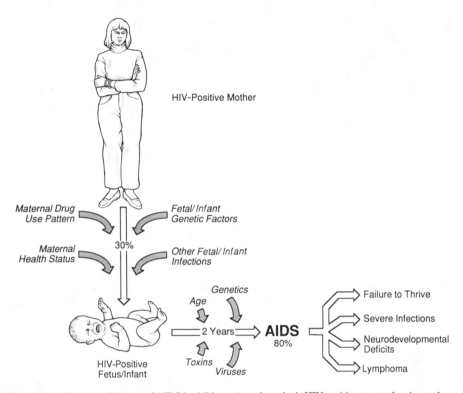

Figure 8.3.   The natural history of AIDS in children. A mother who is HIV positive passes the virus to her fetus. Not all fetuses are infected. Infection depends on multiple factors, including the maternal drug use pattern, maternal health status, and other genetic and infectious factors. The age at which the infant who is HIV positive develops AIDS depends on other genetic and infectious factors, some known, some unknown. The disease itself manifests as recurrent and severe infections and an increased risk of lymphoma.

intercourse because there may be bleeding) or through needle puncture from intravenous drug use (Centers for Disease Control, 1988).

Risk of Transmission of HIV in the Home and School

The most common causes of transmission of HIV must be contrasted with situations that carry a low or negligible risk of transmission. For example, no cases of person-to-person transmission in day care centers or schools have been documented; the risk there is thought to be negligible. The risk of transmission within a household also is thought to be low. Researchers have tried to quantify this risk by looking for family members who, though initially HIV-negative, become HIV-positive after nonsexual exposure to an HIV-positive member (Rogers, White, Sanders, et al., 1990). Over a 15-month observation period, no transmission was identified despite regular kissing, hugging, changing diapers, drooling, bathing, and sharing beds.

Because the risk of HIV infection by school contact is negligible, there is no justification for excluding an infected child from a normal school setting if his or her health permits. However, precautions should be taken if a child with HIV bites another child or teacher or if the child has a skin lesion. Skin exposed to the child's teeth or blood should be washed with soap and water; surgical gloves should be worn when tending to wounds of a child with HIV; blood spills should be cleaned with disinfectants, such as household bleach at dilutions of 1:10 to 1:100 (Task Force in Pediatric AIDS, 1988). Using these few precautions, there are virtually no risks in caring for a child with HIV.

In fact, the major concern about AIDS in a day care center or school is the risk to the child with HIV. These children have a limited ability to fight infection. Thus, even the benign illnesses commonly encountered in childhood can be life-threatening to these children. Parents and physicians must weigh the risks and benefits of placing the child in the school environment. Risks may be minimized by keeping the child isolated during a viral epidemic and by catching infections early so that treatment can be instituted. Outside of those circumstances, most experts feel that the benefits of social contact outweigh the risks of infection, and that from a quality-of-life perspective, children should remain in school as much as possible (Spiegel & Mayers, 1991).

Clinical Features of Pediatric HIV Infection

About 60% of children infected by their mothers develop symptoms in the first year of life and almost 80% by 2 years of age. This incubation period is much shorter than the 8- to 11-year lag between infection and the appearance of symptoms commonly seen in adults (Caldwell & Rogers, 1991). The most usual onset of symptoms in perinatally infected children occurs between 3 and 10 months of age (Meyers & Weitzman, 1991). When first diagnosed, children with HIV infection may have a variety of medical problems. A progressive loss of developmental abilities is the sole complaint in 10%–15% of cases (Belman, Ultmann, Horoupian, et al., 1985). More commonly, the child appears to be chronically ill with symptoms including intermittent fevers, recurrent diarrhea, failure to thrive, and/or acute weight loss. On physical examination, generalized lymph node, liver, and spleen enlargement are often present. As time passes, the children show themselves to be at high risk for bacterial infections, such as sepsis, meningitis, pneumonia, internal organ **abscesses**, and bone and joint infections (Hauger & Powell, 1990). The child is also at risk for life-threatening episodes of common viral illnesses, such as measles and chickenpox (Burroughs & Edelson, 1991). Less severe, but still important, infections include chronic middle ear infections, which can result in hearing loss; infections of the eye, which can lead to visual impairment; and cold sores or mouth **thrush,** which interfere with eating. As a consequence of immune system failure, these children also have an increased risk of developing malignant **lymphomas**. Other body organs are also frequently affected, resulting in congestive heart failure, lymphoid interstitial pneumonia, anemia, and/or kidney failure.

Diagnosis of HIV Infection

Diagnosis of HIV infection is made when antibodies to the virus are detected. In adults, antibodies usually appear within 6–12 weeks of infection. Rarely, persons with HIV may not develop antibodies for as long as 18 months (Steckelberg & Cockerill, 1988).

The diagnosis of HIV infection in infants and young children is complicated by the presence of maternal antibodies to HIV that cross the placenta from mother to fetus. These antibodies are indistinguishable from those produced by the infant and thus, may be present even when the child is not infected. On the average, children lose these maternal antibodies by 9–10 months of age, but, in some cases, maternal antibodies can persist for 15–18 months. Thus, finding HIV antibodies alone is not sufficient to make the diagnosis of HIV infection in children less than 15–18 months. During this period the diagnosis must be based on clinical and additional laboratory evidence, such as the number of T_4 lymphocytes (Arpadi & Caspe, 1991; Pyun, Ochs, Dufford, et al., 1987). Using this combined approach, a diagnosis can often be made by 6 months of age.

Stages of HIV Infection

The spectrum of HIV-related diseases led to the development of a pediatric classification system by the Centers for Disease Control (Table 8.2). Previous terms, such as *AIDS-related complex* (ARC) and *pre-AIDS*, that described less severely ill children have been replaced by this classification. *Class P-O* or *indeterminate infection* refers to children who have acquired the maternal antibody, but not necessarily the virus, via the placenta. These infants are asymptomatic and may test positive to HIV antibody until 15–18 months of age. After this time, a positive HIV antibody test indicates the child is infected. Once HIV infection is confirmed, a child is classified as either asymptomatic (*class P-1*) or symptomatic (*class P-2*) with the appropriately designated subclass.

Medical Management of Pediatric AIDS

Although the litany of medical complications is daunting, recent evidence indicates that survival can be prolonged by early identification and treatment. Major medical

Table 8.2. Pediatric HIV classification system

Class P-O Indeterminate infection

Class P-1 Asymptomatic infection
    Subclass A   Normal immune function
    Subclass B   Abnormal immune function
    Subclass C   Immune function not tested

Class P-2 Symptomatic infection
    Subclass A   Nonspecific findings
    Subclass B   Progressive neurological disease
    Subclass C   Lymphoid interstitial pneumonitis
    Subclass D   Secondary infectious diseases
    Subclass E   Secondary cancers
    Subclass F   Other diseases possibly due to HIV infection

Source: Centers for Disease Control (1987).

advances have included the use of antiretroviral therapy (HIV is a **retrovirus**), pro-phylactic therapy to guard against **Pneumocystis carinii pneumonia**, and immuno-therapy with intravenous immunoglobulin. However, management of AIDS must be truly interdisciplinary to be effective. Comprehensive care should include well-child care, anticipation and planning for management of common childhood illnesses, modification of the immunization schedule, nutritional support, early intervention for developmental disabilities, and psychosocial support.

As of early 1992, zidovudine (AZT) and dideoxyinosine (ddI, Videx) were the only antiretroviral medications approved by the Food and Drug Administration for use in the management of pediatric HIV infection. Based on available data, AZT is currently recommended for treatment of all children who have symptomatic HIV in-fection (Blanche, Duliege, Navarette, et al., 1991; Pizzo & Wilfert, 1988), and is also recommended in asymptomatic HIV-infected children who have evidence of signifi-cant immunodeficiency based on the T_4-lymphocyte count (also called CD_4). Re-searchers are currently trying to determine if asymptomatic HIV-infected children with normal CD_4 lymphocyte counts can also benefit from early initiation of AZT treatment. Early treatment may help reduce the chance of developing the full-blown disease. Evidence also indicates that AZT may improve the neurological outcome in this disease or temporarily reverse some abnormalities (Connor, Bardeguez, & Apuz-zio, 1989). Dideoxyinosine (ddI, Videx) was released in 1991 and may prove valuable as single drug therapy or in combination with AZT (Butler, Hittelman, & Hauger, 1991; Pizzo & Wilfert, 1991). Of particular importance for the treatment of pediatric AIDS is the safety and tolerance profile of these two drugs, as long-term treatment may be necessary. Currently, the long-term effects of these drugs are not entirely known.

Another major advance has been the use of antibiotics (e.g., trimethoprim-sulfa, pentamidine aerosols) that can be given daily to protect against a life-threatening pneumonia caused by the organism pneumocystis carinii. Finally, a na-tional multicenter study has confirmed the effectiveness of using monthly injections of intravenous immunoglobulin (IVIG) to support the immune system. This treat-ment has been shown to reduce the incidence of fever and sepsis and decrease hospi-talizations; but it does not improve survival rates (National Institute of Child Health and Human Developmental Intravenous Immunoglobulin Study Group, 1991).

HIV-infected children should receive routine immunizations but in a modified form. Inactivated injectable polio vaccine (Salk, IPV) should replace the normally administered oral (Sabin) live polio vaccine. In addition, pneumococcal vaccine should be given at 2 years of age to protect against pneumococcal pneumonia. The measles vaccine should be given to all children.

These therapies are most effective if given in child-centered, family-focused, community-based programs. Comprehensive care should be rendered in a culturally appropriate, sensitive, and nonjudgmental manner. One such program, Project STAR in Massachusetts, is a community-based and family-centered program for children from birth through 5 years of age who are at risk for or diagnosed with HIV infection. The project is staffed by a multicultural and multilingual team that provides services to families in their homes and at the STAR Child and Family Center. These services include daycare, early intervention groups, nutritional support, case management, advocacy, family support groups, and coordination of referrals.

Neurodevelopmental Effects of HIV

Developmental abnormalities have been reported in 75%–90% of children with HIV. The common problems include cognitive deficits (Belman, Diamond, Dickson et al., 1988; Pizzo, Eddy, Faloon, et al., 1988), fine and gross motor impairments (Epstein, Sharer, Oleske, et al., 1986; Hittelman, Willoughby, Mendez, et al., 1989; 1990; Mintz, Epstein, & Koenigsberger, 1989), speech and language delays (McCardle, Nannis, Smith, et al., 1991; Nannis, McCardle, Fischer, Conlon, et al., 1991), visual-spatial deficits (Diamond, Kaufman, Belman, et al., 1987), short-term memory problems, and attention difficulties (Hittelman et al., 1990; Mintz et al., 1989). Deficits in social or adaptive behavior have also been documented (Moss, Wolters, Eddy, et al., 1989; Wolters, Moss, Eddy, et al., 1989). Recently, some studies have reported similar deficits in uninfected children who were exposed to HIV prenatally (Koch, Jeremy, Lewis, et al., 1990).

These abnormalities may appear in several distinct patterns. A previously "normal" child may show either rapid or gradual loss of skills. Alternatively, the child's skills may plateau or decline in a step-wise fashion, punctuated by relatively stable periods (Epstein et al., 1986; Pizzo & Wilfert, 1991). In general, cognitive abilities worsen along with the disease, probably reflecting brain infection.

Neurological examination commonly reveals abnormalities, including microcephaly, spasticity, and loss of developmental milestones (Ultmann, Belman, Ruff, et al., 1985). Loss of brain mass has been detected by CT and MRI scans, and there may be a specific abnormality involving calcifications in the basal ganglia and frontal lobes; these signs indicate central nervous system infection *in utero* (Belman, Lantos, Horoupian, et al., 1986). Acute neurological abnormalities may also become evident as a result of infection, stroke, or tumor. These may include paralysis, seizures, or abrupt changes in mental status (Brouwers, Belman, & Epstein, 1991).

Early Identification of and Intervention for Neurodevelopmental Deficits

The development of children with HIV infection may be affected by other confounding environmental and biological factors, such as *in utero* exposure to drugs, prematurity, low birth weight, and failure to thrive. Long-term hospitalizations, chaotic family environments and understimulation may also add to the HIV effects. Finally, parental illness or death, often accompanied by foster care placement, will affect the children's development (Butler et al., 1991).

To identify neurodevelopmental delays as early as possible, children with HIV infection need developmental assessments at regular intervals. In general, infants who are HIV positive should be evaluated by 2 months of age and followed at least every 6 months for the first 2 years of life. After 2 years of age, children should have a neurodevelopmental assessment at least yearly if they remain asymptomatic (Butler et al., 1991). If a developmental delay, a "plateauing" of skills, or a decline is identified, more frequent reevaluation should be undertaken. In older children, neurodevelopmental assessment should include tests of cognition, language, motor development, social and emotional functioning, and attention/memory skills (Brouwers et al., 1991; Schmitt, Seeger, & Kreuz, et al., 1991).

Once delays or deficits are recognized and fully assessed, children with HIV who are younger than 3 years of age should be enrolled in an appropriate early intervention program. Three- to 5-year-old children should be referred to their county school committee for preschool special education placement. Medically related services (e.g., occupational therapy, physical therapy, speech-language therapy) also should be made available to children who have physical deficits. School-age children are also likely to need special education services (Pizzo & Wilfert, 1991).

Psychosocial Aspects of AIDS

The psychological and social issues raised by pediatric AIDS are so devastating and so heartrending that they are almost beyond description. Parents must deal with telling their child that he or she is likely to die. At the same time, parents must come to terms with their own culpability in their child's illness. If the father and/or mother are also infected, they must face the fact that if the child outlives the parents, they will not be around to comfort or care for their dying child. And what of the noninfected children who are likely to be orphaned?

Mothers of children with AIDS go through a grieving process similar to that faced by other mothers of children who are chronically ill or have disabilities (see Chapter 29). An initial period of denial may be followed by anger, bargaining, and finally, acceptance. Individuals go through these stages at various rates, with some backsliding. Some will never reach the acceptance stage. These problems point to the importance of social workers and the need for counseling as part of the therapy plan. Counselors can help parents face their anguish and can provide important information that may give parents hope for the future.

A major problem for families with a child with HIV infection is one of social isolation. Once diagnosed, the mother and child may be ostracized. The father, if not infected, may leave the scene. Grandparents and other family members may feel sorry, but often remain distant out of fear of catching the disease. The mother herself may find it difficult to see her child play with other children of similar ages as the differences in health and development become more obvious. This isolation is amplified when the child is hospitalized for a severe illness.

The child also may exhibit emotional problems. For older children, the need to explain the prognosis and deal with resultant depression may require psychotherapy and the use of antidepressant medication (Spiegel & Mayers, 1991). The child may exhibit behavior problems or even psychiatric illness. These may be situational, but they also may be a neurological manifestation of the disease.

Acceptance is needed not only for the family but also for the health care workers, teachers, and therapists working with the child with HIV infection. Judgments about the parents' behavior must be put aside with the goal of providing the best care for the child. Parents must be treated respectfully so they will return for continuing care.

Outcome

AIDS remains an ultimately fatal disease (Chu, Buehler, Oxtoby, et al., 1991). However, the rate at which it progresses is quite variable. Certain problems are harbingers for good or bad prognoses. The presence of a pneumocystis carinii pneumonia is a poor prognostic sign, with average survival being only a few months after diagnosis (Sanders-Laufer, DeBruin, & Edelson, 1991). Those children who develop neurological problems or kidney disease tend to survive about a year. On the average, children with only recurrent bacterial infections live 6 years after diagnosis. In general, children who are infected in the first year of age have a poorer survival time than those infected at an older age (Scott, Hutto, Makuch, et al., 1989).

In terms of prevention, it is likely that a vaccine will be developed eventually to protect against this disease. However, until that time, the best treatment is avoiding high-risk behavior. This involves teaching adolescent children about safe sex and providing intravenous drug users with clean needles. But, ultimately, society must provide for the needs of our poor, who are the primary target of AIDS.

Manuel: A Child with AIDS

Manuel was born at term to his 26-year-old mother, who was an intravenous drug user. At 4 months of age, he was taken to the emergency department of a hospital in Newark, New Jersey, because of failure to thrive. He had a history of diarrhea and poor feeding. He was also found to have significant developmental delays with most skills at a 2-month level. Although AIDS was suspected, the specific antibody test could not be done because of his young age. However, his mother, who also appeared chronically ill and debilitated, agreed to be tested and was found to be infected with HIV. From this point, his mother had a relentless downhill course despite efforts at treatment with AZT, trimethoprim, intravenous immunoglobulin, and other medications. Her final illness was an episode of meningitis, and she died within 6 months of diagnosis.

Manuel, however, has survived. He received the same treatment noted for his mother and was kept in the hospital until the diarrhea stopped and he started to gain weight. By this time, his mother was so sick that she could no longer care for him. Manuel was placed in a medical foster home. His foster mother had previously taken a special course on caring for children with AIDS. Manuel is examined monthly in a special pediatric AIDS clinic that uses a multidisciplinary approach to treatment. At 10 months of age, a low T_4 lymphocyte count confirmed that Manuel had the HIV infection. Now 2 years old, he attends an early intervention program. He remains developmentally delayed, functioning at a 12-month level, but has not plateaued in skills. He has required hospitalizations for two serious infections, but has survived them.

SUMMARY

Fetal alcohol syndrome, cocaine exposure, and pediatric AIDS have been called the new morbidities. These disorders are new in that they have been recognized as problems only in the past 2 decades. The word "morbidity" is used here because these conditions affect the children's physical appearance, health, and developmental and behavioral status. The prevalence of these disorders is increasing at an alarming rate.

Although independent syndromes, the three disorders have many similarities. Perhaps the most tragic is their prevalence among the poorest of the population, the group least able to cope with this added burden. The other link is substance abuse, which results in infants with fetal alcohol syndrome and "crack" babies, and is the major risk factor in pediatric AIDS. Although these new threats to development have been considered problems of the "underclasses," they affect all of society. Not only should every member of society relate to the human suffering involved with these disorders, but the financial and moral cost to society must be realized. Teachers, therapists, and health care workers will be increasingly affected by these conditions as more of these difficult-to-manage children need care.

The potential bright spot is that these are preventable conditions. It is hoped that improved educational programs about substance abuse and safe sex in grade schools and high schools will decrease the risk of our next generation passing these disorders on to their children. For the present, early intervention and family-centered treatment programs can make a difference in improving the quality of life and outcome in many children. These programs need to involve comprehensive, multidisciplinary, coordinated care that includes educational and drug treatment with special attention to the psychosocial effects on the children and their families.

REFERENCES

Abel, E.L. (1984). *Fetal alcohol syndrome and fetal alcohol effects*. New York: Plenum.

Abel, E.L., & Sokol, R.J. (1987). Incidence of fetal alcohol syndrome and economic impact of FAS-related anomalies. *Drug and Alcohol Dependence, 19*, 51–70.

Abelson, H., & Miller, J. (1985). A decade of trends in cocaine use in the household population. *National Institute of Drug Abuse Research Monograph Series, 61*, 35–49.

American Academy of Pediatrics, Committee on Substance Abuse. (1990). Drug-exposed infants. *Pediatrics, 86*, 639–642.

American Psychiatric Association. (1987). *Diagnostic and statistical manual of mental disorders* (3rd ed.-Rev.). Washington, DC: Author.

Arpadi, S., & Caspe, W.B. (1991). Guidelines for care of children and adolescents with HIV infection: HIV testing. *Journal of Pediatrics, 119*(Supplement 1, Part 2), S8–S13.

Barre-Sinoussi, F., Chermann, J.C., Rey, F., et al. (1983). Isolation of a T lymphotropic retrovirus from a patient at risk for acquired immune deficiency (AIDS). *Science, 220*, 868–871.

Bateman, D.A., & Heagarty, M.C. (1989). Passive freebase cocaine ("crack") inhalation by infants and toddlers. *American Journal of Diseases of Children, 143*, 25–27.

Bauchner, H., Zuckerman, B., McClain, M., et al. (1988). Risk of sudden infant death syndrome among infants with in utero exposure to cocaine. *Journal of Pediatrics, 113*, 831–834.

Becker, M., Warr-Leeper, G.A., & Leeper, H.A., Jr. (1990). Fetal alcohol syndrome: A description of oral, motor, articulatory, short-term memory, grammatical and semantic abilities. *Journal of Communication Disorders, 23*, 97–124.

Belman, A.L., Diamond, G., Dickson, D., et al., (1988). Pediatric acquired immunodeficiency syndrome: Neurological syndromes. *American Journal of Diseases of Children, 142*, 29–35.

Belman, A.L., Lantos, G., Horoupian, D., et al. (1986). AIDS: Calcification of the basal ganglia in infants and children. *Neurology, 36*, 1192–1199.

Belman, A.L., Ultmann, M.H., Horoupian, D., et al., (1985). Neurologic complications in infants and children with acquired immune deficiency syndrome. *Annals of Neurology, 18,* 560–566.

Bingol, N., Fuchs, M., Diaz, V., et al. (1987). Teratogenicity of cocaine in humans. *Journal of Pediatrics, 110,* 93–96.

Blanche, S., Duliege, A-M., Navarette, M.S., et al. (1991). Low-dose zidovudine in children with an human immunodeficiency virus type 1 infection acquired in the perinatal period. *Pediatrics, 88,* 364–370.

Blum, K., Noble, E.P., Sheridan, P.J., et al. (1990). Allelic association of human dopamine D2 receptor gene in alcoholism. *Journal of the American Medical Society, 263,* 2055–2060.

Brouwers, P., Belman, A.L., & Epstein, L.G. (1991). Central nervous system involvement: Manifestations and evaluation. In P. Pizzo & C.M. Wilfert (Eds.), *Pediatric AIDS: The challenge of HIV infection in infants, children, and adolescents.* Baltimore: Williams & Wilkins.

Burroughs, M.H., & Edelson, P.J. (1991). Medical care of the HIV-infected child. *Pediatric Clinics of North America, 38,* 45–67.

Butler, C., Hittelman, J., & Hauger, S.B. (1991). Guidelines for the care of children and adolescents with HIV infection. Approach to neurodevelopmental and neurologic complications in pediatric HIV infection. *Journal of Pediatrics, 119*(Supplement 1, Part 2), S41–S46.

Caldwell, M.B., & Rogers, M.F. (1991). Epidemiology of pediatric HIV infection. *Pediatric Clinics of North America, 38*(1), 1–16.

Centers for Disease Control. (1987). Classification system for human immunodeficiency virus (HIV) in children under 13 years of age. *Journal of the American Medical Association, 260,* 462–465.

Centers for Disease Control. (1988). Update: Universal precautions for prevention of transmission of human immunodeficiency virus, hepatitis B virus, and other blood-borne pathogens in health-care settings. *Morbidity and Mortality Weekly Reports, 37,* 377–388.

Centers for Disease Control. (1991). The HIV/AIDS epidemic: The first 10 years. *Journal of the American Medical Association, 265,* 3228.

Chaney, N.E., Franke, J., & Wadlington, W.B. (1988). Cocaine convulsions in a breast-feeding baby. *Journal of Pediatrics, 112,* 134–135.

Chasnoff, I.J. (1988). Drug use in pregnancy: Parameters of risk. *Pediatric Clinics of North America, 35,* 1403–1412.

Chasnoff, I.J. (1989). Drug use and women: Establishing a standard of care. *Annals of the New York Academy of Science, 562,* 208–210.

Chasnoff, I.J. (1990). *Drug use in pregnancy: Epidemiology and clinical impact.* Paper presented at the Spectrum of Developmental Disabilities XII, Baltimore, MD.

Chasnoff, I.J., Burns, K.A., & Burns, W.J. (1987). Cocaine use in pregnancy: Perinatal morbidity and mortality. *Neurotoxicology and Teratology, 9,* 291–293.

Chasnoff, I.J., Burns, W.J., Schnoll, S.H., & Burns, K.A. (1985). Cocaine use in pregnancy. *New England Journal of Medicine, 313,* 666–669.

Chasnoff, I.J. Bussey, M.E., Savich, R., et al. (1986). Perinatal cerebral infarction and maternal cocaine use. *Journal of Pediatrics, 108,* 456–459.

Chasnoff, I.J., Griffith, D.R., Freir, C., et al., (1992). Cocaine/polydrug use in pregnancy: Two-year follow-up. *Pediatrics, 89,* 284–289.

Chasnoff, I.J., Griffith, D.R., MacGregor, S., et al. (1989). Temporal patterns of cocaine use in pregnancy: Perinatal outcome. *Journal of American Medical Association, 261,* 1741–1744.

Chasnoff, I.J., Landress, H.J., & Barrett, M.E. (1990). The prevalence of illicit drug or alcohol use during pregnancy and discrepancies in mandatory reporting in Pinellas County, Florida. *New England Journal of Medicine, 322,* 1202–1206.

Chasnoff, I.J., Lewis, D.E., & Squires, L. (1987). Cocaine intoxication in a breast-fed infant. *Pediatrics, 80,* 836–838.

Chu, S.Y., Buehler, J.W., Oxtoby, M.J., et al., (1991). Impact of the human immunodeficiency virus epidemic on mortality in children, United States. *Pediatrics, 87,* 806–810.

Connor, E., Bardeguez, A., & Apuzzio, J. (1989). The intrapartum management of the HIV-infected mother and her infant. *Clinics in Perinatology, 16*, 899–908.

Crocker, A.C., Cohen, H.J., & Kastner, T.A. (Eds.). (1992). *HIV infection and developmental disabilities: A resource for service providers.* Baltimore: Paul H. Brookes Publishing Co.

Day, N.L., Richardson, G., Robles, N., et al. (1990). Effect of prenatal alcohol exposure on growth and morphology of offspring at 8 months of age. *Pediatrics, 85*, 748–752.

Daya, M.R., Burton, B.T., Schleiss, M.R., & DiLiberti, J.H. (1988). Recurrent seizures following mucosal application of TAC. *Annals of Emergency Medicine, 17*, 647–648.

Diamond, G.W., Kaufman, J., Belman, A.L., et al. (1987). Characterization of cognitive functioning in a subgroup of children with congential HIV infection. *Archives of Clinical Neuropsychology, 2*, 245–256.

Dixon, S.D., & Bejar, R. (1989). Echoencephalographic findings in neonates associated material cocaine and methamphetamine use: Incidence and clinical correlates. *Journal of Pediatrics, 115*, 770–778.

Dixon, S.D., Bresnahan, K., & Zuckerman, B. (1990). Cocaine babies: Meeting the challenge of management. *Contemporary Pediatrics, 7*(6), 70–92.

Doberczak, T.M., Shanzer, S., Senie, R.T., & Kandall, S.R. (1988). Neonatal neurologic and electroencephalographic effects of intrauterine cocaine exposure. *Journal of Pediatrics, 113*, 354–358.

Dominguez, R., Vilacoro, A.A., Slopsis, J.M., et al. (1991). Brain and ocular abnormalities in infants with *in utero* exposure to cocaine and other street drugs. *American Journal of Diseases of Children, 145*, 688–695.

Dorris, M. (1989). *The broken cord.* New York: Harper Collins.

Epstein, L.G., Sharer, L.R., Oleske, J.M., et al. (1986). Neurologic manifestations of human immunodeficiency virus infection in children. *Pediatrics, 78*, 678–687.

European Collaborative Study. (1988). Mother-to-child transmission of HIV infection. *Lancet, 2*, 1039–1043.

Farrar, H.C., & Kearns, G.L. (1989). Cocaine: Clinical pharmacology and toxicology. *Journal of Pediatrics, 115*, 665–675.

Fauci, A.S. (1988). The human immunodeficiency virus: Infectivity and mechanisms of pathogenesis. *Science, 239*, 617–622.

Finnegan, L.P. (1985). Neonatal abstinence. In N.M. Nelson (Ed.), *Current therapy in neonatal-perinatal medicine, 1985–1986* (pp. 262–270). Saint Louis: C.V. Mosby.

Finnell, R.H., Toloyan, S., VanWaes, M., et al. (1990). Preliminary evidence for a cocaine-induced embryopathy in mice. *Toxicology and Applied Pharmacology, 103*, 228–237.

Frank, D.A., Zuckerman, B.S., Amaro, H., et al. (1988). Cocaine use during pregnancy: Prevalence and correlates. *Pediatrics, 82*, 888–895.

Freeza, M., diPadova, C., Pozzato, G., et al. (1990). High blood alcohol levels in women. The role of decreased gastric alcohol dehydrogenase activity and first pass metabolism. *New England Journal of Medicine, 322*, 95–99.

Freud, S. (1974). *Cocaine papers.* New York: Stonehill Press.

Gallo, R.C., & Streicher, H.Z., (1987). Human T-lymphotropic retroviruses (HTLV—I, II, and III): The biological basis of adult T-cell leukemia, lymphoma and AIDS. In S. Broder (Ed.), *AIDS: Modern concepts and therapeutic challenges.* New York: Marcel Dekker.

Graham, J.M., Jr., Hanson, J.W., Darby, B.L., et al. (1988). Independent dysmorphology evaluation at birth and 4 years of age for children exposed to varying amounts of alcohol in utero. *Pediatrics, 81*, 772–778.

Gwynn, M., Pappaioanou, M., George, J.R., et al. (1991). Prevalence of HIV infection in childbearing women in the United States. Surveillance using newborn blood samples. *Journal of the American Medical Association, 265*, 1704–1708.

Hadeed, A.J., & Siegel, S.R. (1989). Maternal cocaine use during pregnancy: Effect on the newborn infant. *Pediatrics, 84*, 205–210.

Hauger, S.B., & Powell, K.R. (1990). Infectious complications in children with HIV infection. *Pediatric Annals*, *19*, 421–436.

Hett, W.S. (1936). *Aristotle's problemata*. Cambridge, MA: Harvard University Press.

Hittelman, J., Willoughby, A., Mendez, H., et al. (1989). *Prospective neurodevelopmental outcome of infants with perinatally acquired HIV infection and their controls*. Abstract presented at the Fifth Annual Pediatric AIDS Conference, Los Angeles.

Hittelman, J., Willoughby, A., Mendez, H., et al. (1990). *Neurodevelopmental outcome of perinatally acquired HIV infection in the first fifteen months of life*. Abstract presented at the VI International Conference on AIDS, San Francisco.

Hoyme, H.E., Jones, K.L., Dixon, S.D., et al. (1990). Prenatal cocaine exposure and fetal vascular disruption. *Pediatrics*, *85*, 743–747.

Hume, R.F., Jr., O'Donnell, K.J., Stranger, C.L., et al. (1989). In utero cocaine exposure: Observations of fetal behavioral state may predict neonatal outcome. *American Journal of Obstetrics and Gynecology*, *161*, 685–690.

Hutto, C., Parks, W.P., Lai, S.H., et al. (1991). A hospital-based prospective study of perinatal infection with human immunodeficiency virus type 1. *Journal of Pediatrics*, *118*, 347–353.

Jones, K.L., Smith, D.W., Ulleland, C.N., et al. (1973). Pattern of malformation in offspring of chronic alcoholic mothers. *Lancet*, *1*, 1267–1271.

Kapur, R.P., Shaw, C.M., & Shepard, T.H. (1991). Brain hemorrhages in cocaine-exposed human fetuses. *Teratology*, *44*, 11–18.

Koch, T., Jeremy, R.J., Lewis, E., et al. (1990). *Developmental abnormalities in uninfected infants born to HIV infected mothers*. Abstract presented at the VI International Conference on AIDS, San Francisco.

Levy, M., & Koren, G. (1990). Obstetric and neonatal effects of drugs of abuse. *Emergency Medicine Clinics of North America*, *8*, 633–652.

Mahalik, M.P., Gautieri, R.F., & Mann, D.E., (1984). Mechanisms of cocaine induced teratogenesis. *Research Communications in Substance Abuse*, *5*, 279–304.

McCardle, P., Nannis, E., Smith, R., et al. (1991). *Emerging patterns of HIV-related language deficits*. Abstract presented at the VII International Conference on AIDS, Florence.

Meyers, A., & Weitzman, M. (1991). Pediatric HIV disease. The newest chronic illness of childhood. *Pediatric Clinics of North America*, *38*, 169–194.

Mills, J.L., & Graubard, B.I. (1987). Is moderate drinking during pregnancy associated with an increased risk of malformations? *Pediatrics*, *80*, 309–314.

Mintz, M., Epstein, L., & Koenigsberger, R., (1989). Neurologic manifestations of acquired immunodeficiency syndrome in children. *International Pediatrics*, *4*, 161–171.

Moore, T.R., Sorg, J., Miller, L., et al. (1986). Hemodynamic effects of intravenous cocaine on the pregnant ewe and fetus. *American Journal of Obstetrics and Gynecology*, *155*, 883–888.

Moss, H., Wolters, P., Eddy, J., et al. (1989). *The effects of encephalopathy and AZT treatment on the social and emotional behavior of pediatric AIDS patients*. Abstract presented at the V International Conference on AIDS, Montreal.

Myer, D. (1974). *The seven percent solution*. New York: Dutton.

Nannis, E.D., McCardle, P., Fischer, G., Conlon, C., et al. (1991). *Neurodevelopmental findings in military dependent children with HIV disease*. Abstract presented at the Annual Meeting of the American Psychological Association, San Francisco.

The National Institute of Child Health and Human Development Intravenous Immunoglobulin Study Group. (1991). Intravenous immune globulin for the prevention of bacterial infections in children with symptomatic human immunodeficiency virus infection. *New England Journal of Medicine*, *325*, 73–80.

Olegard, R., Sabel, K.G., Aronsson, M., et al. (1979). Effects on the child of alcohol abuse during pregnancy. Retrospective and prospective studies. *Acta Paediatrica Scandinavica*, *275*(Suppl), 112–121.

Oro, A.S., & Dixon, S.D. (1987). Perinatal cocaine and methamphetamine exposure: Maternal and neonatal correlates. *Journal of Pediatrics*, *111*, 571–578.

Pietrantoni, M., & Knuppel, R.A. (1991). Alcohol use in pregnancy. *Clinics in Perinatology*, *18*, 93–111.

Pizzo, P.A., Eddy, J., Faloon, J., et al. (1988). Effect of continuous intravenous infusion of zidovudine (AZT) in children with symptomatic HIV infection. *New England Journal of Medicine*, *319*, 889–896.

Pizzo, P.A., & Wilfert, C. (Eds.). (1991). *Pediatric AIDS: The challenge of HIV infection in infants, children and adolescents*. Baltimore: Williams & Wilkins.

Task Force in Pediatric AIDS. (1988). Pediatric guidelines for infection control of human immunodeficiency virus (acquired immunodeficiency virus) in hospitals, medical offices, schools, and other settings. *Pediatrics*, *82*, 801–807.

Pyun, K.H., Ochs, H.D., Dufford, M.T., et al. (1987). Perinatal infection with human immunodeficiency virus: Specific antibody response by the neonate. *New England Journal of Medicine*, *317*, 611–614.

Rogers, M.F., White, C.R., Sanders, R., et al. (1990). Lack of transmission of human immunodeficiency virus from infected children to their household contacts. *Pediatrics*, *85*, 210–214.

Roland, E.H., & Volpe, J.J. (1989). Effect of maternal cocaine use on the fetus and newborn: Review of the literature. *Pediatric Neuroscience*, *15*, 88–94.

Rosenak, D., Diamant, Y.Z., Yaffe, H., et al. (1990). Cocaine: Maternal use during pregnancy and its effect on the mother, the fetus, and the infant. *Obstetrical and Gynecological Survey*, *45*, 348–359.

Sanders-Laufer, D., DeBruin, W., & Edelson, P.J. (1991). Pneumocystis carinii infections in HIV-infected children. *Pediatric Clinics of North America*, *38*, 69–88.

Schmitt, B., Seeger, J., Kreuz, W., et al. (1991). Central nervous system involvement of children with HIV infection. *Developmental Medicine and Child Neurology*, *33*, 535–540.

Schneider, J.W., & Chasnoff, I.J. (1987). Cocaine abuse during pregnancy: Its effects on infant motor development—A clinical perspective. *Topics in Acute Care and Trauma Rehabilitation*, *2*, 59–69.

Schutzman, D.L., Frankenfield-Chernicoff, M., Clatterbaugh, H.E., et al. (1991). Incidence of intrauterine cocaine-exposure in a suburban setting. *Pediatrics*, *88*, 825–827.

Scott, G.B., Hutto, C., Makuch, R.W., et al. (1989). Survival in children with perinatally acquired human immunodeficiency virus type 1 infection. *New England Journal of Medicine*, *321*, 1791–1796.

Singer, L.T., Garber, R., & Kliegman, R. (1991). Neurobehavioral sequelae of fetal cocaine exposure. *Journal of Pediatrics*, *119*, 667–672.

Spiegel, H., & Mayers, A. (1991). Psychosocial aspects of AIDS in children and adolescents. *Pediatric Clinics of North America*, *38*, 153–167.

Spohr, H.L., & Steinhauser, H.C. (1987). Follow-up studies of children with fetal alcohol syndrome. *Neuropediatrics*, *18*, 13–17.

Steckelberg, J.M., & Cockerill, F.R., III. (1988). Serologic testing for human immunodeficiency virus antibodies. *Mayo Clinic Proceedings*, *63*, 373–380.

Streissguth, A.P., Aase, J.M., Clarren, S.K., et al. (1991). Fetal alcohol syndrome in adolescents and adults. *Journal of the American Medical Association*, *265*, 1961–1967.

Streissguth, A.P., Barr, H.M., Sampson, P.D., et al. (1986). Attention, distraction and reaction time at age 7 years and prenatal alcohol exposure. *Neurobehavioral Toxicology and Teratology*, *8*, 717–725.

Streissguth, A.P., Landesman-Dwyer, S., Martin, J.C., et al. (1980). Teratogenic effects of alcohol in humans and laboratory animals. *Science*, *209*, 353–361.

Tarr, J.E., & Macklin, M. (1987). Cocaine. *Pediatric Clinics of North America*, *34*, 319–331.

Ultmann, M.H., Belman, A.L., Ruff, H.A., et al. (1985). Developmental abnormalities in infants and children with acquired immune deficiency syndrome (AIDS) and AIDS-related complex. *Developmental Medicine and Child Neurology*, *27*, 563–571.

Van de Perre, P., Simonon, A., Msellati, P., et al. (1991). Postnatal transmission of human immunodeficiency virus type 1 from mother to infant. A prospective cohort study in Kigali, Rwanda. *New England Journal of Medicine, 325,* 593–598.

VanDyke, D.C., & Fox, A.A. (1990). Fetal drug exposure and its possible implications for learning in the preschool and school-age population. *Journal of Learning Disabilities, 23,* 160–163.

Wade, N. (1991). Guidelines for the care of children and adolescents with HIV infection. Immunologic considerations in pediatric HIV infection. *Journal of Pediatrics, 119*(Supplement 1, Part 2), S5–S7.

Wolters, P., Moss, H., Eddy, J., et al (1989). *The adaptive behavior of children with symptomatic HIV infection and the effects of AZT therapy.* Abstract presented at the V International Conference on AIDS, Montreal.

Woods, J.R., Jr., Plessinger, M.A., & Clark, K. (1987). Effect of cocaine on uterine blood flow and fetal oxygenation. *Journal of the American Medical Association, 257,* 957–961.

World Health Organization. (1987). Breast-feeding/breast milk and human immunodeficiency virus (HIV). *Weekly Epidemiology Recommendations, 33,* 245–246.

Yazigi, R.A., Odem, R.R., & Polakoski, K.L. (1991). Demonstration of specific binding of cocaine to human spermatozoa. *Journal of the American Medical Association, 266,* 1956–1959.

Zuckerman, B., Frank, D.A., Hingson, R., et al. (1989). Effects of maternal marijuana and cocaine use on fetal growth. *New England Journal of Medicine, 320,* 762–768.

Chapter 9

The Technology-Assisted Child

Susan E. Levy and Sharon L. Pilmer

Upon completion of this chapter, the reader will:
—be knowledgeable about the definition and incidence of the need for technology assistance in children
—be aware of the types of technology assistance and devices
—understand reasons for technology assistance, especially those relating to chronic respiratory failure
—comprehend the difficulties technology-assisted children and their families face due to prolonged hospitalization and/or intensive care in the home
—understand what is involved in dealing with such children in early intervention programs, classrooms, or therapy settings

---

Ray is a 16-year-old who was injured in a motor vehicle accident. He sustained a cervical spinal cord injury that has left him paralyzed from the neck down and unable to breathe without a ventilator. He underwent a **tracheostomy** tube placement to facilitate long-term ventilation and spent the first 6 weeks following the accident in an intensive care unit. His memory of the accident is vague. However, he clearly remembers feeling sadness, fear, and frustration when he realized that he was unable to move or speak. Mouthing words was the only way he could make his needs known. Still, many of his caregivers were unable to read his lips. A nasogastric feeding-tube was placed to supplement his meager oral intake. Ray was frequently tearful and told his parents and many of his caregivers that he wished he had died in the accident.

Six weeks after the accident, Ray was transferred to a pediatric rehabilitation facility with a specialized unit for ventilator-dependent children. The staff made a number of changes in his management. The cuffed tracheostomy tube was replaced

Susan E. Levy, M.D., is Assistant Professor of Pediatrics at The University of Pennsylvania School of Medicine in Philadelphia and is Co-Director of The Respiratory Rehabilitation Unit at Children's Seashore House.

Sharon L. Pilmer, M.D., is Assistant Professor of Anesthesiology and Pediatrics at The University of Pennsylvania School of Medicine in Philadelphia and is Co-Director of the Respiratory Rehabilitation Unit at Children's Seashore House.

with an uncuffed tube, which allowed some of the air from the respirator breaths to pass up and around the tube and through his voice box. This, along with changes in his ventilation, allowed Ray to learn to speak during a respirator breath in a few weeks. He was also placed on a portable ventilator that could be powered by an external battery for up to 12 hours at a time. This ventilator was small enough to be mounted on an electric wheelchair, which Ray was able to learn to control using a chin-operated **microswitch**. Ray's improved ability to communicate and move about the unit greatly lifted his spirits. His appetite improved and his nutritional intake increased to a level permitting the removal of the feeding-tube. Over the next 2 months, classmates visited and brought schoolwork, some of which Ray was able to complete using a personal computer he learned to operate with a stick he held in his mouth. His friends raised money and bought him an environmental control unit that allowed him to activate the room lights, telephone, television, and room temperature by voicing a command.

Ray's family was encouraged to learn and participate in his care. With the guidance of the staff, they eventually were able to be independent with all of his care. Four months after admission to the rehabilitation facility, Ray went home with his family. He was unable to move his arms and legs and was fully dependent on mechanical ventilation, but he was independent in a number of daily living activities with the help of assistive devices.

TECHNOLOGICAL ADVANCES

Thirty years ago, a child like Ray probably would not have survived his injuries. However, advances in medical and surgical care have resulted in improved or prolonged survival of children who have sustained severe spinal cord injury, are born prematurely, and have neuromuscular diseases, cancer, AIDS, and chronic kidney, respiratory, and liver failure. Some of these children become temporarily or permanently dependent on medical assistive devices, such as Ray's mechanical ventilator. In addition to medical technology, nonmedical devices may improve function and enhance independence. In Ray's case, these devices included an electric wheelchair with microswitch controls and an environmental control unit. Like Ray, many children with serious illnesses or disabilities require both medical and nonmedical assistive devices. In this chapter, both types of devices are reviewed, with emphasis on medical assistive technology. The causes of technology dependence and the resulting psychological and socioeconomic impact are also considered.

DEFINITION AND INCIDENCE OF TECHNOLOGY ASSISTANCE

Nonmedical Assistive Technology

Nonmedical assistive technology devices and services are now mandated by Public Law 100-407, the Technology-Related Assistance for Individuals with Disabilities Act of 1988. This legislation defines an assistive technology device as, "any item, piece of equipment, or product system, whether acquired commercially off the shelf, modified, or customized, that is used to increase, maintain, or improve functional capabilities of individuals with disabilities" (PL 100-407). Examples include augmentative communication devices, computers adapted with microswitches, environmental control devices, seating and positioning equipment, power mobility, and adaptive play (Church & Glennen, 1992). This act also provides for assistive technology services that are defined as "directly assisting an individual with a disability in the selection, acquisition, or use of an assistive technology device" (PL 100-407). These services include providing funding to: 1) evaluate an individual's technological needs; 2) purchase or lease equipment; 3) maintain the devices in good repair; 4) train the individual, family members, and professionals in the use of assistive devices; and 5) coordinate the use of assistive devices with other therapies. These devices and services are discussed in detail in the chapters dealing with specific developmental disabilities: vision aids (see Chapter 17), hearing aids (see Chapter 18), augmentative communication devices (see Chapter 19), and computers and environmental control systems (see Chapter 24).

Approximately 2 in 100 children require some type of nonmedical assistive technology (Millner, 1991). The most common of these are hearing aids, wheelchairs, and computers. Although costly, these assistive allow many children with disabilities to be **mainstreamed** and improve their independence.

Medical Assistive Technology

A medical assistive device replaces or augments inadequate vital bodily function. The frequency with which children require medical technology assistance is rather low, occurring in about 1 in 1,000 children (Palfrey, Walker, Haynie, et al., 1991). The Office of Technology Assessment (1987) defines a child who receives medical technology assistance as one who uses such a device and requires substantial daily skilled nursing care to avert death or further disability. These devices include respiratory technology assistance (e.g., oxygen supplementation, mechanical ventilation, positive airway pressure devices), surveillance devices (e.g., cardiorespiratory monitors, pulse oximeters), nutritive assistive devices (e.g., tube-feedings, **ostomies**), intravenous therapy (e.g., **parenteral** nutrition, medication infusion), and kidney dialysis (Office of Technology Assistance, 1987). Approximately half of medically technology-assisted children require some form of respiratory technology assistance (Table 9.1).

REASONS FOR TECHNOLOGY ASSISTANCE

Dependence on technology is associated with a number of childhood diseases, injuries, and disabilities. Some of the more common disorders causing technology dependence are discussed here.

Spinal Cord Injury

Ray's case provides an example of the diverse types of technology assistance that may be required by children who have sustained spinal cord injuries. Medical technology

Table 9.1.   Types of technology assistance

Assistance	Percentage of children
Suction, oxygen, tracheostomy care	31
Cardiorespiratory monitoring	25
Mechanical ventilator support	17
Intravenous medications or nutrition	12
Tube-feedings	10
Kidney dialysis	1
Other	4

Source: Millner (1991).

assistance includes placement of tracheostomy tubes, mechanical ventilation, and tube-feeding. Nonmedical assistive technology includes power wheelchairs, environmental control devices, and computers with microswitches.

Neuromuscular Disorders

Neuromuscular disorders, a group of diseases associated with injury to the central nervous system, spinal cord, peripheral nerves, or the muscles themselves, lead to severe muscle weakness (see Chapter 15). Examples of neuromuscular disorders include polio, Guillain-Barré syndrome, Duchenne muscular dystrophy, and spinal muscular atrophy. If one of these diseases affects the respiratory muscles, mechanical ventilation may be necessary to avert respiratory failure. If the swallowing musculature is involved, tube-feedings may be required. These children may also need nonmedical assistive devices to improve mobility, seating, transferring, and feeding.

Cerebral Palsy

Children with congenital or acquired (i.e., resulting from brain injury or infection) cerebral palsy often require medical and nonmedical technology assistance. **Scoliosis** may occur in children with severe cerebral palsy. The rib cage becomes distorted and stiff, decreasing respiratory muscle power and interfering with lung development. If control of breathing is seriously impaired or if chronic lung disease is severe, assisted ventilation may be required.

Cerebral palsy also predisposes the child to feeding problems, resulting from swallowing dysfunction and **gastroesophageal reflux** (see Chapter 24). Treatment may involve the use of nasogastric or **gastrostomy** tube-feedings with special formulas. Extrapyramidal cerebral palsy may also be associated with a severe **expressive language** disorder. The child's speech may be unintelligible and compensatory sign language or gestures may be impossible because of poor fine motor control. Augmentative communication using a computer that has microswitch-controlled, synthetic voice capacity may be used by children with this type of disability. Computers are also valuable in controlling the environment, such as lights, televisions, curtains, doors, and telephones.

Prematurity

Prematurity is associated with immaturity of many organ systems (see Chapter 7). This underdevelopment may lead to dependence on numerous medical assistive devices. Bronchopulmonary dysplasia, a chronic lung disorder in premature infants, frequently leads to dependence on some form of respiratory technology assistance, such as oxygen supplementation, tracheostomy tube placement, and/or mechanical ventilation (Aylward, Pfeiffer, Wright, & Verhulst, 1989). Unfortunately, some medical technology assistance devices improve one function while interfering with another—for example, a tracheostomy tube may improve ventilation while impairing speech production. In this case, a nonmedical assistive technology device, such as a one-way **speaking valve** attached to the tracheostomy tube, may lessen this impairment.

Another problem for premature infants is immaturity of respiratory control centers in the brain stem. This may lead to periodic cessation of breathing (i.e., apnea). If breathing is not restored quickly, the cardiovascular system may collapse due to lack of oxygen. Continuous electronic surveillance with a cardiorespiratory monitor and alarm may be necessary to alert caregivers to problems when the child is not being directly observed by humans (see Chapter 7).

Tube-feedings may be required by premature infants because of immature sucks or swallows, which prevent adequate oral intake of formula. Total parenteral nutrition (i.e., intravenous nutrition) may be needed after an episode of necrotizing enterocolitis (see Chapter 7). This is a disease of the gastrointestinal tract that may require the surgical removal of a substantial amount of small bowel and the placement of an ostomy (i.e., a direct opening from the gut to the skin surface that permits the evacuation of feces).

Finally, prematurity is associated with an increased risk of developmental disabilities, including cerebral palsy, visual impairments, and hearing loss. These disabilities may require nonmedical assistive technology.

Kidney Failure

Kidney failure can occur in children as a result of a congenital malformation, chronic infection, or disease. Chronic kidney failure leads to the accumulation of fluid in the body and metabolic imbalance. This can result in muscle weakness, coma, brain damage, or death. A cure is possible with kidney transplantation; however, transplantation is not helpful in all cases. Many children who will eventually be eligible for transplants may initially be too young, too small, or lacking a suitable donor organ (Trompeter, 1990). These children require kidney dialysis. Kidney dialysis may be accomplished by **hemodialysis** (i.e., use of infusions through a machine to remove toxins from the blood) or **peritoneal** dialysis (i.e., use of infusions through a special catheter inserted in the abdominal cavity to remove toxins from the peritoneal fluid). Hemodialysis is less commonly used in children, except in preparation for transplantation. Ambulatory peritoneal dialysis is being increasingly used in the home.

Cancer and AIDS

Intravenous medication, nutrition, or blood products may be required for weeks or months in children with certain illnesses. In these situations, a surgically placed **central venous line** may be preferable to repeated **peripheral intravenous lines**. Central venous lines are catheters placed into a vein in the neck and advanced to a position just above the heart. These lines are more stable and can be maintained for months or years with proper care. A child with leukemia may be able to receive intravenous chemotherapy at home, rather than experiencing a series of hospitalizations. Another example is a child with AIDS, who may require prolonged intravenous antibiotics or nutrition.

TYPES OF MEDICAL TECHNOLOGY ASSISTANCE

Federal legislation (PL 100-407) has divided the types of medical technology assistance mentioned previously into four categories for mandated programs (Table 9.2). Type I includes children who require mechanical ventilation for some portion of each day. In Type II are children who require prolonged intravenous therapy either to provide medication or nutrition. Type III includes children who have tracheostomy tubes, feeding-tubes, or require periodic **suctioning** or oxygen supplementation. Finally, Type IV involves children who need cardiorespiratory (CR) monitoring, kidney dialysis, or ostomy care (Office of Technology Assessment, 1987). Of these, the most frequently used technology is cardiorespiratory monitoring. In this chapter, the different categories of medical technology assistance are discussed. Special attention is given to respiratory assistance because of its prevalence and because it can be most frightening to the teacher or therapist caring for a child with a disability.

Respiratory Technology Assistance

Respiratory technology assistance is required by children who have chronic respiratory failure. This is marked by the failure of the respiratory system to maintain normal gas exchange in the lungs, (i.e., the uptake of oxygen [O_2] and elimination of carbon dioxide [CO_2]). Oxygen is an essential fuel for energy-generating chemical reactions in the cells of the body. Carbon dioxide is a waste product of the chemical reactions and must be eliminated by the lungs and kidneys (Figure 9.1).

Table 9.2. Categories of technology assistance

Type	Description
I	Requires mechanical ventilation for at least part of each day
II	Requires prolonged intravenous nutrition or drug therapy
III	Requires support for tracheostomy tube care, suctioning, oxygen supplementation, or tube-feeding
IV	Requires cardiorespiratory monitoring, kidney dialysis, or ostomy care

Source: Office of Technology Assessment (1987).

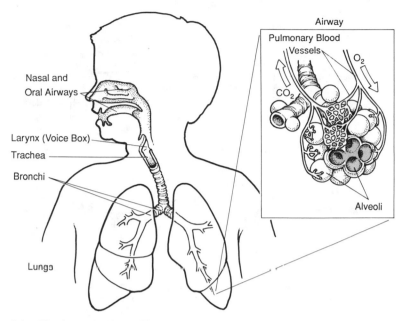

Figure 9.1. The airways and lungs. The airways conduct inhaled gas from the atmosphere to the alveoli. Beginning at the mouth and nose, air enters the nose (and/or mouth), and then the voicebox. It then descends into the chest via the windpipe or trachea. The trachea divides into two bronchi, one serving each lung. The main bronchus to each lung divides repeatedly into a series of progressively smaller tubes that ultimately deliver gas to the alveoli, where gas exchange occurs.

Respiratory failure can be divided into problems with the respiratory muscle pump and problems with the lungs themselves (Figure 9.2). In order for gas exchange to occur, it must be moved in and out of the lungs by the action of the respiratory pump. This consists of the rib cage and the breathing muscles (i.e., diaphragm and intercostal muscles of the chest wall). The pump is driven by the respiratory center in the brain stem (see Figure 9.2). Signals from this center are transmitted via the spinal cord and peripheral nerves to the respiratory muscles, which raise and lower the diaphragm and relax and contract the intercostal muscles of the chest wall. The coordinated action of the respiratory muscles changes the size of the chest cavity and moves gas in and out of the lungs. Dysfunction of any component of the respiratory muscle pump or its neurological control can cause respiratory failure.

In children, respiratory muscle pump failure may be caused by diseases such as spinal cord injury, spinal muscular atrophy, or Duchenne muscular dystrophy. In the pediatric age group, bronchopulmonary dysplasia and cystic fibrosis are primary lung disorders that may result in chronic respiratory failure.

The medical management goals for the child with chronic respiratory failure are to maintain normal O_2 levels in the blood, to prevent ongoing lung injury caused by recurrent infection or collapse, and to promote growth and development. This often can be accomplished using supplemental oxygen, chest physiotherapy, medications, and adequate nutrition. When these are not sufficient to achieve the medical manage-

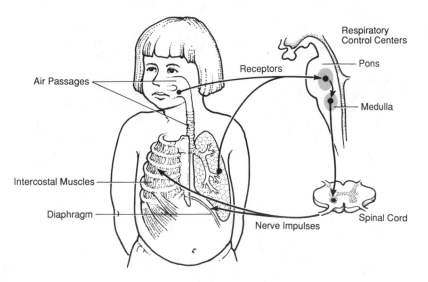

Figure 9.2.   The respiratory muscle pump. Chronic respiratory failure may arise from a defect in any part of the respiratory muscle pump. The respiratory system comprises the respiratory control centers in the brain, the spinal cord and nerves arising from it that transmit signals from the brain, the breathing muscles (diaphragm and intercostal muscles), and the bony and cartilaginous chest cage.

ment goals, mechanical ventilation (Table 9.3) and tracheostomy tube placement are considered.

Oxygen Supplementation   Many children with chronic respiratory failure require supplemental oxygen in order to maintain an oxygen saturation in their blood above 90%, the optimal level for growth and well-being. Room air contains 21% oxygen; additional oxygen may be administered by a nasal cannula (i.e., a tube with prongs inserted into the nostrils), face mask, oxygen tent or hood, or an artificial airway, such as a tracheostomy. A child requiring oxygen goes to school or to a therapy program with an oxygen source and delivery system.

Chest Physiotherapy and Suctioning   Persons with lung disease may produce excessive secretions, and those with pump problems are often unable to cough effectively. Chest physiotherapy and suctioning, which can be performed by any trained professional or parent, can help to clear pulmonary secretions. Chest physiotherapy involves the manual stimulation of the chest to promote coughing and loosening of secretions. Secretions can then be cleared by coughing or, in individuals with tracheostomies, by suctioning. In suctioning, a catheter (i.e., tube) is placed in the trachea and suction is applied to remove secretions. Typically, oxygen is administered before and after suctioning to prevent a decrease in the oxygen saturation level during this procedure. Chest physiotherapy and suctioning are done as often as necessary, typically several times a day.

Positive Airway Pressure   For children with moderate disturbance of pulmonary function who are troubled by recurrent lung collapse, continuous positive air-

Table 9.3.   Components in the care of the ventilator-assisted child

Medical

Ventilation should support physical growth and minimize shortness of breath and fatigue that can interfere with development.

Intercurrent illnesses should be treated aggressively.

Developmental

Children must be thoroughly evaluated on a regular basis by a team of developmental pediatricians, child psychologists, and therapists. Problems are identified, and individualized programs should be designed to enhance developmental functioning.

Early intervention programs with groups of children should be utilized when appropriate.

Physical, occupational, and speech-language therapists should work with children individually as needed.

Environmental

A physical environment that is less restrictive than the typical intensive care unit should be provided.

A regular routine of care, bathing, dressing, mealtimes, play periods, and naps must be provided.

Social

Families may require group and individual psychosocial support.

Families should be encouraged to visit and participate in the child's care.

Families must become an integral part of the caregiving team and should assume an advocacy and decision-making role.

Foster families should be sought when biological families are unable to participate in the child's care.

Primary nursing programs should be used to ensure continuity of care.

way pressure (CPAP) may be employed. CPAP is created by a device that imposes resistance to exhalation. CPAP improves oxygenation by opening alveoli so that they may participate in gas exchange. It may be applied to the child's natural airway via a tight-fitting mask or **nasal pillows** or via a tracheostomy tube. It may also be administered between mechanical breaths if a child is on a mechanical ventilator, in which case it is referred to as positive end expiratory pressure (PEEP).

Mechanical Ventilation and Tracheostomy   Mechanical ventilation is the process by which a device augments or replaces the child's own breaths. Mechanical breaths can be generated by applying negative pressure to the outside of the chest or by delivering positive pressure through the airway. Negative pressure ventilators are used primarily in children with respiratory muscle pump failure. Positive pressure ventilation may be used for "pump failure" or lung disease. Positive pressure ventilation can be noninvasive, applied to the natural airway, or invasive, delivered via a tracheostomy. This chapter focuses on invasive positive pressure ventilation because it is most commonly used in children.

A tracheostomy usually involves the insertion of a polyvinylchloride tube through a surgically created incision in the cartilage of the trachea just below the "Adam's apple." It is secured with adhesive or foam-padded strings around the neck. This open airway is then attached to a ventilator or a CPAP device with tubing that provides humidified air or an air and oxygen mixture. The tracheostomy tube also allows the caregiver to have direct access to the airway, permitting suctioning of secretions or the removal of other blockages.

Accidental displacement of the tracheostomy tube is the most common complication of this assistive device. This can be life-threatening to a child who has a narrowed trachea above the tracheostomy and is totally dependent on the tracheostomy tube. In this instance, a dislodged or blocked tracheostomy tube must be replaced immediately. Children with narrowed tracheas should be closely observed and electronically supervised with cardiorespiratory monitors and/or pulse oximeters when human surveillance is limited (i.e., when the family is sleeping).

Numerous positive pressure ventilators are available and appropriate for children with chronic respiratory failure (Figure 9.3). In general, ventilator selection is determined by the child's underlying disorder and size, where it is to be used (home versus hospital), whether portability is necessary (battery-powered ventilators exist), and other special features that may be helpful to the child.

The ventilator contains an alarm that sounds under conditions of low or high pressure. The most common reason for a low pressure alarm is accidental disconnection of the tracheostomy tube from the ventilator tubing. This may occur when the child is moved from one position to another and is usually not a serious problem; the

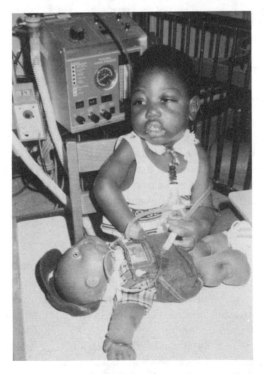

Figure 9.3.   A child with a neuromuscular disease, now 2 years old, with a tracheostomy tube and a ventilator, is participating in an early intervention program.

tube is simply reattached. A high pressure alarm most commonly sounds because something is obstructing the flow of gas into the child. This may be external to the child (i.e., kinked or obstructed tubing), or it may be within the child (e.g., mucous inside the tracheostomy tube, a **bronchospasm**, coughing). Mucous plugging is usually prevented by humidifying the gas mixture that passes through the tubing. If there is a mucous plug, it requires removal by suctioning.

Liberation from Mechanical Ventilation A child's prognosis for liberation from mechanical ventilation depends on the disease causing respiratory failure. If the disorder is not expected to improve with time, such as muscular dystrophy or spinal cord injury, complete liberation from the ventilator may not be a realistic goal. Yet, partial liberation may be possible. In order to promote mobility and independence, the child's schedule can be arranged so that ventilation is provided while the child is resting. For the child who is completely dependent on mechanical ventilation, mobility is still possible using a portable ventilator. These devices, with external batteries capable of powering the ventilator for up to 12 hours, can be mounted on specially designed trays attached to wheelchairs or carts. Though somewhat bulky, they enable the child to attend school and travel with the family.

Complete liberation from mechanical ventilation is usually a realistic goal for children with bronchopulmonary dysplasia. Satisfactory growth, normal gas exchange on the current level of support, sufficient stamina for activities of daily living, and absence of intercurrent illness usually indicate that the child can tolerate a gradual reduction in the level of mechanical support. Weaning occurs over months to years, dictated by the child's clinical status.

Several techniques are used to wean a child from mechanical ventilation. The number of mechanical breaths delivered per minute can be reduced gradually or the child may spend increasingly long periods of time off the ventilator. The "time off" approach has the advantage of allowing the child greater mobility. Nighttime ventilation is usually the last support to be withdrawn. After the child has functioned without ventilation and supplemental oxygen for several months, permanent removal of the tracheostomy tube may be considered.

Developmental Complications of Mechanical Ventilation Developmental complications of long-term mechanical ventilation include language deficits and behavior and feeding problems. A number of studies have pointed to deficits in language production, syntax, and articulation resulting from the presence of a tracheostomy during this period of early language development (Simon, Fowler, & Handler, 1983; Singer, Kercsmar, Legris, et al., 1989). Because of these expressive language difficulties, a speech-language pathologist should provide alternative methods of communication that are developmentally appropriate for the child. These include sign language and the use of nonmedical technology assistance, such as a speaking valve or an **electrolarynx**, esophageal speech, or an augmentative communication system (e.g., language board, computer) (see Chapter 19).

Ventilator-dependent children may have behavior problems (Quint, Chesterman, Crain, et al., 1990). The absence of audible speech leads to frustration in attempts at communication and may result in aggressive or acting out behavior. Noncompliant behavior may also occur because of inconsistencies in caregiving during prolonged hospitalizations. Additionally, some children have developmental disabilities, such as severe-to-profound mental retardation, that are associated with perseverative, self-stimulatory, and self-injurious behaviors (see Chapter 23). Treatment often utilizes behavior management therapy, drug therapy, and supportive counseling for the family or medical caregivers (Levy, 1991).

Behavior problems may also adversely affect nutrition. Children on ventilators are at increased risk for gastroesophageal reflux and resultant vomiting (Sindel, Maisels, & Ballantine, 1989). Over time, the child may associate eating with the subsequent negative experience of vomiting and may refuse to eat. In addition, there may be oral motor dysfunction and frequent interruptions in periods of oral feeding due to acute illnesses (Starrett, 1991). The young child may lose the skills needed for effective feeding. Usually, the feeding disorder is attributable to some combination of these physiological and behavior problems. Effective treatment includes medical management of any underlying disorder (e.g., medical or surgical treatment of gastroesophageal reflux) as well as teaching behavior management skills to the child's parents and caregivers.

Surveillance Devices

Children with disorders that affect the heart or lungs are likely to require the use of surveillance devices. Although these devices provide no direct therapeutic benefit, they give early warning of problems and thereby improve care indirectly. The two most common forms of electronic surveillance are cardiorespiratory monitoring and pulse oximetry. They are used individually or in combination in the hospital and at home (Mallory & Stillwell, 1991).

Oximetry   The oximeter measures oxygen saturation in the blood with a probe that is attached to one of the child's fingers or toes. The probe measures the amount of oxygen bound to hemoglobin, the oxygen-carrying protein in blood cells that gives blood its red color. An alarm can be set to go off below a certain oxygen saturation level. The alarm may be triggered by delivery failure (i.e., the oxygen tank has run out), a disconnected probe, movement, or a change in the child's condition (e.g., an increased oxygen requirement related to a respiratory infection). Under circumstances of illness, oxygen delivery failure, or equipment malfunction, the current activity may need to be curtailed, and the oxygen concentration increased.

Cardiorespiratory Monitoring   The cardiorespiratory monitor has electrodes that are attached to the child's chest to record heart and respiratory rate. An alarm is part of the system and is set off by either high or low rates. If the alarm sounds, the caregiver should examine the child, looking for signs of respiratory distress, heart rate abnormalities, color, and state of alertness. However, the most common cause of an alarm sounding is the inadvertent detachment of the chest electrodes.

In the very rare event that the alarm sounds because of full cardiorespiratory arrest (i.e., cessation of breathing and heart rate), cardiopulmonary resuscitation (CPR) must be instituted. All personnel working with medically fragile children should be trained in the performance of CPR. As respiratory arrest almost always precedes cardiac arrest in children, proper technique for this aspect of resuscitation is essential. In a child with a tracheostomy, breaths of 100% oxygen should be delivered by attaching a resuscitation bag to the tracheostomy tube. For a child without a tracheostomy or a child whose tracheostomy has come out and cannot be reinserted, respiratory resuscitation should be accomplished by using a resuscitation bag and a tight-fitting mask applied to the child's face. For further details, the reader is encouraged to review guidelines for the performance of CPR (American Heart Association, 1986; Zaritsky, 1987).

Nutritional Assistive Devices

Good nutrition is a vital component in the medical management of children with chronic illnesses. Children with bronchopulmonary dysplasia or extrapyramidal cerebral palsy may need 1.5–2 times the normal caloric intake because of the considerable energy expended in breathing or in engaging in involuntary movements (Kurzner, Garg, Bautista, et al., 1988; Markestad & Fitzhardinge, 1981). These children may be unable to ingest even a normal caloric intake because of oromotor deficits, reflux, or behavior problems. Because lung growth parallels linear growth, recovery from bronchopulmonary dysplasia is linked to the child's nutritional status. Similarly, development in children with cerebral palsy is often limited by undernutrition (see Chapter 24).

Tube-Feedings Children with oral intake that is insufficient to maintain normal growth may require tube-feedings either temporarily through a nasogastric tube or chronically by gastrostomy. The latter involves an operation in which a passageway is made between the stomach and the skin to permit insertion of a tube directly into the stomach (see Chapter 12). A similar operation, called a *jejunostomy* can be done to connect the **jejunum** (i.e., the second part of the small intestine) to the skin. This may be used in children who have gastroesophageal reflux. In either case, liquid feedings are administered through the tube. These feedings may consist of specially constituted formulas, such as Jevity and Ensure, or blenderized foods that the family eats (see Chapter 11). The feedings can be given 3–5 times a day or as a continuous drip throughout the day and/or night. The latter requires an electronic pump to deliver a constant flow.

Children with feeding-tubes require certain skills of parents, teachers, and therapists. If the tube falls out, it must be repositioned. It is usually anchored to the stomach by a "button" apparatus or by a bulb that is inflated by water. If the tube comes out, it is often because the bulb has deflated. A trained teacher, therapist, or nurse can thread the tube back in the tunnel a few inches, reinflate the bulb with a syringe that accompanies the tube, and pull the tube back until resistance is met. The gastrostomy tube site must be washed regularly with soap and water. If there is irritation around the gastrostomy site, Vaseline or another occlusive ointment may be applied to protect the area.

Ostomy Care In a sense, gastrostomy tubes are examples of ostomies. However, this term is more commonly applied to openings that permit the evacuation of bowel contents or urine through the abdominal wall. One example is colostomy in a premature infant who has had a section of bowel removed because of necrotizing enterocolitis. In most cases, the bowel can be reattached later after healing has occurred. The care of these ostomy sites, called *stomas* or *openings*, is similar to the care of the gastrostomy site. In addition, special bags are used to collect feces or urine and must be emptied and replaced at routine intervals.

Intravenous Therapy

The premature infant who requires tube-feedings may have previously required total parenteral nutrition (TPN). TPN involves the provision of a high-calorie, high-protein solution directly into the bloodstream by intravenous administration. This is most commonly needed by infants who have a short gut syndrome resulting from necrotizing enterocolitis. TPN may also be required in older children with chronic malabsorption or intestinal inflammation caused by illnesses such as Crohn disease, ulcerative colitis, or AIDS (see Chapter 8). Prolonged intravenous therapy may also be needed to provide medication. The drugs may range from antibiotics to chemotherapy.

The parent or nurse is responsible for administering the solution or medication at the proper intervals and duration. They must be trained in techniques for maintaining the sterile dressings surrounding the central venous catheter and recognizing when the tubing has become detached or contaminated. Most children with a central venous catheter have a **hemostat** that can be clamped over the plastic tubing if it is interrupted. Signs of an infection include redness of the surrounding skin or discharge of pus.

Kidney Dialysis

Home dialysis has been used in the treatment of adults with kidney failure for many years. Now, home peritoneal dialysis is also being used in children with kidney failure. During a hospitalization, a catheter is surgically placed through the abdominal wall and into the abdominal cavity. A dialysis solution can then be run through the catheter, permitted to equilibrate, and then allowed to drain. This eliminates toxins that would normally be eliminated by the kidney. The procedure takes several hours and may be required up to 3–5 days a week. Families can be trained to perform peritoneal dialysis independently at home. Home hemodialysis has been used in adults, but rarely in children.

EFFECTS OF MEDICAL TECHNOLOGY ASSISTANCE ON THE CHILD

Infants with illnesses that require prolonged technology assistance may be hospitalized for prolonged periods of time, isolated among noisy, frightening pieces of machinery. Much of the child's social contact is related to nursing care that may involve unpleasant procedures (Landry, Chapieski, Fletcher, & Denson, 1988). Prolonged hospitalization also isolates the child from his or her family. Even very involved families may find it difficult to spend extended periods of time in the hospital with their child because of distance or work commitments. This may interfere with bonding between the premature infant and the parents or lead to a feeling of abandonment in an older child.

Once home, social isolation may not disappear. Even with school attendance, the child may be recognized as "different" because of the accompanying machinery and medical/nursing needs. Education of classmates and psychological counseling for the child can improve the child's self-image and relationships with peers (Quint et al., 1990).

The child must also learn to deal with the underlying medical problem that led to the technology dependence. This is easier to do if the technology dependence does not span a long time period—for example, intravenous antibiotics to treat a severe infection or a temporary ostomy following abdominal surgery (Quint et al., 1990). However, if the child has a chronic or ultimately fatal disease, such as AIDS, muscular dystrophy, or cystic fibrosis, the adaptation to technology assistance is but one issue among many that must be dealt with by both child and family (see Chapter 29).

Social issues may also adversely influence the child's emotional well-being. Factors known to predispose to prematurity (e.g., young maternal age, low socioeconomic status, maternal substance abuse) may also limit the parents' ability to cope with the stress of caring for a chronically ill child (Burr, Guyer, Todres, et al., 1983). Under these circumstances, parental visitation may be infrequent and home care impossible. Nursing and therapy staff then become the primary emotional as well as medical caregivers. In these instances, a pediatric nursing home or a special medical foster home (individual or group) may be an appropriate alternative to prolonged hospitalization.

If parents are involved and willing, the child should eventually be able to be sent home. From the family's perspective, there are both positive and negative aspects of home care. On one hand, home care enables the entire family to be together, and there may be less disruption. On the other hand, families are frequently stressed by chronic fatigue, financial concerns, and the burden of meeting the technology-dependent child's needs over a prolonged time period (Lichtenstein, 1986). Families may be concerned about making a mistake that could injure or cause the death of the child. For medically fragile children who require ongoing home nursing care, the lack of privacy caused by the presence of shifts of nurses may be an additional stressor. Studies have suggested that families can do well, especially if the technology dependence lasts less than 2 years. More prolonged periods of time are associated with parental burnout (Quint et al., 1990).

FUNDING MEDICAL TECHNOLOGY ASSISTANCE

Technology assistance may be very expensive, depending on the type of technology involved and the extent of disability. Before a child with medical needs can be discharged, a number of financial issues must be addressed (Figure 9.4). The two major issues are nursing care and equipment and supplies. Nursing care can be required for 4–24 hours per day in the case of ventilator assistance; the average is 14 hours (Fields, Rosenblatt, Pollock, et al., 1991). Many insurance policies do not provide

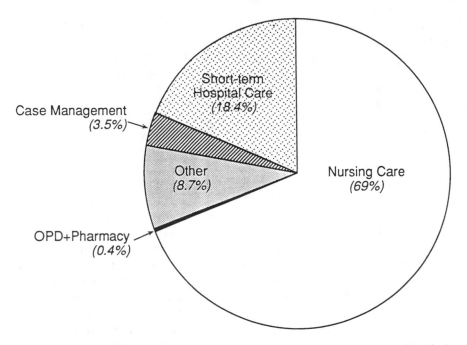

Case Management
(3.5%)

Short-term
Hospital Care
(18.4%)

Other
(8.7%)

OPD+Pharmacy
(0.4%)

Nursing Care
(69%)

Figure 9.4. Distribution of annual home care reimbursements for ventilator-dependent children in the Medicaid model waiver program. Nursing care includes in-home care with an average of 14 hours per day. Short-term hospital care includes all reimbursements for rehospitalizations during the first year after discharge; outpatient department (OPD) includes physician visits and outpatient hospital charges; and other includes durable medical equipment, disposable medical supplies, transportation, and occupational, physical, and speech-language therapies. (Adapted from Fields, Rosenblatt, Pollock, et al., 1991.)

reimbursement for this much nursing care. Even those insurance polices that do reimburse for these needs may have ceilings beyond which they will not pay. Although these ceilings may be many hundreds of thousands of dollars, the benefits can be exhausted in less than a year of intensive care. Yet, the child may require many years of home nursing care and technology assistance.

Prior to 1982, many children who had exhausted their private insurance coverage were not deemed eligible for Medicaid because parental income exceeded Medicaid qualification maximums. In 1982 the case of one ventilator-dependent child, Katie Beckett, was brought to the attention of President Ronald Reagan, who gave an executive order that allowed the rules regarding eligibility requirements to be waived so that she could return home without losing her Medicaid benefits (Murray, 1989). Now each state can apply for up to 200 waiver slots per year (Leonard, Brust, & Choi, 1989; Omnibus Budget Reconciliation Act, 1991). This has helped, but not solved the funding problem. The waiver program limits the number of persons who can be funded per state, frequently has long waiting lists, and is affected by a reluctance on the part of some home health care providers to accept the relatively low reimbursement rates that the waiver program offers (Leonard et al., 1989).

A recent Supreme Court ruling may provide additional relief to financially pressed families by providing Supplemental Security Income (SSI) to more children with disabilities who require technology assistance. The case was a class action suit filed by the family of Brian Zebley, a young child who has congenital brain damage but was not found to qualify under the stringent medical severity standards applied by SSI to all children. In *Sullivan* (the Secretary of the U.S. Department of Health and Human Services) *v. Zebley*, the Justices found that the SSI criteria for children were "manifestly contrary to the statute" (Owen, 1991, p. 42) that had created the program. Now, more individualized criteria are being applied and many more children with disabilities should receive funding for technology assistance under SSI (Perrin & Stein, 1991).

However, there will remain certain out-of-pocket expenses that are not compensated by these federal programs or private insurance policies. These include remodeling of the home, increased utility costs, loss of income from work absences, transportation costs, and child care expenses.

PREPARING FOR HOME CARE

Despite financial and psychosocial problems, more medically technology-assisted children are being reintegrated into the community each year (Andrews & Nielson, 1988). One major incentive is that home care of the technology-assisted child can cost less than half as much as hospital care. But home care, especially for a ventilator-assisted child, is a major undertaking that is a viable option only after a number of requirements have been met (Table 9.4). The family must understand the alternatives to home care—continued hospitalization or nursing home care. If they choose home care, they must master the child's medical and nursing care (Kennely, 1990). Prior to discharge, the family arranges financial support and selects a nursing agency if home nursing services are required. They must also select a durable medical equipment supplier of equipment, disposable supplies, and in-home support (e.g., equipment maintenance, monitoring).

Table 9.4. Criteria to be met prior to sending a child home with medical technology assistance

1. The child's medical condition must be stable.
2. The level of support and intervention the child requires must be able to be safely and practically provided in the home.
3. The family must be willing and have demonstrated proficiency in providing all aspects of the child's care.
4. Financial support must be found to fund equipment, supplies, and personnel in the home.
5. A durable equipment company must be identified to provide oxygen and other respiratory equipment and supplies.
6. Nursing services and therapists must be in place prior to discharge.
7. Adequate emotional and respite care resources must be available.

Source: Kettrick and Donar (1985).

Modifications to the family's home may be needed. Frequently, these consist of changing existing electrical systems and adding ramps for wheelchair or stroller accessibility. Local electric, ambulance, and telephone companies are notified that a person dependent on life support technology will be residing in the family's home so that the household can be placed on a priority list in the event of power failure or medical emergency (Kopacz & Moriarity-Wright, 1984).

A pediatrician or family physician in the community should be identified. The discharging team contacts this individual prior to the child's hospital discharge to introduce the child and encourage the community physician's active participation in the child's care. If the child will require special rehabilitation therapies after discharge, either center-based or home-based providers are arranged. Educational services also need to be identified. Center or school-based education offers the child an opportunity to interact with other children in a stimulating environment, and should be provided if the child's physical condition permits.

RAY: ONE YEAR LATER

All of the necessary considerations were addressed before Ray was discharged from the hospital. One year after the accident, Ray lives at home and is cared for by his family and nurses who come to his house on a daily basis. He attends high school, but has more school absences than before the accident because of his poor tolerance of respiratory illnesses. He is accompanied at all times by his mother or a nurse. He enjoys academics, but his self-esteem sometimes falters because of his disabilities. At times, he feels that he is a burden to his family.

Ray's parents are relieved and happy to have him home, but they are concerned about his safety at home and in school. They worry about his future, when they are too old to care for him. They are often fatigued from providing his care, especially when nursing shifts go unfilled. Remodeling their home to make it wheelchair accessible has cut into their retirement savings. Although they have an excellent health insurance policy, they know that ultimately they will have to turn to the model waiver program and SSI to continue to fund Ray's care at home. Ray's siblings share in the responsibility of his care and are also feeling the fatigue, the limited family freedom that comes with having a family member with a disability, and the decrease in parental attention. Yet, despite these problems, the family remains intact and Ray is an integral part of the family.

OUTCOME

The technology-assisted child's prognosis depends more on the underlying disorder than on the type of technology assistance. Therefore, outcome is best discussed for the individual disorders. As the outcomes for cerebral palsy, neuromuscular disorders, vision and hearing deficits are discussed in other chapters, the ventilator-assisted child is addressed here.

Few studies have been published reporting the developmental outcome of children requiring long-term mechanical ventilation. One of the most extensive studies describes moderate-to-severe developmental delay in almost half of premature infants with bronchopulmonary dysplasia who require long-term ventilation (Schreiner, Downes, Kettrick, et al., 1987). This is about three times the rate of delay in premature infants who do not require ventilator assistance (Kitchen, Ryan, & Rickards, 1987). The question remains whether prolonged mechanical ventilation itself is causally related to the poorer outcome or is a marker for other preexisting neurological deficits that adversely influence development. For example, the premature infant with severe respiratory distress syndrome may have had prolonged hypoxia before intervention was initiated or could have sustained a severe intracerebral hemorrhage. One recent study provides evidence that the neurodevelopmental outcome is a function of previous neurological complications and not the duration of mechanical ventilation (Luchi, Bennett, & Jackson, 1991).

SUMMARY

As the number of technology-assisted children increases, health care professionals, those in allied professions, educators, and administrators will have more frequent contact with them. Some will be involved directly in the care and education of the children. Others will be involved in advocacy and policymaking.

All of these individuals should understand the fundamental issues facing technology-assisted children, so that their needs can be met. First, the underlying disease process must be understood. Second, the risk of discontinuation of therapy should be clear. Third, routine care needs must be identified.

The child's disease and technology dependence will influence how the child grows, develops, learns, and functions in society. Dependence on medical technology will also have an important impact on families with attendant emotional, physical, and financial strain. However, the possibility of home care for the technology-assisted child can improve the lifestyle of these children.

REFERENCES

American Heart Association. (1986). Standards and guidelines for cardiopulmonary resuscitation (CPR) and emergency cardiac care (ECC). *Journal of the American Medical Association, 255*, 2905–2989.

Andrews, M.M., & Nielson, D.W. (1988). Technology-dependent children in the home. *Pediatric Nursing, 14*, 111–114.

Aylward, G.P., Pfeiffer, S.I., Wright, A., & Verhulst, S.J. (1989). Outcome studies of low birth weight infants published in the last decade: A metaanalysis. *Journal of Pediatrics, 115*, 515–520.

Burr, B.H., Guyer, B., Todres, I.D., et al. (1983). Home care for children on respirators. *New England Journal of Medicine, 309*, 1319–1323.

Church, E., & Glennen, S. (1992). *Handbook of assistive technology*. San Diego, CA: Singular Publishing Group.

Fields, A.I., Rosenblatt, A., Pollock, M.M., et al. (1991). Home care cost-effectiveness for respiratory technology-dependent children. *American Journal of Diseases of Children, 145*, 729–733.

Kennelly, C. (1990). Tracheostomy care: Parents as learners. *American Journal of Maternal and Child Nursing, 12,* 264–267.

Kettrick, R.G., & Donar, M.E. (1985). The ventilator-dependent child: Medical and social care. *Critical Care: State of the Art, 6,* 1–38.

Kitchen, W.H., Ryan, M.M., & Rickards, A.L. (1987). A longitudinal study of very low-birthweight infants. IV: Impairments, health and distance growth to 14 years of age. *Australian Paediatrics Journal, 23,* 23211–23212.

Kopacz, M., & Moriarity-Wright, R. (1984). Multidisciplinary approach for the patient on a home ventilator. *Heart & Lung, 13,* 255–262.

Kurzner, S.I., Garg, M., Bautista, D.B., et al. (1988). Growth failure in infants with bronchopulmonary dysplasia: Nutrition and elevated resting metabolic expenditure. *Pediatrics, 81,* 379–384.

Landry, S.H., Chapieski, L., Fletcher, J.M., & Denson, S. (1988). Three-year outcomes for low birth weight infants: Differential effects of early medical complications. *Journal of Pediatric Psychology, 13,* 317–327.

Leonard, B.J., Brust, J.D., & Choi, T. (1989). Providing access to home care for disabled children: Minnesota's medical model waiver program. *Public Health Reports, 104,* 465–472.

Levy, S.E. (1991). Nonpharmacologic management of disorders of behavior and attention. In: A.J. Capute & P.J. Accardo, (Eds.), *Developmental disabilities in infancy and childhood* (pp. 489–494). Baltimore: Paul H. Brookes Publishing Co.

Lichtenstein, M.A. (1986). Pediatric home tracheostomy care: A parents' guide. *Pediatric Nursing, 12,* 41–48, 69.

Luchi, J.M., Bennett, F.C., & Jackson, J.C. (1991). Predictors of neurodevelopmental outcome following bronchopulmonary dysplasia. *American Journal of Diseases of Children, 145,* 813–817.

Mallory, G.B., Jr., & Stillwell, P.C. (1991). The ventilator-dependent child: Issues in diagnosis and management. *Archives of Physical Medicine and Rehabilitation, 72,* 43–55.

Markestad, T., & Fitzhardinge, P.M. (1981). Growth and development in children recovering from bronchopulmonary dysplasia. *Journal of Pediatrics, 98,* 597–602.

Millner, B.N. (1991). Technology-dependent children in New York state. *Bulletin of the New York Academy of Medicine, 67,* 131–142.

Murray, J.E. (1989). Payment mechanisms for pediatric home care. *Caring, 10,* 33–35.

Office of Technology Assessment. (1987). *Technology-dependent children: Hospital v. home care: A technical memorandum* (DHHS Publication No. TM-H-38). Washington, DC: U.S. Government Printing Office.

Omnibus Budget Reconciliation Act. Model 2176. (1991).

Owen, M.J. (1991). What has the Social Security administration done for you lately? *Exceptional Parent, 21*(4), 40–42.

Palfrey, J.S., Walker, D.K., Haynie, M., et al. (1991). Technology's children: Report of a statewide census of children dependent on medical supports. *Pediatrics, 87,* 611–618.

Perrin, J.M., & Stein, R.E. (1991). Reinterpreting disability: Changes in supplemental security income for children. *Pediatrics, 88,* 1047–1051.

Quint, R.D., Chesterman, E., Crain, L.S., et al. (1990). Home care for ventilator-dependent children: Psychosocial impact on the family. *American Journal of Diseases of Children, 144,* 1238–1241.

Schreiner, M.S., Downes, J.J., Kettrick, R.G., et al. (1987). Chronic respiratory failure in infants with prolonged ventilator dependency. *Journal of the American Medical Association, 258,* 3398–3404.

Simon, B.M., Fowler, S.M., & Handler, S.D. (1983). Communication development in young children with long-term tracheostomies: Preliminary report. *International Journal of Pediatric Otorhinolaryngology, 6,* 37–50.

Sindel, B.D., Maisels, M.J., & Ballantine, T.V. (1989). Gastroesophageal reflux to the proximal esophagus in infants with bronchopulmonary dysplasia. *American Journal of Diseases of Children*, *143*, 1103–1106.

Singer, L.T., Kercsmar, C., Legris, G., et al. (1989). Developmental sequelae of long-term infant tracheostomy. *Developmental Medicine and Child Neurology*, *31*, 224–230.

Starrett, A.L. (1991). Growth in developmental disabilities. In A.J. Capute & P.J. Accardo (Eds.) *Developmental disabilities in infancy and childhood* (pp. 181–187). Baltimore: Paul H. Brookes Publishing Co.

Technology-Related Assistance for Individuals with Disabilities Act of 1988, PL 100-407. (August 19, 1988). Title 29, U.S.C. 2201 et seq: *U.S. Statutes at Large, 102*, 1044–1065.

Trompeter, R.S. (1990). Renal transplantation. *Archives of Disease in Childhood, 65*, 143–146.

Zaritsky, A. (1987). Cardiopulmonary resuscitation in children. *Clinics in Chest Medicine, 8*, 561–571.

Chapter 10

Mutant Genes, Missing Enzymes
PKU and Other Inborn Errors

Upon completion of this chapter, the reader will:
—understand what is meant by inborn errors of metabolism
—know the differences between a number of these disorders, including PKU, maple syrup urine disease, and congenital hyperammonemia
—know which of these disorders have newborn screening tests
—be aware of the disorders in this group that are treatable and those for which there is no present treatment
—recognize the different types of treatment for some of these disorders

To receive adequate nutrition, the food we eat must be broken down into fats, proteins, and carbohydrates and then metabolized. This conversion is carried out by enzymes that also work to achieve **homeostasis** (i.e., the maintenance of bodily functions as diverse as blood sugar levels, blood pressure, and rate of growth).

Approximately 1 in 5,000 children is born deficient in an important regulatory enzyme (McKusick, 1990). These children have what are called inborn errors of metabolism, disorders that are inherited as Mendelian traits, usually autosomal recessive ones. Most of these disorders now can be detected prenatally after a mother is known to be at risk (see Chapter 3).

Inborn errors are a relatively recently classified group of diseases. One of the first, *phenylketonuria* (PKU), was described by Fölling in 1934. Most of the others have been identified since 1955, and about five new disorders are recognized each year (McKusick, 1990). This chapter focuses on these inborn errors. Rather than being an exhaustive discussion, this chapter uses examples of different inborn errors to explain some of the recent diagnostic and therapeutic approaches.

INBORN ERRORS OF METABOLISM

Some inborn errors are silent; some explode with symptoms in the newborn period; and some show clinical signs later in childhood. Although developmental disabilities do not occur in all of these children, many develop mental retardation or present a course of progressive neurological deterioration. Recently, the combination of early diagnosis and improved treatment has somewhat improved the prognosis. Nonetheless, a number of these disorders remain resistant to known methods of treatment (Hayes, Costa, Scriver, et al., 1985).

The key to effective treatment is early diagnosis, which is very difficult in silent diseases such as phenylketonuria and hypothyroidism (Fisher, 1987). Symptoms do not appear until later in childhood when treatment will have little effect on the brain damage that has already occurred. These conditions must be caught in the first weeks of life to be treated effectively. Fortunately, newborn screening is now available for these two disorders as well as for some other inborn errors of metabolism (see discussion of Newborn Screening in this chapter).

In disorders that present with severe symptoms in the newborn period, the problem is making the correct diagnosis and treating the child before the crisis leads to irreversible brain damage. Such is the case with *congenital hyperammonemia,* an inborn error in which ammonia, a breakdown product of protein, accumulates and causes brain damage. Children with complete enzyme deficiencies present with vomiting, respiratory distress, and coma in the first week of life (Batshaw, 1984). The disease is fatal if not recognized and treated. Children who have partial defects (i.e., children with 10%–20% normal enzyme activity rather than none) generally function normally in infancy but start to have symptoms of cyclical vomiting and lethargy in childhood. These symptoms are brought on by excessive protein intake or intercurrent infections. Other inborn errors that present similar symptoms include maple syrup urine disease, **multiple carboxylase deficiency,** and *congenital lactic acidoses.* The problem is that these symptoms mimic a severe infection, and if specific metabolic tests, such as ammonia levels, amino acids, and organic acids, are not performed on blood or urine, the disease will go undetected. One study indicated that 60% of persons treated for hyperammonemia had siblings who died of these disorders before the diagnosis was made on the second child with the disorder (Batshaw, 1984).

Other inborn errors are more insidious and lead to progressive neurological disorders within months or years. These disorders are called *storage diseases* because the enzyme deficiency leads to the gradual accumulation of a toxic product in various body organs (Scriver et al., 1989). This is in contrast to the previously described disorders, in which there is acute buildup of toxins but no storage. Examples include Tay-Sachs disease, Hurler disease, and **metachromatic leukodystrophy.** Unfortunately, no effective treatment for this group of disorders currently exists, although organ transplantation and gene therapy hold hopes for the future (see discussion of Importing Genes in this chapter). Yet, even in these untreatable disorders, diagnosis is helpful in giving parents a prognosis and in providing genetic counseling information. Diagnosis of storage disorders relies primarily on blood tests to detect missing enzymes.

A child with developmental disabilities of unknown origin who has either cyclical symptoms or progressive neurological deterioration may have an inborn error of metabolism and should be referred for medical evaluation. The available tests are straightforward and a correct diagnosis can lead to improved therapy and outcome or at least improved genetic counseling.

NEWBORN SCREENING

The most important diagnostic tool for identifying inborn errors has been newborn screening. As noted previously, because toxic accumulation of substances can cause brain damage, early diagnosis is crucial. PKU is the classic example. Occurring with a frequency of 1 in 14,000, PKU presents no symptoms in infancy (Scriver et al., 1989). However, if diagnosis is delayed beyond the first few months of life, the child will develop severe retardation, hyperactivity, and often a seizure disorder, even if he or she is later treated (Partington & Laverty, 1978).

The brain damage in PKU results from a buildup of *phenylalanine*. Normally, much of the phenylalanine humans ingest is used for growth of bone and tissue. The enzyme, phenylalanine hydroxylase, breaks down the remaining phenylalanine and eliminates it in the form of other nontoxic substances. In PKU, phenylalanine is not broken down because the production of this enzyme is deficient.Therefore, the phenylalanine starts to accumulate in the blood and the brain shortly after birth. Before birth, most of the excessive phenylalanine from the fetus passes across the placental membrane, where it is metabolized by the normal maternal enzyme. This is also the case with many other inborn errors. The children appear normal at birth, but soon after the toxins begin to accumulate.

In 1959, Dr. Robert Guthrie developed the first newborn screening test (Guthrie & Susi, 1963). Now, this test and other related tests for congenital hypothyroidism, **galactosemia, homocystinuria, biotinidase deficiency,** and maple syrup urine disease may be routinely performed on all babies prior to discharge from the newborn nursery. Specific tests vary from state to state. To perform the test, a few drops of blood are taken following a heel stick and are placed on filter paper. The blood sample is sent to the state health department, where staff can identify a positive test before a child is 2 weeks old (Figure 10.1). Then, confirmation of the diagnosis and early treatment, which for PKU means a phenylalanine-restricted diet, can be started. Treatments also are available for the other disorders that can be detected by newborn screening. However, these screening tests determine only a few of the many possible causes of mental retardation.

THERAPEUTIC APPROACHES

An inborn error of metabolism blocks the conversion of a toxic compound to a nontoxic product. Potential therapeutic approaches include: 1) limiting intake of the potentially toxic compound; 2) supplementing the deficient product; 3) seeking an

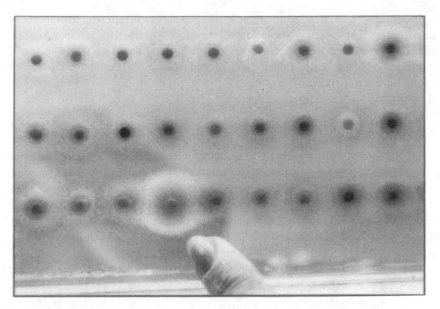

Figure 10.1. PKU spot test. Blood spots are placed in a culture medium containing bacteria that require large amounts of phenylalanine for growth. The finger points to the one blood spot containing excessive bacterial growth. The child who gave this blood has PKU.

alternate pathway; 4) providing vitamin cofactors, which activate enzymes; 5) supplying the enzyme itself or transplanting a body organ containing the missing enzyme; and 6) importing the gene required to code for the enzyme.

Limiting Intake (Dietary Restriction)

If diagnosed early, treatment for PKU is straightforward. Because phenylalanine accumulates and leads to brain damage, the child should be placed on a phenylalanine-restricted diet. An infant with PKU receives a special formula containing only small amounts of phenylalanine and normal amounts of other essential amino acids. As the child grows, he or she is restricted to small quantities of high-protein foods, such as meats, cheeses, and poultry. This diet is not too difficult to enforce when a child is young. However, by the time the child reaches 5 or 6 years of age and is more aware of other good tasting foods and of peer pressure to eat certain foods, it is harder to maintain the diet. Food stealing often becomes a problem.

Because of these difficulties, it has been asked whether it is safe to discontinue the diet when a child reaches 6 years of age, when most brain growth has been completed. Studies suggest that the IQ scores in persons with PKU who stop therapy after 6 years of age do not decrease (Holtzman, Kronmal, van Doorninck, et al., 1986; Waisbren, Mahon, Schnell, et al., 1987). Yet, a matched group of children who were maintained on the diet past this age actually experienced a modest increase in IQ scores between 6 and 10 years, so that the difference in the scores between the two groups became statistically significant (Michals, Azen, Acosta, et al., 1988). Thus, most metabolic specialists believe that the diet should be continued indefinitely (Azen, Koch, Friedman, et al., 1990).

Even in ideally treated PKU children, some deficits remain. Although the IQ scores of these children fall in the normal range, the IQs tend to be somewhat lower than those of their parents (Rylance, 1989). The incidence of attention deficit hyperactivity disorder and learning disabilities is also higher in these children than in the normal population (Smith, Beasley, Wolfe, et al., 1988).

Despite these concerns, it is clear that, when started in infancy, the phenylalanine-restricted diet yields remarkable results. An early study at the University of Toronto showed the difference in IQ scores between children treated within the first month of life compared to their siblings who had been treated later in life (Table 10.1). The children who were treated early had IQ scores around 100 while those treated later in infancy scored between 20–40 (Hanley, Linsao, & Netley, 1971).

Treatment has not been without unanticipated side effects. The most worrisome has been maternal PKU. Before effective early therapy was developed, women with PKU did not have children because such women had severe mental retardation. Now there is a new generation of women with PKU who have normal intelligence and are having babies. As adults, most of these women have stopped following a phenylalanine-restricted diet. These women have been found to produce children with mental retardation, not because the children have PKU but because high maternal phenylalanine levels are toxic to the developing fetus (Hanley, Clarke, & Schoonheyt, 1987). As a result of this finding, it is now suggested that women with PKU go back on the phenylalanine-restricted diet prior to contemplating pregnancy. Preliminary results suggest that lowering the phenylalanine levels in the pregnant mother improves the chances for normal development of her offspring (Krywawych, Haseler, & Brenton, 1991).

Another disorder responsive to dietary restriction therapy is maple syrup urine disease. This disorder is much less common than PKU, occurring in about 1 in 120,000 infants (Scriver et al., 1989). However, among certain groups, especially the Amish, it is far more common (about 1 in 1,600) because maple syrup urine disease is

Table 10.1. Results of treating PKU diagnosed at various stages

	Age at diagnosis (months)				
	0–2	*2–6*	*6–12*	*12–24*	*24+*
Number of cases	38	6	11	19	20
IQ scores:					
90+	27	0	0	1	2
80–89	6	3	0	2	1
70–79	4	1	3	2	0
Under 70	1	2	8	14	17
Mean IQ	93.5	71.6	54.5	55.5	40.8

Reprinted from Hanley, W.B., Linsao, L.S., and Netley, C. (1971). The efficiency of dietary therapy for phenylketonuria by permission of the publisher. *Canadian Medical Association Journal, 104,* June 19, 1971, 1089.

an autosomal recessive disorder, and there is much intermarriage in this closely knit religious sect. Acute symptoms develop in the newborn period that, if undetected, lead to severe brain damage or death. Infants with maple syrup urine disease vomit, are lethargic, and may become comatose. In addition, their urine has an unusual sweet odor reminiscent of maple syrup, hence the name of the disease. This disorder is caused by the accumulation of three amino acids—valine, leucine, and isoleucine—that are not metabolized properly. Treatment consists of a diet that is much more restrictive than the one used to treat PKU because all three amino acids must be regulated. Maintaining the balance is difficult, so the children's health is more fragile. While treatment has been life-saving, it has been somewhat less successful in preventing brain damage than the treatment for PKU (Kaplan, Masur, Field, et al., 1991).

Supplementing the Deficient Product

An example of replacing a missing enzyme product is the use of the thyroid hormone in children with congenital hypothyroidism. Untreated, a lack of the thyroid hormone thyroxine leads to cretinism. Children with this condition are small, floppy, and have severe mental retardation. Occurring in 1 in 6,000 children, hypothyroidism is one of the most common inborn errors of metabolism. Treatment using a thyroid **extract** has been available for over a century. However, newborn screening has existed only in recent years (Fisher, 1987). Early diagnosis now permits early treatment with the deficient hormone. This effectively corrects the metabolic disorder, and children treated in the first months of life develop normally.

Seeking an Alternative Pathway

Equally devastating is a group of inborn errors called the congenital hyperammonemias, which were described previously. Occurring in about 1 in 30,000 children, these disorders result from a child's inability to tolerate a normal protein intake. When protein is broken down into its component amino acids, ammonia, a **neurotoxin,** is released. Normally, the ammonia is converted into a nontoxic product called **urea** through the five enzyme steps in the urea cycle. The urea is then excreted in the urine. If any one of these five enzymes is deficient, ammonia will accumulate and cause severe neurological symptoms. A problem with treating these disorders through diet restriction alone is that the degree of protein restriction required to prevent an accumulation of the ammonia is incompatible with normal growth or prolonged survival. In the past, fewer than 15% of these persons treated with protein-restricted diets survived to 1 year of age (Shih, 1976).

A novel approach has been the use of two drugs, sodium benzoate and sodium phenylacetate, to provide a detour around this enzymatic block and convert the ammonia to nontoxic products that can be excreted in the urine. Using this method, over 90% of children with congenital hyperammonemias have lived longer than 1 year (Batshaw, Brusilow, Waber, et al., 1982). Unfortunately, many of these children have already sustained brain damage before treatment as a result of neonatal coma (Msall,

Batshaw, Suss, et al., 1984). Since no neonatal screening test for these disorders exists, early diagnosis must rely on the diagnostic acumen of the physician.

Providing Vitamin Cofactors

To function effectively, some enzymes require vitamin cofactors—for example, vitamin D is needed to metabolize calcium and form bone. In certain inborn errors, the provision of these cofactors results in amplification of residual enzyme activity and clinical improvement. This approach has been most effective in treating the organic acid disorder multiple carboxylase deficiency. In this disorder, children develop symptoms of acidosis and coma due to deficient activity of four enzymes that require the vitamin **biotin** as a cofactor. If biotin is provided at a very high (but nontoxic) dose, these children recover in a matter of days. They stay healthy if biotin is given and do not require dietary restrictions, but will need vitamin supplements throughout life.

Attempts have been made to treat this disorder with fetal therapy. This approach was successful with a woman who had previously produced a child with multiple carboxylase deficiency. Prenatal diagnosis revealed that she was carrying a second child with the disorder. She elected to take biotin by mouth during the third trimester of pregnancy. At birth, her child looked biochemically normal despite having a complete enzyme deficiency. He continued to be treated with biotin after birth and has remained healthy and has developed normally (Packman, Cowan, Golbus, et al., 1982).

Multiple carboxylase deficiency is a very rare disease and only a few other inborn errors are responsive to vitamin therapy. These include certain cases of **methylmalonic acidemia** (Vitamin B_{12}), homocystinuria (Vitamin B_6), and maple syrup urine disease (thiamin) (Scriver et al., 1989). This quick fix approach to treating inborn errors has unfortunately produced a rash of **megavitamin therapies,** despite clearcut evidence that such therapy is ineffective in treating all but a few rare disorders (Omaye, 1984).

Supplying the Enzyme

All of the previously discussed methods of therapy are indirect attempts at improving the child's condition. The direct approach to treating an inborn error of metabolism would be to supply the missing enzyme. Recent advances have made this a possibility in certain disorders. Enzymes can be provided either alone or by transplanting a body organ that contains the enzyme. Organ transplantation remains a very expensive (more than $100,000) and dangerous procedure; mortality rates are 10%–20%. However, in certain fatal storage disorders, organ transplantation has been attempted with some success. One example is metachromatic leukodystrophy (Krivit, Shapiro, Kennedy, et al., 1990). This disorder is marked by **dementia,** loss of speech, **quadriparesis,** and early death. It is caused by the deficiency of the enzyme arylsulfatase A and is in the same family of disorders as Tay-Sachs disease. Arylsulfatase A is present in cells of the bone marrow. In some persons, bone marrow transplantation has resulted in an arrest of or even improvement in the symptoms. However **graft versus host disease** is common following the transplant. In graft versus host disease, the transplanted cells recognize the child's body as foreign and try to destroy it. This manifests as high fever, diarrhea, and skin rash, and can prove fatal. Until bone marrow transplantation becomes safer and less expensive, it will remain an experimental procedure in treating inborn errors.

Attempts to inject the enzyme itself have been successful in only one disease, **ADA deficiency** (Levy, Hershfield, Fernandez-Mejia, et al., 1988). Severe combined immunodeficiency, or the "bubble baby" disease, results from this deficiency. The immune systems of these children cannot fight off infections and they die at young ages. Recently, the missing enzyme has been produced and can be coated so that it will not be destroyed by the body's defenses against foreign proteins. Enzyme injections are given weekly and have been successful in protecting these children against infections that previously were life-threatening. It is hoped that more enzymes will be able to be used in this fashion for other inborn errors in the future.

Importing Genes

Enzyme therapy is not a cure. The enzyme must be injected at intervals throughout the individual's life, and antibodies can develop against the foreign protein, much as insulin resistance develops in some people with diabetes. Theoretically, the ideal therapy for an inborn error would be the replacement of the defective gene (Ledley, 1987a; 1987b). As mentioned in Chapter 2, each chromosome contains hundreds of genes that direct, among other things, the production of enzymes. In inborn errors of

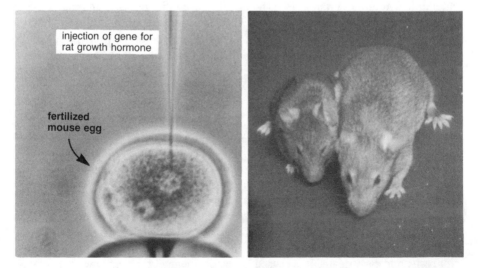

injection of gene for rat growth hormone

fertilized mouse egg

Figure 10.2. A) Microscopic photograph of fertilized mouse egg being injected with the gene for growth hormone. B) The mouse on the left is normal. The mouse on the right received the human growth hormone gene as an embryo and is twice normal size. (Photograph of mice provided by R.L. Brinster, Ph.D., University of Pennsylvania School of Veterinary Medicine, Philadelphia.)

metabolism, a mutation or structural abnormality within the gene causes either the production of a nonfunctional enzyme or no enzyme at all. If the normal gene could be inserted into the person with the inborn error, it should produce the normal enzyme and cure the inborn error.

The first successful insertion of a gene actually occurred in a mouse. In this experiment, the gene for the human growth hormone was injected into a mouse embryo (Palmiter, Norstedt, Gelinas, et al., 1983). The result was a mouse that grew to be twice as large as its siblings (Figure 10.2).

Gene insertion therapy is now a real possibility in treating inborn errors. It is done as follows (Figure 10.3): First, the gene for the defective enzyme is isolated and billions of copies are produced using a process called *polymerase chain reaction (PCR)*. The genes are then spliced onto a *retrovirus*. This virus is little more than DNA surrounded by a capsule. The retrovirus belongs to the same family of viruses as HIV but has been inactivated so that it cannot damage the cell it infects. The retro-

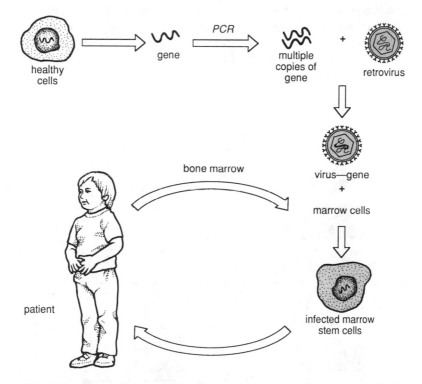

Figure 10.3. Gene therapy. The gene coding for the missing enzyme is obtained from healthy cells. Millions of copies of the gene are generated using a polymerase chain reaction (PCR) machine. These genes are then spliced onto the DNA of a retrovirus. Bone marrow cells are then removed from the child and infected with the virus. The new gene is incorporated into the child's genetic material and can start to code for the production of the missing enzyme. The marrow cells are then reinjected into the child. If things have gone according to plan, the missing enzyme should be produced by the child and the condition cured. At present, this is an experimental procedure.

virus is used as a "taxi" to transport the new gene into the individual's cells. These bone marrow stem cells are removed from the individual and infected with the virus in the test tube. The virus moves into the nucleus of the cell, thus allowing the new gene to incorporate itself into the cell's genetic material and begin to produce the missing enzyme. The cells containing the new gene are then reinjected into the individual. If the procedure is successful, these cells take hold and cure the disease. The first disease being treated with gene therapy is ADA deficiency (ADA human gene therapy clinical protocol, 1990). Cystic fibrosis, **Lesch-Nyhan disease,** and muscular dystrophy are likely candidates for gene therapy in the next few years.

OUTCOME

How effective have these new approaches to treatment been? Most are too recent to have affected long-term outcome. A 1985 study (Figure 10.4) attempted to evaluate the effectiveness of these therapies (Hayes et al., 1985). That study examined a number of parameters: longevity, reproductive ability, growth, intelligence, and ability to work independently. A large number of inborn errors was surveyed. The results were not altogether heartening. In 20%–30% of the disorders, at least some improvement occurred. However, in 70% of the disorders, treatment had little effect on long-term outcome. It is hoped that the new therapeutic approaches will improve this picture in the future.

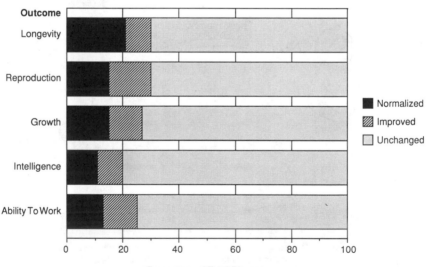

Figure 10.4.   Outcome studies have shown that only about one-quarter of inborn errors of metabolism have benefited from therapy approaches in terms of improved longevity, reproduction, growth, intelligence, or ability to hold a job as adults.

SUMMARY

Although all of the inborn errors of metabolism described here are rare, their consequences are often devastating. Therapy, in the form of dietary restrictions, works for many of these disorders. However, in some instances, the therapy itself can lead to malnutrition. Also, children with these disorders often must continue therapy for the rest of their lives, something that may be difficult to do. In some instances, megavitamin therapy or alternate pathway therapy may yield benefits. In every case, for therapy to succeed at all, it must be started early in life. Researchers continue to look for new therapeutic strategies for these diseases, focusing on gene and enzyme replacement. It is hoped that the next few years will bring more effective therapy and improved outcome.

REFERENCES

ADA human gene therapy clinical protocol. (1990). *Human Gene Therapy, 1,* 327–362.

Azen, C.G., Koch, R., Friedman, E.G., et al. (1991). Intellectual development in 12-year-old children treated for phenylketonuria. *American Journal of Diseases of Children, 145,* 35–39.

Batshaw, M.L.(1984). Hyperammonemia. *Current Problems in Pediatrics, 14*(11), 1–69.

Batshaw, M.L., Brusilow, S., Waber, L., et al.(1982). Treatment of inborn errors of urea synthesis: Activation of alternative pathways of waste nitrogen synthesis and excretion. *New England Journal of Medicine, 306,* 1387–1392.

Fisher, D.A. (1987). Effectiveness of newborn screening programs for congenital hypothyroidism: Prevalence of missed cases. *Pediatric Clinics of North America, 34,* 881–890.

Fölling, A. (1934). Uber ausscheidung von phenylbrennz trauben saure in den harn als stoffwechselanomalie in verbindung mit imbezillitat (Excretion of phenylalanine in urine: An inborn error of metabolism associated with mental retardation.) *Hoppe-Seyler's Z. Physiol. Chemistrie, 227,* 169–176.

Guthrie, R., & Susi, A.(1963). A simple method for detecting phenylketunuria in large populations of newborn infants. *Pediatrics, 32,* 338–343.

Hanley, W.B., Clarke, J.T., & Schoonheyt, W. (1987). Maternal phenylketonuria (PKU)—A review. *Clinical Biochemistry, 20,* 149–156.

Hanley, W.B., Linsao, L.S., & Netley, C. (1971). The efficiency of dietary therapy for phenylketonuria. *Canadian Medical Association Journal, 104,* 1089–1091.

Hayes, A., Costa, T., Scriver, C.R., et al. (1985). The effect of mendelian disease on human health: Response to treatment. *American Journal of Medical Genetics, 21,* 243–255.

Holtzman, N.A., Kronmal, R.A., van Doorninck, W., et al. (1986). Effect of age at loss of dietary control on intellectual performance and behavior of children with phenylketonuria. *New England Journal of Medicine, 314,* 593–598.

Kaplan, P., Mazur, A., Field, M., et al. (1991). Intellectual outcome in children with maple syrup urine disease. *Journal of Pediatrics, 119,* 46–50.

Krivit, W., Shapiro, E., Kennedy, W., et al. (1990). Treatment of late infantile metachromatic leukodystrophy by bone marrow transplantation. *New England Journal of Medicine, 322,* 28–32.

Krywawych, S., Haseler, M., & Brenton, D.P., (1991). Theoretical and practical aspects of preventing fetal damage in women with phenylketonuria. In J. Schaub, F. Van Hoof, & H.L. Vis (Eds.). *Inborn errors of metabolism* (pp. 125–135). New York: Raven Press.

Ledley, F.D. (1987a). Somatic gene therapy for human disease: Background and prospects. Part I. *Journal of Pediatrics, 110,* 1–8.

Ledley, F.D. (1987b). Somatic gene therapy for human disease: Background and prospects. Part II. *Journal of Pediatrics, 110,* 167–174.

Levy, Y., Hershfield, M.S., Fernandez-Mejia, C., et al. (1988). Adenosine deaminase deficiency with late onset of recurrent infections: Response to treatment with polyethylene glycol-modified adenosine deaminase. *Journal of Pediatrics, 113,* 312–317.

McKusick, V.A. (1990). *Mendelian inheritance in man: Catalogs of autosomal dominant, autosomal recessive, and X-linked phenotypes* (9th ed.). Baltimore: The Johns Hopkins University Press.

Michals, K., Azen, C., Acosta, P., et al. (1988). Blood phenylalanine levels and intelligence of 10-year-old children with PKU in the national collaborative study. *Journal of the American Dietetic Association, 88,* 1226–1229.

Msall, M., Batshaw, M.L., Suss, R., et al. (1984). Neurologic outcome in children with inborn errors of urea synthesis. Outcome of urea-cycle enzymopathies. *New England Journal of Medicine, 310,* 1500–1505.

Omaye, S.T. (1984). Safety of megavitamin therapy. *Advances in Experimental Medicine and Biology, 177,* 169–203.

Packman, S., Cowan, M.J., Golbus, M.S., et al. (1982). Prenatal treatment of biotin-responsive multiple carboxylase deficiency. *Lancet, 1,* 1435–1438.

Palmiter, R.D., Norstedt, G., Gelinas, R.E., et al. (1983). Metallothionein—Human GH fusion genes stimulate growth of mice. *Science, 222,* 809–814.

Partington, M.W., & Laverty, T. (1978). Long-term studies of untreated phenylketonuria. Intelligence or mental ability. *Neuropadiatrie, 9,* 245–254.

Rylance, G. (1989). Outcome of early detected and early treated phenylketonuria patients. *Postgraduate Medical Journal, 65*(Suppl. 1), S7–S9.

Scriver, C.R., Beaudet, A.L., Sly, W.S., & Valle, D. (Eds.). (1989). *The metabolic basis of inherited disease* (6th ed.). New York: McGraw-Hill.

Seashore, M.R. (1990). Neonatal screening for inborn errors of metabolism: Update. *Seminars in Perinatology, 14,* 431–438.

Shih, V.E. (1976). Hereditary urea-cycle disorders. In S. Grisolia, R. Baguena, & F. Mayor (Eds.), *The urea cycle* (pp. 367–414). New York: John Wiley & Sons.

Smith, I., Beasley, M.G., Wolff, O.H., et al. (1988). Behavior disturbance in 8-year-old children with early treated phenylketonuria: Report from MRC/DHSS phenyketunuria register. *Journal of Pediatrics, 112,* 403–408.

Waisbren, S.E., Mahon, B.E., Schnell, R.R., et al. (1987). Predictors of intelligence quotient and intelligence quotient change in persons treated for phenylketonuria early in life. *Pediatrics, 79,* 351–355.

Chapter 11

Good Nutrition, Poor Nutrition

Upon completion of this chapter, the reader will:

—know the major food groups and problems that occur if children are deficient in any of them

—be aware of the function of vitamins and minerals, as well as the consequences of their deficiency

—understand the problems of lead poisoning

—know the effects of malnutrition on children, including its effect on brain development

—recognize the complications associated with obesity

—be able to evaluate the merits of various diets, including vegetarian, megavitamin, organic foods, Feingold, and macrobiotic diets.

Most of us have heard the expression, "You are what you eat." This expression highlights the importance of good nutrition, significant to all of us but especially to infants and children, whose growth rate and development are most rapid. To grow well, children need an appropriate mixture of fats, carbohydrates, protein, water, vitamins, and minerals. The optimal caloric distribution of fats, carbohydrates, and protein is: 30% from fat; 55% from carbohydrates; and 15% from protein (Pipes, 1985). These nutrients are metabolized or burned in our bodies to produce energy, the unit of measurement of which is the calorie. How many calories one needs to eat depends on body size, the amount of physical activity, and the rate of growth. Children, whose growth rate and activity are high, need up to 105 calories per kilogram (kg) of body weight each day, while adults require only 30 calories per kilogram (American Academy of Pediatrics, 1985). (One kilogram equals 2.2 pounds.)

This chapter explores the nutritional requirements of children, especially those with disabilities, along with the effects of certain nutritional deficiencies. Also examined are various diets including traditional ones, such as breast- and formula-feeding, and nontraditional ones, such as vegetarian, organic, Feingold, and macrobiotic diets.

171

GROWTH DURING CHILDHOOD

Normally, a newborn loses weight during the first week of life and then gains about 20–30 grams per day for several months (Table 11.1). By 4–6 months of age, the birth weight has doubled and, by 12 months, it has tripled. After this, weight gain slows to about 5 pounds a year until approximately 9–10 years of age, when the adolescent growth spurt begins (Guo, Roche, Fomon, et al., 1991).

Height moves at a slower pace, increasing by 50% during the first year of life and doubling by 4 years of age. When a child reaches 13 years of age, his or her height has usually tripled (Smith, 1977). Normal growth curves for height and weight (Hamill, Drizd, Johnson, et al., 1977) are included at the end of this chapter on pages 194–196. Since children with disabilities, especially those with genetic and metabolic syndromes, often have decreased growth potential, it is especially important to monitor their weight and height (Dietz & Bandini, 1989; Shapiro, Green, Krick, et al., 1986). Some evidence suggests that height potential actually can be increased in children with Down syndrome and Turner syndrome by the use of growth hormone injections (Saenger, 1991).

Besides height and weight gain, the brain grows rapidly during the first year of life. Head circumference increases by 1–2 centimeters a month, and brain weight doubles by 2 years of age (Karlberg, Engstrom, Lichtenstein, et al., 1968) (Table 11.2). At this age, the number of nerve cells is in the adult range, and further growth mainly takes place in the form of increased cell size and intercellular connections.

FAILURE TO THRIVE

To grow normally, a child must have an adequate nutritional intake. Malnutrition remains the leading cause of infant illness and death in developing countries (Grand, Sutphen, & Dietz, 1987). Although cases of severe malnutrition are rare in the United States, an inadequate diet is not uncommon in certain segments of the population, including the impoverished, the food faddists, and persons with developmental disabilities. Early signs of undernutrition include poor weight gain, a decrease in fatty tissue, poor height gain, reduced rate of growth in head circumference, and an increased susceptibility to infections. Later changes include muscle atrophy, hair loss,

Table 11.1. Normal growth during childhood

Age	Weight gain (g/day)	Height gain (mm/day)
0–3 mo.	25–35	1.1
3–6 mo.	15–20	0.7
6–12 mo.	10–13	0.5
1–6 yr.	5–8	0.2
7–10 yr.	5–11	0.15

Source: Fomon, Haschke, Ziegler, et al. (1982).

Table 11.2.   Increase in head circumference

Age (months)	Head circumference increase (cm/month)
0–1	3.0
1–3	3.0
3–6	3.0
6–9	2.0
9–12	1.0
12–18	1.6
18–24	1.0
24–36	1.0

Source: Karlberg, Engstrom, Lichtenstein, et al. (1968).

skin rash, edema, and kidney and liver malfunction. Measurement of the triceps skinfold, using a special caliper, shows decreased thickness, which has been found to correlate with decreased body fat content. Midarm muscle circumference also is reduced, indicating decreased muscle mass. An X ray of the hand shows a delay in the bone age.

When undernutrition becomes severe enough to cause the later signs, it is called *malnutrition*. There are two major forms of malnutrition. One involves a greater deficiency in protein than calories and is called *kwashiorkor*. The other, *marasmus*, is characterized by an equivalent protein-calorie insufficiency. Kwashiorkor is exemplified by the "pot-bellied" starving infants in developing countries. However, health practitioners also may observe this condition in children with chronic diseases, such as cystic fibrosis, and in those with inborn errors of metabolism who require severe protein restriction.

Marasmus has a spectrum of clinical manifestations, ranging from "failure to thrive" to malnutrition. In its mildest form, "failure to thrive" involves a food intake that is inadequate for normal weight gain. Yet, the child with marasmus may continue to grow taller at a fairly normal rate. If the child eats even less, growth in both height and weight is diminished. The child appears thin and wasted with skin rashes and hair loss, and acts irritable and listless (Solomons, 1985). Children with disabilities are at an increased risk for "failure to thrive" for numerous reasons, including increased energy needs and inability to consume an adequate amount of calories because of feeding problems (see Chapter 12). For example, the child with choreoathetoid cerebral palsy uses excessive calories because of involuntary motion. This child also may have feeding problems that interfere with food intake. An example of mild undernutrition may be the child with ADHD who loses his or her appetite when placed on methylphenidate (Ritalin) (Klein & Mannuzza, 1988).

The first line of therapy for malnutrition is to increase caloric intake by providing diets that are high in calories, fat, and protein (Tables 11.3 and 11.4). Malnourished children may require 1.5–2 times the normal caloric intake in order to begin gaining weight. If this strategy fails, nasogastric tube-feedings may become necessary using

Table 11.3.   Foods commonly consumed by children that are good sources of protein

Food	Portion size	Protein content (g)	Caloric content
Pasteurized cheese	1 oz.	6.5	107
Ham and cheese sandwich	1	24.2	372
Scrambled egg (with milk & fat)	1 lg.	6.0	95
Cheese pizza	1 slice	14.6	290
Macaroni and cheese	1 cup	16.8	430
Fish sticks	4 sticks	17.6	304
Hamburger	1	21.1	257
Milk, whole	1 cup	8.0	150

Source: Pennington (1989).

a predigested, **lactose**-free formula (see the discussion of Tube-Feeding in this chapter). Mineral and vitamin supplements also may be needed. By taking ongoing measurements of height, weight, and skinfold thickness, physicians and nutritionists can readily monitor a child's growth.

One much-disputed aspect of malnutrition is its effect on brain growth (Smart, 1991). The question is whether maternal malnutrition during pregnancy influences the growth of the fetus. Studies of the effects of the famine in the Netherlands during World War II on prenatal development (see Chapter 4) suggested that, although the

Table 11.4.   Foods commonly consumed by children that are high in fat content

Food	Portion size	Fat content (g)	Caloric content
Vanilla ice cream	1 cup	23.7	349
Chocolate milk shake	12 oz.	10.5	360
Cream of chicken soup	1 can	17.9	283
Butter	1 tsp.	4.1	36
Whipping cream	1 T.	4.6	44
Peanut butter	3 T.	24	282
Potato chips	3½ oz.	35.4	518
Bologna	1 slice	6.5	73
Sausage	1 patty	8.4	100
French fries	3 oz.	14.2	274
Hot dog	1	13.1	144
Bacon	3 slices	9.4	109
Gravy	4 T.	3.2	47
Chocolate chip cookie	1	2.7	46
Doughnut (cake)	1	5.8	105

Source: Pennington (1989).

birth weight of newborns was decreased, head circumference and intellectual functioning were not affected (Stein & Susser, 1975).

However, if a pregnant woman experiences more severe protein-calorie malnutrition during the last trimester and her baby is malnourished during the first 6 months of life, brain cell count can be decreased by as much as 20% (Crosby, 1991). One study evaluating this phenomenon was done after the Korean War. A number of Korean War orphans were monitored after placement in foster homes in the United States. The physical and intellectual development of all the children fell within normal limits during later childhood. However, the infants who were well-nourished during the first 6 months of life had significantly higher IQs than those who had been malnourished early in life. Because the first year of life is the period of the most rapid brain growth (Winick, 1979), it seems logical that infantile malnutrition would place the child at increased risk for future learning disabilities and attention deficit hyperactivity disorder (Galler, Ramsey, & Solimano, 1984; Galler, Ramsey, Solimano, et al., 1984).

OBESITY

The opposite of malnutrition is obesity, which can be equally devastating. In the United States, it is the most common disorder of nutrition. It has a prevalence of 5%–25% depending on age, sex, and socioeconomic status. Obesity tends to follow children into adulthood, and there is clearly a genetic component. Eighty percent of children with two obese parents become obese, while only 14% of children with two lean parents become obese (Thorp, Peirce, & Deedwania, 1987). The classic example among children with disabilities is the Prader-Willi syndrome. Children with this syndrome have moderate mental retardation and are extremely obese. During sleep, they may have apneic episodes that can be life-threatening (Cassidy & Ledbetter, 1989).

In addition to children with Prader-Willi syndrome, children with Down syndrome, muscular dystrophy, spina bifida, spastic cerebral palsy, and other developmental disabilities that cause decreased activity have a 50% or greater risk of becoming obese (American Dietetic Association, 1987). In these children, obesity may limit mobility by making it more difficult for them to walk or be transported.

Even in children without disabilities, obesity places individuals at increased risk for coronary heart disease, hypertension, and diabetes as adults. Thus, parents should be careful to identify excessive weight gain early and then to institute a weight reduction program. Such a program, directed by a physician or nutritionist, should involve parent management and skill training, physical exercise, and a nutritious, well-balanced, calorie-restricted diet that does not impair linear growth (Epstein, Wing, & Valoski, 1985). Weight reduction counseling must be taught so that the capabilities of the parents as well as the child are considered. Highly structured diets incorporating foods not consumed normally by the household may be too restrictive and ultimately end with failure in compliance. Behavior management of eating habits is equally important to maintain weight reduction. The child must be taught to eat only at meals, to eat slowly, and not to steal food. Food should not be used as a reinforcer for accomplishments or good behavior. Using this approach and a 1,000 calories per day diet in a teenager, the weekly weight loss should average around 2–3 pounds.

NUTRIENTS AND THEIR DEFICIENCIES

To be adequately nourished, a child must receive the proper quantity of proteins, fats, carbohydrates, fiber, and water. Smaller amounts of vitamins and minerals are also necessary.

Proteins

Proteins, contained in such foods as milk, cheese, meat, eggs, and fish (see Table 11.3), are broken down in the digestive tract into amino acids and nitrogen. Amino acids are involved in the synthesis of new tissue, hormones, enzymes, and antibodies; nitrogen is needed to keep existing tissue healthy. There are nine essential amino acids from which all other nonessential amino acids are made. Premature infants actually need 12 essential amino acids, as cystine, taurine, and tyrosine are not able to be produced because of immaturity of metabolic pathways. Thus, formulas for premature infants are supplemented with these amino acids. The quality of a specific protein is measured by the completeness of its essential amino acid content. In general, animal protein contains essential amino acids in greater amounts than plant protein. For example, milk is a complete protein in that it contains all of the essential amino acids. Grains, beans, and seeds, however, are incomplete. The relative requirement for various essential amino acids decreases with age, so adults can be much less careful about their food intake than children. The overall requirement for protein also declines over time. Supplemental protein is not needed during the adolescent growth spurt.

A lack of protein in the diet can lead to a reduction in growth rate as well as a failure to develop normal secondary sexual characteristics, such as pubic hair and breast tissue. An increased incidence of infections and poor digestion, due to deficiencies of certain enzymes, also may result from protein malnutrition (Shils & Young, 1988).

Fats

While proteins are involved primarily in body growth and tissue maintenance, fats produce mainly energy. In addition, two fatty acids, linolenic and arachidonic acids, are essential because they cannot be synthesized in the body. Cow's milk fat (butter) contains much less of the essential fatty acids than human milk. This is why infant formulas are made with skim milk (with the butter removed) and vegetable oils are added. Fatty acid deficiency is rare except in certain chronic diseases, such as cystic fibrosis, where there is impaired fatty acid absorption, or **celiac disease**, where there is diarrhea and malabsorption. A deficiency state increases susceptibility to infection and interferes with blood clotting. Treatment of a malnourished infant may involve the use of a formula supplemented with **medium chain triglycerides (MCT)** and essential fatty acids, such as Portagen and Pregestimil.

Fats in food consist primarily of triglycerides, which are either **saturated** or **unsaturated**. Animal fats also contain cholesterol. Fats yield 9 calories per gram whereas carbohydrates and proteins yield only 4 calories per gram. Foods high in fats include ice cream, nuts, and potato chips (see Table 11.4). In addition to providing energy, fats give food its good taste and make us feel full. This is why dieting on low-fat foods tends to leave one feeling hungry. Most fat is burned as fuel. However, some of it also goes to make vitamins, and some aids in producing tissue.

Recently, much controversy has surrounded the issue of whether diets high in cholesterol or unsaturated fats are unhealthy. Increased risk of heart disease and hypertension have been a major concern. It is clear that individuals with some rare enzyme deficiencies are at risk from high-cholesterol or unsaturated fat diets. However, whether such a diet has an adverse effect on children's health is not completely clear (American Dietetic Association, 1991).

The consensus of several professional organizations is to promote a generally balanced diet for all healthy individuals over the age of 2 years. The diet recommendations are for no more than 30% of the total calories to be derived from fat, less than 10% of energy from saturated fat, and less than 300 milligrams of dietary cholesterol per day (National Cholesterol Education Program, 1990). Examples of suggested types of foods to eat and to avoid are listed in Table 11.5.

This recommendation, however, does not apply to infants, who have a much greater growth rate. Breast milk and infant formulas contain 40%–50% of energy from fat. Poor growth has been associated with lower fat intake in infants. It is generally recommended that infants move from breast milk or commercial formula to whole cow's milk at around 1 year of age (American Academy of Pediatrics, 1985). It is prudent to continue the use of whole milk in the diet until the age of 2 years. At this time, the fat content of the diet can come from more varied sources and fall to the adult 30% figure.

Carbohydrates

Foods high in carbohydrates (Table 11.6) also are used as fuel and provide energy as glucose for brain metabolism. Carbohydrates can be stored in muscles as **glycogen** and released as needed (American Academy of Pediatrics, 1985). There are two classes of carbohydrates: simple sugars and complex carbohydrates. Lactose, the sugar in milk, and sucrose, table sugar, are examples of simple sugars. They are rapidly absorbed and quickly available for use as energy. Polysaccharides, or complex carbohydrates, are present in cereals, grains, potatoes, and corn. These starches are broken down more slowly into simple sugars and fiber.

Fiber

Dietary fiber is that part of food that is not broken down in the digestive tract. Plants, fruits, and grains are the primary sources of fiber in our diet. An advantage of a high-fiber diet is that it increases stool bulk and discourages constipation (see Chapter 12). In addition, low-fiber diets have been implicated in everything from cancer to coronary artery disease, although these assertions remain unproven. In fact, excessive fiber is not necessarily good for young children. It takes up room in a child's small

Table 11.5.   The four food groups and suggested frequency of intake of specific foods shown for children and adults

Anytime	Sometimes	Seldom
Grain group		
Whole-grain breads and cereals	Muffins	Croissants
	Waffles, pancakes	Doughnuts
Brown rice	Heavily sweetened cereals	Danish pastries
Pasta	Granola cereals	
Bagels, rolls		
Fruit and vegetable group		
All fruit and vegetables (except those at right)	Dried and canned fruit	Coconut
	Fruit juice	Pickles
Applesauce, unsweetened	Canned vegetables with salt	Scalloped or au gratin potatoes
Potatoes, white or sweet	French fries, fried in vegetable oil	
Milk group		
Dry-curd cottage cheese	2% low-fat or regular cottage cheese	Soft and hard whole-milk cheeses
Skim milk		
1% low-fat milk products	Reduced-fat or part-skim cheeses	Processed cheeses
Nonfat yogurt	2% low-fat milk, low-fat yogurt	Whole milk, whole-milk yogurt
	Ice milk, frozen nonfat or low-fat yogurt	Ice cream
Fish, poultry, meat, eggs, beans, and nuts group		
	Fish	
All fin fish	Fried fish	
Salmon, canned	Tuna, oil-pack	
Tuna, water-pack	Shrimp	
Shellfish, except shrimp		
	Poultry	
Chicken breast (without skin)	Chicken breast (with skin)	Fried chicken thigh or wing
	Chicken drumstick, thigh	Chicken hot dog
Turkey breast, drumstick, thigh	Fried chicken, except thigh or wing	
Ground turkey (without skin)	Ground turkey (with skin)	
	Red meats	
Pork tenderloin	Bottom round, sirloin steak	Chuck blade, rib roast
Beef eye round and top round	Lean ham	Extra-lean or lean ground beef
	Pork or lamb loin chop	
	Leg of lamb, veal sirloin	Pork or lamb rib chop, bacon
	Veal loin or rib chop	Bologna, salami, hot dog
		Any untrimmed red meat

(continued)

Table 11.5.   *(continued)*

Anytime	Sometimes	Seldom
	Eggs	
Egg white		Whole egg or yolk
	Beans, peas and nuts	
Beans, peas, lentils	Tofu, peanut butter, nuts	

Adapted from Nutrition Action Healthletter, June 1990. Published by the Center for Science in the Public Interest; and The Good Health Magazine, *New York Times*, October 6, 1991, p. 12.

stomach and also can interfere with the absorption of certain vitamins. Probably the best recommendation is to encourage a middle ground, where older infants and children are encouraged to include portions of high-fiber whole grain cereals, breads, fruits, and vegetables in their daily diet.

Table 11.6.   Foods commonly consumed by children that are rich in carbohydrates

Food	Portion size	Carbohydrate content (g)	Caloric content
Coca-Cola	12 oz.	38.0	144
Jelly beans	1 oz.	26.4	104
Milk chocolate (candy bar)	1 bar	27.1	254
Apple Jacks cereal	1 oz.	25.7	110
Cheerios	1 oz.	19.6	111
Spaghetti with tomato sauce	1 cup	37.0	260
Chocolate cupcake (Hostess)	1 bar	29.0	170
Jell-O	½ cup	18.8	81
Chocolate pudding	½ cup	31.7	162
Pancakes and syrup	2	82.2	468
Apple	1 med.	21.1	81
Banana	1 med.	26.7	105
Corn	1 ear	28.7	120
Popcorn (microwave form)	3 cups	18.9	192
Bagel	1	30.9	163
Bread	1 slice	11.7	64
Orange juice	1 cup	26.8	112
Gum	1 stick	2.0	9
Tomato	1 large	5.3	24

Source: Pennington (1989).

Water Requirements

Water is second only to oxygen as an essential for life. The water content in bodies of infants (70%) is higher than that in adults (60%) (American Academy of Pediatrics, 1985). It is replenished by drinking fluids and also is provided in foods. Our requirements for water are related to caloric consumption and average about 1 milliliter of water per 1 calorie in persons of all ages. (One milliliter is 1/30 of an ounce.) Thus, an infant needs to consume far larger amounts of water for weight than an adult because infants take in more calories per kilogram. In young infants, the average intake of fluid should be about 90–150 milliliters per kilogram of weight each day or 1.5–2.5 ounces per pound of weight each day (American Academy of Pediatrics, 1985). In older infants and children, eating solid foods also provides water. Table 11.7 shows the liquid content of various foods.

Treatment of Diarrhea   Special dietary considerations should be made in the event of diarrhea. In stomach flu or **gastroenteritis**, water is lost through vomiting and diarrhea. If it is not replaced, the individual may become dehydrated. This is a particular hazard for a child with multiple disabilities who will become dehydrated more easily. The initial approach to therapy should be to stop milk formulas and give small clear liquid feedings. These may consist of fruit juices, but special formula feedings that contain a balanced electrolyte mixture and glucose are also available. If there is a decrease in stooling in a day or so, soft foods (e.g., rice, apple sauce, bananas) can be added in the next day or so. The child usually can return to a regular diet within a few days. However, if the stooling increases despite this therapy, signs of dehydration, including decreased quantities of concentrated urine, difficulty in forming tears and saliva, sunken eyes, and crinkled skin, should be watched for carefully. These symptoms should receive immediate medical attention. This may require stopping all oral feedings and instituting intravenous therapy with a glucose and electrolyte solution.

Vitamins

Although children need large quantities of fats, proteins, and carbohydrates for normal growth, they require only minute amounts of vitamins. Vitamins are used mainly as cofactors in metabolic reactions and stimulate, or catalyze, the reactions without

Table 11.7.   Liquid content of various foods

Food	Percentage of water
Strained fruits	80–85
Milk	87
Eggs	75
Meats	50–75
Fruits and vegetables	70–90
Breads	35
Cooked cereal	80–88

Source: Watt and Merrill (1963).

being used up themselves. Also, the body can store fat-soluble vitamins so that a deficiency does not become evident until weeks or months after the malnutrition has begun. In the United States, most processed foods are supplemented with vitamins. For example, milk is fortified with vitamin D, vitamin A, and riboflavin, and infant formulas are supplemented with all the essential vitamins. Because of these additives, a normal child over 3 months of age receives at least twice the daily requirement for vitamins in a regular food intake (Table 11.8). However, a child with a disability who does not eat well may need a vitamin supplement. In this instance, the most important vitamins are A, B complex, C, and D (Curtis, 1990).

Vitamin A   Vitamin A, or retinol, is essential for the light-sensitive reaction of the **rods** in the eye. The rods are nerve cells involved in black-and-white vision, and they are responsible for our ability to see in the dark. A deficiency in vitamin A leads to night blindness. However, the administration of too much vitamin A, a possibility with the use of retinol in treating severe acne, can lead to a skin rash, **anorexia**, bone pain, and mildly increased brain pressure (American Academy of Pediatrics, 1985). Retinol, when given to pregnant women, also has been associated with an increased incidence of birth defects, principally spina bifida. Sources of vitamin A include breast milk, infant formulas, fortified cow's milk, liver, carrots, sweet potatoes, greens, peaches, and apricots.

Vitamin B Complex   The vitamin B complex includes thiamine, riboflavin, cyanocobalamin, niacin, folic acid, pantothenic acid, and biotin. Thiamine functions as a cofactor in carbohydrate metabolism. Pork, legumes, and nuts are good sources of thiamine. A lack of thiamine leads to a condition called **beri-beri** (Jukes, 1989). While extremely uncommon in the United States, beri-beri remains a major problem in developing countries. Children with this condition have congestive heart failure, edema, and neurological abnormalities. Unlike vitamin A, an excess of thiamine is nontoxic because it is excreted in the urine.

Another B complex vitamin, B_6, or pyridoxine, aids in the metabolism of certain amino acids. This vitamin also is essential for the adequate functioning of the central nervous system. A deficiency in vitamin B_6 can lead to seizures, anemia, skin rash, and nerve damage. Adequate amounts of it are found in whole grains, liver, and potatoes. Massive doses of pyridoxine (2–6 grams per day, or 1,000 times the requirement) have caused ataxia and sensory loss (American Academy of Pediatrics, 1985).

Vitamin B_{12}, or cyanocobalamin, is vital for the functioning of both the bone marrow and the nerve cells. It is also a cofactor in a number of enzyme reactions. This vitamin is contained in most animal products, including milk and eggs. Deficiencies are rare, except among strict vegetarians. A more common problem associated with a lack of vitamin B_{12} is pernicious anemia, which is due to an inadequate absorption of this vitamin from the digestive tract. This happens either because there is insufficient secretion of a chemical substance in the stomach, called *intrinsic factor*, or as a result of damage to the inner lining of some part of the small intestine. An adult with this disorder develops anemia and progressive neurological symptoms. Treatment consists of administering B_{12} by injection, thus bypassing the defective digestive tract.

Table 11.8. Recommended daily allowances

Age (years)	Minerals				Vitamins					
	Sodium (mg/kg/d)	Potassium (mg/kg/d)	Calcium (mg)	Iron (mg)	A (µg/RE)[a]	Thiamine (mg)	Riboflavin (mg)	Nicotinic acid (mg)	C (mg)	D (i.u.)
Infants:										
0–1	23 to 57.5	39 to 97.5	400 to 600	10	375	0.4	0.5	6	35	400
Children:										
1–3	57.5	97.5	800	10	400	0.7	0.8	9	40	400
3–6	46.0	78.0	800	10	500	0.9	1.1	11	45	400
6–9	34.5	58.5	800	10	700	1.0	1.2	14	45	400
Boys:										
9–12	34.5	58.5	800 to 1200	10 to 12	700 to 1000	1.3 to 1.5	1.2 to 1.5	16	45 to 50	400
12–15	34.5	58.5	1200	12	1000	1.5	1.5 to 1.8	20	50 to 60	400
15–18	34.5	58.5	1200	12	1000	1.5	1.8	22	60	400
Girls:										
9–12	34.5	58.5	800 to 1200	10 to 15	700 to 800	1.0 to 1.1	1.2 to 1.3	15	45 to 50	400
12–15	34.5	58.5	1200	15	800	1.1	1.3	17	50	400
15–18	34.5	58.5	1200	15	800	1.1	1.3	15	60	400

Adapted from Recommended Dietary Allowances (10th ed.). (1989); and U.S. National Research Council (1980).
[a]Retinol equivalents. 1 retinol equivalent = 1 µg retinol or 6 µg betacarotene.

Vitamin B$_{12}$ also has been used to treat some inborn errors of metabolism (see Chapter 10).

The final B vitamin to consider is folate, which plays a role in the metabolism of DNA and certain amino acids as well as in the formation of blood cells (Shils & Young, 1988). Good sources include liver, beans, and leafy green vegetables. A deficiency state is uncommon in the United States, but common in developing countries. It results in poor growth, gastrointestinal disturbances, and anemia. Anemia must be properly diagnosed as it may be caused by either folate or B$_{12}$ deficiency. Treating a B$_{12}$ deficiency with folate will correct the anemia but not the associated neurological disease. Of more concern to children with disabilities is that certain antiepileptic drugs including phenytoin, phenobarbital, and primidone may impair its absorption and metabolism, leading to clinical signs of deficiency. Often a multivitamin supplement that contains folate is recommended for these children.

Vitamin C   The much hailed vitamin C, or ascorbic acid, is needed to form collagen, the connective tissue in tendons and in the walls of blood vessels. It also aids in the metabolism of iron. Scurvy is the condition caused by vitamin C deficiency. Its symptoms include irritability, leg pain, swollen gums, and hemorrhaging. While the disease was quite common during the early exploration of the New World in the 16th century, it is extremely unusual now. Citrus fruits furnish large amounts of vitamin C and protect against scurvy.

The other uses of vitamin C are far more controversial, including its value in treating cancer and in preventing the common cold. Since Linus Pauling's theory concerning vitamin C and the common cold was published (Pauling, 1976), a number of carefully controlled studies have shown that the use of vitamin C has, at best, a small effect on the severity and duration of the symptoms of a cold (Miller, Nance, Norton, et al., 1977). Furthermore, megadoses of vitamin C may have adverse effects. For instance, such doses interfere with the absorption of vitamin B$_{12}$ and may lead to B$_{12}$ deficiency (Herbert & Jacob, 1974). Also, long-term use of such large doses of vitamin C leads to a decrease of this vitamin in the blood. This may explain why a number of infants born to mothers who took 400 milligrams of vitamin C daily throughout pregnancy developed scurvy (Cochrane, 1965). On the basis of these findings, the American Academy of Pediatrics (1985) suggests caution in substantially exceeding the recommended daily allowance of vitamin C for children.

Vitamin D   For people to have healthy bones, vitamin D is necessary. It aids in the absorption of calcium from the digestive tract as well as in the mobilization of calcium from bone. Sunlight is the best natural source of vitamin D. Another good source is cow's milk and infant formulas because they are supplemented with it. Breast milk is a poor source, so breast-fed infants may need to take vitamin D supplements. Whole grain cereals, vegetables, and fruits all contain negligible amounts of vitamin D.

A lack of vitamin D causes rickets (Kainer & Chan, 1989). Signs of rickets include bumps along the rib cartilage, called a **rachitic rosary**, an enlargement of the **anterior fontanel**, the soft spot in the skull, scoliosis, and abnormalities in the long bones and pelvis (Figure 11.1). Treatment consists of the oral administration of large

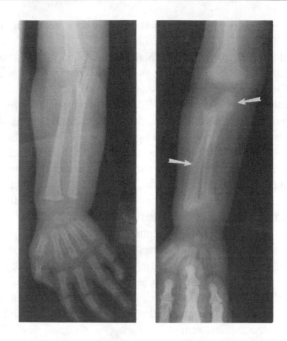

Figure 11.1. X rays of arm in a normal child (left) and in a child with rickets (right). The upper arrow points to the widened, frayed part (metaphysis) of the bone. The lower arrow points to the decreased density of the bone shaft; both of these are typical findings in rickets.

doses of vitamin D. Black children are more likely to develop rickets than white children because their skin absorbs less ultraviolet light from the sun.

Some anticonvulsants, especially the combination of phenobarbital and phenytoin, interfere with the utilization of vitamin D (Hahn & Avioli, 1984). Although the deficit infrequently causes symptoms of rickets, research has suggested that nonam- **bulatory** persons with seizure disorders should receive supplements of vitamin D (Collins, Maher, Cole, et al., 1991). Normally, 1–3 drops per day of Drisdol, an activated vitamin D preparation, prevents the deficit. An excess of vitamin D should be avoided because it can lead to nausea, thirst, and neurological abnormalities.

Vitamins E and K Vitamin E, or tocopherol, is contained in most foods. A deficiency of this vitamin is rare except in premature infants. Supplements of vitamin E now are used in some premature infants to decrease the risk of anemia and intraventricular hemorrhage (Nutrition Reviews, 1988). Vitamin E has been proposed to treat or prevent everything from mental retardation to heart disease and cancer, but none of these claims has substance.

Also unusual is a deficiency of vitamin K, although excessive amounts of vitamin E can interfere with the absorption of vitamin K. Deficiencies also can occur in premature infants and in children with cystic fibrosis or severe developmental disabilities. A deficiency state results in a blood clotting abnormality (American Academy of Pediatrics, 1985). Vitamin K is commonly found in vegetables, soybeans, and alfalfa.

Carnitine   Carnitine is not a vitamin, but it is needed in small amounts for certain enzyme reactions. Carnitine is found in meat and is used in the body to transport fats into the mitochondria of a cell where they can be oxidized to release energy. Carnitine deficiency is associated with low blood sugar, hyperammonemia, and liver dysfunction. Most children receive adequate carnitine in their diets and do not require supplements. However, children with certain inborn errors of metabolism and seizure disorders may benefit from carnitine supplements. The inborn errors associated with carnitine deficiency are the organic acidemias in which carnitine is depleted in conjugating and eliminating the toxins. Carnitine is lost in the urine along with the toxin and may need to be replaced. Certain antiepileptic drugs, including valproic acid, carbamazepine, phenobarbital, and phenytoin, also have been associated with increased carnitine loss (Opala, Winter, Vance, et al., 1991; Winter, Szabo-Aczel, Curry, et al., 1987). It is unclear whether this should be replaced.

Minerals

Children and adults also need various minerals to ensure appropriate body functioning. Some minerals are required in substantial amounts, especially calcium, magnesium, and phosphorus (see Table 11.8). Other elements, such as fluorine, copper, zinc, iodine, iron, and manganese, are needed in very small, or *trace*, amounts.

These diverse minerals perform different functions. For example, calcium, phosphorus, and magnesium are required for the formation of bones and teeth and for normal muscle contraction. These three comprise about 98% of all the mineral content of the body (American Academy of Pediatrics, 1985). Bone minerals are lost during bedrest, muscle paralysis, or immobilization in a cast. A deficiency in these minerals leads to brittle bone structure, rickets, poor muscle tone, and poor growth. For children with disabilities who have borderline nutrition, supplements providing 100% of the recommended daily allowance (RDA) of calcium are useful. This can be given as 4–6 tablets of TUMS a day. The prime source of calcium in infants and young children is milk. Calcium is also found in sardines, salmon, cheese, yogurt, and leafy green vegetables. Magnesium is contained in whole grains, nuts, beans, and leafy greens. Phosphorus is found in milk, milk products, and meats. As a result, supplements of these two minerals are not necessary.

Needed in smaller amounts are potassium, chloride, and sodium. They maintain the body's fluid balance and are found in most foods. An imbalance of these minerals leads to muscle weakness, nausea, states of confusion, and seizures. A deficiency state most commonly occurs during a severe episode of diarrhea.

Trace metals, including iron, zinc, copper, fluoride, iodine, selenium, and manganese, are essential for the activation of certain enzymes. Deficiencies are rare but may occur in premature infants or in chronically ill children who have malabsorption, are fed intravenously, or require dialysis. Zinc deficiency results in growth failure, skin rash, and impaired immunity against infections. Copper deficiency has been linked to anemia and weakened bones. Selenium deficiency has caused heart failure and neurological abnormalities. Although these deficiencies are rare, they have been posited to cause all kinds of problems in the general population ranging from learning difficulties to mental retardation; no scientific evidence supports this thinking.

Deficiencies in two trace elements have been associated with more common diseases: iodine with hypothyroidism, and iron with anemia. Iodine is a component of the thyroid hormone, thyroxine. An insufficiency leads to the development of goiter and hypothyroidism. Iodine is primarily found in shellfish, eggs, and dairy products, and is added to table salt.

Iron is an important constituent of hemoglobin, the respiratory protein of the red blood cell. A person who does not consume enough iron will become anemic. Children who eat insufficient amounts of liver, enriched cereals, legumes, or dried fruits are likely to develop iron-deficiency anemia. This is especially true of children who are raised on milk formulas without iron supplement or without enriched cereals. It occurs most frequently between 6 months and 3 years of age (American Academy of Pediatrics, 1985). Iron supplementation from iron-fortified formula, iron-fortified cereals, or iron compounds should start in full-term infants between 4 and 6 months of age and in premature infants no later than 2 months of age.

LEAD

One mineral that is harmful rather than helpful is lead. It may be present in paint on the walls of some older homes. Combined with **pica** (i.e., the craving of some infants and toddlers for non-nutritive substances), lead poisoning is a major health hazard in inner cities.

Lead paint was outlawed for use in homes after World War II. However, older houses have many layers of paint, the oldest of which still contain lead. If these homes are not well maintained, flaking plaster provides a ready source of lead for the curious child. Minute amounts can result in lead poisoning that may express itself as language delay or other developmental disabilities. Treatment involves both removal of lead from the child's body using the medications **edetate calcium disodium** (**EDTA**) and **penicillamine** and abating the lead from the walls of the house.

There is more controversy about the effects of low-level environmental lead exposure on development. One major study has linked low-level environmental lead exposure with poor school performance (Needleman, Schell, Bellinger, et al., 1990). The removal of lead from gasoline has reduced environmental lead exposure significantly, but more must be done in this area.

TRADITIONAL DIETS

In light of the variety of diets available and recommended, it is important to consider which ones are nutritionally best for children.

Breast-Feeding

For infants, breast milk is the best nourishment. It contains the correct ratio of carbohydrates to fats to protein, and it supplies needed calories and minerals. In addition, breast milk is more easily digestible than commercial infant formulas because of its lower protein and higher carbohydrate content (Winikoff, 1987). It is also presterilized and preheated and provides babies with immunity against certain infections. Finally, it is inexpensive and enhances maternal bonding. In developing countries, breast-feeding often is continued for 18 – 24 months (or until another baby is born). In these places, children develop severe malnutrition only after breast-feeding is terminated. The only time that breast-feeding may not be appropriate is when a disease or drug may be transmitted from mother to child. Although infrequent, this may occur in HIV infection. It definitely happens with alcohol and cocaine exposure (see Chapter 8).

In general, breast-fed infants need supplementation with vitamin D and fluoride (if the water is not fluoridated) in order to be nutritionally complete. Iron supplements are advisable if the introduction of solid foods is to be delayed.

Formula-Feeding

In the United States, although 50% of women breast-feed during their baby's first weeks of life, fewer than 25% nurse after their children reach 5 months of age (Lawrence, 1985; Winikoff, 1990). Usually, women stop breast-feeding as a matter of convenience or because of other demands, such as employment. For these infants, commercial formulas are an appropriate substitute. The most common baby formulas (SMA, Similac, Enfamil) are composed of reconstituted skim milk with a mixture of soy, corn, and other oils added to provide fat (Table 11.9). Lactose is the sugar in these formulas. In children who appear to be lactose intolerant, with episodes of vomiting and diarrhea, a soy-based formula (e.g., Isomil or Nursoy) can be used. Soy contains sucrose (corn oil) rather than lactose as its carbohydrate.

Proprietary formulas supply an adequate amount of calories, vitamins, minerals, proteins, fats, and carbohydrates. No additional vitamin supplements are needed (Curtis, 1990). The average infant ingests about 3–5 ounces per kilogram of weight per day of formula. Cereals and fruits often are added at 4–6 months of age, although they are not really needed until 6–9 months (Fomon, 1974) (Figure 11.2). Introduction of foods into the infant's diet should be done using single ingredient foods in order to detect possible intolerance. Rice cereal is generally added first, followed by vegetables, egg yolks, fruits, and meats, although the order doesn't really matter. The average infant usually is fed completely on solid table foods and whole milk by 1–2 years of age (American Academy of Pediatrics, 1985).

Tube-Feeding

Some children with developmental disabilities may not make the transition to solid foods in the normal fashion as a consequence of motor dysfunction or anatomical problems (see Chapter 12). If the child is unable to take adequate amounts of food by mouth, feedings by a nasogastric or gastrostomy tube may be necessary to maintain adequate nutrition (Moore & Greene, 1985). The nutrition given through the tube can be puréed everyday foods, provided they maintain the proper nutritive value. Alternatively, there are complete formula-feedings available, such as Ensure and Jevity

Table 11.9.   Commercial formulas used in infancy and childhood

Formula	Source	Use	Calories/100 ml
Milk, cow	Cow's milk	Routine	67
Milk, human	Human milk	Infant formula	67
Similac, SMA, Enfamil	Nonfat cow's milk, corn oil, coconut oil, soy oil	Infant formula	67
Prosobee, Isomil	Soy protein, corn syrup solids, soy and coconut oils	Lactase intolerance infant formula	67
Portagen, Pregestimil	Glucose, medium chain triglyceride, protein hydrolysale	Malabsorption in infants	67
Pedialyte, Lytren,	Oral electrolyte formula, glucose	Diarrhea in infants and children	10
Ensure	Corn syrup solids, sucrose, casein, corn oil, soy protein (lactose free)	High-caloric tube-feeding for children	106
Osmolite, Jevity	Medium chain triglyceride, corn starch, casein, corn oil (lactose free)	High-protein, high caloric tube-feeding for undernourished children	106

(see Table 11.9). These formulas differ from infant formulas in containing an increased concentration of calories and protein so that more nutrition can be given in a smaller volume.

NONTRADITIONAL DIETS

In recent years, many nontraditional diets have become popular (Hanning & Zlotkin, 1985). Some of these, such as "health food" and vegetarian diets, provide adequate nutrition. A few, such as the Feingold diet, are of unproven value. Others, such as megavitamin and macrobiotic diets, may harm children.

Vegetarian Diets

Vegetarian diets can be classified as lacto-ovo-vegetarian (vegetables plus dairy products and eggs) or vegan (plant foods only). People in many societies have practiced vegetarianism for centuries and have remained healthy, especially when they have supplemented their diet with milk or eggs. In fact, in many ways, the lacto-ovo-vegetarian diet is nutritionally similar to diets containing meats. In older children, vegan diets can be equally nourishing, as long as vegetarians select their foods carefully and make sure they receive sufficient calories, essential amino acids, and vi-

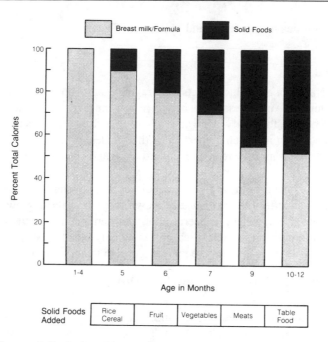

Figure 11.2. Suggested distribution of breast milk/formula and solid foods during first year of life. (*Source: Service Master Diet Manual* [2nd ed.], 1990.)

tamins (Jacobs & Dwyer, 1988). Advantages of a vegetarian diet include a low incidence of obesity and low cholesterol levels.

Yet, there are problems with a vegetarian diet for small children. If a nursing mother follows a vegan diet, her infant may develop deficiencies in calcium, vitamin D, vitamin B_{12}, and iron. The child needs supplements of these vitamins and minerals. The fat content of the mother's milk also will be low. For a toddler, vegetarian diets are so high in bulk that the child may be unable to eat a sufficient quantity of fruits and vegetables to obtain adequate calories. The protein content is also low, although this can be countered by using increased quantities of legumes (beans, peas, and soy). An older child can eat legumes, wheat germ products, nuts, seeds, and dark green leafy vegetables to achieve an adequate caloric intake. Even for this child, a multivitamin/mineral supplement is necessary.

Macrobiotic Diets

While a vegetarian diet may permit normal growth and development, a macrobiotic diet is definitely detrimental to growing children. The goals of such a diet are largely spiritual. One must follow 10 stages of dietary restriction beginning with the gradual elimination of animal products and leading to the elimination of fruits and vegetables. The highest level diets allow only cereals; their caloric intake is very low. Strict adherence to such a diet may result in scurvy, rickets, anemia, hypocalcemia, malnutrition, and even death in infancy and childhood (Dagnelie, Vergote, van-Staveren, et al., 1990).

Health Foods

Unlike vegetarian or macrobiotic diets, natural or organic food diets are not restricted in their content. The main restriction here is in how the plants are grown or in how the animals are raised. To qualify as organic, plants must be grown in soil enriched with humus and compost in which no pesticides, herbicides, or inorganic fertilizers have been used. Animals must be reared on natural feeds and not treated with hormones or antibiotics.

While proponents of these diets laud their results, no long-term study has shown the nutritional superiority of organically grown crops over those grown under standard conditions. Nevertheless, concerns about hormones and additives are valid and, for some individuals, are sufficient reason to buy only organic foods. One important consideration is that these foods are more expensive than ordinary foods.

The Feingold or Kaiser-Permanente (K-P) Diet

Many individuals are concerned about the additives present in today's foods. An additive is defined as a blend of substances deliberately added to basic foodstuffs (American Academy of Pediatrics, 1985). The largest group of additives are flavors, food colors, texture agents, and preservatives. Flavors are either extracted from natural sources or synthesized. Most food colors are synthesized. Preservatives, often chemicals, are added to prevent spoilage.

All additives must receive approval from the federal Food and Drug Administration (FDA) before they are used. Yet questions remain about their safety, especially in children's diets. Dr. Benjamin Feingold (1975) linked additives with hyperactive behavior in children. He asserted that almost half of the children who are labeled as hyperactive would improve if synthetic colors, flavors, and natural **salicylates** were removed from their diets. Foods containing salicylates include oranges, apples, grapes, cucumbers, and tomatoes. Studies investigating Feingold's claims have found no clinically significant differences between groups of hyperactive children treated versus not treated with the Feingold diet. There is little evidence to support Feingold's contention that this diet has merit for treating a large percentage of hyperactive children and children with learning disabilities (National Institutes of Health, 1982; Wolraich, Mitich, Stumbo, et al., 1985). In various research studies, fewer than 10% of the children responded to the Feingold diet (Valey, 1984; Wolraich et al., 1985).

Megavitamin Diets (Orthomolecular Therapy)

While the Feingold diet is restrictive, megavitamin diets involve supplementation. Large doses of certain vitamins, usually 10 times or more the recommended daily allowance, are advocated.

The basis for megavitamin diets, or **orthomolecular therapy**, is the finding that certain persons with rare inborn errors of metabolism benefit from high doses of specific vitamins (see Chapter 10). Studies have found that some persons born with defective enzymes require a much higher intake of a certain vitamin than normal to stimulate enzyme activity. Others have expanded this finding to suggest that individuals with disorders ranging from learning disabilities to mental retardation and childhood psychosis can successfully be treated with megavitamin therapy (Cott, 1972). Such usage is unsubstantiated (Nutrition Committee, Canadian Pediatric Society, 1990). Furthermore, certain risks are inherent with ingesting large amounts of vitamins. For example, taking large doses of vitamin A can lead to nausea and increased intracranial pressure. Excessive use of vitamin B_6 produces muscle weakness, and too much vitamin D results in hypercalcemia. Finally, an overdose of vitamin E can cause stomach pain and an increased risk of bleeding. Children receiving a normal diet do not need vitamin supplementation.

SUMMARY

Considerable latitude exists in what parents safely can feed their children to ensure adequate nutrition. However, before embarking on any specialty diet, parents would be wise to consult a nutritionist or a physician. Some of the newer diets are dangerous for healthy children and may be devastating for children with disabilities.

REFERENCES

American Academy of Pediatrics. (1985). *Pediatric nutrition handbook* (2nd ed.). Evanston, IL: American Academy of Pediatrics, Committee on Nutrition staff.

American Dietetic Association. (1987). Nutrition in comprehensive program planning for persons with developmental disabilities: Technical support paper. *Journal of the American Dietetic Assocition, 87,* 1069–1074.

American Dietetic Association. (1991). Timely statement on NCEP report on children and adolescents. *Journal of the American Dietetic Association, 91,* 983.

Cassidy, S.B., & Ledbetter, D.H. (1989). Prader-Willi syndrome. *Neurologic Clinics, 7,* 37–54.

Cochrane, W.A. (1965). Overnutrition in prenatal and neonatal life: A problem? *Canadian Medical Association Journal, 93,* 893–899.

Collins, N., Maher, J., Cole, M., et al. (1991). A prospective study to evaluate the dose of vitamin D required to correct low 25–hydroxyvitamin D levels, calcium, and alkaline phosphatase in patients at risk of developing antiepileptic drug-induced osteomalacia. *Quarterly Journal of Medicine, 78,* 113–122.

Cott, A. (1972). Megavitamins: The orthomolecular approach to behavioral disorders and learning disabilities. *Academic Therapy, 7,* 245–249.

Crosby, W.M. (1991). Studies in fetal malnutrition. *American Journal of Diseases of Children, 145,* 871–876.

Curtis, D.M. (1990). Infant nutrient supplementation. *Journal of Pediatrics, 117,* S110–S118.

Dagnelie, P.C., Vergote, F.J., van-Staveren, W.A., et al. (1990). High prevalence of rickets in infants on macrobiotic diets. *American Journal of Clinical Nutrition, 51,* 202–208.

Dietz, W.H., & Bandini, L. (1989). Nutritional assessment of the handicapped child. *Pediatrics in Review, 11*(4), 109–115.

Epstein, L.H., Wing, R.R., & Valoski, A. (1985). Childhood obesity. *Pediatric Clinics of North America, 32,* 363–379.

Feingold, B.F. (1975). *Why your child is hyperactive.* New York: Random House.

Fomon, S.J. (1974). *Infant nutrition* (2nd ed.). Philadelphia: W.B. Saunders.

Fomon, S.J., Haschke, F., Ziegler, E.E., et al. (1982). Body composition of reference children from birth to age 10 years. *American Journal of Clinical Nutrition, 35*(5 Suppl.), 1169–1175.

Galler, J.R., Ramsey, F., & Solimano, G. (1984). The influence of early malnutrition on subsequent behavioral development. III. Learning disabilities as a sequel to malnutrition. *Pediatric Research, 18,* 309–313.

Galler, J.R., Ramsey, F., Solimano, G., et al. (1984). The influence of early malnutrition on subsequent behavioral development. IV. Soft neurologic signs. *Pediatric Research, 18,* 826–832.

Grand, R.J., Sutphen, J.L., & Dietz, W.H. (1987). *Pediatric nutrition: Theory and practice.* Stoneham, MA: Butterworth-Heinemann.

Guo, S., Roche, A.F., Fomon, S.J., et al. (1991). Reference data on gains in weight and length during the first two years of life. *Journal of Pediatrics, 119,* 355–362.

Hahn, T.J., & Avioli, L.V. (1984). Anticonvulsant-drug-induced mineral disorders. In D.A. Roe & T.C. Campbell (Eds.), *Drugs and nutrients—The interactive effects* (pp. 409–427). New York: Marcel Dekker.

Hamill, P.V., Drizd, T.A., Johnson, C.L., et al. (1977). NCHS growth curves for children, birth–18 years. In *Vital & Health Statistics,* Series 11, No. 165 (pp. 56–61). Hyattsville, MD: U.S. Department of Health, Education & Welfare, Public Health Service.

Hanning, R.M., & Zlotkin, S.H. (1985). Unconventional eating practices and their health implication. *Pediatric Clinics of North America, 32,* 429–445.

Herbert, V., & Jacob, E. (1974). Destruction of vitamin B_{12} by ascorbic acid. *Journal of the American Medical Association, 230,* 241–242.

Jacobs, C., & Dwyer, J.T. (1988). Vegetarian children: Appropriate and inappropriate diets. *American Journal of Clinical Nutrition, 48* (Suppl. 3), 811–818.

Jukes, T.H. (1989). The prevention and conquest of scurvy, beri-beri, and pellagra. *Preventive Medicine, 18,* 877–883.

Kainer, G., & Chan, J.C. (1989). Hypocalcemic and hypercalcemic disorders in children. *Current Problems in Pediatrics, 19,* 489–545.

Karlberg, P., Engstrom, I., Lichtenstein, H., et al. (1968). The development of children in a Swedish urban community. A prospective longitudinal study. III. Physical growth during the first three years of life. *Acta Paediatrica Scandinavica, 187*(Suppl.), 48–66.

Klein, R.G., & Mannuzza, S. (1988). Hyperactive boys almost grown up. III. Methylphenidate effect on ultimate height. *Archives of General Psychiatry, 45,* 1131–1134.

Miller, J.Z., Nance, W.E., Norton, J.A., et al. (1977). Therapeutic effects of vitamin C: A co-twin control study. *Journal of the American Medical Association, 237,* 248–251.

Moore, M.C., & Greene, H.L. (1985). Tube feeding of infants and children. *Pediatric Clinics of North America, 32,* 401–417.

National Center for Health Statistics. (1977). *NCHS growth curves for children, birth to 18 years (U.S.).* Hyattsville, MD: Author.

National Cholesterol Education Program. (1990). *Report of the expert panel on population strategies for blood cholesterol reduction* (DHHS Publication No. NIH 90-3046). Washington, DC: U.S. Government Printing Office

National Institutes of Health. (1982). Consensus conference: Defined diets and childhood hyperactivity. *Journal of the American Medical Association, 248,* 290–292.

Needleman, H.L., Schell, A., Bellinger, D., et al. (1990). The long-term effects of exposure to low doses of lead in childhood. An 11-year follow-up report. *New England Journal of Medicine, 322,* 83–88.

Nutrition Committee, Canadian Paediatric Society. (1990). Megavitamin and megamineral therapy in childhood. *Canadian Medical Association Journal, 143,* 1009–1013.

Nutrition Reviews. (1988). Vitamin E supplementation of premature infants. *Nutrition Reviews, 46,* 122–123.

Opala, G., Winter, S., Vance, C., et al. (1991). The effect of valproic acid on plasma carnitine levels. *American Journal of Diseases of Children, 145*, 999–1001.

Pauling, L.C. (1976). *Vitamin C, the common cold and the flu.* San Francisco: W.H. Freeman & Co.

Pennington, J.A.T. (1989). *Bowes and Church's food values of portions commonly used* (15th ed.). Philadelphia: J.B. Lippincott.

Pipes, P.L. (Ed.). (1988). *Nutrition in infancy and childhood* (3rd ed.). St. Louis: Times-Mirror Mosby.

Saenger, P. (1991). Use of growth hormone in the treatment of short stature: Boon or abuse? *Pediatrics in Review, 12*, 355–363.

Service Master Company, L.D. (1990). *Service Master diet manual* (2nd ed. rev.). Downers Grove, IL: Author.

Shapiro, B.K., Green, P., Krick, J., et al. (1986). Growth of severely impaired children: Neurological versus nutritional factors. *Developmental Medicine and Child Neurology, 28*, 729–733.

Shils, M.E., & Young, V.R. (1988). *Modern nutrition in health and disease* (7th ed.). Philadelphia: Lea & Febiger.

Smart, J.L. (1991). Critical periods in brain development. *CIBA Foundation Symposium, 156*, 109–124.

Smith, D.W. (1977). *Growth and its disorders: Basics and standards, approach and classifications, growth deficiency disorders, growth excess disorders, obesity.* Philadelphia: W.B. Saunders.

Solomons, N.W. (1985). Assessment of nutritional status: Functional indicators of pediatric nutriture. *Pediatric Clinics of North America, 32*, 319–334.

Stein, Z., & Susser, M. (1975). The Dutch famine 1944–45, and the reproductive process. I. Effects on six indices at birth. *Pediatric Research, 9*, 70–76.

Thorp, F.K., Peirce, P., & Deedwania, C. (1987). Nutrition in the infant and the young child. In S.L. Halpern (Ed.), *Quick reference to clinical nutrition* (2nd ed. pp. 72–101). Philadelphia: J.B. Lippincott.

Valey, C.K. (1984). Diet and the behavior of children with attention deficit disorder. *Journal of the American Academy of Child Psychiatry, 23*, 182–185.

Watt, B.K., & Merrill, A.L. (1963). *Composition of foods—Raw processed, prepared.* Washington, DC: U.S. Department of Agriculture, Agriculture Handbook No.8.

Winick, M. (Ed.). (1979). *Nutrition: Pre- and postnatal development.* New York: Plenum.

Winikoff, B. (1990). Breastfeeding. *Current Opinion in Obstetrics and Gynecology, 2*, 548–555.

Winikoff, B., Myers, D., Laukaran, V.H., et al. (1987). Overcoming obstacles to breastfeeding in a large municipal hospital: Applications of lessons learned. *Pediatrics, 80*, 423–433.

Winter, S.C., Szabo-Aczel, S., Curry, C.J.S., et al. (1987). Plasma carnitine deficiency: Clinical observations in 51 pediatric patients. *American Journal of Children, 141*, 660–665.

Wolraich, M., Mitich, R., Stumbo, P., et al. (1985). Effects of sucrose ingestion in the behavior of hyperactive boys. *Journal of Pediatrics, 106*, 675–682.

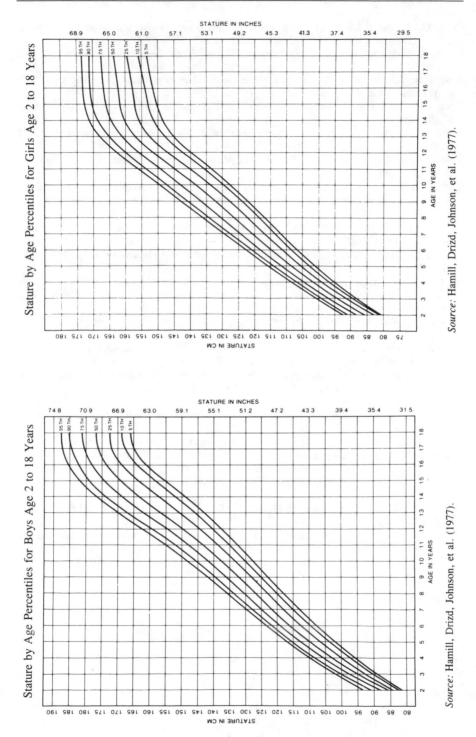

Source: Hamill, Drizd, Johnson, et al. (1977).

Source: Hamill, Drizd, Johnson, et al. (1977).

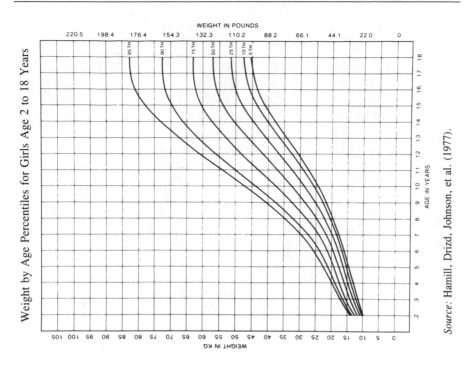

Source: Hamill, Drizd, Johnson, et al. (1977).

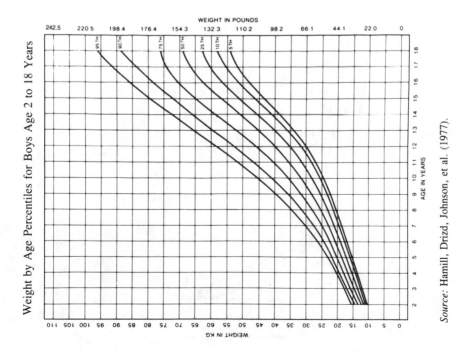

Source: Hamill, Drizd, Johnson, et al. (1977).

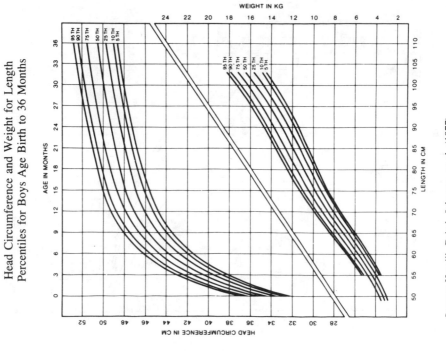

Head Circumference and Weight for Length Percentiles for Boys Age Birth to 36 Months

Source: Hamill, Drizd, Johnson, et al. (1977).

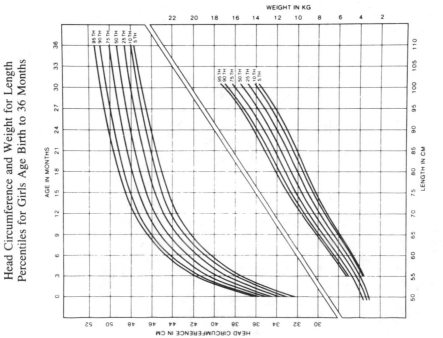

Head Circumference and Weight for Length Percentiles for Girls Age Birth to 36 Months

Source: Hamill, Drizd, Johnson, et al. (1977).

Chapter 12

Feeding the Child with Disabilities

Peggy Monahan Eicher

Upon completion of this chapter, the reader will:
—understand the function and structure of the gastrointestinal tract
—be aware of the feeding problems of children with disabilities
—know some of the ways to treat these problems

Children with developmental disabilities may face special problems in obtaining adequate nutrition. Some have medical conditions that interfere with the ability of the gastrointestinal tract to tolerate or digest food. Others have motor dysfunction that makes it difficult to accept new food textures or interferes with the preparation of food for swallowing. The continuous pressures on these children and their caregivers to maintain adequate nutrition often lead to behavior problems, making mealtimes even more stressful. In this chapter, the normal anatomy and function of the gastrointestinal tract are explained so that the influences of various medical and developmental conditions can be understood. Specific feeding and digestive disorders are discussed, along with approaches to therapy.

THE GASTROINTESTINAL TRACT

For adequate nutrition to take place, the gastrointestinal tract must be able to perform its three major functions: the controlled movement of food from the mouth to the anus, the digestion of food, and the absorption of nutrients.

The digestive process begins in the oral cavity, where food is prepared for its journey down the gastrointestinal tract. The action of taking food into the mouth by

Peggy Monahan Eicher, M.D., is Director of the Pediatric Feeding Program at Children's Seashore House and Assistant Professor of Pediatrics at The University of Pennsylvania School of Medicine in Philadelphia.

bottle or spoon and then breaking it up into a small parcel of **bolus** collected at the mid-tongue region is accomplished through a series of complex motor movements of the lips, tongue, and jaw. Once a bolus is formed, the tongue is signalled to propel it backward into the pharynx. This triggers a swallow, an involuntary cascade of highly coordinated motor movements of the pharyngeal and esophageal musculature. The swallow enables continued propulsion of the bolus past the airway, down the **esophagus,** and into the stomach (Figure 12.1). With each swallow, respiration ceases as the **nasopharynx** and trachea are covered by the soft palate and **epiglottis,** respectively, so that food is not **aspirated** into the airway.

As the bolus of food travels to the stomach, the esophageal muscle works as a one-way valve to prevent the backward flow, or reflux, of food after it has entered the stomach (Figure 12.2). Meanwhile, the stomach secretes acids to further break down the food. Contractions of the stomach wall mix the food, acids, and added fluids and push this mass gradually into the **duodenum,** the upper part of the small intestine (Figure 12.3). (Incidentally, the intestines are referred to as small or large because of their diameter, not their length.)

Enzymes and other substances from the pancreas and bile ducts are released into the duodenum and aid in the breakdown of food particles into their major components: proteins, fats, and carbohydrates. These compounds are further simplified into sugars, such as lactose, fatty acids, amino acids, and vitamins. The **ileum,** or lower small intestine, absorbs these digested nutrients. The water and electrolytes added in the stomach are recycled when they are reabsorbed by the ileum.

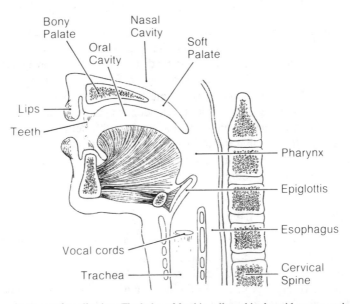

Figure 12.1.   Anatomy of swallowing. The bolus of food is collected in the mid-tongue region. It is then pushed backward to the pharynx. As swallowing begins, the epiglottis normally folds over the opening of the trachea to direct food down the esophagus and not into the lungs. Defective closure results in aspiration into the trachea.

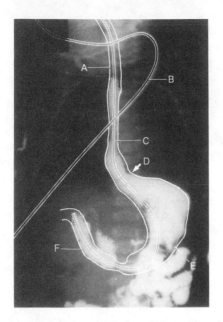

Figure 12.2.   Food passes down the espohagus (A), through the esophageal sphincter (D), and into the stomach (E), and duodenum (F). If the sphincter does not remain closed after the passage of food, reflux (C) occurs as shown in this barium study in a child with a nasogastric tube (B) in place F.

The leftovers, including the remaining water and electrolytes, then pass to the large intestine or colon (see Figure 12.3). In the adult, the colon receives about 50 ounces of fluid a day but discharges only about 3–6 ounces as stool. The rest of the fluid is normally reabsorbed. It is in the colon that bacteria alter nondigestible residues to form substances that give the stool its odor. The absence of bacteria in an infant's colon accounts for the lack of smell in the stool during the first few months of life. A change in the content of nondigestible residues presented to the bacteria also can result in changed odors. Blood, for example, when broken down by bacteria, accounts for the extremely malodorous smell of stool in individuals with stomach ulcers.

Movement through the colon is much slower than through the rest of the digestive tract and depends on the volume of nonabsorbable nutrients, often called **bulk** or fiber, that is contained in the food. While movement from the stomach to the end of the ileum may take only 30–90 minutes, passage through the colon may require 1–7 days. Rapid movement, which happens, for example, during a stomach flu, leads to diarrhea. Conversely, slower movement causes more water to be absorbed and results in hard stools and constipation. Constipation can lead to slower transit through the entire system and even vomiting. For proper bowel movement to take place, an individual needs fluid, fiber, and coordinated propulsive muscle activity. This includes control of the rectal sphincter muscles that facilitate voluntary defecation.

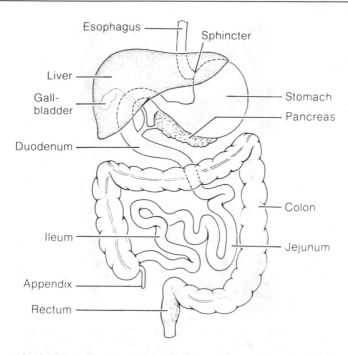

Figure 12.3. After food enters the stomach, it is mixed with acid and is partially digested. Then it passes through the three segments of the small intestine (duodenum, jejunum, and ileum). There, digestive juices are added, and nutrients are removed. The remaining water and electrolytes pass through the colon where water is removed. Voluntary stooling is controlled by the rectal sphincter muscle.

FEEDING PROBLEMS IN CHILDREN WITH DISABILITIES

Effective feeding depends on: 1) the ability to take in food, form a bolus, and swallow; 2) the absence of aspiration of food into the airway; 3) the lack of reflux of food once it enters the stomach; and, 4) the normal digestion and movement of food through the intestines. Problems can occur at one or more of these steps.

Taking in Food

Eating skills are acquired in a sequential fashion, driven in part by practice. If a child has not had adequate experience with one oral stage, he or she may have trouble moving on to the next stage, even if the physiological problem that had prevented practice has been resolved. Therefore, the child's medical and developmental history is important in understanding a feeding problem, since past conditions may be influencing the current status.

Suckling   Suckling is the most primitive oral movement and has been seen in fetuses as early as 12 weeks. However, suckling is not combined with swallowing until 34 weeks gestation, and only at full term does the pattern become coordinated with breathing to allow functional feeding. This is why premature infants generally require tube-feedings.

The suckle pattern involves a rhythmic up and down motion of the jaw, with the tongue riding in and out with a stripping wave motion. Initially, suckling is a reflexive activity that is elicited involuntarily whenever something enters the child's mouth. With brain maturation, the reflex is inhibited and the pattern is refined to the voluntary act of sucking.

Sucking During sucking the lips purse, the jaw movements are better controlled, and the tongue is raised and lowered independently. This creates a vacuum that pulls food into the mouth. Once an up-down sucking pattern replaces the in-out stripping wave pattern of suckling, the child can progress to spoon-feeding. This usually occurs around 5 months of age, and the child can begin to eat puréed foods. If spoon-feeding is tried earlier, the food will ride out of the mouth on the tongue instead of being swallowed.

For children with disabilities, especially children with cerebral palsy, a number of problems may interfere with the normal development and performance of these oral motor skills. Abnormal muscle tone often is expressed as abnormal patterns of lip or tongue retraction and poor jaw closure. When the lips are retracted or tightly drawn back, they are more difficult to purse, to make the seal necessary for sucking. Similarly, retracting the tongue bunches it up and hinders the creation of a vacuum. It is also less well suited for the collection and propulsion of the bolus required to initiate an effective swallow. This decreases the child's control over bolus movement and increases the risk of aspiration. In addition, abnormal body muscle tone or primitive reflex activity may drive the child into an arched, extended posture. This also makes feeding more difficult and aspiration more likely and increases the likelihood of vomiting because of elevated abdominal pressure.

Spoon-Feeding Advancing to eating from a spoon may be frustrating for these children and their caregivers. In order to be spoon-fed, a child must be able to respond appropriately to the touch of a spoon to his or her lips, clean the spoon of food, and collect the bolus at the mid-tongue level, prior to propelling it backward to the pharynx. Problems can develop at any of these stages.

One problem is persistence of the primitive suckle pattern, which prevents the movements necessary to clear food from the spoon. A second problem is tongue thrusting, which often is associated with extrapyramidal cerebral palsy. This leads to the expulsion of food from the mouth rather than down the throat. A tongue thrust also may be voluntary. Some children with gastroesophageal reflux or aspiration use a tongue thrust in an attempt to avoid the pain or discomfort associated with swallowing food. This can be confused with movements inherent to cerebral palsy.

A third problem in spoon-feeding relates to the presence of a tonic bite reflex. Also associated with cerebral palsy, this primitive reflex leads to the sudden closure of the jaw when the teeth or gums are lightly touched. If this happens, the bite does not release for some time. As a result, the spoon is stopped before it even delivers the food. The child also may be hypersensitive to the touch of the spoon or food and may refuse to open his or her mouth in the first place. Sometimes the jaw fails to close around the spoon; the food then slides out of the mouth.

A final problem is lack of practice. Often, for medical reasons, oral feeding is prohibited for prolonged periods of time in children with disabilities. Without ongoing practice, these children are at risk of losing their oral motor skills.

Munching and Chewing   Once a child is able to be spoon-fed, the next developmental step is munching, followed by chewing. Munching begins with the development of a normal bite-and-release pattern. The emergence of tongue lateralization at this stage enables the child to move food from side to side and collect the bolus of food in the midline. Munching then consists of a rhythmical bite-and-release pattern with a series of well-graded jaw openings and closings. Small pieces of food can then be broken off or flattened and then collected in preparation for swallowing. Chewing of the food into smaller pieces does not occur until the child acquires a rotary component to jaw movement. This can be seen as early as 9 months but is gradually modified to the adult pattern, which is reached at around 3 years of age in normal children.

Some children with disabilities never gain the skills needed to chew. Even those who have this potential may be delayed in chewing because of abnormalities in muscle tone, involuntary tongue movement, or the persistence of primitive reflexes, such as the tonic bite or tongue thrust.

Aspiration

Swallowing   The final step is swallowing, which has three phases: oral, pharyngeal, and esophageal. The child must be able to form a bolus and then coordinate the contraction of the muscles to move the food from the back of the tongue to the pharynx and then down the esophagus (see Figure 12.1). The epiglottis must then fold over the opening of the trachea to prevent the food from being inhaled into the lungs. Poor coordination or weakening of these muscle contractions may interfere with adequate food intake or increase the risk of aspiration of food into the lungs, a problem that leads to recurrent pneumonia.

Gastroesophageal Reflux

Gagging, vomiting, and **rumination** provide further problems for children with developmental disabilities. These problems interfere with adequate nutrition. One contributing factor to these symptoms is gastroesophageal reflux (GER) (Figure 12.2). GER is the backward flow of stomach contents up into the esophagus. GER can result from the dysfunction of many mechanisms (Sutphen, 1990). The most common involves a weakened muscle at the end of the lower esophagus. As a result, the sphincter does not work properly to prevent food from backing up into the esophagus. Alternatively, abdominal pressure may be increased because of increased muscle tone or posturing. This can push food up through even a normally functioning sphincter. A third problem is delayed stomach emptying, usually caused by poor intestinal motility or air swallowing. Both result in a swelling of the stomach, which increases sphincter relaxation and resultant reflux.

The result of each of these mechanisms is gastroesophageal reflux. Food and stomach acid juices can surge up from the stomach after a meal and cause vomiting or aspiration into the lungs. In addition, the escape of stomach acid can cause an inflammation of the esophagus that makes eating uncomfortable.

Not all vomiting is a consequence of reflux. It also can result from a behavior disorder called *rumination*. This term refers to a digestive process observed in cows, in which the cow swallows food and then brings it up again from its rumen to rechew it. Some people with severe mental retardation experience rumination. Shortly after swallowing, they vomit and then chew and swallow again. This is inefficient as well as socially offensive. It can often be controlled using behavior management techniques.

Digestion

The Small Intestine While problems of sucking and swallowing are common in children with disabilities, they usually are able to absorb nutrients after the food reaches the small intestine. Occasionally, however, there may be malabsorption that interferes with adequate nutrition (Brady, Rickard, Fitzgerald, et al., 1986).

The most common malabsorptive disorder is lactose intolerance. Approximately 10%–20% of black and Jewish children have this problem (Heitlinger & Lebenthal, 1988). Symptoms include vomiting and diarrhea after swallowing milk products. The cause of the intolerance is an inherited deficiency of the enzyme **lactase,** which normally breaks down milk sugar (lactose) and allows its absorption. Unabsorbed lactose irritates the gastrointestinal wall and causes vomiting and diarrhea. An individual with this disorder can prevent or at least decrease the symptoms by taking lactase in a capsule form before ingesting a milk product.

The function of the small intestine also can be compromised by "dumping." This occurs with too rapid emptying of the stomach or too rich a meal. Children receiving high-calorie supplements are particularly at risk. Dumping results in an altered pancreatic response, insulin swings, pallor, sweating, and sometimes diarrhea.

Constipation

The Large Intestine For children with disabilities, the major problem with the function of the large intestine or colon is constipation. This is due to an inadequate fluid and fiber intake combined with uncoordinated muscle contractions and poor rectal sphincter control. The result is the retention of stool for prolonged periods of time. The longer the stool remains in the colon, the more water is absorbed, and the harder and more immobile the stool becomes. The end result is constipation (Fitzgerald, 1987).

Diarrhea also can be a problem. It may be caused by dumping or by overaggressive bowel cleaning. If diarrhea or constipation is a problem, the child's diet and bowel regimen should be evaluated and adjusted as described below.

Diagnostic Procedures

If aspiration or gastroesophageal reflux is suspected, three tests may be performed to define the problem: an upper gastrointestinal (GI) study, a milk scan, and a pH probe. In the upper GI series a milk-like susbtance is either ingested by the child or given by nasogastric tube. The barium in this substance is visible on X ray film. The radiologist can follow the fluid as it courses through the stomach and small intestine, helping to identify structural abnormalities in the esophagus, stomach, and intestine. Reflux from the stomach into the esophagus also may be seen (see Figure 12.2).

The second study, a milk scan, also involves the child swallowing a liquid. However, this fluid contains small amounts of radioactivity, enabling the radiologist to scan the child's body and determine where the radioactivity has settled. If evidence of radioactivity is seen in the lung, this suggests aspiration. The scan also may reveal a delay in the emptying of stomach contents, predisposing the child to reflux.

The final test, a pH probe, provides sensitive evidence of gastroesophageal reflux (Ross, Haase, Reiley, et al., 1988). In this study, a nasogastric-like tube is placed just above the junction of the stomach and esophagus. At the tip of the tube is a pH probe that measures the acidity above the gastroesophageal junction. If acid in the stomach refluxes through an incompetent valve, the pH probe records a sudden drop in the pH level, signaling gastroesophageal reflux (Figure 12.4). Reflux is most likely to occur in the hour following a meal or during sleep because the child is reclining. For this reason, the pH probe records for 24 hours to indicate the presence of reflux and the circumstances of its occurrence. This may have important therapeutic implications in terms of positioning after feeding.

MANAGING FEEDING PROBLEMS

Because feeding difficulties in children with disabilities usually result from the interaction of multiple problems, managing them can be difficult, time consuming, and frustrating (Crane, 1987; Helfrich-Miller, Rector, & Straka, 1986). The following are some recommendations to facilitate mealtimes:

Make Mealtimes Distinct and Inviting

Let the child know that mealtime is coming so he or she can prepare for the "work" to be done. This may entail a premeal routine of going to a special corner of the room and putting on a bib or napkin, or some relaxation therapy followed by oral stimulation to get the needed muscles ready for eating. Children with feeding difficulties usually eat better in one-to-one situations or in small groups because there is less

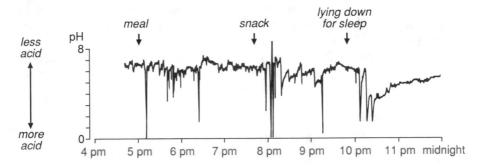

Figure 12.4.   A pH probe study is done by passing a tube containing a pH electrode down the esophagus and positioning it just above the stomach. If there is reflux, the pH should drop as the acid contents of the stomach reach the lower esophagus where the probe is placed. Shown here is an abnormal study with multiple episodes of low pH occurring about half an hour after feedings or when the child is laid down to sleep. (From Batshaw, M.L. [1991]. *Your child has a disability: A complete sourcebook of daily and medical care*. Boston: Little, Brown; reprinted by permission.)

distraction and they are better able to focus on the eating process. Undivided attention also makes mealtimes more reinforcing.

Understand that Eating Is Work

Eating is a motor activity that requires more coordination between muscle groups than any other motor activity. Failure to perform the work competently may result in aspiration, which is both unpleasant and frightening. For children with motor problems, this increases the work demanded of them while eating. Therefore, it is important to make eating as easy as possible (Lamm & Greer, 1988). This can be accomplished by increasing their focus on the meal and increasing the satisfaction they get from eating. This is done by giving social attention or a favorite food after the meal is completed.

Promote Appetite

Some children have little appetite or are unable to communicate that they are hungry. If speech is impaired or limited, signing or a communication board may prove helpful. If this does not work, try feeding the child at different times of the day to find out at which hour he or she eats best. The child may eat his or her largest meal at breakfast or lunch rather than at dinner. Foods the child likes can be paired with less favored ones (Iwata, Riordan, Wohl, & Finney, 1982). Some medications such as cyproheptadine (Periactin) have been used to stimulate appetite. They have had varying success but are clearly no cure.

Individualize Dietary Intake

While the required ratio of fats to carbohydrates and proteins is the same for all children, the caloric requirements of children with disabilities are different from those of other children. In these children, the requirements are more appropriately calculated per unit of height than per unit of weight (Thommessen, Heiberg, & Kase, 1991). In general, ambulatory children who have various types of motor dysfunction require about the same number of calories per unit of body height as those who do not have motor dysfunction. However, if the child is nonambulatory, only about 75% of the normal caloric intake is required. Children with movement disorders, such as **choreoathetosis**, may have increased caloric requirements because of the increased activity level.

Ensure Proper Positioning

Although it is not possible to hasten the neurological maturation of oral motor patterns, practice makes a newly acquired skill more automatic and thereby easier to perform. Physical therapists, occupational therapists, and speech-language pathologists each have developed approaches to handling children with disabilities that facilitate practice of new skills (Christensen, 1989).

The first step involves the appropriate positioning of the child (Nwaobi & Smith, 1986). Feeding is a flexor activity that requires good breath support. The child should be firmly supported though the hips and trunk to provide a stable base. The head and neck should be aligned in a neutral position, which decreases extension through the oral musculature while maintaining an open airway. Such positioning allows better coordination and control of the steps in oral motor preparation and transport.

Facilitating jaw and lip closure when necessary may help make the child's oral pattern more effective, as well as accustom him or her to the proper positions. Spoon placement with gentle pressure on the mid-tongue region can help remind the child to keep the tongue inside the mouth. Chewing may be enhanced by placing food between the upper and lower back teeth. This encourages the child to move the jaw and use the tongue in an effort to dislodge the food.

Alter Food Textures

Food textures can be manipulated to facilitate safe, controlled swallowing (Gisel, 1991). Thickening of liquids slows their rate of flow, allowing more time for the child to organize and initiate a swallow. Thickening agents (such as Thickit) can transform even water into a pudding-like texture. This enables children who have difficulty drinking to use alternative means to ensure adequate hydration.

It is important to remember that the primary goal of eating is to achieve adequate nutrition. Thus, when a child is first learning to accept a higher texture of foods, these foods should be presented during snack time, when volumes are smaller. At mealtimes, easier textures should be used to ensure consumption of adequate calories during this transition period.

Use Adaptive Equipment

Uncoordinated movements or weakness may make it difficult for a child with disabilities to handle a fork or spoon accurately, so that food, if it can be picked up at all, does not reach the mouth. The effort needed to obtain food may be so great that the child avoids eating altogether. A number of adaptive devices can help the child to become independent in feeding. These include bowls with high sides, spoons with curved handles, and cups with rocker bottoms (Figure 12.5).

Decrease Reflux

After food is swallowed, vomiting, gagging, and rumination may present additional problems. A number of approaches, including positioning, meal modification, medications, surgery, and behavior management, may be needed to control these difficulties (Orenstein, Whitlington, & Orenstein, 1983). The goal of each of these interventions is to protect the esophagus from reflux of stomach acid, either by decreasing the amount of food in the stomach at any one time or by decreasing the acid in the stomach.

Small, frequent meals and/or medications that promote stomach emptying help to decrease the volume of food in the stomach. Upright positioning and thickened feedings employ gravity to help keep stomach contents from refluxing into the esophagus. Medications, such as urecholine (Bethanechol) and metoclopramide (Reglan) (Temple, Bradby, O'Connor, et al., 1983), increase the tone in the esophageal sphincter, making it harder for reflux to occur. Cimetidine (Tagamet) and ranitidine (Zantac)

Figure 12.5. An adaptive cup for drinking.

often are added to decrease stomach acidity and thereby lower the risk of inflammation of the esophagus from reflux (Sontag, 1990).

Sometimes gastroesophageal reflux cannot be controlled by positioning or medication. Prolonged reflux can lead to failure to thrive, recurrent aspiration pneumonia, and/or gastroesophageal bleeding. Surgery may be necessary. A **fundal plication** (Boix-Ochoa & Cassasa, 1989; Davidson, Hurd, & Johnstone, 1987) is an operation in which the top of the stomach is wrapped around the opening of the esophagus (Figure 12.6). This decreases reflux while permitting continued oral feeding.

Consider Alternative Methods of Feeding

In some cases, oral feeding may be insufficient to permit adequate nutrition because of an inadequate suck, a swallowing problem, or frequent bouts of aspiration pneumonia. For these children, nasogastric tube-feedings or the placement of gastrostomy tubes often is required. With nasogastric tube-feedings, a tube is passed through the nose down the esophagus and into the stomach. Once it is inserted, a small amount of air is pushed into the tube to check placement. The caregiver should listen for rumbling in the stomach. If no rumblings are heard, the tube has not been placed correctly. After the nasogastric tube has been correctly placed, the child can receive a liquid feeding through it. A commercially available formula, such as Ensure or Pediasure (see Table 11.9), or blended feedings composed of a regular diet combined with milk can be used.

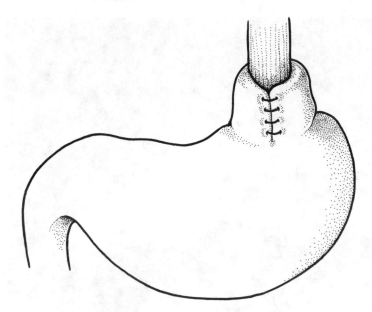

Figure 12.6.   In the surgical procedure of fundal plication, the upper stomach is wrapped around the lower esophagus to create a muscular valve that prevents reflux.

The main problem with nasogastric tube-feeding is that it can be used for only a few months at a time because the tube irritates the esophagus and can cause aspiration if incorrectly placed. Therefore, in children for whom adequate oral feeding becomes impossible, a gastrostomy tube (G-tube) is placed. A small hole is made in the abdominal and stomach walls, and a tube is placed through the hole into the stomach (Figure 12.7). Feeding then can be done through the gastrostomy tube in a manner similar to nasogastric tube-feeding. The placement of a gastrostomy tube does not preclude oral feeding.

Placement of a tube in the jejunum (the second section of the small intestine) also can decrease reflux and improve nutrition. The jejunal, or J-tube, bypasses the stomach and uses the **pylorus** (i.e., the valve connecting the stomach to the duodenum) to prevent reflux of the nutrients. Unfortunately, for both G-tube and J-tube feeding, the primary nutrient source does not pass through the mouth. This often leads to the loss of residual feeding skills.

With any of these tubes in place, a liquid formula or blenderized food can be given. The feedings can be given as single large volumes of 3–8 ounces every 3–6 hours, or as a continuous drip throughout the day or over night. The advantage of large volume feedings is that they do not interfere with normal daily activities. The feeding itself takes about 30 minutes. However, the large volume may be difficult for the child to tolerate and may lead to vomiting or abdominal discomfort. If this happens, continuous drip feedings can be used. A Kangaroo or similar type pump is used to deliver the formula at a set rate (see Figure 12.7). Sometimes tube-feedings are

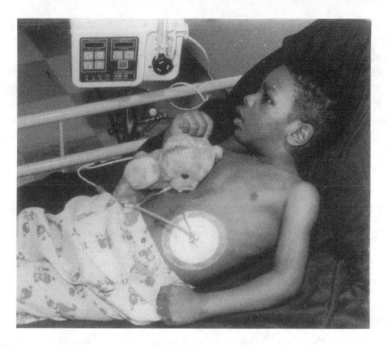

Figure 12.7. A gastrostomy tube is placed if the child cannot eat enough by mouth. A replaceable tube is inserted surgically through the skin and abdominal muscle into the stomach. This child is receiving his feedings by continuous drip using a Kangaroo pump.

used to supplement oral feedings. In this case, the tube-feedings generally are used at night, so that the child's stomach is not filled with the tube-feeding during the day.

Once a gastrostomy or jejunal tube has been placed, it must be maintained properly. The area surrounding the tube should be washed daily and the tube changed every few months. If the skin area around the tube bleeds, it may need to be cauterized using silver nitrate sticks. If formula leaks around the outside of the tube, the tube can be removed for a few hours at a time, and the hole will shrink in size so there is a better fit. Finally, if the area is inflamed, it means that the area is infected or that stomach acid is leaking. If the child's doctor has ruled out infection, the use of Duoderm or another occlusive dressing, such as Vaseline, should help.

Avoid and Treat Constipation

Constipation is a chronic problem for most children with developmental disabilities. Constipation is uncomfortable and may decrease the child's appetite and increase gastroesophageal reflux. While no cures for constipation are known, the following suggestions may be helpful.

As much fluid as possible should be added to the diet. Bulky and high-fiber foods, such as whole grain cereals, bran, and raw fruits and vegetables, should be included in the diet to increase movement through the gastrointestinal tract (Liebl, Fischer, Van Calcar, et al., 1990). Prune or apricot juice can be given to act as a mild laxative. Stool softeners, such as Colace or Kondremul, may be used regularly to help coat the stool and facilitate its movement through the intestines. Active or passive physical exercise also is important to aid the movement of the stool.

When constipation is present, additional measures may be needed. Laxatives and suppositories include Milk of Magnesia, Maltsupex, Senokot, Dulcolax, or glycerine suppositories. Enemas, such as Fleet's pediatric enema, also may help, but constant use of enemas can interfere with normal rectal sphincter control and should be avoided. A combination of these approaches may be needed to establish regular bowel movements. Keep in mind, however, that not all children need to produce one stool each day; one every 3 days may suffice.

SUMMARY

Feeding a child with a disability often requires the implementation of a number of creative approaches and the involvement of a variety of health care professionals. When effective, these methods enable the children to receive the necessary combination of nutrients and fluids to help them grow and remain healthy.

REFERENCES

Boix-Ochoa, J., & Cassasa, J.M. (1989). Surgical treatment of gastroesophageal reflux in children. *Surgical Annual, 21,* 97–118.

Brady, M.S., Richard, K.A., Fitzgerald, J.F., et al. (1986). Specialized formulas and feedings for infants with malabsorption or formula intolerance. *Journal of the American Dietetic Association, 86,* 191–200.

Christensen, J.R. (1989). Developmental approach to pediatric neurogenic dysphagia. *Dysphagia, 3,* 131–134.

Crane, S. (1987). Feeding the handicapped child—A review of intervention strategies. *Nutrition and Health, 5,* 109–118.

Davidson, B.R., Hurd, D.M., & Johnstone, M.S. (1987). Nissen fundoplication and pyloroplasty in the management of gastro-oesophageal reflux in children. *British Journal of Surgery, 74,* 488–499.

Fitzgerald, J.F. (1987). Constipation in children. *Pediatrics in Review, 8,* 299–302.

Gisel, E.G. (1991). Effect of food texture on the development of chewing of children between 6 months and 2 years of age. *Developmental Medicine and Child Neurology, 33,* 69–79.

Heitlinger, L.A., & Lebenthal, E. (1988). Disorders of carbohydrate digestion and absorption. *Pediatric Clinics of North America, 35,* 239–255.

Helfrich-Miller, K.R., Rector, K.L., & Straka, J.A. (1986). Dysphagia: Its treatment in the profoundly retarded patient with cerebral palsy. *Archives of Physical Medicine and Rehabilitation, 67,* 520–525.

Iwata, B.A., Riordan, M.M., Wohl, M.K., & Finney, J.W. (1982). Pediatric feeding disorders: Behavioral analysis and treatment. In P.J. Accardo (Ed.), *Failure to thrive in infancy and early childhood* (pp. 297–329). Baltimore: University Park Press.

Lamm, N., & Greer, R.D. (1988). Induction and maintenance of swallowing responses in infants with dysphagia. *Journal of Applied Behavior Analysis, 21,* 143–156.

Liebl, B.H., Fischer, M.H., Van Calcar, S.C., et al. (1990). Dietary fiber and long-term large bowel response in enterally nourished, nonambulatory, profoundly retarded youth. *Journal of Parenteral and Enteral Nutriton, 14,* 371–375.

Morris, S.E. (1977). *Program guidelines for children with feeding problems.* Edison, NJ: Childcraft Education Corp.

Morris, S.E. (1981). *The normal acquisition of oral feeding skills: Implications for assessment and treatment.* New York: Therapeutic Media.

Nwaobi, O.M., & Smith, P. D. (1986). Effect of adaptive seating on pulmonary function of children with cerebral palsy. *Developmental Medicine and Child Neurology, 28,* 351–354.

Orenstein, S.R., Whitington, P.F., & Orenstein, D.M. (1983). The infant seat as treatment for gastroesophageal reflux. *New England Journal of Medicine, 309,* 760–763.

Ross, M.N., Haase, G.M., Reiley, T.T., et al. (1988). The importance of acid reflux patterns in neurologically damaged children detected by four-channel esophageal pH monitoring. *Journal of Pediatric Surgery, 23,* 573–576.

Smith, M.A.H. (Ed.). (1976). *Guides for nutritional assessment of the mentally retarded and the developmentally disabled.* Memphis: University of Tennessee Center for the Health Sciences, Child Development Center.

Sontag, S.J. (1990). The medical management of reflux esophagitis: Role of antacids and acid inhibition. *Gastroenterology Clinics of North America, 19,* 683–712.

Sutphen, J.L. (1990). Pediatric gastroesophageal reflux disease. *Gastroenterology Clinics of North America, 19,* 617–629.

Temple, J.G., Bradby, G.V., O'Connor, F.O., et al. (1983). Cimetidine and metoclopramide in oesophageal reflux disease. *British Medical Journal, 286,* 1863–1864.

Thommessen, M., Heiberg, A., & Kase, B.F. (1991). Feeding problems, height and weight in different groups of disabled children, *Acta Paediatrica Scandinavica, 80,* 527–533.

U.S. Maternal and Child Health Service, Children's Bureau. (1970). *Feeding the child with a handicap.* Washington, DC: U.S. Government Printing Office, Publication No. 2091.

Wilson, J.M. (1978). *Oral-motor function and dysfunction in children.* Chapel Hill: University of North Carolina, Department of Medical Allied Health Professionals, Division of Physical Therapy.

Chapter 13

Dental Care

Upon completion of this chapter, the reader will:
—understand the development and structure of the teeth
—recognize malformations such as cleft lip and palate and their effect on nutrition and speech
—be aware of the effects of habits, such as teeth grinding and tongue thrusting, on oral health
—know how dental decay and periodontal disease occur and what prophylactic steps can be taken to prevent these problems
—understand the specific dental problems common to children with disabilities
—understand what procedures are commonly used during routine dental checkups and dental surgery

---

Our teeth are essential for the preparation of food for swallowing and digestion. In children, the emergence of teeth also stimulates the growth of the jaw. Besides these functions, teeth help in the production of certain sounds during speech. Children with disabilities are at an increased risk for both dental malformations and dental disease. Thus, those who care for these children need to be careful to provide them with appropriate dental care.

In this chapter, teeth formation and the problems that may occur during this process are addressed. Various types of dental disorders are discussed, followed by a consideration of the appropriate kinds of dental care.

THE FORMATION OF TEETH

Tooth buds first appear when the human embryo is only 6 weeks old. As the pregnancy progresses, the outer layer of these buds, made up of **epithelial** cells, forms the dental enamel. This enamel is deposited over the softer inner tissue, or dentin (Stewart, Barber, Troutman, et al., 1982) (Figure 13.1). The dentin is gradually **calcified;** nerves, blood, and lymph vessels develop to form the pulp of the mature tooth. Ten primary, or **deciduous** (baby), teeth are formed in what is to become the upper jaw (the **maxilla**) and 10 more in the lower jaw (the mandible). These primary teeth also keep the proper spacing in the dental arch that is needed for the later development of

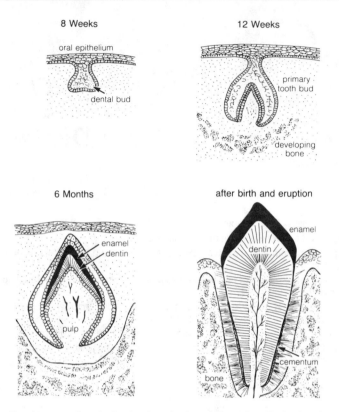

Figure 13.1. Development of teeth. By the time the fetus is 8 weeks old, the dental (tooth) bud has formed, and by 12 weeks it is beginning to assume a tooth-like shape. At 6 months gestation, the layers of the tooth—enamel, dentin, and pulp—are evident. After birth, when the child is about 16 months old, the primary cuspid, completely formed, erupts.

permanent teeth. If there is a disturbance in the formation of dentin or enamel, or if foreign material is incorporated in this process, the texture, thickness, or color of the teeth can be affected (Schaefer, Hine, & Levy, 1983).

By the third month of gestation, the permanent tooth buds have started to form under the primary teeth. After birth, these teeth begin to calcify. When a child is around 6 years of age, the permanent teeth begin to emerge. During their eruption, the roots of the primary teeth are reabsorbed. Thus, the primary teeth have a life cycle that begins with their formation early in fetal life and ends with their shedding during childhood.

PROBLEMS AFFECTING THE DEVELOPMENT OF TEETH

In most children, dental development moves along smoothly. However, a number of problems may affect tooth development. Evidence of disturbances is revealed in the crown of the developing tooth. Abnormalities appear on the upper parts of the teeth that are forming at the time of the disturbance. These abnormalities can be caused by nutritional deficits, congenital infections, and drugs, including the use of the antibiotic, tetracycline, by a woman when she is pregnant. If tetracycline is taken between the fourth and the last month of pregnancy, the infant's teeth may have a brownish-yellow discoloration, and the enamel may be thinned (Pinkham, 1988). This discoloration is unattractive, and the thinned enamel also makes the teeth more susceptible to decay. If a child takes tetracycline between 4 months and 8 years of age, his or her permanent teeth also may be discolored. Thus, it is suggested that pregnant women and young children avoid tetracycline.

Other conditions also can cause tooth discoloration (Nowak, 1976). For example, in Rh incompatibility, bilirubin causes pigment deposits in the dental enamel (Stewart & Poole, 1982).

More serious are the dental malformations associated with certain genetically inherited syndromes (Poole & Redford-Badwal, 1991). Anodontia, the absence of all teeth, or hypodontia, the absence of one or several teeth, is found in ectodermal dysplasia, a disorder of skin and its products, **Ellis-van Creveld syndrome**, and **Hallermann-Streiff syndrome** (Jones, 1988). Hypodontia is also seen in Down syndrome and cleft palate. Thinly enameled, abnormally shaped teeth are found in the **mucopolysaccharidoses** and tuberous sclerosis (Buyse, 1990). These abnormalities may increase both the risk of tooth decay and malocclusion.

MALFORMATIONS OF THE JAW—CLEFT PALATE

Abnormalities of the jaw can affect the development of the teeth. The **Robin sequence** describes a malformation in which the child has a small mandible and a relatively large recessed tongue. This abnormality may be associated with fetal alcohol syndrome (see Chapter 8), fetal Dilantin syndrome (see Chapter 4), and trisomy 18 (see Chapter 2). It leads to airway obstruction and feeding problems. Additionally, the teeth are crowded.

The most common malformation affecting the jaw region is cleft lip and palate. The defects occur when normal fusion of the palatal shelves fails to occur during the sixth to eighth week of fetal development (Figure 13.2). In about 1 out of 700 live-born infants, the cells that should grow together to form the lips and palate do not move in the proper direction (Jones, 1988). This creates a cleft, or opening. Such a defect may be an isolated one, unassociated with mental retardation or other disabilities, or it may be part of a more complex syndrome. However, in the isolated condition, an increased incidence of learning disabilities and attention deficit hyperactivity disorder accompanies cleft lip and palate (Richman, Eliason, & Lindgren, 1988). Stature also tends to be short (Duncan, Shapiro, Soley, et al., 1983). The isolated condition has a recurrence risk of 1%–3%.

Cleft lip and palate create a number of dental problems including extra or missing teeth. Malocclusion may result from missing segments of bone. This can appear

Figure 13.2.   Cleft lip and palate result from incomplete fusion of the palatal arches.

as a collapse of the posterior or anterior parts of the dental arches. Cases of cross bite (i.e., the upper incisors are behind the lower incisors) may be evident (Dahllof, Ussisoo-Joandi, Ideberg, et al., 1989).

Cleft palate also can affect speech and nutrition. The formation of various speech sounds may be more difficult, and errors in speech production may follow. Speech problems are accentuated if the **adenoids** have been removed as a result of frequent middle ear infections (Mason & Warren, 1980) (see Chapter 18). If hypernasal speech develops following adenoid removal, surgical correction may be required. Before the cleft is repaired, it also interferes with the baby's ability to breast- or bottle-feed because it prevents the development of negative pressure needed to suck (Clarren, Anderson, & Wolf, 1987).

As a result of these problems, surgical correction of a cleft lip and/or palate should begin in infancy. The first surgery, occurring at 2–3 months of age, involves closure of the cleft lip. This results in improved sucking because the infant can now exert pressure against the nipple. At about 1 year of age, the soft and hard palates are repaired (Dorf & Curtin, 1982). Those repairs are not done earlier because precipitating the fusion of the maxilla can alter facial structure. However, later closure adversely affects the development of normal articulation.

Multiple surgical procedures may need to be performed over time to correct various abnormalities (Kaufman, 1991). Bone grafting may be required to enhance the jaw size and dental arch stability. Orthodontic work is generally needed to improve tooth position and occlusion (Shaw & Semb, 1989). Finally, middle ear tubes are often placed to prevent the frequent ear infections that accompany this malformation as a result of **eustachian tube** malfunction (Grant, Quiney, Mercer, et al., 1988).

THE EMERGENCE OF TEETH

A baby's first tooth, the lower central incisor, appears around 6 months of age (Figure 13.3A). In rapid succession, the child sprouts another incisor; a cuspid, or pointed tooth; and two molars on either side of the mouth, in the upper and lower jaws. By 18–30 months of age, the child has 20 primary teeth. When the child is about 6 years old, the first of these teeth is shed and is replaced shortly by an adult central incisor (Table 13.1). Over the next 6 years, the rest of the primary teeth are shed and perma-

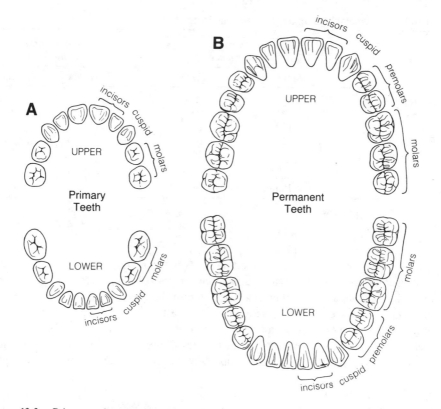

Figure 13.3. Primary and permanent teeth. A) There are 20 primary teeth: 4 incisors, 2 cuspids, and 4 molars on the top and on the bottom of the mouth. B) There are 32 permanent teeth: 4 incisors, 2 cuspids, 4 premolars, and 6 molars on the top and on the bottom.

nent teeth emerge. Ultimately, there are 32 permanent teeth (Figure 13.3B) (Stewart & Poole, 1982).

Children who have developmental delays also may have delays in tooth eruption. Thus, this timetable may not hold true for them (Wessels, 1979).

DENTAL PROBLEMS

The most common dental problems in childhood are dental decay, **periodontal** disease, malocclusion, and dental injuries. Each of these problems occurs more frequently in children with developmental disabilities than in nondisabled children: dental decay in cerebral palsy, periodontal disease in Down syndrome, malocclusion in cleft palate, and dental injuries associated with self-injurious behavior.

Dental Decay

Dental decay (or caries), which causes cavities, occurs mainly in children and adolescents. Dental caries begins with plaque formation. Plaque is composed of bacteria,

Table 13.1. Timetable for emergence and shedding of teeth

	Age (months) at emergence		Age (years) at shedding	
	Lower	Upper	Lower	Upper
Central incisor	6	7½	6–7	7–8
Lateral incisor	7	9	7–8	8–9
Cuspid	16	18	9–10	11–12
First molar	12	14	6–7	6–7
Second molar	20	24	11–13	12–13
Incisors	Range = ±2 months			
Molars	Range = ±4 months			

Source: Lunt and Low (1974).

bacterial byproducts, saliva, and food particles that combine to form a clear, sticky mass that clings to the teeth and gums (Johnsen, 1991). The bacteria in plaque ferment the food sugars that come into contact with the teeth. Acids are then released that can destroy the enamel and the dentin of the tooth. Over months, this process may demolish the tooth gradually. In addition, unremoved plaque calcifies as tartar (calculus) and can cause tenderness and swelling of the gums. The associated inflammation eventually can destroy bony supports of the tooth and, thus, may loosen teeth as well.

In infants, tooth decay often takes the form of *nursing caries* (Ripa, 1988). Here, the baby goes to sleep with a bottle of milk or juice or sucks on a honey-coated pacifier. The result is prolonged contact of the sugar-containing liquid with bacteria on the teeth. The bacteria produce acid from the sugar and the process of tooth decay begins. This emphasizes the importance of cleaning the infant's mouth as soon as the first tooth emerges. It also suggests weaning a baby from the bottle by 12 months of age. Caries is also commonly seen in older children, especially those who do not drink fluorinated water and those with physical disabilities that interfere with toothbrushing.

Periodontal Disease

Periodontal disease is a continuum. It starts as gum inflammation and, if unchecked, the supports of the teeth are damaged. Gum disease is generally considered to be a much more common disorder in older adults. Yet, almost 70% of children above 7 years of age have had an episode of mild gum inflammation, and 10% have periodontal bone disease (Bimstein, 1991). Gum disease and periodontal bone disease can be particular problems in children with disabilities. For example, a high incidence of gum disease has been found in children with Down syndrome, probably related to their pattern of poor oral hygiene and malocclusion. The best **prophylaxis** against periodontal diseases is thorough daily toothbrushing and flossing.

Malocclusion

Malocclusion is the improper fitting together of the upper and lower teeth. It is common in the general population but occurs even more frequently in children with disabilities (Smith, 1991). Treatment of these irregularities falls under the domain of the pediatric dentist or **orthodontist.** Although the correction of this improper alignment of the teeth often is thought of as being simply cosmetic, the use of braces to separate and properly space the teeth also decreases the incidence of dental decay and periodontal disease by making routine oral hygiene easier.

Dental Injuries

Tooth fractures occur in approximately 25% of all children (Fonseca & Walker, 1990). These fractures usually result from injuries sustained in sports, fights, or falls, or from thrown objects. The most commonly injured teeth are the maxillary incisors, or front teeth, especially in the first 2–3 years after their emergence and particularly when they are flared or protruded (buck teeth) (Ferguson & Ripa, 1979). The severity of the damage to the tooth correlates with the prognosis (Josell & Abrams, 1991). A crown fracture involving only the enamel and dentin will probably heal so long as the pulp has not been traumatized. Even a tooth that has been completely knocked out can be reimplanted within an hour of the accident if the tooth has been kept moist. This is done by placing the tooth in milk, saliva, or tap water. The tooth should not be cleaned as this could remove tissue useful in reattachment (American Dental Association, 1982).

In any kind of tooth injury, one must be careful that the child does not inhale the tooth or tooth fragments. The best treatment of dental injuries is prevention. Children who play in contact sports should wear mouth guards for protection during falls and collisions.

DENTAL CARE AND TREATMENT

Dental care and treatment consist of preventive dental care in the home, routine dental checkups, and dental treatment. This is particularly important for children with disabilities who are at increased risk for dental disease.

Preventive Dental Care

Good oral hygiene depends on removing bacterial plaque, modifying the diet to reduce the presence of sugars around the teeth, and using fluoride therapy to decrease the vulnerability of the teeth to caries. Four forms of prophylactic dental care can reduce the likelihood of caries and periodontal disease significantly. These are: 1) healthful eating habits, 2) toothbrushing and flossing, 3) fluoridation, and 4) regular professional dental care (Griffen & Goepferd, 1991).

In terms of diet, if possible, children should eat sweets sparingly. Between-meal snacks should include cheese, milk, and fresh fibrous vegetables and nuts (e.g., carrots, peanuts) rather than candies, soft drinks, and other sweets (American Dental

Association, 1983). Some foods that are good to eat as snacks are listed in Table 13.2. Sweets that tend to stick to the teeth are a particular problem. These include caramels, raisins, and other dried fruits, and sugar-containing gum.

Besides a proper diet, toothbrushing and flossing are essential ingredients for preventing periodontal disease. However, these have a limited influence on dental decay. Ideally, the child should brush after every meal, but realistically, a thorough toothbrushing and flossing once a day is probably sufficient. For children, a small, soft, multibristle nylon brush should be used, held at a 45° angle to the gums. Brushing is done in a circular motion for a few minutes. After brushing, the child should use dental floss, a waxed or unwaxed nylon filament. This is gently pulled between the teeth in a back-and-forth, sawlike manner. The floss removes foreign matter and plaque that accumulates between the teeth and cannot be removed by a toothbrush.

The single most important impact on dental caries has been fluoridation of water (Newbrun, 1980). Fluoride reacts with certain chemical compounds in tooth enamel to form a more acid-stable enamel that resists decay. It also interferes with bacterial growth. Finally, it promotes remineralization of the enamel. Many water supplies are now fluoridated, but some are not. Also, many brands of toothpaste contain fluoride. Thus, in most cases, it is unnecessary to take daily fluoride tablets or vitamins that contain fluoride. Fluoridation has resulted in nearly halving the incidence of dental cavities (Epidemiology and Oral Disease Prevention Program, NIDAR, 1989).

Routine Dental Checkups

Besides practicing preventive dental care in the home, children should start visiting their dentists regularly for "preventive maintenance" by 2 years of age or within 6 months of the eruption of the first tooth. These visits generally involve a visual inspection of the soft tissue and teeth, while looking for signs of decay, gum inflammation, and the position of the teeth (Cooley & Sanders, 1991). The teeth are cleaned using a brush to remove plaque; often, a fluoride treatment also is given. The dentist

Table 13.2. Foods that are good to use as snacks to maintain dental health

Raw vegetables	
Carrot sticks	Green pepper rings
Celery sticks	Lettuce wedges
Cauliflower bits	Radishes
Cucumber sticks	Tomatoes
Drinks	
Milk	
Sugar-free carbonated beverages	Unsweetened vegetable juices
Other snacks	
Nuts	Unsweetened peanut butter
Popcorn	Cheese
Unsweetened plain yogurt	Sugarless gum or candy

Source: American Dental Association (1983).

or dental hygienist also probes for cavities. Periodically, an X ray may be taken to look for hidden decay and for the development of the secondary teeth.

A major advance in preventive dental treatment involves the use of pit and fissure sealant on permanent teeth (Ripa, 1985). In this technique, the biting surface of the molars and premolars is etched with a mild acid and coated with a plastic material. This covering bonds to the tooth surface, providing protection to the pit and grooved surfaces of the teeth that are most susceptible to cavities (Johnsen, 1991).

Despite the rather benign nature of the visit to the dentist, many children—and adults—express fear about going. Children may learn from their frightened parents that the dentist is someone to avoid. To decrease anxiety, it is helpful to explain before the visit what will happen. The child should be told that the dentist is someone who will help him or her, will count the teeth, clean them, and apply tooth nourishment—fluoride. Often dentists use music or cartoons to allay fears; some reward children with small gifts after the visit. Once the pattern of a pleasant visit has been established, most children trust the dentist, and future treatment becomes easier to administer. However, this will not be the case for some children with disabilities who may not understand explanations and may remain frightened and agitated. In these instances, gentle restraints and mouth props may be needed to complete the dental examination. These are only used if positive reinforcement techniques have proven unsuccessful (Musselman, 1991).

Dental Surgery

The most common type of dental surgery is the filling of a cavity. To do this, the dentist begins by using a high-speed drill to remove the decay. This creates a larger hole, which is filled, often with a silver amalgam compound. Normally, the procedure takes less than 10 minutes.

To make the procedure feel more comfortable, a local anesthetic, usually Xylocaine, is used to temporarily deaden the nerve of the tooth being repaired. After the treatment, the child's mouth will feel numb for about 2 hours, but he or she should feel no pain. If the child is anxious, the dentist may administer nitrous oxide ("laughing gas") to relax the child (Frassica & Miller, 1989). Other useful drugs include Valium and chloral hydrate. Valium is used as an antianxiety agent and chloral hydrate as a sedative.

If the individual has a congenital heart defect, the dentist may need to treat him or her with antibiotics prior to surgery. This is done to prevent the occurrence of subacute bacterial **endocarditis** (SBE), an infection of the lining of the heart that may be induced by bacteria released during dental treatment (Holbrook, Willey, & Shaw, et al., 1983).

Dental Problems and Care for Children with Disabilities

Children with disabilities are at increased risk for virtually every dental problem. Some relate to behavior problems and others result from facial malformations or physical disabilities (Feigal & Jensen, 1982). The remainder of this chapter discusses certain dental problems in specific disabilities and approaches to treatment.

Seizure Disorders   Children with seizure disorders are likely to develop gum problems if treated with the antiepileptic phenytoin (Dilantin). Of children who receive phenytoin, 35% develop enlarged gums that are prone to infection, trauma, and bleeding (Figure 13.4) (Stinnett, Rodu, & Grizzle, 1987). Stopping phenytoin usually causes the gums to gradually shrink. If the gums become very enlarged, the dentist may have to trim them surgically (Jones, Weddell, & McKown, 1988). Interestingly, none of the other antiepileptic medications causes this complication.

The other concern in seizure disorders is the risk of dental injury from falls during convulsions. Some children who have uncontrolled seizures wear mouth guards or hockey helmets to avoid these injuries.

Mental Retardation   Children who have mild mental retardation generally do not have dental problems that are significantly different from children without disabilities. They simply need to be treated according to their mental age rather than their chronological age in terms of expectations for independence in dental self-care skills.

Children with more severe retardation do have specific dental problems. They may have a syndrome, such as Down syndrome, that predisposes them to dental disease. Children with Down syndrome have a flattened facial appearance as a result of malocclusion (Cooley & Sanders, 1991). In addition, their teeth may be abnormal in size and number, also increasing the risk of malocclusion and plaque formation. Their open-mouth posture with mouth breathing is also a problem. Over time, it can lead to inflammation of the gums and other periodontal disease.

In addition to specific problems of disease, there may be habits that predispose children with disabilities to caries or periodontal disease. These include **bruxism,** self-injurious behavior, being accident prone, and pouching food. Tooth grinding, or bruxism, occurs in over half of children with severe mental retardation. For these children, tooth grinding is a form of self-stimulatory behavior. Grinding of the molar teeth may lead to enamel and dentin abrasion, fracture, and abnormal mobility of the teeth (Peterson & Schneider, 1991). For nighttime bruxism, the use of an occlusal

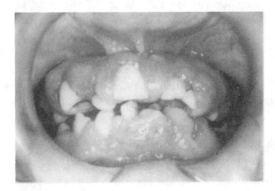

Figure 13.4.   Enlarged, inflamed gums associated with chronic ingestion of phenytoin for control of seizures. (Photograph courtesy of Dr. Seth Canion.)

splint to keep the teeth from touching has proven helpful (Okeson, 1987). Some behavior management techniques, including rewarding the child for periods of time when he or she does not engage in the troublesome behavior, also have met with a measure of success for daytime bruxism (Musselman, 1991). Children with severe-to-profound mental retardation may have additional disabilities, including cerebral palsy, that combine to predispose the child to dental disease and at the same time interfere with preventive dental care (Gallagher, 1980).

Cerebral Palsy Children with cerebral palsy have many problems that affect dental care (Rosenstein, 1978). Poor oral motor control and tongue thrusting not only interfere with eating because food is pushed out of the mouth, but also lead to malocclusion because the tongue repeatedly pushes forward against the front teeth. Tongue thrusting is an involuntary behavior and usually does not respond to behavior management techniques.

A second problem is the need for increased carbohydrate intake to maintain weight. These supplements tend to replace more highly textured foods. As a consequence, the teeth do not receive as much natural cleansing with fiber and may be exposed to more sugars, placing them at risk for dental caries.

This predisposition to caries is made worse by a decreased intake of fluoride. Because of feeding problems and the inability to handle secretions, these children tend to drink less water and may not use toothpaste in cleaning the teeth. Thus, the intake of fluoride may be insufficient to be an effective deterrent of tooth decay. Toothbrushing and flossing also may be difficult for the child and he or she may need to rely entirely on a parent or caregiver. These difficulties, combined with a possible predisposition to caries and periodontal disease, malocclusion, or other teeth malformations, increase the risk of tooth decay and periodontal disease in children with cerebral palsy (American Dental Association, 1982).

Approaches to treatment must address each of these problems (Sanger & Casamassimo, 1983). Children who are receiving inadequate fluoride in water or toothpaste can be given daily fluoride tablets or drops. Fluoride treatments at a dentist's office every 6 months also help to restore needed minerals to the tooth enamel. Toothbrushing can be performed once a day before bedtime. Occupational therapists can adapt the handles of toothbrushes to help children who lack fine motor dexterity. Another option is the use of a washcloth, a piece of gauze, or a cotton-tipped applicator treated with a mild abrasive. Electric toothbrushes also may be used. The use of an oral irrigating device, such as a Water-Pic or similar tool, may help to remove food and foreign bodies, but does not take the place of proper toothbrushing. When responsibility for toothbrushing falls to a parent or caregiver, appropriate positioning of the child also must be considered (Barnett, Ziring, Friedman, et al., 1988).

SUMMARY

Oral health is important for adequate nutrition, speech, and aesthetics. For a child with a disability, the maintenance of healthy teeth is complicated because of malformations, malocclusion, diet, and medication. Dental trauma is a further complication, especially in individuals with seizure disorders. These problems accentuate the importance of preventive dental care and routine dental checkups.

REFERENCES

American Dental Association. (1982). *Caring for the disabled child's dental health.* Chicago: American Dental Association, Bureau of Health Education and Audiovisual Services.

American Dental Association. (1983). *Diet and dental health.* Chicago: American Dental Association, Bureau of Health Education and Audiovisual Services.

Barnett, M.L., Ziring, P., Friedman, D., et al. (1988). Dental treatment program for patients with mental retardation. *Mental Retardation, 26,* 310–313.

Bimstein, E. (1991). Peridontal health and disease in children and adolescents. *Pediatric Clinics of North America, 38,* 1183–1207.

Buyse, M.I. (1990). *Birth defects encyclopedia.* Dover: Center for Birth Defects Information Services, Inc.

Clarren, S.K., Anderson, B., & Wolf, L.S. (1987). Feeding infants with cleft lip, cleft palate, or cleft lip and palate. *Cleft Palate Journal, 24,* 244–249.

Cooley, R.O., & Sanders, B.J. (1991). The pediatrician's involvement in prevention and treatment of oral disease in medically compromised children. *Pediatric Clinics of North America, 38,* 1265–1288.

Dahllof, G., Ussisoo-Joandi, R., Ideberg, M., et al. (1989). Caries, gingivitis, and dental abnormalities in preschool children with cleft lip and/or palate. *Cleft Palate Journal, 26,* 233–237.

Dorf, D.S., & Curtin, J.W. (1982). Early cleft palate repair and speech outcome. *Plastic and Reconstructive Surgery, 70,* 74–81.

Duncan, P.A., Shapiro, L.R., Soley, R.L., et al. (1983). Linear growth patterns in patients with cleft lip or palate or both. *American Journal of Diseases of Children, 137,* 159–163.

Epidemiology and Oral Disease Prevention Program, NIDAR. (1989). *Oral health of United States children, 1986–1987* (NIH Publication No.89-2247). Washington, DC: U.S. Government Printing Office.

Feigal, R.J., & Jensen, M.E. (1982). The cariogenic potential of liquid medications: A concern for the handicapped patient. *Special Care in Dentistry, 2,* 20–24.

Ferguson, F.S., & Ripa, L.W. (1979). Prevalence and type of traumatic injuries to the anterior teeth of preschool children. *Journal of Pedodontics, 4,* 3–8.

Fonseca, R.J., & Walker, R.V. (Eds.). (1990). *Oral and maxillofacial trauma.* Philadelphia: W.B. Saunders.

Frassica, J.J., & Miller, E.C. (1989). Anesthesia management in pediatric and special needs patients undergoing dental and oral surgery. *International Anesthesiology Clinics, 27,* 109–115.

Gallagher, F.E. (1980). Dental care of the developmentally disabled child. In A.P. Scheiner & I.F. Abroms (Eds.), *The practical management of the developmentally disabled child.* St. Louis: C.V. Mosby.

Grant, H.R., Quiney, R.E., Mercer, D.M., et al. (1988). Cleft palate and glue ear. *Archives of Diseases of Childhood, 63,* 176–179.

Griffen, A.L., & Goepferd, S.J. (1991). Preventive oral health care for the infant, child, and adolescent. *Pediatric Clinics of North America, 38,* 1209–1226.

Holbrook, W.P., Willey, R.F., & Shaw, T.R. (1983). Prophylaxis of infective endocarditis. *British Dental Journal, 154,* 36–39.

Johnsen, D.C. (1991). The role of the pediatrician in identifying and treating dental caries. *Pediatric Clinics of North America, 38,* 1173–1181.

Jones, J.E., Weddell, J.A., & McKown, C.G. (1988). Incidence and indications for surgical management of phenytoin-induced gingival overgrowth in a cerebral palsy population. *Journal of Oral Maxillofacial Surgery, 46*, 385–390.

Jones, K.L. (1988). *Smith's recognizable patterns of human malformation.* Philadelphia: W.B. Saunders.

Jones, M.C. (1988). Etiology of facial clefts: Prospective evaluation of 428 patients. *Cleft Palate Journal, 25*, 16–20.

Josell, S.D., & Abrams, R.G. (1991). Managing common dental problems and emergencies. *Pediatric Clinics of North America, 38*, 1325–1342.

Kaufman, F.L. (1991). Managing the cleft lip and palate patient. *Pediatric Clinics of North America, 38*, 1127–1147.

Lunt, R.L., & Low, O.B. (1974). A review of the chronology of eruption of deciduous teeth. *Journal of the American Dental Association, 89*, 872–879.

Mason, R.M., & Warren, D.W. (1980). Adenoid involution and developing hypernasality in cleft palate. *Journal of Speech and Hearing Disorders, 45*, 469–480.

Massler, M., & Schour, I. (1958). *Atlas of the month.* Chicago: American Dental Association.

McDonald, R.E., & Avery, D.R. (1987). *Dentistry for the child and adolescent.* St. Louis: C.V. Mosby.

Musselman, R.J. (1991). Considerations in behavioral management of the pediatric dental patient. *Pediatric Clinics of North America, 38*, 1309–1324.

Newbrun, E. (1980). Achievements of the seventies: Community and school fluoridation. *Journal of Public Health Dentistry, 40*, 234–247.

Nowak, A.J. (Ed.). (1976). *Dentistry for the handicapped patient.* St. Louis: C.V. Mosby.

Okeson, J. P. (1987). The effects of hard and soft occlusal splints on nocturnal bruxism. *Journal of the American Dental Association, 114*, 788–791.

Peterson, J.E., Jr., & Schneider, P.E. (1991). Oral habits: A behavioral approach. *Pediatric Clinics of North America, 38*, 1289–1307.

Pinkham, J.R. (1988). *Pediatric dentistry: Infancy through adolescence.* Philadelphia: W.B. Saunders.

Poole, A.E., & Redford-Badwal, D.A. (1991). Structural abnormalities of the craniofacial complex and congenital malformations. *Pediatric Clinics of North America, 38*, 1089–1125.

Richman, L.C., Eliason, M.J., & Lindgren, S.D. (1988). Reading disability in children with clefts. *Cleft Palate Journal, 25*, 21–25.

Ripa, L.W. (1985). The current status of pit and fissure sealants. *Journal of the Canadian Dental Association, 51*, 367–380.

Ripa, L.W. (1988). Nursing caries: A comprehensive review. *Pediatric Dentistry, 10*, 268–282.

Rosenstein, S.N. (1978). *Dentistry in cerebral palsy and related handicapping conditions.* Springfield, IL: Charles C Thomas.

Sanger, R.G., & Casamassimo, P.S. (1983). The physically and mentally disabled patient. *Dental Clinics of North America, 27*, 363–385.

Schaefer, W.G., Hine, M.K., & Levy, B.M. (1983). *A textbook of oral pathology* (4th ed.). Philadelphia: W.B. Saunders.

Shaw, W., & Semb, G. (1989). Current approaches to the orthodontic management of cleft lip and palate. *Journal of the Royal Society of Medicine, 83*, 30–33.

Smith, R.J. (1991). Identifying normal and abnormal development of dental occlusion. *Pediatric Clinics of North America, 38*, 1149–1171.

Starks, D., Market, G., Miller, C.B., et al. (1985). Day to day dental care: A parents' guide. *The Exceptional Parent, 15*(4), 10–17.

Stewart, R.E., Barber, T.K., Troutman, K.C., et al. (1982). *Pediatric dentistry: Scientific foundations and clinical practice.* St. Louis: C.V. Mosby.

Stewart, R.E., & Poole, A.E. (1982). The orofacial structures and their association with congenital abnormalities. *Pediatric Clinics of North America, 29*, 547–584.

Stinnett, E., Rodu, B., & Grizzle, W.E. (1987). New developments in understanding phenytoin-induced gingival hyperplasia. *Journal of the American Dental Association, 114*, 814–816.

Wessels, K.E. (Ed.). (1979). *Dentistry and the handicapped patient*. Littleton, MA: John Wright—PSG.

Chapter 14

The Brain and Nervous System
Our Computer

Upon completion of this chapter, the reader will:
— be able to trace the development of the central nervous system
— know the structure of the neuron, how it operates, and how messages are transmitted
— be aware of the regions of the cerebrum and their function
— know the location and purpose of the basal ganglia
— understand the interaction between the cerebellum and the cerebrum
— comprehend the workings of the peripheral nervous system and how it aids in movement
— know the function of the autonomic nervous system
— be able to describe the flow of the cerebrospinal fluid in addition to knowing its origin and function

---

The nervous system is the body's computer; it coordinates and directs various body functions. Its major components are the **central nervous system (CNS)**, consisting of the brain and spinal cord, the **peripheral nervous system**, and the **autonomic nervous system**. Each component controls some aspect of behavior and affects our understanding of the world around us. For example, the brain not only is involved in perception and thought; it also initiates voluntary movement. An impairment of any part of this system makes us less able to adapt to the environment and can lead to disorders as varied as mental retardation, learning disabilities, cerebral palsy, spina bifida, and seizure disorders. This chapter provides an overview of the structure and function of this intricate system.

DEVELOPMENT OF THE CENTRAL NERVOUS SYSTEM

The central nervous system begins to form during the third week after fertilization, when the embryo is merely 1.5 millimeters long (Garoutte, 1987). Part of the ectodermal layer forms an elongated, shoe-shaped body called the *neural plate*. With further development, this plate expands and rises to become the *neural fold*, later taking the form of the *neural tube* (Figure 14.1). At this time, the central nervous system looks like a closed tubular structure with a tail and a head. The tail portion becomes the spinal cord, and the broader head portion forms the brain. Lack of closure of the neural tube at this stage leads to the development of spina bifida or anencephaly (see Chapter 25).

By the third week of gestation, the head portion of this tubular structure has three distinct bulges that eventually form the basic subdivisions of the brain: the *cerebral hemispheres*, the *brain stem*, and the *cerebellum* (Figure 14.2). Within about 3 more weeks, these parts of the brain start to bend into their adult shape. The cerebral hemispheres rest on top of the brain stem, and the cerebellum lies behind it. The cerebellum is the last part of the central nervous system to be formed and is still immature at birth (see Figure 14.2).

When the fetus is 4 months old, all of the basic brain structures are in place. Yet, internally, enormous changes continue to occur.

THE NERVE CELL

The *neuron*, or nerve cell, is the basic functional unit of the nervous system (Noback, 1991). Similar to other cells, the neuron has a cell body consisting of a nucleus and cytoplasm. Unlike other cells, it also has a long fiber—called an *axon*—extending from the cell body and many, shorter, jutting tendrils called *dendrites* (Figure 14.3).

Axons and dendrites have different functions. The axon carries impulses away from the nerve cell body, while the dendrites receive impulses from other neurons

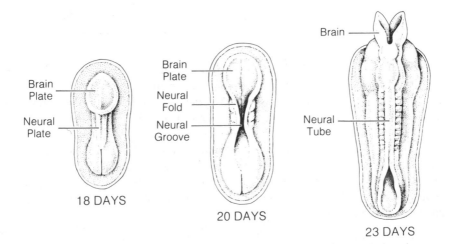

Figure 14.1.   Development of the central nervous system during the first month of fetal life. This is a longitudinal view showing the gradual closure of the neural tube to form the spinal column and the rounding up of the head region to form the primitive brain.

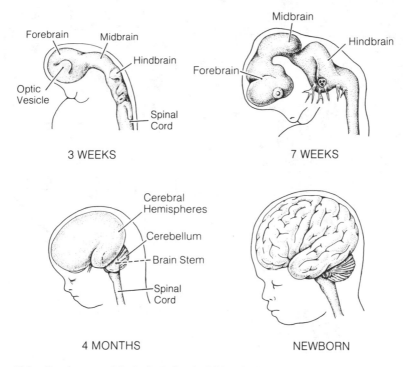

Figure 14.2. Development of the brain during fetal life. This is a side view illustrating the increasing complexity of the brain over time. The forebrain develops into the cerebral hemispheres, the midbrain into the brain stem, and the hindbrain into the cerebellum. Although all brain structures are formed by 4 months, the brain grows greatly in size and complexity during the final months of prenatal development.

and carry them toward the cell body. Attached along the length of the dendrites are tiny projections, or spines, that increase the surface area of the dendrites and enable a more elaborate transmission of messages. It is interesting to note that children with Down syndrome have dendritic spines that are fewer in number and narrower than those of children who do not have Down syndrome (Purpura, 1974). The more narrow the spine, the more difficult it is to communicate messages because the resistance to electrical current is increased (see Figure 14.3).

Arrangement of Nerve Cells in the Brain and Spinal Cord

While there is only one cell layer during early fetal life, nerve cells in the adult brain are arranged in six layers. As the brain expands in size, so do the number and complexity of the nerve cell layers. The nerve cell bodies migrate from the bottom layer toward the top layer (Figure 14.4). Incomplete migration of nerve cell bodies has been discovered in a number of types of severe mental retardation. Why such cells do not complete their migration is unknown.

Besides being divided into layers, the neurons of the brain and spinal cord are further separated into two distinct regions called the *gray* and the *white matter*. The

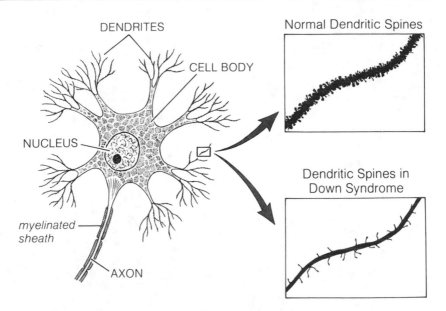

Figure 14.3.   Idealized picture of a nerve cell showing its component elements. The enlargements show the minute dendritic spines that increase the number of synapses or junctures between nerve cells. Note the diminished size and number of dendritic spines in a child with Down syndrome.

gray matter contains the nerve cell bodies; it appears grayish in color. The white matter is made up of axons sheathed with a protective covering called *myelin*.

During fetal life, most of the axons have no myelin coating. After birth, the axons gradually develop this glistening sheath that aids in more rapid conduction of nerve impulses. The dendrites also change, increasing in number and expanding in complexity. During the first 2 years of life, the proliferation of the nerve fibers

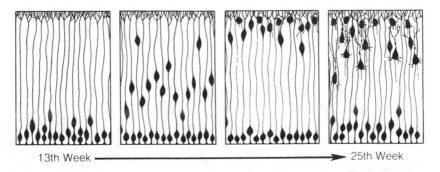

Figure 14.4.   Growth of nerve cells in the cortex between 3 and 6 months gestation. The cell bodies climb toward the upper layers of the cortex and sprout dendrites. There is an increase both in the number of cells and in the complexity of their projections.

changes the appearance of the neural network from that of a barren sapling to an arboreal structure of great beauty and complexity.

Transmission of Messages

Impulses jump from one neuron to another across a junction, or **synapse**. Here the terminal of the axon of one neuron almost touches either the dendrite or the cell body of another neuron (Figure 14.5). When a nerve cell generates an electrical impulse, that impulse can travel down the axon only as far as the end of the axon, called the *presynaptic membrane* (see Figure 14.5). It cannot cross without a bridge. In this case, the bridge consists of a chemical called a **neurotransmitter**. Each neuron has a specific neurotransmitter. These substances include norepinephrine, acetylcholine, dopamine, serotonin, and GABA; they are contained in small pouches near the presynaptic membrane. Upon stimulation by an electrical impulse, the pockets open and release the neurochemical into the opening or *synaptic cleft*. The nerve impulse's electrical energy is first transformed into chemical energy and then back again to electrical energy at the receptor on the tip of the other neuron, called the *postsynaptic membrane* (Gilman & Winans-Newman, 1987). It then can continue on its way to the next synapse, eventually reaching its final destination.

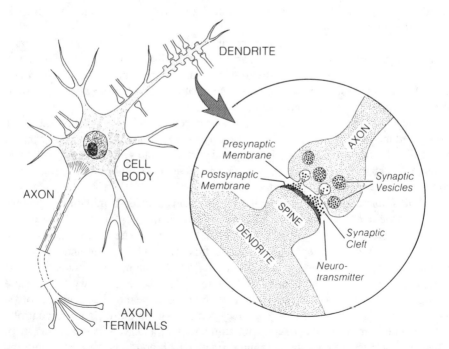

Figure 14.5.   Central nervous system synapse. The enlargement shows the abutting of an axon against a dendritic spine. The space separating the two is the synaptic cleft. Neurotransmitter bundles are released into the cleft from vesicles in the presynaptic membrane. These permit transmission of an impulse across the juncture.

THE CENTRAL NERVOUS SYSTEM: BRAIN AND SPINAL CORD

The central nervous system consists of the brain and the spinal cord. In an adult, the brain weighs about 3 pounds; it has four main components: the *cerebrum*, the *diencephalon*, the *brain stem*, and the *cerebellum*.

The Cerebrum

The cerebrum is the largest part of the brain. It contains two hemispheres joined together in the middle by the fibrous tissue of the **corpus callosum** (Figure 14.6A). The corpus callosum permits the exchange of information between hemispheres. The importance of this exchange is emphasized by the results of a surgical procedure called a **corpus callosotomy**. In this operation, a portion of the corpus callosum is cut in an attempt to control a severe seizure disorder. It has proven quite effective in decreasing seizure activity, but in some adults, it has resulted in a decline in language and in manual dexterity, probably because the operation interferes with interhemispheric compensatory mechanisms (Sass, Spencer, Spencer, et al., 1988). This procedure is discussed in more detail in Chapter 26.

Each cerebral hemisphere is functionally divided into four lobes. The *frontal lobe* occupies the front, or anterior, third of the hemisphere, and the *occipital lobe* takes up the back, or posterior, fourth of each hemisphere. The *parietal lobe* sits in the middle-upper part of the cerebrum, while the *temporal lobe* is in the lower-middle region (see Figure 14.6B).

In the fetus, the cerebral surface appears smooth. As the complexity of the brain increases, indentations gradually appear. By late childhood, the surface of the cerebrum has become very convoluted with many furrows and humps, called **sulci** and **gyri**. In an adult, a smooth, unconvoluted cerebrum, called *lissencephaly*, is associated with some forms of severe mental retardation.

The substance underlying the surface of the cerebrum is called the *cortex* and is composed mainly of nerve cell bodies, or gray matter. Below the gray matter lie the nerve fibers, or the white matter. The cerebral cortex initiates motion and thought and adds to the capability of the more reflexive and involuntary brain stem. Each cortical lobe takes care of particular activities and functions.

The Frontal Lobe The frontal lobe is involved in both initiating voluntary muscle movement and cognition. The motor strip of the frontal lobe, lying just in front of the parietal lobe, controls voluntary motor activity. The different areas of the body are represented topographically along this strip. The tongue and larynx, or voice box, are at the lowest point. They are followed in an upward sequence by the face, hand, arm, trunk, thigh, and foot (Figure 14.7). The tongue, larynx, and hand occupy a particularly large area along this strip because the motor activities involved in speech and fine motor dexterity are very complex and require elaborate control.

Voluntary movement is begun with stimulation of a nerve impulse in this strip. This impulse passes down the pyramidal tract, which connects the cortex with the diencephalon, the brain stem, and the spinal cord. At the spinal cord, the impulse is passed across a synapse to a peripheral nerve that leads to some body part. The end result is muscle movement. This movement in turn sets off a sensory, or **afferent**, communication back to the cerebrum to complete the circuit.

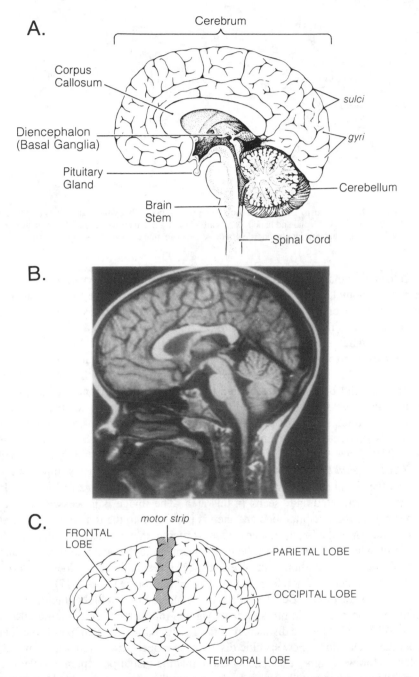

Figure 14.6. A) Lateral view of the brain showing the component elements: cerebrum, diencephalon, cerebellum, brain stem, and spinal cord. B) Lateral view of brain by MRI scan. Note the excellent reproduction of the structures of the brain. C) Side view of the left hemisphere. The cortex is divided into four lobes: frontal, parietal, temporal, and occipital. The motor strip, lying at the back of the frontal lobe, is highlighted. It initiates voluntary movement and is damaged in spastic cerebral palsy.

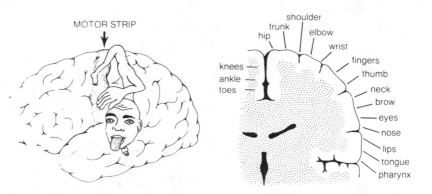

Figure 14.7. The motor strip. The cartoon shows a representation of body parts at various points on the strip. Note that the areas of facial and hand muscles are very large. This is because of the intricate control necessary for speech and fine motor coordination. A cross-sectional view of the motor strip is shown at right.

If there is damage to either the motor cortex or the pyramidal tract, **spastic** paralysis results. Voluntary movement becomes difficult, and muscle tone is increased. Conversely, if the entire motor strip, rather than a specific area, is stimulated at one time, a massive, simultaneous contraction of all muscles, called a *tonic seizure*, occurs. This is what happens in a tonic-clonic seizure (see Chapter 26).

Besides controlling voluntary movement, the frontal lobe also contains areas that are involved in abstract thinking. Years ago, some persons with severe **psychosis** or with antisocial behavior were treated by undergoing a prefrontal leukotomy, an operation in which part of the frontal lobe was cut. This diminished the number of aggressive outbursts, but the persons became messy, lost some of their initiative, were easily distracted, and demonstrated poor judgment (Benson, Stuss, Naeser, et al., 1981). Because of these side effects, leukotomies are now rarely performed.

The Occipital Lobe The occipital lobe is primarily concerned with vision. It is here that the visual stimuli terminate in what is called the *visual-receptive area*. Images are reconstructed and "seen" in this area. The image is processed further in another part of the occipital lobe and then is passed on to the temporal and parietal lobes. In the parietal lobe, the images are integrated with what has been heard and felt so an intelligent interpretation can be made. Damage to the occipital region leads to "cortical blindness." Although the eyes can see, the occipital lobe does not receive the image. The person, therefore, is functionally blind (see Chapter 17).

The Parietal Lobe Besides aiding in vision, the parietal lobe integrates other stimuli, making a whole impression from various inputs received from the different senses. Within this lobe are distinct areas for visual, auditory, touch, pain, smell, and temperature sensations. Few specific diseases have been associated with damage to this lobe. However, some researchers believe that the visual-perceptual problems experienced by children with learning disabilities are the result of abnormal functioning in this lobe (Obrzut & Hynd, 1991). In addition, the difficulty that a child with attention deficit hyperactivity disorder has in performing fine motor tasks may result from changes in this area of the brain.

The Temporal Lobe   The temporal lobe of the cerebrum is mainly involved in communication and sensation. In the dominant hemisphere (usually the left side), it helps to form and understand language and stores visual and auditory experiences. When the temporal lobe malfunctions, a number of disorders may result. The two most common are **receptive aphasia** and complex partial seizures.

In receptive aphasia, which is basically an adult disorder, the temporal lobe is damaged by a tumor, stroke, or traumatic injury (Brown, 1972). The person cannot understand the words he or she hears (see Chapter 19).

Complex partial seizures also arise from the temporal lobe (Hermann & Seidenberg, 1989). Before the seizure begins, the individual may experience a "déjà vu," or flashback phenomena caused by stimulation of this area of the brain. The person also may see strange images, smell unpleasant odors, or hear bizarre sounds (see Chapter 26). In some children whose seizures have been resistant to antiepileptic drugs, a portion of the temporal lobe is removed. The results have been encouraging in improving seizure control and side effects have been few (Duchowny, 1989). This differs from adults who have received the same surgery for intractible seizures for they have experienced memory loss and/or decreased spontaneous speech if the surgery was performed on the dominant hemisphere (Walczak, Radtke, McNamara, et al., 1990). This suggests that the child's brain, in which the nondominant hemisphere can take over some of the language functions of the damaged area, is more flexible than the adult's.

The Diencephalon

Resting beneath the cortex in the center of the brain is an area called the *diencephalon* (see Figure 14.6A). It contains the basal ganglia and related structures. In lower vertebrates, this area controls motor activity. In human beings, however, this primitive part of the brain modifies and alters the instructions from the motor cortex that call for voluntary movement.

Besides the basal ganglia, the **labyrinth** in the inner ear and the cerebellum also affect voluntary movement. Together, these three parts of the nervous system serve as a series of checks and balances on motor activity and balance.

Damage to the diencephalon leads to abnormalities in movement. The most common of these disorders is called *extrapyramidal cerebral palsy* (see Chapter 24). Other diseases involving this region are **Parkinson disease**, **Huntington disease**, and **torsion dystonia**.

The Brain Stem

The brain stem lies between the cerebral hemispheres and the spinal cord. It has three regions: the medulla, the pons, and the midbrain (Figure 14.8). These parts together contain 12 cranial nerves that control such diverse functions as breathing, swallowing, seeing, and hearing. These nerves also affect facial expression, eye and tongue movement, and salivation. Besides these cranial nerves, the brain stem also contains sections of the pyramidal and extrapyramidal tracts as well as other nerve tracts that flow from the cortex to the spinal cord.

Children with cerebral palsy often have damage to the brain stem or to pathways

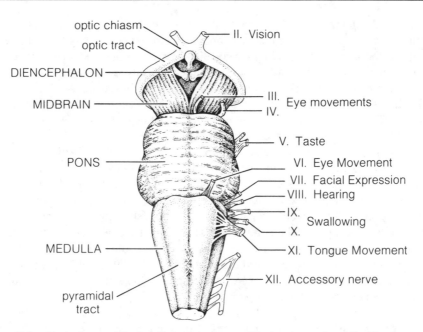

optic chiasm
optic tract
DIENCEPHALON
MIDBRAIN
PONS
MEDULLA
pyramidal tract

II. Vision
III. Eye movements
IV.
V. Taste
VI. Eye Movement
VII. Facial Expression
VIII. Hearing
IX.
Swallowing
X.
XI. Tongue Movement
XII. Accessory nerve

Figure 14.8. The brain stem. The three regions are shown: midbrain, pons, and medulla. The placement and function of 11 of the 12 cranial nerves are illustrated. (The first cranial nerve [smell] is not shown. It lies in front of the second cranial nerve, below the frontal lobe.) Note that the pyramidal tract runs from the cortex into the brain stem. The pyramidal fibers cross over in the medulla. Thus, the right hemisphere controls left-sided movement.

that end in the brain stem. This explains why these children have a high incidence of sucking and swallowing problems, strabismus, excessive salivation, and speech disorders.

The Cerebellum

The last of the major parts of the brain, the cerebellum, hangs over the brain stem and rests just below the cerebral hemispheres (see Figure 14.6A). The cerebellum coordinates the action of the voluntary muscles and times their contractions so that movements are performed smoothly and accurately.

For us to move efficiently, the work of the cerebellum must be integrated with the work of the cerebral hemispheres and the basal ganglia. While voluntary movement can occur without the presence of the cerebellum, such movement is clumsy and disorganized. The walk of a person with abnormal cerebellar functioning is called **ataxic** and is most commonly seen in an inebriated person. Also, the hands of a person with cerebellar damage tremble, the eyes twitch (also called nystagmus), and the individual overshoots the mark when reaching for an object.

In childhood, the most common cause of cerebellar dysfunction is drug intoxication (Menkes, 1990). For example, a child with a seizure disorder who receives too much phenytoin (Dilantin) weaves while walking and has difficulty reaching precisely. This is because phenytoin has a direct effect on cerebellar function. When the drug level returns to normal, these problems disappear.

The Spinal Cord

Below the brain lies the spinal cord. It is a cylindrical structure that extends from the brain stem to the lower back. Surrounding both the brain and the spinal cord are three layers of covering called the **meninges** (Figure 14.9). The spinal cord is enlarged in the neck, or **cervical**, region and in the **lumbar**, or lower back area. These enlarged areas contain **anterior horn cells**, which send messages to the peripheral nerve fibers that lead to the arms and legs.

Primarily a conduit, the spinal cord transmits motor and sensory messages. If the spinal cord is damaged—for example, because of an injury or a congenital malformation such as spina bifida—the messages from the brain to the peripheral nerves below the lesion or area of injury are short-circuited. The result may be the loss of both sensation and movement in the affected limbs.

Damage to the spinal cord also can come from an infection. The polio virus, now virtually eradicated in the United States, led to paralysis in many children during the 1950s because it destroyed the anterior horn cells of the spinal cord. While the sensory pathways remained intact, the motor path was interrupted (Menkes, 1990).

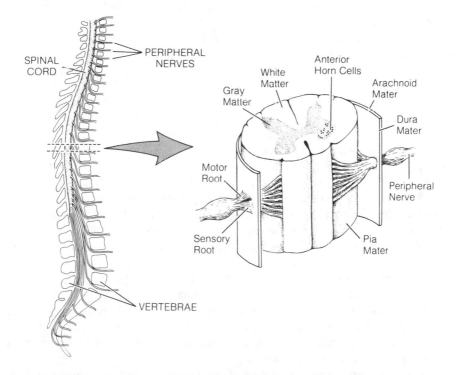

Figure 14.9. The spinal column. The spinal cord extends from the neck to the lower back. It is protected by the bony vertebrae that form the spinal column. The enlargement to the right shows a section of the cord taken from the upper back region. Note the meninges (the dura, arachnoid, and pia mater) surrounding the cord and the peripheral nerve on its way to a muscle. This nerve contains both motor and sensory components. The spinal cord, like the brain, has both gray and white matter. The gray matter consists of various nerve cells, most important of which are the anterior motor horn cells. These are destroyed in polio. The white matter contains nerve fibers wrapped in myelin that gives the cord its glistening appearance.

The child could feel touch and pain but could not move. Another infection affecting the spinal column is meningitis, caused by either a virus or bacteria. In meningitis, the infectious agent attacks the meninges. Except in infants, the effects of meningitis are usually reversible. In **encephalitis**, a virus invades the brain tissue itself, causing a much more dangerous type of infection (Bell & McCormick, 1981).

THE PERIPHERAL NERVOUS SYSTEM

For voluntary movement to occur, the nerve impulse that passes from the motor cortex to the anterior horn cells in the spinal cord must connect with a peripheral nerve. This nerve then takes the impulse from the spinal cord to the muscle. Actually, peripheral nerves have fibers that run in both directions. The motor, or **efferent**, fibers bring signals from the brain to the muscles and cause movement. The sensory, or afferent, fibers carry signals from the muscle to the brain that indicate the position of a joint and the tone of the muscle following the movement. The interaction between these two types of nerves allows smooth movement.

For normal muscle tone to occur, the proper relationship between the motor and the sensory fibers must exist. Even when at rest, muscles have some tone because of this constant interchange between the motor and sensory nerves. In other words, it is not the muscle itself, but rather the activity of the nervous system, that maintains muscle tone. For example, if a muscle is stimulated by moving a joint, a person feels resistance to this movement (i.e., an increase in muscle tone). The activity of the muscle at rest and the involuntary reaction that opposes the stretch of the muscle are characteristics of muscle tone. This tone is decreased when the motor fibers from the spinal cord are cut, or when the sensory fibers are abnormal.

When either the anterior horn cells or the motor fibers of the peripheral nervous system are injured, an individual may lose both the voluntary and the reflexive qualities of the muscle and become paralyzed. Besides the paralysis, the affected muscle loses its tone and becomes floppy, or **hypotonic**. After a while, the affected muscle and limb begin to shrink, or atrophy, from lack of use. This is what happens to a person who has spina bifida or a severe spinal cord injury.

If there is damage to either the pyramidal tract or the extrapyramidal tract, muscle tone again is affected. When the pyramidal tract is injured, the tone and reflexes actually increase. Muscle resistance is strong at the beginning of movement but then gives way in a sudden, clasped-knife fashion as more force is applied. Also, a quick stretch of a tendon will produce **clonus**, a sustained series of rhythmic jerks. The combination of these characteristics is called *spasticity* and is the hallmark of pyramidal or spastic cerebral palsy (see Chapter 24) because it arises from an abnormality in the motor cortex or pyramidal tract.

The changes resulting from damage to the extrapyramidal tract are quite different. With damage to this system, voluntary movement is possible, but it may be exaggerated in a twisting, squirming pattern called choreoathetosis. In addition, a plastic or "lead pipe" rigidity rather than spasticity characterizes the changes in tone and is the hallmark of extrapyramidal cerebral palsy (see Chapter 24).

THE AUTONOMIC NERVOUS SYSTEM

While the preceding discussion has focused on control of voluntary movement, an entirely different nervous system takes care of involuntary activities—the autonomic nervous system. This system controls the functioning of the cardiovascular, respiratory, digestive, endocrine, urinary, and reproductive systems. The tracts of this system start in either the diencephalon or the spinal cord and move on to the particular organ with which they are involved.

While the voluntary nervous system is concerned with individual muscle movements, the autonomic nervous system has an all or none effect. The best example of this is the "fight or flight" response (Figure 14.10). When a person is frightened, several physiological changes take place simultaneously. The pupils dilate, the hair stands on end, and the functioning of the digestive system is suspended so that blood can be diverted to more important areas, such as the brain. Heart rate and blood pressure increase, and the bronchioles of the lung expand in size. All of these changes are controlled by the autonomic nervous system and prepare the individual to react to the emergency.

A more common function of the autonomic nervous system is the control of bowel and bladder function. In infants, this function is purely reflexive. When the bladder or bowel fills, the outlet muscles release and the child urinates or defecates. Between the ages of 12 and 18 months, the child gradually gains control over these

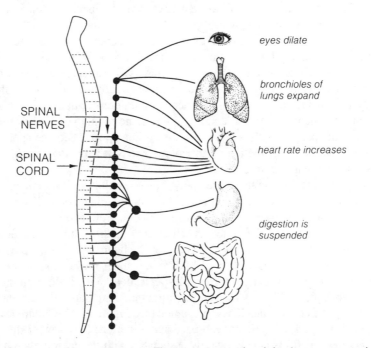

SPINAL NERVES

SPINAL CORD

eyes dilate

bronchioles of lungs expand

heart rate increases

digestion is suspended

Figure 14.10. Autonomic nervous system. These nerves control such involuntary motor activities as breathing, heart rate, and digestion. This system is involved in "fight or flight" reactions.

activities. The cerebral cortex sends fibers to the spinal cord and, from there, to the muscles of the bowel and bladder. These fibers inhibit the autonomic nervous system's response so that the reflexive action of urinating or defectating is reduced. Thus, when an older child feels the need to urinate or defecate, he or she can tighten the necessary muscles until he or she reaches a bathroom. Damage to the pyramidal tract or the spinal cord causes a loss of this inhibition of the autonomic nervous system. This is why most children with cerebral palsy, spina bifida, or severe mental retardation have great difficulty controlling bladder and bowel function.

THE CEREBROSPINAL FLUID AND HYDROCEPHALUS

The cerebrospinal fluid is a clear, watery liquid that bathes the spinal cord and flows through the ventricles, or cavities, within the brain (Figure 14.11). Totaling about 4 ounces in an adult, this fluid serves as a buffer for the central nervous system against sudden pressure changes and also helps to provide this system with nutrition. Produced in a tangle of cells that hang from the roof of the ventricles, called the **choroid plexus**, and absorbed on the surface of the brain, this fluid is constantly recirculated.

After it is produced in the roof of the **lateral ventricles**, the cerebrospinal fluid flows through the third ventricle toward the fourth ventricle via a narrow passageway called the *aqueduct*. Three openings in the roof of the fourth ventricle allow some of the cerebrospinal fluid to flow into the small space surrounding the brain. Much of the fluid, however, goes from the fourth ventricle down the meninges surrounding the spinal cord to the base of the spine.

If this flow is obstructed, it backs up in the ventricles and leads to increased intracranial pressure. This condition is called *hydrocephalus* (see Figure 25.6) (Milhorat, 1972). In an infant, a significant increase in intracranial pressure is prevented because the brain can expand by pushing open the unfused bones of the skull. This results in an increase in the infant's head circumference. In an older child, however, the cranial bones are fused, and the brain has no room to expand. If untreated, this intracranial pressure builds and cause the child to vomit, become lethargic, and go into a coma. Such a situation requires emergency treatment at the first sign of increased intracranial pressure.

The causes of hydrocephalus are many. In some children, it is congenital (e.g., spina bifida) (see Chapter 25). In others, it follows meningitis or an intraventricular hemorrhage. The infection or bleeding causes a blockage either of the openings on the surface of the brain or of the aqueduct. Both abnormalities hinder the flow of the cerebrospinal fluid. In some cases, the cause of the hydrocephalus is unknown.

Treatment of hydrocephalus usually involves either medication or the surgical placement of a bypass, usually a **ventriculo-peritoneal** (V-P) **shunt** (Vintzileos, Ingardia, & Nochimson, 1983), which allows intracranial pressure to be decreased, and further enlargement of the head to be prevented (see Figure 25.6). Children who have these ventriculo-peritoneal shunts can participate in all activities other than contact sports. Hydrocephalus is not necessarily associated with mental retardation or other disabilities, and many of these children grow up to lead normal lives (Prigatano,

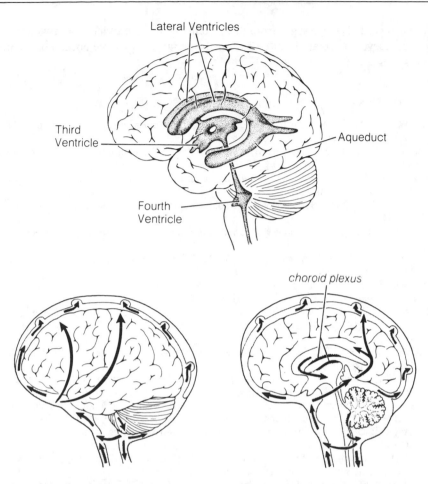

Figure 14.11. The ventricular system of the brain. The major parts of the ventricular system are shown above. The flow of cerebrospinal fluid is shown below. The fluid is produced by the choroid plexus in the roof of the lateral and third ventricles. Its primary route is through the aqueduct, into the fourth ventricle, and then into the spinal column, where it is absorbed. A secondary route is around the surface of the brain. A blockage, most commonly of the aqueduct, leads to hydrocephalus. (Lower illustration redrawn with permission from Milhorat, T.H. [1972]. *Hydrocephalus and the cerebrospinal fluid*. Baltimore: Williams & Wilkins Co. Copyright © 1972, The Williams & Wilkins Co., Baltimore.)

Zeiner, Pollay, et al., 1983). Hydrocephalus and its treatment is discussed further in Chapter 25.

SUMMARY

The nervous system has three major subunits: the central nervous system, the peripheral nervous system, and the autonomic nervous system. Within the central nervous system are the cerebrum, the diencephalon, the brain stem, the cerebellum, and the spinal cord. The messages from these components control the other two nervous systems. Developmental disabilities result from damage to some portion of the nervous system.

REFERENCES

Bell, W.E., & McCormick, W.F. (1981). *Neurologic infections in children* (2nd ed.). Philadelphia: W.B. Saunders.

Benson, D.F., Stuss, D.T., Naeser, M.A., et al. (1981). The long-term effects of prefrontal leukotomy. *Archives of Neurology, 38,* 165–169.

Brown, J.W. (1972). *Aphasia, apraxia, and agnosia: Clinical and theoretical aspects.* Springfield, IL: Charles C Thomas.

Duchowny, M.S. (1989). Surgery for intractable epilepsy: Issues and outcome. *Pediatrics, 84,* 886–894.

Garoutte, B. (Ed.). (1987). *Survey of functional neuroanatomy* (2nd ed.). St. Louis: C.V. Mosby.

Gilman, S., & Winans-Newman, S. (Eds.). (1987). *Manter & Gatz's essentials of clinical neuroanatomy and neurophysiology* (7th ed.). Philadelphia: F.A. Davis.

Hermann, B.P., & Seidenberg, M. (1989). *Childhood epilepsies: Neurophysical, psychosocial, and intervention aspects.* New York: John Wiley & Sons.

Menkes, J.H. (1990). *Textbook of child neurology* (4th ed.). Philadelphia: Lea & Febiger.

Milhorat, T.H. (1972). *Hydrocephalus and the cerebrospinal fluid.* Baltimore: Williams & Wilkins Co.

Noback, C.R. (1991). *The human nervous system: Introduction and review* (4th ed.). Philadelphia: Lea & Febiger.

Obrzut, J.E., & Hynd, G.W. (Eds.). (1991). *Neuropsychological foundations of learning disabilities: A handbook of issues, methods and practice.* New York: Academic Press.

Prigatano, G.P., Zeiner, H.K., Pollay, M., et al. (1983). Neuropsychological functioning in children with shunted uncomplicated hydrocephalus. *Child's Brain, 10,* 112–120.

Purpura, D.P. (1974). Dendritic spine "dysgenesis" and mental retardation. *Science, 186,* 1126–1128.

Sass, K.J., Spencer, D.D., Spencer, S.S., et al. (1988). Corpus callosotomy for epilepsy II. Neurology and neuropsychological outcome. *Neurology, 38,* 24–28.

Vintzileos, A.M., Ingardia, C.J., & Nochimson, D.J. (1983). Congenital hydrocephalus: A review and protocol for perinatal management. *Obstetrics and Gynecology, 62,* 539–549.

Walczak, T.S., Radtke, R.A., McNamara J.O., et al. (1990). Anterior temporal lobectomy for complex partial seizures. Evaluation, results, and long-term follow-up of 100 cases. *Neurology, 40,* 413–418.

Chapter 15

Bones, Joints, and Muscles
Support and Movement

Upon completion of this chapter, the reader will:
—be able to explain the structure and development of bone
—know some of the most common bony deformities and their treatment
—recognize the various types of joints
—be aware of what happens when a person has arthritis
—know the function of tendons and ligaments
—understand how the musculoskeletal and nervous systems work together
—be able to identify some of the major diseases affecting movement, including muscular dystrophy and torsion dystonia

---

Although the nervous system initiates movement, without bones, joints, and muscles to respond to the signals, nothing would happen. We would be immobile. Muscles, joints, and bones, or the musculoskeletal system, assist with movement through the interworkings of the bone, cartilage, ligaments, tendons, and muscles. This chapter explores how these various tissues function and examines what can go wrong.

TYPES OF MOVEMENT

Before discussing how the musculoskeletal system works, it is important to understand the terms used to describe different kinds of movement. These terms are illustrated in Figure 15.1.

Flexion refers to the bending of a part of the body at a joint. *Extension*, the opposite of flexion, means to straighten. *Abduction* is the moving of a part of the body away from the midline, or middle segment, of the body, while *adduction* is the movement toward the midline. The midline is also called the *median plane*. The outer parts of the body are the lateral sections. To illustrate, the umbilicus is in the median plane while the breasts are in the lateral sections of the body. *Anterior* refers to the top of a

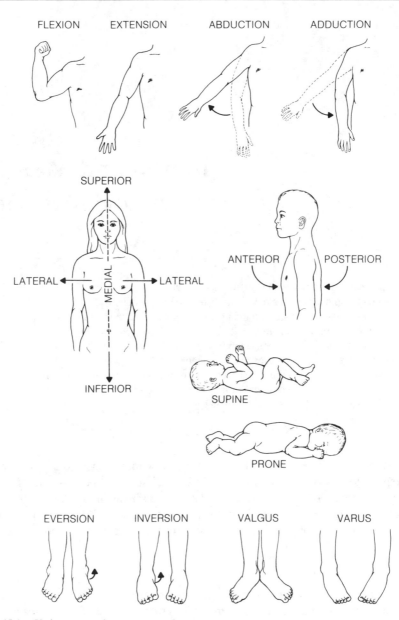

Figure 15.1. Various types of movements and postures.

flat surface, whereas *posterior* is the rear or under part. Thus, the chest is anterior, while the back is posterior. The word *superior* means up or above; *inferior* means below. The head is superior, and the feet are inferior, to the shoulders.

When you lie on your back, you are in a *supine* position. You are *prone* when you lie on your stomach. A foot is *everted* when the sole faces outward and *inverted* when the sole turns inward. *Valgus* denotes a deformity in which the angulation of the body part is away from the midline of the body. An example is talipes valgus where the heal is turned outward from the midline of the leg (see Figure 15.1). A *varus* deformity is the opposite.

Equinus refers to a deformity in which the sole of the foot is flexed, such that the child walks like a horse. This is often combined with scissoring of the legs and is a sign of spasticity. *Dislocation* refers to the displacement of a bone from its normal joint. *Subluxation* is an incomplete or partial dislocation of a joint. *Athetosis* refers to slow, writhing, involuntary movements, especially in the hands. This accompanies certain forms of extrapyramidal cerebral palsy. *Ataxia* implies an incoordination of muscular movement, usually resulting from abnormalities in the cerebellum.

BONE

Bone forms our skeleton, the internal structure of our body. Our bones range in size from the 0.5-inch **phalanges** of the finger to the roughly 18-inch femur, or thigh bone. Some bones, such as the skull, are flat; others, such as the femur, are tubular. Even though bones are hard and immobile, they are actively growing and changing. Just as the body is dependent on the skeleton for support, so the skeletal system relies on the body for its maintenance and growth.

Structure and Development of Bone

The height of a child increases because of growth of the long, tubular bones. To understand how this works, it is helpful first to examine the structure of a bone. Consider the femur as an example. This bone consists of a shaft or *diaphysis*, a spongy, upper portion called a *metaphysis*, the end of the bone called the *epiphysis*, and a growth plate that separates the metaphysis and epiphysis (Figure 15.2). Surrounding the bone is a tough, fibrous, protective layer called the **periosteum**. Calcium crystals embedded in a protein compound make up about one-third of a bone. It is this mineral-protein mixture that lends strength to the bone. The central core, the bone marrow, is where blood cells are formed. Weaving through the bone's structure are blood vessels that supply oxygen and nutrition necessary for growth.

Bone grows from the growth plate. Here, cartilage cells are laid down and are then invaded by bone-forming cells, or **osteoblasts**. These cells contain calcium and gradually transform the cartilage into bone. This process is called **enchondral ossification**. Both ends of the long bone then lengthen, and the child grows taller (see Figure 15.2).

As growth takes place, the bone undergoes different stresses, and it begins to remodel or change in shape. This increases its strength and stability. If bone were not capable of this reshaping, it would be more susceptible to fracture. This growth process involves both the osteoblast cells, which form or lay down bone, and the **osteoclast** cells, which resorb bone. The osteoblast adds calcium crystals, and the osteoclast removes the crystals from already formed bone and returns them to the blood stream. A part of the bone, therefore, is constantly disappearing, and new bone is

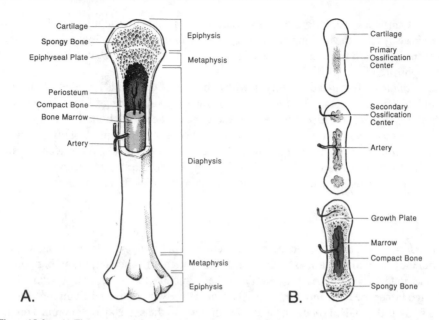

Figure 15.2. A) The structure of a typical long bone, the humerus. New bone grows from the epiphysis, and the arm lengthens. The upper portion of the bone is the metaphysis, and the shaft is called the diaphysis. The bone marrow, which produces blood cells, lies in the center of the shaft. Surrounding the bone is a fibrous protective sheath, the periosteum. The bone facing the joint space is covered by flexible cartilage. B) The long bone starts off as a mass of cartilage in fetal life. Gradually the center is invaded by osteoblasts. These cells lay down minerals that form bone. The ossification centers spread and the bone enlarges and hardens. After birth, further bone growth occurs only from the epiphysis.

being laid down in its place. This reshaping results in a sleeker, longer bone. On the average, a section of a child's bone lasts about a year and is then replaced by new bone. Thus, bone is a living organ that constantly grows and reshapes to increase its effectiveness. In an adult, the reshaping continues even though growth has stopped. The average bone segment of an adult lasts about 7 years (Tachdjian, 1990).

Osteopetrosis, an inherited disorder of bone, involves an abnormality of the osteoclasts (Bollerslev, 1987). The bone becomes very dense and sclerotic because the osteoclasts fail to resorb the bone. The skull and long bones become very thick, and the bone marrow becomes very narrow. This results in progressive enlargement of the head, impingement of the cranial nerves causing blindness and deafness, and severe anemia. Growth is delayed and most affected children have died at young ages. However, recently it has been shown that bone marrow transplantation (see Chapter 10) is effective in providing normal osteoclasts to children with osteopetrosis, reversing many of the symptoms and permitting prolonged survival. This procedure is not without significant dangers, including graft versus host disease, which carries a 10%–20% mortality rate (Fischer, Griscelli, Friedrick, et al., 1986).

Bony Deformities

Bony deformities may occur *in utero* or after birth. Two of the most common prenatal types are club foot and congenital dislocation of the hip.

In most cases, club foot, or *talipes equinovarus*, comes from a malformation of the foot (see Figure 4.4). In most cases the cause is unknown; the incidence is approximately 1 in 1,000 infants. There are three components of the deformity: equinus, hindfoot varus, and forefoot adductus (Morrissy, 1990). However, club foot also may result from deformity of a normally shaped foot. This can occur in a fetus who has spinal muscular atrophy (see below), is caught in an abnormal position *in utero*, and is too weak to move. It also may result from "packing syndromes," such as oligohydramnios, where there has been leakage of amniotic fluid, resulting in abnormal pressure on the foot (see Chapter 4). One or both feet may be affected. The club foot deformity can be corrected either through serial casting or with **orthopedic** surgery.

While club foot is more common in boys, congenital dislocation of the hip occurs more frequently in girls. This condition seems to be associated with breech delivery, although a hereditary predisposition may contribute to the defect. Whatever the cause, the result is a misshapen pelvis that has an abnormal **acetabulum**, or bony socket (Bernard, O'Hara, Bazin, et al., 1987). Thus, the "ball"-shaped head of the femur does not fit properly into the shallow socket of the abnormal acetabulum (Figure 15.3). Spreading back the hips in flexion and abduction when the child is an infant, which can be accomplished by using either a **Pavlik harness** or a **Spica cast**, often prevents the need for corrective surgery.

While club foot and congenital hip dislocation represent isolated deformities, other bony disorders may involve the entire skeleton. One such example is achondroplasia, an autosomal dominantly inherited form of short-limbed dwarfism. In a child with this disorder, all of the long bones are short and stubby so he or she has shortened arms and legs and a disproportionately large head (Figure 15.4). The incidence is about 1 in 10,000 (Buyse, 1990).

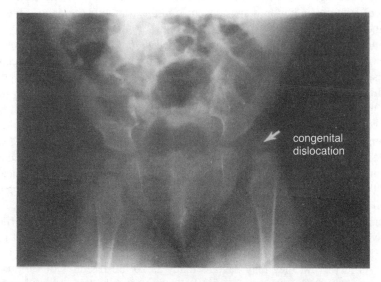

congenital
dislocation

Figure 15.3. Congenital dislocation of the hip. The arrow indicates the point of dislocation. (X ray courtesy of Dr. Sandra Kramer, Department of Pediatric Radiology, The Children's Hospital of Philadelphia.)

Figure 15.4.   Achondroplasia, an autosomal dominant form of short-limbed dwarfism.

Bony deformities also may develop after birth. For example, in cerebral palsy, abnormal muscle balance due to spasticity may cause scoliosis or dislocations of the limbs.

Fractures

Any person may fracture, or break, a bone. A fracture occurs when sufficient force is brought to bear against the bone, causing it to break (Figure 15.5). The most common causes of fractures in children are household and automobile accidents, sports injuries, and child abuse.

Some children experience fractures, called *pathological fractures*, even when there does not seem to be sufficient force to break the bone. For example, such a child might sustain a broken leg merely by being lifted from a lying to a sitting position. Nonambulatory children with disabilities have frail bones and are more likely to experience these fractures. As discussed in Chapter 11, it may be important to add vitamin D and calcium supplements to the diets of these children. Fractures also may occur in children who have leukemia or other tumors that invade the bone marrow and weaken the internal structure of the bone. Children with rickets who have not formed normal calcium/phosphorus mineral deposits are more prone to sustain pathological fractures. This is also a problem in nonambulatory children are who are receiving certain antiepileptic drugs.

In addition, *osteogenesis imperfecta* (OI), an autosomal dominant inherited disorder with an incidence of 1 in 20,000, is associated with brittle bones that fracture easily (Marini, 1988). These children may sustain multiple fractures during their delivery. As they grow, they may have as many as 20–30 fractures of various bones (Sillence, 1988). No specific treatment is presently available for this disorder, but rehabilitation treatment and bracing is helpful in keeping the children ambulatory.

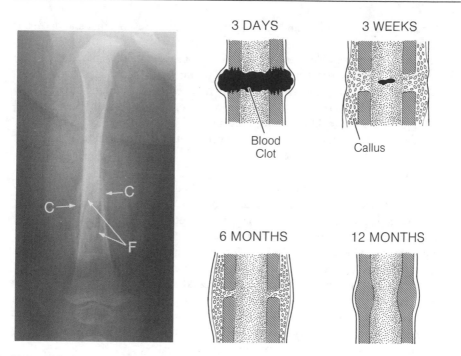

Figure 15.5. Bone fracture. The X ray shows the fracture line (F). This was taken 3 weeks after the accident, and callus formation can be seen (C). The mechanism of healing is outlined to the right. Initially, there is bleeding from bone capillaries damaged in the accident. Soon this blood clot is invaded by osteoblasts that lay down extensive bony tissue forming a callus. By 6 months, the bones are almost fused, but the bone structure is still enlarged. At 12 months, fusion is complete, and the bone is strong and looks fairly normal. Further reshaping over time will make all signs of fracture disappear.

For proper healing to occur and to avoid deformity, fractures must be aligned properly and immobilized. Children's bones usually heal in 4–6 weeks. Casts are made of plaster in a fashion similar to papier mâché. Lighter and stronger casts now can be made of fiberglass. The cast serves to stabilize the bone fragments and hold them together after they have been properly realigned by an orthopedic surgeon. This allows the bone to heal in the normal position. Healing takes place by a process called **callus** formation (see Figure 15.5). The callus begins as a blood clot, the result of bleeding from tiny blood vessels inside and around the bone. Cartilage subsequently forms, and within a few weeks, osteoblasts start to lay down new bone on the cartilage framework. After 4–6 weeks, weight can be placed on the bone, and it usually can function again. The remodeling process, however, continues. Eventually, the bulging callus remodels and disappears. Within 6–12 months, a bone that appears to be normal is seen on an X ray (Morrissy, 1990).

JOINTS

A joint is defined as the connection of two or more bones. It is made up of the epiphysis and cartilage of the two connecting bones, the small, lubricated space called the *joint cavity*, and the ligaments and muscles that bind the bones together and make the joint stable (Figure 15.6).

Joints may be immobile, partly mobile, or completely mobile. The sutures of the skull (where the bones meet) are the examples of immobile joints. The hand is composed of slightly mobile joints and completely mobile joints, including hinge, pivot, and ball-and-socket joints. The knee is an example of a hinge joint that can flex and extend (see Figure 15.6). At this joint, movement of 145° back and forth is possible. At the elbow (which is a pivot and hinge joint), rotation as well as hinge movement occurs. The hip, a ball-and-socket joint, can move in all three planes—flexion, rotation, and abduction.

A common affliction of joints is arthritis. Actually, arthritis is a group of disorders, each with its own characteristics and problems. In all cases, however, the cartilage surrounding the joint space is damaged. The bones grind against each other and become inflamed; sometimes, they fuse. The result is pain and loss of motion. In older people and in individuals with disabilities, the most common form of arthritis is **osteoarthritis** (see Figure 15.6). Arthritis is particularly likely to occur as a result of dislocated joints. Thus, a child with spastic cerebral palsy may develop a dislocation of the hip as a result of unbalanced muscle forces acting across this joint. He or she may not only experience a loss of movement at the various joints but also may experience painful arthritis. Surgery is directed at correcting the dislocation and lessening the risk of arthritis and pain (see Chapter 24).

LIGAMENTS AND TENDONS

As noted previously, ligaments are the fibrous tissues that attach one bone to another across a joint (see Figure 15.6). Tendons are similar in composition and function to ligaments, but they have looser fibers. They attach muscles to bones rather than connecting two bones (Figure 15.7). Both ligaments and tendons are flexible, resilient, and are essential to keep joints moving properly. Unlike bone, these tissues have a limited ability to regenerate. Thus, damage to tendons or ligaments (all too common in athletes) often requires surgical repair. Even then, success is not guaranteed. Movement in the joint after such an injury may be limited and painful.

MUSCLES AND THE NEUROMUSCULAR JUNCTION

In order for a muscle to move across a joint, a signal that begins in the brain passes through the spinal cord and ends in a peripheral nerve. Since the sole function of the muscle is to contract, its structure is very different from other body organs. The cell of a muscle is called the *muscle fiber* (see Figure 15.7). This fiber's chief components are two proteins, **actin** and **myosin**, that form highly organized subunits, called **sarcomeres**, within the muscle fibers. These subunits are stimulated by nerve impulses to contract.

Such stimulation occurs at the neuromuscular junction, where the peripheral nerve reaches the muscle fiber. At this point, the nerve and muscle are separated by a

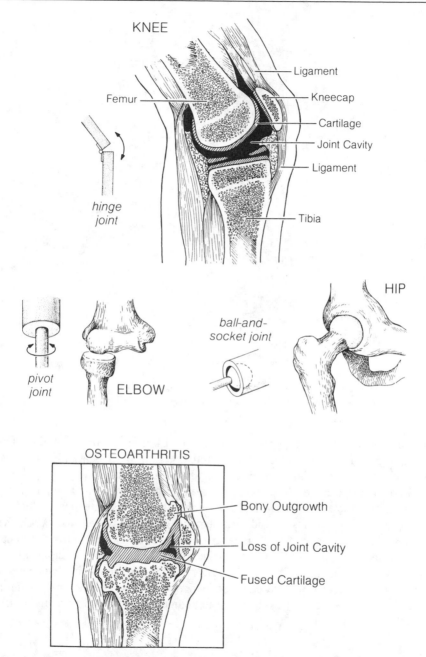

Figure 15.6. Joints. A normal knee joint is shown above as compared to an arthritic knee joint below. Normally there is a lubricated joint cavity separating the femur and tibia bones. Muscles cross the joint attached to the ligaments. In the diseased joint, the cavity has disappeared, and there is fusion of the opposing bones. This severely limits movement. The different types of joints are also illustrated: hinge (knee), pivot (elbow), and ball-and-socket (hip).

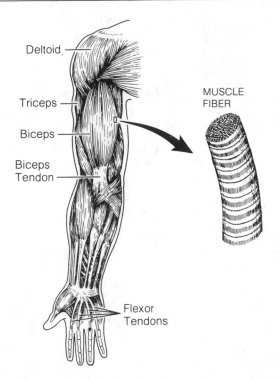

Deltoid

Triceps

Biceps

Biceps
Tendon

MUSCLE
FIBER

Flexor
Tendons

Figure 15.7. Muscles. The major muscles in the arm. Note that the biceps and triceps are antagonists. The enlargement shows a muscle fiber, which is the unit of muscle tissue.

synaptic gap (see Chapter 14). The electrical impulse from the brain can jump this gap using a neurotransmitter that is released into this gap. The message then moves to the muscle fiber, stimulating it to contract, and movement occurs.

Smooth movement results as long as all the muscle groups around the joint act in concert. Each muscle has *agonists* and *antagonists*. Antagonists are muscles that oppose the movement of a muscle, and agonists are muscles that work in concert with a given muscle. So, for example, when the arm is flexed, the biceps contracts, as does the brachialis (an agonist to the biceps). The triceps (the antagonist muscle), however, relaxes (see Figure 15.7). If both muscle groups contracted simultaneously, a painful muscle spasm would develop. So, when the brain tells the arm to move, it actually sends a series of messages that tell some muscles to contract and others to relax.

NEUROMUSCULAR DISEASES

Neuromuscular diseases affect movement because of damage to the spinal cord (see Chapter 25), the anterior horn cells of the spinal cord, the peripheral nerves, the neuromuscular junction, or the muscle itself (Brooke, 1986). Other disorders, such as cerebral palsy, also affect movement, but the primary abnormalities in these cases are in the brain rather than in the musculoskeletal system. The normal inhibiting signals from the brain that suppress reflex arcs are lost so abnormal reflex activity results, including the expression of primitive reflexes (see Chapter 24).

Diseases of the Anterior Horn Cells

When an impulse leaves the brain to signal movement, it passes along the spinal cord to a point near the particular joint to be moved. Here it reaches an anterior horn cell (see Figure 14.9), which, in turn, passes the impulse to the peripheral nerve.

The two diseases most commonly associated with damage to the anterior horn cells are polio and the spinal muscular atrophies (Wessel, 1989). The polio virus selectively destroys the anterior horn cells and creates a gap between the central nervous system and the peripheral nerves. Paralysis takes place below the part of the spinal column that has been damaged by the infection. Polio has not been a significant health problem in the United States since the polio vaccine was first introduced in 1955 by Dr. Jonas Salk. Later, Dr. Albert Sabin developed an oral vaccine that is used worldwide. Now, the immunizations that infants receive include three doses of oral polio vaccine in addition to their series of diphtheria, whooping cough (pertussis), and tetanus (DPT) shots (Kimpen & Ogra, 1990). Unfortunately, polio remains a major health problem throughout developing countries in spite of this effective vaccine.

Spinal muscular atrophy also attacks the anterior horn cells in the spinal cord and brain stem. This is an autosomal recessive inherited disorder of unknown origin. Children with the severe form of this disorder are inactive *in utero* and very floppy after birth. Life expectancy is short because of breathing problems caused by a weak diaphragm and recurrent pulmonary infections. Microscopic examination of the spinal cord reveals a severe deficiency of anterior horn cells. No specific treatment is available although rehabilitative therapy using adaptive seating can make these children more functionally active.

Disease of the Peripheral Nerves

Guillain-Barré syndrome is an example of an illness affecting the peripheral nerves. Its incidence is rare, approximately 1 in 100,000 (Evans, 1986). Also called **acute polyneuropathy**, this disease causes paralysis similar to that seen in polio. It generally occurs a few weeks after a viral illness and, unlike polio, involves both sides of the body equally. It usually starts in the lower extremities and moves upward for about 1–2 weeks. The upper extremities and diaphragm also may be affected, and as a result, breathing may be impaired. Mechanical ventilation may be required for a time. However, recovery tends to be as dramatic as the onset of the illness, with complete recovery often occurring within 2 months (McKhann, 1990). Yet, some individuals are left with residual problems, most commonly weakness of the facial muscles or lower extremities. During the recovery phase, physical therapy is necessary.

Guillain-Barré syndrome results from an **autoimmune** response to a viral infection. The body mistakenly identifies infected nerve roots as foreign bodies and tries to destroy them. A new treatment directed at the autoimmune response, called *plasma-*

pheresis, has lessened the duration and improved the outcome of the disease (Epstein & Sladky, 1990; French Cooperative Group on Plasma Exchange in Guillain-Barré Syndrome, 1987). This procedure involves removing some of the individual's blood plasma and replacing it with unaffected plasma. In this way, the autoantibodies in the plasma are removed.

Disease of the Neuromuscular Junction

Another disease involving the body's immune response is *myasthenia gravis*. This inherited disorder affects neurochemical transmission at the neuromuscular junction of skeletal muscles. It occurs most frequently in women, but adolescent girls also may be affected (Fenichel, 1989).

Muscle weakness is the main characteristic of myasthenia. Initially, it affects the eyelids, making them droopy. Then it progresses to involve other muscle groups. A person with myasthenia gravis usually feels strong in the morning and increasingly weakens as the day passes. The weakness can affect speech, eating, walking, and even breathing.

This disease results from antibodies blocking the receptors for the neurotransmitter acetylcholine (Linton & Philcox, 1990). Consequently, when the nerve impulse moves down the peripheral nerve to the neuromuscular junction, it can go no further. Acetylcholine cannot be released into the synaptic opening, and muscle movement is either weak or nonexistent.

Treatment of myasthenia has focused on either removing the offending antibody or increasing the level of acetylcholine in the synaptic cleft. The first approach has employed plasmapheresis and the surgical removal of the thymus gland. Plasmapheresis rapidly removes the circulating antibodies, in this case directed against the acetylcholine receptor. Plasmapheresis is used on an emergency basis in an individual with myasthenia who is having difficulty breathing because of weak respiratory muscles. Yet, unlike Guillain-Barré, which is a self-limited postinfectious disease, myasthenia gravis is a chronic illness. Thus, plasmapheresis is not a permanent solution. In many cases, the solution has been to perform a *thymectomy*, an operation in which the thymus is removed. This small gland, resting in the neck region, is home to the white blood cells that produce the offending anti-acetylcholine antibody. After the thymus has been removed, the antibody is no longer produced, and the myasthenia usually goes into remission within 3 years.

In less severe cases, a medication called *neostigmine* may sufficiently control the myasthenia to avoid surgery. This drug delays the breakdown of acetylcholine so that more of the chemical is available to aid in the transmission of the nerve impulse. Strength improves within minutes of taking this drug. Using this treatment approach, individuals with myasthenia can lead quite normal lives.

Diseases of the Muscle

Diseases of the muscle itself obviously affect movement. The best known of these disorders is muscular dystrophy. The most common form of this disease is *Duchenne muscular dystrophy*. Inherited as a sex-linked disorder (see Chapter 2), Duchenne affects males and has an incidence of about 2 in 10,000 (Buyse, 1990).

Parents are usually unaware of any problem until the child is around 3 years of age. Then the child's ambulation skills deteriorate; he develops a waddling gait and has difficulty climbing steps or getting up from a lying down position. Over a period of time, ranging from months to years, the child becomes weaker and less mobile, eventually requiring a wheelchair. Pain, especially in the legs, is common, and the calf muscles become overdeveloped but weak (Hyser & Mendell, 1988). The muscles closest to the torso are most affected, and the legs are more affected than the arms.

Approaches to therapy are directed at minimizing **contractures**, maximizing muscle strength, and compensating for weakness. The child should be encouraged to avoid the use of a wheelchair for as long as possible and to be involved in an active exercise program. Even when a wheelchair is necessary, the child should spend time daily in a standing brace to maintain bone strength. Adaptive skills also should be stressed. This may require the use of assistive devices to maintain independence. An orthopedic surgeon works with occupational and physical therapists to determine the need for bracing or surgery. The most common procedure is spinal fusion for scoliosis and release of contracted tendons at the elbows, heels, legs, and hips. These children often have learning problems.

Gradually, all the muscle groups become weak. Besides causing flaccid weakness in the voluntary muscles, this disease also damages the involuntary muscles of the heart and diaphragm, often leading to respiratory and heart failure. At this point, a decision of whether to prolong life by mechanical ventilation must be made (see Chapter 29). Unfortunately, children with muscular dystrophy usually do not live to adulthood.

Diagnosing muscular dystrophy depends on finding a markedly elevated level of **creatine kinase (CK)** in the blood. This enzyme is released by dying muscle cells. A muscle biopsy may show that the muscle fibers are in disarray and contain excessive fat and fibrous tissue (Figure 15.8).

Recently the gene for Duchenne was isolated and the deficient gene product identified as *dystrophin* (Hoffman, Fischbeck, Brown, et al., 1988). Dystrophin is a protein that surrounds and protects muscle fibers. In its absence the muscle degenerates. Unfortunately, no effective treatment for muscular dystrophy exists. However, the use of **steroids** may hold some promise (Mendell, Moxley, Griggs, et al., 1989). They appear to slow the progression of the disease and improve lung function and walking in some persons.

Another group of muscle diseases in childhood is called the *congenital myopathies*. As in muscular dystrophy, these disorders are marked by decreased muscle tone and strength. However, they are distinguished from muscular dystrophy by having normal levels of creatine kinase and a different pattern of abnormalities on muscle biopsy and electromyography, a test of electrical activity at the neuromuscular junction.

There are many types of these diseases and the causes of most remain unknown.

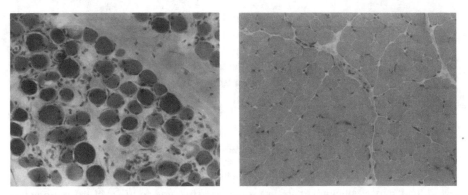

Figure 15.8. Example of a muscle biopsy from a child with Duchenne muscular dystrophy (left), and from a child who does not have the disorder (right). Note that the muscle biopsy from the child with muscular dystrophy has decreased numbers of muscle fibers and increased fat and fibrous tissue compared to the normal biopsy. (Photos courtesy of John Sladky, M.D., The Children's Hospital of Philadelphia.) (From Batshaw, M.L. [1991]. *Your child has a disability: A complete sourcebook of daily and medical care*. Boston: Little, Brown; reprinted by permission.)

However, a fair amount is known about one group of disorders called the *mitochondrial myopathies*. They are named after an organelle within the cell called the mitochondria. The mitochondria may have been an independent organism in ancient times (Thomas, 1972). At some point in the distant past, it appears to have invaded the human body to become part of the genetic makeup and live symbiotically with human beings. Mitochondria are inherited maternally rather than equally from both parents and have their own DNA.

Mitochondria serve as power plants; they convert fatty acids in the diet to high-phosphate energy. This involves a complex series of enzymatic steps, and a deficiency in any of the enzymes in this pathway impairs energy production. Because muscles use enormous amounts of energy to contract, one result of a mitochondrial defect is muscle weakness (Pavlakis, Rowland, DeVivo, et al., 1988).

Children with mitochondrial disorders may have catastrophic illnesses beginning at birth and leading to death in the first month of life. Alternatively, they may have milder disorders that impair normal muscle function. At this point, little is known about therapy for these disorders.

MOVEMENT DISORDERS—TORSION DYSTONIA

In addition to the previously mentioned neuromuscular diseases, a number of other disorders affect movement. Their origins, however, are not in the musculoskeletal system, but in the brain. The most important of these is cerebral palsy, which is discussed at length in Chapter 24. Another example of a movement disorder is *torsion dystonia*.

Like muscular dystrophy, dystonia starts in childhood and is an inherited disease. Usually the first symptom is an inversion of one foot while walking. This unnatural position gradually becomes more pronounced and is accentuated by movement (Marsden & Quinn, 1990). Eventually, sustained muscle contractions cause twisting or other abnormal postures of the entire body.

The underlying problem in this disorder seems to involve the basal ganglia, although no structural abnormalities have been identified in this or any other brain region. It is likely that a neurochemical imbalance causes the unusual movements characteristic of dystonia.

Treatment has focused on restoring the neurochemical balance in the basal ganglia by using medications that affect various neurochemical levels in the brain. These drugs include L-dopa (Sinemet), trihexyphenidyl (Artane), and diazepam (Valium) (Burke, Fahn, & Marsden, 1986). Approximately half of the children treated with medication have some benefit, although significant improvement is rare.

SUMMARY

The musculoskeletal system both supports the physical structure and helps to carry out normal movement. Abnormalities of the bone lead to deformities such as club foot or short-limbed dwarfism, or diseases such as arthritis. Muscle diseases cause weakness and low tone, while peripheral nerve and anterior horn cell diseases result in paralysis. Because many of these diseases are difficult to treat, it is consoling to note that their incidence is rare.

REFERENCES

Bernard, A.A., O'Hara, J.N., Bazin, S., et al. (1987). An improved screening system for the early detection of congenital dislocation of the hip. *Journal of Pediatric Orthopedics, 7*, 277–282.

Bollerslev, J. (1987). Osteopetrosis: A genetic and epidemiologic study. *Clinical Genetics, 31*, 86–90.

Brooke, M.H. (1986). *A clinician's view of neuromuscular disease* (2nd ed.). Baltimore: Williams & Wilkins.

Burke, R.E., Fahn, S., & Marsden, C.D. (1986). Torsion dystonia: A double-blind, prospective trial of high-dosage trihexyphenidyl. *Neurology, 36*, 160–164.

Buyse, M.L. (Ed.). (1990). *Birth defects encyclopedia*. Dover, MA: Center for Birth Defects Information Services.

Epstein, M.A., & Sladky, J.T. (1990). The role of plasmapheresis in childhood Guillain-Barré syndrome. *Annals of Neurology, 28*, 65–69.

Evans, O.B. (1986). Guillain-Barré syndrome in children. *Pediatrics in Review, 8*, 69–74.

Fenichel, G.M. (1989). Myasthenia gravis. *Pediatric Annals, 18*, 432–438.

Fischer, A., Griscelli, C., Friedrick, W., et al. (1986). Bone-marrow transplantation for immunodeficiencies and osteopetrosis: European survey 1968–1985. *Lancet, 2*, 1080–1084.

French Cooperative Group on Plasma Exchange in Guillain-Barré Syndrome. (1987). Efficiency of plasma exchange in Guillain-Barré syndrome: Role of replacement fluids. *Annals of Neurology, 22*, 753–761.

Hoffman, E.P., Fischbeck, K.H., Brown, R.H., et al. (1988). Characterization of dystrophin in muscle-biopsy specimens from patients with Duchenne's or Becker's muscular dystrophy. *New England Journal of Medicine, 318*, 1363–1368.

Hyser, C.L., & Mendell, J.R. (1988). Recent advances in Duchenne and Becker muscular dystrophy. *Neurologic Clinics, 6*, 429–453.

Kimpen, J.L., & Ogra, P.L. (1990). Poliovirus vaccines. A continuing challenge. *Pediatric Clinics of North America, 37*, 627–649.

Linton, D.M., & Philcox, D. (1990). Myasthenia gravis. *Disease a Month, 36*, 593–637.

Marini, J.C. (1988). Osteogenesis imperfecta: Comprehensive management. *Advances in Pediatrics, 35*, 391–426.

Marsden, C.D., & Quinn, N.P. (1990). The dystonias. *British Medical Journal, 300*, 139–144.

McKhann, G.M. (1990). Guillain-Barré syndrome: Clinical and therapeutic observations. *Annals of Neurology, 27*(Suppl), S13–S16.

Mendell, J.R., Moxley, R.T., Griggs, R.C., et al. (1989). Randomized, double-blind six-month trial of prednisone in Duchenne's muscular dystrophy. *New England Journal of Medicine, 320*, 1592–1597.

Morrissy, R.T. (1990). *Lovell and Winter's pediatric orthopaedics* (3rd ed.). Philadelphia: J.B. Lippincott.

Pavlakis, S.G., Rowland, L.P., DeVivo, D.C., et al. (1988). Mitochondrial myopathies and encephalomyopathies. In F. Plum (Ed.), *Advances in contemporary neurology* (pp. 95–123). New York: F.A. Davis.

Sillence, D.O. (1988). Osteogenesis imperfecta: Nosology and genetics. *Annals of the New York Academy of Science, 543*, 1–15.

Tachdjian, M.O. (1990). *Pediatric orthopedics* (2nd ed.). Philadelphia: W.B. Saunders.

Thomas, L. (1972). Organelles as organisms. *New England Journal of Medicine, 287*, 294–295.

Wessel, H.B. (1989). Spinal muscular atrophy. *Pediatric Annals, 18*, 421–427.

Chapter 16

Normal and Abnormal Development
Mental Retardation

with Bruce K. Shapiro

Upon completion of this chapter, the reader will:
— know the developmental milestones children attain
— be acquainted with Piaget's theory of intellectual development
— understand the definition and implications of the term *mental retardation*
— be aware of the various causes of mental retardation, focusing especially on Down syndrome and fragile X syndrome
— know the advantages and disadvantages of the principal intelligence tests used with children
— recognize the various approaches to intervention in mental retardation
— be aware of the different levels of functioning and independence individuals with mental retardation can achieve

---

At birth, a newborn responds in an involuntary, or reflexive, way to the environment. Over the next 2 years, a combination of brain growth and learning experiences enables the child to move from complete dependence on parents to active participation in the world. This development occurs in a sequential, step-by-step fashion. Yet, some of the steps are steeper than others, and some children cannot manage all of them. This chapter discusses the principles of normal development and developmental delay. It also identifies different causes of mental retardation, focusing on Down syndrome and fragile X syndrome, and reviews some of the approaches to intervention in mental retardation.

Bruce K. Shapiro, M.D., is Director of the Center for Learning and Its Disorders at The Kennedy Krieger Institute and is Associate Professor of Pediatrics at The Johns Hopkins University School of Medicine in Baltimore.

THE DEVELOPMENTAL SEQUENCE

The sequence of development has a number of characteristics. First, development is an ongoing process that begins with embryogenesis and continues throughout a person's life. Second, this process is closely linked to the maturation of the central nervous system. Consequently, the most rapid intellectual development takes place when the brain is growing rapidly, during the first few years of life (Illingworth, 1987). Third, development progresses from head to foot, or in a cephalocaudal fashion. A child first gains head control, then sits, then crawls, and finally walks. Fourth, development follows a fixed sequence. Children usually roll before sitting, sit before crawling, and crawl before walking. This fourth characteristic of development permits the assessment of children by comparing rates of attaining developmental milestones to norms and thereby provides a means of early identification of developmental delay.

When discussing development, four major types of skills are usually considered: *gross motor*, *fine motor*, *language*, and *social-adaptive*. Language, the best predictor of future intellectual functioning, consists of expressive and receptive skills. **Receptive language** involves understanding what is said, while expressive language entails communicating with others—usually by talking (see Chapter 19).

The case of Michael, the child born of a normal pregnancy, as discussed in Chapter 6, is used here to illustrate the sequence of developmental milestones children pass as they grow from birth to 2 years of age (Table 16.1).

Gross Motor Development

As is generally true of children, Michael's activity during the first 3 months of life reflected the influence of primitive reflexes. During early infancy, when Michael's mother, Jessica, stroked the side of his lips, he rooted, or turned toward her. When she placed her breast at his lips, he began to suck vigorously. If Michael turned his head to the right, his right arm and leg shot out involuntarily while his left arm and leg flexed. Michael usually held his hands in a clenched position and, when pried open, his fingers automatically grasped Jessica's fingers.

Yet, fairly quickly, he began to gain some control over his movements. For example, when pulled to a sitting position, he managed to hold his head upright for a few seconds before it fell to rest on his chest. Also, when placed face down, Michael turned his head to one side or the other as if to breathe more comfortably.

As Michael grew, his actions became more purposeful. This development corresponded with the rapid growth and **myelination**, or sheathing, of the nerve tracts in the central nervous system. This myelination allowed more rapid communication between the brain and the body and initiation of more complex movements. Thus, Michael was able to roll over from stomach to back at 5 months of age. To perform this action, his brain had to suppress certain primitive reflexes (Capute, Palmer, Shapiro, et al., 1984). If Michael had brain damage, the primitive reflexes would have persisted and interfered with rolling. Such persistence is a clue to the presence of cerebral palsy (see Chapter 24).

Continuing to develop on schedule, Michael next progressed to sitting up without support at 7 months of age. To accomplish this, he had to pass through a series of

Table 16.1. Development in the first 2 years of life (approximate ages of skill attainment)

Month	Gross motor	Fine motor	Social-adaptive	Language
1	Partial head control Primitive reflexes predominate	Clenched fists	Fixates objects and follows 90°	Alerts to sound Makes small sounds
2	Good head control Lifts chin in prone		Follows 180° Smiles responsively	
3	Lifts chest off bed Primitive reflexes less prominent	Hands held open Reaches toward objects Pulls at clothing	Follows 360° Recognizes mother	Coos
4	Swimming movements	Hands come to midline	Shakes rattle Anticipates food Belly laughs	Laughs aloud Produces different sounds for different needs
5	Rolls over stomach to back Holds head erect		Frolics when played with	Orients toward sound Gives a "raspberry"
6	Anterior propping response	Transfers objects Holds bottle Palmar grasp	Looks after lost toy Mirror play	Babbles Recognizes friendly and angry voices
7	Bounces when standing Sits without support	Feeds self cookie	Drinks from cup	Imitates noise Responds to name
8	Lateral propping responses	Rings bell Radial raking grasp	Separation anxiety begins Tries to gain attention	Uses nonspecific "Mama" Understands "no"
9	Crawls	Mouths objects		Recognizes familiar words

(continued)

Table 16.1. *(continued)*

Month	Gross motor	Fine motor	Social-adaptive	Language
10	Stands with support	Plays with bell Claps	Waves "bye-bye" Plays pat-a-cake	Says specific "Da-da, Ma-ma"
11	Cruises around objects	Uses pincer grasp		Follows gesture command
12	Makes first steps	Throws objects Puts objects in containers	Aids in dressing Turns papers Takes turns	Says 2–3 specific words
15	Climbs up stairs	Marks with pencil	Indicates when wet Spoon-feeds Builds tower with blocks Gives kisses Imitates chores	Speaks low jargon Follows 1-step commands Speaks 4–6 words Identifies 1 body part
18	Runs stiffly Handedness is determined	Constructive play with toys Scribbles Imitates lines Places objects in formboard	Places formboard Turns pages Parallel play Takes off shoes Does puzzles	Speaks high jargon Follows 2-step commands Points to 1 picture in book Uses 10 words
24	Walks up and down steps, both feet on each step	Imitates vertical lines	Puts on and takes off shoes Plays alongside other children Is negativistic Uses fork Indicates toileting needs	Uses "I" Identifies 4 body parts Can form 3-word sentences Says "yes" and "no"

developmental steps. Initially, Michael had been unable to sit because he could not maintain his balance. A primitive reflex, called the *tonic labyrinthine response*, interfered by making Michael retract his shoulders and extend his arms whenever he lifted his head. He would then fall over. At 5 months of age, this reflex had been suppressed, and Michael could sit with support. The next step was to develop propping responses in which his hands would reach out to help him balance himself whenever he began to topple over as he sat. Once this was perfected, he could sit with confidence.

Not satisfied with his sedentary existence, Michael next began the evolution to walking. At 7 months, he could stand when held, bearing weight on his feet. Then, at 9 months, he began to crawl, alternating both feet. He was able to pull himself up to a standing position at 10 months and started to walk around objects, or cruise, at 11 months. At last, at 13 months, Michael took his first independent steps. Five months later, he was running and, by 2 years of age, he could jump and walk up steps (Caplan, 1978).

Fine Motor Development

Michael's fine motor development paralleled his gross motor development. During his first 2–3 months, he could do very little with his hands because they were usually in a clenched position. Once they opened at 3 months, Michael started to reach toward his colorful mobile and pull at his clothing. In the fourth month, he would clasp his hands together and then put them in his mouth, often chortling when he did this.

By 6 months of age, Michael could transfer objects from one hand to the other (Shapiro, 1991). At this age, he was slightly more independent; he could feed himself a cookie and hold a bottle. Over the next few months, he started to explore his environment actively, reaching out to anything in sight and examining it. For example, if placed near a bell, Michael would grab it and ring it until one of his parents successfully substituted a quieter instrument. When he could crawl, at 9 months, he explored all the nooks and crannies of his house. At 11 months, his pincer grasp (i.e., using his thumb and forefinger) was refined and enabled him to pick up small objects. These objects usually ended up in his mouth, whether they were edible or not. When he reached 18 months of age, he could scribble with a pencil, creating many abstract works of art.

Communication Skills

Almost from birth, Michael began to explore the world with his eyes. If Jessica were lucky, she could hold his attention for a few seconds. He responded to loud noises by stopping his movement for an instant and then returned to his seemingly random movements. When Michael was 2 months old, he rewarded his father's attention with a smile.

As a newborn, Michael communicated his needs mainly by crying. As time went on, he quickly developed more complex communication skills. He cooed in the third month and gave a "raspberry" in the fourth. A month later, Michael started to turn his head toward a conversation as if to take part in it. In the sixth month, he started making babbling sounds. Four weeks later, he tried to imitate the sounds his parents made and responded to his name with a smile and a turn of the head. By the time Michael was 8 months old, he understood the command "no," although understanding it did not ensure his following it for very long. He began saying "mama" to everything and everyone in sight. At 11 months, Michael spoke a few specific words (ma, bye) and could follow a simple command if it were accompanied by a gesture.

Unlike the development of motor skills that were simply refined during the second year of life, Michael's language skills exploded between 12 and 24 months. At 15 months, he had a 5- to 10-word vocabulary and used jargon or double-talked all the time. He also closed the door or sat down when commanded without a gesture as a guide. When he was 18 months old, Michael could point to different parts of his body when asked to name them. He spoke unintelligible monologues, interspersing real words with jargon. By 2 years of age, he could name some pictures in a book, follow 2-step commands such as "take the bell and put it on the table." and referred to himself as "I." Soon, he began to put together 3-word phrases such as "I am hungry" or "I go outside." He was well on his way to having good communication skills.

Social-Adaptive Skills

Besides gaining motor and communication skills, Michael developed the ability to relate to the important people in his life and to differentiate some of their emotional responses. By the time he was 2 months old, Michael started to distinguish Jessica from other people, giving her his best smiles. During his fourth month, he began to laugh heartily. By 6 months he would reach for his bottle when it was brought into sight.

Michael's social interactions also became more sophisticated. Before he was a year old, he could play "peek-a-boo" and "pat-a-cake," wave "bye-bye," and throw a ball. During the second year, Michael started to help push his arms through a shirt and take off most of his clothes. He also began to play alongside other children, not yet wanting to share with them (Illingworth, 1987). When he was separated from his parents, he became upset. By age 2, he became quite independent, feeding himself with a spoon and fork. Like his communication skills, his social skills had become much more refined.

PIAGET'S THEORY OF INTELLECTUAL DEVELOPMENT

The example of Michael illustrates that development involves a series of steps that build to eventually enable a person to reason and solve problems. It is the inability to complete all of the steps that defines mental retardation. The problem in mental retardation is not so much that a child with mild retardation attains a mental age of only 10 years instead of, for example, 16 years, but that certain abilities to understand information are beyond the grasp of that individual. This lifelong limitation interferes with the person's ability to adapt to his or her world.

To explain normal and abnormal intellectual development, the Swiss educator

Jean Piaget divided the process into four stages: 1) *the sensorimotor period* that lasts from birth to approximately 18 months; 2) *the preoperational stage* that lasts from 2 to 7 years of age; 3) *the stage of concrete operations* that extends from ages 7 to 12 years; and 4) *the period of formal operations*, after 12 years of age (Gruber & Voneche, 1977). The progression through these stages is sequential with more abilities added at each stage. Although some theorists have objected to Piaget's classifications, such delineations provide a framework to help in understanding both the sequence of intellectual development and the limitations at the different levels of mental retardation.

The Sensorimotor Stage

During the sensorimotor stage, primitive forms of intelligence are evident. Even before a child is able to use language well, he or she exhibits some complex behavior. The child begins to coordinate activities to reach certain goals, such as pulling a string to reach a brightly colored ring attached to it. In addition, the child gradually becomes more interested in the world and less self-absorbed. In exploring the environment, the child, through experimentation, finds ways of acting and relating to achieve goals. For example, an 18-month-old child may want something out of reach. To do this, he or she finds a chair or stool and climbs on it to reach the desired object. The child is beginning to find solutions to concrete problems. However, the child still cannot generalize what is learned to new situations. Most "discoveries" are made through trial and error. A child with severe retardation usually does not progress beyond this stage.

The Preoperational Stage

The preoperational stage is characterized by the use of meaningful language. In the sensorimotor stage, the child deals with objects that are visible. With the use of language, beginning around 2 years of age, the child can use symbols to represent objects that are not present. For example, at this age, a child may pretend a mud pie is a chocolate bar and also may pretend to eat it. A child at age 3 can make up a story and may reconstruct the recent past and project into the very near future.

Even with the use of language and the ability to think in more abstract terms, the preoperational stage of development remains a relatively primitive type of intelligence. Although the child is beginning to be able to classify and group objects, he or she is not yet proficient at it. Also, while the child can distinguish between certain quantities—for example, big versus little—he or she is not yet able to perform the operation of conservation. A child of 4, for example, believes that when water is poured from a tall, thin glass into a wide-mouthed, shorter glass, there is less water. He or she is taken in by the appearance of more water. The ability to understand that quantity cannot be judged by appearance alone is refined during the stage of concrete operations. A child with moderate retardation rarely progresses beyond this second stage.

The Stage of Concrete Operations

During the stage of concrete operations, a child becomes better able to order and classify objects and to see relationships between different items. For example, a 9-year-old can speak of one object as being wider than another and shorter than something else. A child at this point also can arrange objects according to size or weight and can divide something into its parts. Children in this stage of development are able to solve some mathematical problems and to read well. They also are able to generalize learning to new situations and to begin to appreciate another person's point of view. However, these children still have difficulty dealing with hypothetical problems. In addition, although children in this stage are better able to understand the concept of past and future, this understanding is somewhat limited. Individuals with mild retardation usually remain at this level of development.

The Stage of Formal Operations

Piaget's final stage of intellectual development proceeds from age 12 throughout one's life. During the stage of formal operations, individuals are able to project themselves into the future and to think about long-term goals. They also develop a sensitivity to the feelings of others and become, at the same time, increasingly self-conscious. A notable characteristic is the development of an ability to reason using hypotheses. A classic example is Cyril Burt's test (Burt, 1959): If Edith is fairer than Susan and darker than Lilly, who is the darkest of all three? To solve this problem, a child must be able to form a system that includes all possible combinations of each element. As another example, a child may be asked to determine how many combinations can be formed with three colors. Once again, the child must be able to figure out all the possible combinations of the three colors to arrive at an answer. This ability is developed during the stage of formal operations. The use of higher mathematics is also possible. In other words, development of formal thought involves an ability to isolate a problem, to review it systematically, and to figure out all possible solutions to that problem.

Thus, Piaget's perspective on intellectual development involves the addition of more complex and abstract abilities with each stage. The child progresses from one stage to another. A person who is unable to progress through all the stages is limited in his or her ability to adapt as an adult. Such a person would have mental retardation.

MENTAL RETARDATION

To be classified as having mental retardation, a person must: 1) have significantly subaverage intellectual functioning; 2) have mental retardation as a result of an injury, disease, or abnormality that existed before age 18; and 3) be impaired in his or her ability to adapt to the environment (Grossman, 1983). In May of 1992, the American Association on Mental Retardation (AAMR) voted to expand this definition, particularly in its focus on assessing adaptive skills and implementing a multidimensional matrix of support (Luckasson, in press).

The first part of the definition involves a statistical interpretation of normal intellectual functioning. Consider the average, or mean, intellectual functioning in a population to be the apex of a bell-shaped curve. Two standard deviations on either side of the mean encompass 95% of a population sample and approximately define the range of normal (Figure 16.1). Since the average intelligence quotient, or IQ score, is 100, and the standard deviation of most IQ tests is 15 points, a person scoring two standard deviations below the mean would be considered to have mental retardation (American Psychiatric Association, 1980) if he or she also meets the other criteria of mental retardation. (The 1992 AAMR definition allows a range of 70–75 rather than an exact cut-off.) Figure 16.1 also has a second, small curve within the range of severe mental retardation, marking a subgroup. This subgroup is the population that has mental retardation because of organic causes—for example, birth injuries, genetic diseases, trauma, and infections. The existence of this subgroup means that the incidence of severe mental retardation is higher than is predicted by the normal distribution curve.

The second part of the definition, concerning age of onset, is illustrated by the following example: If a 3-year-old boy were in a car accident resulting in severe brain damage, he would be considered to have mental retardation because the injury occurred during his developmental years. However, if his father sustained the same injury in this accident, he would have organic brain damage, not mental retardation, since he was no longer in his developmental years.

Finally, individuals with mental retardation not only have limitations in their

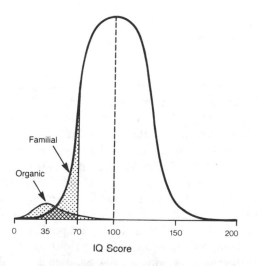

Figure 16.1. Bimodal distribution of intelligence. The mean IQ is 100. An IQ score of less than 70, or two standard deviations below the mean, can indicate mental retardation. The second, smaller curve takes into account those individuals who have mental retardation because of birth trauma, infection, inborn errors, or other "organic" causes. This explains why more individuals have severe mental retardation than are predicted by the "familial" curve alone. (From Zigler, E. [1967, January]. Familial retardation: A continuing dilemma. *Science, 155*, 292–298, Figure 1; reprinted by permission. Copyright © 1967 by the American Association for the Advancement of Science.)

intellectual abilities but also are impaired in their ability to adapt or function in society. This impairment may range from mild to severe.

According to statistical definitions, approximately 2.5% of the population has mental retardation, and another 2.5% has superior intelligence (see Figure 16.1). In the United States, this means that roughly 6 million people have mental retardation and more than 85% of people with mental retardation have IQ scores between two and three standard deviations below the mean. According to the historical definitions (Grossman, 1983), each lower stage of mental retardation refers to an additional 15 points, or one standard deviation, below the mean, and these levels are categorized as mild, moderate, severe, and profound. The 1992 AAMR definition de-emphasizes classification in favor of a focus on level of support needed, and therefore suggests using only mild and severe categories.

In fact, the actual incidence of mental retardation may be somewhat lower than the statistical predictions. Recent studies (McLaren & Bryson, 1987) suggest a much lower rate of mild mental retardation and consequently a lower overall rate of mental retardation, somewhere between 0.8% and 1.2% rather than the predicted 2.5%. This difference between expectation and empirically derived data is probably due to differences in ascertainment. For example, individuals from poor socioeconomic environments and those with English as a second language tend to have IQs skewed toward mild mental retardation.

Psychological Testing

IQ scores are derived from psychological tests that are standardized for various age groups. The most commonly used tests for children are the Bayley Scales of Infant Development, the Stanford-Binet Intelligence Scale, and the Wechsler Intelligence Scales for Children (Goldman, Stein, & Guerry, 1983; Weaver, 1984; Wodrich & Kush, 1990).

The McCarthy Scales and the Bayley Scales are used to assess fine motor, gross motor, language skills, and visual problem-solving skills of children between 2 months and 2½ years of age. The McCarthy Scales offer a "general cognitive index" that is roughly equivalent to an IQ score and is derived from a variety of language and nonlanguage thinking tasks (Wodrich & Kush, 1990). It also assesses memory and motor tasks. In the Bayley Scales, a mental development index (MDI) (similar to an IQ) and a psychomotor development index (PDI) (a measure of motor competence) are derived from the results. However, one must be cautious about placing too much emphasis on this test's results because it is primarily dependent on nonlanguage items (Bayley, 1958). Language items best predict future IQ. The Bayley scales permit the differentiation of infants with severe retardation from infants who are normal; it is less helpful in drawing the line between a typical child and a child with mild retardation or between an average and an above average child (Shapiro et al., 1989).

The Stanford-Binet Intelligence Scale is used to test children older than 2 years of age. In the past, it was criticized because it yielded a single mental age rather than providing a profile of strengths and weaknesses. The 1986 edition remedies these drawbacks by using 15 tests to assess four areas of intelligence: verbal abilities, abstract/visual thinking, quantitative reasoning, and short-term memory. This permits the evaluator to determine, using some caution, areas of relative strength and weakness.

Because of the criticisms of the earlier editions of the Stanford-Binet test, the Wechsler scales have been the preferred psychological tests for children over 4½ years of age. The Wechsler Preschool and Primary Scale of Intelligence (WPPSI) was revised in 1989 and is used for children with mental ages of 3–7 years; the Wechsler Intelligence Scale for Children (WISC–III, revised in 1991) is used for children who function above a 6-year level. Both scales contain a number of subtests in the areas of verbal and performance skills, allowing the examiner to determine a series of IQs in different areas, thereby obtaining a more accurate picture of a child's strengths and weaknesses. Although children with mental retardation usually score below normal on all subscale scores, they occasionally score in the normal range in one or more performance areas.

In addition to the various IQ tests, tests that assess social-adaptive abilities are available. Two commonly used tests are the Vineland Social Maturity Scale and the American Association on Mental Deficiency Adaptive Behavior Scale (ABS) (Wodrich & Kush, 1990). The Vineland Scale is older and is used more frequently. It tests self-help skills (e.g., eating, dressing), interaction and cooperation with others, judgment, and self-control. The ABS has two parts, one similar in content to the Vineland and the other concerned with emotional adjustment.

Identifying a Child with a Developmental Delay

The most common presentation of mental retardation is the failure to achieve age appropriate developmental skills (Meisels, 1989; Shapiro, Palmer, & Capute, 1987). In the first months of life, abnormal development is indicated by an inadequate sucking response, floppy or spastic muscle tone, and/or a lack of visual or auditory response. Later in the first year, motor delays in sitting and walking may suggest a developmental delay. By the second and third years, language and behavioral abnormalities suggest possible problems.

To illustrate, consider the story of David, Maria's child who is discussed in Chapter 6. David was born by cesarean section as a result of an abruptio placenta, a complication that led to brain damage. Maria noticed many of the signs in David's development that were indicative of developmental delay. (In the following paragraphs, the normal ages for these developmental milestones are indicated in parentheses after the age at which David achieved them.)

Maria noticed that David, as a tiny infant, showed little interest in his environment and was not very alert. He would sit in an infant seat for hours without complaint. Although Maria tried to breast-feed him, his suck was weak, and he frequently regurgitated his formula. He was floppy, and he had poor head control. His cry was high-pitched, and he was difficult to comfort. In gross motor development, David could hold his head up at 4 months (1 month), roll over at 8 months (5 months), and sit up at 14 months (7 months). He pulled himself to a standing position at 20 months (10 months).

In social and fine motor development, David also lagged behind the norm. He smiled at 5 months (2 months) and, generally, was not very responsive to his parents' attention. He transferred objects at 15 months (6 months). He did not start babbling until 13 months (6 months) and said "mama" at 24 months (10 months).

David's parents, concerned about their child's progress, consulted their pediatrician who suspected David had mental retardation as early as 6 months of age. When given a Bayley scale at 24 months, David's mental age was found to be 10 months, and he received an MDI (Mental Developmental Index) of 40. He began attending an early intervention program shortly after the testing.

When David was 6 years old, he was retested on the Stanford-Binet Intelligence Scale and achieved a mental age of 2 years 8 months, IQ of 40.

David's case illustrates a number of points. First, David was a high-risk newborn who was followed closely for signs of developmental delay. Second, David's development did not follow a typical pattern, making the diagnosis of mental retardation more likely. Third, David's development in motor, language, and social-adaptive skills all progressed at about half the normal rate throughout infancy and into childhood. Because of this, David fell farther and farther behind his peers and was identified as functioning at a subaverage level (Palfrey, Singer, Walker, et al., 1987).

Causes of Mental Retardation

David's case illustrates that cases of severe mental retardation are likely to have identifiable causes; in David's case a perinatal complication. In children with mental retardation, the chance of discovering the origins of the condition is about 50%. The odds of discovering the causes of mild mental retardation are significantly lower even though these children account for almost 90% of all cases of mental retardation. In these children, there is often a familial pattern, and an overrepresentation in the lower socioeconomic classes. However, only about 10% of these children carry specific causal diagnoses (Illingworth, 1987).

Given this information, it seems wiser to seek the origins of mental retardation in children with severe mental retardation and not to search as hard for the causes of the mild cases. Yet, even for children with severe mental retardation, one could argue that most of the identifiable disorders are not amenable to specific intervention. Therefore, many ask why scarce resources should be spent looking for a cause that cannot be cured? A search for the causes of mental retardation can be justified for several reasons. First, an identifiable cause may permit more complete prognostic information. Second, some of the underlying disorders are inherited and therefore carry an increased risk of recurrence; if the cause is known, prenatal diagnosis may be possible (see Chapter 3). Third, parents want to know why their child has mental retardation (see Chapter 29). Finally, approaches to intervention vary according to the origins of the disorders.

Actually, no single method for detecting all causes of mental retardation exists. Instead, evaluations must be tailored to the history and physical findings of each child. For example, those children with unusual appearances may be evaluated for chromosomal syndromes (see Chapter 1). Those with positive family histories and loss of milestones may have an inborn error of metabolism, and amino acid or enzyme studies should be performed (see Chapter 10). Children with abnormal head size (too big or too small) may be evaluated for gross brain abnormalities by CT or MRI scan; and those with seizures should undergo EEGs.

The list of tests that can be performed to rule out disorders associated with mental retardation is almost endless. Unfortunately, most of these tests are expensive and provide little information; even CT and MRI scans, which provide substantial information about brain structure, tell little about brain function. However, occasionally a "fishing expedition" is fruitful. These tests should not be summarily dismissed if the child's history is suggestive of a particular diagnosis.

As noted previously, diagnostic searches are more likely to bear fruit in children with severe mental retardation. The most common causes are listed in Table 16.2 (Moser, 1985). Ten percent of the known causes of severe mental retardation is attributable to intrauterine influences such as congenital infections, fetal alcohol syndrome (see Chapter 8), and other teratogens (see Chapter 4). Another 10% is associated with perinatal complications, such as intracranial hemorrhage or anoxia (see Chapter 5). Six percent are the result of postnatal trauma, most commonly traumatic brain injury from falls or motor vehicle accidents (see Chapter 27). Environmental toxins, such as lead, account for 3% of cases, while postnatal infections, including meningitis and encephalitis, result in another 6% (see Chapter 6).

While these problems are theoretically preventable, the majority of identifiable causes of severe mental retardation (65%) are attributable to congenital anomalies and genetic disorders. Congenital anomalies, including brain malformations, such as hydrocephalus and microcephaly, account for 20% of cases (see Chapter 14). The largest group (45%) consists of genetic causes, approximately 15% of which are caused by Down syndrome, and 10% of which are attributable to fragile X syndrome. As a result of their prevalence, these two disorders are discussed in some detail.

Table 16.2. Known causes of severe mental retardation

Cause		Percent of people affected
Intrauterine influences		10
Perinatal trauma		10
Postnatal trauma		6
Environmental toxins		3
Infections		6
Congenital anomalies		20
Genetic causes		45
Down syndrome	15	
Fragile X syndrome	10	
Other	20	

Source: Moser (1985).

Down Syndrome   Down syndrome (DS), or trisomy 21, (i.e., having three rather than two copies of chromosome #21) was one of the first conditions to be associated with mental retardation. Although the chromosomal abnormality was not identified until 1959, initial descriptions of the syndrome appeared in the mid 19th century. These descriptions were based on a rather characteristic appearance, consisting of hypotonia, short stature, a foreshortened skull with occipital flattening, small underdeveloped ears, obliquely placed eyes, underdeveloped iris, excessive skin about the neck, abnormal finger prints, widely spaced nipples, and cardiac, gastrointestinal, and skeletal malformations (Figure 16.2).

The incidence of Down syndrome is about 1 in 700 live births. Even in the years before the chromosomal abnormality was identified, the association between Down syndrome and advanced maternal age was known. The risk of a 35- to 39-year-old woman having a child with Down syndrome is approximately 6.5 times that of a 20- to 24-year-old. This figure climbs to 20.5 times for mothers between 40 and 44 years of age (see Figure 3.1). The age effect relates to the mechanism of formation of trisomy 21. Nondisjunction (i.e., unequal division) accounts for 95% of all cases and most commonly occurs during the first meiotic division. This phenomenon is far more likely to occur in older parents (see Chapter 1). The defect originates in the egg 85% of the time, and in the sperm 15% of the time (Dagna-Bricarelli, Pierluigi, Grasso, et al., 1990).

Much has been learned in the past decade about the embryology and neuropathology of Down syndrome. There appears to be a "critical region" on chromosome #21 that, if present, produces Down syndrome, and if absent, even in the presence of the rest of chromosome #21, does not. Thus, the genes coding for Down syndrome seem to reside in this lower region of chromosome #21 (Korenberg, Kawashima, &

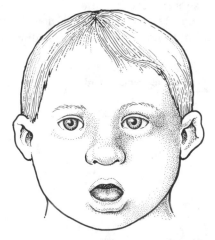

Figure 16.2.   The physical features of a child with Down syndrome include a small head with flattening of the back and face. The nose is recessed, and there is an upward slant to the eyes with epicanthal folds at the inner corners. The ears and mouth are small, as are the hands and feet. The fingers are short and stubby, with incurving of the fifth digit. There is often a simian crease on the palm. The neck is broad and the skin may appear mottled.

Pulst, 1990). It is likely that genes in this region lead to malformations as a consequence of incomplete embryogenesis rather than deviant development. For example, the heart is basically normally formed, but the wall separating the two sides of the heart may not close completely, resulting in an *endocardial cushion defect*. Similarly, the separation of the trachea and esophagus may be incomplete, so there exists a tracheo-esophageal fistula or connection. This leads to aspiration of food into the lungs and must be corrected surgically.

In terms of neuropathology, examination of brain tissue of individuals with Down syndrome reveals an immaturity of neurons and their synaptic connections. Similar abnormalities are evident in an animal model of Down syndrome, the trisomy 16 mouse (Sweeny, Hohmann, Oster-Granite, & Coyle, 1989). Chromosome #16 in the mouse contains many of the same genes found in chromosome #21 in human beings. Lastly, a gene for amyloid, an abnormal protein found in the brain of individuals with Alzheimer disease, is located on chromosome #21 (Rumble, Retallack, Hilbich, et al., 1989). This may relate to the increased risk of Alzheimer disease in adults with Down syndrome (Fishman, 1986). As more is learned about the contents of chromosome #21, it is likely that the origins of the clinical manifestations of Down syndrome also will be better understood.

Because there is no known cure for Down syndrome, efforts have focused on decreasing its incidence. Prenatal diagnosis of Down syndrome can be accomplished by detecting a third #21 chromosome in fetal tissue obtained by amniocentesis or chorionic villus sampling (see Chapter 3). This is offered to all women over 35 years of age. Yet, although Down syndrome is far more likely to occur in these women, they comprise such a small fraction of all pregnant women that the majority of children with Down syndrome are born to mothers under age 30. Because these women do not undergo prenatal diagnosis routinely, other methods have been evaluated to screen for Down syndrome. It has been found that the level of alpha-fetoprotein in maternal blood, measured during the second trimester of pregnancy to screen for spina bifida, is also useful in screening for Down syndrome. While high levels of alpha-fetoprotein suggest spina bifida, low levels suggest Down syndrome (DiMaio, Baumgarten, Greenstein, et al., 1987) (see Figure 3.6). Of fetuses with Down syndrome, 20%– 30% can be identified in this manner with confirmation being made by amniocentesis (Ashwood, Cheng, & Luthy, 1987). Ultrasound also has been suggested as a means of identifying fetuses with Down syndrome by noting excessive skin fold thickness in the neck region. (Benacerraf, Gelman, & Frigoletto, 1987).

If not detected prenatally, the clinical diagnosis of Down syndrome should be evident at birth because these infants have a distinctive appearance (Pueschel, 1990). Their heads are small and flattened at the back. Also, the face is flattened with a recessed bridge of the nose, and the eyes slant upward giving the children an oriental appearance. The ears and mouth are small, and the tongue is large. There is often a skin fold at the inner corner of the eye, and the irises may have flecks of light color in the periphery. The children's hands and feet are short, and the fingers are stubby with incurving of the fifth digit. In over half of these children, there are a single creases across the palms and soles of the feet. The neck is broad and stocky, and there are loose skin folds at the nape. The chest may be funnel-shaped or pigeon-breasted. The skin appears fair and mottled.

Despite the presence of these distinctive physical features, a diagnosis of Down syndrome should be confirmed by chromosome analysis. This is important because about 5% of these children have either a mosaic picture, in which not all cells are affected and the mental retardation is less severe, or a translocation, which increases the risk of recurrence in future siblings (see Chapter 1).

The hallmark of the early development of the child with Down syndrome is motor delay. The infant has markedly decreased muscle tone and appears floppy. Associated feeding problems may result in the infant failing to thrive. Gross motor skills are delayed with the average child not sitting until 1 year of age or walking until 2 years. Not all children with Down syndrome experience difficulty in these areas, and those who have severe hypotonia improve over time so that significant physical disabilities are rarely evident by school age.

In the first 2 years of life, the child with Down syndrome looks better cognitively than he or she will appear later in life (Cicchette & Beeghly, 1990). This has been attributed to their happy personalities, responsiveness, and attentiveness to their parents. However, significant language delays become evident by 1 year of age; their first word is often delayed until 24 months. Children with Down syndrome usually learn to talk by 4–5 years, although they may have unusual speech patterns with articulation errors. Formal psychological testing at school age usually reveals an IQ in the 40–60 range.

In addition to cognitive deficits, children with Down syndrome are at increased risk for a number of medical problems that are more extensive than in other children with moderate mental retardation. These problems can affect virtually every body organ and may appear at any time from birth to adulthood (Table 16.3). Thus, children with Down syndrome need periodic medical checkups.

In the newborn period, the most common medical concerns are congenital heart disease and gastrointestinal blockage. Forty percent of children with Down syndrome have congenital heart defects, commonly an endocardial cushion defect or A-V canal (i.e., a connection between the atria and ventricles). Other heart lesions include ventricular septal defects and **tetralogy of Fallot**. These defects can lead to heart failure and usually require open heart surgery.

Congenital gastrointestinal malformations lead to blockage in 12% of cases. Clinical symptoms include vomiting, poor feeding, and **aspiration pneumonia**. The anatomical defects may involve persistence of an embryonical connection between the trachea and esophagus (tracheoesophageal fistula), blockage of the stomach outlet (pyloric stenosis) or small intestine (duodenal atresia), or an **imperforate** anus. These malformations can be successfully corrected surgically.

In early childhood a number of new problems may develop affecting the eyes, ears, and teeth (Rogers & Roizen, 1991). Virtually all children with Down syndrome have some vision problem, including refractive errors (70%), strabismus (50%), nystagmus (35%), and cataracts (3%). Hearing problems result from narrow ear canals and a subtle immune deficiency, which predisposes these children to recurrent

Table 16.3. Characteristics of Down syndrome

Finding	Percent of people affected
Mental retardation	100
Congenital heart disease	40
Gastrointestinal tract defect	12
Hypodontia, malocclusion	60–100
Leukemia	1
Alopecia (hair loss)	10
Hypothyroidism	10–20
Joint laxity	15
Short stature	100
Obesity	50
Vision abnormalities	
Cataracts	3
Refractive errors	70
Strabismus	50
Nystagmus	35
Seizures	6
Hearing loss	60–80
Psychiatric disorders in adolescence	13
Alzheimer disease after 40 years	15–30

Source: Pueschel (1990).

middle ear infections. Of children with Down syndrome, 60%–90% have a mild-to-moderate conductive hearing loss resulting from chronic middle ear infections (see Chapter 18). These children also may have sleep apnea as a consequence of upper airway obstruction from enlarged tonsils and adenoids. Sleep studies can be performed to document this problem, and if antibiotic treatment is unsuccessful in shrinking the adenoids, they may need to be removed. Dental problems, most prominently malocclusion and periodontal disease, are consequences of delayed eruption and absence of some teeth. About 10% of children develop **alopecia,** or scalp hair loss. The origin of this is unclear, but the hair usually grows back in time. There is also about a 1% risk of the child with Down syndrome developing acute leukemia either in infancy or later in life (Kalwinsky, Raimondi, Bunin, et al., 1990).

In later childhood, additional medical problems may develop, the most common being obesity, short stature, hypothyroidism, seizures, joint dislocations, and depression. The most common of these are short stature and obesity. Over half of children with Down syndrome demonstrate excessive weight gain from overeating and inactivity (Pueschel, Tingey, Rynders, Crocker, & Crutcher, 1987). All children with Down syndrome are short, with the average male reaching a height of 5 feet and the average female 4.5 feet (Cronk, Crocker, Pueschel, et al., 1988). Studies have suggested that injections of the human growth hormone can significantly increase the height potential of children with Down syndrome (Torrado, Bastian, Wisniewski, et al., 1991). This is a controversial issue, as is the use of plastic surgery to alter the children's facial appearance.

About 10%–20% of children with Down syndrome develop hypothyroidism (Cutler, Benezra-Obeiter, & Brink, 1986). This may lead to excessive weight gain and make the child appear mentally slow. The diagnosis is made by measuring levels of the thyroid hormone (T_4) and the thyroid stimulating hormone (TSH). Treatment involves daily thyroid supplementation.

There is also an increased prevalence (6%) of nonfebrile seizures (Stafstrom, Patxot, Gilmore, et al., 1991). Most are generalized tonic-clonic in nature, but infantile spasms also have been reported. The seizures normally respond to antiepileptic drugs (see Chapter 26).

Another problem relates to joint laxity. In infancy, this presents as floppiness. In older children, it can lead to joint dislocations, most commonly at the hips or in the upper spine. Partial dislocation of the upper spine (atlanto-occipital or atlanto-axial subluxation) occurs in about 15% of children with Down syndrome but only becomes symptomatic in 1.5% (Pueschel & Scola, 1987) (Figure 16.3). However, because these dislocations can lead to spinal cord compression, they must be detected early. Symptoms of spinal cord compression include a head tilt, increasing clumsiness,

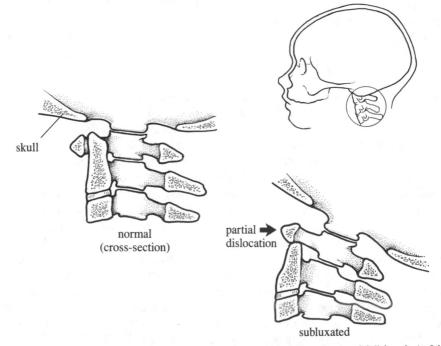

skull

normal
(cross-section)

partial ➤
dislocation

subluxated

Figure 16.3.   Children with Down syndrome are at risk to develop subluxation (partial dislocation) of the atlanto-axial or atlanto-occipital joint, shown in this illustration. A normal neck region is shown for comparison. This subluxation predisposes these children to spinal injury with trauma. This abnormality can be detected by X ray or MRI scan of the neck.

limping or refusing to walk, and weakness of an arm. Because symptoms primarily involve the motor system, the deterioration of function may be confused with degeneration. Because of this concern, an X ray of the neck is advisable before the child participates in contact sports or gymnastics. Surgical fusion of the upper vertebral column may be needed if the child becomes symptomatic.

A final problem is deterioration of cognitive or psychological functions, which may become evident first in adolescence with worsening of behavior or academic performance. Most of the known causes of this in adolescence are reversible. One possibility is unrecognized hypothyroidism. A second is depression, which occurs in approximately 13% of adolescents with Down syndrome. Depression may respond to supportive counseling and mood-elevating medications. In the fourth to fifth decade of life, deterioration is likely to be a sign of Alzheimer disease (Cork, 1990). It appears that virtually all individuals with Down syndrome over the age of 50 have pathological plaques and tangles in the brain, which are the hallmarks of Alzheimer disease. However, only 15%–25% of individuals with Down syndrome over the age of 40 demonstrate clinical signs of Alzheimer disease (i.e., loss of memory, impaired speech, decreased cognitive abilities) (Franceschi, Comola, Piattoni, et al., 1990).

Having focused on medical problems, it is important to emphasize that the majority of individuals with Down syndrome have long and fully functional lives. The congenital heart defects, if present, are usually successfully repaired. The hypotonia gets better over time, and persistent physical disabilities are rare. Hearing and vision problems are usually mild and can be corrected with eyeglasses and hearing aids, and hypothyroidism can be treated with the thyroid hormone. Obesity is a life-long problem, but it can be addressed by decreasing dietary intake and increasing activity.

Although these therapies are effective in improving the medical problems, many parents still consider nontraditional therapies, seeking a "cure." These have included the use of megavitamin and trace metal supplements, "cell therapy," and amino acids. Controlled studies have shown that there is no scientific evidence to support the use of these therapies (Bidder, Gray, Newcombe, et al., 1989; VanDyke, Lang, van Duyne, et al., 1990).

Currently, the most common life experience of the child with Down syndrome is to remain at home until young adulthood, when he or she enters a small group home (Pueschel, 1988). Education is usually received in a self-contained class for children with moderate mental retardation. Outcome for individuals who have grown up at home has been much better than for those who were institutionalized. Individuals with Down syndrome who grew up at home have markedly better adaptive abilities and an increased life span (Schroeder-Kurth, Schaffert, Koeckritz, et al., 1990). As adults, most individuals with Down syndrome can function in supported employment situations and are generally perceived as good workers (Tingey, 1987).

The life span for individuals with Down syndrome is somewhat shorter than normal. The presence of congenital heart disease has particular impact. Survival to 1 year of age is 76% for children with congenital heart disease as compared to 91% for those without heart defects. Survival to age 30 is 50% for children with heart defects versus 80% for those without heart defects (Baird & Sadovnick, 1987). The major causes of death, in addition to heart disease, are leukemia, severe infections, and Alzheimer disease. It is likely that life span will increase in the future with improved medical care.

Fragile X Syndrome It has been recognized for many years that severe mental retardation occur more frequently in males than females. It now seems likely that fragile X syndrome is responsible for much of this excess. The discovery of fragile X syndrome was accidental. Researchers at a genetics laboratory in Australia were performing chromosomal studies on residents in a mental retardation facility. They happened to be using a new media, which was low in folic acid, and found that a number of the residents, all men, had a previously unrecognized abnormality of the X chromosome. The bottom tip of the long arm of the X chromosome was pinched off, appearing fragile (Figure 16.4). Interestingly, only about half of the cells were affected. When the cells were grown in media with a folic acid supplement, the abnormality disappeared. Normally, folic acid supplements are used to grow cells for chromosome analyses, explaining why this abnormality had not been detected previously.

Once identified as a discrete entity, it soon became clear that men with fragile X syndrome tend to look remarkably alike. They have elongated faces, prominent jaws, and long ears (see Figure 16.4). Almost all have enlarged testicles and many have a prolapse of the mitral heart valve. The degree of mental retardation usually falls into the severe range, and many have aggressive behavior (Wisniewski, French, Fernando, et al., 1985). It also became clear that this disorder is inherited as a sex-linked trait, with many men with fragile X syndrome having family histories of the syndrome in male siblings or maternal uncles (see Chapter 2).

Since its discovery, the importance of fragile X syndrome has grown rapidly.

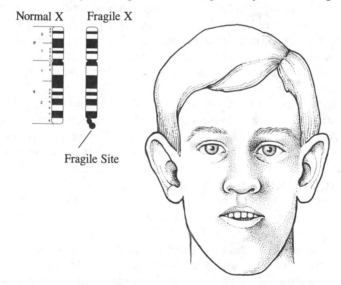

Figure 16.4.   An adolescent with fragile X syndrome has an unusual, elongated face, large ears, and a prominent jaw. He usually develops enlarged testicles. Younger children have more subtle facial alterations. The fragile X chromosome is shown, with the terminal pinched off portion.

Studies now show that it has an incidence of between 0.6–1.0 per 1,000 in men. It probably represents between 6%–14% of all males with severe mental retardation (Chudley & Hagerman, 1987). Furthermore, approximately 10% of boys who carry the diagnosis of autism have fragile X syndrome, and 50% of young men with mental retardation and large testicles have this disorder. Fragile X syndrome is now second to Down syndrome as the single most commonly identifiable cause of mental retardation (Hagerman, 1987).

Compared to adult men with this disorder, boys have more subtle facial changes and no testicular enlargement. However, their heads are large and their ears protrude; palates are high and arched, and the nasal bridges are narrow (Table 16.4). Like children with Down syndrome, they may have epicanthal folds and simian creases. The children also tend to be hypotonic and clumsy.

More prominent than the physical appearance are the cognitive, communicative, and behavioral deficits. Boys with fragile X syndrome have mental retardation, and their communication skills are more delayed than other cognitive and motor abilities (Table 16.5). Speech tends to be echolalic, perseverative, and dysfluent (Curfs, Schreppers-Tijdink, Wiegers, et al., 1989; Wolf-Schein, Sudhalter, Cohen, et al., 1987). There is poor auditory memory and auditory reception (Ho, Glahn, Ho, et al., 1988). Overall, these boys have the greatest difficulty processing new, sequential information, especially when short-term memory and flexibility in problem solving are required (Reiss & Freund, 1990). Also, their IQ scores tend to decrease over time, probably due to initial overestimation of nonverbal skills (Prouty, Rogers, & Stevenson, 1988). Seizures occur in about 20% of cases. Behavior problems include both self-stimulatory behavior, such as hand flapping, and self-injurious behavior, such as head banging. Other behavioral alterations include marked hyperactivity, attention deficits, and disciplinary problems (Hagerman & Sobesky, 1989). The combination of mental retardation, a communication disorder, a lack of sociability, and self-

Table 16.4.   Physical findings in males with fragile X syndrome

Finding	Percent of males affected
Prepubescent[a]	
Protruding ears	70
High arched palate, flattened nasal bridge	50
Macrocephaly	40
Epicanthal folds/Simian creases	40
Poor coordination	50
Hyperextensible joints/hypotonia	20
Postpubescent[b]	
Elongated face/prominent jaw	48
Long ears	80
Macroorchidism	92
Mitral valve prolapse	80

Source: [a] Simko, Hornstein, Soukups et al. (1989); [b] Hagerman (1987).

Table 16.5. Cognitive and behavioral characteristics of fragile X syndrome in young children

Parental concern	Percent of children affected
Boys	
Mental retardation	80
Communication disorder	95
Hyperactivity	65
Poor eye contact	80
Self-stimulatory/autistic-like behavior	60
Discipline problems	60
Seizures	20
Girls	
Cognitive deficits	
Learning disability	20
Mild mental retardation	10
Abnormal speech patterns	30
Emotional disturbance	30

Source: Simko, Hornstein, Soukups, et al. (1989).

stimulatory behavior define many of these children as having autism (see Chapter 22) or another pervasive developmental disorder.

Another intriguing aspect of this syndrome relates to its inheritance pattern. Although it is clearly inherited as a sex-linked trait, some men with fragile X chromosomes are asymptomatic, and many women who are carriers are symptomatic. We are now beginning to understand the complicated mechanism of inheritance in this disorder, aided by the recent discovery that the fragile region of the X chromosome actually contains the defective gene causing this disorder (Sutherland & Mulley, 1990). Prenatal diagnosis is now possible (Rousseau, Heitz, Biancalana, et al., 1991).

Approximately 20% of males carrying the fragile X chromosome are asymptomatic but can transmit the trait to their children or grandchildren, who may be symptomatic. In addition, approximately 30% of carrier girls express the disorder in a milder form than boys with the syndrome (see Table 16.5). These girls have only a slightly abnormal appearance. However, they do have cognitive deficits that range from learning disabilities (20% of carriers) to mild mental retardation (10% of carriers) (Borghgraef, Fryns, & van den Berghe, 1990). It is now believed that about 7% of mild mental retardation in girls is attributable to fragile X syndrome. On WISC-R IQ tests, girls with fragile X syndrome tend to score particularly low in arithmetic, digit span, and block design, and they may have visual-spatial processing deficits. They also have unusual speech patterns, which are high-pitched, repetitious, and cluttered, and they may have attention problems. Their personalities tend to be shy and withdrawn, and psychiatric illnesses have been diagnosed in 20% of these individuals (Reiss & Freund, 1990).

Intervention approaches for boys and girls with fragile X syndrome are directed at the various cognitive, communicative, and behavioral deficits. The boys do best in self-contained classrooms for children with comparable degrees of mental retardation. Behavior management techniques are used to control hyperactive, self-stimulatory, and self-injurious behaviors. They also benefit from speech-language therapy and social skills training. Some improvement has been reported from using stimulant medication to control hyperactivity.

The needs of girls with fragile X syndrome depend on the degree of deficits. Girls with learning disabilities usually can be mainstreamed with resource help. Those with mild mental retardation do well in classes directed at this degree of retardation (Hagerman, Jackson, Amiri, et al., 1992).

Folic acid has been proposed to treat boys and girls with fragile X syndrome based on the finding that it prevents the fragile X change in their chromosomes. There has been controversy about whether this works because studies do not demonstrate consistent benefit to behavior or cognition (Fisch, Cohen, Gross, et al., 1988; Hagerman, 1987).

In terms of long-term outcome, studies are incomplete because this is a newly recognized disorder. However, it is likely that boys with fragile X syndrome will do less well than children with Down syndrome because of the associated communicative, behavioral, and social skills deficits.

Intervention Approaches for Mental Retardation

As described in reference to Down syndrome and fragile X syndrome, the most useful approach to intervention for children with mental retardation consists of multidisciplinary efforts directed at many aspects of the child's life—education, social and recreational activities, behavior problems, and associated deficits (Colozzi & Pollow, 1984). Genetic and supportive counseling also is offered to the parents and siblings (see Chapters 3 and 29).

Early diagnosis is a prerequisite for effective intervention. Children with severe retardation demonstrate developmental delays at very young ages. However, many children with mild retardation do not have significant developmental delays recognized during the first years of their lives. Problems may not become evident until they reach preschool age. Premature children, children who are small for gestational age, and children who have had difficulties as newborns should be watched closely in early intervention programs because they are at greater risk for mental retardation than other children (see Chapters 6 and 7).

Interdisciplinary Evaluation After the diagnosis is made, the child should be referred to an interdisciplinary team at a public school, a state or private diagnostic and evaluation (D & E) center, or a university affiliated program (UAP). Ideally, the evaluation should include an examination by a developmental pediatrician, a clinical psychologist, and a social worker. The child also may need to be seen by a special education teacher, speech-language therapist, audiologist, and behavioral psychologist. An individualized intervention plan is then developed (Menolascino & Stark, 1988).

Education The educational component of the intervention plan should be based on the child's developmental level and his or her goals for independence (Johnson & Werner, 1977). For instance, the child with mild retardation needs to gain basic academic and vocational skills, while the child with severe retardation needs "survival" skills that can be used in supported employment and alternate living units.

In the past, this educational program began in the primary grades. However, as a result of the Education of the Handicapped Act Amendments of 1986 (Public Law 99-457), these programs are now initiated in the preschool years. In 1991, this act was reauthorized as PL 102-119, the Individuals with Disabilities Education Act Amendments. Early identification and intervention programs are available both to children who have been identified as having disabilities and to children at risk for developmental disabilities (Simeonsson, Cooper, & Scheiner, 1982). Each eligible child undergoes a multidisciplinary assessment that results in an individualized family service plan (IFSP). The IFSP must contain: 1) a statement of the child's present level of development; 2) a statement of the family's strengths and needs related to enhancing the child's development; 3) a statement of major outcomes expected to be achieved for the child and family and the criteria, procedures, and timelines for determining progress; 4) the specific early intervention services required to meet the needs of the child and family, including the frequency, intensity, and expected duration; 5) the name of the case manager responsible for implementing the plan; and 6) the procedures for transition from early intervention to preschool services. The plan requires annual review, and targets children from 2 to 5 years of age. A discretionary program deals with infants with special needs from birth through 2 years, but this is not yet being implemented in all states.

Social and Recreational Needs   Besides education, the team needs to address the child's social and recreational needs. Participation in sports is beneficial in many ways, including weight management, development of physical coordination, maintenance of cardiovascular fitness, and improvement of self-image (Committee on Sports Medicine, 1987). In general, children and adolescents with mental retardation do better in individual or small group activities than in team sports. They generally perform better in sports that require gross motor skills than they do in sports requiring fine motor coordination. Examples of these include track and field, swimming, and hiking. The Special Olympics provides many children with a framework for such activities. Some children with mental retardation should take precautions before participating in certain activities. As noted previously, children with Down syndrome must be checked for abnormalities in the upper neck vertebrae before participating in gymnastics or contact sports.

Social activities are equally important. These include dances, trips, dating, and other normal social and recreational events.

Control of Behavior   To facilitate the child's socialization, behavior problems must be addressed. Although most children with mental retardation do not have behavior disorders, problems occur with a greater frequency in such children than in children with normal intelligence. The causes may be simple or complex. They may result from inappropriate parental expectations, organic problems, and/or family difficulties, or they may represent attempts by the child to get attention or avoid frustration. In assessing the behavior of a child with mental retardation, one must consider whether the behavior is inappropriate for the child's mental age, rather than his or her chronological age. The "terrible 2s" in a 4-year-old child with severe retardation may be age-appropriate and may not require professional intervention. Environmental change, such as a more appropriate classroom setting, may improve certain behavior problems. With others behavior management techniques and/or the use of medication may be necessary.

The theory behind applied behavior management is explained in greater detail in Chapter 21. The techniques involve the reinforcement of appropriate behaviors and the discouragement of inappropriate behaviors. For children with retardation, this approach is often used to encourage compliance with instructions or to treat self-stimulatory or self-injurious behavior.

Self-injurious behavior, which includes head banging, eye gouging, scratching, and biting, occurs most frequently in children with severe mental retardation. Management techniques, such as extinction, time-out, aversive conditioning, overcorrection, and/or differential reinforcement of other behaviors, may be needed to discourage these behaviors. In extinction, the relationship between a behavior and a subsequent reward is broken. For instance, if an undesirable behavior resulted in parental attention, such attention would be withdrawn. It should be noted that extinction causes an initial increase in the behavior, which subsequently tapers off. Using time-out involves removing the child from social contacts, usually in a separate room, after the occurrence of the problem behavior. Overcorrection, a mild punishment procedure, requires the child to exaggerate the correction of the behavior. One example would be to forcibly hold a child's hand for 1 minute following the self-injurious behavior. Overcorrection and other approaches are often combined to teach a child a new skill that is physically incompatible with the injurious behavior. For instance, a child cannot hit him- or herself while stringing beads. It should be emphasized that overcorrection and other punishment procedures should only be used if more positive techniques have been ineffective and the target behaviors carry a significant risk of injury. If used consistently and with good judgment, behavior management techniques are quite successful in controlling these behavior problems.

Use of Medication   Although it is not necessary in most cases, some children need to receive medication in addition to educational programming and behavior management techniques to facilitate learning or to help suppress certain behaviors. Drugs are never an appropriate substitute for effective programming.

The medications most commonly used to control behavior problems in children with mental retardation fall into three groups: **phenothiazines**, **butyrophenones**, and stimulants (Platt, Campbell, Green, et al., 1984; Zimmermann & Heistad, 1982). Phenothiazines include chlorpromazine (Thorazine), thioridazine (Mellaril), and trifluoperazine (Stelazine). These drugs are sedatives and cause decreased levels of motor activity, anxiety, and combativeness. However, they also decrease attention span and may thus interfere with academic learning. The range of dosage in childhood for Thorazine or Mellaril is 25–200 milligrams/day. Common side effects include excessive appetite and drowsiness. Uncommon toxic effects include abnormal liver function, skin eruptions, and increased occurrence of seizures.

The second group of drugs, the butyrophenones, includes haloperidol (Haldol). These medications have therapeutic and toxic effects similar to those of the phenylthiazines. The usual dose of haloperidol is 1–5 milligrams/day.

Unusual movements, sometimes simulating Parkinson disease, may be seen in children receiving long-term treatment with phenylthiazines or butyrophenones. The most common movement disorder is *tardive dyskinesia*, which is characterized by involuntary, repetitive movements of the face and mouth including sticking out the tongue, licking the lips, chewing, and eye blinking (Burke, 1984; Sprague, Kalachnik, Breuning, et al., 1984). These abnormal movements may interfere with eating and speaking. They may not stop for weeks or months after use of the drug has been discontinued.

The third group of drugs, stimulants, includes methylphenidate (Ritalin) and dextroamphetamine (Dexedrine). They have been shown to be effective for the short-term control of hyperactivity and attention problems in children with normal intelligence (see Chapter 21). They appear to be somewhat less effective in controlling these problems in children with mental retardation, particularly those with IQs of less than 50 (Handen, Breaux, Gosling, et al., 1990). Because they have fewer and milder side effects than phenothiazines, stimulants are worth trying.

A host of drugs has been reported to be successful in individual cases but only inconsistently successful for groups of persons. These include carbamazepine (Tegretol), clonidine (Catapres), lithium, propranolol (Inderal), tricyclic antidepressants (e.g., imipramine [Tofranil]), and valproic acid (Valproate) (Kastner, Friedman, Plummer, et al., 1990). Such agents do not constitute "first line" agents but may, in selected cases, prove helpful for specific behaviors.

Other medications remain experimental at present. Examples include naloxone (Narcan) and naltrexone (Trexan), which have been used to control self-injurious behavior. Evidence suggests that some forms of self-injurious behavior result from an alteration in the receptors for **endorphins**, the body's own opiates or "pleasure producers." Children may engage in self-injurious behavior to "turn themselves on" by stimulating endorphin release. If this is true, drugs such as naloxone or naltrexone, which block endorphin receptors, may help to treat this type of behavior.

Preferably, trials of any of the above medication should be made prior to onset of long-term therapy. Ideally, the teacher should not be informed that a medication is being tried. During this "blind" trial, the teacher should keep a record of attention, behavior, and activity level (e.g., using the Conners rating scale) (Conners & Wells, 1986). Even if a medication proves successful, the child should be taken off the medication at least once a year to evaluate the need for continued treatment.

Evaluating Associated Disabilities The team also must assess the child for any associated disabilities (Shapiro & Batshaw, 1992). Mental retardation frequently occurs in conjunction with other developmental disabilities, such as cerebral palsy; visual deficits; seizure disorders; speech disorders; autism; and other disorders of language, behavior, and perception. The severity and frequency of these associated deficits tend to be correlated with the severity of mental retardation. Failure to adequately identify and treat these problems may result in unsuccessful **habilitation** and may heighten behavior problems.

Periodic Reevaluation   Annual reviews are necessary throughout childhood. Although the degree of mental retardation does not change over time, the needs of the child and his or her family do. As the child grows, more information must be provided to parents, goals must be reassessed, and programming may need to be adjusted. A review should include information about the child's health status and his or her functioning both at home and at school.

Prognosis

The prognosis for individuals with mental retardation obviously depends on the degree of mental retardation and associated deficits.

Many people with mental retardation are able to gain economic and social independence with the equivalent of up to a fourth grade education. Eighty percent of people with mild mental retardation find work, mainly in unskilled or semiskilled jobs. More than 80% marry, usually to a spouse with normal intelligence. As adults, they have mental ages ranging between 9 and 11 years of age, compared to adults with normal intelligence having a mental age of about 16 years (Illingworth, 1987).

For other individuals, the goal of education is to enhance adaptive skills, functional academics, and vocational skills so they are better able to live in the adult world. Not so many years ago, most of these people were institutionalized. Now it is recognized that many are able to manage well in caring home environments or in small living units with only modest supervision. Individuals with Down syndrome generally fit in this group.

Beginning in the 1980s, major initiatives have been started to enhance the independence of people with mental retardation. One example is the concept of supported employment. Here, the focus is on teaching individuals how to do specific jobs in specific settings, aided by "job coaches." Using this approach, many adults have been able to bypass the sheltered workshop stage and perform well in regular unskilled jobs, such as a janitor or maid. However, other individuals, in addition to having mental retardation, have associated deficits, such as cerebral palsy and sensory deficits, that further impair their functioning. An institutional setting may be needed for certain children with associated medical problems, severe behavioral disturbance, or familial dissolution. Life span appears to be somewhat shortened in these individuals (Eyman, Grossman, Chaney, et al., 1990).

SUMMARY

Development is a step-by-step process that is related to the maturation of the central nervous system. With mental retardation, development is altered so that adaptive and intellectual skills are impaired. Causes of mental retardation range from newborn trauma to infectious disease and from chromosomal abnormalities to inborn errors of metabolism. The most common genetic causes are Down syndrome and fragile X syndrome. In most cases, the cause of mental retardation is unclear.

Most people with mental retardation have mild retardation and are able to achieve economic and social independence. The early identification of a developmental delay is important to ensure appropriate treatment and to enable the child to develop and use all of his or her capabilities.

REFERENCES

American Psychiatric Association. (1980). *Diagnostic and statistical manual of mental disorders (DSM III)* (3rd ed.). Washington, DC: Author.

Ashwood, E.R., Cheng, E., & Luthy, D.A. (1987). Maternal serum alpha-fetoprotein and fetal trisomy 21 in women 35 years and older: implications for alpha-fetoprotein screening programs. *American Journal of Medical Genetics, 26*, 531–539.

Baird, P.A., & Sadovnick, A.D. (1987). Life expectancy in Down syndrome. *Journal of Pediatrics, 110*, 849–854.

Bayley, N. (1958). Value and limitations of infant testing. *Children, 5*, 129–133.

Benacerraf, B.R., Gelman, R., Frigoletto, F.D., Jr. (1987). Sonographic identification of second-trimester fetuses with Down's syndrome. *New England Journal of Medicine, 317*, 1371–1376.

Bidder, R.T., Gray, P., Newcombe, R.G., et al. (1989). The effects of multivitamins and minerals on children with Down syndrome. *Developmental Medicine and Child Neurology, 31*, 532–537.

Borghgraef, M., Fryns, J.P., & van den Berghe, H. (1990). The female and the fragile X snydrome: Data on clinical and psychological findings in 7 fra(x) carriers. *Clinical Genetics, 37*, 341–346.

Burke, R.E. (1984). Tardive dyskinesia: Current clinical issues. *Neurology, 34*, 1,348–1,353.

Burt, C. (1959). General ability and special aptitudes. *Educational Research, 1*, 3–16.

Caplan, F. (Ed.). (1978). *The first twelve months of life.* New York: Bantam Books.

Capute, A.J., Palmer, F.B., Shapiro, B.K., et al. (1984). Primitive reflex profile: A quantitation of primitive reflexes in infancy. *Developmental Medicine and Child Neurology, 26*, 375–383.

Chudley, A.E., & Hagerman, R.J. (1987). Fragile X syndrome. *Journal of Pediatrics, 110*, 821–831.

Cicchette, D., & Beeghly, M. (Eds.). (1990). *Children with Down syndrome: A developmental perspective.* Cambridge: Cambridge University Press.

Colozzi, G.A., & Pollow, R.S. (1984). Teaching independent walking to mentally retarded children in a public school. *Education and Training of the Mentally Retarded, 19*, 97–101.

Committee on Sports Medicine. (1987). Exercise for children who are mentally retarded. *Pediatrics, 8*, 447–448.

Conners, C.K., & Wells, A.C. (1986). *Hyperactive children.* Beverly Hills: Sage Publications.

Cork, L.C. (1990). Neuropathology of Down syndrome and Alzheimer disease. *American Journal of Medical Genetics, 7*(Suppl.), 282–286.

Cronk, C., Crocker, A.C., Pueschel, S.M., et al. (1988). Growth charts for children with Down syndrome—1 month to 18 years of age. *Pediatrics, 81*, 102–110.

Curfs, L.M., Schreppers-Tijdink, G., Wiegers, A., et al. (1989). Intelligence and cognitive profile in the fra(X) syndrome: A longitudinal study in 18 fra(X) boys. *Journal of Medical Genetics, 26*, 443–446.

Cutler, A.T., Benezra-Obeiter, R., & Brink, S.J. (1986). Thyroid function in young children with Down syndrome. *American Journal of Diseases of Children, 140*, 479–483.

Dagna-Bricarelli, F.D., Pierluigi, M., Grasso, M., et al. (1990). Origin of extra chromosome

21 in 343 families: Cytogenetic and molecular approaches. *American Journal of Medical Genetics, 7*(Suppl.) 129–132.

DiMaio, M.S., Baumgarten, A., Greenstein, R.M., et al. (1987). Screening for fetal Down syndrome in pregnancy by measuring maternal serum alpha-fetoprotein levels. *New England Journal of Medicine, 317*, 342–346.

Eyman, R.K., Grossman, H.J., Chaney, R.H., et al. (1990). The life expectancy of profoundly handicapped people with mental retardation. *New England Journal of Medicine, 323*, 584–589.

Fisch, G.S., Cohen, I.L., Gross, A.C., et al. (1988). Folic acid treatment of fragile-X males: A further study. *American Journal of Medical Genetics, 30*, 393–399.

Fishman, M.A. (1986). Will the study of Down syndrome solve the riddle of Alzheimer disease? *Journal of Pediatrics, 108*, 627–629.

Franceschi, M., Comola, M., Piattoni, F., et al. (1990). Prevalence of dementia in adult patients with trisomy 21. *American Journal of Medical Genetics, 7*(Suppl.), 306–308.

Goldman, J., Stein, C.L., & Guerry, S. (1983). *Psychological methods of child assessment.* New York: Brunner/Mazel.

Grossman, H.J. (Ed.). (1983). *Classification in mental retardation.* Washington, DC: American Association on Mental Deficiency.

Gruber, H.E., & Voneche, J.J. (Eds.). (1977). *The essential Piaget.* New York: Basic Books.

Hagerman, R.J. (1987). Fragile-X syndrome. *Current Problems in Pediatrics, 17*, 621–674.

Hagerman, R.J., Jackson, C., Amiri, K., et al. (1992). Girls with fragile-X syndrome: Physical and neurocognitive status and outcome. *Pediatrics, 89*, 395–400.

Hagerman, R.J., & Sobesky, W.E. (1989). Psychopathology in fragile-X syndrome. *American Journal of Orthopsychiatry, 59*, 142–152.

Handen, B.L., Breaux, A.M., Gosling, A., et al. (1990). Efficacy of methylphenidate among mentally retarded children with attention deficit hyperactivity disorder. *Pediatrics, 86*, 922–930.

Ho, H.Z., Glahn, T.J., & Ho, J.C. (1988). The fragile X syndrome. *Developmental Medicine and Child Neurology, 30*, 257–261.

Illingworth, R.S. (1987) *The development of the infant and young child: Normal and abnormal* (9th ed.). New York: Churchill Livingstone.

Johnson, V.M., & Werner, R.A. (1977). *A step-by-step learning guide for older retarded children.* Syracuse, NY: Syracuse University Press.

Kalwinsky, D.K., Raimondi, S.C., Bunin, N.J., et al. (1990). Clinical and biological characteristics of acute lymphocytic leukemia in children with Down syndrome. *American Journal of Medical Genetics, 7*(Suppl.), 267–271.

Kastner, T., Friedman, D.L., Plummer, A.T., et al. (1990). Valproic acid for the treatment of children with mental retardation and mood symptomatology. *Pediatrics, 86*, 467–472.

Kavanagh, J.F. (Ed.). (1988). *Understanding mental retardation: Research accomplishments and new frontiers.* Baltimore: Paul H. Brookes Publishing Co.

Korenberg, J.R., Kawashima, H., & Pulst, S.M. (1990). Molecular definition of a region of chromosome 21 that causes features of the Down syndrome phenotype. *American Journal of Human Genetics, 47*, 236–246.

Luckasson, R. (Ed.). (in press). *Mental retardation definition, classifications, and systems of support* (9th ed.). Washington, DC: American Association on Mental Retardation.

McLaren, J., & Bryson, S.E. (1987). Review of recent epidemiological studies of mental retardation: Prevalence, associated disorders, and etiology. *American Journal of Mental Retardation, 92*, 243–254.

Meisels, S.J. (1989). Can developmental screening tests identify children who are developmentally at risk? *Pediatrics, 83*, 578–585.

Menolascino, F.J., & Stark, J.A. (Eds.). (1988). *Preventive and curative intervention in mental retardation.* Baltimore: Paul H. Brookes Publishing Co.

Moser, H.M. (1985). *Prenatal/perinatal factors associated with brain disorders* (NIH Publication T5–1149). Washington, DC: U.S. Government Printing Office.

Palfrey, J.S., Singer, J.D., Walker, D.K., et al. (1987). Early identification of children's special needs: A study in 5 metropolitan communities. *Journal of Pediatrics, 111*, 651–659.

Platt, J.E., Campbell, M., Green, W.H., et al. (1984). Cognitive effects of lithium carbonate and haloperidol in treatment-resistant aggressive children. *Archives of General Psychiatry, 41*, 657–662.

Prouty, L.A., Rogers, C., & Stevenson, R.E. (1988). Fragile-X syndrome: Growth, development, and intellectual function. *American Journal of Medical Genetics, 30*, 123–142.

Pueschel, S.M. (Ed.). (1988). *The young person with Down syndrome: Transition from adolescence to adulthood*. Baltimore: Paul H. Brookes Publishing Co.

Pueschel, S.M. (1990). Clinical aspects of Down syndrome from infancy to adulthood. *American Journal of Medical Genetics, 7*(Suppl.), 52–56.

Pueschel, S.M., & Scola, F.H. (1987). Atlantoaxial; instability in individuals with Down syndrome: Epidemiologic, radiographic and clinical studies. *Pediatrics, 80*, 555–560.

Pueschel, S.M., Tingey, C., Rynders, J.E., Crocker, A.C., & Crutcher, D.M. (Eds.). (1987). *New perspectives on Down syndrome*. Baltimore: Paul H. Brookes Publishing Co.

Reiss, A.L., & Freund, L. (1990). Fragile-X syndrome. *Biological Psychiatry, 27*, 223–240.

Rogers, P.T., & Roizen, N.J. (1991). A life-cycle approach to the management of Down syndrome. In A.J. Capute, & P.J. Accardo, (Eds.), *Developmental disabilities in infancy and childhood* (pp. 441–453). Baltimore: Paul H. Brookes Publishing Co.

Rousseau, F., Heitz, D. Biancalana, V., et al. (1991). Direct diagnosis by DNA analysis of the fragile-X syndrome of mental retardation. *New England Journal of Medicine, 325*, 1673–1681.

Rumble, B., Retallack, R., Hilbich, C., et al. (1989). Amyloid A_4 protein and its precursor in Down's syndrome and Alzheimer's disease. *New England Journal of Medicine, 320*, 1446–1452.

Schroeder-Kurth, T.M., Schaffert, G., Koeckritz, W., et al. (1990). Quality of life of adults with trisomy 21 living in mental retardation homes compared with those staying under parental care. *American Journal of Medical Genetics, 7*(Suppl.), 317–321.

Shapiro, B.K. (1991). The pediatric neurodevelopmental assessment of infants and young children. In A.J. Capute & P.J. Accardo (Eds.), *Developmental disabilities in infancy and childhood* (pp. 139–149). Baltimore: Paul H. Brookes Publishing Co.

Shapiro, B.K., & Batshaw, M.L. (in press). Mental retardation. In F.D. Burg (Ed.), *Current pediatric therapy* (14th ed.). Philadelphia: W.B. Saunders.

Shapiro, B.K., Palmer, F.B., Antell, S.E., Bilker, S., Ross, A., & Capute, A.J. (1989). Giftedness: Can it be predicted in infancy? *Clinical Pediatrics, 28*, 205–209.

Shapiro, B.K., Palmer, F.B., & Capute, A.J. (1987). The early detection of mental retardation. *Clinical Pediatrics, 26*, 215–220.

Simeonsson, R.J., Cooper, D.H., & Scheiner, A.P. (1982). A review and analysis of the effectiveness of early intervention programs. *Pediatrics, 69*, 635–641.

Simko, A., Hornstein, L., Soukup, S., et al. (1989). Fragile X syndrome: Recognition in young children. *Pediatrics, 83*, 547–552.

Sprague, R.L., Kalachnik, J.E., Breuning, S.E., et al. (1984). The dyskinesia identification system—Coldwater (DIS-Co): A tardive dyskinesia rating scale for the developmentally disabled. *Psychopharmacology Bulletin, 20*, 328–338.

Stafstrom, C.E., Patxot, O.F., Gilmore, H.E., et al. (1991). Seizures in children with Down syndrome: Etiology, characteristics, and outcome. *Developmental Medicine and Child Neurology, 33*, 191–200.

Sutherland, G.R., & Mulley, J.C. (1990). Diagnostic molecular genetics of the fragile-X. *Clinical Genetics, 37*, 2–11.

Sweeny, J.E., Hohmann, C.F., Oster-Granite, M.L., & Coyle, J.T. (1989). Neurogenesis of the basal forebrain in euploid and trisomy 16 mice: An animal model for developmental disorders in Down syndrome. *Neuroscience, 31*, 413–425.

Tingey, C. (1987). *Down syndrome: A resource handbook*. San Diego: College-Hill Press.

Torrado, C., Bastian, W., Wisniewski, K.E., et al. (1991). Treatment of children with Down syndrome and growth retardation with recombinant human growth hormone. *Journal of Pediatrics, 119*, 478–483.

VanDyke, D.C., Lang, D.J., van Duyne, S., et al. (1990). Cell therapy in children with Down syndrome. A retrospective study. *Pediatrics, 85*, 79–84.

Weaver, S.J. (Ed.). (1984). *Testing children: A reference guide for effective clinical and psychoeducational assessments*. Kansas City, MO: Test Corporation of America.

Wisniewski, K.E., French, J.H., Fernando, S., et al. (1985). Fragile X syndrome: Associated neurological abnormalities and developmental disabilities. *Annals of Neurology, 18*, 665–669.

Wodrich, D.L., & Kush, S.A. (1990). *Children's psychological testing: A guide for nonpsychologists* (2nd ed.). Baltimore: Paul H. Brookes Publishing Co.

Wolf-Schein, E.G., Sudhalter, V., Cohen, I.L., et al. (1987). Speech-language and the fragile-X syndrome: Initial findings. *Asha, 29*, 35–38.

Zigler, E. (1967, January). Familial retardation: A continuing dilemma. *Science, 155*, 292–298.

Zimmermann, R.L., & Heistad, G.T. (1982). Studies of the long-term efficacy of antipsychotic drugs in controlling the behavior of institutionalized retardates. *Journal of the American Academy of Child Psychiatry, 21*, 136–143.

Chapter 17

Vision

Upon completion of this chapter, the reader will:
— be able to describe the anatomy of the eye
— know the function of the major parts of the eye and some common problems associated with them
— be aware of some of the tests used to determine visual acuity
— understand how a child develops visual skills
— know the definition and some of the causes of blindness in children
— recognize some of the ways in which a blind child's development differs from a sighted child's and some approaches for treating a blind child

Vision may be the most important sense for interpreting the world around us. When sight is impaired, it can have a detrimental effect on a child's physical, neurological, and emotional development. Even as an isolated disability, blindness causes delays in walking and talking and necessitates dependence on others. However, if visual loss is identified early, various methods of treatment may improve the prognosis.

This chapter explores the embryonic development of the eye along with its structure and function. It also examines diseases of the eye and common visual problems of the child with disabilities. Finally, the effects of blindness on a child's development are discussed.

STRUCTURE OF THE EYE

Reflected rays of light from an object strike the eye and are **refracted** at the surfaces of the **cornea** and the **lens**. This refraction yields a focused image on the retina. The image is then transmitted to the occipital lobe of the brain, where it is interpreted. A problem anywhere along this pathway causes some degree of visual loss.

In many ways, the structure of the eye is similar to that of a camera (Figure 17.1). The case of the eyeball is a thick, white fibrous covering called the **sclera**. The shutter is the **iris**, the colored speckled area that opens and closes according to light conditions. The **pupil** is the aperture in the center of the iris. The cornea covers and protects the iris and is also the first and most important refracting surface of the eye. The

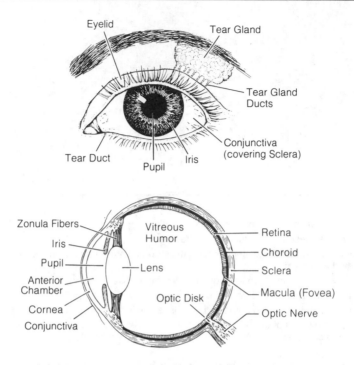

Figure 17.1.   The structure of the eye is similar to that of a camera.

lens, the second refracting surface, transmits and further deflects the light rays toward the retina. The retina is the photographic film, a light-sensitive surface that records the image in an upside-down, back-to-front format. Near the center of the retina lies the **fovea centralis**, or **macula**, which is composed completely of **cone cells** and is the one area of the retina that has 20/20 vision. As a result, we tend to turn our eyes so that the object viewed is focused directly on the fovea.

The region between the cornea and the iris is called the *anterior chamber* and contains a watery fluid, the **aqueous humor**. Between the lens and the retina is a space filled with a translucent jelly-like substance, called the **vitreous humor**. These fluids maintain the shape of the eye and nourish it.

The eye itself sits in a bony socket of the skull. The *extraocular muscles*, small fibers that turn the eyeball, and the *optic nerve,* which sends images from the eye to the brain, also lie in this space. A series of layers protects the surface of the eyeball. First, a thin, transparent layer called the *conjunctiva* covers the sclera and contains tiny blood vessels that give a "bloodshot" appearance to the eye when it is inflamed or infected. Next, the *eyelids* intermittently sweep across the eye, wiping dust and other foreign bodies from the eye. The *eyelashes* protect the eye from airborn debris. Tears are released from the **lacrimal** glands at the outer edge of the eye and are collected in the *tear ducts* in the inner corner of the eye.

DEVELOPMENT OF THE EYE

In the fetus, the eyes first appear at 4 weeks gestational age as two spherical bulbs at the side of the head (Figure 17.2). These bulbs gradually indent to form the *optic cups*. The three cell layers in these cups then develop into the various parts of the eye. The ectoderm forms part of the lens and cornea. The **neuroectoderm** produces the retina and inner eye muscles, while the mesoderm forms the optic nerve, blood vessels, and muscles of the eyeball, and the eyelids. By 7 weeks gestational age, when the embryo is only 1 inch long, the eyes have already assumed their basic form (Isenberg, 1988).

As fetal growth continues, the eyes gradually move from the side of the head to the center of the face. Malformations during the first trimester may lead to many defects—for example, *anophthalmia*, a lack of eyes, and *microphthalmia*, or small eyes. They also may prevent the complete fusion of the retina or the iris, a condition called a *coloboma* (Langman & Sadler, 1991). One syndrome resulting from such malformations is the **CHARGE association** (Goldson, Smith, & Stewart, 1986). Characteristics of this syndrome include coloboma (C), congenital heart disease (H), **atresia** of nasal passage (A), retarded growth (R), genital abnormalities (G), ear

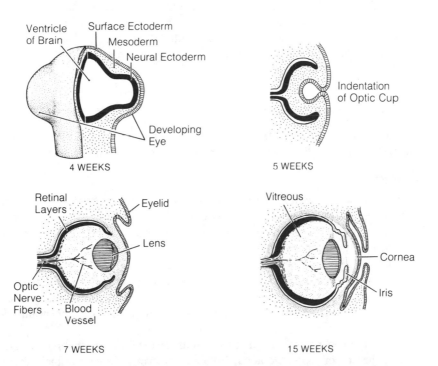

Figure 17.2. Embryonic development of the eye. The eyes first appear at 4 weeks gestational age as two spherical bulges at the side of the head. They indent in the next week to form the optic cups. By 7 weeks, the eyes have already assumed their basic form. The eye is completely formed by 15 weeks.

anomalies and/or deafness (E). Trisomy 13 and trisomy 18 syndromes also are frequently accompanied by coloboma. Abnormalities occurring later in fetal life may lead to ocular **hypertelorism,** or widely spaced eyes. Finally, intrauterine infections, such as rubella and toxoplasmosis (see Chapter 4), can invade the eye and cause **chorioretinitis** (an inflammation of the retina and **choroid**), **cataracts,** and/or **glaucoma**. Each of these conditions may produce severe visual loss and abnormal facial features (Table 17.1).

DEVELOPMENT OF VISUAL SKILLS

Like the acquisition of language and other skills, vision also has developmental milestones (Greenwald, 1983). A newborn can focus on a human face and follow the movement of the face 90° across a visual field (Adams, Maurer, & Davis, 1986). By 1 month of age, an infant can follow an object horizontally 180°, and by 2 months, he or she can follow the same object vertically. At this age, the child also can imitate a smile. At 3 months, he or she can distinguish colors and follow an object in a complete circle. A month later, the child can reach for and grab an object anywhere in the visual field. Normal visual acuity appears to be about 20/600 at birth, 20/100 at 6 months, 20/30 by 3 years, and 20/20 (the standard for normal vision) by 5 years (Figure 17.3) (Boothe, Dobson, & Teller, 1985). **Binocular vision** begins at around 4 months of age and is well developed by 6 months. Because of the lack of binocular vision and accommodation prior to 4 months, strabismus is not uncommon nor necessarily abnormal in infancy.

FUNCTION AND DISEASES OF THE EYE

In this section, the functions of the cornea, lens, retina, optic nerves, and eye muscles are discussed, along with some of the common disorders that affect them.

The Cornea

The cornea, which is the most powerful refractive surface in the eye, focuses an image on the most light-sensitive part of the retina, the fovea centralis. This is accomplished in the following manner. When a person looks at a tree, the eyes see a series of parallel rays of light that leave the tree and reach the surface of the cornea. If these rays continued unfocused, they would each project to a different part of the retina, and the image would be blurred. However, as the parallel rays hit the **spherical convex** surface of the cornea, they are turned or refracted. If everything works properly, the rays focus on the fovea, and a sharp image is transmitted to the brain (Figure 17.4).

For this to happen correctly, the eyeball must be the right length, and the cornea must have the proper shape (Pernoud, 1990). If the eye is too long or the refractive surfaces of the eye (i.e., cornea and lens) are too strong, the focused image (where all lines converge) is in front of the retina, and the picture is blurred (see Figure 17.4). This is called *myopia*, or nearsightedness. When the eye is too short or the cornea and

Table 17.1. Selected genetic syndromes associated with eye abnormalities

Syndrome	Eye abnormality
Lowe	Cataracts, glaucoma
Zellweger	Cataracts, retinitis pigmentosa
Marfan	Dislocated lens
Homocystinuria	Dislocated lens
Osteogenesis imperfecta	Blue sclera, cataract
Osteopetrosis	Cranial nerve palsies, optic atrophy
Aicardi	Retinal abnormalities
Sturge-Weber	Glaucoma, choroidal hemangioma
Tuberous sclerosis	Retinal defects, iris depigmentation
Tay-Sachs disease	Cherry red spot of macula, optic nerve atrophy
Hurler	Cloudy cornea
Galactosemia	Cataract
CHARGE association	Coloboma, microphthalmos
Trisomy 13, trisomy 18	Microphthalmos, corneal opacities, coloboma

lens are too weak, the image is formed behind the retina, also producing a blurred image (see Figure 17.4). In this instance, the person has *hyperopia*, or farsightedness. Hyperopia is the most common refractive error of childhood (Tongue, 1987). The other common refractive problem is *astigmatism* (see Figure 17.4). Astigmatism typically occurs when the surface of the cornea has the shape of a football rather than a sphere. Because of this change in shape, as parallel rays of light enter the eye, they do not focus on one point, and the image is blurred.

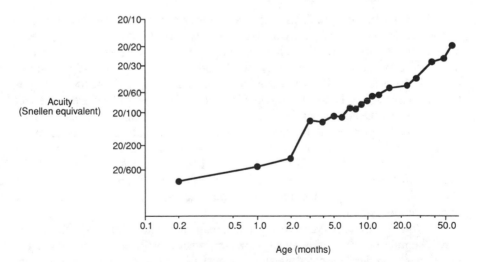

Figure 17.3.   Change in visual acuity during the first 4 years of life as measured by preferential looking (From Stager, D.R., Birch, E.E., & Weakley, D.R. [1990]. Amblyopia and the pediatrician. *Pediatric Annals, 19,* 301–315; reprinted by permission.)

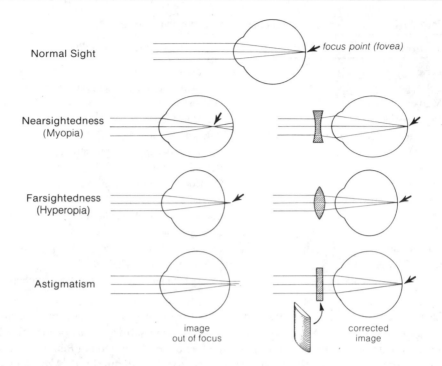

Figure 17.4. Refractive errors. If the eyeball is too long, images are focused in front of the retina (myopia). A concave lens deflects the rays, correcting the problem. If the eyeball is too short, the image focuses behind the retina and is again blurred (hyperopia). A convex lens corrects this. In astigmatism, the eyeball is the correct size, but the cornea is misshapen. A cylindrical lens is required to compensate.

When any of these problems exists, people may have to wear eyeglasses or contact lenses. Myopic people wear **concave** (inwardly curved) lenses to move the focal point farther back, whereas the farsighted person wears **convex** (outwardly curved) lenses to move the focal point closer (see Figure 17.4). To correct astigmatism, a cylindrical lens is used with different angles of bending, compensating for the irregular cornea (see Figure 17.4). For individuals with astigmatism, a beneficial side effect of aging is that the cornea flattens, making astigmatism less apparent.

Corneal Clouding Refraction also can be affected if the cornea is not clear. A clouded cornea can result from glaucoma as well as certain metabolic disorders, such as Hurler disease. Refraction also is abnormal if the cornea has been damaged, for example by trauma or as a result of riboflavin deficiency. If rapid correction of the corneal abnormality is not possible, corneal transplantation may be required in order to prevent **amblyopia**.

Refraction Errors Very young infants can wear glasses, and should if they have a significant visual impairment. However, what constitutes a significant visual loss varies with age. As noted previously, most 6-month-old infants have a visual acuity of about 20/100, so glasses are not necessary unless visual acuity is significantly worse than 20/100, or unless there is strabismus or unequal refractive errors placing the infant at risk for amblyopia (see below).

Refraction correction can be done without the child's cooperation using a **retinoscope**. The ophthalmologist looks through this apparatus and adjusts combinations of lenses until the correct refraction is obtained. Correction of refraction errors is described in units called **diopters.** Thus, a prescription might indicate a -3.0 diopter correction, indicating a concave spherical lens for correction of myopia, or a $+2.5$ diopter correction for a convex lens to correct hyperopia. Astigmatism requires a cylindrical lens and correction is also indicated by diopters, but specifying the direction or the long axis of the "football" in degrees from the horizontal axis. The left eye is designated OS, and the right eye is designated OD on the prescription. Unequal refractive errors have different prescriptions for each eye.

Glasses are generally used for young children, while contact lens often are preferred by teenagers. The age at which contacts can be worn depends on the child's commitment and ability to accept responsibility for cleaning and inserting the lenses. Contacts are preferred for treatment after a cataract has been removed. Soft contact lenses are most commonly used for myopia and hyperopia; gas-permeable "hard" lenses are used for astigmatism; and extended wear lenses are used following cataract surgery. Complications associated with contacts include red eyes, discomfort, itching, corneal ulcers, and infection. These are generally avoidable if the lenses are not worn overnight and good hygiene is used.

If glasses are chosen, they should be made of polycarbonate plastic rather than glass. Although plastic lenses scratch more easily, they are lighter, safer, and last longer. Frames with cable temples and eyepieces with hinges tend to fit best. For young children, head bands to hold on the glasses are useful.

Whether glasses or contacts are used, refraction should be repeated at least once a year because the child's eyes are likely to grow and the prescription will change.

The Anterior Chamber

In the anterior chamber behind the cornea, pressure is kept within normal limits by the drainage of fluid through a passageway at the angle of the eye, called Schlemm's canal (Figure 17.5). If this canal is blocked, the intraocular pressure rises and causes glaucoma.

Glaucoma In children, glaucoma most commonly represents a congenital abnormality, but it also may occur as a consequence of a cataract, congenital infection, or retinopathy of prematurity. Glaucoma also has been observed in certain syndromes, including chromosomal abnormalities, homocystinuria, Lowe syndrome, and Sturge-Weber syndrome. Finally, glaucoma can develop following eye trauma or chronic inflammation.

Glaucoma causes approximately 4% of all blindness in children (Nelson, Calhoun, & Harley, 1991). Signs of glaucoma include a large hazy cornea and excessive tearing. The individual experiences eye pain and discomfort in bright light. Diagnosis is made by measuring the intraocular pressure using a **tonometer**. If glaucoma

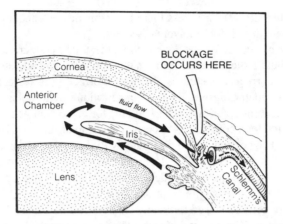

Figure 17.5. Glaucoma. Fluid normally drains from the anterior chamber through Schlemm's canal. A blockage in this passage leads to the accumulation of fluid and pressure, a condition called glaucoma.

is found, a medication, acetazolamide (Diamox), or eye drops (Timoptic) may be used to decrease the pressure until surgery can be performed. A microsurgical procedure, a **goniotomy**, or a **trabeculotomy** is performed, in which the meshwork in the anterior chamber angle is cut to open a passageway to permit drainage of the aqueous humor. If not treated, glaucoma usually causes blindness in the affected eye. Early treatment results in successful preservation of vision in the affected eye in 90% of children (Franks & Taylor, 1989).

The Lens

The lens, the second refracting surface of the eye, is a globular body located between the cornea and retina. It can change its shape to accommodate changes in the distance of an object from the eye by being stretched or relaxed by its **ciliary** (zonular) **muscles** (see Figure 17.1). This accommodation permits most young children to compensate for their natural hyperopia without the use of glasses.

The lens is convex on both sides and translucent. When light comes from a distant object, the rays are close together and well-focused. Because little refraction is needed, the ciliary muscles tighten and pull the lens so that it minimally refracts the light rays (Figure 17.6). To see a nearby object where the rays are dispersed, the ciliary muscles relax to allow the lens to become globular in shape with greater refractive power. The rays are sharply focused on the fovea. As a person ages, the lens becomes less flexible and less able to accommodate, a condition called **presbyopia**. The individual's near vision becomes blurred. Wearing bifocals or reading glasses helps to compensate for the loss of flexibility.

Cataracts   The major disease affecting the lens is the cataract, which refers to any defect in clarity of the lens. Small cataracts often remain stable and do not need to be removed. However, a cataract more commonly becomes dense enough to be visible as a white object in the pupil; at this point, it is likely to significantly obscure vision (Figure 17.7). Although this disorder is much more common in adults, it ac-

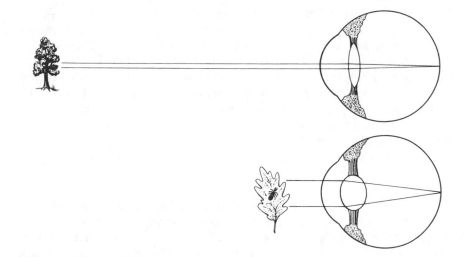

Figure 17.6. Accommodation. The lens changes shape to focus on a near or far object. The lens becomes thin and less refractive for distant objects, but rounded and more refractive for near vision.

counts for about 15% of blindness in children and occurs in about 1 in 250 births (Nelson et al., 1991). It may be an isolated abnormality or part of a syndrome or disease. For example, children with galactosemia, congenital rubella, or eye trauma may develop cataracts (Endres & Shin, 1990).

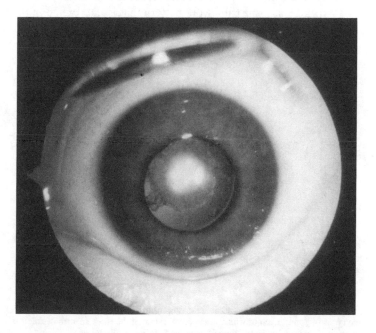

Figure 17.7. Photograph of a cataract, the white body seen through the pupil.

If a cataract is large enough to interfere with vision, it should be removed shortly after its appearance to avoid permanent visual loss due to amblyopia. A congenital cataract, for example, should be removed in the first months of life. The cataract is removed using a microsurgical method in which the contents of the lens are cut and aspirated, leaving only the outer membrane intact. The procedure is quite safe and can be done in a day surgery unit. However, by removing the lens, a significant refractive surface of the eye is eliminated. Thick glasses, a contact lens, or an experimental intraocular lens must be used to compensate for the loss of the natural lens. Contact lenses are preferred (Epstein, 1991). The outcome depends on how long the cataract has been affecting vision (Birch & Stager, 1988).

The Retina

The retina is the light-sensitive "film" of the eye. Visual images are focused on it and then projected to the brain. Two layers, the sclera and the choroid, surround the retina and support, protect, and nourish it (see Figure 17.1). Within the retina are two types of sensory cells, the *rods* and the *cones*. Both types of cells respond to light by undergoing a chemical reaction. Also, both contain a pigment called *retinol*, which is stored in the body as vitamin A. Retinol is bound to another molecule called **opsin**. Although the amount of retinol is the same in both rods and cones, the type of opsin differs (Nelson et al., 1991).

For detailed vision, such as reading, seeing distant objects, and color vision, cones are needed. Each cone is sensitive to one of three distinct colors: red, green, or blue (Figure 17.8). The light from a colored object causes a different response from each type of cone and leads to a patchwork pattern that is interpreted in the brain as shades of color and shape. The macula, the portion of the retina that contains the area of clearest vision, contains only cones.

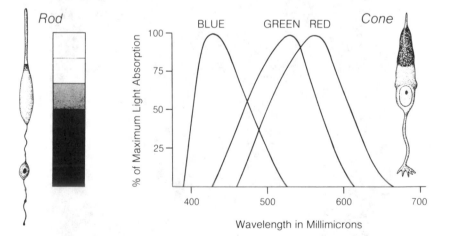

Figure 17.8.   Rods react in low light conditions, allowing night vision. Cones are needed for color vision. There are three types of cones, each of which is sensitive to one of the three spectra of color: red, blue, or green. The absence of or damage to one type of cone leads to color blindness.

In the more peripheral areas of the retina, the rods predominate. Rods function in conditions of diminished light and are therefore necessary for night vision (see Figure 17.8). Unlike human beings, some animals have only rods or only cones. For instance, bats, which have only rods, fly at night. Squirrels have only cones and hunt in daylight.

A number of disorders involve abnormalities in the rods or cones. Some are birth defects. For example, color blindness affects about 8% of men and 1% of women and is typically an X-linked disorder (see Chapter 2) in which one of the three types of cones is either abnormal or missing at birth. The disorder has been shown to involve a reduced number of green pigment genes and/or a partial deletion of the red color pigment gene (Nathans, Piantanida, Eddy, et al., 1986). With this disorder, a person may be unable to discriminate red from green or may confuse shades of red and green. Simple color blindness does not cause a decrease in vision and is not associated with educational disabilities.

Other diseases damage the cones or rods after they have been formed. For example, a dietary deficiency of vitamin A depletes the supply of retinol and initially impairs night vision. If untreated, such a deficiency leads to blindness. **Retinitis pigmentosa**, a group of inherited diseases including Leber amaurosis, gradually destroys the rods and/or cones (Lambert, Kriss, Taylor, et al., 1989). Initially, it causes night blindness and then generalized visual impairment (Pagon, 1988).

The retina also can be damaged by trauma that results in a retinal hemorrhage or tear. This may produce visual loss in the affected eye. Progressive nervous system disorders, such as Tay-Sachs disease, are associated with deposits of toxic material on the choroid and retina, also causing blindness. Diagnosis of a retinal disorder is made by an ophthalmologic examination and electroretinogram (see section on Vision Tests in this chapter).

Retinopathy of Prematurity   Retinopathy of prematurity (ROP) occurs principally in premature infants. It has an incidence of 7% in infants weighing less than 1.2 kilograms (approximately 2.5 pounds) at birth (DeVoe, 1988; Gallo & Lennerstrand, 1991). Although the incidence of this disorder has not changed in recent years, there is now a greater number of infants with ROP because of the increased survival of very small premature babies (Valentine, Jackson, Kalina, et al., 1989).

Retinopathy of prematurity results from the disruption of normal blood vessel development in the retina followed by the later proliferation of vascular membranes reaching into the vitreous humor (Figure 17.9). These membranes may lead to traction and the ultimate detachment of a portion of the retina and distortions of the macula (Avery & Glass, 1988). This will affect both eyes, although one may be more damaged than the other. During fetal development, the formation of blood vessels in the retina progresses outwardly from the optic nerve. Because the macula rests near the optic nerve, the very premature infant (28–30 week gestation) is likely to have ROP involving more areas of the retina, impairing vision. The formation of blood vessels is complete by 40 weeks gestation, at which time the risk of ROP disappears.

The causes of ROP are not completely known. However, it is clear that oxygen supplementation used to treat respiratory distress syndrome is one of the major fac-

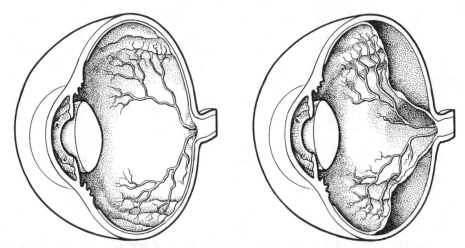

Figure 17.9.   Retinopathy of prematurity. Blood vessels in the retina proliferate. Eventually they stop growing, leaving a fibrous scar that contracts and, in the most severe cases, pulls the retina away from the back of the eye, causing blindness. (From Batshaw, M.L. [1991]. *Your child has a disability. A complete sourcebook of daily and medical care*. Boston. Little, Brown; reprinted by permission.)

tors. As a result, newborn intensive care units now use the lowest concentrations of oxygen possible. Attempts to prevent ROP using vitamin E, an antioxidant, have not proven successful (Johnson, Quinn, Abbasi, et al, 1989). The best approach to therapy is prevention by delaying delivery of a premature infant so that the retina has more time to develop and by treating respiratory distress syndrome with surfactant replacement treatment (see Chapter 7).

If ROP cannot be prevented, it can at least be detected early so treatment can be instituted. An ophthalmologist should examine the retina of the premature infant at frequent intervals during the first months of life. If abnormal blood vessel development and buckling of the retina are observed, laser or cryotherapy may be used to prevent retinal detachment. Cryotherapy involves placing a cold source against the sclera overlying the affected area of the retina (Phelps & Phelps, 1989). Lasers are used to cauterize the abnormal area of the retina. This reduces the likelihood of traction and retinal detachment. This treatment has reduced blindness resulting from ROP significantly (Gallo & Lennerstrand, 1991). The most likely residual abnormality of ROP now is high myopia, which can be corrected with glasses. Other complications of ROP may include macular distortions, glaucoma, and strabismus.

Retinoblastoma   The retina also may be damaged by a tumor, the most common being *retinoblastoma*. About 40% of these malignant tumors are inherited as an autosomal dominant disorder linked to a deletion in the long arm of chromosome #13 (Abramson, 1990). The portion deleted is thought to contain a gene that normally suppresses the development of retinoblastoma. In this form of retinoblastoma, the tumor develops in both eyes.

Retinoblastoma has an incidence of about 1 in 17,000 and is usually diagnosed between 1–2 years of age (Abramson, 1990). When the tumor forms, it is attached to the retina, but it subsequently grows into the vitreous humor. The most common finding is a white pupil that may simulate a cataract. However, the tumor can be distinguished through an ophthalmoscopic examination and on a CT, MRI, or ultrasound scan of the eye. In the noninherited form of this disease, there is usually a unilateral tumor, and the surgeons may choose to remove the affected eye. In bilateral tumors, the more severely affected eye is removed, while the other eye is treated with chemotherapy, radiotherapy, or laser therapy. There is a 90% cure rate, although vision in the affected eye is usually compromised or lost (Amendola, Lamm, Markoe, et al., 1990). There is also an increased risk of the later development of nonocular malignant tumors.

The Optic Nerve

Deep within the retina, the rods and cones are connected to the cells of the optic nerve via bipolar neurons. Over a million of these nerve cells join to form the optic nerve. The part of the eye where this junction occurs is called the *optic disc*, or the blind spot of the eye (see Figure 17.1). If you cover one eye, stare straight ahead, and move one finger across the field of vision of your other eye, the finger will disappear at one point. This corresponds to the optic disc on the retina. Because this place contains nerve fibers but neither rods nor cones, no vision occurs.

One optic nerve emerges from behind each eye. A portion of the fibers of each crosses at a point called the *optic chiasm* (Figure 17.10). This point rests within the skull, just before the nerves enter the brain. The nerve tract continues through the cerebral hemisphere to the occipital lobes (see Figure 17.10). There the image received by the retina is perceived and coordinated with the sounds transmitted from the ear to form a complete message that can be interpreted.

Damage to various parts of the pathway or the occipital lobe brings about different kinds of vision loss. For instance, damage to the right occipital lobe or to the right optic pathway itself will make a person blind to objects in the left visual field of each eye (see Figure 17.10). By identifying the part of a visual field a person cannot see, an ophthalmologist often can determine where the damage has occurred.

Amblyopia Amblyopia is the term used to describe a reduction in visual acuity without overt signs of eye abnormality. In other words, vision is impaired despite a normal cornea, lens, retina, and optic nerve, and the vision loss cannot be corrected by glasses or contact lenses. Amblyopia occurs as a consequence of prolonged blurred or absent retinal images in children younger than 9 years of age. The incidence is about 2% in this population of children (Stager, Birch, & Weakley, 1990).

Amblyopia has been associated with a number of conditions, including cataracts, corneal clouding, strabismus, and unequal refraction errors. Cataracts and corneal clouding lead to amblyopia as a consequence of "deprivation" while strabismus and refractive errors cause amblyopia because of "suppression." If a child has a cataract or corneal clouding that severely obscures vision, there is a lack of stimulation of the cortical visual pathways. In a young child, this lack of stimulation leads to a regression of this neural pathway, much as a lack of movement of a spastic limb leads to its atrophy. For example, if a congenital cataract is not removed before 3 months of

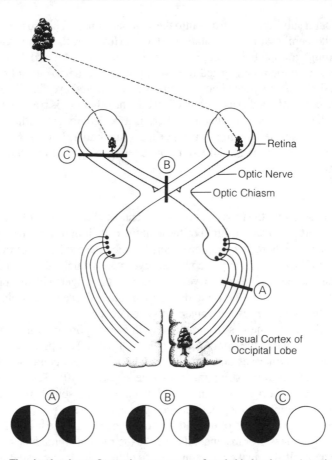

Figure 17.10. The visual pathway. One optic nerve emerges from behind each eye. A portion of the fibers of each crosses at the optic chiasm. An abnormality at various points along the route (upper figure) will lead to different patterns of visual loss (lower figure). These are illustrated: A) abnormality at the cortical pathway; B) damage to the optic chiasm; C) retinal damage.

age, vision in the eye is likely to be restricted to 20/200 or less, even if it is subsequently removed. However, if it is removed within 2 months, vision is likely to be 20/80 or better (Stager et al., 1990). Evidence in support of this cause of amblyopia was provided in the Nobel prize-winning work of Drs. David Hubel and Thorsten Wiesel (1979). These investigators showed, in infant monkeys, that prolonged covering of one eye led to an actual decrease in the number of nerve cells in the occipital cortex.

When amblyopia is associated with strabismus and unequal refractive errors, it involves suppression of a double or blurred image. Normally, when a person focuses on an object, the image of the object falls simultaneously on the fovea of each eye. The impulses carrying these two identical images then travel along the optic pathway to the occipital cortex, where they are fused into a **stereoscopic** picture (Friendly, 1987). If one eye points in one direction and the other in a different direction, two different images fall on the foveas, and the occipital cortex perceives two separate pictures. If this persists, in order to avoid double vision resulting from strabismus or blurred vision created by unequal refractive errors, the brain will suppress the image from the weaker eye. This suppression has the same effect as deprivation on the weaker visual pathway, leading to its atrophy and resultant amblyopia.

Amblyopia occurs only in preadolescent children. Once the visual pathways have fully formed, they will not regress. Thus, an adolescent who develops strabismus as a result of an accident will not become amblyopic, even if the strabismus is not corrected. However, he or she will have persistent double vision.

Because amblyopia cannot be effectively corrected later in life, the best approach is prevention in early childhood. This involves proper refraction of unequal refractive errors, early removal of a cataract that is impairing vision, and correction of strabismus. Once these treatments have been administered, the child still may need therapy to strengthen vision in the "lazy eye." By using an occlusive patch on the stronger eye and/or glasses or contact lenses on the weaker eye, the child is forced to fixate with the weaker eye. In general, the younger the child, the more effective and rapid the response to occlusive therapy. Adhesive-backed gauze pads are generally worn during the waking hours for a treatment period of a few weeks to a few months. Behavior management techniques may be required to keep the child from pulling off the pad. If successful, the patching time can be reduced gradually, although the patch may need to be worn for some time each day for many months or even years. Most children will improve with occlusive patching, but approximately half will have a recurrence later in childhood and require a second period of patching.

The Eye Muscles

Six eye muscles direct the eye toward an object and maintain binocular vision (Figure 17.11). Four of these muscles rest along the four sides of the eye. The other two are placed obliquely and help to rotate the eye. The complex, coordinated movement of these eye muscles allows us to look in all directions without turning our heads. The loss of this coordinated movement leads to squint, or strabismus.

Strabismus   Abnormal alignment of the eyes occurs in about 3%–4% of children but in 15% of former premature infants and in 40% of children with cerebral palsy (Nelson et al., 1991). Strabismus usually becomes evident between 18–36 months of age (Fielder, 1989). Two main forms of strabismus exist: *esotropia* and *exotropia*. When a child has esotropia, the eyes turn in. If the child has exotropia, the eyes turn out (see Figure 17.11). Esotropia is more common. The improper alignment may be apparent all the time or only intermittently, such as when the child tires. Intermittent eye deviations are unlikely to cause visual problems, whereas uncorrected, ongoing deviations in a child under the age of 9 years may lead to amblyopia.

Strabismus may result from an abnormality in eye focusing, in the nerves supplying the eye muscles, or in the brain. In some children, farsightedness may be the reason for the esotropia. By wearing glasses to correct the farsightedness, the child's esotropia also is corrected (Catalano, 1990). In cerebral palsy, brain damage may alter the brain's signals to the eye muscles and cause strabismus. Here, glasses are

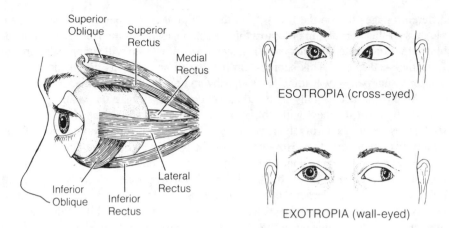

Figure 17.11. The eye muscles. Six muscles move the eyeball. A weakness of these muscles causes strabismus, or squint. In esotropia, the eye turns in, while in exotropia, the eye turns out. Esotropia and exotropia of the left eye are illustrated.

usually not sufficient. Corrective eye muscle surgery may be necessary to realign the eyes (Deutsch & Nelson, 1990). This is also true of the child with hydrocephalus who develops strabismus from nerve palsy relating to increased intracranial pressure. The child also may need to wear an occlusive patch over the good eye for some time after strabismus surgery. Approximately 75% of children show significant improvement following surgery (Fielder, 1989).

VISION TESTS

Because infants normally have a number of visual skills, it is not difficult to identify children who are totally blind. Determining a partial visual loss in infancy is more difficult. Furthermore, there is the possibility of mistakenly identifying a child with mental retardation as having a severe visual loss. Such a child may be delayed in the development of visual skills; however, other developmental skills should be equally delayed.

Different tests are used to evaluate visual acuity at various ages. Four approaches have been used to assess visual acuity in infants and young children: 1) fixing and following, 2) checking the **opticokinetic** response, 3) performing preferential looking tests, and 4) measuring visual evoked responses (VERs) (Birch, 1989).

Testing of fixing and following is best accomplished by standing in front of the infant. The infant should be observed to determine if he or she looks at the person and visually follows the person as he or she walks around the room. As noted previously, a full-term newborn should fixate on a face, while a 1- to 2-month-old infant should begin to follow. The absence of fixing and following suggests a severe vision loss. However, the absence also may be a consequence of inattention or severe mental retardation.

The opticokinetic response is determined by twirling a black and white striped cylinder in front of the child. Similar to the effect of watching a picket fence from a passing car, the child's eyes should jiggle as they rapidly focus first on one stripe and then on another. If the child's eyes do not move, he or she may have a significant vision problem. However, it also may mean that the child is simply not focusing on the stripes. Thus, this test is not a very accurate measure.

Another approach, preferential looking, involves alternating the position and size of a round checkerboard placed on a wall in front of the child. This test is based on the observation that children have a natural preference for images that have texture and character. They prefer a grid of black and white stripes to a solid color. This test can be performed in children from 6 months to 3 years of age. Two hidden examiners are required; one changes the position of the grids while the second observes the child's eye movements. The child's visual acuity is then determined by varying the size of the grid. A variation of this procedure is the Teller acuity test (Teller, McDonald, & Preston, 1986), in which a series of cards are held in front of the child, one with black and white stripes and the other with a solid color (Figure 17.12). The child should look toward the card with stripes until the grids become too narrow and close together to be discriminated from a solid color.

A final approach to vision testing is measuring what are called visual evoked

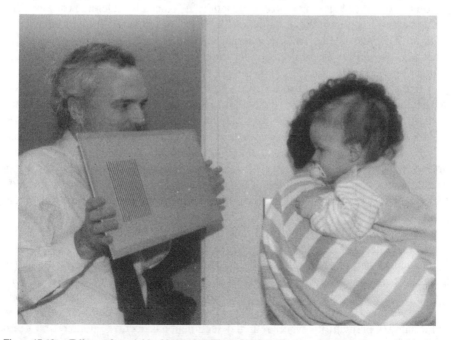

Figure 17.12. Teller preferential looking cards. The infant is held and a grated pattern on a card is shown on one side and a single color card on the other. The baby prefers the grate to a plain color. The sides are switched to ensure the baby is looking at the pattern. Successively smaller grates are shown until the child no longer shows a preference, indicating that he or she cannot differentiate the grate from the solid color. The smallest discriminable size grate determines visual acuity.

responses. This technique ascertains the electrical reaction of the occipital cortex to a visual stimulus. In this test, electrodes are placed on the back of the child's head, and a flash of light or a checkerboard pattern is displayed in front of the child's eyes. Within a split second, the electrode that rests over the occipital lobe should record an electrical impulse. If this does not happen, the abnormality in vision lies somewhere between the eye and the occipital cortex. However, the child simply may not be focusing on the display so this is not always a very accurate measurement.

For older children, the simplest approach to visual screening is to ask the child what he or she sees. In school-age children, this involves the use of the Snellen eye charts, which contain letters of various sizes. This card is placed 20 feet away from the person who covers one eye and reads from the largest letter down to the smallest line he or she can distinguish. Normal vision is defined as 20/20. If an individual can only read down to the 20/40 line, he or she is assumed to have a mild visual deficiency. This means that the smallest letter he or she can identify can be seen by a person with normal vision from 40 feet away. A person with a severe visual deficiency cannot read the 20/100 line even with glasses.

Because a Snellen eye chart can only be used for children old enough to know the letters of the alphabet, a modification of this chart is used for children age 4–6 years (Hall, Pugh, & Hall, 1983). This is called the tumbling "E" chart. Instead of having various letters, the chart contains only the letter "E" placed in different positions. The child is asked to point in the direction of the "legs" of the letter. A variation used in children 2–4 years is the Allen Kindergarten Chart. Pictures of animals, toys, or other familiar objects are projected on a screen and the child is asked to name them (Birch, 1989) (Figure 17.13).

A thorough eye exam also involves other tests. An ophthalmologist uses a slit lamp to examine the front part of the eye and an **ophthalmoscope** to examine the back portion. The slit lamp, a machine that produces a high-intensity band of light, is used to look for damage to the cornea and the lens. The ophthalmoscope, a device consisting of a series of magnifying lenses and a light source, is used to examine the retina, optic nerve, and retinal blood vessels (Figure 17.14). With it, an ophthalmologist can detect tumors, abnormalities of the optic nerve, and damage to the retina or its blood supply. Finally, the tonometer is used to measure pressure in the eyeball to rule out glaucoma.

In a blind child, these tests still may not locate the source of the problem. For such a child, the electroretinogram (ERG) or the previously mentioned VER measuring may prove helpful. In the ERG, a contact lens containing an electrode is applied to the child's cornea. A light is then flashed in front of the child's eyes. The electrode registers the retina's response to light. No electrical current after the light is flashed indicates that the retina is damaged. This test is abnormal in children with severe retinopathy of prematurity, where retinal detachment has occurred, or in retinitis pigmentosa. If the child appears to be blind but the ERG is normal, the diagnosis may be cortical blindness. In this instance, the abnormality rests either in the occipital lobe of the brain or in the pathway leading from the retina to the brain. The VER measurement should be abnormal in these instances.

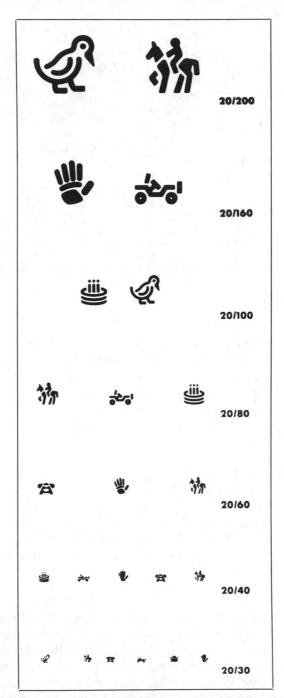

Figure 17.13.   Allen Kindergarten Chart. The child names the various pictures down as far as he or she can go. The smallest line that can be named indicates visual acuity (Courtesy of Richmond Products, Inc.)

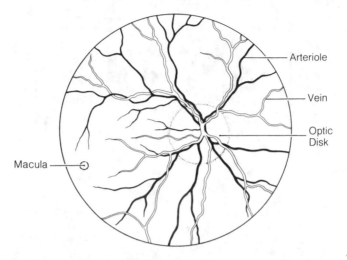

Figure 17.14. Looking through an ophthalmoscope, an ophthalmologist can examine a portion of the retina, including the optic nerve or disc, the macula, and blood vessels.

BLINDNESS

Legal blindness is defined as visual acuity in both eyes of less than 20/200 or a visual field of less than 20° despite the best correction with glasses. The normal visual field is about 105°. A partially sighted person is one who has visual acuity ranging from 20/70 to 20/200 with correction (Buncic, 1987). Many children who are legally blind still can distinguish shades of light. Totally blind people do not have light and dark perception. Visual efficiency also must be considered. A child who has a visual loss and myopia, for example, has more limited functional vision than a child with visual loss alone.

The overall incidence of blindness in children is 1 in 3,000; 46% of these children were born blind, and an additional 38% lost their sight before 1 year of age (Foster, 1988). Among blind children, approximately 25% are totally blind, 25% have some light perception, and the remaining 50% may have enough vision to read enlarged type (Buncic, 1987). The most common sites of the visual impairment are the retina (36%), the optic nerve or pathways to the brain (22%), the lens (17%), and the eye (16%) (Nelson et al., 1991).

Causes of Blindness

In childhood, the causes of blindness are many and varied (Williamson, Desmond, Andrew, et al., 1987). The most common congenital causes are intrauterine infections and malformations. Intrauterine infections, such as rubella and toxoplasmosis, may cause severe retinal damage. Malformations of the visual system range from colobomas of the retina to optic nerve hypoplasia and cerebral malformations. Other causes of blindness include retinopathy of prematurity, head trauma, anoxic events, eye infections, and tumors. Blindness is far more prevalent in developing countries where nutritional disorders, such as vitamin-A deficiency, infections such as **trachoma**, and measles and tuberculosis are common (Foster & Johnson, 1990). Public health measures, such as the use of silver nitrate drops at birth to prevent infections in infants' eyes and immunization programs, are gradually making an inroad into this tragic situation.

Cortical Blindness   When blindness is unassociated with abnormalities in the eye itself, it is termed *cortical blindness* (Whiting, Jan, Wong, et al., 1985). It is, in a sense, a profound case of amblyopia. Cortical blindness implies that there is a problem somewhere along the visual pathway leading from the optic nerve to the occipital lobe of the brain. In this case, the ERG should be normal while the VER is abnormal. Causes of cortical blindness include brain infections, such as meningitis and encephalitis, anoxia, and traumatic brain injury. Unlike retinal blindness, cortical blindness can improve over time, although the reason for this is unclear. It has been hypothesized that alternate neuronal pathways or cortical areas take over the vision function. As a result of these adaptations, it is difficult to predict the ultimate visual abilities of a young child with cortical blindness (Wong, 1991).

Identifying the Blind Child

Blindness can be an isolated disability or part of a condition involving multiple disabilities. For example, blindness caused by ROP is often an isolated finding, while blindness caused by congenital rubella usually is associated with congenital heart disease, hearing loss, cerebral palsy, and mental retardation. About half of totally blind children have other developmental disabilities (Warburg, Frederiksen, & Rattleff, 1979).

Considering the infant who has blindness as an isolated disability, several clues may point to the loss of vision. The child does not visually fixate on a parent's face or show interest in following brightly colored objects. Parents also may notice abnormalities in the movement of the child's eyes. The eyes have random, jerky, uncoordinated movements called **nystagmus**. Nystagmus may even occur in children with less severe visual loss. There also may be roving eye movements, as the child neither focuses on an object nor follows it. Strabismus is often present. When a threatening gesture is made, the infant does not blink or cry. Any of these findings should lead to the child's being examined by an ophthalmologist.

Development of the Blind Child

Even with normal intelligence, a child who is blind from birth or early childhood is delayed developmentally (Dekker & Koole, 1992; Teplin, 1983). Muscle tone is decreased, partly because its maintenance depends on visual perception. Because of this, gross motor skills are delayed. The child may not sit until after 8 months and usually does not crawl at all (Figure 17.15). The child may not take steps until 2–2½ years of age. A blind child tends to have a wide-based gait to help provide support in the absence of visual cues. Fine motor skills are also delayed or unusual.

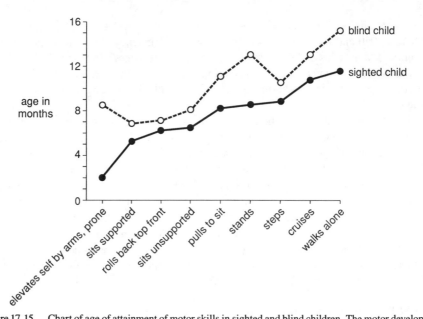

Figure 17.15.   Chart of age of attainment of motor skills in sighted and blind children. The motor development of a blind child is delayed (adapted from Fraiberg, 1977). (From Batshaw, M.L. [1991]. *Your child has a disability: A complete sourcebook of daily and medical care.* Boston: Little, Brown; reprinted by permission.)

Reaching for objects occurs at 9 months rather than 4 months, and the child reaches toward a sound rather than turning toward it. Self-feeding skills are similarly delayed (Fraiberg, 1977).

Since speech is learned by imitating mouth movements as well as by listening to sounds, language development is delayed (Pring, 1984). The blind child must learn to speak using auditory means alone. This is a slow, painstaking process, often accompanied by **echolalia.** The child also may imitate noises in the environment (e.g., cars, flushing toilets) and have difficulty differentiating "I" from "you." In the child with normal intellect, speech and language become more normal by school age. However, speech is accompanied by less body and facial expression, and there is little nonverbal communication (Greenwald, 1983).

In addition to developmental delays, the blind child may exhibit unusual behaviors. Self-stimulatory behaviors may include eye pressing, blinking forcefully, gazing at lights, waving fingers between the face and a strong light, rolling the head, and swaying the body (Good & Hoyt, 1989). Eye pressing seems to occur only in children with retinal disease in whom it produces visual stimulation. Self-stimulatory behaviors occur most commonly when the child is bored or tired. This behavior can be controlled using behavior management techniques, and tends to decrease by 4 years of age in children with normal intelligence. However, it usually persists in children who also have mental retardation or hearing loss (Jan, 1991).

Since the Bayley Scales of Infant Development and other infant developmental scales are based primarily on performance of visual skills, they are not very useful for evaluating blind infants. IQ testing for these children is difficult before they reach a cognitive level of 5 years. After that, the verbal subtests of the Wechsler Intelligence Scale for Children may give a fairly accurate picture of the child's intelligence and help in educational planning. A special test, the Perkins-Binet Intelligence Scale for the Visually Handicapped, also can be used (Wodrich & Kush, 1990). There is evidence that blind children have more difficulty with abstract concepts than sighted children, but they do well with computation.

Stimulating the Blind Child

The primary ways for the blind child to explore the world are through touch and sound (Ferrell, 1985). Therefore, parents and therapists should place toys within or just outside the child's reach, and they should encourage the child to explore the environment without fear (Heiner, 1986). Toys that are textured or make sounds are particularly favored; dolls carry little interest. Finger foods are useful in teaching independent feeding. Blind children generally do not like mushy or sticky food because they prefer to keep their hands clean and sensitive to touch.

As an infant, the blind child should be placed on the stomach rather than on the back to strengthen neck and trunk muscles. Cradle gyms are good to promote the use of muscles in pulling. Once a toddler, the child also should be urged to walk despite the risks of scrapes and bruises. Poor peripheral vision (tunnel vision) is more of a problem in walking than the loss of central vision. However, any residual vision is better than none, and its use should be stimulated as much as possible. The use of aids for walking is in dispute. Generally, children who can see fingers 12 inches away are able to travel independently. For children with more severe visual impairments, teachers and therapists advocate the use of seeing eye dogs, canes, or laser-guided obstacle devices. The laser device provides information about the size and distance of obstacles. Most of these professionals believe that a child should use whatever works best to attain the greatest degree of independence (Sonksen, Petrie, & Drew, 1991).

Self-dressing should be encouraged by using Velcro straps for shoes, pants, and shirts. It is important for parents to talk to their child, explaining and describing the world, and to allow the child to touch and smell many things. Parents should try not to be discouraged by slow development and not to overprotect the child (Fraiberg, 1977). Parents must realize that until the congenitally blind child reaches 4–5 years of age, the child does not realize he or she is different from other children.

The play of blind children is also different. Interactive play develops more slowly, as do other social interactions. Also, their play tends to lack imagination and be stereotypic (Parsons, 1986). Preschool and kindergarten programs are very helpful in expanding these skills.

Educating the Blind Child

The definition of blindness from a federal educational standpoint (PL 101-476, the Individuals with Disabilities Education Act) is the same as that stated previously in this chapter: visual acuity in both eyes of less than 20/200 or a visual field of less than 20° despite the best correction with glasses (Bishop, 1991). Partially sighted students are defined as having a visual acuity better than 20/200 but worse than 20/70 with correction. Specific educational placement for a child depends on age, extent of visual loss, and presence of other disabilities (Scott, Jan, & Freeman, 1985).

For the partially sighted or blind child, it is important to start an infant stimulation program by 6 months of age. Usually, this involves a home-based program in which the teacher visits and works with the parent and child once a week. Besides language and exploration, the teacher works on motor skills (Sonksen et al., 1991).

By 2 years of age, the child is usually ready for a special preschool program. Listening and conversation skills need to be emphasized. Work on self-help skills, such as dressing and feeding, and social skills, such as controlling self-stimulatory behavior and improving participation in communal activities, is important.

By the time the child with visual impairment reaches school age, the extent of the visual loss is usually clear. A child with better than 20/200 vision may be able to read large print books. This child often can be mainstreamed into a regular school classroom with the use of visual aids and resource help. The child should be placed in the front of the classroom and do schoolwork and assignments on a computer. By high school, technical and vocational training generally is incorporated into the curriculum. Many colleges now accept and make accommodations for students with visual impairments.

The partially sighted child, with 20/200 vision, can get around a room without assistance, but reading is difficult. However, this child may be able to read using a ViewScan, a machine that employs a camera to project an image onto a screen in any size print and contrast required (Jan & Robinson, 1989).

Children who are totally blind need to learn braille and use talking books, computers, and tutors (Jan, Sykanda, & Groenveld, 1990). Braille is a written language formed as a series of raised dots on a page and read from left to right. Text can be converted to braille using a machine, called an Optacon, that changes typed text into a tactile stimulus of vibrating "pins." Another system, VersaBraille, can convert material received by a computer into braille. Computer printouts can also be converted into speech using a Kurzweil Reading Machine, and TotalTalk and other programs provide speech capacity to a personal computer. There is even a Talking Calculator that reacts with spoken numbers as calculations are performed. In addition, books on tape are generally available at bookstores and libraries. With these tools, blind children with normal intelligence often can follow a normal curriculum as well as receive special services.

The Blind Child with Multiple Disabilities

The incidence of blindness in children with multiple disabilities is more than 200 times that found in the normal population (Warburg et al., 1979). One-third of partially sighted and two-thirds of blind children have other disabilities including mental retardation, hearing impairments, seizure disorders, congenital heart disease, and cerebral palsy. Sixty-five percent of the children have two or more disabilities besides blindness (Curtis & Donlon, 1984).

In the study conducted by Warberg et al. (1979), the most common causes of blindness in these children with multiple disabilities were malformations of the central nervous system (35%), prenatal and postnatal infections (13%), genetic disorders (17%), and prematurity (12%). The most frequent causes of visual impairments were optic atrophy (39%), cortical blindness (20%), retinal abnormalities (15%), cataracts (7%), and malformations of the eye (6%).

Treatment of these children must address all the disabilities and must use all the senses and abilities that remain. A multidisciplinary approach involving a range of health care professionals is essential.

Beth: A Blind Child

Beth was born prematurely at 32 weeks gestation and weighed 2½ pounds. Because she had a severe case of respiratory distress syndrome, she received high levels of oxygen for many weeks. When she was discharged at 2 months of age, her parents were delighted with her progress. She was alert, active, and fed eagerly.

Since the doctors had warned Beth's parents that her development might lag because of her prematurity, they were not initially concerned when she neither seemed to focus her eyes nor smile. They did become concerned, however, when, at 3 months of age, she still showed no interest in brightly colored mobiles and would not smile socially. Beth's pediatrician also became concerned. She was aware of a condition, retrolental fibroplasia (now called retinopathy of prematurity), that was common among premature infants. When she examined Beth, she confirmed that the child neither fixated nor followed objects. She examined Beth's retina with an ophthalmoscope and found a partial detachment of the retina in both eyes. Since no therapy was then available, all the pediatrician could do was advise the parents that the extent of Beth's loss of vision would become more apparent as she grew.

As was to be expected, Beth continued to develop slowly. She had decreased muscle tone and did not sit until 12 months of age. Her speech was also delayed, although her understanding of language was appropriate for her age.

By 2 years of age, Beth's behavior became a definite problem. She was very reluctant to try new things, and when frustrated, she would often hold her breath or scream. She also rocked, banged her head, and pressed on her eyes.

At this time, Beth's parents knew she had some perception of light and dark. She did move toward a bright light and would reach in the general direction of the light. But they also recognized that she would not reach toward a large object placed as close as 1 foot away from her.

Until this time, Beth's parents had been guilt-ridden and depressed over their child's condition and had catered to her every whim. Beth, at 3 years of age, was a tyrant. Feeling that something had to be done, Beth's parents consulted their pediatrician. She convinced them that their guilt feelings were felt by all parents of children with disabilities and were a normal reaction. At the same time, she encouraged them to be strict and consistent with Beth and not to give in to her demands. She also advised them to enroll Beth in a preschool program.

This was a turning point in Beth's life. Her parents' responses to her changed. When she screamed, they carried her to her room where they left her for a few minutes until she composed herself. When she started rocking and banging her head, her parents would ignore her or would involve her in other tasks. Soon this behavior stopped. She entered a small nursery school program with sighted children. Gradually, she adapted and became more independent. Her parents also attended classes to learn to teach Beth at home.

Things went smoothly until Beth was 8 years old. After a fall, her retinas completely detached. Her world became completely dark. Without light perception, Beth had to make new adaptations. For some time, she was terribly depressed. She tried using a seeing eye dog, but eventually gave him up because she felt this labeled her as being abnormal. Instead, she chose to use a cane and memorized the location of objects and steps in her home and her school.

In high school, Beth did very well. By this time she had learned braille and also used talking books and tutors. Although she had to spend 4–5 hours a night doing homework, she graduated with honors. She subsequently attended college, married, and has two children.

PROGNOSIS FOR SEVERE VISUAL IMPAIRMENT

The prognosis for the child with severe visual impairment or blindness depends most on the amount of residual vision and the child's intellectual function (Warburg, 1983). The less the visual impairment and the higher the IQ, the better the prognosis. In one study of 82 children who were blind (18 also had mental retardation), 33 did well in a mainstreamed school setting, 41 had a mixed school performance, and 8 did poorly. At 25 years of age, 17 were married, and 43 still lived at home. Sixty-six traveled independently, and 27 were gainfully employed.

SUMMARY

Our eyes help us to perceive and to understand our world. Indirectly, they also affect the development of muscle tone, language, and other developmental skills. The causes of blindness are many, ranging from cataracts to retinopathy of prematurity and from infections to tumors. When the visual acuity is less than 20/200 with correction, the person is considered to be legally blind. A person with 20/70 to 20/200 vision with correction can read large type books. A totally blind person must rely on braille or other aids. As an isolated disability, blindness is compatible with an independent and successful lifestyle. However, when combined with other developmental disabilities, the outcome is generally not good. To a great extent, the prognosis for a blind child depends on the extent of the visual loss, the child's intelligence and motivation, parental involvement, and the skill of his or her teachers.

REFERENCES

Abramson, D.H. (1990). Retinoblastoma 1990: Diagnosis, treatment, and implications. *Pediatric Annals, 19*, 387–395.

Adams, R.J., Maurer, D., & Davis, M. (1986). Newborns' discrimination of chromatic from achromatic stimuli. *Journal of Experimental Child Psychology, 41,* 267.

Amendola, B.E., Lamm, F.R., Markoe, A.M., et al. (1990). Radiotherapy of retinoblastoma. A review of 63 children treated with different irradiation techniques. *Cancer, 66,* 21–26.

Avery, G.B., & Glass, P. (1988). Retinopathy of prematurity: What causes it? *Clinics in Perinatology, 15,* 917–928.

Birch, E.E. (1989). Visual acuity testing in infants and young children. *Ophthalmology Clinics of North America, 13,* 369–389.

Birch, E.E., & Stager, D.R. (1988). Prevalence of good visual acuity following surgery for congenital unilateral cataract. *Archives of Ophthalmology, 106,* 40–43.

Bishop, V.E. (1991). Preschool visually impaired children: A demographic study. *Journal of Visual Impairment and Blindness, 85,* 69–74.

Boothe, R.G., Dobson, V., & Teller, D.Y. (1985). Postnatal development of vision in human and nonhuman primates. *Annual Review of Neuroscience, 8,* 495–545.

Buncic, J.R. (1987). The blind child. *Pediatric Clinics of North America, 34,* 1403–1414.

Catalano, J.D. (1990). Strabismus. *Pediatric Annals, 19,* 289, 292–297.

Curtis, W.S., & Donlon, E.T. (1984). A ten-year follow-up study of deaf-blind children. *Exceptional Child, 50,* 449–455.

Dekker, R., & Koole, F.D. (1992). Visually impaired children's visual characteristics and intelligence. *Developmental Medicine & Child Neurology, 34,* 123–133.

Deutsch, J.A., & Nelson, L.B. (1990). Diagnosis and management of childhood strabismus. *Pediatrician, 17,* 152–162.

DeVoe, W.M. (1988). Prevention of retinopathy of prematurity. *Seminars in Perinatology, 12,* 373–380.

Endres, W., & Shin, Y.S. (1990). Cataract and metabolic disease. *Journal of Inherited Metabolic Disease, 13,* 509–516.

Epstein, R.J. (1991). Contact lenses for the correction of pediatric aphakia. *International Ophthalmology Clinics, 31,* 53–60.

Ferrell, K.A. (1985). *Reach out and teach: Materials for parents of visually handicapped and multihandicapped young children.* New York: American Foundation for the Blind.

Fielder, A.R. (1989). The management of squint. *Archives of Disease in Childhood, 64,* 413–418.

Foster, A. (1988). Childhood blindness. *Eye, 2* (Suppl), S27–S36.

Foster, A., & Johnson, G.J. (1990). Magnitude and causes of blindness in the developing world. *International Ophthalmology, 14,* 135–140.

Fraiberg, S. (1977). *Insights from the blind.* New York: Basic Books.

Franks, W., & Taylor, D. (1989). Congenital glaucoma—A preventable cause of blindness. *Archives of Disease in Childhood, 64,* 649–650.

Friendly, D.S. (1987). Amblyopia. *Pediatric Clinics of North America, 34,* 1389–1402.

Gallo, J.E., & Lennerstrand, G. (1991). A population-based study of ocular abnormalities in premature children aged 5 to 10 years. *American Journal of Ophthalmology, 111,* 539–547.

Goldson, E., Smith, A.C., & Stewart, J.M. (1986). The CHARGE association: How well can they do? *American Journal of Diseases of Children, 140,* 918–921.

Good, W.V., & Hoyt, C.S. (1989). Behavioral correlates of poor vision in children. *International Ophthalmology Clinics, 29,* 57–60.

Greenwald, M.J. (1983). Visual development in infancy and childhood. *Pediatric Clinics of North America, 30,* 977–993.

Hall, S.M., Pugh, A.G., & Hall, D.M. (1982). Vision screening in under 5s. *British Medical Journal, 285,* 1096–1098.

Heiner, D. (1986). *Learning to look. A handbook for parents of low vision infants and young children.* Lansing, MI: International Institute for the Visually Impaired.

Hubel, D.H., & Wiesel, T.N. (1979). Brain mechanisms of vision. *Scientific American, 241*(3), 150–162.

Isenberg, S.J. (1988). *The eye in infancy*. Chicago: Yearbook Medical Publishers.

Jan, J.E. (1991). Head movements of visually impaired children. *Developmental Medicine and Child Neurology, 33,* 645–647.

Jan, J.E., & Robinson, G.C. (1989). A multidisciplinary program for visually impaired children and youths. *International Ophthalmology Clinics, 29,* 33–36.

Jan, J.E., Sykanda, A., & Groenveld, M. (1990). Habilitation and rehabilitation of visually impaired and blind children. *Pediatrician, 17,* 202–207.

Johnson, L., Quinn, G.E., Abbasi, S., et al. (1989). Effect of sustained pharmacologic vitamin E levels on incidence and severity of retinopathy of prematurity: A controlled clinical trial. *Journal of Pediatrics, 114,* 827–838.

Lambert, S.R., Kriss, A., Taylor, D., et al. (1989). Follow-up and diagnostic reappraisal of 75 patients with Leber's congenital amaurosis. *American Journal of Ophthalmology, 107,* 624–631.

Nathans, J., Piantanida, T.P., Eddy, R.L., et al. (1986). Molecular genetics of inherited variations in human color vision. *Science, 232,* 203–210.

Nelson, L.B., Calhoun, J.H., & Harley, R.D. (1991). *Pediatric ophthalmology (3rd ed.)*. Philadelphia: W.B. Saunders.

Pagon, R.A. (1988). Retinitis pigmentosa. *Survey of Ophthalmology, 33,* 137–177.

Parsons, S. (1986). Function of play in low-vision children. *Journal of Visual Impairment and Blindness, 80,* 777–782.

Pernoud, F.G., III. (1990). Inherited and developmental corneal disorders. *Pediatric Annals, 19,* 326–333.

Phelps, D.L., & Phelps, C.E. (1989). Cryotherapy in infants with retinopathy of prematurity. A decision model for treating one or both eyes. *Journal of the American Medical Association, 261,* 1751–1756.

Pring, L. (1984). A comparison of the word recognition processes of blind and sighted children. *Child Development, 55,* 1865–1877.

Sadler, T.W. (1990). *Langman's medical embryology* (6th ed.). Baltimore: Williams & Wilkins.

Scott, E.P., Jan, J.E., & Freeman, R.D. (1985). *Can't your child see?* (2nd ed.). Austin, TX: PRO-ED.

Sonksen, P.M., Petrie, A., & Drew, K.J. (1991). Promotion of visual development of severely visually impaired babies: Evaluation of a developmentally based programme. *Developmental Medicine and Child Neurology, 33,* 320–335.

Stager, D.R., Birch, E.E., & Weakley, D.R. (1990). Amblyopia and the pediatrician. *Pediatric Annals, 19,* 301–305, 309–315.

Teller, D.Y., McDonald, M.A., Preston, K., et al. (1986). Assessment of visual acuity in infants and children. *Developmental Medicine and Child Neurology, 28,* 779–789.

Teplin, S.W. (1983). Development of blind infants and children with retrolental fibroplasia: Implications for physicians. *Pediatrics, 71,* 6–12.

Tongue, A.C. (1987). Refractive errors in children. *Pediatric Clinics of North America, 34,* 1425–1437.

Valentine, P.H., Jackson, J.C., Kalina, R.E., et al. (1989). Increased survival of low birth weight infants: Impact on the incidence of retinopathy of prematurity. *Pediatrics, 84,* 442–445.

Warburg, M. (1983). Why are the blind and severely visually impaired children with mental retardation much more retarded than the sighted children? *Acta Ophthalmologica, 157* (Suppl.), 72–81.

Warburg, M., Frederiksen, P., & Rattleff, J. (1979). Blindness among 7,720 mentally retarded children in Denmark. *Clinical Developmental Medicine, 73,* 56–67.

Whiting, S., Jan, J.E., Wong, P.K., et al. (1985). Permanent cortical visual impairment in children. *Developmental Medicine and Child Neurology, 27,* 730–739.

Williamson, W.D., Desmond, M.M., Andrew, L.P., et al. (1987). Visually impaired infants in the 1980s. A survey of etiologic factors and additional handicapping conditions in a school population. *Clinical Pediatrics, 26,* 241–244.

Wodrich, D.L., & Kush, S.A. (1990). *Children's psychological testing: A guide for nonpsychologists* (2nd ed.). Baltimore: Paul H. Brookes Publishing Co.

Wong, V.C. (1991). Cortical blindness in children: A study of etiology and prognosis. *Pediatric Neurology, 7,* 178–185.

Chapter 18

Hearing

Upon completion of this chapter, the reader will:
—be able to describe the anatomy of the ear
—know the different types of hearing losses and their causes
—be aware of the different hearing tests and their uses
—understand the ways to treat a child with hearing loss
—be able to discuss the prognoses for different hearing impairments

---

Even when alone in the woods, a person is surrounded by meaningful sounds. A gurgling brook indicates water is near. Chirping birds announce daybreak. Rustling leaves may indicate the presence of wind or the approach of an animal. Through hearing, we perceive and understand our surroundings. In this chapter, hearing impairment, its effect on a child's ability to communicate, and its treatment are discussed.

DEFINING SOUND

When we hear a sound, we are actually interpreting a pattern of vibrations that originates somewhere in our surroundings. Similar to what happens when a stone is thrown into a pond, sound waves start at one point and spread out in concentric circles or waves. These waves have both a frequency, or **pitch,** and an *intensity,* or loudness (Figure 18.1).

The closer the waves are to each other, the higher the frequency of the sound. To measure frequency, the number of cycles per second is counted. One cycle is the distance from the top of one wave to the top of the next wave. Humans can hear frequencies ranging from 20 to 20,000 cycles per second, whereas dogs can hear frequencies above 40,000 cycles per second. The unit of measurement of frequency is called a hertz (Hz) and is equal to one cycle per second. Low-pitched sounds have a frequency less than 500 Hz and have a bass quality. High-pitched sounds have a frequency above 2,000 Hz and a tenor quality. Middle C equals 256 Hz. Virtually all speech frequencies are in the range of 250–6,000 Hz (Bess, 1988).

While the frequency of the wave determines its pitch, intensity is defined by the height of the wave. The intensity produced by a sound is measured in decibels (dB).

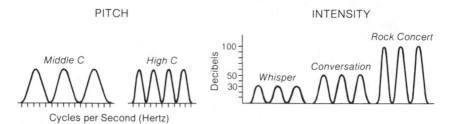

Figure 18.1. Pitch and intensity of sound waves. The pitch of a sound, or its frequency, is expressed as cycles per second, or Hertz (Hz). Middle C is 256 Hz; one octave above is 512 Hz. Intensity of sound is expressed as decibels (dB) and varies from a whisper at 30 dB to a rock music concert at 100 dB or more.

The softest sound a person with normal hearing can perceive is defined as 0 dB hearing level (HL). To put these intensities in context, the sound of a person whispering a few feet away would register 30 dB HL. The normal level of conversation measures 40–60 dB HL, a bell rung near the ear registers around 80 dB, and a rock concert can measure 100 dB HL or more.

What makes things more complicated is that speech does not occur at a single intensity or frequency. In general, vowel sounds have a low frequency while consonant sounds have a high frequency; vowel sounds are also more intense. Furthermore, during a conversation, the speaker will change the intensity of speech by talking in a louder or softer voice to express emotion or emphasis. This adversely affects an individual with a hearing loss, especially if the loss is not consistent along all frequencies. This individual hears only parts of words and often is unable to follow a conversation.

THE HEARING SYSTEM

The mechanism for hearing is a beautifully designed and complex system. It is divided into a peripheral auditory mechanism, which starts at the outer ear and ends at the auditory nerve, and a central auditory system, which runs from the auditory nerve to the brain. A defect in the peripheral system results in a hearing loss, while a central auditory problem interferes with the interpretation of what is heard. The most visible part of this system, the outer ear or *auricle,* is the least important.

Sound waves enter the ear through the auricle, and pass through the 1-inch long ear canal. At the end of this canal lies the *tympanic membrane* or eardrum, which separates the outer and middle ear. The ear canal protects the delicate structures of the middle ear. Glands inside the canal produce a wax that traps debris and moves it away from the ear drum and out of the ear.

When sound waves wash up against the tympanic membrane, they make it vibrate (Figure 18.2). These vibrations are transmitted through the middle ear by means of three tiny bones, or **ossicles.** The first of these bones is the *malleus,* or hammer. Then comes the *incus,* or anvil, followed by the *stapes,* or stirrup. The stapes lies next to the *oval window,* a membrane that serves as the gateway to the inner ear.

In addition to transmitting sound, the tympanic membrane and ossicles amplify

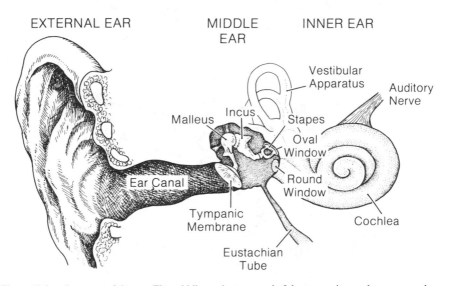

EXTERNAL EAR   MIDDLE   INNER EAR
EAR

Vestibular
Apparatus

Auditory
Nerve

Malleus   Incus   Stapes

Oval
Window

Ear Canal   Round
Window

Cochlea

Tympanic
Membrane

Eustachian
Tube

Figure 18.2.   Structure of the ear. The middle ear is composed of the tympanic membrane, or eardrum, and the three ear bones, the malleus, the incus, and the stapes. The stapes lies next to the oval window, the gateway to the inner ear. The inner ear contains the cochlea and the vestibular apparatus, collectively called the labyrinth.

it by about 30 dB. This amplification does not occur when there is fluid in the middle ear due to a middle ear infection. In addition, an infection usually causes blockage of the eustachian tube, which connects the middle ear to the back of the throat. This tube normally opens and closes with swallowing, allowing the air pressure within the middle ear to equilibrate with the pressure in the back of the throat. It also prevents the accumulation of fluid. When the eustachian tube is not functioning correctly, the middle ear is at risk for infection, fluid collection, and hearing loss.

Even if there is blockage or inflammation of the external or middle ear, sounds can be heard, although they are muffled and have lower intensity. Under these circumstances, sound is heard by bone-conducted vibrations of the temporal bone, which rests behind the ear. These vibrations bypass the external and middle ear and directly stimulate the inner ear.

In the inner ear, sound is transformed from mechanical to electrical energy. To understand how this happens, one must appreciate the complexity of the *labyrinth*. This structure, no bigger than a pea, contains the **vestibular apparatus** and the **cochlea.** The vestibular apparatus helps maintain our balance in walking. The cochlea, a membranous, snail-shaped structure with three chambers, makes hearing possible. The outer and inner chambers, the scala vestibuli and scala tympani, communicate with each other at the end of the cochlear coils and contain a fluid called *perilymph* (Figure 18.3). The middle chamber houses the **organ of Corti** and is bathed in a different fluid called *endolymph*. The organ of Corti consists of multiple rows of delicate hair cells, numbering about 20,000, that are receptors for the auditory nerve. The hair cells near the oval window respond to high-frequency sounds

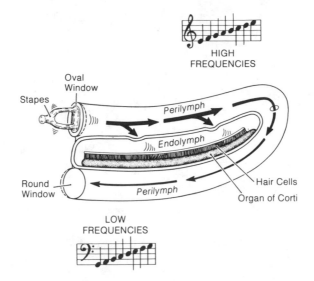

Figure 18.3. The cochlea. The cochlea has been "unfolded" for simplicity. Sound vibrations from the stapes are transmitted as waves in the perilymph. This leads to the displacement of hair cells in the organ of Corti. These hair cells lie above and attach to the auditory nerve, and the impulses generated are fed to the brain. Low-frequency sounds stimulate hair cells close to the oval window, while high-frequency sounds stimulate the end of the organ. The sound wave in the perilymph is rapidly dissipated through the round window, and the cochlea is ready to accept a new set of vibrations.

(above 2,000 Hz), while those in the middle and end of the cochlear coil react to low-frequency sounds. When the vibrations from the stapes hit the oval window, the window bulges outward. This creates a change in pressure in the inner ear and sets off a wave in the perilymph that is transmitted to the endolymph. This, in turn, causes a slight movement of some of the hair cells. The extent of movement depends on the frequency and intensity of the stimulus.

The mechanical energy generated by this movement is converted into electrical energy, and a nerve impulse is produced in the auditory nerve. The structure of the auditory nerve is orderly; its core contains fibers from the end of the cochlear coils, and the other regions are represented around this core. About half of the fibers respond to frequencies above 2,000 Hz, so that our hearing is most acute for higher pitched sounds. Because of the individual characteristics of the nerve fibers, a majority of the fibers must be damaged before there is an observable effect on hearing. If only half of the fibers are functioning, hearing will still be fairly normal, although high-frequency sounds may be affected.

From the inner ear, sound is carried to the auditory cortex in the temporal lobe of the brain. The route from ear to cortex is complex and includes four transmitting stations (Figure 18.4). The first stop is the cochlear nucleus of the brain stem. Between here and the next stop, the superior olive, most of the nerve fibers cross over, permitting stereophonic hearing. Higher relay stations are located in the inferior colliculus and the medial geniculate body in the midbrain, where fine tuning of sound

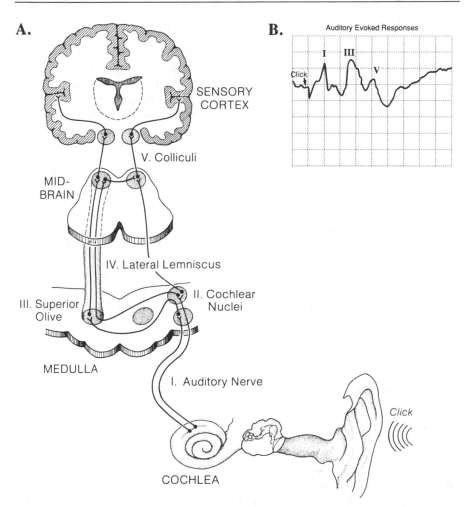

A.

SENSORY
CORTEX

V. Colliculi

MID-
BRAIN

IV. Lateral Lemniscus

III. Superior
Olive

II. Cochlear
Nuclei

MEDULLA

I. Auditory Nerve

Click

COCHLEA

B. Auditory Evoked Responses

I   III

Click   V

Figure 18.4. A) The auditory pathway, and B) auditory evoked responses (AER). The auditory nerve carries sounds to the cochlear nuclei in the medullary portion of the brain stem. Here most impulses cross over to the superior olive and then ascend to the opposite inferior colliculus and ultimately the sensory cortex, where the sound is perceived. The function of this pathway can be measured by auditory evoked responses. Each wave corresponds to a higher level of the pathway (denoted by Roman numerals). AER has been used to test hearing in infants and children with severe disabilities.

occurs including inhibition of background noise. The final destination is the auditory cortex, where the sound is combined with other sensory information and memory to permit perception and interpretation.

The auditory cortex is not needed to "hear" pure tones, but it is needed to interpret language. In fact, destruction of all of the brain stem above the inferior colliculus only results in a 40 dB hearing loss. This principle underlies the finding that an anencephalic infant, who lacks an upper brain stem, midbrain, and auditory cortex, does not appear to have a severe hearing loss.

EMBRYONIC DEVELOPMENT OF THE HEARING APPARATUS

The embryologic development of the hearing apparatus is important in that about one-third of all cases of deafness are congenital in origin (i.e., resulting from abnormal development or damage to the hearing apparatus prior to birth). The outer and inner portion of the ear develop from ectodermal tissue, while the middle ear comes from mesodermal tissue. The first signs of ear development are evident in the middle of the 3rd week after conception (Figure 18.5). By 4½ weeks the primitive labyrinth is recognizable, and by the 6th week the beginnings of the cochlea are evident. The auricle begins to develop during the 7th week, and by the 8th week, the ossicles are present. By 20 weeks the hearing apparatus is functional although not completely mature.

The type of damage that results from a prenatal problem depends on when the **insult** occurred. As noted previously, the most critical period of ear development occurs in the first trimester of pregnancy.

HEARING LOSS

When some part of the hearing apparatus is malformed or malfunctions, hearing loss results. Not only does this affect hearing, it often hinders a child's ability to speak, especially if the damage occurs prior to 2 years of age (the prelingual period).

Incidence of Hearing Loss

Approximately 10% of preschool children fail hearing tests. However, only about 1% of all children have a persistent hearing loss. Among children who have a persistent hearing loss, approximately 40% have a mild loss, 20% a moderate loss, 20% a severe loss, and 20% a profound loss (Glorig & Roberts, 1977). Thus, a profound loss or deafness affects approximately 2 in 1,000 children. Of these children, 65% are born deaf and an additional 12% develop deafness during the first 3 years of life. In the United States, about 22,000 infants are born with or acquire permanent hearing loss each year (Northern & Downs, 1991). Approximately one-third of these children have one or more additional disabilities, including visual impairments, learning disabilities, and mental retardation (Karchmer, 1985).

Types of Hearing Loss

Damage to the external or middle ear causes a *conductive hearing loss*. If the cochlea or auditory nerve malfunctions, a *sensorineural loss* results. A *mixed type hearing loss* occurs when there is both a conductive and a sensorineural component to the loss.

The maximum conductive hearing loss is 60 dB. Conductive losses can often be cured with medication (i.e., antibiotics) and/or surgery (i.e., tympanoplasty/ adenoidectomy). Sensorineural losses cannot be completely corrected medically or surgically, but can be treated with amplification, language tutoring, and speech therapy.

The effect of a hearing loss on speech and language depends on its severity, stability, age of onset, age of discovery, and age of intervention. A hearing loss may affect one ear (i.e., unilateral loss) or both ears (i.e., bilateral loss). A unilateral

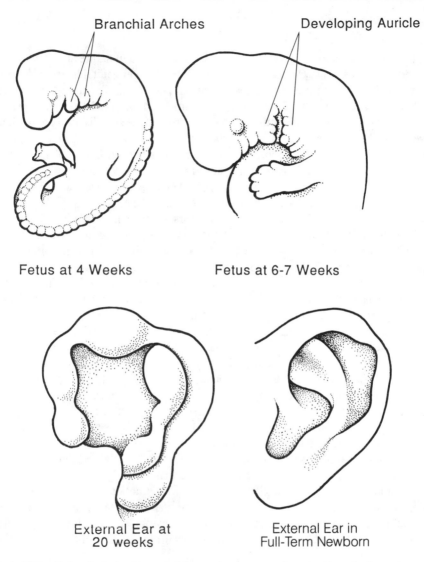

Figure 18.5. Embryologic development of the ear showing stages from the 4th week of gestation to the newborn period. The ear is functional by 20 weeks gestation.

hearing loss is less incapacitating than a bilateral one, but accounts for less than 20% of children with hearing impairments (Bess & Tharpe, 1984). In general, low-frequency losses are less of a problem than high-frequency losses. Some hearing losses get progressively worse over time while others remain stable. For example, the cochlea may gradually degenerate and ossify after an episode of meningitis, resulting in a progressive loss of hearing. Hearing losses beginning after speech has been established have less of an effect on speech and language development and later academic achievement than hearing losses occurring in infancy.

Causes of Hearing Loss

Of all acquired hearing loss in children, 95% is conductive in nature and attributable to middle ear infections (Northern & Downs, 1991). For congenital hearing loss and the remainder of acquired hearing loss, approximately one-third are genetic, one-third acquired, and one-third have unknown causes (Peckham, 1986). The genetic causes of hearing loss include some in which deafness is the sole disability and others in which the hearing loss is but part of a spectrum of abnormalities. Among acquired conditions, causes of hearing loss include both prenatal and postnatal infections, anoxia, prematurity, certain antibiotics, and trauma. Because middle ear infections have been shown to contribute to so many cases of conductive hearing loss (Bluestone & Klein, 1988), they are discussed in an upcoming subsection.

Genetic Causes Hereditary deafness occurs in approximately 1 in 2,000 to 1 in 6,000 children. There are well over 70 inherited syndromes associated with deafness. About 90% of children who have hereditary deafness inherit it as an autosomal recessive disorder; often a child's sibling is also affected (Konigsmark & Gorlin, 1976).

Hereditary disorders can affect the formation or function of any part of the hearing mechanism (Buyse, 1990). A number of examples follow. Children with Treacher-Collins syndrome, an autosomal dominant disorder, have an abnormal facial appearance, deformed auricles, and defects in the ear canal and middle ear. As a result, these children have a conductive hearing loss. Another autosomal dominant disorder is Waardenberg syndrome. Individuals with this syndrome have an unusual facial appearance, irises of different colors, a white forelock, and a stable sensorineural hearing loss. The organ of Corti may be absent in these individuals. In Laurence-Moon-Biedl syndrome, an autosomal recessive disorder, there is retinitis pigmentosa (see Chapter 17) associated with a progressive sensorineural hearing loss. These children also have mental retardation, obesity, and extra fingers or toes. Another autosomal recessive disorder, Pendred syndrome, is associated with goiter and moderate-to-profound sensorineural hearing loss. Usher syndrome, also inherited as a recessive disorder, includes sensorineural deafness and progressive loss of vision. Some of these children have mental retardation. Finally, in the CHARGE association, there is usually a mixed hearing loss associated with a variety of eye, gastrointestinal, and other malformations. The occurrence of this disorder appears to be sporadic.

Children with chromosomal disorders also frequently have hearing losses. For example, children with Down syndrome have small auricles, narrow ear canals, and a high incidence of middle ear infections (Dahle & McCollister, 1986) (see Chapter 16). A majority of these children have some hearing loss, usually conductive. Other chromosomal disorders, including trisomy 13 and trisomy 18, have also been associated with hearing loss, more commonly sensorineural.

Cleft Palate Cleft palate, in which the roof of the mouth is partially open, is a malformation associated with a conductive hearing loss. It has a multifactorial inheritance pattern, and an incidence of about 1 in 900. It may occur alone or together with cleft lip. Of children with a cleft palate, 50%–90% are susceptible to severe and persistent middle ear infections (Grant, Quiney, Mercer, et al., 1988; Hubbard, Paradise, McWilliams, et al., 1985) because the absence of closure of the palate hinders middle ear drainage through the eustachian tubes. More than 30% of children with cleft palate develop a conductive hearing loss, and an additional 25% have sensorineural or mixed type hearing losses (Northern & Downs, 1991). In order to prevent hearing impairment in these children, **myringotomy** and pressure equalization tube insertions are frequently performed. These procedures are discussed in subsequent sections of this chapter. (See Chapter 13 for further discussion of cleft palate.)

Neonatal Complications and Prematurity During delivery or in the newborn period, a number of complications may cause a hearing loss (Thiringer, Kankkunen, Liden, et al., 1984). Asphyxia may damage the cochlea (Salamy, Eldredge, & Tooley, 1989). This is a particular problem in children with **persistent fetal circulation,** one-quarter of whom develop a progressive sensorineural loss (Northern & Downs, 1991). Hyperbilirubinemia may cause a high-frequency sensorineural loss. Intracranial hemorrhage has also been a cause of sensorineural hearing loss. Premature infants, especially those born weighing less than 1,500 grams, have an increased susceptibility to all three of these problems. Of these babies, 2%–5% demonstrate significant hearing loss (Kenworthy, Bess, Stahlman, et al., 1987). (See Chapters 6 and 7 for further discussion of neonatal complications and prematurity.)

Trauma Trauma to the cochlea, as might occur following a blow to the temporal bone, may lead to a severe sensorineural hearing loss. Mild-to-moderate sensorineural hearing losses may result from traumatic noise levels, the most common source of which is heavy industry. Noise intensity levels greater than 120 dB have been recorded in some work settings. Riveters, airplane maintenance personnel, and press operators are particularly at risk for hearing loss. Individuals in these occupations should wear ear protectors to prevent hearing loss. Rock concerts are a cause of brief sensorineural hearing loss. Noise levels of above 90 dB are painful, and during concerts, levels of 100–110 dB are often present. Noise level has also been a concern in premature infants placed in incubators. The surrounding noise level can range from 60–80 dB (Northern & Downs, 1991). Fortunately the noise is low-frequency, and there is no evidence that this causes a persistent hearing loss.

Infections and Antibiotics Infections, both intrauterine and after birth, can also cause hearing loss. A mother who contracts rubella during the first trimester of her pregnancy has about a 30% risk of bearing an infant who has a severe, high-frequency sensorineural hearing loss, microcephaly, retinal abnormalities, and other disabilities (Miller, Cradock-Watson, & Pollock, 1982). Other infections during pregnancy, including toxoplasmosis, herpesvirus, syphilis, and cytomegalovirus (CMV), may cause similar hearing losses (Sever, Ellenberg, Ley, et al., 1988; Stagno, Pass, Cloud, et al., 1986). The most prevalent of these is CMV with an incidence of 2–20 per 1,000 in newborn infants (Johnson, Hosford-Dunn, Paryani, et al., 1986). Sensorineural loss occurs in 30% of symptomatic babies and in 10% of asymptomatic children. The loss is symmetrical and high-frequency and may worsen over time (Williamson, Percy, Yon, et al., 1990).

During infancy and childhood, certain infections can also lead to a sensorineural hearing loss. Bacterial meningitis carries a 10% risk of hearing loss from damage to the cochlea (Cohen, Schenk, & Sweeney, 1988). Like CMV damage, the hearing loss may develop gradually and worsen over time as the cochlea degenerates. Among viral diseases of childhood, unilateral hearing loss has been reported after mumps, while bilateral involvement has occurred after measles and chickenpox.

Certain antibiotics used to treat severe bacterial infections also may be toxic to the cochlea (Harada, Iwamori, Nagai, et al., 1986). This is especially true of the aminoglycosides: neomycin, kanamycin, gentamicin, vancomycin, and tobramycin (listed in descending order of toxicity). They destroy the outer row of hair cells. Fortunately, physicians can measure antibiotic blood levels during treatment to avoid the development of toxic levels.

Middle Ear Infections   As noted previously, the most common type of hearing impairment is a mild-to-moderate conductive hearing loss resulting from a chronic middle ear infection that has lasted more than 2 months. Middle ear infection, or otitis media, is most common in very young children. Of all children, 76%–95% have at least one middle ear infection during their first 2 years of life (Bluestone & Klein, 1988). However, certain populations are at greater risk than normal to develop recurrent or chronic otitis media. Children with Down syndrome and cleft palate are at particular risk. Certain cultures are also at increased risk, most notably the Native Americans and Eskimos. In these children, the risk of developing a persisting conductive hearing loss is significant (Bluestone & Klein, 1988). Thus, rapid detection and treatment of middle ear infections are important.

In most cases, fever or irritability is the first sign of the infection. Frequently, the child pulls at the ears and fluid may drain from the ear. Hearing may be impaired, and there may be a loss of balance. On examination with an otoscope, the eardrum looks red and opaque rather than white and translucent. Fluid or effusion is usually present behind the eardrum. The diagnosis can be confirmed by tympanometry that shows a flat rather than "tented" pattern, resulting from the drainage.

Medical Treatment of Middle Ear Infections   Treatment of middle ear infections involves the use of an antibiotic, usually amoxicillin or ampicillin, for 1 week. Although decongestants have been used in the past, experimental studies indicate that they make little difference in the duration or outcome of a middle ear infection (Bluestone, 1989). They are no longer recommended. Clinical improvement generally occurs in 48–72 hours, but the ears should be rechecked in 1–2 weeks to make certain the fluid is gone.

Complications of Middle Ear Infections   If hearing is tested during an infection, a mild-to-moderate conductive hearing loss is frequently found. This usually clears up within a week or two. However, if the fluid buildup persists or recurs, it may cause a permanent hearing loss. This loss actually may be a mixed type with a sensorineural loss superimposed on the initial conductive loss. The sensorineural loss may result from damage to the organ of Corti from bacterial toxins. This mild-to-moderate hearing loss can affect speech and language development and scholastic achievement.

Less common complications include the formation of a **cholesteatoma** and the development of **mastoiditis.** A cholesteatoma can develop during a chronic middle ear infection in which a perforation of the tympanic membrane has occurred. Under these conditions skin tissue lining the ear canal can migrate through the perforated ear drum into the middle ear forming a mass. If not surgically removed, this cholesteatoma can destroy the ossicles, causing a permanent conductive hearing loss.

The second complication, mastoiditis, can lead to a permanent sensorineural hearing loss by damaging the cochlea. Mastoiditis involves the extension of the middle ear infection into the mastoid air cells of the temporal bone, which contains the cochlea. Treatment involves antibiotics and, if antibiotics are unsuccessful, surgical drainage of the abscessed mastoid air cells. Although a major cause of hearing loss in the preantibiotic era (i.e., before 1950), mastoiditis is now very uncommon.

These complications point to the importance of aggressive treatment and follow-up of a middle ear infection. If the infection is recurrent or persistent, it often must be treated with a 1–2 month course of antibiotics. This is particularly true if the first infection occurred before 6 months of age, if there have been 3 episodes of otitis media within a 6-month period, or if the child has had fluid in the middle ear for at least 3 months.

Surgical Management of Middle Ear Infections If antibiotic treatment is not effective in preventing future infections, an ear, nose, and throat (ENT) surgeon may need to perform a myringotomy, a minor surgical procedure in which the eardrum is cut and a small plastic tube inserted into the middle ear (Gebhart, 1981) (Figure 18.6). This tube serves in place of the clogged eustachian tube and equalizes the pressure between the middle ear and the ear canal, enabling fluid to drain from the middle ear. Over a number of months, as the eustachian tube becomes unclogged, the tube gradually works its way into the ear canal and drops out or can be removed. The eardrum closes over the incision. The use of these tubes has significantly reduced the incidence of permanent hearing loss in children with chronic otitis media (Bluestone & Klein, 1988). There is also some evidence that removal of the adenoids (but not the tonsils) decreases the risk of recurrent middle ear infections in children who have enlarged adenoids (Paradise, Bluestone, Rogers, et al., 1990). Therefore, the performance of myringotomy and tube placement may be combined with an adenoidectomy. These day surgery procedures require general anesthesia; the complications are few but include bleeding and infection.

Identification of Hearing Loss

Unfortunately there is often a considerable delay in identifying a child with hearing impairment (Coplan, 1987). Hearing loss is considered a silent disorder in young children because it is not usually accompanied by pain, fever, or physical abnormalities. Furthermore, during the first 6 months of life, there is little difference in the development of the normal hearing and deaf child. Finally, infants and young children cannot tell us that they are having difficulty hearing.

There are, however, certain signs that can be used for early identification by parents and professionals. Some groups of children, such as premature infants, those

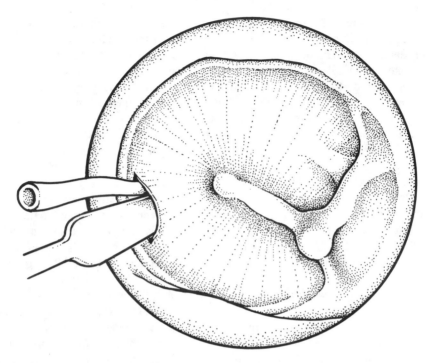

Figure 18.6. The procedure of myringotomy and tube placement involves the surgical incision of the tympanic membrane. The effusion is withdrawn and a plastic tube is then inserted through the opening to permit ongoing drainage of fluid and equilibration of air pressure.

with complicated pregnancies or newborn periods, and children with family histories of deafness, should be watched carefully for signs of hearing loss. These children should have routine hearing tests performed before 6 months of age. The pediatrician also should routinely check developmental language milestones (see Table 16.1) and obtain a hearing test in any child who is lagging in speech and language development.

The importance of early identification of a hearing loss is analogous to the need for early detection of a vision loss (see Chapter 17). The brain pathways for both of these senses are still immature at birth. They only develop normally when stimulated. It is therefore not surprising that the infant with a hearing impairment who receives amplification early in life develops much better speech and language skills than the child with a similar hearing loss who receives amplification after 2 years of age.

Hearing Milestones There are specific "language" milestones that are helpful in detecting a hearing loss (see Table 16.1). As noted in the discussion of the embryogenic development of the ear, the hearing mechanism is functional by 20 weeks gestation, particularly for low-pitched sounds. A microphone placed inside a uterus at term can record understandable speech spoken at 45 dB HL from 6 feet away. This means that the "old wives tale" of being able to teach a fetus to enjoy classical music by playing it repeatedly in the mother's presence during the last trimester of pregnancy has some basis in reality. It has been shown that newborn infants will suck a non-nutritive formula in order to hear a recording of his or her mother's voice but will not suck to hear a recording of another woman's voice. The infant will also awaken from sleep to the loud voice of his or her parent but not to the voice of others (Northern & Downs, 1991).

The newborn infant clearly prefers to listen to speech as opposed to other environmental sounds, just as the infant prefers to fixate visually on a face rather than an object. By 2 months of age, the infant can distinguish vowel from consonant sounds, and by 4 months the infant shows a preference for speech patterns that have varied rhythm and stress. The child prefers listening to prolonged discourse rather than repetitive baby talk. Between 4–7 months of age the child will turn toward a sound out of sight and begins to babble. Between 9–13 months, the child starts to make consonant sounds like "Da" that carry meaning. Between 12–24 months the child develops an increasing vocabulary and the ability to string words together into ideas (Northern & Downs, 1991).

Up to 5 months of age, the speech sounds a baby makes are not influenced by the sounds the baby hears. This is why the early babbling of infants from different countries sounds alike. However, after 5 months of age, the infant's babbling starts to imitate the parents' speech patterns (Northern & Downs, 1991). The babbling of a French-speaking infant becomes different from that of an English-speaking child. The important point is that listening to spoken language during early life is a critical prerequisite for the normal development of speech. This is why a child who becomes deaf after learning to speak has far better speech and language than the child with congenital deafness. Helen Keller was an example of a child who lost hearing (and vision) as a result of meningitis at 18 months of age and ultimately developed effective speech.

Signs of Hearing Impairment   With the normal milestones in mind, the variations in development found in deaf infants is easier to understand. An early sign of severe hearing loss is a sleeping infant who does not awaken to loud noises. However, between 3–4 months of age, these children coo and laugh normally, and babbling begins at around 6 months of age. The difference is that normally, as babbling develops, it becomes more complex and eventually simulates words. For example, "Da" may start out at 8 months as a babble but by 10 months becomes attached to the concept of the man who is "Da." In contrast, the babbling of a deaf child remains fairly monotonous, containing only vowel sounds. Instead of becoming more specific and acquiring meaning, the deaf child babbles less and less over time, becoming mute by 1 year of age. Without the ability to imitate, repeat, and associate sounds with meaning, vocalizations decline.

Receptive language also lags. By 4 months of age, the hearing child turns toward his or her parents' voices; the deaf child does not do this. At around 12 months of age, infants receive verbal instructions accompanied by gestures. The deaf child of this age can often figure out the command by watching mouth movements and following the gestures. However, by 16 months of age, the child is expected to start responding to more complex instructions by words alone. The deaf child cannot do this and stops following instructions unless they are accompanied by gestures. Children with mental retardation and normal hearing are also delayed in the achievement of these language milestones. However, in these children, speech, motor, and cognitive skills are similarly delayed, while the child with hearing impairment has slow development of speech and language skills but not of other abilities.

Early Identification of Children with Hearing Impairments Although these differences in development seem fairly clear, they are only fully evident in children with profound hearing impairment. Children with less severe hearing losses have more normal developments. In general, the less severe the hearing impairment, the later it is discovered. There may be a delay of 2 or more years before moderate-to-severe losses are detected, and mild impairments or unilateral losses may not be detected until kindergarten.

For children at high risk of having a hearing loss, careful ongoing assessment of language development is essential. Periodic hearing tests of high-risk infants and children are equally important (Kramer, Vertes, & Condon, 1989). Seven factors have been identified as precursors of significant hearing loss: 1) a positive family history of deafness; 2) an intrauterine infection; 3) a postnatal infection, such as meningitis; 4) congenital malformations of the head and neck; 5) prematurity, with a birthweight of less than 1,500 grams; 6) anoxia; and 7) admission to a newborn intensive care unit (NICU) for more than 48 hours (American Speech-Language-Hearing Association, 1990). Among this group of children the most common indicators of hearing loss are family history (43%), admission to an NICU (24%), anoxia (18%), and infection (12%) (Epstein, 1987). This approach to determining which children should undergo hearing tests before 6 months of age has been shown to result in an improvement in the age of identification of severe hearing loss (Northern & Downs, 1991). Yet half of the children who are later diagnosed with severe hearing losses do not fall into one of the high-risk categories and are therefore missed by this screening approach.

Another screening procedure is the audiometric testing performed in elementary schools. However, school tests are just screens and many children who fail them do not have persistent hearing impairments. These children may have been tested when they had a short-term hearing loss caused by a middle ear infection. For every 10 children who fail a school hearing screening, only one will have a persistent sensorineural hearing loss (FitzZaland & Zink, 1984).

Hearing Tests Formal hearing testing is performed to: 1) determine whether there is a hearing loss, 2) differentiate a conductive hearing loss from a sensorineural loss, 3) confirm the degree of the hearing impairment in each ear, and 4) identify whether the loss is of high or low frequency or both frequencies. A child of any age can be tested for hearing loss. However, the particular hearing test, or **audiometry**, that is used must vary according to the age of the child. In children with mental retardation, the test chosen should be based on the child's mental, rather than chronological, age. Hearing tests range from *behavioral observation audiometry* and *auditory brain stem responses* in infants, to *visual reinforced audiometry* in toddlers, and *conditioned play audiometry* in preschool-age children. In addition, *impedance audiometry* has proven invaluable for detecting conductive hearing loss related to middle ear infections.

Testing Infants Under 6 Months of Age   In infants, behavioral observation tests can often detect whether hearing is impaired. However, these tests cannot determine precisely the degree of the impairment or its type. A low-pitched sound, such as a horn, is generally sounded near a sleeping baby, and the observer looks for limb movements or eye blinking. A positive response rules out deafness but does not distinguish between a mild-to-moderate bilateral hearing loss and a unilateral impairment because the horn or bell sounds are quite loud, often in the range of 80–90 dB. These tests also do not distinguish between conductive and sensorineural hearing loss. Furthermore, the absence of a response does not necessarily mean that the child has a severe hearing loss. Infants rapidly adjust to repeated loud environmental noises. This is called *auditory habituation* and is a mark of good cortical function. However, this habituation limits the interpretation of behavioral observation audiometry.

The Crib-o-Gram is an automated behavioral audiometric testing device that emits a sound and records subsequent body movement. This apparatus is useful in testing newborn infants, but is not very helpful in testing high-risk infants because of the high incidence of false positive results (Durieux-Smith, Picton, Edwards, et al., 1985).

A better method of testing infant hearing is to record auditory brain stem responses (ABR), also called *brain stem response audiometry* (BSRA), and *brain stem auditory evoked response* (BAER) (Northern & Gerkin, 1989; American Speech-Language-Hearing Association, 1989). This test does not require the infant's cooperation and is also used in testing older children with multiple disabilities who are unable to respond to behavioral audiometric testing. EEG electrodes are pasted to the forehead and behind the ears of the sleeping child. Using earphones, tones at frequencies of 200–6,000 Hz are presented first to one ear and then to the other. Following the click, a burst of neural activity should occur. A computer averages the intensity of the responses and presents the ABR on a viewing screen. These responses take the form of waves, numbered I, III, and V (see Figure 18.4). Each wave represents successively higher levels of the brain stem pathway. An absence of one or more of the waves suggests an abnormality somewhere in the hearing pathway from the inner ear to the brain (Warren, 1989).

Testing Children from 6 Months to 2 Years of Age   Between 6 months and 2 years of age, a child can be tested using visual reinforcement audiometry, which is more accurate than ABR in defining the degree of hearing loss. In a small child, audiometric testing is done in sound fields with loudspeakers. These infants do not tolerate earphones, so the test signals are projected through loudspeakers. The tones presented have frequencies ranging from 250 to 4,000 Hz and intensities from 0 to 110 dB. Hearing losses from slight to profound can be detected. The weakness of this approach is that it does not discriminate between hearing loss in the two ears; it gives the result of the better ear. Also, it does not differentiate between a conductive and sensorineural hearing loss.

An underlying challenge in using audiometry is to get the child to give consistent responses. This is where visual reinforcement is helpful. The child is taught to associate a sound with a visual occurrence. For example, a Donald Duck mask with a light placed in the eyes is positioned in front of the child. The audiologist pairs a sound with turning on the light. After a few trials, the child consistently turns toward Donald every time a sound is audible, in anticipation of seeing the eyes light up. Then comes the trick. The audiologist turns on a sound but does not immediately light up Donald's eyes. However, if the child, having heard the sound, looks in expectation at Donald, the audiologist then turns on the light, reinforcing this behavior.

The limitation of using sound field testing is eliminated by the time the child reaches about 2 years of age and will tolerate earphones. Then, a variation of the above paradigm can be used. One toy is placed to the right of the child and another to the left. The sound is now presented to one ear at a time and paired with lighting the toy on that side. Again, the child looks in anticipation of the toy lighting up and testing of both ears can be completed. Using earphones, the audiologist not only can test for different hearing intensities in each ear, but also can distinguish sensorineural losses from conductive losses (Figure 18.7). The sounds are first presented through the earphones (i.e., air conduction) and then through a vibrator placed behind the ear (i.e., bone conduction) (Figure 18.8). Children with sensorineural loss have the same hearing loss for both air and bone conduction signals; those with conductive loss show a difference, hearing normally by bone conduction because the test sound by-passes the outer and the middle ear where the conductive hearing loss resides.

Testing Children Older Than 2 Years of Age Conditional play audiometry can be used for testing children 2–5 years of age. In this approach, the child wears ear-phones and is asked to perform a play task whenever he or she hears a sound. For example, the audiologist could ask the child to stack blocks, or put rings on a peg. By 5 years, the play component can usually be dropped and testing is virtually identical to that in adults. The child is simply asked to press a button or signal when he or she hears the sound.

Assessing Middle Ear Function To better understand the functioning of the middle ear, a test called **impedance audiometry** is used. It detects excessive negative pressure behind the eardrum or middle ear fluid, both of which occur during episodes of otitis media. This test is used in combination with audiometry in all children older than 7 months. It evaluates middle ear pressure, mobility of the ear drum, eustachian tube function, mobility of the middle ear ossicles, and acoustic reflex thresholds. To perform impedance audiometry, a small microphone attached to a probe is sealed in the ear canal, creating an airtight chamber. Air is then either pumped in or removed from the canal so that the pressure ranges from -300 to $+200$ millimeters of water. A low-frequency tone, around 220 Hz, is presented and by measuring how well that sound bounces off the eardrum at different pressures, the eardrum's elasticity can be estimated. The eardrum is normally flexible so the *tympanogram,* the graph of this test, has a tent shape (Figure 18.9). If the tympanic membrane is immobile, as it is when there is fluid in the middle ear, a flattened line is obtained, indicating that sound is not being conducted (see Figure 18.8). Usually, the tympanogram returns to its normal shape within a week or two after medical treatment of an infection. Persistence of a flattened pattern suggests that the ear is retaining fluid, and the physician may need to treat the child further. Tympanometry detects about 85% of middle ear effusions (Paparella, Fox, & Schachern, 1989).

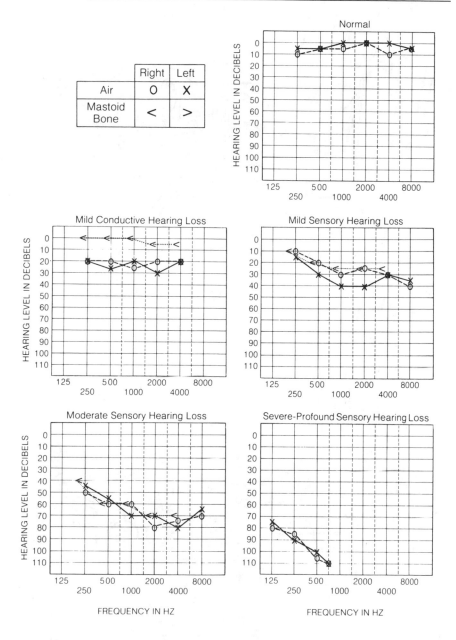

Figure 18.7. Audiograms showing normal hearing and various degrees of hearing loss. Note that, in most cases, both ears are equally affected. In a conductive hearing loss, bone conduction is found to be better than air conduction because it bypasses the outer and the middle ear where the damage lies. In sensorineural hearing loss, bone and air conduction produce similar results because the problem lies near the inner ear. The range of hearing loss is as follows: slight: 16–25 dB; mild 26–40 dB; moderate 41–55 dB; moderate-severe 56–70 dB; severe 71–90 dB; profound > 90 dB. (Audiograms courtesy of Brad Friedrich, Ph.D.)

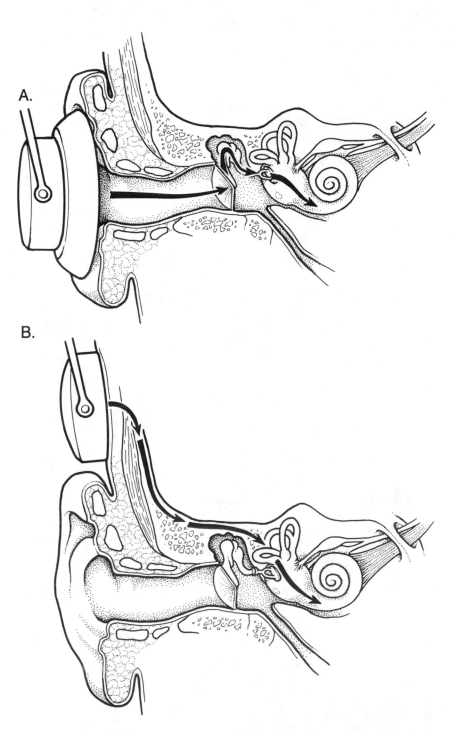

Figure 18.8.   Approaches to testing air and bone conduction of sound. A) In air conduction, the sound comes through the ear canal and middle ear to reach the inner ear. B) In bone conduction, the sound bypasses the outer and middle ear and comes directly to the inner ear.

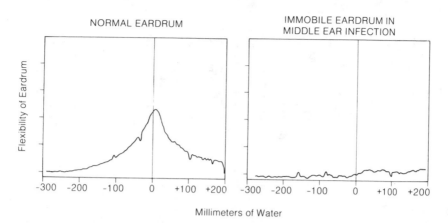

NORMAL EARDRUM

IMMOBILE EARDRUM IN
MIDDLE EAR INFECTION

Flexibility of Eardrum

-300   -200   -100   0   +100   +200   -300   -200   -100   0   +100   +200

Millimeters of Water

Figure 18.9.   Tympanogram. During otitis media (middle ear infection), the eardrum loses its elasticity, and a flat-line tympanogram is recorded. Once the infection clears, a normal, tent-shaped typanogram should be obtained. If it is not, a myringotomy and placement of PE tubes may be necessary to correct the impairment. (Courtesy of Brad Friedrich, Ph.D.)

Impedance audiometry also tests the acoustic reflex, which is produced by the tightening of the muscle that is attached to the stapes bone. It functions as a damper for sound waves so they do not damage the eardrum. However, if there is a greater than 30 dB conductive hearing loss, the sound will not produce this reflex.

Assessing Cortical Hearing Function   A final group of tests assess cortical reception of auditory messages. These are rather complex psycholinguistic tests that generally are used in older children and adults. They attempt to identify central auditory processing disorders, most often found in children with learning disabilities or traumatic brain injury (see Chapters 20 and 27). There are tests for auditory memory, discrimination of like-sounding words, perception of whole words when parts are missing, attention, word association, and blending of sounds (see Chapter 19). Abnormalities of these higher cortical processes do not imply a hearing loss as the previous tests do. They instead indicate deficits in the interpretation or retention of what is heard. Conventional audiometric tests of these children usually yield normal findings.

Degrees of Hearing Loss

Hearing loss detected by audiometry ranges from slight to profound (Table 18.1). The degree of hearing loss is determined by measuring the softest sound that can be perceived at three different frequencies and then averaging these measurements. A slight loss (i.e., threshold of 16–25 dB HL) is usually associated with a middle ear infection and should have no significant effect on development. However, the child may have difficulty hearing faint or distant speech, missing up to 10% of speech when the teacher is at a distance of greater than 3 feet or when the classroom is noisy (Anderson & Matkin, 1991). This should be monitored, and if there is evidence of problems in school or in social interactions, a hearing aid or personal FM system (see discussion of Amplification in this chapter) may be necessary. At the minimum, these children

Table 18.1. Effects of varying degrees of hearing loss on function, treatment, and educational needs

Hearing level (dB)	Degree of loss	Type	Missed sounds	Effect	Intervention
16–25	Slight	C, SN	10% speech signal	Miss fast-paced peer interactions, fatigue in listening	Hearing aids or FM system, seating in front, antibiotics, myringotomy
26–40	Mild	C, SN	25%–40% speech signal, distant sounds, unvoiced consonants, plurals, and tenses	Miss 50% of class discussion, has problem supressing background noise	Seating in front, hearing aids or FM system, language therapy, antibiotics, myringotomy
41–55	Moderate	C, SN	50%–80% speech signal	Articulation deficits, limited vocabulary, learning dysfunction	Hearing aids or FM system, resource help, speech-language therapy, speech reading
56–70	Moderate-severe	SN or mixed	100% of speech information	Delayed language, syntax, atonal voice, reduced speech intelligibility	Full-time amplification, special education, special education class, speech-language therapy
71–90	Severe	SN or mixed	All speech sounds; can hear loud environmental noises	Speech not developed or deteriorates, learning deficits	Full-time program for deaf, signing or total communication, amplification
>90	Profound	SN or mixed	All speech and other sounds; feels vibrations	As above	As above, cochlear implant

Source: Anderson and Matkin (1991).
C = Conductive; SN = Sensorineural.

should be seated in the front of the classroom. They may also need resource help with vocabulary and speech.

A child with a mild hearing impairment can hear only sounds that are at least 26–40 dB in intensity. This condition is also most commonly associated with chronic otitis media. For this child speech is usually normal, but the child has difficulty hearing distant sounds or soft speech, missing 25%–40% of speech. The child has the most difficulty perceiving the unvoiced consonants s,p,t,k,th,f, and sh, which have high frequencies and contain minimal sound energy. As a result, the child may miss half of class discussions. *Prosody* (i.e., intonation and stress patterns of speech) may also be difficult for the child to learn if there is a significant loss of tone in the low frequencies. The child should be reevaluated at 3–6 month intervals, and if there are speech and language delays, he or she should be fitted with hearing aids, use an FM system in the classroom, and receive auditory language therapy (Davis, Elfenbein, Schum, et al., 1986).

Sounds must register at least 41–55 dB to be heard by children with moderate hearing loss. This amount of loss affects the ability to hear even loud conversation. These children are also likely to have limited vocabulary, imperfect speech production, and an atonal voice quality (Anderson & Matkin, 1991). By school age, there may be learning problems related to difficulty in understanding grammatical rules. As a result, they may need resource help in language-based subjects, such as literature and social studies. These children benefit from hearing aids and classroom amplification as well as speech-language therapy and academic tutoring.

In the absence of amplification, a child with a moderate-to-severe loss (56–70 dB) misses almost all conversation. Speech delay is even greater than with a moderate loss, with severe deficits in syntax and speech intelligibility. Full-time use of amplification is essential. Education should focus on language skills, pragmatics, reading, and writing.

A child with a severe hearing loss requires sound to register at least 71–90 dB to be heard. The child can hear certain close loud environmental sounds without amplification but not words (Geers & Moog, 1987). Even with amplification, consonant sounds are missed. If the loss occurred before 2 years of age, language and speech do not develop spontaneously. Speech can be taught provided there is early and consistent use of amplification, but the child's vocabulary is limited and the voice quality atonal. If the hearing loss occurs later in childhood, there is a deterioration in speech quality. In educating children with severe hearing loss, auditory language skills, speech reading, concept development, and speech should be emphasized (Anderson & Matkin, 1991).

A profound hearing impairment involves a loss greater than 91 dB. While a child with this loss may react to very loud sounds, hearing will not be the primary avenue by which the child learns and communicates. The child is more aware of vibrations than tonal patterns. With amplification, this child may learn to distinguish rhythm and accent patterns of speech and to recognize environmental sounds, but generally he or she cannot comprehend speech. Cochlear implants may be appropriate for selected children. Speech can be taught but, at best, only about one-quarter of the speech will be intelligible to classmates (Northern & Downs, 1991). At 5 years of age, the child may have a vocabulary of 200 words, as compared to a hearing child's vocabulary of 5,000–26,000 words at this age. These children are likely to depend on manual communication and often attend self-contained classes or schools for the deaf. By 16 years of age, reading achievement is rarely above a fifth-grade level. Social interactions in the hearing world are also limited by the child's severe communication deficits.

TREATMENT OF HEARING LOSS

Treatment of the child with hearing impairment must be multidisciplinary. It must include amplification, speech-language therapy, special education, and often psychological counseling. For optimal outcome, therapy should be started as soon as a significant hearing loss has been identified, with parents included as partners in the intervention plan.

Amplification

The most frequently used approach to helping a child with a significant hearing loss is amplification. Hearing aids can be used in children of any age and should be fitted as soon as a persistent hearing loss has been identified. As mentioned previously, even a mild hearing loss in early childhood may interfere with normal speech and language development.

Hearing aids have three components: a microphone that changes sound waves into electrical signals, an amplifier/power supply that increases the intensity of the signal, and a receiver/loudspeaker that converts the signal back to an amplified sound wave. This amplified sound is transmitted to the middle ear through an earmold placed in the ear canal (Figure 18.10). Children's hearing aids also have the capacity for direct audio input (DAI) so that sound can be transmitted to the student from a wireless FM microphone. For example, this type of device might be worn by a teacher.

As hearing aids have become increasingly sophisticated, they have become more flexible and can be adjusted to the specific characteristics of a hearing loss. Two categories of hearing aids exist: *body aids* and *ear-level aids* (Pollack, 1988). Body aids are rarely used except for infants and children with malformed external ears or multiple disabilities. The disadvantage of this type of aid is that it is bulky and cosmetically less appealing. The reception is also at chest level rather than at the normal ear level. Ear-level aids can be used for infants and toddlers as well as school-age children. Behind-the-ear aids are used for younger children, and in-the-ear aids are sometimes used for older children who become concerned with the visibility of their hearing aids.

A hearing aid with a broad range of adjustable controls is chosen to provide adaptability as the child's needs change over time (Matkin, 1985). Bilateral aids are used in most instances. Problems associated with the use of hearing aids include the requirement of frequent adjustments and a child's initial dislike of wearing them. Behavior management techniques are often required to get the child to consistently

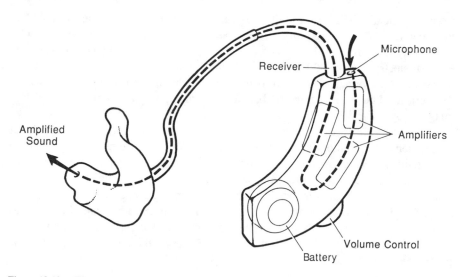

Figure 18.10. The components of a behind-the-ear hearing aid. The aid consists of a microphone, an amplifier/power supply, and a receiver that projects the amplified sound through the ear mold into the ear canal.

wear the aid rather than destroying or ignoring it. This points to the importance of parental involvement. Parents must accept that the child needs the hearing aid, be willing to care for it, and make sure their child wears it.

Hearing aids are unlikely to completely correct a hearing loss, but they benefit the majority of children with hearing impairments. Functionally, hearing aids raise the range of sound children can hear by 10–60 dB (Sandlin, 1988). However, training is needed for the child to learn to use this amplified sound effectively. Even with optimal amplification, children with hearing impairments are likely to require ongoing speech-language therapy. The adverse side effects of hearing aids are few. There is no evidence that the hearing mechanism can be significantly damaged by "over amplification," but if the ear mold is not properly fitted, the ear canal may become inflamed. Also, constant squealing or feedback may be a major annoyance for parents and teachers.

Surgical Treatment

The most commonly performed ear surgery is myringotomy and pressure equalizing (PE) tube placement (Balkany & Pashley, 1987). As noted previously, this is done to treat children who have persistent middle ear effusions and resultant hearing loss. This procedure may be combined with the removal of the adenoids if there is evidence of chronic infection of this tissue. Both procedures have been shown to be effective and have few complications. Tonsils are no longer removed, as they have been shown to be an important part of the immune system.

Cochlear implants are new devices that have been released for implantation in individuals over 2 years of age who have profound hearing loss and have not benefited from amplification (Kreton & Balkany, 1991). The rationale for the use of cochlear implants is that many auditory nerve fibers remain functional in persons with cochlear-type deafness. These auditory nerve fibers can be stimulated by applying external electric currents through the cochlear implant. It acts as a substitute for the hair cells of the organ of Corti. In one study of adults, 80% of individuals whose deafness resulted from meningitis benefited from the implant with improved language recognition (House, Berliner, & Luxford, 1987).

The cochlear implant is surgically attached to the cochlea and provides direct stimulation of the auditory nerve. The device has four components: a receiver buried in the temporal bone, an external microphone attached to a transmitter, a signal processor that captures and electronically codes incoming sounds, and the cochlear implant. The nerve impulse generated by the cochlear implant is relayed to the brain and the artificial potential is interpreted as speech. The complication rate of this procedure is low, about 3%, with the most common problems being infection, pain, and delayed wound healing (House et al., 1987). However, the degree of hearing improvement is quite variable.

Speech-Language Therapy

The amount and type of speech-language therapy required depends on the degree of hearing impairment. The child with mild-to-moderate hearing loss should work to improve articulation and syntax. This approach is especially effective if started early in life. The child with severe-to-profound deafness may have little understandable speech. For these children, auditory/oral and manual techniques are available. The controversy over the use of spoken language-only versus sign language-only communication methods is long-standing. Proponents of the manual communication method suggest the use of sign language (American Sign Language [ASL]) and fingerspelling rather than any attempt at attaining imperfect oral communication skills (see Chapter 19). However, because sign language is not known by most people, these children are limited in their ability to communicate. In fact, fewer than 2% of hearing parents of deaf children learn ASL well enough to communicate effectively with their school-age children (Matkin & Matkin, 1985). Proponents of the auditory/oral approach discourage the use of sign language and work toward developing speech. Unfortunately, the articulation and voice quality of children with a profound degree of hearing loss may be so affected that their speech is unintelligible to people other than family members and teachers. Their paucity of vocabulary and problems with speech structure are also limiting.

A compromise position is the philosophy of "total communication" that individualizes communication for each child (Matkin & Matkin, 1985). With this approach, a child's language program may consist of a combination of hearing aids, natural gestures, pantomime, sign language, fingerspelling, lipreading, and body language with or without oral speech. In other words, the child learns to use whatever tools provide the best possible means of communication. The majority of speech pathologists use total communication techniques (Rutter & Martin, 1972), and most parents prefer it (Matkin & Matkin, 1985).

Education

Hearing impairment, from an education perspective, has been divided into "deaf," defined as having a hearing loss of 70 dB HL or greater in the better ear, and "hard-of-hearing," defined as having a loss of 35–69 dB. PL 94-142, PL 99-457, and PL 101-476 mandate early intervention and educational services for all infants and children with hearing impairments (Ferguson, Hicks, & Pfau, 1988). The mandated services include hearing testing, hearing aid fittings, speech-language therapy, and special education. Services start in infancy with a speech therapist or teacher of students with hearing impairments coming to the house once a week (Musselman, Lindsay, & Wilson, 1988). After the child reaches 2 years of age, he or she probably will be entered into a center-based program for a number of days of therapy a week. After the child reaches school age, he or she will be eligible for whatever special education services are needed (Lewis & Gallico, 1991).

Psychological-Behavioral Therapy

It is not uncommon for children who have severe hearing impairments to have some associated behavioral and psychological issues. Such a child may become frustrated by an inability to communicate effectively (Schwartz, 1987). The child may also feel different and isolated because of wearing hearing aids and/or attending special classes. This may translate into temper tantrums, noncompliance, or depression. If present, these problems must be dealt with effectively for the child to be able to reach his or her potential. Behavior management techniques have proven very successful in both controlling temper tantrums and teaching compliance in wearing hearing aids. Psychotherapy may be needed for the older child who exhibits depression or other emotional problems. Support of the parents is equally important (see Chapter 29). These therapeutic approaches have often eased the adjustments of children who previously had psychological problems that were interfering with learning and social interactions.

AMY: A CHILD WITH DEAFNESS

Amy is an extremely pretty child with wide blue eyes, a rush of blonde hair, and dainty features. She had no difficulties during her newborn period, and she went home with her parents on the third day of her life. She fed well and looked around with interest. She also slept well no matter how much noise surrounded her. She rarely awakened to her mother's voice but woke quickly if touched or picked up. She seemed to look at faces and to follow expressions closely. Amy smiled at 2 months and cooed at 3 months. Although her parents were concerned about her lack of response to sound, they felt relieved when Amy started to babble. Developmentally, she did well. She sat at 6 months and crawled at 8 months; she also fed herself a cookie at 8 months. Yet, by 9 months, the babbling decreased. Her parents banged pans behind her, and she did not respond.

When her parents took Amy to the pediatrician, she, too, was concerned because Amy did not turn toward a loud bell noise. Otherwise, Amy's physical examination was normal. The pediatrician referred her to an audiologist. Testing revealed that Amy had a hearing loss of 100 dB in both ears. Her parents were distraught, but they were determined to help her. They were referred to a speech-language pathologist, who began a total communication approach with Amy.

By 2 years of age, Amy was able to communicate using many signs and gestures. At 5 years of age, she began to attend a special class for children with hearing impairments. Psychological testing showed an IQ of 120. She learned mathematics quickly and drew beautifully. However, reading and social studies were much more difficult. Although she had a rich language of gestures and signs, her speech remained unintelligible. As she grew up, Amy became quite proficient in the use of her own communication methods, and is now entering high school. Except for English, her coursework is at grade level.

PROGNOSIS

How successfully children like Amy will function is determined both by the severity of their hearing loss and by the presence of other disabilities. Most cases of hearing loss are unassociated with mental retardation or other developmental disabilities. For these children, the extent of their hearing problem and when it occurred are critical. Children with conductive hearing losses tend to do well. They have no more than a moderate hearing loss and are able to communicate verbally and understand speech with the use of amplification. This is also true of children who have mild-to-moderate sensorineural losses.

For children with severe-to-profound sensorineural hearing losses, the prognosis is different. Rarely can these children speak clearly. The one exception to this is the child who loses hearing after 2 years of age, when he or she has already learned to talk. However, even this child will lose some speech skills. For children who are deaf from birth or infancy, the problem involves difficulty both in communication and in reasoning. The thinking pattern of deaf children appears to be different from that of children who can hear. Education for these children must take this into account. For example, although deaf children may do well in mathematics and science, reading will remain a difficult problem. Even bright deaf children may not be able to read beyond a fifth grade level by the time they graduate from high school (Northern & Downs, 1991). However, many colleges have special programs for individuals with hearing impairments, and Gallaudet College in Washington, D.C., was founded over 100 years ago specifically to provide a college education for deaf students.

SUMMARY

Among the senses, hearing is equaled only by vision in its importance to our understanding of the world around us. A hearing deficit, therefore, is a major disability. Hearing losses may be conductive, involving the outer or middle ear, sensorineural, affecting the cochlea or auditory nerve, or mixed, with components of both. A hearing loss can range from slight to profound, and may be unilateral or bilateral. Such a loss may exist alone or as part of a multiple disability condition. Defining the type and severity of loss is important for treatment.

If a hearing loss is an isolated disability, the child tends to do well, often going to college and having a professional career. This can be true even for the profoundly deaf child, provided he or she is identified early and develops alternative methods of communication.

REFERENCES

American Speech-Language-Hearing Association. (1989). Audiologic screening of infants who are at risk for hearing impairment. *Asha, 31,* 89–92.

American Speech-Language-Hearing Association. (1990). Guidelines for screening for hearing impairments and middle ear disorders. *Asha, 32*(Suppl 2) 17–24.

Anderson, K.L., & Matkin, N.D. (1991). Hearing conservation in the public schools revisited. *Seminars in Hearing, 12,* 340–364.

Balkany, T.J., & Pashley, N.R.T. (Eds.). (1987). *Clinical pediatric otolaryngology.* St. Louis. C.V. Mosby.

Bess, F.H., & Tharpe, A.M.(1984). Unilateral hearing impairment in children. *Pediatrics, 74,* 206–216.

Bess, F.H. (Ed.). (1988). *Hearing impairment in children.* Parkton, MD: York Press.

Bluestone, C.D. (1989). Modern management of otitis media. *Pediatric clinics of North America, 36,* 1371–1387.

Bluestone, C.D., & Klein, J.O. (1988). *Otitis media in infants and children.* Philadelphia: W.B. Saunders.

Buyse, M.L. (Ed.). (1990). *Birth defects encyclopedia.* Dover, MA: Center for Birth Defects Information Services.

Capute, A.J., & Accardo, P.J. (1978). Linguistic and auditory milestones during the first two years of life: A language inventory for the practitioner. *Clinical Pediatrics, 17,* 847–853.

Church, M.W., & Gerkin, K.P. (1988). Hearing disorders in children with fetal alcohol syndrome: Findings from case reports. *Pediatrics, 82,* 147–154.

Cohen, B.A., Schenk, V.A., & Sweeney, D.B. (1988). Meningitis-related hearing loss evaluated with evoked potentials. *Pediatric Neurology, 4,* 18–22.

Coplan J. (1987). Deafness: Ever heard of it? Delayed recognition of permanent hearing loss. *Pediatrics, 79,* 206–213.

Dahle, A.J., & McCollister, F.P. (1986). Hearing and otologic disorders in children with Down syndrome. *American Journal of Mental Deficiency, 90,* 636–642.

Davis, J.M., Elfenbein, J., Schum, R., et al. (1986). Effects of mild and moderate hearing impairments on language, educational, and psychosocial behavior of children. *Journal of Speech and Hearing Disorders, 51,* 53–62.

Durieux-Smith, A., Picton, T., Edwards, C., et al. (1985). The Crib-O-Gram in the NICU: An evaluation based on brain stem electric response audiometry. *Ear and Hearing, 6,* 20–24.

Ferguson, D.G., Hicks, D.E., & Pfau, G. (1988). Education of the hearing impaired learner. In N.J. Lass, L.V. McReynolds, J.L. Northern, et al.(Eds.), *Speech, language and hearing* (pp. 1265–1277). Toronto: B.C. Decker.

FitzZaland, R.E., & Zink, G.D. (1984). A comparative study of hearing screening procedures. *Ear and Hearing, 5,* 205–210.

Gebhart, D.E. (1981). Tympanostomy tubes in the otitis media prone child. *Laryngoscope, 91,* 849–866.

Geers, A.E., & Moog, J.S. (1987). Predicting spoken language acquisition of profoundly hearing-impaired children. *Journal of Speech and Hearing Disorders, 52,* 84–94.

Glorig, A., & Roberts, J. (1977). *Hearing levels of adults by age and sex.* (Series II, No. 11. U.S. Vital Health Statistics). Bethesda, MD: National Center for Health Statistics.

Grant, H.R., Quiney, R.E., Mercer, D.M., et al. (1988). Cleft palate and glue ear. *Archives of Diseases of Childhood, 63,* 176–179.

Harada, T., Iwamori, M., Nagai, Y., et al. (1986). Ototoxicity of neomycin and its penetration through the round window membrane into perilymph. *Annals of Otology, Rhinology, & Laryngology, 95,* 404–408.

House, W.F., Berliner, K.I., & Luxford, W.M. (1987). Cochlear implants in deaf children. *Current Problems in Pediatrics, 17,* 345–388.

Hubbard, T.W., Paradise, J.L., McWilliams, B.J., et al. (1985). Consequences of unremitting middle-ear disease in early life: Otologic, audiologic, and developmental findings in children with cleft palate. *New England Journal of Medicine, 312,* 1529–1534.

Johnson, S.J., Hosford-Dunn, H., Paryani, S., et al. (1986). Prevalence of sensorineural hearing loss in premature and sick term infants with perinatally acquired cytomegalovirus infection. *Ear and Hearing, 7,* 325–327.

Karchmer, M.A. (1985). A demographic perspective. In E. Cherow, N.D. Matkin, R.J. Trybus (Eds.), *Hearing-impaired children and youth with developmental disabilities* (pp. 36–58). Washington, DC: Gallaudet College Press.

Kenworthy, O.T., Bess, F.H., Stahlman, M.T., et al. (1987). Hearing, speech and language outcome in infants with extreme immaturity. *American Journal of Otolaryngology, 8,* 419–425.

Konigsmark, B.W., & Gorlin, R.G. (1976). *Genetic and metabolic deafness.* Philadelphia: W.B. Saunders.

Kramer, S.J., Vertes, D.R., & Condon, M. (1989). Auditory brain stem responses and clinical follow-up of high-risk infants. *Pediatrics, 83,* 385–392.

Kreton, J., & Balkany, T.J. (1991). Status of cochlear implantation in children. *Journal of Pediatrics, 118,* 1–7.

Lewis, M.E.B., & Gallico, R. (1991). Educational programs for your child. In M.L. Batshaw, *Your child has a disability: A complete sourcebook of daily and medical care* (pp. 285–307). Boston: Little, Brown.

Matkin, N.D. (1985). Hearing aids for children. In W.R. Hodgson (Ed.), *Hearing aid assessment and use in audiologic habilitation* (3rd ed.) (pp. 170–190). Baltimore: Williams & Wilkins.

Matkin, A., & Matkin, N. (1985). Benefits of total communication as perceived by parents of hearing-impaired children. *Language, Speech & Hearing Services in Schools, 16,* 64–74.

Miller, E., Cradock-Watson, J.E., & Pollock, T.M. (1982). Consequences of confirmed maternal rubella at successive stages of pregnancy. *Lancet, 2,* 781–784.

Musselman, C.R., Lindsay, P.H., & Wilson, A.K. (1988). An evaluation of recent trends in preschool programming for hearing-impaired children. *Journal of Speech and Hearing Disorders, 53,* 71–88.

Northern, J.L., & Downs, M.P. (1991). *Hearing in children* (4th ed.). Baltimore: Williams & Wilkins.

Northern, J.L., & Gerkin, K.P. (1989). New technology in infant hearing screening. *Otolaryngologic Clinics of North America, 22,* 75–87.

Paparella, M.M., Fox, R.Y., & Schachern, P.A. (1989). Diagnosis and treatment of sensorineural hearing loss in children. *Otolaryngologic Clinics of North America, 22,* 51–74.

Paradise, J.L., Bluestone, C.D., Rogers, K.D., et al. (1990). Efficacy of adenoidectomy for recurrent otitis media in children previously treated with tympanostomy-tube placement. *Journal of the American Medical Association, 263,* 2066–2073.

Peckham, C.S. (1986). Hearing impairment in childhood. *British Medical Bulletin, 42,* 145–149.

Pollack, M. (1988). *Amplification for the hearing-impaired* (3rd ed.). New York: Grune & Stratton.

Rutter, M., & Martin, J.A.M. (1972). *The child with delayed speech*. Philadelphia: J.B. Lippincott.

Salamy, A., Eldredge, L., & Tooley, W.H. (1989). Neonatal status and hearing loss in high-risk infants. *Journal of Pediatrics, 114*, 847–852.

Sandlin, R.E. (Ed.). (1988). *Handbook of hearing aid amplification*. Boston: College-Hill Press.

Schwartz, S. (1987). *Choices in deafness: A parents' guide*. Montgomery, MD: Woodbine House.

Sever, J.L., Ellenberg, J.H., Ley, A.C., et al. (1988). Toxoplasmosis: Maternal and pediatric findings in 23,000 pregnancies. *Pediatrics, 82*, 181–192.

Stagno, S., Pass, R.F., Cloud, G., et al. (1986). Primary cytomegalovirus infection in pregnancy: Incidence, transmission to fetus, and clinical outcome. *Journal of the American Medical Association, 256*, 1904–1908.

Thiringer, K., Kankkunen, A., Liden, G., et al. (1984). Perinatal risk factors in the aetiology of hearing loss in preschool children. *Developmental Medicine and Child Neurology, 26*, 799–807.

Warren, M.P. (1989). The auditory brainstem response in pediatrics. *Otolaryngologic Clinics of North America, 22*, 473–500.

Williamson, W.D., Percy, A.K., Yow, M.D., et al. (1990). Asymptomatic congenital cytomegalovirus infection: Audiologic, neuroradiologic, and neurodevelopmental abnormalities during the first year. *American Journal of Diseases of Children, 144*, 1365–1368.

Chapter 19

Language and Communication

Development and Disorders

with Ken Bleile

Upon completion of this chapter, the reader will:
—be able to define speech and language and their different elements
—be aware of the normal development of speech and language in childhood
—understand a neuropathological model of language in the brain
—know the major types of speech and language disorders
—recognize treatment approaches to these communication disorders

---

Language is a code, a means of representing ideas using symbols (Lyons, 1979). It is the major way we express ideas to each other and is the primary skill that distinguishes human beings from lower animals. In young children, language development is the best predictor of future intellectual functioning (Blackstone & Painter, 1985). Delayed or deviant development of language may be a symptom of many developmental disabilities, including communication disorders, mental retardation, cerebral palsy, hearing impairment, hydrocephalus, and autism (Rescorla, 1989; Waterhouse & Fein, 1982). Such a delay should lead to early consultation among a pediatrician, psychologist, speech-language pathologist, and audiologist. In this chapter, language development and the diagnosis and treatment of communication disorders are discussed.

Ken Bleile, Ph.D., is Assistant Professor of Otorhinolaryngology and Human Communication and Director of Speech-Language Pathology at Children's Seashore House in Philadelphia.

THE DEVELOPMENT OF LANGUAGE

By the meaningful use of words and gestures, we relate our needs and desires to those around us. Major milestones in language development during the first 3 years of life are listed in Table 16.1. Language development begins in the first months of life. By 4 months, different sounds are produced for different needs. At 7 months, the child reacts when called by name. By 12 months, a few specific words are spoken and understood.

The second year of life is a period of rapid development. The child begins this period by being able to respond to simple requests, such as "give me," if the request is accompanied by a gesture. By 16 months, the child understands 10–15 words and says five or more words. The child responds to simple spoken commands even if the requests are not accompanied by gestures. The primary means of communication at this age is a combination of gestures, sounds, and words. By 18 months, the child knows five or more body parts, points to a few pictures, hands a book to an adult to have a story read, and uses words as the primary means of communication. At the end of the second year, 2-word sentences are spoken and the vocabulary is greatly expanded.

The child continues to make rapid advances in language development during the third year of life. By 30 months, the child comprehends the concept of "I" and can remember two numbers given in sequence. He or she understands a few prepositional commands (e.g., "put the doll on the chair"). At 36 months, 3 or 4 prepositions and several colors are known, and sentences containing 3 or 4 words are spoken. By the end of the third year, the child can answer simple "if, then" questions, such as, "If you fell down, what would you do?" Sentences are longer and more grammatically complex.

PRINCIPLES OF SPEECH

Speech involves *articulation, resonance, rhythm,* and *voice.* Articulation is the production of speech sounds (i.e., consonants and vowels) by the articulators in the oral cavity. For example, the word "bit" has three speech sounds, and the word "bleak" has four speech sounds. As in the case of the word "bleak," the number of speech sounds in a word is not always the same as its number of letters. *Syllables* are combinations of consonants and vowels. The word "banana," for example, has three syllables, and the word "absolutely" has four syllables.

Resonance refers to the flow of air between the oral and nasal tract. The nasal consonants "m," "n," and "ng" are made as air flows from the oral tract into the nose (i.e., the nasal tract). All other English sounds are oral consonants and vowels, and are made as air flows out of the mouth (i.e., the oral tract).

Rhythm is the music of speech. Rhythm is made by rising and falling changes in pitch that occur in sentences. Rhythm is planned by the brain. Speech with little rhythm sounds flat and dull, and speech with a great deal of rhythm sounds excited and exuberant. Voice refers to the activities of the larynx, or voice box. Besides being the mechanism that produces the rhythm of speech, the larynx determines whether a person's voice sounds high, deep, hoarse, or smooth.

PRINCIPLES OF LANGUAGE

Language has three components: *form, content,* and *use* (Bloom & Lahey, 1978). The form of language is its structure. In school, when we learn grammar and **phonics,** we are studying the form of language. Form is further broken down into **phonemes, morphemes,** and **syntax**. The phoneme is the smallest unit of sound that distinguishes one utterance from another. The vowel and consonant sounds are phonemes. The morpheme is the smallest unit of meaning (e.g., the -s at the end of a word that makes it plural, the -ed at the end of a word that denotes past tense). Syntax refers to grammar, the order in which words are put together to make phrases and sentences. Active and passive voice are examples: "We studied this problem" versus "This problem was studied by us."

Clearly, these elements relate closely to the content, or meaning, of language, the study of which is called *semantics*. The vocabulary that forms the basis of semantics is called a *lexicon*. It is knowledge of the meaning of words that allows effective communication. A conversation that is completely accurate in syntax but devoid of meaning has little, if any, communicative value. An example of language that has form but no content is *echolalia,* where a person repeats automatically what is said without attaching any meaning to it.

The third component is the use of language in a social context (Prizant et al., 1990). Melody, gesture, and facial expression help to convey emotion and meaning, the part of language called *prosody*. Furthermore, different language is used in different social settings. For instance, one talks with friends in one way and in job interviews in another. The adaptation of language and behavior to various life situations is called *pragmatics*.

A NEUROPATHOLOGICAL MODEL OF COMMUNICATION

The brain mechanisms involved in language remain somewhat of a mystery. Most of what is known comes from studies of adults who have experienced strokes or have undergone neurosurgical procedures with **cortical mapping**. Strokes cause damage to specific areas of the cortex. Models of language are developed by correlating the loss of certain brain tissue with various language impairments. The classic model postulated that two specific regions of the brain controlled expressive and receptive language (Figure 19.1). Broca's area in the left frontal lobe was believed to be responsible for expressive language while Wernicke's area in the left temporal lobe produced receptive language. They are connected by a nerve tract called the **arcuate fasciculus**.

It now appears that this model is too simplistic. While Broca's and Wernicke's areas are important language centers in most people, additional language areas now are believed to reside in other parts of the temporal and parietal lobes in patterns that vary according to the individual (Ojemann, 1991). This *convergence model* suggests that the various aspects of language may be processed in different areas of the brain. Then, instead of all of the information being sent to one area of the brain, different brain areas are activated together in time (Damasio, 1990). For example, when a per-

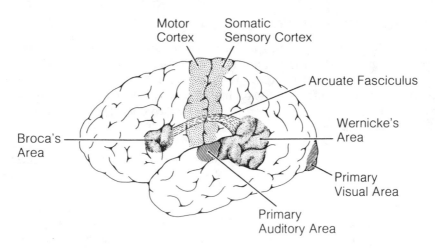

Figure 19.1.   An adult neuropathological model of language. Sounds are received in Wernicke's area and passed on to Broca's area via nerve fibers of the arcuate fasciculus. Expressive language is formed here, and the motor cortex is then stimulated to produce speech.

son thinks of a ball, groups of neurons that store knowledge about color, shape, and texture are activated. These neurons project the information onto a common "convergence zone," which then forms the word "ball."

Damage to the language areas of the brain not only affects speech and understanding of language, it also interferes with writing and reading. In order to write a word, the "thought" of the word is passed back to the visual area of the occipital lobe where a specific pattern is formed. This visual image is then passed to the language area and then to the motor strip that controls the actual writing of the word. The process of reading involves the reverse route. As a result, damage to the language pathway may affect all language-related activities. This is also why **dyslexia** is considered a language-based disorder.

In more than 90% of people, the control of language rests in the left hemisphere of the brain (Yule & Rutter, 1987). This is why a stroke that affects the left cerebral hemisphere impairs language, while a stroke on the right side usually leaves language intact. Following a stroke in an adult, the deficit in language, called **aphasia,** is often permanent because of the loss of brain tissue.

The localization of language in a child's brain appears to be similar to that found in adults. A child who is involved in a motor vehicle accident or has a brain tumor that damages the left temporal lobe is more likely to experience language problems than a child whose injury alters the right hemisphere. However, a child's brain can recover from injury or disease more completely than an adult brain (Campbell & Dollaghan, 1990). This is probably a consequence of the continued growth of neurons in the child's brain. Regions of the brain not normally used for language may be able to take over language function, a phenomenon termed **plasticity** (Bach-y-Rita, 1990).

This plasticity also may explain why young children are much better at learning second languages than adults. In the first 2 years of life, there is a proliferation of synaptic connections that aid in the development of language. It is speculated that, as with vision (see Chapter 17), these connections must be used or they are lost. This loss of synaptic connections may explain why second languages are difficult to learn later in life, why deaf children have language deficits, and why infants with tracheostomy tubes (see Chapter 9) may have speech deficits (Hill & Singer, 1990; Locke & Pearson, 1990).

CAUSES OF CHILDHOOD COMMUNICATION DISORDERS

Approximately 2%–4% of children have speech or language disorders. Boys are affected about twice as frequently as girls (Shewan & Malm, 1990). In the majority of cases, the causes of these disorders are unknown. However, some instances can be attributed to the same circumstances that cause other developmental disabilities: prematurity, birth trauma, serious infections, malformations, and chromosomal and other genetic disorders (Table 19.1).

Speech Disorders

Speech disorders are the most common type of communication disorder. They affect the ability to produce speech, but not the ability to express or understand language. Because speech develops very rapidly and the anatomy of speech production is complex, there is much opportunity for abnormality. Even in casual speech, 14 sounds per second are made; a decreased rate interferes with speech production. Furthermore, the parts of the body involved in speech range from the various nerve tracts leading from the brain, to the voice box, throat, nose, and mouth. A defect anywhere along this path affects speech.

Speech disorders can be isolated disabilities or part of a more complex developmental disorder, such as cerebral palsy (Ruscello, St. Louis, & Mason, 1991). The most common speech disorders involve problems of articulation, rhythm, resonance, and voice. They present in children as articulation errors, stuttering, or resonance abnormalities. Articulation errors are by far the most common speech disorder. To articulate well, a child must progress through a series of milestones. For example, the "b" sound is spoken before the "t," and the "sh" and "th" sounds are some of the last sounds to be mastered (Van Dyke, Yeager, McInerney, et al., 1984). Most children who have articulation problems tend to improve without any treatment. However, the persistence of such problems indicates an articulation disorder. Articulation errors are also evident in children with severe hearing impairments, especially when the hearing impairments occurred before the children were 2 years of age. Rhythm disorders usually involve stuttering, where the production of individual words is disrupted by syllable or sound repetition or sound prolongation. Resonance disorders occur in children with abnormalities of the oral or nasal tract, the most common cause being cleft palate (Pannbacker, 1988b). The pitch is too low, too high, too loud, or too soft. An extreme example of a voice disorder is the premature infant who has prolonged placement of an endotracheal tube. This child may be unable to speak because the tube bypasses the vocal cords.

Table 19.1. Communication disorders of childhood

Type	Description of disorder	Common causes
Speech disorders		
Articulation disorders	Deficits in forming certain sounds, leading to substitutions, omissions, additions, or distortions	Isolated deficit
Stuttering	Rhythm disorder, production of individual words disrupted by syllable or sound repetition or sound prolongation	Isolated deficit
Resonance abnormalities	Speech production altered by abnormality of oral or nasal tract leading to volume that is too high or too low or abnormal sounding speech	Cleft palate
Voice disorders	Speech production altered by abnormalities affecting the larynx	Tracheostomy tube, vocal abuse
Motor speech disorders		
Dysarthric speech	Abnormal articulation caused by impaired oral motor muscle control	Cerebral palsy
Verbal dyspraxia	Impairment of voluntary speech activity despite normal oral motor muscle control; mute or speech articulation severely impaired	Developmental abnormality
Language delay		
Delay in language development	Delayed development of expressive and/or receptive language	Prematurity, mental retardation
Language disorders		
Lexical-syntactic disorder	Word-finding problems, immature sentence structure; spontaneous language better than elicited speech	Traumatic brain injury, meningitis or encephalitis, brain tumor
Semantic-pragmatic disorder	Verbose; echolalia; impaired conversational use of language; impaired understanding of discourse	Learning disabilities, hydrocephalus, blindness, deafness
Nonverbal and verbal communication impairments	Limited speech or mute; limited comprehension of language	Autism

Unlike speech disorders, motor speech disorders are more common in children with developmental disabilities and include **dysarthria** and **dyspraxia** (Kent, Weismer, Kent, et al., 1989). In dysarthria, articulation is impaired because of poor oral motor muscle control (Bishop, Brown, & Robson, 1990). The child has difficulty moving the tongue both when speaking and when eating. As a result, speech may be slurred, monotone, hoarse, or strangled. Cerebral palsy (see Chapter 24), with its impaired motor control, is an example of a disorder that predisposes individuals to dysarthria.

In dyspraxia, there is a discrepancy between what the child seems physically capable of articulating and what is said. The child may be able to imitate words but unable to form them spontaneously. The impairment is of voluntary but not reflexive activity, while dysarthria affects both types of activity. A child with dyspraxia has trouble positioning the structures involved in speech and has difficulty producing vowels and consonants (Aram & Horwitz, 1983). These children may be mute, but their understanding of language is normal. The cause is unknown.

Language Disorders

If speech is the act of producing words, language implies having something to say. The usual consequence of early brain damage is to produce a developmental delay in language, rather than to produce a language disorder. The most common cause of a language delay is mental retardation (see Chapter 16). Here, speech may be normal but communication is delayed. Another cause of generalized delay in language development is prematurity (Aram, Hack, & Burchinal, 1991). However, unless the language delay is greater than the delay in other cognitive areas, it is not thought of as a true language disorder. Thus, a 4-year-old who is functioning at a 2-year level in both language and other cognitive areas is said to have mental retardation, not a communication disorder. However, a 4-year-old child with an overall mental age of 2 years but a language age of 1 year is considered to have a communication disorder superimposed on mental retardation.

Fragile X syndrome is an example of a disorder in which the combination of mental retardation and language disorder occurs (Hagerman & Sobesky, 1989) (see Chapter 16). In fact, all disorders of the X chromosome are associated with language disorders. For example, in XXY syndrome (Kleinfelter syndrome), verbal IQ is significantly lower than performance IQ on the Wechsler Scales of Intelligence (Graham, Bashir, Stark, et al., 1988). These children have word-finding and syntactical problems, but receptive language is unimpaired.

A child with a language disorder has a significant delay or abnormality in expressive and/or receptive language compared to other developmental milestones (see Table 16.1) (Kamhi & Johnston, 1982). A *receptive language disorder* implies that the child has difficulty comprehending what is heard; it does not mean the child cannot hear. Similarly, an *expressive language disorder* does not mean the child cannot make speech sounds; it means that the child cannot use language effectively for self-expression (Flower, 1981; Silva, 1980). The term *specific language impairment* (SLI) is used to refer to difficulty with spoken receptive and expressive language that is not the result of mental retardation, autism, or other etiologies.

Expressive Language Disorders Expressive language disorders have been divided into lexical-syntactic disorders and semantic-pragmatic disorders (Rapin & Allen, 1988). The former may be congenital (e.g., due to fragile X syndrome or Kleinfelter syndrome) or acquired as a result of a traumatic brain injury, a brain infection, or a tumor. These children have word-finding problems and immature speech structure. Their spontaneous language is better than elicited speech. Fortunately, most children with acquired disorders improve significantly over time, although many are left with mild language problems (Johnston & Mellits, 1980). Children with congenital, rather than acquired disorders, in which the expressive language is significantly delayed from infancy, show less improvement over time. In semantic-pragmatic dysphasia, the child's speech may range from echolalic to verbose. The underlying problem is the impaired conversational use of language and the understanding of discourse. A child with hydrocephalus often has a fairly prominent deficit, while a child with a learning disability has more subtle problems. Children with sensory deficits tend to be in the middle. The speech of a child with hydrocephalus often consists of "cocktail party language"; although the articulation is good, speech lacks meaning (i.e., semantics) or, at best, is only slightly related to the subject.

Children with blindness and/or deafness may have difficulty acquiring word meanings and learning the pragmatics of conversation. The child with a learning disability has more subtle deficits that interfere with the functional use of language (Lapadat, 1991). This may involve a delay in learning certain syntactical forms, such as the verb "to be." The child may also talk in circles, be verbose, and have difficulty using language properly and accurately. For example, instead of asking for a glass of water when thirsty, the child with a learning disability might ask if there is water in the house. The listener then must interpret what the child really wants to communicate.

Receptive Language Disorders An isolated receptive language disorder is rare; it is usually accompanied by an expressive language component (Lass, McReynolds, Northern, et al., 1982). In children with learning disabilities, the receptive component of a language disorder is associated with discourse—for example, having difficulty understanding the plot to a story (German & Simon, 1991). This understanding also is impaired in children with hydrocephalus. In autism, there is a severe combination of an expressive and receptive semantic disorder, stereotypic behavior, cognitive deficits, and problems with social interactions, further interfering with communication (see Chapter 22).

DIAGNOSIS AND TESTING

Early identification of communication disorders is essential for early intervention and an optimal outcome. A communication disorder is initially suspected in a child because his or her speech or language development is slow or aberrant. The next step is to identify whether a discrepancy between communication and other developmental skills exists. A severe language disorder is more likely to be diagnosed early than a mild disorder. A mild deficit may be missed for many years. A thorough developmental history, with special attention paid to language milestones, is helpful in making a diagnosis.

Communication is very complex, and no single test adequately evaluates all its components. Among the language screening tests used by pediatricians are the Early Language Milestone Scale (ELM), the Clinical Linguistic and Auditory Milestones Scale (CLAMS), and the Receptive-Expressive Emergent Language Scale (REEL). The ELM is similar in design to the Denver Developmental Screening Test and separates language skills into visual, auditory, receptive, and auditory expressive subsets (Coplan & Gleason, 1990). The CLAMS lists 1–3 tasks that should be accomplished at each month of development between 2 and 24 months of age (Capute & Accardo, 1978). The REEL evaluates verbal abilities through parent interviews. Comprehensive assessment instruments used by speech-language pathologists include the Sequenced Inventory of Communication Development (SICD) and the Preschool Language Scale (PLS). The SICD lists a range of speech and language milestones from 0 to 4 years (Hedrick, Prather, & Tobin, 1984). The PLS, though less comprehensive than the SICD, lists milestones from 1 to 7 years (Zimmerman, Steiner, & Pond, 1979).

For older children, it is advisable to use a battery of standardized tests to assess different areas of language abilities. These abilities include: 1) understanding and expressing single words, 2) comprehending and using grammar and syntax, 3) handling language as it increases in complexity and length, and 4) reading. One test used to evaluate these items is the Illinois Test of Psycholinguistic Abilities (ITPA), which includes a battery of tests that assesses a multitude of language abilities (Wodrich & Kush, 1990) (see Chapter 20). Another test, the Wepman Auditory Discrimination Test asks the child to discriminate between the sounds of two similar words (Machowsky & Meyers, 1975). The Peabody Picture Vocabulary Test (PPVT) deals with single-word recognition (Wodrich & Kush, 1990). And, finally, the verbal subtests of various IQ tests—for example, the Wechsler Preschool and Primary Scale of Intelligence (WPPSI) and the Stanford-Binet Intelligence Scales—measure various aspects of language comprehension and use (Wodrich & Kush, 1990). Using these tests combined with an interview and direct observation of a child's communication patterns, a speech-language pathologist can obtain a profile of a child's strengths and weaknesses. Part of the evaluation also should include an audiology screening test to make sure that an undetected hearing loss is not contributing to the communication disorder (see Chapter 18).

SPEECH-LANGUAGE THERAPY

Once identified, a child who has a speech-language disorder needs an individualized treatment program aimed at his or her developmental level. This program must be integrated with the other educational and rehabilitative needs of the child. Speech-language therapy is typically offered in a treatment room, a classroom, or at home. Individual and group therapy is generally available and should occur 2–3 times a week for 30-minute periods.

Treatment of speech disorders generally involves articulation therapy. The child is taught to produce phonemes, words, phrases, and sentences. For children with isolated articulation disorders, this approach works well. It is less effective, however, in children with more complex physical disabilities (e.g., cerebral palsy, severe hearing loss, cleft palate) (Blackstone & Painter, 1985). In these instances, oral motor therapy may be used, involving the physical stimulation of the mouth, face, and throat to improve oral motor abilities in children with cerebral palsy or to decrease the excessive escape of air through the nose of children with cleft palate.

For children who have combined expressive and receptive language disorders, language facilitation and direct teaching of vocabulary, grammar, and language usage seem to work best (Conant, Budoff, & Hecht, 1983; Conant, Budoff, Hecht, et al., 1984; Pannbacker, 1988a). Until approximately 15 years ago, direct language teaching was used by itself. At present, few professionals rely on drilling grammatical rules or word meaning as the sole means of helping a child to learn language. In addition to direct teaching, they commonly use *language facilitation therapy,* which involves providing opportunities to use language to communicate. For example, the child in an early intervention program may be encouraged to tell stories or play games while using language appropriately. A second form of facilitation is called *oral motor therapy* and is used with children who have problems with the physical act of speaking. The child with a cleft palate, for example, would be taught to speak without allowing excessive amounts of air to escape through the nose. In a child with cerebral palsy, therapy may involve physical stimulation of the mouth, face, and throat to improve oral motor abilities.

ALTERNATE MEANS OF COMMUNICATION

In some instances, speech is not sufficient to permit adequate communication. This may occur in children with cerebral palsy whose speech is unintelligible or in children who have severe expressive dysarthria, hearing loss, severe mental retardation, or autism. In these instances, oral communication must be supplemented with augmentative communication or replaced by alternative methods of communication, such as sign language.

American Sign Language (ASL), the language of the deaf, is the most commonly used sign language (see Chapter 18). The child must have a mental age of at least 10–12 months to begin to learn signing (deVilliers & deVilliers, 1978). In children who are unable to speak, signing has been found to increase communication and reduce frustration. A few functional signs can enable some children with severe retardation to communicate daily needs, such as hunger or a wish to go outside. Significant improvement in behavior has resulted from teaching basic functional signs to such children.

In addition to signing, there are many types of alternative communication devices. The simplest are flat boards with squares containing pictures or words (Figure 19.2). The child points to the square containing the word or picture that is of interest. With the advent of computers, such communication boards are typically used only in

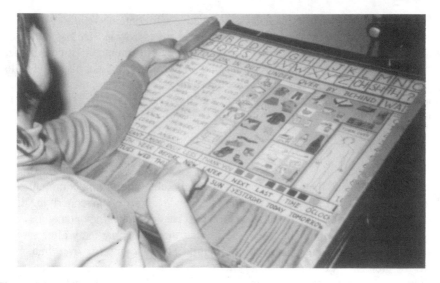

Figure 19.2. A communication board is being used by a child with cerebral palsy. A combination of pictures, letters, and words is used to allow the child to communicate with others.

temporary situations. Electronic, computerized communication boards have many advantages over the older "flat" boards. They can be equipped with voice synthesizers that say aloud whatever appears on the screen. Computers also permit more rapid communication because a single touch can activate a long sentence. They are also very flexible in being able to be reprogrammed to include new words and sentences as the child's vocabulary and interests change. Besides typing, there are alternate means of controlling the board, including light and toggle switches. A problem is that these devices can be quite expensive.

JAMAL: A CHILD WITH A COMMUNICATION DISORDER

Jamal, who is now 8 years old, was slow to develop speech compared to his older brother and sister. Yet, in other developmental areas he progressed quite normally— for example, walking when he was 11 months old. At 4 years of age, Jamal had fairly significant articulation problems and began speech therapy. By the time he started school, his articulation was normal, but his development of sentence structure was still delayed.

Jamal did not do well in first grade. His teacher noted that he had difficulty learning to read words and following instructions. However, he was not hyperactive or inattentive, and he did well in mathematics. His teachers and parents decided that Jamal might benefit from special education so they gave him a battery of formal psychological tests that revealed an IQ of 105. On subtests of the Illinois Test of Psycholinguistic Abilities, Jamal showed significant deficits in both expressive and receptive language. He had particular difficulty with auditory memory and speech closure. He was diagnosed as having a learning disability.

As a result of these tests, Jamal was placed in a self-contained learning disability class and received speech-language therapy three times a week. He has done very well, excelling in math and eventually learning to read by phonics. His communication skills also have improved with language therapy, and with them his social skills. However, Jamal still has some difficulty expressing complex ideas and understanding stories. His prognosis is quite good, but he is likely to carry certain aspects of his language disorder into adulthood.

OUTCOME

It is difficult to make blanket statements about the outcome of any communication disorder other than to indicate that prognosis depends largely on the underlying disorder. Isolated stuttering and articulation problems may disappear spontaneously over time, and the speech of a child with cleft palate improves markedly after surgical correction. Dysphasia due to traumatic brain injury tends to improve over time, especially in preteens. Comprehension generally returns before expressive language. Children with cerebral palsy may improve or may need to use alternative means of communication. The prognosis for language development in children with autism is not entirely clear (see Chapter 22).

In a study of children with expressive language delays at 2 years of age, one-third had developed normal language when retested 5 months later, one-third showed mild improvement, and one-third demonstrated no improvement (Fischel, Whitehurst, Caulfield, et al., 1989). In a study of 4-year-old children with language impairments who were followed for 18 months, children with isolated phonological disorders developed good language. IQ was the best predictor of outcome in these children (Bishop & Edmundson, 1987). However, children with multiple deficits had persistent language problems. Finally, Aram, Ekelman, and Nation (1984) tested 20 adolescents who had been diagnosed with language disorders as preschoolers. Although persistent language problems were subtle, they were sufficient to cause learning problems and subaverage school achievement. Only 3–4 children performed above the 15th percentile on achievement tests.

In summary, outcome depends on the origin of the communication disorder and on its severity. Many children will show improvement, especially if receiving appropriate therapy. However, it is likely that remaining deficits will interfere with functioning in school and in social situations.

SUMMARY

The spectrum of speech-language deficits ranges from mild speech defects to severe communication disorders that affect both expressive and receptive language. Children with developmental disabilities such as cerebral palsy, autism, hydrocephalus, and learning disabilities are at increased risk to have speech and language problems. Early identification is important to facilitate effective treatment and to help the child to develop fully.

REFERENCES

Aram, D.M., Ekelman, B.L., & Nation, J.E. (1984). Preschoolers with language disorders: 10 years later. *Journal of Speech and Hearing Research, 27,* 232–244.

Aram, D.M., Hack, M., & Burchinal, M.R. (1991). Very-low-birth weight children and speech and language development. *Journal of Speech and Hearing Research, 34,* 1169–1179.

Aram, D.M., & Horwitz, S.J. (1983). Sequential and non-speech praxic abilities in developmental verbal apraxia. *Developmental Medicine and Child Neurology, 25,* 197–206.

Bach-y-Rita, P. (1990). Brain plasticity as a basis for recovery of function in humans. *Neuropsychologica, 28,* 547–554.

Bishop, D.V., Brown, B.B., & Robson, J. (1990). The relationship between phoneme discrimination, speech production, and language comprehension in cerebral-palsied individuals. *Journal of Speech and Hearing Research, 33,* 210–219.

Bishop, D.V., & Edmundson, A. (1987). Language-impaired 4 year olds: Distinguishing transient from persistent impairment. *Journal of Speech and Hearing Disorders, 52,* 156–173.

Blackstone, S.W., & Painter, M.J. (1985). Speech problems in multihandicapped children. In J.K. Darby (Ed.), *Speech and language evaluation in neurology: Childhood disorders* (pp. 219–242). New York: Grune & Stratton.

Bloom, L., & Lahey, M. (1978). *Language development and language disorders.* New York: John Wiley & Sons.

Brown, J.W. (1979). *Aphasia, apraxia, and agnosia: Clinical and theoretical aspects.* Springfield, IL: Charles C Thomas.

Campbell, T.F., & Dollaghan, C.A. (1990). Expressive language recovery in severely brain-damaged children and adolescents. *Journal of Speech and Hearing Disorders, 55,* 567–581.

Capute, A.J., & Accardo, P.J. (1978). Linguistic and auditory milestones during the first two years of life: A language inventory for the practitioner. *Clinical Pediatrics, 17,* 847–853.

Conant, S., Budoff, M., & Hecht, B. (1983). *Teaching language-disabled children. A communication games intervention.* Cambridge, MA: Brookline Books.

Conant, S., Budoff, M., Hecht, B., et al. (1984). Language intervention: A pragmatic approach. *Journal of Autism and Developmental Disorders, 14,* 301–317.

Coplan, J., & Gleason, J.R. (1990). Quantifying language development from birth to 3 years using The Early Language Milestone Scale. *Pediatrics, 86,* 963–971.

Damasio, A.R. (1990). Category-related recognition defects as a clue to the neural substrates of knowledge. *Trends in Neuroscience, 13,* 95–98.

deVilliers, J., & deVilliers, P. (1978). *Language acquisition.* Cambridge, MA: Harvard University Press.

Fischel, J.E., Whitehurst, G.J., Caulfield, M.B., et al. (1989). Language growth in children with expressive language delay. *Pediatrics, 83,* 218–227.

Flower, R.M. (1981). Neurodevelopmental disorders in childhood. In J.K. Darby (Ed.), *Speech evaluation in medicine* (pp. 309–340). New York: Grune & Stratton.

German, D.J., & Simon, E. (1991). Analysis of children's word-finding skills in discourse. *Journal of Speech and Hearing Research, 34,* 309–316.

Graham, J.M., Bashir, A.S., Stark, R.E., et al. (1988). Oral and written language abilities of XXY boys: Implications for anticipatory guidance. *Pediatrics, 81,* 795–806.

Hagerman, R.J., & Sobesky, W.E. (1989). Psychopathology in fragile X syndrome. *American Journal of Orthopsychiatry, 59,* 142–152.

Hedrick, D., Prather, E., & Tobin, A. (1984). *Sequenced Inventory of Communication Development.* Seattle: University of Washington Press.

Hill, B.P., & Singer, L.T. (1990). Speech and language development after infant tracheostomy. *Journal of Speech and Hearing Disorders, 55,* 15–20.

Johnston, R.B., & Mellits, E.D. (1980). Pediatric coma: Prognosis and outcome. *Developmental Medicine and Child Neurology, 22,* 3–12.

Johnston, R.B., Stark, R.E., Mellits, E.D., et al. (1981). Neurological status of language-impaired and normal children. *Annals of Neurology, 10,* 159–163.

Kamhi, A.G., & Johnston, J.R. (1982). Towards an understanding of retarded children's linguistic deficiencies. *Journal of Speech and Hearing Research, 25,* 435–445.

Kent, R.D., Weismer, G., Kent, J., et al. (1989). Toward phonetic intelligibility testing in dysarthria. *Journal of Speech and Hearing Disorders, 54,* 482–499.

Lapadat, J.C. (1991). Pragmatic language skills in students with language and/or learning disabilities: A quantitative synthesis. *Journal of Learning Disabilities, 24,* 147–158.

Lass, N.J., McReynolds, L.V., Northern, J.K., et al. (Eds.). (1982). *Speech, language, and hearing: Normal processes and clinical disorders.* Philadelphia: W.B. Sanders.

Locke, J., & Pearson, D. (1990). Linguistic significance of babbling: Evidence from a tracheostomized infant. *Journal of Child Language, 17,* 1–16.

Lombardino, L.J., Stein, J.E., Kricos, P.B., et al. (1986). Play diversity and structural relationships in the play and language of language-impaired and language-normal preschoolers: Preliminary data. *Journal of Communication Disorders, 19,* 475–489.

Lyons, J. (1979). *Semantics* (Vol. 1). New York: Cambridge University Press.

Machowsky, H., & Meyers, J. (1975). Auditory discrimination, intelligence, and reading achievement at grade 1. *Perceptual and Motor Skills, 40,* 363–368.

Manter, J.T., Gatz, A.J., Gilman, S., et al. (1982). *Manter and Gatz's essentials of clinical neuroanatomy and neurophysiology* (6th ed.). Philadelphia: F.A. Davis.

Ojemann, G.A. (1991). Cortical organization of language. *Journal of Neuroscience, 11,* 2281–2287.

Pannbacker, M. (1988a). Management strategies for developmental apraxia of speech: A review of the literature. *Journal of Communication Disorders, 21,* 363–371.

Pannbacker, M. (1988b). Prevention of communication problems associated with cleft palate. *Journal of Communication Disorders, 21,* 401–408.

Prizant, B.M., Audet, L.R., Burke, G.M., Hummel, L.J., Maher, S.R., & Theadore, G. (1990). Communication disorders and emotional/behavioral disorders in children and adolescents. *Journal of Speech and Hearing Disorders, 55,* 179–192.

Rapin, I., & Allen, D.A. (1988). Syndromes in developmental dysphasia and adult aphasia. In F. Plum (Ed.), *Language communication, and the brain* (pp. 57–75). New York: Raven Press.

Rescorla, L. (1989). The language development survey: A screening tool for delayed language in toddlers. *Journal of Speech and Hearing Disorders, 54,* 587–599.

Ruscello, D.M., St. Louis, K.O., & Mason, N. (1991). School-aged children with phonologic disorders: Coexistence with other speech/language disorders. *Journal of Speech and Hearing Research, 34,* 236–242.

Shewan, C.M., & Malm, K.E. (1990). The prevalence of speech and language impairments. *American Speech-Language-Hearing Association, 32,* 108.

Silva, P.A. (1980). The prevalence, stability and significance of developmental language delay in preschool children. *Developmental Medicine and Child Neurology, 22,* 768–777.

Van Dyke, D.C., Yeager, D.J., McInerney, J.F., et al. (1984). Speech and language disorders in children. *American Family Physician, 29,* 257–268.

Waterhouse, L., & Fein, D. (1982). Language skills in developmentally disabled children. *Brain and Language, 15,* 307–333.

Wodrich, D.L., & Kush, S.A. (1990). *Children's psychological testing: A guide for nonpsychologists* (2nd ed.). Baltimore: Paul H. Brookes Publishing Co.

Yule, W., & Rutter, M. (1987). *Language development and disorders.* Oxford: MacKeith Press.

Zimmerman, I., Steiner, V., & Pond, R. (1979). *Preschool language scale.* Columbus, Ohio: Charles E. Merrill.

Chapter 20

Learning Disabilities

Robin Gallico and M.E.B. Lewis

Upon completion of this chapter, the reader will:
— know the definition of learning disability
— understand some of the ways to identify children with learning disabilities at young ages
— be aware of the various intervention approaches for children with learning disabilities

---

A child may have trouble learning for many reasons. As other chapters in this book illustrate, mental retardation, cerebral palsy, seizure disorders, and hearing and vision impairments may interfere with normal learning. This chapter focuses on the child who has none of these disorders but still fails to learn effectively in school: the child with learning disabilities.

DEFINITION OF LEARNING DISABILITIES

The term *learning disability* is difficult to define precisely. Most definitions arrive at what a learning disability is by describing what it is not. For example, a child with learning disabilities does not have mental retardation, nor does he or she have any disabling physical, emotional, or social problem. Usually, the child has had normal cultural advantages and adequate learning opportunities. Yet, despite the lack of any other developmental disability and the presence of a normal environment, the child fails to learn according to his or her abilities (Feagans, 1983). There is a spectrum of learning disabilities, ranging from variations of normal to severe disability (Shaywitz, Escobar, Shaywitz, et al., 1992).

In the Individuals with Disabilities Education Act (PL 101-476, the Education of

---

Robin Gallico, Ed.D., is Director of Special Education at The Kennedy Krieger Institute in Baltimore.

M.E.B. Lewis, Ed.D., is Principal of The Kennedy Krieger School at The Kennedy Krieger Institute in Baltimore.

the Handicapped Act Amendments of 1990, which reauthorized PL 94-142, the Education for All Handicapped Children Act of 1975, and retitled both acts IDEA), learning disability is defined as "a disorder in one or more of *the basic psychological processes* involved in understanding or in using language, spoken or written, which may manifest itself in an *imperfect ability* to listen, speak, read, write, spell, or do mathematical calculations" (Office of Education, 1977; 1990) (italics added). According to this definition, children with learning disabilities have at least average potential, but have some problems that interfere with normal learning. However, the definition fails to provide guidelines regarding what the "basic psychological processes" are or how marked an "imperfect ability" to learn must be to be considered a disability. Consequently there has been much debate, confusion, and inconsistency in the identification of children with learning disabilities. Furthermore, the exclusionary clause requires that all other possible causes for the learning problems be ruled out. This raises serious question as to whether learning disabilities can occur concomitantly with other disabilities. In an attempt to deal with these limitations, the National Joint Committee on Learning Disabilities proposed the following amended definition:

> Learning disability is a generic term that refers to a heterogeneous group of disorders manifested by significant difficulties in the acquisition and use of listening, speaking, reading, writing, reasoning, or mathematical abilities. These disorders are intrinsic to the individual and are presumed to be due to central nervous system dysfunction. Even though a learning disability may occur concomitantly with other disabling conditions (e.g., sensory impairment, mental retardation, social and emotional disturbance) or environmental influences (e.g., cultural differences or insufficient/inappropriate instruction), it is not the direct result of those conditions or influences. (Hammill, 1990, pp. 77–78)

The most common approach for determining the existence of a specific learning disability is to demonstrate a severe ability-achievement discrepancy (i.e., a significant difference between a child's potential to learn or IQ and his or her actual achievement). Unfortunately, the definition of what constitutes such a discrepancy varies from state to state (Berk, 1984). Until the mid 1980s, a 2-year disparity between chronological age and school achievement level was often used as a criterion. The problem with this approach is that it overestimates the existence of learning disabilities in children with IQ scores lower than 100 and underestimates such disabilities in children with higher IQ scores. For example, a 9-year-old child with an IQ of 80 is expected to function at a 7-year-old level in school. Using this criterion, he or she would be classified as having a learning disability because of the 2-year discrepancy between age and achievement. However, a 9-year-old with an IQ of 130 who is functioning at a 9-year-old level in school would not be classified as having a learning disability because he or she is functioning at age level. Yet, this child's IQ score indicates that he or she should be able to function at a higher age level. In fact, a 9-year-old level of achievement would be significantly below this child's potential. This child may, in fact, have a learning disability. In an attempt to address this problem, current methods employ a regression model to determine the severe discrepancy component of learning disabilities based on the child's potential and achievement (Evans, 1990).

PREVALENCE OF LEARNING DISABILITIES

Shaywitz and Shaywitz (1987) reported an estimated prevalence of learning disability among children at the end of first grade of 11.0%. This figure increased to 12.6% one year later when the same children were studied. Included in this number are children with attention deficit hyperactivity disorder and learning disabilities (see Chapter 21). As with ADHD, the traditional view of learning disabilities has been that it occurs in boys more frequently than girls (Weiss & Hechtman, 1979). Recent studies, however, question the validity of this view (Berry, Shaywitz, & Shaywitz, 1985; Shaywitz & Shaywitz, 1987). Because girls manifest attention and learning problems differently than boys and tend not to exhibit the "acting out" behaviors of boys, they have been able to "hide" in the back of classrooms without coming to the teachers' attention. In the future, it may be determined that learning disabilities and attention problems affect boys and girls equally but in different ways.

SUBGROUPS OF CHILDREN WITH LEARNING DISABILITIES

The federal government has issued regulations that specify seven areas in which a child might exhibit a specific learning disability (Office of Education, 1977): oral expression, written expression, listening comprehension, basic reading skills, reading comprehension, math calculation, and math reasoning. Reading disabilities are by far the most common form of learning disability. Since reading is the first skill in the development of the language arts, reading problems temporally precede spelling and written expression problems. A child with language arts problems often has problems with handwriting and arithmetic as well. When children have difficulty in several areas of learning, they are thought to have global learning disabilities.

Thus, a child may have an isolated learning disability (e.g., in reading, writing, spelling, or mathematics), a combined problem (e.g., in reading and writing), or a global one (e.g., in reading, writing, and mathematics). As a result, learning disabilities have been divided into a number of subgroups primarily to help in the selection of appropriate intervention programs.

Reading disability itself has been subdivided in a number of ways. Rutter, Graham, and Yule (1970) divided children with reading disabilities into those with reading retardation, commonly called *dyslexia*, and those with reading backwardness, usually called *slow learning*. They noted that children with dyslexia basically had a language disorder and a specific reading problem. Children with reading backwardness, however, tended to have low IQ scores, a history of birth injury, and other developmental problems. Interestingly, the children with dyslexia had more trouble developing reading skills than the group with reading backwardness, even though they had higher IQs (Yule, 1973).

Within the group with dyslexia, researchers have proposed further subdivisions. For instance, Boder has suggested classifying children with reading disabilities by the types of reading errors (Boder, 1973; Boder, 1976; Fried, Tanguay, Boder, et al., 1981). Using this method of categorization, three groups are described: *dyseidetic, dysphonetic,* and *mixed.* The dyseidetic group is unable to identify groupings of letters in patterns. Such children would read and spell words by their sounds (Figure 20.1); "laugh" might be "laf," and "bagel," "bagl." These children read very slowly because they must sound out each word instead of relying on a repertoire of visually recognized words. As they proceed in school, these children generally remain slow readers, but they can become relatively good spellers. The dysphonetic group is unable to relate symbols to sounds and thus cannot develop **phonetic** word analysis skills. The child makes bizarre spelling errors, unrelated to the sound of the word (Figure 20.2). The dysphonetic reader can identify words he or she has memorized but cannot use phonetics to sound out new words. This child may be able to approach grade level in reading, but is usually a poor speller. Finally, the child with a mixed type of dyslexia has the worst of both worlds.

Since Boder's work was published, a number of studies have challenged this distinction between linguistic and visuo-spatial subtypes (Hooper & Hynd, 1985; Liberman, 1983; Vellutino, 1983). Felton and Wood (1989) suggest that deficits in rote verbal learning and memory occur as a function of attention deficits rather than reading disability. They found that Boder's subtyping scheme was strongly dependent on whether the child had ADHD, and they suggest that attention deficits interact with the type and degree of cognitive deficit to produce reading disabilities.

This concept of behavior affecting learning has been studied by investigators at the Frank Porter Graham Child Development Center, who have identified different types and prevalence of behavior problems in children with learning disabilities (McKinney, 1987; McKinney & Feagans, 1984): attention deficits (29%), conduct problems (14%), withdrawal (17%), global behavior problems (5%), no significant

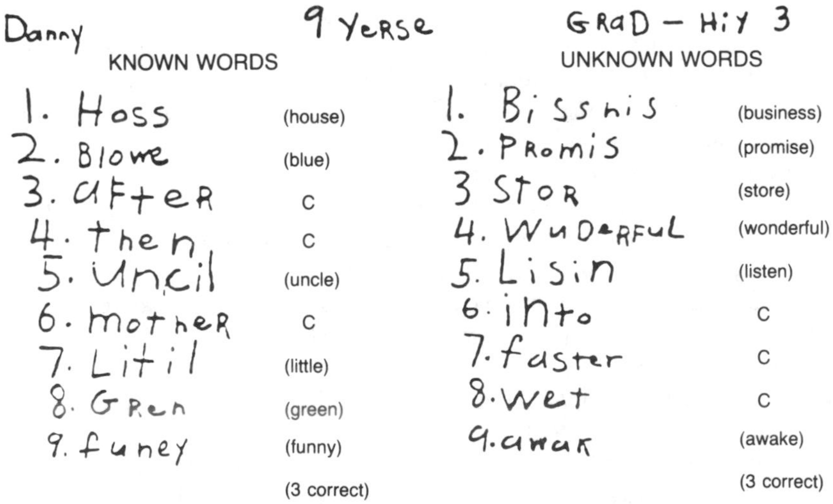

Danny	9 YeRSe	GRaD – HiY 3
KNOWN WORDS		UNKNOWN WORDS

1. Hoss	(house)		1. Bisshis	(business)
2. Blowe	(blue)		2. PRomiS	(promise)
3. aFteR	c		3 StoR	(store)
4. then	c		4. WuDaRFuL	(wonderful)
5. Uncil	(uncle)		5. Lisin	(listen)
6. motheR	c		6. into	c
7. Litil	(little)		7. faster	c
8. GRen	(green)		8. wet	c
9. funey	(funny)		9. awak	(awake)
	(3 correct)			(3 correct)

Figure 20.1.   Example of a dyseidetic child's spelling; the errors are generally phonetically correct. (From Boder, E., & Jarrico, S. [1982]. *The Boder Test of Reading-Spelling Patterns*, p. 51. New York: Grune & Stratton; reprinted by permission of The Psychological Corporation.)

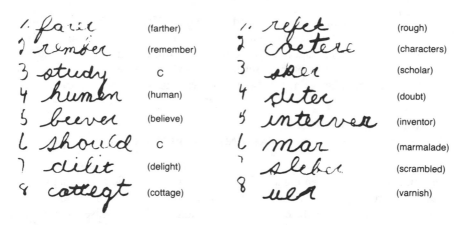

1. _farie_ (farther)
2. _remoder_ (remember)
3. _study_ c
4. _humen_ (human)
5. _beever_ (believe)
6. _should_ c
7. _dilit_ (delight)
8. _cottegt_ (cottage)

1. _refek_ (rough)
2. _coetere_ (characters)
3. _saer_ (scholar)
4. _duter_ (doubt)
5. _interver_ (inventor)
6. _mar_ (marmalade)
7. _slebe_ (scrambled)
8. _uer_ (varnish)

Figure 20.2. Example of a dysphonetic child's spelling. The spelling errors bear little resemblance to the word and are phonetically incorrect. (From Boder, E. [1973]. Developmental dyslexia: A diagnostic approach based on three atypical reading-spelling patterns. *Developmental Medicine and Child Neurology, 15,* 663–687; reprinted by permission. Copyright © 1973 by Spastics International Medical Publications.)

behavior problems (35%). This study found that problems that bring the child in conflict with the environment represent the largest percentage of subtype membership. The prognosis for children with these subtypes (e.g., conduct disorders, attention deficits) was significantly worse in that as they got older, a higher percentage developed juvenile delinquency. In addition, although all students were measured to be academically equal at the outset of the study, over a 3-year period, those students belonging to one of the maladaptive subtypes made less academic gain than students belonging to a more acceptable subtype, such as withdrawal or low self-esteem. Thus, it may be most appropriate to categorize children not only on the basis of their learning deficits but also on their associated perceptual-cognitive, language, and behavior problems (McKinney & Feagans, 1984).

CAUSES OF LEARNING DISABILITIES

The origin of learning disabilities remains unclear. Children with these disabilities do not seem to have an increased incidence of birth trauma or other environmental influences, and they tend to develop as rapidly as their siblings except in the area of language. Because of their difficulties with language, children with learning disabilities are thought to have a type of language disorder (Zuckerman & Chase, 1984). In support of this hypothesis are studies of brain pathology in adults with learning disabilities who have been found to have developmental abnormalities in the parietal lobe of the brain, which is involved with auditory processing and language syntax (Duffy, Denckla, McAnulty, & Holmes, 1988; Livingstone, Rosen, Drislane, et al., 1991). However, recent research has also implicated the central visual pathways in the brain, which may mean that the occipital lobe is involved (Rumsey, Berman, Denckla, et al., 1987). Finally, genetics appears to play a role; often several members in a family have learning disabilities, although the pattern does not follow the classic types of Mendelian inheritance described in Chapter 2 (Childs & Finucci, 1983). Children with certain genetic syndromes may also have learning disabilities. Girls with Turner syndrome or fragile X syndrome, boys with Kleinfelter syndrome, and children with neurofibromatosis have severe visual-perceptual problems and learning disabilities (Eldridge, Denckla, Bien, et al., 1989; Reiss & Freund, 1990).

DISORDERS AND PSYCHOSOCIAL
SITUATIONS THAT SIMULATE LEARNING DISABILITIES

Many medical conditions can adversely influence learning and may simulate learning disabilities. If a child has an unidentified hearing or vision deficit, learning may be impaired. Poorly controlled seizures may adversely influence learning. Children with chronic illnesses, such as diabetes, arthritis, and kidney or liver disease, may perform poorly in school because of the disease or because of psychosocial problems related to it. Finally, children with psychiatric disorders often fail in school. After these medical conditions have been brought under control, learning may improve.

Environmental influences are as important as the child's physical and emotional health. A child who is hungry cannot pay attention and does not learn well (Durkin, 1989). A child who comes from a home that does not emphasize learning rarely achieves well in school. Finally, a home beset with family problems or abuse has an adverse effect on the child's school performance (Coles, 1987; Maslow, 1970). Improvement in these psychosocial issues should result in improved school performance.

CHARACTERISTICS OF CHILDREN WITH LEARNING DISABILITIES

There is a spectrum of characteristics of children with learning disabilities (Foundation for Children with Learning Disabilities, 1984) (Table 20.1). In some children, learning disabilities do not influence aspects of the child's life other than academics, but more commonly the child has associated deficits that interfere with functioning at school and at home. These problems involve memory deficits, perceptual-motor impairments, emotional lability, and speech-language disorders. Other deficits may include hyperactivity, impulsivity, clumsiness associated with neurological **soft signs,** and attention problems.

Children with learning disabilities usually have difficulty from the time they enter formal school programs. The structure of new learning activities frequently brings out their weaknesses in comprehending abstract linguistic processes and actions, including a range of activities from telling time to sharing. In kindergarten, a child with learning disabilities often has trouble distinguishing shapes and sizes and finds it difficult to learn the alphabet and letter sounds. Writing may be no easier. However, working with numbers may be a strength if the child has an isolated reading disability.

If the child is in a kindergarten program that emphasizes socialization rather than academic readiness skills, he or she may appear academically able but socially immature. The child may be rejected by peers because of inappropriate attempts to get attention. As a result, the child may appear to be depressed, develop a poor self-

Table 20.1. Common characteristics of children with learning disabilities

Specific academic skills deficits: Children may have difficulties with any or all of the following: acquiring basic reading skills (e.g., learning letter names and sounds, blending, applying phonetic and structural analysis), reading comprehension, writing, written expression, spelling, mathematical calculation, and mathematical reasoning.

Perceptual-motor impairments: Children may have difficulty distinguishing shapes and sizes and have difficulty with fine motor activities, such as writing, coloring, and cutting. They may lack established handedness and may make letter, word, and/or number reversals.

Memory and thinking disorders: Children may be deficient in the use of strategies for memorization and haphazard in their approaches to learning. They may have poor language skills, which hinder memory, difficulty with short-term auditory and visual memory, and a lack of awareness of skills and strategies needed to solve problems and perform tasks.

Speech-language disorders: Language development may be delayed. Children may have difficulty with the grammar (syntax), meaning (semantics), or social use (pragmatics) of language.

Attention disorders: Children may have difficulty concentrating and remaining "on task." They rarely finish what is started, frequently jump from one activity to another, and are easily distracted by competing stimuli.

Hyperactivity: Children have difficulty sitting still, are constantly in motion, are fidgety, and are driven by an "inner motor."

Impulsiveness: Children often act without thinking, have poor planning and organizational skills, respond quickly and make many errors, and lack self-regulation skills.

Emotional lability: Children are moody and often isolated or rejected by peers. They may have low self-esteem and are more likely to violate social norms. They may exhibit inappropriate ways of getting attention, elicit more negative reactions from others, and be lacking in social cognition skills. Also, they may have difficulty with reading nonverbal social cues and with motivation. They may be passive, rather than active, learners.

General coordination deficits: Children may be clumsy and have difficulty with fine and/or gross motor skills (e.g., tying shoes, running, hopping, skipping), and depth perception.

Neurological soft signs: Soft signs may include poor fine motor coordination, balance, and tactile discrimination. They also may have strabismus and poor visual-motor coordination.

image, and withdraw from participating in class. Eventually, the child may avoid going to school or act out in class to obtain the attention he or she does not receive through good grades.

An exception to this picture is the gifted child who has an IQ over 130 and has learning disabilities. This child's innate capacity often will allow good progress through the early elementary grades. However, the child may begin to experience difficulties upon entering the intermediate grades or middle school where the demands for organization, study skills, and writing for a variety of content areas increase.

EARLY IDENTIFICATION

Since most definitions of learning disability are based on the existence of significant differences between intellectual potential and school achievement, the identification of students with learning disabilities has usually not occurred until after school entry.

Efforts are underway to develop tools and definitions to better identify children with learning disabilities before they reach school age. Unfortunately, items most often asked on school readiness education tests, such as the Metropolitan Readiness Test and the Gates-MacGinitie Reading Test, have poor track records of predicting which students will develop specific learning disabilities (Badian, McAnulty, Duffy, et al., 1990). However, newer tests of language and memory function employ **grapheme**-phoneme associations and rapid retrieval from long-term memory, and they appear to be helpful in differentiating normal readers from dyslexic readers (Badian et al., 1990). Difficulties in semantic-syntactic aspects of language development have been found to predict poor reading skills (Catts, 1991) (see Chapter 19). Finally, short-term auditory memory skills and the ability to pay attention and follow sequential commands have been good markers for future learning deficits (Felton & Wood, 1989).

Deficits in visual-perceptual skills, which are common in children with learning disabilities, are more difficult to diagnose at a young age than language delays. However, tests can indicate problems in drawing and understanding shape concepts. For example, a 3-year-old should be able to draw a circle and a cross and to match colors. A 4-year-old normally can draw a "stick figure," and a 6-year-old should be able to copy a number of the pictures in the Bender-Gestalt test (Figure 20.3). Many kindergarten and first grade teachers feel that difficulty with certain perceptual-motor tasks, such as tying shoes and skipping, are red flags in predicting poor academic success. However, other visual-perceptual signs may not show up until a child is older than 7 years. For example, although letter reversal is common in children with learning disabilities, it is not uncommon for children under 7 years of age to reverse letters such as "b" for "d." While an inability to distinguish right from left may be a marker for learning disability (Accardo, 1980), it is not until 6 years of age that an average child can accomplish this task consistently. Other so-called soft neurological signs do not appear until after 6 years of age, and their importance in diagnosing a learning disability at any time is questionable.

A final problem with early identification is that children who are labeled as having learning disabilities at 4 or 5 years of age may simply have a developmental delay and ultimately turn out to have normal abilities. There is also the concern of creating a self-fulfilling prophecy, that of producing children with learning disabilities by tests. In one study, deHirsch, Jansky, and Langford (1966) accurately identified approximately 75% of the children in a kindergarten class who later developed learning disabilities. However, they also labeled as having a learning disability a large number of the children who later had normal learning patterns. The important point here is that traditional means of diagnosing learning disabilities in young children must be cautiously applied. As the newer approaches described earlier are applied outside of the research arenas, the future for early detection of learning disabilities should continue to improve.

EVALUATION OF CHILDREN WITH LEARNING DISABILITIES

Before performing a battery of psychological and educational tests on a child who is having trouble learning, a complete medical and social history should be taken to

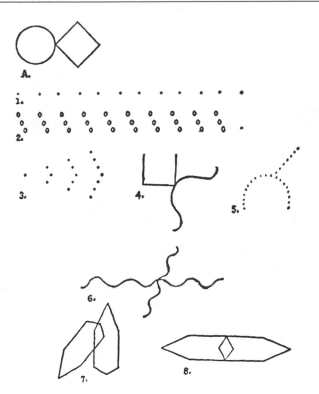

Figure 20.3. Figures used in the Bender-Gestalt test of visual-perceptual abilities. The individual is asked to copy the nine figures. (From Bender, L. [1946]. *Instructions for the use of Visual Motor Gestalt Test*, Plate I. New York: American Orthopsychiatric Association, 1946; reprinted by permission. Copyright © 1946 by Lauretta Bender and The American Orthopsychiatric Association, Inc.)

consider other confounding diagnoses. Questions to the parents might include: Is your child overactive? Is your child easily distracted or inattentive? Does your child have any chronic illnesses? Does your child receive any medication that might affect learning? Does your child have any problem behaviors? Does your child avoid going to school, sometimes using sickness as an excuse? Is there or has there ever been a problem with vision or hearing? Do you think that any recent changes in your home may have upset your child? Are you having any problems with your child outside of school? The answers to these and other questions provide information about other medical and psychosocial influences on learning. The next step is to consider the child's educational history. A child with learning disabilities can usually be recognized by the time he or she is in the second grade. If, for example, a 10-year old who has previously done well academically suddenly begins to fail, the problem is probably not a learning disability, unless the child is gifted.

After deficits other than learning disabilities have been eliminated, formal testing can be done to assess cognitive, visual-perceptual, and psycholinguistic strengths and weaknesses. An assessment is also made of the level of achievement in different academic areas. This leads to the diagnosis of a potential-achievement discrepancy and to a strategy for intervention. Most children are not tested with the battery of tests discussed below until they have completed kindergarten.

The most commonly used cognitive or IQ test is the Wechsler Intelligence Scale for Children–III (WISC-III). This test contains measures of both language abilities and performance tests of eye-hand skills that require minimal verbal responses (Dudley-Marling, Kaufman, & Tarver, 1981). It is divided into six verbal and six performance subtests, none of which requires reading or spelling. These subtests consist of a series of increasingly difficult questions ranging from a 6- to 16-year-old level. On each, the child is asked to perform up to the level at which he or she consistently fails. Each subtest is then scored, with 10 being an average score. It is possible to determine a child's strengths and weaknesses by examining the results of the subtests. A variation of this test, used for children 3 years and older, is called the Wechsler Preschool and Primary Scale of Intelligence–Revised (WPPSI-R) (Wodrich & Kush, 1990).

The verbal subtests of the Wechsler scales include: information, comprehension, arithmetic, similarities, vocabulary, and digit span. The performance subtests include: picture completion, picture arrangement, block design, object assembly, coding, and mazes. The child with a learning disability may have a scattering of abilities similar to the child with ADHD (Ackerman, Peters, & Dykman, 1971), and the WISC-III is useful in evaluating various strengths and weaknesses. For example, the examiner may find specific strengths in verbal areas or particular weaknesses in the visual-performance area. Such information is helpful in setting up an individualized education program (IEP).

Psychologists have identified a number of patterns of WISC-III performance indicative of reading and/or learning disabilities. One such pattern is the *ACID profile,* named because it includes the subtests of arithmetic, coding, information, and digit span (Wodrich & Kush, 1990). Children with reading disabilities have been found to be weak in these tasks. Other indications of learning disability based on WISC-III profiles have centered around variability in performance on individual subtests and differences between verbal IQ scores and performance IQ scores. A difference of greater than 15 points is considered significant. Caution must be exercised, however, against relying too heavily on such "profile" or "scatter" analyses, as a significant amount of scatter has been found in the non–learning disabled population as well (Berk, 1983).

Wechsler scales are usually combined with educational batteries, including tests listed in Table 20.2. These include measures of visual-perceptual abilities, such as the Bender-Gestalt figures (see Figure 20.3) or the Goodenough-Harris Drawing Test, and psycholinguistic tests such as the Illinois Test of Psycholinguistic Abilities (ITPA) (Wodrich & Kush, 1990). Finally, there is a range of academic achievement tests of oral reading and comprehension, spelling, and arithmetic. The results of the combined psychoeducational testing indicate the child's IQ, visual-perceptual and language abilities, and levels of achievement in various areas of learning. From these findings, discrepancies between potential and achievement are quantified and IEPs are developed. Retesting at the end of each school year is important to determine the progress the child has made and the effectiveness of the program.

Table 20.2. Commonly used tests for evaluating the child with learning disabilities

Name of test	Consists of	Assesses
Visual-Perceptual Tests[a]		
Bender-Gestalt Test	9 drawings the child is asked to copy	Visual-perceptual skills; eye-hand coordination
Goodenough Draw-a-Person Test	Points given for number of body parts, accuracy, and detail in a drawing (of a person) by the child	Visual-perceptual skills; child's self-image
Psycholinguistic Tests		
Illinois Test of Psycho-linguistic Abilities (ITPA)	Two groups of 6 subtests	Auditory reception: visual reception; auditory/visual association; visual-motor association; verbal expression; manual expression (first 6 tests); auditory expression: grammar, auditory sequential memory, visual sequential memory; sound comprehension; specific language deficiencies
Wepman Auditory Discrimination Test	Spoken words that sound similar	Ability to differentiate similar sounding words
Academic Achievement Tests[b]		
The Wide Range Achievement Tests (WRAT) Battery (useful for determining rate of learning)	3 subtests; grade level is obtained on each subtest.	Spelling, reading, math abilities
Woodcock-Johnson Psycho-educational Battery	Subtests in areas covering reading skills, mathematics, writing, science, social studies, humanities	General ability, academic achievement, personal interest
Metropolitan Readiness Test (taken during second half of kindergarten)	Screening test for entering first grade; may be first standardized measure of learning problem	Counting, number concepts, alphabet, phonetics, visual discrimination
Gates-MacGinitie Reading Test	Vocabulary words; stories and questions about the stories	Silent comprehension and vocabulary
Durrell Reading Test	Stories	Oral reading
Word Recognition Test	List of words of varying difficulty. "Flash score": Percentage of words recognized instantly; "Untimed score": Percentage described without a time limit	Sight-reading vocabulary; word skills

(continued)

Table 20.2.   *(continued)*

Name of test	Consists of	Assesses
Detroit Test of Learning Aptitude	19 subtests	Prerequisite skills (short-term recollection, memory, ability to follow oral directions, etc.) for reading and other school subjects; ability to understand opposites
Informal Reading Inventory (IRI)	Tests that yield four levels of reading ability[c]	"Independent" reading ability; "Instructional" level; "Frustration" level; "Hearing capacity" level
Key Math Diagnostic Arithmetic Test	Several subtests; yields grade equivalent	Computational skills and concepts; identifies types of errors made

[a]Wodrich and Kush (1990).
[b]Taylor (1984), Taylor and Warren (1984).
[c]Wilson (1981).

TREATMENT AND INTERVENTION

Learning disabilities have no cure. While the best approach seems to be one that teaches the child methods of compensating for the disability, professionals continue to debate the most effective intervention strategies. In teaching the child with learning disabilities, a main consideration is whether to strive to overcome the child's weaknesses or to develop the child's strengths. Little evidence supports the superiority of one approach over another, and no single educational method works well for all children (Warren & Taylor, 1984). Some teachers prefer certain methods, and different approaches are popular at various times. Cognitive, attention, perceptual, and sensory deficits, together with hyperactivity, immaturity, and poor motivation play roles in determining the child's needs and potentially useful approaches to remediation. Strategies, such as the use of advanced organizers (i.e., relating material to what has been previously learned), verbal rehearsal (i.e., self-instruction through oral verbal processing of tasks), and the use of computers can be of assistance (Church & Bender, 1989). In reviewing methods of instructional intervention, the areas of reading, writing, and mathematics are emphasized.

Reading

The perception and processing of symbols and their sounds are the bases for reading. In elementary school, reading instruction includes methods that increase vocabulary, phonics, syntax, and comprehension (Zintz & Maggart, 1989) (Table 20.3). Regardless of which method is chosen, the development of reading is accomplished by the combination of word recognition and comprehension. Word recognition can be taught by analyzing new words for sound (phonics and phonetics) or structure (visual configuration), or by encountering the word and memorizing it as a total entity (whole-word approach). Comprehension strategies center on developing the ability to draw meaning from text, often using a basal approach in which there is careful sequencing of books that permits gradual progression of reading skills. Meaning is easier to teach in the primary and intermediate grades as compared to high school grades, where meaning may become buried in nuances of language, such as humor, sarcasm, and metaphor (Englert & Hiebert, 1984).

A student with a reading disability needs an adjustment in the curriculum or placement in a specialized class setting (Lewis, 1982). Some of the curricular approaches that can be adapted for the child with learning disabilities are the Orton-Gillingham technique (Orton, 1937), the Fernald method (Silberberg, Iversen, & Goins, 1975) (both of which are multisensory approaches to learning), whole language techniques (in which a spectrum of language arts is reinforced), individualized reading (in which the student chooses materials to read), functional skills approaches (in which daily living skills and minimum competency standards are addressed), programmed approach (stressing pre-assessment, practice, and posttesting), and the language experience approach (in which the student generates stories for purposes of instruction).

Writing

Students with **dysgraphia** are those with specific disabilities in processing and reporting information in written form. Writing is firmly connected to reading and spelling because comprehension and exposition of these skills are demonstrated through writing. While writing is a representation of oral language (Zintz & Maggart, 1989), it also must convey meaning without vocal intonation or stress, making organizational demands on the writer.

Problems in writing may result from an inability to manipulate a pen and paper to produce a legible representation of ideas or an inability to express oneself on paper. The former can be addressed with the introduction of a word processor. Problems

Table 20.3. Types of reading remediation techniques

Phonics offer a highly structured system requiring the reader to apply rules and cues to analyze words and speak with increasing speed and accuracy.

Basals employ carefully sequenced books and supplemental materials that offer gradual progression through vocabulary and comprehension activities. Basals are often utilized to introduce phonics as the key to developing the building blocks of reading individual words.

Individualized reading stresses the independence of the reader in selecting and recording materials read from an extensive selection within the classroom or school library. The student and teacher meet on a regular schedule to discuss progress.

Language experience methods utilize the reader's daily experiences to generate vocabulary and syntax.

Programmed reading stresses study using pre-assessment, diagnosis, practice, and posttesting.

Modified writing systems, such as the initial teaching alphabet (i/t/a) or rebus reading systems, assist children in making connections between symbolic representation and the actual reading process. Such a method leads to later writing skills, but tends to lend an additional level of complexity to the process.

with composition and exposition can be treated with a variety of remedial techniques, such as: 1) the use of open-ended sentences (Mercer, Hughes, & Mercer, 1985), 2) the Fernald approach for the development of vocabulary, 3) the keeping of journals and diaries, 4) modified writing systems using **rebus symbols** such as using a picture of a knot to mean the word "not" (Newcomer, Nodine, & Barenbaum, 1988), and 5) the use of newspapers to demonstrate writing styles and organization.

Mathematics

Students whose learning disabilities center around arithmetic functioning are called **dyscalculic.** This problem involves an inability to perform basic math functions (i.e., addition, subtraction, multiplication, division) or to apply those operations to daily situations. If math functions remain a problem, a calculator may prove helpful as an aid. However, often the problem is in understanding the abstract concepts of mathematical usage. When students with dyscalculia have only written math problems to solve, the concepts remain vague; but when functional applications are used (e.g., involving money or time), they can connect the concepts to their practical application and demonstrate greater understanding (Schwartz & Budd, 1983). Thus, teaching may focus on the use of money in fast food restaurants (e.g., making change), grocery shopping (e.g., comparing prices per unit of weight), banking (e.g., balancing a checkbook, calculating interest), cooking (e.g., measurement), and transportation (e.g., reading, keeping to schedules).

For many students with mathematical disabilities, the more abstract levels of mathematics, such as algebra, geometry, and calculus, may remain mysteries forever, but they can still become facile with basic mathematical functions in daily life. Many schools teach students how and when to use calculators so that more complex problems may be simplified or homework can be checked for accuracy.

Educational Approaches

Education for children with learning disabilities should consist of three components: general education, vocational training, and career education. General education teaches children about the world and provides basic academic skills in addition to physical education, music, art, and so on. Vocational training, which usually begins in high school, consists of counseling, assessment, and education for the hands-on skills that future jobs require. Finally, career education focuses on the awareness of and preparation for the various roles, settings, and events that are important for the world of work (Brolin, Elliott, & Corcoran, 1984).

Individualized education programs (IEPs) are designed by teams of professionals, in consultation with parents, for any child diagnosed with a learning disability. As originally mandated in 1975 by PL 94-142, the Education for All Handicapped Children Act (reauthorized in 1990 as PL 101-476, the Individuals with Disabilities Education Act), IEP implementation should occur in the "least restrictive environment." While states can determine how these services are delivered (e.g., students with learning disabilities might receive services along a continuum of environments, ranging from regular class settings to resource rooms or self-contained classes of students with similar needs), the goal is always mainstreaming or education with peers in community schools. A child's IEP is evaluated annually, at which time changes are made to reflect the student's progress and ongoing strengths and needs; parents, who are involved in this process, have the right to appeal if they do not agree with the goals and objectives of their child's IEP.

Career education can begin as early as elementary school with learning how to complete forms (a skill vital to later employment), or how to perform a task in sequence. As adults, individuals with learning disabilities continue to have poor retention of verbal instructions and other problems that may interfere with effectiveness in their jobs. They also may be hesitant to ask questions and seek assistance. Social immaturity, clumsiness, and poor judgment make interactions more difficult. Colleges and job placement agencies are often unprepared to help with their special learning problems (Foundation for Children with Learning Disabilities, 1984). In order to deal in advance with these issues, career education includes developing a student's knowledge about jobs in broad work categories, such as health occupations (e.g., physician, dentist, nurse, technician, dental assistant, nurse's aide). Although career training was developed for children with learning disabilities, it is appropriate and important for all children with disabilities.

Medication

Although treatment of children with learning disabilities has primarily focused on educational approaches, the use of medication may be helpful for some children. Yet, medication should never be a substitute for sound educational programming. Stimulant medications have been used in children with ADHD to decrease hyperactivity and increase attention span. Such medication may also help to improve attention in children with learning disabilities who are not physically hyperactive (Dykman, Ackerman, & McCray, 1980). In addition to stimulant medication, some students with learning disabilities may require other psychotropic drugs to treat accompanying anxiety or depression (Gallico, Burns, & Grob, 1988). If any of these drugs is used, its effectiveness must be monitored carefully.

Nontraditional Treatment Approaches

Because there is no cure for learning disabilities, it is not surprising that a host of nontraditional therapies have gained advocates from time to time. The most commonly used nontraditional approaches have been directed at correcting an underlying perceptual deficit. These treatment methods include **patterning,** optometry, and sensory integration.

Proposed in 1966 by Doman and Delacato, "patterning" is based on the theory that development is patterned after the evolution of humans from lower primates (Delacato, 1966). Doman and Delacato assume that the failure to pass through a proper sequence of developmental stages in motor ability, language, visual, auditory, and other sensory areas leads to poor neurological organization of the brain (Delacato, 1966). Treatment, or reprogramming, is carried out by following a rigorous series of physical and breathing exercises as well as by restricting the intake of fluids, salt, and sugar. No studies have supported the effectiveness of this approach, and the American Academy of Pediatrics (1982) and other educational and medical organizations have expressed concern about the use of this method.

Some optometrists propose that children with dyslexia should use visual training exercises to overcome visual-perceptual deficits. Yet, no research has found that eye muscle exercises have any beneficial effect on reading (Metzger & Werner, 1984). Another visual hypothesis focuses on scotopic sensitivity of the retina. Investigators speculated that certain children are highly sensitive to particular frequencies and wavelengths of the white light spectrum. This deficit is postulated to cause fatigue and trauma, resulting in reading disability, poor coordination and depth perception, eye strain, and sensitivity to glare (O'Connor, Sofo, Kendall, et al., 1990). They reported that symptoms of dyslexia can be eliminated by colored lenses that filter out offending light frequencies. Research conducted on the colored lenses has not proven them to be effective (Hoyt, 1990).

Another approach attempts to overcome perceptual problems by sensory integration training (Ayres, 1972). This theory suggests that the ability of the cortex to respond to auditory and visual stimuli depends on the organization of the stimuli in the brain stem. Ayres noted that other abnormalities connected with the functioning of the brain stem are apparent in children with learning disabilities. These include clumsiness and poor eye muscle coordination. To deal with this, she proposed activities that involve balancing and fine motor coordination aimed at improving brain stem functioning. Initial studies suggest that this method is not successful in treating learning disabilities (Golden, 1984).

To summarize, little evidence supports nontraditional approaches to treatment of children with learning disabilities. However, until more effective traditional treatment approaches are developed, it is likely that new fads and controversial treatments will continue to appear and be used by families hoping for a cure.

CASE STUDIES OF CHILDREN WITH LEARNING DISABILITIES

David: A Child with Dyslexia

David developed normally as a young child and seemed as bright and alert as his sisters. He was not hyperactive, nor did he seem particularly clumsy. However, in kindergarten, he began to have some difficulties. He got along well with the other children but had trouble with his schoolwork. He had particular problems learning the alphabet and how each letter sounded. On the Metropolitan Readiness Test, he scored well below average in reading skills, although his math skills fell within the average range.

In first grade, David entered a regular class and soon began to fail. He could not learn phonetic skills, and reading remained a mystery. His spelling errors were bizarre. Yet, he learned how to add and subtract easily. David went through a battery of tests that confirmed dyslexia. His full-scale IQ on the WISC-III was 120.

The school decided to keep David in a regular class for the remainder of the school year and to have an itinerant special education teacher give him extra help. This approach did not work well. David fell farther and farther behind the other children in language skills. He started misbehaving in school and avoiding going to school, using headaches as an excuse. At the end of first grade, his reading was more than 1 year delayed, while his arithmetic skills were at an age-appropriate level.

When he entered second grade, David was still anxious and unhappy. This time, he went to a reading resource room daily for 45 minutes, where he found only five other children. The reading specialist was kind but firm; the approach was very structured. Soon David began to learn. It was a slow, arduous process. Besides the special class in school, his parents worked with him at night. He remained a poor reader, but he could feel the excitement of gaining new knowledge. Friendships developed among him and the other children in the resource room. Yet, his less sensitive schoolmates still teased him.

At the end of second grade, David was retested and found to have made 1 year's progress during the previous school year. He remained a little more than a year behind in reading, but his rate of learning had accelerated. He continued to attend the resource room daily for 2 more years. By this time, he was an expert mathematician, which helped to offset his difficulty with reading and spelling. He still found school difficult, but he stopped avoiding it. Behavior problems faded. With the continued support of his teachers and parents, David has a good prognosis. He is bright, and the early help he received kept significant emotional problems from developing.

Maria: A Child with Dysgraphia and Dyscalculia

Maria is a 12-year-old who attends a regular middle school in her neighborhood. She has received resource services since the second grade. Although Maria has always maintained adequate grades, especially in reading, her teachers have noted her struggle with note taking, written assignments, and copying from the board. Maria also has had difficulty in arithmetic instruction, finding it impossible to memorize math facts and apply them. These weaknesses were documented through a comprehensive educational assessment. The evaluator predicted that as Maria entered middle school, her deficits in written expression would have an increasing impact on her academic functioning because more writing and study strategies would be required. This has proven to be the case.

Maria's abilities as measured by the WISC-III showed verbal skills of 105 and performance skills of 90, yielding a 15 point difference between these areas. The evaluator noted a high degree of frustration whenever Maria had to contend with written demands or math calculations. This has begun to manifest itself in the classroom with a falling attendance rate and at home with more frequent somatic complaints, such as stomachaches or headaches.

The school decided to provide Maria with specific resource assistance in the area of organization and study skills. She began using a word processor for longer written assignments, and a calculator during math class. Maria was also assigned a "buddy" to take notes for her whenever she could not keep up with the demands of the written work. In addition, teachers were advised not to penalize her for spelling errors but rather require her to correct them.

Maria's difficulties seem manageable because the school staff has been willing to be flexible and creative in accommodating her needs. Since this program was implemented, Maria's attendance has improved and her increasing willingness to attempt more difficult assignments has met with success. As she progresses through middle school and enters high school, she will continue to need assistance in organizing her study skills, in using word processing, and in developing math coping strategies. Given these compensations, her prognosis is good.

PROGNOSIS

The prognosis for most children with learning disabilities is good. Many go on to college and professional careers. However, they frequently achieve less as adults than children without learning disabilities who have similar IQs. Most retain some degree of learning disability as adults. In one study, 74% of the children who had reading impairments when they were 7 years old continued to have reading impairments years later (Watson, Watson, & Fredd, 1982). Prognosis appears to depend less on the method used to help the child than on the severity of the learning disability, the age at diagnosis and intervention, the IQ score of the child, the motivation to learn, and family support systems.

SUMMARY

A learning disability is a disorder in which a healthy child with normal intelligence fails to learn up to his or her intellectual potential. The underlying cause of this disorder is unknown. It may involve abnormal functioning in the parietal and/or occipital lobes of the brain and may have a genetic component. Whatever the cause, early detection is important because, if not helped, the child may develop emotional problems that hinder progress. If a learning disability is suspected, a psychoeducational evaluation should be performed to identify areas of strengths and weaknesses. Then the school can develop an individualized education program. Results of the program must be assessed at the end of each year and appropriate changes made. No one treatment method is best for all children, so a trial-and-error approach may be needed to find the most useful method for each child. Career and vocational education should be integrated into the general educational program. The prognosis for the child with a learning disability is generally good, but he or she usually takes the processing difficulties into adulthood.

REFERENCES

Accardo, P.J. (1980). *A neurodevelopmental perspective on specific learning disabilities*. Baltimore: University Park Press.

Ackerman, P.T., Peters, J.E., & Dykman, R.A. (1971). Children with specific learning disabilities: WISC profiles. *Journal of Learning Disabilities, 4,* 150–166.

American Academy of Pediatrics. (1982). The Doman-Delacato treatment of neurologically handicapped children. *Pediatrics, 70,* 810–812.

Ayres, A.J. (1972). Improving academic scores through sensory integration. *Journal of Learning Disabilities, 5,* 338–343.

Badian, N.A., McAnulty, G.B., Duffy, F.H., et al. (1990). Prediction of dyslexia in kindergarten boys. *Annals of Dyslexia, 40,* 152–169.

Bender, M., & Church, G. (1984). Developing a computer-applications training program for the learning disabled. *Learning Disabilities, 3,* 91–102.

Berk, R.A. (1983). The value of WISC-R profile analysis for the differential diagnosis of learning disabled children. *Journal of Clinical Psychology, 39,* 133–136.

Berk, R.A. (1984). *Screening and diagnosis of children with learning disabilities.* Springfield, IL: Charles C Thomas.

Berry, C.A., Shaywitz, S.E., & Shaywitz, B.A. (1985). Girls with attention deficit disorder: A silent minority? A report on behavioral and cognitive characteristics. *Pediatrics, 76,* 801–809.

Boder, E. (1973). Developmental dyslexia: A diagnostic approach based on three typical reading-spelling patterns. *Developmental Medicine and Child Neurology, 15,* 663–687.

Boder, E. (1976). School failure—Evaluation and treatment. *Pediatrics, 58,* 394–403.

Brolin, D.E., Elliott, T.R., & Corcoran, J.R. (1984). Career education for persons with learning disabilities. *Learning Disabilities, 3,* 1–14.

Catts, H.W. (1991). Early identification of dyslexia: Evidence from a follow-up study of speech-language impaired children. *Annals of Dyslexia, 41,* 163–177.

Childs, B., & Finnuci, J. (1983). Genetics, epidemiology, and specific learning disability. In M. Rutter (Ed.), *Developmental neuropsychiatry* (pp. 507–519). New York: Guilford Press.

Church, G., & Bender, M. (1989). *Teaching with computers: A curriculum for special education.* Boston: College-Hill Press.

Coles, G. (1987). *The learning mystique: A critical look at learning disabilities.* New York: Fawcett.

deHirsch, K., Jansky, J., & Langford, W. (1966). *Predicting reading failure.* New York: Harper & Row.

Delacato, C.H. (1966). *Neurological organization and reading.* Springfield, IL: Charles C Thomas.

Division of Educational Services, Special Education Programs. (1987). *Ninth annual report to Congress on the Education of the Handicapped Act.* Washington, DC: U.S. Department of Education.

Dudley-Marling, C.C., Kaufman, N.J., & Tarver, S.G. (1981). WISC and WISC-R profiles of learning disabled children: A review. *Learning Disabilities Quarterly, 4,* 307–319.

Duffy, F.H., Denckla, M.B., McAnulty, G.B., & Holmes, J.A. (1988). Neurophysiological studies in dyslexia. In F. Plum (Ed.), *Language, communication, and the brain* (pp. 149–170). New York: Raven Press.

Durkin, D. (1989). *Teaching them to read.* Boston: Allyn & Bacon.

Dykman, R.A., Ackerman, P.T., & McCray, D.S. (1980). Effects of methylphenidate on selective and sustained attention in hyperactive, reading-disabled, and presumably attention-disordered boys. *Journal of Nervous and Mental Disease, 168,* 745–752.

Eldridge, R., Denckla, M.B., Bien, E., et al. (1989). Neurofibromatosis type I (Recklinghausen's disease): Neurologic and cognitive assessment with sibling controls. *American Journal of Diseases of Children, 143,* 833–837.

Englert, C.S., & Hiebert, E.H. (1984). Children's developing awareness of text structure in expository material. *Journal of Education Psychology, 76,* 65–74.

Evans, L.D. (1990). A conceptual overview of the regression discrepancy model for evaluating severe discrepancy between IQ and achievement scores. *Journal of Learning Disabilities, 23(7),* 406–412.

Feagans, L. (1983). A current view of learning disabilities. *Journal of Pediatrics, 102,* 487–493.

Felton, R.H., & Wood, F.B. (1989). Cognitive deficits in reading disability and attention deficit disorder. *Journal of Learning Disabilities, 22(1),* 3–22.

Foundation for Children with Learning Disabilities (FCLD). (1984). *The FLCD guide for parents of children with learning disabilities*. New York: Education Systems.

Fried, I., Tanguay, P.E., Boder, E., et al. (1981). Development of dyslexia: Electrophysiological evidence of clinical subgroups. *Brain and Language, 12*, 14–22.

Gallico, R.P., Burns, T.J., & Grob, C.S. (1988). *Emotional and behavioral problems in children with learning disabilities*. Boston: College-Hill Press.

Gillett, J.W., & Temple, C. (1990). *Understanding reading problems—Assessment and instruction* (3rd ed.). Boston: Little, Brown.

Golden, G.S. (1984). Symposium on learning disorders. Controversial therapies. *Pediatric Clinics of North America, 31*, 459–469.

Hammill, D.D. (1990). On defining learning disabilities: An emerging consensus. *Journal of Learning Disabilities, 23*(2), 74–84.

Hooper, S.C., & Hynd, G.W. (1985). Differential diagnosis of developmental dyslexia with the Kaufman Assessment Battery for Children (K-ABC). *Journal of Clinical Child Psychology, 14*, 145–152.

Hoyt, C.S. (1990). Irlen lenses and reading difficulties. *Journal of Learning Disabilities, 23*, 624–627.

Lewis, M.E.B. (1982). Use of thematic curriculum in development for learning disabled students: Assumptions and applications. *Learning Disabilities—An Interdisciplinary Journal, 1*(3), 25–33.

Liberman, I.Y. (1983). A language-oriented view of reading and its disabilities. In H.R. Myklebust (Ed.), *Progress in learning disabilities* (pp. 81–102). New York: Grune & Stratton.

Livingstone, M.S., Rosen, G.D., Drislane, F.W., et al. (1991). Physiological and anatomical evidence for a magnocellular defect in developmental dyslexia. *Proceeding of the National Academy of Sciences (U.S.A.), 88*, 7943–7947.

Maslow, A. (1970). *Motivation and personality*. New York: HarperCollins.

McKinney, J.D. (1987). Research on conceptually and empirically derived subtypes of specific learning disabilities. In M.C. Wang, M.C. Reynolds, & H.J. Walberg (Eds.), *Handbook of special education: Research and practice* (Volume II) (pp. 253–282). New York: Pergamon.

McKinney, J.D., & Feagans, L. (1984). Academic and behavioral characteristics: Longitudinal studies of learning disabled children and average achievers. *Learning Disability Quarterly, 7*, 251–265.

Mercer, C.D., Hughes, C.A., & Mercer, A.R. (1985). Learning disabilities definitions used by state education departments. *Learning Disability Quarterly, 8*, 45–55.

Metzger, R.L., & Werner, D.B. (1984). Use of visual training for reading disabilities: A review. *Pediatrics, 73*, 824–829.

Newcomer, P., Nodine, B., & Barenbaum, E. (1988). Teaching writing to exceptional children: Reaction and recommendations. *Exceptional Children, 54*, 559–564.

O'Connor, P.D., Sofo, F., Kendall, L., et al. (1990). Reading disabilities and the effects of colored filters. *Journal of Learning Disabilities, 23*, 597–603.

Office of Education. (1990). *Education of individuals with disabilities* (IDEA). 20 U.S.C. §§1401(1)(15) p. 4.

Orton, S.T. (1937). *Reading, writing, and speech problems in children: A presentation of certain types of disorders in the development of the language faculty*. New York: W.W. Norton.

Reiss, A.L., & Freund, L. (1990). Fragile-X syndrome. *Biological Psychiatry, 27*, 223–240.

Rumsey, J.M., Berman, K.F., Denckla, M.B., et al. (1987). Regional cerebral blood flow in severe developmental dyslexia. *Archives of Neurology, 44*, 1144–1150.

Rutter, M., Graham, P., & Yule, W. (1970). *A neuropsychiatric study in childhood*. Philadelphia: J.B. Lippincott.

Schwartz, S.E., & Budd, D. (1983). Mathematics for handicapped learners: A functional approach for adolescents. In E. Meyer, G.A. Vergason, & B.P. Whelan (Eds.), *Promising practices for exceptional children—Curriculum implications* (pp. 321–340). Denver: Love Publishing.

Shaywitz, S.E, Escobar, M.D., Shaywitz, B.A., et al. (1992). Evidence that dyslexia may represent the lower tail of a normal distribution of reading ability. *New England Journal of Medicine, 326,* 145–150.

Shaywitz, S.E., & Shaywitz, B.A. (1987). Attention deficit disorder: Current perspectives. *Pediatric Neurology, 3,* 129–135.

Silberberg, N.E., Iversen, I.A., & Goins, J.T. (1975). Which reading method works best? *Journal of Learning Disabilities, 6,* 547–556.

Taylor, R.L. (1984). *Assessment of exceptional students. Educational and psychological procedures.* Englewood Cliffs, NJ: Prentice Hall.

U.S. Office of Education. (1977). Assistance to states for education for handicapped children: Procedures for evaluating specific learning disabilities. *Federal Register, 42*(250), 62,082–62,085.

Vellutino, F.R. (1983). Childhood dyslexia: Language disorder. In H.R. Myklebust (Ed.), *Progress in learning disabilities* (pp. 135–173). New York: Grune & Stratton.

Warren, S.A., & Taylor, R.L. (1984). Education of children with learning problems. *Pediatric Clinics of North America, 31,* 331–343.

Watson, B.U., Watson, C.S., & Fredd, R. (1982). Follow-up studies of specific reading disability. *Journal of American Academy of Child Psychiatry, 21,* 376–382.

Weiss, G., & Hechtman, L. (1979). The hyperactive child syndrome. *Science, 205,* 1348–1354.

Wodrich, D.L., & Kush, S.A. (1990). *Children's psychological testing: A guide for nonpsychologists* (2nd ed.). Baltimore: Paul H. Brookes Publishing Co.

Yule, W. (1973). Differential prognosis of reading backwardness and specific reading retardation. *British Journal & Educational Psychology, 43,* 244–248.

Zintz, M.V., & Maggart, Z.R. (1989). *The reading process: The teacher and the learner* (5th ed.). Dubuque, IA: William C. Brown.

Zuckerman, B.S., & Chase, C. (1984). Specific learning disability and dyslexia: A language-based model. *Advances in Pediatrics, 30,* 249–280.

Chapter 21

Attention Deficit Hyperactivity Disorder

with Marianne Mercugliano

Upon completion of this chapter, the reader will:
—be able to define attention deficit hyperactivity disorder
—recognize some of the problems associated with this disorder
—understand what is known about the various causes of inattention and hyperactivity
—know the different approaches to management

A short attention span, impulsivity, distractibility, and hyperactivity are common childhood behavior characteristics that tend to occur together. These are symptoms, rather than a disease, with many causes. Some children with this cluster of symptoms meet the diagnostic criteria of attention deficit hyperactivity disorder (ADHD) (Table 21.1). Other disorders associated with these symptoms include unrecognized learning disabilities, hearing or visual impairments, and certain medical, neurological, and psychiatric disorders. In order to make the diagnosis of ADHD, a physician must find the characteristics of this disorder *and* determine that other causes of similar behaviors are not present.

These symptoms require investigation and intervention because they interfere with learning, interpersonal relationships, and self-esteem. Coping with such difficulties on a chronic basis is stressful and exhausting for the child and his or her family. This chapter focuses on children diagnosed with ADHD and discusses the management and prognosis for this disorder.

Marianne Mercugliano, M.D., is Assistant Professor of Pediatrics at The University of Pennsylvania School of Medicine in Philadelphia and is a Co-Director of the Attention Deficit Hyperactivity Disorder Evaluation and Treatment Program at Children's Seashore House.

Table 21.1. Diagnostic criteria for ADHD[a]

- Does the child often fidget with hands or feet or squirm in seat?
- Does the child have difficulty remaining seated when required to do so?
- Is the child easily distracted by extraneous stimuli?
- Does the child have difficulty awaiting his or her turn in games or group situations?
- Does the child often blurt out answers to questions before they have been completed?
- Does the child often have difficulty following instructions from others?
- Does the child have difficulty sustaining attention in tasks or play activities?
- Does the child often shift from one uncompleted activity to another?
- Does the child have difficulty playing quietly?
- Does the child often talk excessively?
- Does the child often interrupt or intrude on others?
- Does the child often not seem to listen to what is being said to him or her?
- Does the child often lose things necessary for tasks or activities at school or at home?
- Does the child often engage in physically dangerous activities without considering possible consequences?

Source: American Psychiatric Association (1987).

[a]The child must experience a disturbance for at least 6 months and exhibit 8 of the 14 symptoms.

MATTHEW: A CHILD WITH ADHD

The story of Matthew provides an illustration of a child with ADHD. Matthew was the third child in his family. Although the labor and delivery were uncomplicated, as an infant Matthew did not feed well. He would suck greedily at his mother's breast for a few minutes and then lose interest. He did not like to be held or cuddled, and he slept fitfully. During the first 3 months of his life, Matthew had colic, crying as if in pain after each feeding. He was a cranky, unhappy infant.

Developmentally, Matthew reached the various milestones at the normal times, although his development was somewhat slower than that of his two siblings. Both his sister and his brother had spoken in phrases by 2 years of age, but Matthew did not do this until several months later.

By the time he was 2 years old, Matthew's parents were quite concerned about his marked hyperactivity. He was not merely curious; he was a terror, running aimlessly from one room to the next. He would pull out all the pots and pans, tear the curtains, and write on the walls. Matthew would cover three or four rooms in a matter of minutes, wrecking each as he passed through. His parents, always worn out, nicknamed him "The Little Hurricane."

As he grew up, Matthew knew no fears. He could not be left alone, even for a few moments. He was just as likely to turn on the stove as he was to run outside and into the street. Matthew also had trouble sharing things. He showed little interest in playing cooperatively and was easily frustrated in his dealings with other children. He was soon recognized as a loner.

In first grade, Matthew did poorly. His printing was messy, and many letters were reversed. He didn't know his alphabet. His memory for numbers was poor, and he frequently forgot lessons he had been taught only moments earlier. Socially, he was ostracized by the other children, who called him "retarded." At home, he did no better. He was punished constantly for his uncontrollable behavior and poor school performance. Matthew was unhappy most of the time and had many mood swings.

Fortunately, at the end of the first grade, Matthew was evaluated for a special education placement. On the Wechsler Intelligence Scale for Children-Revised (WISC-R), Matthew earned an IQ of 105. A neurological exam showed clumsiness and other "soft neurological signs." Psychoeducational testing found visual-perceptual problems and a scattering of scores ranging from a 4- to a 7-year-old level. He was particularly poor at remembering numbers and instructions that were spoken to him. His ability to pay attention was markedly decreased. Also, it was clear that Matthew had a poor self-image and expected to fail at everything he tried.

This information, in combination with a thorough medical history and physical examination, led to a diagnosis of ADHD and the beginning of a coordinated effort to help Matthew. The intervention plan involved: 1) enrollment in a small, self-contained learning disability class; 2) behavior management therapy; and 3) stimulant medication. The results of these efforts are reviewed later in this chapter.

ATTENTION DEFICIT HYPERACTIVITY DISORDER

Matthew's problem has been called by many names: *minimal brain damage, minimal cerebral dysfunction, hyperactive child syndrome, attention deficit disorder with* or *without hyperactivity,* and the current name, *attention deficit hyperactivity disorder.* The names have been changed over the years as understanding of the disorder has improved, although there is still much to be learned. For example, it is now recognized that a decreased ability to concentrate is often more functionally relevant than physical hyperactivity. Also known is that ADHD usually occurs in the absence of any history of brain damage and, in fact, is often passed on as a trait from parent to child. While this trait may not come from brain damage, it does relate to how the brain functions to regulate behavior. Not all children with ADHD are as hyperactive as Matthew, but most are restless or fidgety. A few are quiet and introverted. These children are more likely to have their attention problems go unnoticed because they are not disruptive to others. For most children with ADHD, a combination of their inborn behavior characteristics and external factors, such as negative responses from others and academic frustration, contribute to the overall picture (Figure 21.1). Estimates of prevalence have ranged from 2% to 10% in the United States (Shaywitz & Shaywitz, 1988).

As toddlers, many children with ADHD are in constant motion, getting into everything from dawn to dusk. These children remain hyperactive as they grow older. In elementary school, they may fidget so much that they fall out of their chairs. They may walk around the classroom, disrupting other students. This hyperactivity frequently decreases to fidgeting or restlessness or disappears entirely by adolescence (Hechtman, Weiss, & Perlman, 1984b).

Children with ADHD also have decreased attention spans. Unlike the hyperactivity, this often persists throughout life. They may move from one project to another,

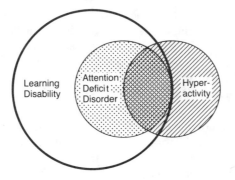

Figure 21.1.   Interrelationships among attention deficit disorder, learning disabilities, and hyperactivity. Children with attention deficit disorder tend to have learning disabilities; some are also hyperactive (ADHD). However, not all children with hyperactivity or learning disabilities have attention deficit disorder.

rarely staying with one task long enough to complete it. Attention may be normal, however, in highly motivating situations, such as while watching exciting television shows or playing video games. This variability in performance is confusing to parents, teachers, and the children themselves. "If my child can pay attention to a game, why can't he (or she) pay attention in class?" is a question frequently posed to professionals. There is an increasing recognition that this variability is characteristic of ADHD. These children are now thought to have a lower internal degree of motivation for, and reinforcement from, routine activities compared to children without ADHD (Barkley, 1990). In school, children with ADHD may have trouble concentrating on their work. They are easily distracted, seem not to listen, and often fail to finish what they start (American Psychiatric Association, 1987). Inattention makes it difficult for children with ADHD to follow more than one command at a time. Older children may have trouble planning and organizing work or daily activities for themselves.

Many children with ADHD have some difficulty with achievement in school. For some, the symptoms of ADHD are the main cause of underachievement. For others, additional deficits in the processing of auditory or visual information result in concurrent learning disabilities (see Chapter 20). These learning difficulties may be compounded by the child's poor impulse control and low tolerance for frustration. Impulsivity may be reflected in cognitive style, temperament, or behavior. In learning situations, their cognitive style may be reckless, and they may take a wild guess at a word after simply looking at the first letter. There are often temperament problems, with sudden mood swings and anger. Gradually, as they continue to have difficulty in a variety of situations, they may stop trying and/or become oppositional. Oppositional defiant disorder, characterized by noncompliance with authority, often occurs with ADHD (American Psychiatric Association, 1987), children with ADHD may take unnecessary risks and exhibit aggressive behavior.

Upon physical examination, a large proportion of children with ADHD demonstrate "soft neurological signs," which are neurological findings usually seen in younger children (Rapoport & Ismond, 1984). For example, a child might be unable to stand on one foot without falling, or he or she may have difficulty distinguishing the right from the left hand or moving the fingers of one hand while keeping the fingers of the other hand still. While soft neurological signs are not specific or diagnostic for ADHD (see the Diagnosing ADHD section in this chapter), they can help physicians to identify children who have poor motor organization and coordination as contributing factors to difficulty with certain complex tasks.

Thus, children with ADHD are beset with many problems (see Figure 21.1). They may think of themselves as being "stupid" because of problems in school. They may fail in social relationships and in physical activities such as sports. Furthermore, they may receive little encouragement at home because of disruptive behavior. Eventually, these children may develop poor self-concepts, expect to fail at everything, and stop trying.

Psychoeducational testing of these children helps to reveal their current level of academic achievement, intellectual potential, areas of strengths and weaknesses, and how they respond to various teaching techniques. The results of these tests help educators to develop school programs that can best meet their needs (see Chapter 20). The goal of early identification and intervention is to maximize long-term potential by improving academic and interpersonal functioning. The long-term efficacy of current intervention approaches, however, is as yet unproven.

CAUSES OF ADHD

Exactly what causes ADHD is unknown. Often there is a genetic component (Biederman, Faraone, Keenan, et al., 1990; Goodman, 1989). For example, the father of a child with ADHD may have done poorly in school and may have been hyperactive as a child. It is known that ADHD occurs more frequently in boys than in girls (American Psychiatric Association, 1987), but this may simply reflect that girls may not display the behavior problems associated with ADHD and thus go undiagnosed (Berry, Shaywitz, & Shaywitz, 1985).

Although the term *minimal brain damage* has been used to describe this disorder, children with ADHD do not usually have histories of birth trauma or brain damage. However, certain conditions known to affect brain development may predispose a child to developing this disorder. These include prenatal exposure to lead (Bellinger & Needleman, 1983), excessive alcohol (Abel, 1984), and probably to cocaine (Giacoia, 1990); prematurity; low birth weight at term (Hawdon, Hey, Klovin, et al., 1990); brain infections; inborn errors of metabolism (Shaywitz & Shaywitz, 1988); sex chromosome abnormalities, such as Kleinfelter syndrome, Turner syndrome, and fragile X syndrome (Borghgraef, Fryns, & van den Berghe, 1990); and certain other genetic syndromes such as neurofibromatosis and Tourette syndrome (Comings & Comings, 1990; Shaywitz & Shaywitz, 1988). The disparate group of disorders associated with ADHD suggests that many factors present during development may influence the way the brain later functions to organize thinking and behavior.

In addition to not knowing exactly what causes ADHD in most cases, relatively little is understood about the brain mechanisms that underlie this syndrome. Several areas of the brain are involved in the control of attention, including the frontal lobes of the cortex and the **reticular activating system/locus ceruleus** (Raskin, Shaywitz, Shaywitz, et al., 1984).

The frontal lobe of the brain is important in planning, organization, and feelings (Solanto, 1984). As is true of all parts of the brain, the stimulation of these areas requires chemicals called *neurotransmitters,* which act as chemical messengers between brain cells. Recent research suggests that children with ADHD have neurotransmitter abnormalities (Shaywitz & Shaywitz, 1988). They may have less activity than others in the parts of the brain important in the control of attention (Lou, Henriksen, & Bruhn, 1990; Zametkin, Nordahl, Gross, et al., 1990). This underlies the rationale for using stimulant medications to treat ADHD, since these drugs increase the activity of neurotransmitters in certain areas of the brain.

The reticular activating system/locus ceruleus in the midbrain region allows screening out of distracting sounds and images so concentration on a particular task can occur. For example, people in theaters are able to listen to their neighbors' conversation only after blocking out the conversations of the other people surrounding them. In a similar way, children can learn effectively only if they pay attention to the teacher and are not distracted by other images that come into their lines of vision. In effect, the reticular system puts "mental blinders" on a person, allowing the individual to pay attention.

OTHER CAUSES OF HYPERACTIVITY AND ATTENTION DEFICITS

Other disorders can have symptoms that simulate ADHD or a child may have additional, coexistent disabilities. These disorders include mental retardation, learning disabilities, seizure disorders, sensory impairments, and psychiatric disorders. A child who is not recognized as having mental retardation may be thought to have ADHD when, in fact, the caregivers have inappropriate behavioral expectations. Yet, children with mental retardation also may have ADHD. In this instance, the combination of hyperactivity, short attention span, impulsive behavior, frustration intolerance, and poor school performance is beyond that expected for the children's cognitive ages. Medications used to treat children with ADHD are also effective in treating children with mild mental retardation who have ADHD, but these drugs are less effective in children with more severe mental retardation (Handen, Breaux, Gosling, et al., 1990).

Unrecognized learning disabilities, even in children with normal to superior intelligence, can lead to restless and inattentive behavior if they cannot absorb material as it is taught in class. However, learning disabilities also may coexist with ADHD.

Inattentiveness and hyperactivity may be apparent in children who have seizure disorders. If seizures are poorly controlled, the children are inattentive during the seizures and for a while after them. Behavior problems may also occur as side effects to antiepileptic medications; for example, 20% of children who take phenobarbital become hyperactive (Livingston, 1972). To further complicate matters, the same central nervous system pathology that precipitated the seizure disorder also may have led to the expression of ADHD (Feldman, Crumrine, Handen, et al., 1989).

Children with hearing impairments also may be hyperactive or have other behavior problems. These problems may be the result of the same insult that caused the hearing loss or a consequence of frustration resulting from an undetected or ineffectively treated hearing impairment.

Finally, children with psychiatric disorders, such as depression, primary anxiety disorders, obsessive-compulsive disorder, and pervasive developmental disorders, must be differentiated from those with ADHD (American Psychiatric Association, 1987) (see Chapter 23).

DIAGNOSING ADHD

Unfortunately, no test exists that specifically diagnoses ADHD. Brain wave tests (i.e., electroencephalograms [EEGs]) are mildly abnormal in about half of these children, but these alterations are also seen in about a quarter of children without ADHD (Caresia, Pugnetti, Besana, et al., 1984). Computerized brain scans have failed to reveal any abnormalities (Shaywitz, Shaywitz, Byrne, et al., 1983). **Positron emission tomographic** (PET) scanning, a new, primarily experimental, brain imaging technique that quantifies cerebral metabolism, has revealed decreased glucose utilization in multiple brain regions of adults who had ADHD with the largest decrease noted in the frontal cortex (Zametkin et al., 1990). Soft neurological signs often exist, but their absence does not rule out ADHD (Gillberg, 1985; Vitiello, Stoff, Atkins, et al., 1990). Finally, psychoeducational testing may suggest that a child has specific cognitive deficits, although symptoms are usually minimized in one-to-one situations. There are no specific test result patterns that are diagnostic of ADHD.

Ultimately, the diagnosis of ADHD relies on the exclusion of other diagnoses and the presence of the clinical symptoms of attention deficit, impulsive behavior, distractibility, and often hyperactivity. According to the *DSM-III-R* definition, to be diagnosed as having ADHD the child must experience a disturbance lasting at least 6 months and exhibit 8 of the 14 symptoms listed in Table 21.1 (American Psychiatric Association, 1987). Onset must be before 7 years of age.

Proper diagnosis is important because it dictates the type of therapy used. A positive response to stimulant medications cannot be used to make a diagnosis because individuals without ADHD also have improved concentration and productivity when receiving medications (Rapoport, Buchsbaum, Zahn, et al., 1978). Most often, standardized rating scales, completed by parents and teachers, are used to determine whether a child has the symptoms of ADHD in greater proportion than would be expected for his or her age (Table 21.2).

Table 21.2. Representative questions from the Conners Teacher Rating Scale and the Conners Parent Rating Scale[a]

- Does the child make inappropriate noises when he or she should not?
- Does the child make demands that must be met immediately?
- Is the child easily distracted or troubled by a poor attention span?
- Does the child disturb other children?
- Does the child daydream at inappropriate times?
- Does the child's mood change quickly and drastically?
- Is the child restless and always "up and on the go"?
- Is the child excitable and impulsive?
- Does the child make excessive demands for teachers' attention?
- Does the child fail to finish things that he or she starts?
- Does the child exhibit childish and immature behavior?
- Is the child easily frustrated in efforts?
- Is the child uncooperative with teachers?
- Does the child have difficulty in learning?

Source: Conners and Wells (1986). These questions are reproduced with permission of Sage Publications, Inc.

[a]Each behavior is rated "not at all," "just a little," "pretty much," or "very much." Responses are examined for substantial change after medication or trials of behavior management.

MANAGEMENT OF ADHD

The management of children with ADHD is most effective when a combination of approaches is used. These may include educational intervention, counseling, behavior management, and medication.

Educational Approaches

Appropriate school programs are extremely important in the management of children with ADHD. These children often have coexisting learning disabilities that are accentuated by hyperactivity and decreased attention span (Klein & Rapin, 1990). There is no substitute for a well-trained and caring teacher who provides special help and an educational program suited to the needs of specific children. Assistance in the form of structured or self-contained special education classrooms and resource help may also be useful, but many children do not qualify for such services (see Chapter 20). Tutoring can be extremely helpful for those who do not qualify for special education services through the school system but nonetheless feel frustrated by their difficulty with mastering new material.

Counseling

Counseling for both the child and the family is a key element in the intervention program. A social worker, school counselor, psychologist, or psychiatrist can provide this help and support. Children with ADHD must understand what ADHD is and that they are not stupid, sick, or alone (Kelly, Cohen, Walker, et al., 1989). Counseling can provide a place for children and other family members to talk about their anxieties, frustrations, and anger. Parents and siblings may need help in understanding the implications that ADHD may have for them (Silver, 1989). Parents may need guidance in how to set limits on the child's behavior and how to develop realistic expectations. They must also understand that they are not to blame for their child's disorder. Everyone in the family can benefit from thoughtful support, information, and an objective forum for working out problems. Ideally, this should be provided not merely when a crisis hits, but as an ongoing process. Stress in the family and in the marriage can exacerbate behavior problems and should be addressed for everyone's benefit (see Chapter 29).

A number of national and local parent groups exist to provide support and education for individuals with ADHD and their families. Membership in such organizations can be extremely helpful in supplementing what is provided by professionals and in providing parents an organized forum to advocate for their children's needs (see Resources for Children with Disabilities, Appendix C).

Behavior Management Techniques

One of the most effective approaches to improving the behavior of children with ADHD is the use of behavior management techniques. This method involves reinforcement of behavior that is appropriate and the consistent management of inappropriate behavior (Hersher, 1985). Behavior management helps children with ADHD to keep in mind what they should and should not do and motivates them to demonstrate desirable behavior. The basic premise is that behavior is controlled by its consequences. Thus, if a behavior results in reinforcement, it will occur with a greater frequency in the future. If the behavior is unrewarded, it is less likely to recur. This premise leads to three basic methods of managing behavior: reinforcement, differential attention, and punishment.

Reinforcement The most effective behavior management approach for children with ADHD appears to be positive reinforcement (Craighead, Kazdin, & Mahoney, 1981). The way it works is illustrated by the following example (Figure 21.2A). To improve attention in a classroom, a teacher might tell a student to maintain eye contact. If the student does this for a given period of time, he or she is reinforced in some way. The reinforcement might be social in the form of approval or a hug, or it might be material, such as candy or a happy face symbol. Also, a delayed reinforcement may be used. The child may receive a token or a star each time he or she exhibits the desired behavior. Then, after a certain number of tokens are collected, the child can trade them in for a privilege or a gift.

Sometimes, an even more formal type of positive reinforcement, involving an oral or written contract, is used. The child may agree to do certain things—for example, remain in the seat, refrain from calling out, or complete homework assignments. At the end of an hour or a day, the child receives a special reward for adhering to the contract. The parents, for instance, might provide the reward at home, reinforcing the teacher's efforts.

Because hyperactive children are so infrequently rewarded and so often punished, positive reinforcement is especially helpful. Not only does behavior improve, but the child also learns that he or she can succeed. It is important that rewarded behaviors be clearly defined and within the child's capability. For example,

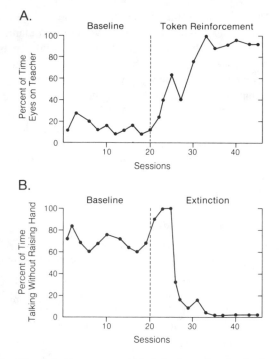

Figure 21.2. Effects of two behavior management techniques on changing the frequency of a behavior. A) Positive reinforcement results in an increase in the percentage of time a child keeps his or her eyes on the teacher. B) A differential attention procedure results in a decrease in the percentage of time a child talks out of turn.

"remaining on task" may be the ultimate goal, but it is too broad and ill-defined for the child to keep in mind. If the child feels that there is little chance of success, he or she will not be motivated to try to adhere to the contract. As success becomes routine for the simpler goals, the contract should evolve to include new ones.

Differential Attention Sometimes it is effective to simply withhold attention previously provided to the child for disruptive but nondangerous behavior. The prior relationship between the behavior and the consequence is thereby disconnected. An example is ignoring disruptive behavior (see Figure 21.2B). A teacher who does not call on a child who consistently speaks without raising a hand is practicing differential attention. The child eventually learns to use appropriate behavior to gain attention. The child stops speaking out, raises a hand, and the teacher starts to call on the child.

Usually, the previously reinforced behavior (e.g., speaking out) initially increases when the differential attention is introduced. Rather than raising a hand, the child may yell or scream more and be very disruptive. If the teacher gives in and calls on the child at this point, the teacher will have taught the child to get attention by screaming and yelling. In other words, the teacher will have positively reinforced inappropriate behavior. Thus, consistency is the key. With time, the disruptive behavior should diminish or disappear. The child will eventually learn the more appropriate thing to do through proper instruction and modeling by the teacher.

Punishment Punishment differs from reinforcement in that it reduces the frequency of a behavior by the use of aversive consequences. Punishments, such as scolding and spanking, generally do not work well with hyperactive children. A more effective form of punishment for these children may be the temporary withholding of a privilege, followed by its reinstatement contingent upon the child's demonstration of more acceptable behaviors. Although removal of privileges may help, it is no substitute for catching the child being "good" and acknowledging his or her efforts.

How To Implement Behavior Management Knowing the theory behind behavior management is simpler than putting it into practice. It is helpful to keep in mind some rules. First, one must obtain baseline data. The only way to know if a procedure works is to have data before the management procedure is begun. A baseline period of nonintervention should occur, during which records of the frequency of the inappropriate behavior are kept (see Figure 21.2). Then, an intervention method is begun. If this works, and the child's behavior improves, the procedure can then be used on a long-term basis, although modifications will be introduced to maintain the child's interest and an appropriate degree of challenge. The technique must also be administered consistently and immediately after the behavior occurs. This is the only way to guarantee that the child makes the proper connection between the behavior and its consequence (Patterson, 1975).

Often, good behavior doesn't occur spontaneously. Any child, and especially a hyperactive child, must learn a series of behaviors that make him or her more socially acceptable and better able to learn. These behaviors are acquired in much the same way that a new play in sports is learned. Step by step, a coach goes over the component elements of the play and rewards an athlete as each step is perfected. Eventually, the athlete masters all the steps and combines them into the complete play. This process of teaching behavior step by step is called *shaping*. Shaping can be effective with hyperactive children. One rewards the behavior that most closely approximates what is socially acceptable or what improves attention. As this behavior occurs more frequently, it can be shaped into even more appropriate responses. Besides shaping, one must use teaching strategies that help the child to generalize learned behaviors, transferring them from the school environment to the home, playground, and other situations.

Techniques of behavior analysis can also be applied to improve attention span, organizational abilities, and problem-solving skills. This approach is called *cognitive therapy* and involves teaching the child to regulate his or her own behavior. Initially, this is done by modeling after the trainer, but eventually it is self-initiated. Problem-solving can be trained by breaking problems down to their component elements and then solving each step in turn until a complete solution is evident.

Most ADHD experts recommend that parents learn the strategies for behavior management and how to apply them by joining a parent training group or working with a psychologist in individual sessions. Adopting new strategies, knowing how and when to alter them, and applying them consistently are critical, yet difficult to do without guidance and support.

Medication

Medication may be used in addition to educational and behavioral strategies for children who continue to have difficulty with ADHD symptoms. The most common class of medication used to treat children with ADHD is the stimulant group. Stimulants include methylphenidate (Ritalin), dextroamphetamine (Dexedrine), and pemoline (Cylert). These medications are likely to increase attention and decrease motor activity and impulsive behavior. However, they will not remedy the other problems associated with ADHD—for example, learning disabilities and poor self-image. Less frequently used and generally less effective drugs include antidepressants, clonidine, and phenothiazines.

Stimulants   In both hyperactive and normal children, stimulants reduce the extent of physical activity, decrease impulsive behavior, and improve attention span. Although no drug exists that can alleviate all the problems associated with ADHD, stimulants can certainly provide these children some short-term gains. It was by chance that stimulants were first used to treat hyperactivity. In 1937, Dr. Charles Bradley used one type of stimulant medication, amphetamine, to treat children with various behavior disorders and found incidentally that this drug also reduced hyperactivity and increased attention span. Over the next 30 years, the use of stimulants spread widely. Not only were they being prescribed for hyperactivity, but they were also being used to treat many other kinds of behavior and psychiatric problems. In addition to treatment-related uses, stimulants were being taken by college students to "pull all-nighters," by truckers to maintain vigilance while driving, and by dieters to curb their appetites. The high levels of misuse eventually led to the passage of federal legislation that classified certain stimulant medications as "controlled substances." This legislation also limited the use of methylphenidate, dextroamphetamine, and pemoline to the treatment of hyperactivity and narcolepsy (i.e., a rare neurological disorder with sudden, uncontrolled bouts of sleeping during the daytime hours). Presently, 1%–2% of children receive some stimulant medication for ADHD (Shaywitz & Shaywitz, 1988; Stevenson & Wolraich, 1989).

The two most commonly used stimulants are methylphenidate and dextroamphetamine. The usual dosage for methylphenidate ranges from 10 to 60 milligrams/day (0.3–0.6 milligrams/kilogram/dose). This may be given 2 or 3 times per day (McBride, 1988; Sebrechts, Shaywitz, Shaywitz, et al., 1986; Swanson, Sandman, Deutsch, et al., 1983), or it can be given in 1 or 2 doses of a "timed-release" capsule (Barkley, DuPaul, & McMurray, 1991; Pelham, Greenslade, Vodde-Hamilton, et al., 1990). For dextroamphetamine, the daily dosage is about half that amount and comes as a liquid, tablet, or sustained release capsule. Generally, these drugs begin working in 30–45 minutes. The effects of the tablets last about 4 hours, and the sustained release capsule works for roughly 8 hours. The third stimulant, pemoline, is given once a day and lasts for about 8 hours (Collier, Soldin, Swanson, et al., 1985).

Before starting the medication, the physician may use a teacher/parent behavior report to document the problem behaviors that the medication is intended to affect (Blondis, Accardo, & Snow, 1989a, 1989b; Cohen, Kelly, & Atkinson, 1989) (see Table 21.2). Improvement often occurs the same day as starting methylphenidate or dextroamphetamine, while it may take a few days to a few weeks for pemoline to be effective. Children do not usually develop tolerance to the medication (i.e., the medication does not stop being effective during long-term therapy) (Safer & Allen, 1989). Although children may continue to take these medications for many years, they are often discontinued as the children reach adolescence. However, it is now clear that some adults with ADHD continue to benefit from stimulants (Wender, Wood, & Reimherr, 1985).

As with other drugs, there are side effects, but they are rarely serious. The most common side effect is loss of appetite after taking the medication. Children may also experience some decrease in rate of weight and height gain during treatment. When the medication is stopped (e.g., during the summer) a rapid gain of weight and height follows. Final height need not be affected as a result of long-term therapy with stimulants (Klein & Mannuzza, 1988). Besides the impact on appetite and growth pattern, these drugs may cause insomnia if they are taken late in the day. In addition, about 10%–20% of children who take stimulants develop stomach discomfort, which usually decreases over time (Golinko, 1984). A larger percent may have difficulty with irritability or mood swings at the end of the day as the medication wears off. This phenomenon is called *rebound* because the child may seem to have a temporary worsening of symptoms (Johnston, Pelham, Hoza, ct al., 1988). In less than 4% of children side effects are severe enough to require discontinuation of therapy (Barkley, McMurray, Edelbrock, et al., 1990).

A rare side effect that may require stopping treatment is the development of *tics,* which are brief repetitive movements, such as eye blinks or throat clearing, that resemble nervous habits. Stimulants are known to bring out tics in susceptible individuals, perhaps because of overstimulation of the parts of the brain responsible for these motor behaviors. Tics are common in childhood and may range in severity from very mild and transient to more severe and permanent. The most severe tic disorder is called *Tourette syndrome,* which consists of multiple motor and vocal tics that vary in nature and severity over time. This disorder is frequently associated with additional diagnoses including ADHD, learning disabilities, and anxiety or obsessive-compulsive behaviors (Matthews, 1988).

Because of the possibility of an exacerbation of tics, stimulants are not generally used in children with family histories of tics, Tourette syndrome, or obsessive-compulsive disorders. Many physicians are beginning to use clonidine rather than stimulants as a first choice medication for children with ADHD who are susceptible to tics because clonidine does not exacerbate, and, in fact, may decrease tic frequency. However, if other strategies fail, and ADHD is a more functionally relevant problem for the child than the tics, a judicious trial of stimulants may be warranted (Cohen & Leckman, 1989).

Another concern is whether the use of stimulants predisposes hyperactive children to future drug abuse. Amphetamines have street names, such as "speed" and "uppers," and are commonly abused drugs. Long-term follow-up studies have not supported this concern (Hechtman, Weiss, & Perlman, 1984a, 1984b). Although amphetamines cause euphoric effects in large doses, therapeutic doses do not produce "highs" in children with ADHD.

To alleviate some of the concerns about adverse effects, many physicians suggest that the child be given the medication only on weekdays during the school year. For most children, this works well. However, for some, the hyperactivity is so severe that family and peer relationships are seriously compromised without the assistance of the medication. Thus, no blanket rule can be written about who should receive these drugs and when. The decision must be made according to the needs of each child and family. However, every year or so, the child should be given a drug "holiday" to determine if medication is still needed.

Evaluating the long-term benefits of stimulant treatment is extremely difficult. For the most part, only short-term follow-up studies have been done. These studies have shown improvement in over 80% of the children (Abikoff & Gittelman, 1985; McBride, 1988). Teachers rate both the children's behavior and their attention span as improved. Impulsive behavior is also less evident (Rapoport et al., 1978). The children perform better on visual-motor tasks, such as puzzles and penmanship. The few long-term studies suggest, however, that these benefits may be short-lived. In comparing one group of children who were treated for 2 years or more with stimulants with an untreated group, no difference in achievement between the two groups existed 10 years later (Hechtman et al., 1984a, 1984b). However, the medication may have helped the children to be better accepted by their peers and have improved self-images. Trying to assess the validity of these various studies raises numerous questions and problems. Because it is very difficult to match for variables, such as severity of hyperactivity or the effect of behavior management at home, a comparison of results across studies may not be valid. Recent studies are beginning to indicate better outcomes for children who have been treated with a combination of behavioral, educational, and pharmacological approaches (Gittelman, Mannuzza, Shenker, et al., 1985).

Antidepressants   Antidepressants are similar to stimulants in that they increase neurotransmitter activity in certain parts of the brain. A particular subgroup of antidepressants, called the *tricyclic antidepressants,* has been studied and found effective in treating ADHD symptoms (Zametkin, Rapoport, Murphy, et al., 1985). The most commonly used are imipramine (Tofranil) and desipramine (Norpramin) (Donnelly, Zametkin, Rapoport, et al., 1986). Although effective, these medications are usually reserved for older children who have symptoms of ADHD accompanied by low self-esteem, anxiety, or depression. They are also used in children who experience significant side effects from stimulants. Antidepressants are advantageous in that they are effective continuously and therefore do not cause the mood swings and rebound behavior sometimes seen with stimulants. They must be given 2–4 times per day and may take several days to show an effect. Also, unlike stimulants, they must be given every day, including weekends, in order to maintain effective blood levels. Antidepressants can have significant but rare side effects on heart function, necessitating periodic monitoring with blood tests and electrocardiograms (Shaywitz & Shaywitz, 1988). A few isolated cases of sudden death, presumably from cardiac arrythmias, have occurred in children taking desipramine (Riddle, Nelson, Kleinman, et al., 1991).

Clonidine Clonidine (Catapres) works differently from stimulants and antidepressants, but exactly how it works in ADHD is not clear. While it has only recently come into use for ADHD, it has been used for some time to treat high blood pressure in adults. Clonidine has been shown to improve hyperactivity (Hunt, Minderaa, & Cohen, 1985) but its effect on attention and concentration is not proven. It is perhaps most useful for children who have tics because it does not seem to exacerbate them and may decrease their frequency. Like antidepressants, clonidine works more slowly than amphetamines and may take more time to know if it will be effective.

Phenothiazines Phenothiazines (including thioridazine [Mellaril], and chlorpromazine [Thorazine])are drugs that are used most often to treat psychosis. However, these drugs may also help in the treatment of certain types of hyperactivity. They have a sedating effect and so decrease hyperactivity; but they also reduce concentration and, as a result, may interfere with academic progress. Therefore, phenothiazines are not appropriate therapy for children with ADHD with normal intellectual function. These drugs have proven useful in certain children with mental retardation and severe hyperactivity. Half of these children show a significant decrease in hyperactivity when taking this type of medication (Biederman & Jellinek, 1984).

Unfortunately, phenothiazines have a considerable number of side effects. These drugs increase the risk of seizures in persons with seizure disorders. They have also been associated with liver dysfunction and excessive weight gain. These drugs may cause a condition called *tardive dyskinesia* in which a person has continual restless movements of the arms and legs. Most of these side effects are uncommon and disappear once the therapy is stopped, but the tardive dyskinesia may be permanent.

MATTHEW GROWS UP

Matthew's treatment program involved a combination of the various therapies described in this chapter. In first grade, because his hyperactivity was so severe, he began to take methylphenidate, 15 milligrams, before school and at lunchtime. His behavior improved. Together, Matthew's teacher and parents outlined a behavior management program. He also received extra help in reading and mathematics. Within 6 months, Matthew changed from a withdrawn, rather somber child to one who was interested in making friends and attending school.

In physical activities, he had other problems. Since Matthew's clumsiness persisted, it was difficult for him to do well in sports, and the other children teased him. His father took him to special physical education classes to help improve his coordination. There, he met other children with similar problems. This discovery helped Matthew feel less alone and encouraged him to keep trying. He did particularly well in swimming. Even so, he continued to have "two left feet" and to be accident prone over the years.

Matthew continued in a small class setting throughout his elementary school years. He began to meet regularly with a counselor at school who helped him better understand and cope with his problems and frustrations. His parents frequently participated in these discussions. Some years were better than others. By 12 years of age, he no longer required methylphenidate or special class placement. He was much less hyperactive, but his short attention span and impulsive behavior persisted. He maintained a "C" average. Matthew received tutoring throughout junior and senior high school to help him master new material by improving his organization and study skills.

Now Matthew is entering the job market. He will make it in society but how well is uncertain. He continues to be at a disadvantage because of his disabilities. Yet he has tasted success and is willing to work hard to make a go of it. Matthew's story may well end happily.

ADHD IN YOUNG ADULTS

The story of Matthew is typical of many children with ADHD. As adolescents, over half of these children improve, if they have not developed motivation and conduct problems (Klein & Mannuzza, 1991). They are less hyperactive, although they still have problems with organization and planning (Thorley, 1988; Wender, 1987). The majority become well-adjusted, well-functioning adults, but they often do not attain as high an academic level as their siblings (Weiss & Hechtman, 1986). Hyperactive persons may have problems with maintaining stability in their interpersonal relationships and jobs and may exhibit a higher incidence of antisocial behavior and psychiatric disorders as adults (Barkley, 1990; Satterfield, Satterfield, & Schell, 1987). When identification and intervention are begun early, the likelihood of preventing future problems improves.

SUMMARY

Attention problems and hyperactivity are symptoms common to many disorders. The cause of the symptoms must be determined before effective intervention is possible. If the diagnosis is ADHD, a program combining behavior management techniques, educational intervention, stimulant medication, and counseling usually is helpful. If the symptoms stem from a problem such as mental retardation, a neurological disease, deafness, or a psychiatric disturbance, the underlying disorder determines the kind of intervention and the prognosis. For the child with ADHD who is diagnosed early and treated comprehensively, the likelihood of a favorable outcome is good.

REFERENCES

Abel, E.L. (1984). Prenatal effects of alcohol. *Drug and Alcohol Dependence, 14*, 1–10.
Abikoff, H., & Gittelman, R. (1985). The normalizing effects of methylphenidate on the classroom behavior of ADDH children. *Journal of Abnormal Child Psychology, 13*, 33–44.

American Psychiatric Association. (1987). *Diagnostic and statistical manual of mental disorders (DSM-III-R)*. Washington, DC: Author.

Bain, L. (1991). *The Children's Hospital of Philadelphia—A parent's guide to attention deficit disorders*. New York: Dell.

Barkley, R.A. (1990). *Attention deficit hyperactivity disorder—A handbook for diagnosis and treatment*. New York: Guilford Press.

Barkley, R.A., DuPaul, G.J., & McMurray, M.B. (1991). Attention deficit disorder with and without hyperactivity: Clinical response to three dose levels of methylphenidate. *Pediatrics, 87*, 519–531.

Barkley, R.A., McMurray, M.B., Edelbrock, C.S., et al. (1990). Side effects of methylphenidate in children with attention deficit hyperactivity disorder: A systematic, placebo-controlled evaluation. *Pediatrics, 86*, 184–192.

Bellinger, D.C., & Needleman, H.L. (1983). Lead and the relationship between maternal and child intelligence. *Journal of Pediatrics, 102*, 523–527.

Berry, C.A., Shaywitz, S.E., & Shaywitz, B.A. (1985). Girls with attention deficit disorder: A silent minority? A report on behavioral and cognitive characteristics. *Pediatrics, 76*, 801–809.

Biederman, J., Faraone, S.V., Keenan, K., et al. (1990). Family genetic and psychosocial risk factors in DSM-III attention deficit disorder. *Journal of the American Academy of Child and Adolescent Psychiatry, 29*, 526–33.

Biederman, J., & Jellinek, M.S. (1984). Current concepts. Psychopharmacology in children. *New England Journal of Medicine, 310*, 968–972.

Blondis, T.A., Accardo, P.J., & Snow, J.H. (1989a). Measures of attention deficit. Part I: Questionnaires. *Clinical Pediatrics, 28*, 222–228.

Blondis, T.A., Accardo, P.J., & Snow, J.H. (1989b). Measures of attention deficit. Part II: Clinical perspectives and test interpretation. *Clinical Pediatrics, 28*, 268–276.

Borghgraef, M., Fryns, J.P., & van den Berghe, H. (1990). The female and the fragile X syndrome: Data on clinical and psychological findings in 7 fra (x) carriers. *Clinical Genetics, 37*, 341–346.

Caresia, L., Pugnetti, L., Besana, R., et al. (1984). EEG and clinical findings during pemoline treatment in children and adults with attention deficit disorder. An 8-week open trial. *Neuropsychobiology, 11*, 158–167.

Cohen, D.J., & Leckman, J.F. (1989). Methylphenidate treatment of attention-deficit hyperactivity disorder in boys with Tourette's syndrome. Commentary. *Journal of the American Academy of Child and Adolescent Psychiatry, 28*, 580–582.

Cohen, M.L., Kelly, P.C., & Atkinson, A.W. (1989). Parent, teacher, child. A trilateral approach to attention deficit disorder. *American Journal of Diseases of Children, 143*, 1229-1233.

Coleman, W.S. (1988). *Attention deficit disorders, hyperactivity & associated disorders: A handbook for parents and professionals* (5th ed.). Madison, WI: Calliope Books.

Collier, C.P., Soldin, S.J., Swanson, J.M., et al. (1985). Pemoline pharmacokinetics and long term therapy in children with attention deficit disorder and hyperactivity. *Clinical Pharmacokinetics, 10*, 269–278.

Comings, D.E., & Comings, B.G. (1990). A controlled family history study of Tourette syndrome. I: Attention deficit hyperactivity disorder and learning disorders. *Journal of Clinical Psychiatry, 51*, 275–280.

Conners, C.K., & Wells, K.C. (1986). *Hyperkinetic children*. Newbury Park, CA: Sage Publications.

Craighead, W.E., Kazdin, A.E., & Mahoney, M.J. (1981). *Behavior modification: Principles, issues, and applications* (2nd ed.). Boston: Houghton Mifflin Co.

Donnelly, M., Zametkin, A.J., Rapoport, J.L., et al. (1986). Treatment of childhood hyperactivity with desipramine: Plasma drug concentration, cardiovascular efforts, plasma and urinary catecholamine levels, and clinical response. *Clinical Pharmacology and Therapeutics, 39,* 72–81.

Feldman, H., Crumrine, P., Handen, B.L., et al. (1989). Methylphenidate in children with seizures and attention-deficit disorder. *American Journal of Diseases of Children, 143,* 1081–1086.

Galvin, M.R. (1988). *Otto learns about his medicine: A story about medication for hyperactive children.* New York: Magination Press.

Giacoia, G.P. (1990). Cocaine in the cradle: A hidden epidemic. *Southern Medical Journal, 83,* 947–951.

Gillberg, I.C. (1985). Children with minor neurodevelopmental disorders. III: Neurological and neurodevelopmental problems at age 10. *Developmental Medicine and Child Neurology, 27,* 3–16.

Gittelman, R., Mannuzza, S. Shenker, R., et al. (1985). Hyperactive boys almost grown up. I. Psychiatric status. *Archives of General Psychiatry, 42,* 937–947.

Goldstein, S., & Goldstein, M. (1990). *Managing attention disorders in children: A guide for practitioners.* New York: John Wiley & Sons.

Golinko, B.E. (1984). Side effects of dextroamphetamine and methylphenidate in hyperactive children—A brief review. *Progress in Neuro-psycho-pharmacology and Biological Psychiatry, 8,* 1–8.

Goodman, R. (1989). Genetic factors in hyperactivity. *British Medical Journal, 298,* 1407–1408.

Handen, B.L., Breaux, A.M., Gosling, A., et al. (1990). Efficacy of methylphenidate among mentally retarded children with attention deficit hyperactivity disorder. *Pediatrics, 86,* 922–930.

Hawdon, J.M., Hey, E., Klovin, I., et al. (1990). Born too small—Is outcome still affected? *Developmental Medicine and Child Neurology, 32,* 943–953.

Hechtman, L., Weiss, G., & Perlman, T. (1984a). Hyperactives as young adults: Past and current substance abuse and antisocial behavior. *American Journal of Orthopsychiatry, 54,* 415–425.

Hechtman, L., Weiss, G., & Perlman, T. (1984b). Young adult outcome of hyperactive children who received long-term stimulant treatment. *Journal of the American Academy of Child Psychiatry, 23,* 261–269.

Hersher, L. (1985). The effectiveness of behavior modification on hyperkinesis. *Child Psychiatry and Human Development, 16,* 87–96.

Hunt, R.D., Minderaa, R.B., & Cohen, D.J. (1985). Clonidine benefits children with attention deficit disorder and hyperactivity: Report of a double-blind placebo-crossover therapeutic trial. *Journal of the American Academy of Child Psychiatry, 24,* 617–629.

Johnston, C., Pelham, W.E., Hoza, J., & Sturges, J. (1988). Psychostimulant rebound in attention deficit disordered boys. *Journal of the American Academy of Child and Adolescent Psychiatry, 27,* 806–810.

Kelly, P.C., Cohen, M.L., Walker, W.O., et al. (1989). Self-esteem in children medically managed for attention deficit disorder. *Pediatrics, 83,* 211–217.

Klein, R.G., & Mannuzza, S. (1988). Hyperactive boys almost grown up. III. Methylphenidate effects on ultimate height. *Archives of General Psychiatry, 45,* 1131–1134.

Klein, R.G., & Mannuzza, S. (1991). Long-term outcome of hyperactive children: A review. *Journal of the American Academy of Child and Adolescent Psychiatry, 30*(3), 383–387.

Klein, S.K., & Rapin I. (1990). Clinical assessment of pediatric disorders of higher cerebral function. *Current Problems in Pediatrics, 20,* 1–60.

Livingston, S. (1972). *Comprehensive management of epilepsy in infancy, childhood, and adolescence.* Springfield, IL: Charles C Thomas.

Lou, H.C., Henriksen, L., & Bruhn, P. (1990). Focal cerebral dysfunction in developmental learning disabilities. *Lancet, 335,* 8–11.

Matthews, W.S. (1988). Attention deficits and learning disabilities in children with Tourette's syndrome. *Pediatric Annals, 17,* 410–411, 414, 416.

McBride, M.C. (1988). An individual double-blind crossover trial for assessing methylphenidate response in children with attention deficit disorder. *Journal of Pediatrics, 113,* 137–145.

Moss, R., & Dunlap, H. (1990). *Why Johnny can't concentrate.* New York: Bantam Books.

Patterson, G.R. (1975). *Families: Application of social learning to family life.* Champaign, IL: Research Press.

Pelham, W.E., Jr., Greenslade, K.E., Vodde-Hamilton, M., et al. (1990). Relative efficacy of long-acting stimulants on children with attention deficit-hyperactivity disorder: A comparison of standard methylphenidate, sustained-release methylphenidate, sustained-release dextroamphetamine, and pemoline. *Pediatrics, 86,* 226–237.

Rapoport, J.L., Buchsbaum, M.S., Zahn, T.P., et al. (1978). Dextroamphetamine: Cognitive and behavioral effects in normal prepubertal boys. *Science, 199,* 560–563.

Rapoport, J.L., & Ismond, D.R. (1984). *DSM-III training guide for diagnosis of childhood disorders.* New York: Brunner/Mazel.

Raskin, L.A., Shaywitz, S.E., Shaywitz, B.A., et al. (1984). Neurochemical correlates of attention deficit disorder. *Pediatric Clinics of North America, 31,* 387–396.

Riddle, M.A., Nelson, J.C., Kleinman, C.S., et al. (1991). Sudden death in children receiving norpramin: A review of three reported cases and commentary. *Journal of the American Academy of Child and Adolescent Psychiatry, 30,* 104–108.

Safer, D.J., & Allen, R.P. (1989). Absence of tolerance to the behavioral effects of methylphenidate in hyperactive and inattentive children. *Journal of Pediatrics, 115,* 1003–1008.

Satterfield, J.H., Satterfield, B.T., & Schell, A.M. (1987). Therapeutic interventions to prevent delinquency in hyperactive boys. *Journal of American Academy of Child and Adolescent Psychiatry, 26,* 56–64.

Sebrechts, M.M., Shaywitz, S.E., Shaywitz, B.A., et al. (1986). Components of attention, methylphenidate dosage, and blood levels in children with attention deficit disorder. *Pediatrics, 77,* 222–228.

Shaywitz, B.A., Shaywitz, S.E., Byrne, T., et al. (1983). Attention deficit disorder: Quantitative analysis of CT. *Neurology, 33,* 1500–1503.

Shaywitz, S.E., & Shaywitz, B.A. (1988). Attention deficit disorder: Current perspective. In J.F. Kavanagh & T.J. Truss, Jr. (Eds.), *Learning disability: Proceedings of the national conference* (pp. 369–523). Parkton, MD: York Press.

Silver, L.B. (1989). Psychological and family problems associated with learning disabilities: Assessment and intervention. *Journal of the American Academy of Child and Adolescent Psychiatry, 28,* 319–325.

Solanto, M.V. (1984). Neuropharmacological basis of stimulant drug action in attention deficit disorder with hyperactivity: A review and synthesis. *Psychological Bulletin, 95,* 387–409.

Stevenson, R.D., & Wolraich, M.L. (1989). Stimulant medication therapy in the treatment of children with attention deficit hyperactivity disorder. *Pediatric Clinics of North America, 36,* 1183–1197.

Swanson, J.M., Sandman, C.A., Deutsch, C., et al. (1983). Methylphenidate hydrochloride given with or before breakfast. I. Behavioral, cognitive, and electrophysiologic effects. *Pediatrics, 72,* 49–55.

Taylor, E.A. (Ed.). (1986). *The overactive child.* London: Spastics International Medical Publishers, Blackwell Scientific Publications Ltd.

Thorley, G. (1988). Adolescent outcome for hyperactive children. *Archives of Disease in Childhood, 63,* 1181–1183.

Vitiello, B., Stoff, D., Atkins, M., et al. (1990). Soft neurological signs and impulsivity in children. *Journal of Developmental and Behavioral Pediatrics, 11,* 112–115.

Weiss, G., & Hechtman, L. (1986). *Hyperactive children grown up.* New York: Guilford Press.

Wender, P.H. (1987). *The hyperactive child, adolescent, and adult: Attention deficit disorder through the life span.* Oxford University Press.

Wender, P.H., Wood, D.R., & Reimherr, F.W. (1985). Pharmacological treatment of attention deficit disorder, residual type (ADD, RT, "minimal brain dysfunction," "hyperactivity"), in adults. *Psychopharmacology Bulletin, 21,* 222–231.

Zametkin, A.J., Nordahl, T.E., Gross, M., et al. (1990). Cerebral glucose metabolism in adults with hyperactivity of childhood onset. *New England Journal of Medicine, 323,* 1361–1366.

Zametkin, A., Rapoport, J.L., Murphy, D.L., et al. (1985). Treatment of hyperactive children with monoamine oxidase inhibitors. I. Clinical efficacy. *Archives of General Psychiatry, 42,* 962–966.

Chapter 22

Autism

with Mark Reber

Upon completion of this chapter, the reader will:
—be able to define autism
—understand the characteristics of this disorder
—know how to distinguish autism from other developmental disabilities
—be acquainted with the various intervention approaches to this disorder

---

Like mental retardation, autism is a brain-based developmental disability with multiple causes. Autism differs from mental retardation in that its characteristic feature is not a delay in development, but a series of striking deviations from normal developmental patterns that become apparent by 3 years of age. Autism involves disturbances in cognition, interpersonal communication, social interactions, and behavior (in particular, the presence of obsessional, ritualistic, stereotyped, and rigid behaviors) (American Psychiatric Association, 1987; Cohen, Donnellan, & Paul, 1987; Gillberg, 1990). Deviant development in all of these areas is necessary for a diagnosis of autism, thus giving rise to its classification as a pervasive developmental disorder.

Autism is a rare condition. Studies have determined its prevalence to be about 4 in 10,000 (Lotter, 1966; Ritvo, Freeman, Pingree, et al., 1989), and boys with autism outnumber girls 4:1. There appears to be a genetic component, as a family with one child with autism has about a 9% risk of having a second child with autism (Ritvo, Jorde, Mason-Brothers, et al., 1989).

A HISTORICAL PERSPECTIVE

Despite its rarity, autism has been the focus of considerable research since it was first described in 1943. Dr. Leo Kanner published the first description of what he called "autistic disturbances of affective contact" (Kanner, 1943, p. 217). He identified a group of children who exhibited symptoms that isolated them from their environment

Mark Reber, M.D., is Clinical Assistant Professor of Psychiatry at The University of Pennsylvania School of Medicine, Children's Seashore House, in Philadelphia.

and had abnormal language or did not speak at all. In his view, the fundamental disturbance in these children was "an inability to relate themselves in the ordinary way to people and situations from the beginning of life" (p. 242). He observed that as infants, these children did not seek to be held, ignored or shut out any social approaches, treated people as objects, and made minimal eye contact. In addition, children with autism required such a sameness in their environment that even a minor change—for example, the repositioning of a chair—threw them into a rage. Among those children who could speak, unusual features of language included parrot-like repetition of phrases, sometimes uttered long after they were heard (delayed echolalia); literalness of usage; and a tendency to repeat pronouns as heard (e.g., using "you" to refer to oneself). Play was repetitive and stereotyped, with little imaginative use of toys and other objects. Kanner noted that the parents of these children tended to be cold and formal in their interpersonal relationships, but speculated that the disorder was an "inborn disturbance" (p. 250).

In the 2 decades after Kanner's description, "cold" and "aloof" parents were increasingly blamed for causing autism. More recently, autism has been viewed as a disturbance that arises early in life and originates in the child's own biology. Controversy still remains, however, over the symptoms that constitute the core features of the disorder. Kanner emphasized the child's inability to relate, while other researchers have suggested that the language disorder, cognitive disturbance, or a certain group of sensory abnormalities is the essential feature. Definition of the fundamental psychological deficit is important, as it will help to direct research toward uncovering the specific brain disturbance that underlies autism.

CHARACTERISTICS OF AUTISM

In order to be diagnosed with autism, a child must meet 8 of the 16 criteria listed in the *Diagnostic and Statistical Manual of Mental Disorders* (*DSM-III-R*) (American Psychiatric Association, 1987) (Table 22.1). These criteria fall into three broad categories: 1) impairment in reciprocal social interaction, 2) impairment in communication and imaginative activity, and 3) markedly restricted repertoire of activities and interests. While not included in the diagnostic criteria, other behavioral, cognitive, and neurological disturbances are recognized as part of the disorder. The severity of this disorder is based on intellectual and associated deficits. Autism can occur in children with average intelligence, who have severe problems with communication skills, social interactions, and behavior, and in children with mental retardation and stereotypic behaviors (Rapin, 1991).

Social Interactions

Kanner's view that problems with social interactions represent the fundamental problem in autism is also supported by Wing (1988), who has described three types of social interaction impairments: impaired social recognition, communication, and understanding or imagining.

Impaired social recognition, in its mild form, appears as lack of interest in the feelings and thoughts of others and an absence of eye contact. Individuals with severe

Table 22.1.   Diagnostic criteria for autism

At least 8 of the following 16 items should be present. The child should exhibit at least two items from Group A, one from Group B, and one from Group C. (The examples are arranged so that those first mentioned are more likely to apply to younger children or children with more severe autism, and the later examples are more likely to apply to older children or children with less severe autism.)

Group A
Qualitative impairment in social interaction as manifested by the following:
1. Marked lack of awareness of the existence of others or their feelings
2. No effort or an abnormal effort to seek comfort at times of distress (e.g., does not come for comfort even when ill, hurt, or tired); seeks comfort in a stereotyped way (e.g., says "cheese, cheese, cheese" whenever hurt)
3. No imitation or impaired imitation (e.g., does not wave bye-bye, does not copy mother's domestic activities, mechanically imitates others' actions out of context)
4. No social play or abnormal social play (e.g., does not actively participate in simple games, prefers solitary play activities, involves other children in play only as "mechanical aids")
5. Gross impairment in ability to make peer friendships (e.g., no interest in making peer friendships; lacks understanding of conventions of social interaction [e.g., reads telephone book to uninterested peer])

Group B
Qualitative impairment in verbal and nonverbal communication and in imaginative activity as manifested by the following:
1. No mode of communication
2. Markedly abnormal nonverbal communication (e.g., does not anticipate being held, stiffens when held, does not look at the person or smile when making a social approach, does not greet parents or visitors, stares fixedly in social situations)
3. Absence of imaginative activity (e.g., no playacting of adult roles, fantasy characters, or animals; lack of interest in stories about imaginary events)
4. Marked abnormalities in speech production, including volume, pitch, stress, rate, rhythm, and intonation (e.g., monotonous tone, question-like melody, high pitch)
5. Marked abnormalities in the form or content of speech, including stereotyped and repetitive use of speech (e.g., immediate echolalia, mechanical repetition of television commercial); use of "you" when "I" is meant (e.g., using "You want cookie?" to mean "I want a cookie"); idiosyncratic use of words or phrases (e.g., "Go on green riding" to mean "I want to go on the swing"); or frequent irrelevant remarks (e.g., starts talking about train schedules during a conversation about sports)
6. Markedly impaired ability to initiate or sustain conversations with others, despite adequate speech (e.g., lengthy monologues on one subject regardless of interjections from others)

Group C
Markedly restricted repertoire of activities and interests as manifested by the following:
1. Stereotyped body movements (e.g., hand flicking, hand twisting, spinning, head banging, complex whole-body movements)
2. Persistent preoccupation with parts of objects (e.g., sniffing or smelling objects, repetitive feeling of texture of materials, spinning wheels of toy cars) or attachment to unusual objects (e.g., insists on carrying around a piece of string)
3. Marked distress over changes in trivial aspects of environment (e.g., when a vase is moved from usual position)
4. Unreasonable insistence on following routines in precise detail (e.g., insisting that exactly the same route be followed when shopping)
5. Markedly restricted range of interests and a preoccupation with one narrow interest (e.g., aligning objects, amassing facts about meteorology, pretending to be a fantasy character)

Adapted from American Psychiatric Association (1987).

autism demonstrate extreme aloofness and total indifference to other people. The second component, impaired social communication, is characterized by an absence of pleasure in the exchange of smiles and feelings (i.e., body language). This characteristic may be obvious as early as the first 2–3 months of life, though it often goes unrecognized until other deficits become more obvious (Stone, Lemanek, Fishel, et al., 1990). Impaired social communication also implies a lack of desire to communicate with others or communication that is limited to the simple expression of needs. The third component, impaired social imagination and understanding, refers to the inability to imitate others and engage in pretend play or to imagine another's thoughts and feelings. For example, infants with this deficit do not copy their mothers' facial expressions.

Other social deficits associated with autism include not seeking comfort when hurt and lacking interest in forming friendships. It is unclear whether children with autism do not display normal attachment behavior or do not understand relationships and want to form them (Hertzig, Snow, & Sherman, 1989; Shapiro, Frosch, & Arnold, 1987; Sigman & Mundy, 1989).

Communication Disorders

In children with autism, the development of language is severely delayed and deviant, hindering both expressive and receptive communication (Ferrari, 1982). Cooing and babbling may develop normally in the first 6 months of life, but then may regress. Speech may develop late or not at all. About half of children with autism remain mute throughout their lives and may even be unable to use gestures or signs to communicate (Rutter, 1985a). Those who develop language do not use it creatively or spontaneously. Their voices are often high-pitched, with unsual speech rhythm and intonation, which makes their speech sound sing-song or monotonous. They tend to use language in a very stereotyped, rote fashion, exhibiting excellent memorization skills but actually communicating very little, if any, meaning. They tend to repeat phrases and long commercial jingles. While it may seem that they are understanding what they are saying, they are usually parroting what they have heard. Despite good articulation and an adequate vocabulary, these children have a severe expressive language disorder.

Receptive language is affected as well. Children with autism may respond to brief phrases, but they find it very difficult to understand more complex commands. They learn better with visual than with auditory cues. At one point, language deficits were thought to be the primary cause of social withdrawal in children with autism, but these deficits are now regarded as secondary to the brain abnormality that causes the more fundamental disorder in relating to other people (Paul, 1987). Development of language is an important prognostic feature in autism. Children who develop language fare much better than those who do not (Schreibman, 1988).

Behavior Problems

The behavior problems in autism, particularly the restricted behavior repertoire and distressed response to environmental change, are among the most striking features of the disorder. Obsessive rituals and strict adherence to routines are common; including, for example, rigid insistence in eating at the same time every day and eating a restricted menu of foods, sitting in exactly the same position at the table, placing objects in a particular location, and touching every door knob one passes. Young children with autism may show intense attachment to unusual objects, such as a piece of plastic tubing, rather than a cuddly item like a teddy bear. They may not use toys in their intended manner, but focus instead on a part of a toy, such as the wheels on a toy truck, which they may spin incessantly. A common form of play is to line objects up in rows. Shining surfaces, rotating fans, and people's hair or beards may fascinate these young children. Older, more cognitively advanced individuals may become intensely preoccupied with train schedules, calendars, or particular patterns of numerical relationships. They will focus on these things to the exclusion of other activities.

Frequently, children with autism become upset and have intense tantrums if anything interferes with these rituals and preoccupations. Similar tantrums may be provoked by trivial departures from daily routines or changes in the environment. Stereotyped movements and self-stimulating behaviors, such as rocking, hand waving, arm flapping, toe walking, head banging, and other forms of self-injurious behavior are also common, especially among children with autism who have low IQs (Howlin & Rutter, 1987).

Other behavior problems associated with autism include sleep disturbances (especially in younger children), short attention spans, hyperactivity, tantrums, and aggressiveness. These behaviors, while not specific to autism, may be as difficult to manage as the characteristics of autism.

Intellectual Functioning

Children with autism function at various levels in the intellectual spectrum. However, about 70% have mental retardation: 35% have mild retardation, 15% have moderate retardation, and 20% have severe or profound retardation. Twenty-five percent fall in the borderline-to-normal range of intelligence (IQ 70–100) and about 5% have IQs over 100 (Minshew & Payton, 1988).

Psychological testing can be performed on children with autism, and the resultant IQs appear to be fairly accurate, providing the testing is done by a psychologist who is experienced in working with such children. The tests may need to be adapted, or nonverbal tests may be needed because the performance of children with autism is uneven. They tend to perform better on tests of visual-spatial skills and rote memory, and poorer on tasks requiring symbolic and logical reasoning. Some children with autism have restricted areas of higher functioning, called *islets of ability* or *splinter skills*. These include musical skills, such as perfect pitch, exceptional rote memory, an unusual capacity for jigsaw puzzles, or the ability to do rapid calculations of a specific kind, such as finding the day of the week for distant dates. Usually, these splinter skills relate to the individual's selected area of preoccupation and do not help them to solve problems in daily life. Even if the splinter skill involves some useful function, the child with autism is often not able to apply the skill to real life events.

Other Problems

Because children with autism are a heterogeneous group, there is no consistent pattern of physical or neurological abnormalities. A range of sensory disturbances has been reported, including both under- and oversensitivity to certain sounds, indifference to pain, and a preference for certain sensations, such as those that appeal to taste and smell rather than touch or sound. Most children with autism are clumsy and some have abnormalities of posture and movement (DeMyer, 1976). EEG abnormalities occur in approximately 80% of children with autism, but the incidence of seizures is not significantly different from the incidence in children with communication disorders (Minshew, 1991; Tuchman, Rapin, & Shinnar, 1991).

CAUSES OF AUTISM

There is, at present, nearly universal agreement that autism is caused by some form of brain damage or abnormality in brain development (Coleman & Gillberg, 1985; Lord, Mulloy, Wendelboe, et al., 1991; Nelson, 1991). The evidence for this includes: 1) the high incidence of EEG abnormalities; 2) the increased incidence of autism in certain diseases that are known to cause brain damage, such as untreated phenylketonuria (PKU) (see Chapter 10) and congenital infections; 3) the high frequency of mental retardation in autism (Wing, 1988); and 4) the high incidence of prenatal infections, prematurity, birth trauma, and so on (Bryson, Smith, & Eastwood, 1988; Mason-Brothers, Ritvo, Pingree, et al., 1990). These observations suggest that autism may result from brain damage sustained in a number of ways, including genetic abnormalities and environmental influences, and that the damage may be anatomical, physiological, and/or biochemical.

Neuroanatomical studies, based on imaging studies and examinations of the brains of persons with autism who have died, have identified abnormalities in the development of the cerebellum (Courchesne, 1991; Courchesne, Yeung-Courchesne, Press, et al., 1988; Ritvo, Freeman, Scheibel, et al., 1986) and the cerebral cortex (Piven, Berthier, Starkstein, et al., 1990). Findings such as these may provide information about when in the course of brain development the abnormalities developed.

Neurochemical studies have implicated various neurotransmitter disturbances in autism, although none consistently (Volkmar & Cohen, 1988). Some recent research has noted similar behaviors between children with autism and animals given opiates (Panksepp & Sahley, 1987), suggesting that abnormalities in these levels may play a role in autism (Weizman, Gil-Ad, Dick, et al., 1988; Young, Leven, Newcorn, et al., 1987).

A genetic basis for autism has been suggested by studies that have identified subgroups of children with autism who have a known genetic cause of brain injury, such as fragile X syndrome (Bregman, Leckman, & Ort, 1988; Reiss & Freund, 1990). Other studies have shown that autism occurs at higher rates among identical twins than among fraternal twins (Folstein & Piven, 1991; Smalley, Asarnow, & Spence, 1988) and that the risk of autism is much higher in families with one child with autism than in the general population. Taken together, these studies indicate a genetic predisposition to autism.

DISTINGUISHING AUTISM FROM OTHER DEVELOPMENTAL DISABILITIES

Since intervention strategies vary according to diagnosis, it is important to distinguish autism from other developmental disabilities. The most common disorders that are mistaken for autism are mental retardation, childhood psychosis, sensory impairments, developmental language disorders, and progressive nervous system disorders.

Autism is distinguished from mental retardation by its characteristic social and behavior problems and by a somewhat different pattern of cognitive deficits. Children with autism shun social interactions and treat everyone, even parents, as objects; children with mental retardation generally enjoy social contacts. Children with mental retardation usually have equal delays in language, cognitive, and visual-perceptual skills, whereas children with autism have more prominent language impairments. However, most children with autism also have mental retardation, and many individuals with severe mental retardation display autistic features, such as stereotyped movements and self-injury (Capute, Derivan, Chauvel, et al., 1975).

Autism may also be confused with psychiatric disorders, such as schizophrenia (American Psychiatric Association, 1987). The key difference between the two syndromes is age of onset. Autism begins in the first 3 years of life, while schizophrenia rarely starts before adolescence. Furthermore, while the child with autism may behave in a bizarre manner, he or she will not have the delusions and hallucinations that are characteristic of schizophrenia. In addition, while a child with autism lacks imagination, a child with schizophrenia may live in a fantasy world. Finally, children with schizophrenia do not usually have mental retardation (see Chapter 23).

Children with sensory impairments may also demonstrate autistic features. Children with visual impairment often display self-stimulatory behaviors and lack the skills necessary for interpersonal interactions. They do not have the global language disorder that distinguishes children with autism, and their intelligence is usually normal. Furthermore, if there is improvement in their sensory function, the autistic features disappear. This makes it extremely important for the vision and hearing of children with autistic behaviors to be tested before the diagnosis of autism is confirmed.

Similarly, children with developmental language disorders may display shyness, echolalia, and some social withdrawal (see Chapter 19), but they typically do not show the deviant language features of autism, such as stereotyped utterances, abnormal social interactions, bizarre behaviors, and absence of a desire to communicate (Rutter, 1985a).

Finally, a group of progressive neurological diseases initially may be misdiagnosed as autism. Children with these disorders develop normally in infancy, then start to lose both intellectual and motor skills, and fall behind (Menkes, 1990). One example is Rett syndrome (Hagberg, Aicardi, Dias, et al., 1983; Percy, Zoghbi, Lewis, et al., 1987). Although children with autism may also seem to regress in their development, their loss of skills is usually restricted to language. Furthermore, most children with autism have problems in social development that can be traced to the first year of life. The diagnosis of a progressive neurological disorder becomes evident as abilities continue to deteriorate over time.

Testing for Autism

There is no specific medical test for autism. Blood tests and EEGs may be abnormal, but are nonspecific. However, tests may be conducted to identify syndromes commonly associated with autism and to rule out other explanations for abnormal behavior. For example, a chromosome study would be performed if fragile X syndrome is suspected (see Chapter 16); metabolic studies might be ordered to test for PKU or other inborn errors of metabolism; and an MRI scan may be done to look for abnormalities in the cortex or cerebellum.

TREATMENT AND INTERVENTION APPROACHES

Michael Rutter, an eminent British child psychiatrist, has outlined five main goals of the treatment of autism: 1) the fostering of normal development, 2) the promotion of learning, 3) the reduction of rigidity and stereotypy, 4) the elimination of nonspecific maladaptive behaviors, and 5) the alleviation of family distress (Rutter, 1985b).

These goals are best met through a comprehensive educational and behavior management program that includes a highly structured education setting, language training, behavioral interventions, positive social experiences, and intensive parent involvement (Howlin & Rutter, 1987; Rogers & Lewis, 1989; Schreibman, 1988). Treatment should begin as early as possible, as there is some evidence that early intervention to promote acquisition of communication skills can lessen later maladaptive behaviors (Prizant & Wetherby, 1988).

Behavior therapy may be needed to modify behaviors that might otherwise interfere with development and learning. Reduction in stereotypical, rigid, ritualistic, and maladaptive behaviors (e.g., tantrums, aggression, self-injury) may be accomplished through a number of behavioral strategies. For example, behavior shaping can help to systematically positively reinforce approximations of desired communicative behavior and withdrawal of reinforcement can help to extinguish self-stimulatory behaviors. Other behavioral interventions attempt to increase social interaction (Schreibman, 1988). Parents are often used as co-therapists in these forms of intervention.

Fostering normal development must include language therapy with an emphasis on the pragmatics of language (i.e., using it to accomplish social goals) (Schuler & Prizant, 1987). Interactive and meaningful conversations should be modeled and practiced, and echolalia discouraged. With children with autism who are mute, attempts should be made to train verbal utterances, such as babbling or jargoning (Howlin & Rutter, 1987; Schuler & Prizant, 1987). Sign language can also be attempted, but it is often difficult for children with autism to learn. A novel approach, termed *facilitated communication*, is now being evaluated. The basic element of facilitated communication is providing physical support to the child's arm as he or she attempts to type messages on a keyboard or communication board (Biklen, 1990).

This is done to overcome dyspraxia that may underlie the child's inability to use a communication device independently. Art and music therapy have also been used in attempts to communicate with children with autism nonverbally.

The education of children with autism usually requires highly structured programs with predictable routines and presentation of material in graded steps (Rogers & Lewis, 1989; Rutter, 1985a). Children with autism should be enrolled in preschool early intervention programs that stress communication skills and social interactions. By school age, many children with autism learn effectively in public school special education classes with children who function at similar developmental levels. Class sizes should be small, and activities should be broken into simple subunits to hold the children's interest and decrease stereotypical behavior. One-to-one interactions with teachers and fellow students are encouraged so that children with autism may develop social skills. Higher functioning children with autism may be integrated into regular education settings.

Medications play a limited role in the treatment of autism, as there is no pharmacological remedy for the disorder (Minshew & Payton, 1988). Certain medications, however, have been used to relieve some of the symptoms, including hyperactivity, irritable mood, social withdrawal, and aggression. The best studied of these medications is haloperidol (Haldol), a high-potency antipsychotic drug that has been shown to be effective in decreasing stereotypical behaviors, withdrawal, aggression, negativism, and irritability, as well as increasing performance on learning tasks (Anderson, Campbell, Grega, et al., 1984; Joshi, Capozzoli, & Coyle, 1988). Unfortunately, haloperidol is also associated with a high incidence of movement abnormalities (Perry, Campbell, Adams, et al., 1989). A medication that once looked promising in autism, fenfluramine, has more recently been shown to be largely ineffective. In addition, it interferes with discrimination learning and is poorly tolerated (Campbell, Adams, Small, et al., 1988; Stern, Walker, Sawyer, et al., 1990; Varley & Holm, 1990). Opiate antagonists, such as naltrexone, are being studied to see if they alleviate any of the hyperactive and maladaptive behaviors associated with autism. Preliminary reports show mild benefits (Campbell, Anderson, Small, et al., 1990).

Stimulants, used to treat hyperactivity, were formerly thought to aggravate stereotyped behaviors. But, methylphenidate (Ritalin) has been shown to be helpful in controlling hyperactivity in some children with autism (Birmaher, Quintana, & Greenhill, 1988; Strayhorn, Rapp, Donina, et al., 1988). Clonidine (Catapres), a newer medication for hyperactivity, which was developed to treat hypertension in adults, may also be useful for treating hyperactivity in children with autism. Lithium has also been used to treat the manic-like symptoms of autism (Steingard & Biederman, 1987).

Parents need emotional support and advocacy and, most of all, should be brought into the treatment process as teachers and co-therapists of their children. There is no doubt that having a child with autism is enormously stressful for the family. In addition to the normal stresses of having a child with disabilities, there are many additional demands as well as the frustration of caring for a child who provides few emotional rewards, requires intense supervision, has disturbed sleep, and exhibits behavior that is difficult to manage. If emotional problems arise, family counseling is indicated.

KENNY: A CHILD WITH AUTISM

Kenny had problems from infancy. His early development was delayed, and his parents were quite concerned that Kenny would have mental retardation. They noticed that he did not "coo" or respond to sounds. He did not reach out to be picked up, and he seemed stiff and uncomfortable when they held him. Soon, his motor development improved. He sat by 8 months and walked by 15 months. His parents became hopeful that he did not have "brain damage." He also showed good visual-perceptual skills, being able to put together simple puzzles by 2 years of age and to build intricate block towers by 2½.

Yet, his parents remained concerned about his language, behavior, and relationships with other people. At 2 years of age, he neither spoke nor consistently followed 1-step commands. He was a loner. He showed no interest in playing with other children and barely acknowledged his parents. He still did not like to be held. Kenny exhibited no warmth and maintained no eye contact with others. He had many strange, ritualistic behaviors. He spun around, rocked, and constantly played with a string. He would fly into a rage when the furniture was moved or when he encountered new situations.

By 4 years of age, Kenny had developed some language, but it was very strange. He had an extraordinary memory for numbers and commercials. He would constantly carry a detergent bottle around the house singing its advertising jingle, and he would endlessly repeat strings of numbers. However, he still basically communicated with no one. He could not follow 2-step commands and spoke in only 1- or 2-word phrases. More often than not, he pointed to what he wanted.

At this time, psychological testing was performed. Kenny's IQ was 37, indicating he functioned around the level of an 18-month-old. However, he could build block towers and solve puzzles at a 4-year-old level. Because of his strange behavior, withdrawal, and reactions of rage, he was referred to a child psychiatrist. These symptoms, combined with good gross motor and visual-perceptual skills and severe mental retardation, led to a diagnosis of autism. His parents, in a sense, were relieved; they had a diagnosis, some place to start.

Even more important, Kenny was enrolled in an intervention program. He received the drug haloperidol to decrease his anxiety. His reactions of rage decreased. He entered a special school program where language and other reasoning skills were taught at an 18-month-old level. Behavior management techniques were used to help Kenny with new social situations and to reduce self-stimulatory behavior. At the same time, Kenny's parents received counseling from a social worker and followed through on a behavior management program set up by a behavioral psychologist.

By 6 years of age, Kenny had improved substantially. He could now form 3-word sentences, and the automatic repetition of words decreased. His behavior was better, and he could be brought into new situations without difficulty.

Kenny's eventual outcome is still unclear. He will continue to gain new skills, but his cognitive function will likely remain in the range of mental retardation. It is hoped that he will gain increased communication and social skills that will permit him to function in supported employment when he is an adult.

PROGNOSIS

Autistic features generally become less pronounced as the child grows, and stereotypic behavior decreases. By adolescence, the child's function will principally depend on his or her intelligence and speech skills Only about one-half of children with autism gain socially useful speech, usually by 5 years of age (Rutter, 1985a). The child with autism and moderate-to-severe mental retardation will function in a manner similar to other children with mental retardation, although he or she will have poorer language skills, possibly better problem-solving abilities, and a decreased interest in social interactions. Even among higher functioning individuals with autism, abnormalities of verbal expression, concrete thought processes, social awkwardness, and stereotyped and inappropriate social behaviors tend to persist (Wing, 1988). Overall, about 15% of children with autism have a good outcome, 15% a fair outcome, and 70% a poor outcome in terms of functioning independently in society as an adult. The majority live at home or in supervised living situations (Rumsey, Rapoport, & Sceery, 1985). Most individuals with autism are independent in self-care skills and can participate in activities of daily living (Wing, 1985). Some young adults can engage in supported employment, especially in jobs that require the use of their visual-motor skills. Those with normal intelligence can often live and work independently.

SUMMARY

Autism appears to be a distinct syndrome. Its principal characteristics are a global language disorder, abnormal behavior patterns, social isolation, and, usually, mental retardation. Its causes are many. Differentiation from other disabilities, such as mental retardation, psychiatric illness, sensory impairments, and progressive neurological disorders, is essential for proper therapy to be possible. Therapy consists of an interdisciplinary approach that includes psychiatry, speech-language pathology, behavioral psychology, and social work. At this point, the value of medication is uncertain. In adolescents and adults, the bizarre behavior is less apparent, but prognosis is generally poor. The children with the best hope for the future are those with the higher IQ scores.

REFERENCES

American Psychiatric Association. (1987). *Diagnostic and statistical manual of mental disorders (DSM-III-R)* (3rd ed.). Washington, DC: Author.

Anderson, L.T., Campbell, M., Grega, D.M., et al. (1984). Haloperidol in the treatment of infantile autism: Effects on learning and behavioral symptoms. *American Journal of Psychiatry, 141,* 1195–1202.

Biklen, D. (1990). Communication unbound. Autism and praxis. *Harvard Educational Review, 60,* 291–314.

Birmaher, B., Quintana, H., & Greenhill, L.L. (1988). Methylphenidate treatment of hyperactive autistic children. *Journal of The American Academy of Child and Adolescent Psychiatry, 27,* 248–251.

Bregman, J.D., Leckman, J.F., & Ort, S.I. (1988). Fragile-X syndrome: Genetic predisposition to psychopathology. *Journal of Autism and Developmental Disorders, 18,* 343–354.

Bryson, S.E., Smith, I.M., & Eastwood, D. (1988). Obstetrical suboptimality in autistic children. *Journal of The American Academy of Child and Adolescent Psychiatry, 27,* 418–422.

Campbell, M., Adams, P., Small, A.M., et al. (1988). Efficacy and safety of fenfluramine in autistic children. *Journal of The American Academy of Child and Adolescent Psychiatry, 27,* 434–439.

Campbell, M., Anderson, L.T., Small, A.M., et al. (1990). Naltrexone in autistic children: A double-blind and placebo-controlled study. *Psychopharmacology Bulletin, 26,* 130–135.

Capute, A.J., Derivan, A.T., Chauvel, P.J., et al. (1975). Infantile autism. I: A prospective study of the diagnosis. *Developmental Medicine and Child Neurology, 17,* 58–62.

Cohen, D.J., Donnellan, A.M., & Paul, R. (Eds.). (1987). *Handbook of autism and pervasive developmental disorders.* New York: John Wiley & Sons.

Coleman, M., & Gillberg, C. (1985). *The biology of the autism syndrome,* New York: Praeger.

Courchesne, E. (1991). Neuroanatomic imaging in autism. *Pediatrics, 87,* 781–790.

Courchesne, E., Yeung-Courchesne, R., Press, G.A., et al. (1988). Hypoplasia of cerebellar vermal lobules VI and VII in autism. *New England Journal of Medicine, 318,* 1349–1354.

DeMyer, M.K. (1976). Motor, perceptual-motor and intellectual disabilities in autistic children. In L. Wing (Ed.), *Early childhood autism* (2nd ed.). Elmsford, NY: Pergamon.

Ferrari, M. (1982). Childhood autism: Deficits of communication and symbolic development. I. Distinctions from language disorders. *Journal of Communication Disorders, 15,* 191–208.

Folstein, S.E., & Piven, J. (1991). Etiology of autism: Genetic influences. *Pediatrics, 87,* 767–773.

Gillberg, C. (1990). Autism and pervasive developmental disorder. *Journal of Child Psychology and Psychiatry and Allied Disciplines, 31,* 99–119.

Gillberg, C. (1991). Outcome in autism and autistic-like conditions. *Journal of the American Academy of Child and Adolescent Psychiatry, 30,* 375–382.

Hagberg, B., Aicardi, J., Dias, K., et al. (1983). A progressive syndrome of autism, dementia, ataxia, and loss of purposeful hand use in girls: Rett's syndrome: report of 35 cases. *Annals Neurology, 14,* 471–479.

Hertzig, M.E., Snow, M.E., & Sherman, M. (1989). Affect and cognition in autism. *Journal of The American Academy of Child and Adolescent Psychiatry, 28,* 195–199.

Howlin, P., & Rutter, M. (1987). *Treatment of autistic children.* New York: John Wiley & Sons.

Joshi, P.T., Capozzoli, J.A., & Coyle, J.T. (1988). Low-dose neuroleptic therapy for children with childhood-onset pervasive developmental disorder. *American Journal of Psychiatry, 145,* 335–338.

Kanner, L. (1943). Autistic disturbances of affective contact. *Nervous Child, 2,* 217–250.

Lord, C., Mulloy, C., Wendelboe, M., et al. (1991). Pre- and perinatal factors in high-functioning females and males with autism. *Journal of Autism and Developmental Disorders, 21,* 197–219.

Lotter, V., (1966). Epidemiology of autistic conditions in young children. I. Prevalence. *Social Psychiatry, 1,* 124–137.

Mason-Brothers, A., Ritvo, E.R., Pingree, C., et al. (1990). The UCLA-University of Utah epidemiologic survey of autism: Prenatal, perinatal and postnatal factors. *Pediatrics, 86,* 514–519.

Menkes, J.H. (1990). *Textbook of child neurology* (4th ed.). Philadelphia: Lea & Febiger.

Minshew, N.J. (1991). Indices of neural function in autism: Clinical and biological implications. *Pediatrics, 87,* 774–780.

Minshew, N.J., & Payton, J.B. (1988). New perspectives in autism. Part I: The clinical spectrum of autism. Part II: The differential diagnosis and neurobiology of autism. *Current Problems in Pediatrics, 18,* 561–694.

Nelson, K.B. (1991). Prenatal and perinatal factors in the etiology of autism. *Pediatrics, 87,* 761–766.

Panksepp, J., & Sahley, T.L. (1987). Possible brain opioid involvement in disrupted social intent and language development of autism. In E. Schopler & G.B. Mesibov (Eds.), *Neurobiological issues in autism.* New York: Plenum.

Paul, R. (1987). Communication. In D.J. Cohen, A.M. Donnellan, & R. Paul (Eds.), *Handbook of autism and pervasive developmental disorders* (pp. 61–84). New York: John Wiley & Sons.

Percy, A.K., Zoghbi, H.Y., Lewis, K.R., et al. (1987). Rett syndrome: Qualitative and quantitative differentiation from autism. *Journal of Child Neurology, 3(Suppl.),* 565–567.

Perry, R., Campbell, M., Adams, P., et al. (1989). Long-term efficacy of haloperidol in autistic children: Continuous versus discontinuous drug administration. *Journal of The American Academy of Child and Adolescent Psychiatry, 28,* 87–92.

Piven, J., Berthier, M.L., Starkstein, S.E., et al. (1990). Magnetic resonance imaging evidence for a defect of cerebral cortical development in autism. *American Journal of Psychiatry, 147,* 734–739.

Prizant, B.M., & Wetherby, A.M. (1988). Providing services to children with autism (ages 0 to 2 years) and their families. *Topics in Language Disorders, 9,* 1–23.

Rapin, I. (1991). Autistic children: Diagnosis and clinical features. *Pediatrics, 87,* 751–760.

Reiss, A.L., & Freund, L. (1990). Fragile-X syndrome, DSM-III-R, and autism. *Journal of The American Academy of Child and Adolescent Psychiatry, 29,* 885–891.

Ritvo, E.R., Freeman, B.J., Pingree, C., et al. (1989). The UCLA–University of Utah epidemiologic survey of autism: Prevalence. *American Journal of Psychiatry, 146,* 194–199.

Ritvo, E.R., Freeman, B.J., Scheibel, A.B., et al. (1986). Lower purkinje cell counts in the cerebella of four autistic subjects: Initial findings of the UCLA-NSAC autopsy research report. *American Journal of Psychiatry, 143,* 862–866.

Ritvo, E.R., Jorde, L.B., Mason-Brothers, A., et al. (1989). The UCLA-University of Utah epidemiologic survey of autism: Recurrence risk estimates and genetic counseling. *American Journal of Psychiatry, 146,* 1032–1036.

Rogers, S.J., & Lewis, H. (1989). An effective day treatment model for young children with pervasive developmental disorders. *Journal of The American Academy of Child and Adolescent Psychiatry, 28,* 207–214.

Rumsey, J.M., Rapoport, J.L., & Sceery, W.R. (1985). Autistic children as adults: Psychiatric, social and behavioral outcomes. *Journal of The American Academy of Child Psychiatry, 24,* 465–473.

Rutter, M. (1985a). Infantile autism and other pervasive developmental disorders. In M. Rutter & L. Hersov (Eds.), *Child and adolescent psychiatry: Modern approaches* (pp. 545–566). Oxford: Blackwell Scientific Publications.

Rutter, M. (1985b). The treatment of autistic children. *Journal of Child Psychology and Psychiatry and Allied Disciplines, 26,* 193–214.

Schreibman, L. (1988). *Autism.* Newbury Park, CA: Sage Publications.

Schuler, A.L., & Prizant, B.M. (1987). Facilitating communication: Pre-language approaches. In D.J. Cohen, A.M. Donnellan, & R. Paul (Eds.), *Handbook of autism and pervasive developmental disorders* (pp. 301–315). New York: John Wiley & Sons.

Shapiro, T., Frosch, E., & Arnold, S. (1987). Attachment in autism and other developmental disorders. *Journal of The American Academy of Child and Adolescent Psychiatry, 26,* 480–484.

Sigman, M., & Mundy, P. (1989). Social attachments in autistic children. *Journal of The American Academy of Child and Adolescent Psychiatry, 28,* 74–81.

Smalley, S.L., Asarnow, R.F., & Spence, M.A. (1988). Autism and genetics: A decade of research. *Archives of General Psychiatry, 45,* 953–961.

Steingard, R., & Biederman, J. (1987). Lithium responsive manic-like symptoms in two individuals with autism and mental retardation. *Journal of The American Academy of Child and Adolescent Psychiatry, 26,* 932–935.

Stern, L.M., Walker, M.K., Sawyer, M.G., et al. (1990). A controlled crossover trial of fenfluramine in autism. *Journal of Child Psychology and Psychiatry and Allied Disciplines, 31,* 569–585.

Stone, W.L., Lemanek, K.L., Fishel, P.T., et al. (1990). Play and imitation skills in the diagnosis of autism in young children. *Pediatrics, 86,* 267–272.

Strayhorn, J.M., Jr., Rapp, N., Donina, W., et al. (1988). Randomized trial of methylphenidate for an autistic child. *Journal of The American Academy of Child and Adolescent Psychiatry, 27,* 244–247.

Tuchman, R.F., Rapin, I., & Shinnar, S. (1991). Autistic and dysphasic children. II: Epilepsy. *Pediatrics, 88,* 1219–1225.

Varley, C.K., & Holm, V.A. (1990). A two-year follow-up of autistic children treated with fenfluramine. *Journal of The American Academy of Child and Adolescent Psychiatry, 29,* 137–140.

Volkmar, F.R., & Cohen, D.J. (1988). Neurobiologic aspects of autism. *New England Journal of Medicine, 318,* 1390–1392.

Weizman, R., Gil-Ad, I., Dick, J., et al. (1988). Low plasma immunoreactive beta-endorphin levels in autism. *Journal of The American Academy of Child and Adolescent Psychiatry, 27,* 430–433.

Wing, L. (1985). *Autistic children: A guide for parents.* New York: Brunner/Mazel.

Wing, L. (1988). The continuum of autistic characteristics. In E. Schopler & G.B. Mesibov (Eds.), *Diagnosis and assessment in autism* (pp. 91–110). New York: Plenum.

Young, J.G., Leven, L.I., Newcorn, J.H., et al. (1987). Genetic and neurobiologic approaches to the pathophysiology of autism and the pervasive developmental disorders. In H.Y. Meltzer (Ed.), *Psychopharmacology: The third generation of progress* (pp. 825–836). New York: Raven Press.

Chapter 23

Dual Diagnosis
Psychiatric Disorders and Mental Retardation

Mark Reber

Upon completion of this chapter, the reader will:
—understand the risk factors that can contribute to the higher prevalence of psychiatric disorders in individuals with mental retardation
—be able to describe the types and symptoms of some of these disorders
—be knowledgeable about diagnostic and treatment approaches

Children with mental retardation may be affected not only by their cognitive deficits, but also by emotional and behavioral disturbances that limit their ability to adapt, learn, develop socially, and become independent. Although these disturbances were at one time attributed to mental retardation itself, they are now understood to be the same psychiatric disorders that occur in persons without mental retardation. This chapter reviews the prevalence and causes of psychiatric disorders in children with mental retardation, provides clinical descriptions of several psychiatric disorders, and reviews commonly used intervention approaches.

PREVALENCE OF PSYCHIATRIC DISORDERS IN INDIVIDUALS WITH MENTAL RETARDATION

A psychiatric disorder is a specific, clinically significant disturbance of thought, behavior, or emotions that can be described as a syndrome (i.e., a cluster of symptoms) or a pattern. Studies of psychiatric disorders among children with mental retardation have shown a higher prevalence in this group than among children without mental

Mark Reber, M.D., is Clinical Assistant Professor of Psychiatry at The University of Pennsylvania School of Medicine, Children's Seashore House, in Philadelphia.

retardation. In the landmark Isle of Wight study of children's psychiatric disorders, Rutter and colleagues found that 30%–42% of children with mental retardation had emotional disturbances, compared to 7%–10% of the general population (Rutter, Graham, & Yule, 1970; Rutter, Tizard, & Whitmore, 1970). Among children with severe mental retardation, 50% were found to have a psychiatric disorder. This is a four- to five-fold increase in the prevalence of psychiatric disorders over communities of children without mental retardation. It has been confirmed in subsequent community studies (Bregman, 1988; Russell, 1985). The Isle of Wight study also documented an inverse correlation between IQ and incidence of psychiatric disorder, with frequency of psychiatric disturbance being greatest among children with severe mental retardation.

While the prevalence is higher, the kinds of psychiatric disorders among this population are the same as those diagnosed in children without mental retardation and include psychoses, disruptive behavior disorders, hyperactivity, personality disorders, **neuroses,** and **transient situational disorders** (Philips & Williams 1975, 1977; Menolascino, Levitas, & Greiner, 1986). Clearly recognizable mood disorders—depression, **mania,** and **manic-depressive** illness—have also been reported in individuals with mental retardation, including those with severe mental retardation (Carlson, 1979; Menolascino, Lazer, & Stark, 1989; Sovner & Hurley, 1983). Only among individuals with severe and profound mental retardation does one encounter a few psychiatric disorders that are uncommon in the general population. These include stereotypy-habit disorder (i.e., repetitive, self-stimulating, or self-injurious behavior) and pica (i.e., the eating of nonfood items).

CAUSES OF PSYCHIATRIC DISTURBANCES

One may ask why psychiatric disorders are more common among persons with mental retardation. Do both the mental retardation and psychiatric disturbance result from a common cause, such as brain damage? Is it mental retardation itself or something associated with it that increases the risk of developing psychiatric disorders?

Clearly, one possible cause of psychiatric disturbance is brain dysfunction, and there is evidence that some children with mental retardation—including the majority of children with IQs of less than 50—have brain abnormalities (see Chapter 16). The relationship between brain damage and emotional or behavioral disturbance, however, is not direct cause-and-effect. Even in conditions with manifest destruction of brain tissue and cognitive impairment (e.g., following traumatic brain injury), the occurrence of a psychiatric disorder is influenced by numerous family, environmental, and psychosocial factors, including how the family understands and copes with the child's injury (Russell, 1985). Brain damage thus appears to be a risk factor for psychiatric disturbance, not an immediate cause.

Experiences that often accompany mental retardation, such as traumatic social experiences (e.g., stigmatization, rejection by age mates and society at large), certain temperamental features (e.g., inadequate adaptability to new situations, poor concentration), medical illnesses (e.g., seizures), educational failure, and associated communication disorders, have been implicated as contributing to increased vulnerability to psychiatric disorders (Russell, 1985) (Figure 23.1). It is likely that several of these risk factors act in concert to account for the increased prevalence of psychiatric disturbance among individuals with mental retardation.

It has also been suggested that the kinds of family dysfunction and social adversity that contribute to emotional disturbances in nonretarded children have a greater impact on children with mental retardation because of their limited understanding and problem-solving abilities, their greater need for support, and temperaments that make them less able to cope with such stress. Their families, in turn, may be more vulnerable because of the experience of having a child with mental retardation (Corbett, 1985).

Present knowledge does not permit identification of the exact "cause" of any psychiatric disorder. Psychiatric disturbances appear to have multiple causes, including inherited biological vulnerability, abnormalities in early brain development, stressful or traumatic life experiences, family dysfunction, acute alterations in brain functioning, and maladaptive patterns of thought and behavior (Bregman, 1991).

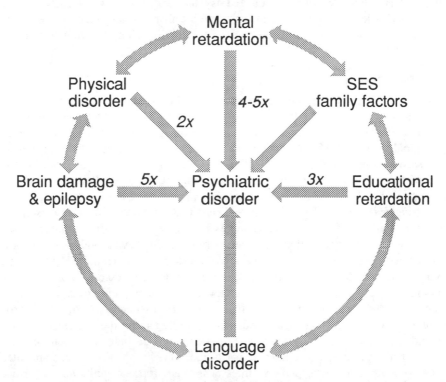

Figure 23.1.   The risk of psychiatric disorders is higher in children with various developmental disabilities. The highest risk (4–5 times greater than normal) is found in children with mental retardation or seizure disorders. A 2- to 3-fold increased risk is found in children with other physical disabilities, learning disabilities, and speech-language disorders. Low socioeconomic status and other family factors also increase the risk of psychiatric disorders.

Every child has some degree of vulnerability to psychiatric disturbance. In addition, however, the child with mental retardation experiences stresses and limitations that other children are usually spared. The developmental crises, failure, social rejection, scapegoating, and shame that can be part of having mental retardation, the frequent inadequacy of social supports, and the stress on the family no doubt constitute a major additional risk factor for a child with mental retardation to develop a psychiatric disorder (Corbett, 1985).

TYPES OF DISORDERS

Children and adolescents with mental retardation are an extremely diverse group, with widely varying skills and deficits, an enormous number of accompanying medical and neurological disorders (or no organic illness at all) from all kinds of families and backgrounds. It is no exaggeration to say that each person with mental retardation is unique. The ways in which psychiatric disturbances manifest themselves also vary with the individual. Certain general descriptions can, however, be provided. The discussion that follows describes: 1) selected psychiatric disorders with clearly defined symptoms, 2) certain genetic diseases associated with abnormal patterns of behavior, and 3) a few serious behavior disorders found primarily among individuals with severe mental retardation.

Psychiatric Disorders

Researchers have reported on the following psychiatric disorders in persons with mental retardation: bipolar (i.e., manic-depressive) disorder (McCracken & Diamond, 1988; Steingard & Biederman, 1987), **schizophrenia** (Menolascino, Ruedrich, Golden, et al., 1985), major depression with psychotic features (Carlson, 1979), **obsessive-compulsive disorder** (Vitiello, Spreat, & Behar, 1989), attention deficit hyperactivity disorder (Handen, Breaux, Gosling, et al., 1990; Payton, Burkhart, Hersen, et al., 1989), and **anxiety disorders** (Parsons, May, & Menolascino, 1984).

Bipolar Disorder Bipolar disorder refers to a condition in which a person experiences episodes of both mania and depression (Table 23.1). During a manic phase, an individual experiences an altered state of mood and behavior, which occurs for a distinct period of time and includes an elevated, expansive, or irritable mood. Symptoms include inflated self-esteem, decreased need for sleep, excessive or pressured talking, distractibility, feeling that one's thoughts are racing, and excessive involvement in pleasurable activity with potentially harmful consequences (e.g., sexual promiscuity) (American Psychiatric Association, 1987). During the depressive phase, the individual may experience a major depression, which includes symptoms of emotional withdrawal, diminished interest in activities, problems with sleep and appetite, poor concentration, feelings of worthlessness, inappropriate guilt, and recurrent thoughts of death or suicide. Some individuals with bipolar disorder predominantly have manic episodes while others experience mostly recurrent depressions. Psychosis can occur with both mania and major depression.

The occurrence of bipolar disorder in children and adolescents with mental re-

Table 23.1.   Symptoms of psychiatric illness

Bipolar disorder

Major depression
1. Depressed or irritable mood
2. Markedly diminished interest or pleasure in activities
3. Significant weight gain or loss or failure to make expected weight gains
4. Insomnia or excessive sleeping
5. Psychomotor agitation or retardation
6. Fatigue or loss of energy
7. Diminished ability to concentrate
8. Recurrent thoughts of death or suicide

Mania
1. Period of abnormal and persistently elevated, expansive, or irritable mood
2. Presence of at least three of the following symptoms during mood disturbance: inflated self-esteem, decreased need for sleep, talkativeness, racing thoughts, distractibility, increased goal-directed and pleasure-seeking activity

Recurrent and intermixed or alternating episodes of mania and depression

Schizophrenia

1. Delusions (e.g., thought broadcasting)
2. Hallucinations (e.g., a voice giving a running commentary on the person's behavior or thoughts)
3. Incoherence or marked loosening of associations
4. Catatonic behavior
5. Flat or grossly inappropriate emotions

Obsessive-compulsive disorder

Obsessions
1. Recurrent and persistent ideas, thoughts, impulses, or images that are experienced, at least initially, as intrusive and senseless
2. Attempts to ignore, suppress, or neutralize thoughts or impulses with other thoughts or actions
3. Understanding that the obsessions are products of the mind, not imposed from outside

Compulsions
1. Repetitive, purposeful, and intentional behaviors that are performed in response to obsessions, according to certain rules, or in a stereotyped fashion
2. Behavior designed to neutralize or to prevent discomfort or some dreaded event or situation; however, the activity is not realistically connected with what it is designed to neutralize or prevent or it is clearly excessive

The obsessions or compulsions cause marked distress, are time-consuming, or significantly interfere with the person's normal routine or social activities or relationships

Dementia[a]

1. Impairment in short- and long-term memory[b]
2. At least one of the following:
    - Impairment in abstract thinking
    - Impaired judgment
    - Other disturbances of brain function, such as not understanding spoken language and having difficulty in planning motor acts
    - Personality change

Source: American Psychiatric Association (1987).

[a]As in Alzheimer disease.

[b]Short-term memory permits the learning of new information. Long-term memory permits the retention of information that was known in the past, such as name and address.

tardation appears to be independent of their cognitive level and is related, as in other people, to heredity. Bipolar disorder is rare in young children, usually beginning in adolescence or early adult life (Parsons et al., 1984). Diagnosing this condition in individuals who are not able to report on their mood state and thought processes depends on evidence of cyclic alteration in mood over time, family history of mood disorders, and observable symptoms (e.g., sudden, momentary shifts in mood, changes in sleep and eating, changes in rate of speech, altered level of activity). The diagnosis of bipolar disorder can explain symptoms, such as periodic sleeplessness or aggression, and provide an avenue for relief. There are a number of medications that can alleviate the severity of the depressive and manic states and, in some cases, prevent their recurrence (see of Pharmacotherapy subsection in this chapter).

Depression   Depression comprises several disorders. Major depression (see Table 23.1) can occur independently or as part of bipolar disorder and is not rare. At any one time, 2% of preadolescent school children and 5% of adolescents have this disorder (Kashani, Carlson, Beck, et al., 1987; Kashani, McGee, Clarkson, et al., 1983). It is a severe condition and can be associated with psychosis and suicidal behavior. Major depression has a genetically determined biological basis, but psychological factors are also important in the genesis of depression.

A milder, but chronic form of depression is **dysthymia,** which is characterized by depressed mood that is usually present during a period of at least 1 year, low self-esteem, feelings of hopelessness, poor concentration, low energy, and changes in school performance, sleep, and appetite. Because of life experiences that have a damaging effect on self-esteem, persons with mental retardation are at particular risk of developing dysthymia. Another type of depression is *adjustment disorder with depressed mood*. This is a time-limited depression that follows a stressful event and constitutes a maladaptive response to that event. Maladaptive responses to stress can also occur as disturbed and defiant behavior, anxiety, and inhibited capacity to work or study. Each of these is a different adjustment disorder.

Psychosis   The defining symptoms of psychosis are confused thinking, **hallucinations, delusions,** and agitation or stupor. A number of psychiatric disorders can cause a clinical picture of psychosis. In addition to major depression with psychotic features and mania, these include schizophrenia and **delirium.** Signs and symptoms of schizophrenia include deterioration in functional level, prominent hallucinations, delusions (i.e., false beliefs, often quite bizarre), incoherence, catatonia (i.e., muscle rigidity and stupor), and grossly inappropriate emotional expression (see Table 23.1). These more severe manifestations are usually preceded by a period of social withdrawal, apparent loss of skills, peculiar behavior, altered thought and speech, poor self-care, lack of initiative, and odd ideas. Schizophrenia is a chronic condition and symptoms must be present for at least 6 months to make a diagnosis. It characteristically begins in adolescence or young adult life; occurrence in younger children is rare (Russell, 1985). Among individuals with mild mental retardation, schizophrenia is not difficult to diagnose. However, in people with more severe mental retardation who have difficulty describing their thoughts, behavioral deterioration and severe disorganization may be the only clues to the presence of the disorder, which may then be called *psychotic disorder, not otherwise specified*. The individual's family history may suggest the diagnosis.

Organically Based Psychiatric Disorders: Delirium and Dementia In contrast to schizophrenia, delirium usually has an acute, rather than insidious, onset. It is a kind of psychosis characterized by impaired attention, disorganized thinking, altered and fluctuating levels of consciousness, perceptual disturbances, changes in sleep-wake cycle, agitation or slowing of movements and memory impairment (American Psychiatric Association, 1987). Delirium *always* has an organic cause—for example, encephalitis, diabetes, or intoxication—and is usually reversed by treating the individual for the medical disorder or overdose. It is extremely important to make the diagnosis of delirium in individuals with mental retardation and search for the underlying medical cause, and not simply to attribute symptoms to mental retardation or to some functional psychiatric illness.

Some individuals with mental retardation exhibit signs of dementia, although rarely during childhood. The aging process of the brain seems to be accentuated to some extent, making Alzheimer disease a more common occurrence. Symptoms of dementia include memory loss, impairment in abstract thinking and judgment, other disturbances of higher cortical function, and personality change (see Table 23.1). Individuals with dementia may also be combative and irritable. Dementia is most common in individuals with Down syndrome. It is hypothesized that the presence of an extra #21 chromosome leads to the excessive production of amyloid because the gene for amyloid is located on this chromosome. It is the laying down of amyloid plaques in the brain that is thought to be the cause of Alzheimer disease. No specific preventive measures or treatment for this disorder exist. Fortunately, less than 15% of individuals with Down syndrome develop this disorder, although a much larger percentage develop amyloid plaques in the brain (Wisniewski, Wisniewski, & Wen, 1985).

Attention Deficit Hyperactivity Disorder Attention deficit hyperactivity disorder (ADHD) has long been described in children with mental retardation but has only recently been systematically studied in this population. Symptoms include decreased attention span, impulsiveness, and hyperactivity beyond that expected for the child's mental age. Stimulant medications appear to be helpful in treating children who have mild mental retardation and ADHD (Handen et al., 1990; Payton et al., 1989). They appear to be less effective in children with more severe forms of mental retardation, although this varies with the individual. Behavior management techniques are both important and effective in these children. ADHD is discussed in detail in Chapter 21.

Somatoform and Anxiety Disorders Another group of psychiatric conditions are **somatoform** and anxiety disorders. They are among the most common psychiatric disorders found in children and adolescents. These include conversion reactions (i.e., psychosomatic conditions involving unusual neurological disabilities with psychological causes), panic attacks, phobias (i.e., irrational fears), generalized anxiety, separation anxiety disorder, obsessive-compulsive disorder, and posttraumatic stress disorder.

A number of these conditions (e.g., panic attacks, obsessive-compulsive disorder) result in part from a biological predisposition. Stressful experience and psychological factors precipitate and aggravate these disorders. In the case of obsessive-compulsive disorder, there are recurrent and persistent thoughts and ideas that cannot be suppressed. These are associated with repetitive behaviors performed in response to the obsession. The obsessions or compulsions cause distress, are time-consuming, and interfere with social interactions. In a child with severe mental retardation it may be difficult to distinguish compulsive behavior from self-stimulatory behavior (see discussion of Self-Stimulatory Behavior in this chapter).

Other anxiety disorders are environmental in origin. For example, posttraumatic stress disorder is precipitated by an unanticipated, psychologically devastating event, such as a physical attack and/or sexual abuse, a severe car accident, or the sudden loss of a close family member. Symptoms include reexperiencing the traumatic event or, alternatively, amnesia for the event, numbing of emotions, sleep disturbances, and other symptoms of depression and anxiety. This disorder is not uncommon in children with developmental disabilities, who are known to be at increased risk for physical abuse.

Psychoactive Substance Use Disorders Among people with mental retardation, substance abuse (involving alcohol and drugs) is a problem, as it is in the general population, particularly in adolescents with mild mental retardation. These children do not have any inborn reason to be more susceptible to substance abuse, but their immature judgment, impulsiveness, and desire for social acceptance may lead them to experiment with drugs or alcohol. However, there is no evidence that the prior use of psychoactive drugs, such as stimulant medications for ADHD, increases the risk of later substance abuse. The best treatment is prevention through education, starting in elementary school.

Genetic Syndromes Associated with
Mental Retardation and Abnormal Behaviors

Certain abnormal behavior patterns may occur as symptoms of genetic syndromes that also cause developmental disabilities. Previously discussed is the relationship of Down syndrome to dementia. Other inherited mental retardation syndromes associated with abnormal behavior patterns include fragile X syndrome, Rett syndrome, Prader-Willi syndrome, and Lesch-Nyhan syndrome. These syndromes are all rare, and the majority of children with mental retardation and psychiatric or behavior disorders do not have specific genetic disorders. However, if one of these disorders is suspected, there are specific medical tests that can help to diagnose them and permit genetic counseling to the family.

Fragile X Syndrome Although there is wide variation in the symptoms demonstrated by persons with fragile X syndrome (see Chapter 16), there have been reports of characteristic behaviors. These children may exhibit poor eye contact with other people, deficits in communication and speech (e.g., repeating things over and over, echoing other people's words), and self-stimulating and stereotyped body movements, such as rocking and hand flapping (Bregman, 1988). These behaviors represent a subset of the abnormalities seen in autism (Reiss & Freund, 1990).

Rett Syndrome Rett syndrome, an X-linked, dominant progressive neurological disorder, occurs in girls. These children tend to develop normally during the first year of life but then begin losing mental capacity and motor skills. There is an arrest in head growth, and the onset of spasticity and seizures. Like children with fragile X syndrome, these children display certain autistic features. The most prominent behavior is a loss of purposeful hand movements and the onset of stereotypical hand wringing and hand flapping, often accompanied by hyperventilation (Hagberg, Aicardi, Dias, et al., 1983; Naidu, Murphy, & Moser, 1986). There is a gradual worsening of neurological status, such that by later childhood they are usually nonambulatory and nonverbal.

Prader-Willi Syndrome A third example is the Prader-Willi syndrome, a disorder often associated with a defect in chromosome pair #15, resulting in a missing band, a translocation, or another anomaly (Butler, 1992). Usual physical features include decreased muscle tone, short stature, obesity, moderate mental retardation, underdeveloped gonads, and a particular facial appearance with almond-shaped, upslanting eyes, and a narrow forehead. Behavioral symptoms relate to the striking obesity seen in these children. They will demand, steal, and even forage for food, and these feeding behaviors are often accompanied by impulsiveness, obstinacy, and disinhibition (Bray, Dahms, Swerdloff, et al., 1983). Research indicates that the insatiable overeating results from a lack of a feeling of satiation derived from an abnormality in the hypothalamic region of the brain. Their overeating has proved very resistant both to diet and behavior modification.

Lesch-Nyhan Syndrome Lesch-Nyhan syndrome is inherited through the X chromosome and is manifested in boys. Its biological basis is a disturbance in the metabolism of purines, the building blocks of DNA. In addition to having mental retardation and a progressive neurological disorder, boys with Lesch-Nyhan syndrome compulsively bite their lips and fingers. Studies of brain chemistry have found abnormalities in the neurotransmitters dopamine and serotonin, but treatment strategies based on these findings have not achieved much success (Nyhan, Johnson, Kaufman, & Jones, 1980).

Severe Abnormal Behaviors: Self-Injury and Pica

Children other than those with Lesch-Nyhan syndrome may also demonstrate repetitive self-injury. This behavior occurs most commonly in individuals with severe-to-profound mental retardation and may be accompanied by additional repetitive, stereotyped behaviors, such as hand waving and body rocking. When these behaviors interfere with adaptive activities or result in significant injury to the individual, a diagnosis of *stereotypy-habit disorder* is made. Some children with this disorder also demonstrate aggressive behavior. Although serious aggression and self-injury occur in fewer than 5% of people with mental retardation, these behaviors are important because they cause enormous distress to these individuals and their caregivers, can result in severe bodily injury, and may lead to the separation of the individual from the family or from other social contacts (Sulkes & Davidson, 1989).

Evidence from the psychological literature indicates that the expression of self-injurious behavior (SIB) is influenced by prior and consequent environmental events (National Institutes of Health, 1989). SIB may also be a manifestation of psychiatric disorders, such as autism, depression, mania, schizophrenia, and other psychoses; or medical disorders, such as epilepsy. Alternately, SIB may be a nonspecific expression of distress or pain in a nonverbal person. Individuals who engage in SIB may bang their heads, bite themselves, pick their skin, hit themselves with their hands, or scratch at their eyes. They may do this once or twice a day in association with tantrums or up to several hundred times an hour. Tissue destruction, infection, internal injury, loss of vision, and even death may result.

The causes of SIB vary among individuals and include both biological and environmental factors. SIB may begin as a symptom of a medical or psychiatric disorder and then persist even when that disorder has resolved. While the brain mechanisms underlying SIB are unknown, several neurotransmitters are thought to be involved. These include dopamine, which mediates certain reinforcement systems in the brain; serotonin, depletion of which is sometimes associated with violent behavior; and gamma-aminobutyric acid (GABA), an inhibitory neurotransmitter. Recent theories have also suggested that opioids, the brain's natural painkillers, may be secreted excessively during SIB (Herman, Hammock, Arthur-Smith, et al., 1987). It is hypothesized that opioid production may be higher to begin with in people with SIB, or that painful self-injury may stimulate opioid production and thus reinforce the behavior. Treatment has included the use of medication acting on the neurotransmitter systems and behavior management techniques.

Pica, the craving and ingesting of nonfood items, is a normal behavior in toddlers. However, it should fade after 2 years of age. Both psychiatric disorders and nutritional deficiencies may lead to pica. It may also persist or develop later in childhood in a small number of individuals with severe and profound mental retardation (Sachdev & McNiff, 1989). This behavior may necessitate medical procedures and operations to locate and remove objects from the gastrointestinal system. Furthermore, poisoning with lead or other substances, infection with parasites, and internal injuries may result. Behavior management techniques have been found to be effective in decreasing this behavior.

MAKING A DIAGNOSIS

The goals of assessment are to clarify a diagnosis and describe specific problems so that a treatment plan addressing them can be developed. The context of the problems—including parents' or caregivers' behavior and attitudes, the child's strengths and level of adaptive functioning, and the availability of educational, social, and vocational resources—must be clearly defined. Psychiatric diagnosis is important because detection of a specific medical or psychiatric disorder may explain a range of problem behaviors and point the way to particular treatments. Assessment of a child or adolescent with emotional or behavior problems should always be conducted by a mental health professional (i.e., psychiatrist, psychologist, social worker) who is familiar with the range of mental disorders, modern diagnostic categories, and especially children and adolescents with mental retardation.

Comprehensive diagnostic assessment includes the following: 1) an interview with the parents or caregivers covering developmental, medical, and educational history, a thorough description of behavior problems, and an assessment of parents' feelings and attitudes; 2) an interview with the child; 3) a review of prior medical and psychological assessments; and 4) a neurodevelopmental examination. Assessment may also include the use of structured interviews and rating scales, direct observation of the child's behavior in the home or school, and quantitative measurement of observed behaviors, as well as previous and consequent events.

Experienced mental health professionals have found that the same interviewing techniques used with other persons can be utilized, with minimal modification, in persons with mild-to-moderate mental retardation (Szymanksi, 1977, 1985). Modifications include providing more overt support and reinforcement so that the child does not regard the interview as another test likely to be failed, being more directive without asking leading questions, and taking time to develop rapport. As in other child psychiatric assessments, play behavior, and nonverbal communication are important sources of data.

With children who are limited in their ability to communicate verbally, data normally gained from interviews must be derived from direct observations by the mental health professional, parents, or teachers. A number of assessment approaches based on identifying and quantifying mood states, abnormal behaviors, and sleep patterns have been proposed (Sovner & Lowry, 1990). Only a handful of rating scales have been developed and normed specifically for individuals with mental retardation (Aman & Singh, 1988; Matson & Frame, 1985).

APPROACHES TO INTERVENTION

The foundation for treating a child or adolescent with mental retardation and a psychiatric disorder is a comprehensive plan that addresses rehabilitation and education, the child's emotional needs, family support, the specific psychiatric diagnosis, and behavior problems. This kind of multilevel approach is essential because a person's vulnerability to psychiatric disturbances may derive from skill deficits, inappropriate school placement, lack of stimulation in the environment, excessive parental expectations, and other conditions. These stressors must be effectively relieved if directed therapies are to be effective.

Education

The educational setting can help or hinder therapy. If the child is in a small class with the availability of one-to-one supervision, the teacher can record behaviors, incorporate behavior therapy, and provide emotional support. The guidance counselor may also be able to provide supportive therapy. The curriculum can be modified to decrease stress and give the student a positive experience. Yet, if the class is large and the teacher is unaware of the child's emotional problems, school failure may result in adverse consequences on behavior and emotions. Thus, it is essential that the school be part of the therapy program and that there be good communication among teacher, parents, and therapists.

Rehabilitation

Rehabilitative therapy programs can also have a positive impact on children with disabilities who have emotional disturbances. These may include speech-language therapy, physical therapy, and occupational therapy. There is some evidence that language deficits are a significant factor in the development of certain behavior problems. Some aggressive and self-injurious behaviors have been linked to the inability to communicate needs. When such children have been taught signing or provided augmentative communication aids, their behavior problems have lessened (Poulton & Algozzine, 1980). Thus, speech-language therapy may be an important part of the therapy program. Similarly, pain from contractures, an inability to ambulate, or difficulty reaching for desired objects may lead to behavior and mood alterations in the child with a physical disability. Physical and occupational therapy may result in an improvement in motor function with associated improvement in behavior and mood.

Behavior Management

Perhaps the most widely researched type of therapeutic intervention in children and adolescents with mental retardation is behavior therapy. This approach comprises many different types of treatment that complement and enhance education and rehabilitation. The foundation of behavior treatment is data-based assessment of individual behaviors as they occur in a person's natural social environment, with attention to prior conditions and subsequent events. A fundamental assumption in this approach is that the behavior is maintained by environmental variables, which can include antecedents (i.e., specific stimuli and events in the setting that precede or accompany the behavior) and consequences (i.e., responses that are contingent upon the behavior and may serve to reinforce it). A type of assessment called *functional analysis* attempts quantitatively to identify the variables that maintain the behavior, then manipulate these variables experimentally to demonstrate that they, in fact, control the behavior. Interventions can then be based on the functional analysis.

Behavioral interventions have been used to treat problematic behaviors, such as self-injury, as well as to teach self-help, vocational, leisure, social, and community survival and communication skills. After a functional analysis has been completed, the most common behavioral approaches utilize positive reinforcement of desired behaviors or withdrawal of reinforcement for undesired behaviors.

Examples of positive reinforcement approaches include differential reinforcement of other behavior (DRO) and differential reinforcement of incompatible behavior (DRI). In DRO, a reward (reinforcement) is offered when a period of time has elapsed in which a behavior other than the undesired behavior occurs. Reinforcement causes the alternative behavior to increase in frequency and to replace the undesired behavior. DRI involves selective reinforcement of a behavior that is incompatible with the undesired behavior. A DRO approach to treating a child who head slaps might involve offering a reward whenever the child has played (the desired other behavior) for a set amount of time without slapping. A DRI approach with the same child might involve systematically rewarding the child for drawing, a behavior that would occupy the hands and thus be incompatible with slapping.

In situations where the functional analysis indicates that a problem behavior is followed naturally by specific reinforcers, the systematic removal of these reinforcers can lead to a reduction of the undesired behavior—a process called *extinction*. Extinction procedures are sometimes combined with DRI and DRO.

Punishments also may have a place in behavioral intervention. They can be an effective treatment as long as they are humanely and consistently applied. Punishment is seldom used alone; it is usually combined with positive reinforcement procedures. Types of punishment may include overcorrection (in which, for example, the destructive effects of an individual's aggression are cleaned up and desirable behaviors are repeatedly practiced immediately following an aggressive act), time-out (i.e., removal of the individual from sources of reinforcement), response cost (i.e., loss of an earned reward, such as tokens or points), and more aversive responses, such as spraying with water mist.

The use of aversive punishments is highly controversial and presents many ethical dilemmas (National Institutes of Health, 1989). Some institutions do not permit the use of aversive punishments and those that do use them generally employ community-based ethics committees to supervise their use.

There is extensive literature supporting the effectiveness of behavioral approaches in psychiatric disorders (National Institutes of Health, 1989). When used in a context of comprehensive assessment, medical and psychiatric diagnosis, and programmatic intervention, behavior management is among the most powerful therapeutic approaches. However, like psychotherapy and pharmacotherapy, it should be used only by licensed professionals who have been specifically trained in this methodology. Behavior management techniques must also be used consistently to be effective. Therefore, the entire family and the school must "buy into" the program for it to be effective. This is often difficult and may limit the value of this approach.

Psychotherapy

There is ample evidence that **psychotherapy**—individual, group, and family—can benefit children and adolescents with mental retardation (Bregman, 1988; Sigman, 1985; Szymanski & Doherty, 1989). Psychotherapy must be adapted to the child's mental age and communication abilities. Regrettably, individuals with mental retardation are seriously underserved with these traditional therapies, which can provide a supportive relationship, restore self-esteem, promote social skills, and enhance the capacity to recognize and master emotional conflicts and solve problems.

Pharmacotherapy

Medication is indicated when a psychiatric condition known to benefit from specific drugs has been diagnosed. Most guidelines for using psychoactive medicines come from studies performed in adults without mental retardation. Since the 1970s, pharmacotherapy has become an established mode of treatment for psychiatric disorders in children and adolescents. Studies of children and adolescents without mental retardation have demonstrated the clinical usefulness of medicines, such as stimulants (e.g., methylphenidate [Ritalin]) for the treatment of ADHD, lithium for bipolar disorder, clomipramine (Anafranil) for obsessive-compulsive disorder, and antipsychotics (e.g., thioridazine [Mellaril]) for schizophrenia (Campbell & Spencer, 1988). The helpfulness of antidepressant medication (e.g., fluoxetine [Prozac], nortriptyline [Pamelor]) in major depressive disorder has not yet been documented in well-designed, controlled research studies with adolescents, but is suggested by clinical experience (Ambrosini, 1987).

Well-controlled studies of the pharmacological treatment of psychiatric disorders among individuals with mental retardation are relatively few. Although these medications have not been extensively tested, there is nothing to suggest that an individual with mental retardation would respond differently to standard treatments. People with mental retardation experience the same psychiatric disorders as other people and can be expected to respond to the same medicines.

It is, furthermore, important to recognize that this rationale for using medication has nothing to do with so-called "chemical restraint" or the administration of medicine to control behavior. Appropriate use of pharmacotherapy assumes that a comprehensive medical and psychiatric evaluation has been completed, a psychiatric diagnosis has been made, and that a medication has been selected because of its known effects in relieving target symptoms associated with that diagnosis. As indicated previously, this use of medicine should be only one part of a comprehensive treatment plan including education, rehabilitation, family counseling, psychotherapy, and behavior therapy.

With regard to behaviors such as self-injury, pica, and certain forms of high-frequency or destructive aggression in persons with severe and profound mental retardation, the use of pharmacotherapy has been controversial. The use of medications to control these behaviors, particularly in institutional settings, has been criticized as excessive (National Institutes of Health, 1989). With persons who manifest these behaviors, the ideal clinical approach should be to use drugs only if they are treating symptoms of a specific psychiatric diagnosis (e.g., prescribe lithium for a person with symptoms of mania who may be hitting other people during the manic state).

Yet, it may be very difficult to make accurate diagnoses for nonverbal persons with severe and profound mental retardation. It is therefore not uncommon for physicians to prescribe medication with the aim of reducing the frequency of dangerous behaviors, such as self-injury. Among the medications that have been used with self-injury are antipsychotics (also called *major tranquilizers* or *neuroleptics*), lithium, and opiate antagonists. The antipsychotic medications appear to exert their effects by reducing activity level and stereotyped behaviors (Farber, 1987). However, they have many side effects, including movement abnormalities that can appear with long-term use. Lithium has been shown to have antiaggressive properties (Campbell & Spencer, 1988). The use of opiate antagonists (e.g., naloxone [Narcan], naltrexone [Trexan]) derives from theories of excessive opioid production by the brain in individuals who engage in self-injurious behavior (Bernstein, Hughes, Mitchell, & Thompson, 1987; Herman et al., 1987). Studies of their use have yielded equivocal results. Medications commonly used in the treatment of psychiatric and behavior disorders are shown in Table 23.2.

MARY: AN ADOLESCENT WITH MENTAL RETARDATION AND DEPRESSION

Mary was referred for psychiatric evaluation at age 16 primarily because of episodic wandering from her special education classroom at school. Mary had first been determined to have learning disabilities when she was 5 years old because she could not keep up with her classmates. She was tested by a psychologist, found to have mild mental retardation, and placed in a special education program in her local public school. She did well in this setting and worked very hard in school, but always worried that her performance was not good enough. She was also very emotionally dependent on her mother and did not like to be separated from her. These anxieties became more evident at age 8, following the separation of her parents.

At age 14, Mary entered high school. She continued in special education classes, but these were now departmentalized. Mary had to relate to several teachers and move from class to class. She had difficulty with this adjustment and her separation anxiety became severe. She worried about her mother when she was at school and shadowed her at home. After school holidays and brief illnesses, she did not want to return to school. Mary and her mother then began psychotherapy, which focused on developing ways for Mary to cope with her anxiety and supporting her mother's effort to put some appropriate distance between them. Therapy was helpful, but at age 15 Mary began to wander from the classroom and appear confused.

Mary was referred to a neurologist to make sure that these wandering episodes were not the result of seizures. The neurologist found no evidence of seizures, but detected a mass in Mary's belly. This mass, an ovarian cyst, was surgically removed and Mary returned to school. Her mood at school was now noted to be different. She seemed more withdrawn; the wandering behavior returned and became more frequent; there were occasional angry outbursts in the classroom and at home. She began compulsively to collect paper and stuff it behind her dresser. She experienced difficulty falling asleep, had diminished energy, and appeared apathetic.

Mary was referred to a psychiatrist. In an interview, she attributed leaving the classroom to an intolerable "frustrated" feeling and spoke of feeling angry and crying all the time. She expressed shame over her temper outbursts. She appeared depressed and anxious, moved slowly and stiffly. There were long pauses before she answered questions and she fingered her belly as she spoke.

The psychiatrist diagnosed Mary as having a major depression. It was recommended that she continue in psychotherapy and, in addition, she was started on an antidepressant medicine. Her school participation, compulsive behaviors, sleep, and mood improved, but 8 months later, without any changes in her life at home or school, she had another episode of depressed mood with compulsive behaviors and

Table 23.2. Medications used to treat psychiatric and behavior disorders in children with mental retardation

Generic name	Trade name	Drug category/ common uses	Preparations[a]	Side effects
Alprazolam	Xanax	Antianxiety	T	Depression, drowsiness, confusion
Chlorpromazine	Thorazine	Antipsychotic/ psychosis, mania, last resource for severe aggression and self-injury	T, C, L, injection	Dry mouth, constipation, weight gain, drowsiness, decreased attention, movement disorder, low blood pressure, lower seizure threshold, liver toxicity
Clomipramine	Anafranil	Anti-obsessive-compulsive disorder	C	Nausea, constipation, anorexia, dizziness, sleepiness; overdose can be fatal
Fluoxetine	Prozac	Antidepressant	C	Skin rash, insomnia, weight loss, nausea, seizures, irritability
Haloperidol	Haldol	Antipsychotic/ psychosis tic disorders	T, L	Same as chlorpromazine, but with less sedation and less effect on blood pressure; restlessness; muscle tightness
Imipramine	Tofranil	Antidepressant/ bedwetting, hyperactivity, depression	T, C	Drowsiness, rapid heart rate, dry mouth, skin rash; overdose can be fatal
Lithium carbonate	Eskalith Lithobid	Antimania/behavior disorders, mania, prevention of relapses in bipolar disorder	T, C	Hand tremor, excessive thirst and urination, nausea, muscular weakness, diarrhea; overdose can be fatal

(continued)

Table 23.2. (continued)

Generic name	Trade name	Drug category/ common uses	Preparations[a]	Side effects
Methylpheni- date	Ritalin	Stimulant/ hyperactivity and attention deficits	C, T, L	Anorexia, upset stomach, irritability, increased heart rate, insomnia
Naltrexone	Trexan	Narcotic antagonist/ substance abuse, self-injurious behavior	T	Low blood pres- sure, nausea
Nortriptyline	Pamelor	Antidepressant, depression	C, L	Same as imi- pramine
Propranolol	Inderal	Beta blocker/rage reactions, aggres- sion, self-injury	T, C	Dizziness, low blood pressure, fatigue, wheezing
Thioridazine	Mellaril	Antipsychotic	T, L	Same as chlor- promazine, but with less effect on seizures

Source: Physicians' Desk Reference (1992).
[a]T = tablet; C = capsule; L = liquid/suspension.

began to hallucinate. She was admitted for a brief psychiatric hospitalization. She recovered when treated with both antidepressant and antipsychotic medicine and then switched from public school to a special school for students with mental retardation and emotional problems. Mary stayed on antidepressant treatment for a year, contin- ued in therapy, and began to achieve better academically and make friends in her new school. She became less focused on her mother and more interested in "teenage" activities, such as school dances and cheerleading. She graduated, at age 21, winning academic awards.

Unfortunately, when Mary completed high school, she had to wait 18 months for a place in a vocational training program. She participated in activities, such as the Special Olympics, but found herself home and idle during most days. She lost some of the feelings of self-confidence and independence that she had gained in high school. About 4 months into this waiting period, Mary again experienced a major depression. Once again, she responded to antidepressant and antipsychotic medica- tion. When she recovered, she was placed on lithium, with careful supervision for side effects, to try to prevent recurrent depression. She entered vocational training at age 22, on lithium and continuing in psychotherapy, working on becoming a more self-sufficient adult.

SUMMARY

This chapter has reviewed a range of disorders that may bring children or adolescents with mental retardation to the attention of mental health professionals. The types of emotional disturbances are similar, for the most part, to those found in individuals without mental retardation. The exceptions are self-injury and pica, which are seen most often in individuals with severe-to-profound mental retardation. Early assessment and treatment of a child with mental retardation who is exhibiting an emotional disorder is essential to permit the individual to reach his or her potential. Treatment should be multidisciplinary and include education, rehabilitation, counseling, behavior management, and possibly medication.

REFERENCES

Aman, M.G., & Singh, N.N. (1988). Patterns of drug use, methodological considerations, measurement techniques and future trends. In M.G. Aman & N.N. Singh (Eds.), *Psychopharmacology of the developmental disabilities* (pp. 1–28). New York: Springer-Verlag.

Ambrosini, P.J. (1987). Pharmacology in child and adolescent major depressive disorder. In H.Y. Meltzer (Ed.), *Psychopharmacology: The third generation of progress* (pp. 1274–1254). New York: Raven Press.

American Psychiatric Association. (1987). *Diagnostic and statistical manual of mental disorders (DSM-III-R)*. Washington, DC: Author.

Bernstein, G.A., Hughes, J.R., Mitchell, J.E., & Thompson, T. (1987). Effects of narcotic antagonists on self-injurious behavior: A single case study. *Journal of The American Academy of Child and Adolescent Psychiatry, 26*, 886–889.

Bray, G.A., Dahms, W.T., Swerdloff, R.S., et al. (1983). The Prader-Willi syndrome: A study of 40 patients and a review of the literature. *Medicine, 62*, 59–80.

Bregman, J.D. (1988). Treatment approaches for the mentally retarded. In R. Michels, A.M. Cooper, S.B., Guze, et al. (Eds.), *Psychiatry* (pp. 1–11). Philadelphia: J.B. Lippincott.

Bregman, J.D. (1991). Current developments in the understanding of mental retardation. Part II: Psychopathology. *Journal of the American Academy of Child and Adolescent Psychiatry, 30*, 861–872.

Butler, M. (1992, March). A genetic and molecular perspective on Prader-Willi syndrome. In A. Tfadt (Chair), *Biopsychosocial perspectives on psychopathology in persons with Prader-Willi syndrome*. Symposium conducted at the meeting of the Gatlinburg Conference on Research and Theory in Mental Retardation and Developmental Disabilities, Gatlinburg.

Campbell, M., & Spencer, E.K. (1988). Psychopharmacology in child and adolescent psychiatry: A review of the past five years. *Journal of The American Academy of Child and Adolescent Psychiatry, 27*, 269–279.

Carlson, G. (1979). Affective psychoses in mental retardates. *Psychiatric Clinics of North America, 2*, 499–510.

Corbett, J.A. (1985). Mental retardation: Psychiatric aspects. In M. Rutter & L. Hersov (Eds.), *Child and adolescent psychiatry: Modern approaches* (2nd ed.) (pp. 661–678). Oxford: Blackwell Scientific Publications.

Farber, J.M. (1987). Psychopharmacology of self-injurious behavior in the mentally retarded. *Journal of The American Academy of Child and Adolescent Psychiatry, 26*, 296–302.

Hagberg, B., Aicardi, J., Dias, K., et al. (1983). A progressive syndrome of autism, dementia, ataxia and loss of purposeful hand use in girls: Rett's syndrome: Report of 35 cases. *Annals of Neurology, 14*, 471–479.

Handen, B.L., Breaux, A.M., Gosling, A., et al. (1990). Efficacy of methylphenidate among mentally retarded children with attention deficit hyperactivity disorder. *Pediatrics, 86*, 922–930.

Herman, B.H., Hammock, M.K., Arthur-Smith, A., et al. (1987). Naltrexone decreases self-injurious behavior. *Annals of Neurology, 22*, 550–552.

Kashani, J.H., Carlson, G.A., Beck, N.C., et al. (1987). Depression, depressive symptoms, and depressed mood among a community sample of adolescents. *American Journal of Psychiatry, 144*, 931–934.

Kashani, J.H., McGee, R.O., Clarkson, S.E., et al. (1983). Depression in a sample of 9-year-old children. Prevalence and associated characteristics. *Archives of General Psychiatry, 40*, 1217–1223.

Matson, J.L., & Frame, C.L. (1985). *Psychopathology among mentally retarded children and adolescents.* Beverly Hills: Sage Publications.

McCracken, J.T., & Diamond, R.P. (1988). Bipolar disorder in mentally retarded adolescents. *Journal of the American Academy of Child and Adolescent Psychiatry, 27*, 494–499.

Menolascino, F.J., Lazer, J., & Stark, J.A. (1989). Diagnosis and management of depression and suicidal behavior in persons with severe mental retardation. *Journal of the Multihandicapped Person, 2*, 89–103.

Menolascino, F.J., Levitas, A., & Greiner, C. (1986). The nature and types of mental illness in the mentally retarded. *Psychopharmacology Bulletin, 22*, 1060–1071.

Menolascino, F.J., Ruedrich, S.L., Golden, C.J., et al. (1985). Diagnosis and pharmacotherapy of schizophrenia in the retarded. *Psychopharmacology Bulletin, 21*, 316–322.

Naidu, S., Murphy, M., Moser, H.W., et al. (1986). Rett syndrome—Natural history in 70 cases. *American Journal of Medical Genetics, 1*(Suppl.), 61–76.

National Institutes of Health. (1989). Treatment of destructive behaviors in persons with developmental disabilities. *NIH Consensus Development Conference Statement, 7*(9), 1–14.

Nyhan, W.L., Johnson, H.G., Kaufman, I.A., & Jones, K.L. (1980). Serotonergic approaches to the modification of behavior in Lesch-Nyhan syndrome. *Applied Research in Mental Retardation, 1*, 25–40.

Parsons, J.A., May, J.G., & Menolascino, F.J. (1984). The nature and incidence of mental illness in mentally retarded individuals. In F.J. Menolascino & J.A. Stark (Eds.), *Handbook of mental illness in the mentally retarded* (pp. 3–43). New York: Plenum.

Payton, J.B., Burkhart, J.E., Hersen, M., et al. (1989). Treatment of ADDH in mentally retarded children: A preliminary study. *Journal of the American Academy of Child and Adolescent Psychiatry, 28*, 761–767.

Philips, I., & Williams, N. (1975). Psychopathology and mental retardation: A study of 100 mentally retarded children: I. Psychopathology. *American Journal of Psychiatry, 132*, 1265–1271.

Philips, I., & Williams, N. (1977). Psychopathology and mental retardation: A statistical study of 100 mentally retarded children treated at a psychiatric clinic: II. Hyperactivity. *American Journal of Psychiatry, 134*, 418–419.

Poulton, K.T., & Algozzine, B. (1980). Manual communication and mental retardation: A review of research and implications. *American Journal of Mental Deficiency, 85*, 145–152.

Reiss, A.L., & Freund, L. (1990). Fragile X syndrome, DSM-III-R, and autism. *Journal of the American Academy of Child and Adolescent Psychiatry, 29*, 885–891.

Russell, A.T. (1985). The mentally retarded, emotionally disturbed child and adolescent. In M. Sigman (Ed.), *Children with emotional disorders and developmental disabilities: Assessment and treatment* (pp. 111–136). New York: Grune & Stratton.

Rutter, M. (1981). Psychological sequelae of brain damage in children. *American Journal of Psychiatry, 138*, 1533–1544.

Rutter, M., Graham, P., & Yule, W. (1970). *A neuropsychiatric study in childhood.* Philadelphia: J.B. Lippincott.

Rutter, M., Tizard, J., & Whitmore, K. (1970). *Education, health and behavior.* London: Longman-Krieger.

Sachdev, A., & McNiff, C. (1989). Pica. In I.L. Rubin & A.C. Crocker (Eds.), *Developmental disabilities: Delivery of medical care for children and adults* (pp. 361–366). Philadelphia: Lea & Febiger.

Sigman, M. (1985). Individual and group psychotherapy with mentally retarded adolescents. In M. Sigman (Ed.), *Children with emotional disorders and developmental disabilities* (pp. 259–276). New York: Grune & Stratton.

Sovner, R., & Hurley, A. (1983). Do the mentally retarded suffer from affective illness? *Archives of General Psychiatry, 40,* 61–67.

Sovner, R., & Lowry, M.A. (1990). A behavioral methodology for diagnosing affective disorders in individuals with mental retardation. *The Habilitative Mental Healthcare Newsletter, 9,* 55–61.

Steingard, R., & Biederman, J. (1987). Lithium responsive manic-like symptoms in two individuals with autism and mental retardation. *Journal of the American Academy of Child and Adolescent Psychiatry, 26,* 932–935.

Sulkes, S.B., & Davidson, P.W. (1989). Self-injurious behavior. In I.L. Rubin & A.C. Crocker (Eds.), *Developmental disabilities: Delivery of medical care for children and adults* (pp. 354–361). Philadelphia: Lea & Febiger.

Szymanski, L.S. (1977). Psychiatric diagnostic evaluation of mentally retarded individuals. *Journal of the American Academy of Child Psychiatry, 16,* 67–87.

Szymanski, L.S. (1985). Diagnosis of mental disorders in mentally retarded persons. In M. Sigman (Ed.), *Children with emotional disorders and developmental disabilities: Assessment and treatment* (pp. 249–258). New York: Grune & Stratton.

Szymanski, L.S., & Doherty, M.B. (1989). Mildly and moderately retarded persons. In I.L. Rubin & A.C. Crocker (Eds.), *Developmental disabilities: Delivery of medical care for children and adults* (pp. 334–341). Philadelphia: Lea & Febiger

Vitiello, B., Spreat, S., & Behar, D. (1989). Obsessive compulsive disorder in mentally retarded patients. *Journal of Nervous and Mental Disease, 177,* 232–236.

Wisniewski, K.E., Wisniewski, H.M., & Wen, G.Y. (1985). Occurrence of neuropathological changes and dementia of Alzheimer's disease in Down's syndrome. *Annals of Neurology, 17,* 278–282.

Zipf, W.B., & Bernstein, G.G. (1987). Characteristics of abnormal food-intake patterns in children with Prader-Willi syndrome and study of effects of naloxone. *American Journal of Clinical Nutrition, 46,* 277–281.

Chapter 24

Cerebral Palsy

with Lisa A. Kurtz

Upon completion of this chapter, the reader will:
—be aware of some early clues to the diagnosis of cerebral palsy
—know the various types of cerebral palsy and their characteristics
—understand how cerebral palsy is diagnosed
—understand the role of primitive reflexes and automatic movement reactions in motor function
—be able to identify various treatment and management approaches to cerebral palsy, including occupational and physical therapy, medication, and surgery
—understand the prognoses for the different forms of cerebral palsy

---

Cerebral palsy refers to a disorder of movement and posture that is due to a non-progressive abnormality of the immature brain. The brain damage that causes cerebral palsy also may produce a number of other disabilities, including mental retardation, seizures, visual and auditory deficits, and behavior problems. A child who has severe brain injury at birth may show abnormal movements and posture during his or her first months of life. A previously healthy child may experience brain injury in a car accident and show symptoms of this disorder during recovery from a coma. Both of these children have cerebral palsy, although the causes are quite different. In both cases, the damage occurred before the child's brain had fully developed (the age of brain maturation is usually designated as being 16 years of age). Also, the damage was not ongoing, as would be the case with a brain tumor or a progressive neurological disorder. Thus, the basic distinctions of cerebral palsy are the age of onset and the lack of progression.

This chapter presents an outline of the causes, types, and treatment of cerebral palsy. Also discussed are other developmental disabilities commonly associated with cerebral palsy and the prognosis for children with this disorder.

Lisa A. Kurtz, M.Ed., OTR/L, is Director of Occupational Therapy at Children's Seashore House in Philadelphia.

CAUSES OF CEREBRAL PALSY

Many diseases may affect the developing brain and lead to cerebral palsy (Naeye, Peters, Bartholomew, & Landis, 1989; Stanley & Alberman, 1984). Some of these are discussed in the earlier chapters on fetal development and the birth process (Chapters 4 and 5). Conditions that lead to the motor impairments characteristic of cerebral palsy tend to be grouped together not because they are presumed to share a common cause, but because they share problems requiring similar clinical management (Paneth, 1986).

The most common causes of cerebral palsy are listed in Table 24.1. Until the 1980s, it was thought that most cases of cerebral palsy resulted from birth trauma. However, it is now clear that only a small fraction of cases actually results from this cause (Nelson & Ellenberg, 1986). Problems during intrauterine development account for the majority of known causes of cerebral palsy (Scher, Belfar, Martin, et al, 1991). Although children with cerebral palsy are more likely to have had difficult deliveries, this appears to be the result of preexisting brain damage rather than the cause of it.

Events during the first trimester of pregnancy that may cause cerebral palsy include exposure to radiation, exposure to teratogenic drugs, intrauterine infections, developmental brain abnormalities, and chromosomal abnormalities (see Chapter 4). In later pregnancy, abruptio placenta and other abnormalities in the fetal–placental unit place the child at risk. Complications during labor and delivery also are risk

Table 24.1.   Causes of cerebral palsy

	Causes	Percentage of cases
Prenatal		44
1st trimester:	Teratogens Genetic syndromes Chromosomal abnormalities Brain malformations	
2nd–3rd trimester:	Intrauterine infections Problems in fetal/placental functioning	
Labor and delivery	Preeclampsia Complications of labor and delivery	19
Perinatal:	Sepsis/central nervous system infection Asphyxia Prematurity	8
Childhood:	Meningitis Traumatic brain injury Toxins	5
Not obvious		24

Adapted from Hagberg and Hagberg (1984).

factors, although they have been overstated. The remaining cases result from neonatal illness or early childhood disorders, such as meningitis, head trauma, and poisonings. In some cases the cause is multifactional—for example, the low birth weight infant is both more likely to experience asphyxia during labor and is more vulnerable to its effects (Paneth, 1986; Pidcock, Graziani, Stanley, et al., 1990). While diagnostic approaches are improving, in over 40% of persons with cerebral palsy, a specific cause cannot be determined (Russman & Gage, 1989).

TYPES OF CEREBRAL PALSY

Many classification systems of cerebral palsy exist. For the purposes of this book, a simplified three-group model is used: *pyramidal, extrapyramidal,* and *mixed type.* The overall incidence of these three groups ranges from 0.6 to 2.4 per 1,000, depending on the study, and varies little across industrialized countries (Paneth & Kiely, 1984). The incidence appears to have held fairly steady between 1970 and 1990. However, a significant upward trend in the prevalence among low birth weight infants suggests that advances in obstetric and neonatal care may be permitting the survival of a greater number of very small infants who have an increased risk of neurological deficits (Hagberg, Hagberg, & Zetterstrom, 1989; Pharoah, Cooke, Rosenbloom,

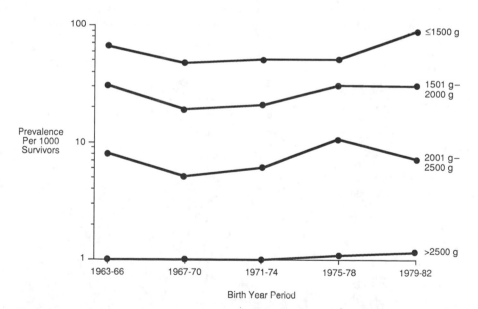

Figure 24.1.   Incidence of cerebral palsy. The occurrence of cerebral palsy is much more common in premature infants (less than 2,500 grams birth weight) than in full-term infants (7–70/1,000 versus 1/1,000). Very small premature infants (less than 1,500 grams) have a higher prevalence (70/1,000) than larger prematures (7–20/1,000). Interestingly, the overall prevalence of cerebral palsy has not decreased significantly despite improved neonatal intensive care (Hagberg, Hagberg, & Zetterstrom, 1989).

et al., 1987) (Figure 24.1). Cerebral palsy in these infants usually presents as spastic diplegia, accounting for the increase in the relative incidence of spastic cerebral palsy. This is contrasted with the marked decrease in the incidence of athetoid cerebral palsy, which had been associated with the now rare high bilirubin condition, kernicterus.

Pyramidal (Spastic) Cerebral Palsy

In children with pyramidal cerebral palsy, there is damage to the motor cortex or to the pyramidal tract of the brain. As noted in Chapter 14, the motor strip of the frontal lobe passes its signals for voluntary movement to the spinal cord via the pyramidal tract. Damage to any part of this pathway leads to spasticity. In spasticity, muscle tone is increased with a characteristic clasped-knife quality. When the arm or leg is moved, the initial resistance is strong, but it gives way abruptly, as would a closing pocket knife blade. These changes in muscle tone interfere with normal movement.

Depending on where the damage occurs, different parts of the body are affected. In the premature infant, a fragile area exists in the part of the pyramidal tract that passes near the lateral ventricles (see Chapter 14). The blood vessels that feed this region hemorrhage easily (Pidcock et al., 1990). Because this area includes those fibers that primarily control movement of the legs, the legs are affected more than the arms, a condition termed *spastic diplegia* (Figure 24.2).

Hemiplegia is a second type of spastic cerebral palsy and causes one-sided abnormalities (Uvebrant, 1988). Since the pyramidal nerve fibers cross over before they enter the spinal cord, damage to one side of the brain causes abnormalities in the other

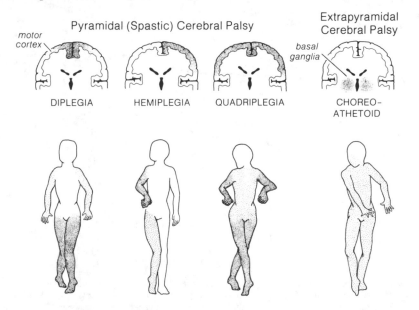

Figure 24.2.   Different regions of the brain are affected in various forms of cerebral palsy. The darker the shading, the more severe the involvement.

side of the body. If the child experiences a head injury that leads to bleeding into the area of the left pyramidal tract, the right side of the body is affected. This child is said to have a *right spastic hemiplegia* (see Figure 24.2). In contrast to diplegia, in hemiplegia, the arm is usually more affected than the leg (Uvebrant, 1988).

Quadriplegia is the third type of spastic cerebral palsy. When there is diffuse and severe damage to the cerebral cortex, *spastic quadriplegia* results (see Figure 24.1). In this condition, all four limbs are affected and the prognosis is worse. Severe mental retardation, seizures, and visual or auditory deficits are very common. Overall, diplegia accounts for about 25% of pyramidal tract cerebral palsy, quadriplegia for 30%, and hemiplegia for 45% (Eiben & Crocker, 1983).

Extrapyramidal Cerebral Palsy

In extrapyramidal cerebral palsy, damage occurs to the pathways outside the pyramidal tract. These other tracts pass through the basal ganglia or emanate from the cerebellum (see Chapter 14), and it is here that most of the damage seems to occur. The most common type of extrapyramidal cerebral palsy is called *choreoathetoid cerebral palsy* (see Figure 24.2). It is marked by the presence of abrupt, involuntary movements of the extremities. Unlike pyramidal cerebral palsy, in which the problem is one of initiating movement, in choreoathetoid cerebral palsy, the difficulty is one of regulating movement and maintaining posture.

A child with this form of cerebral palsy has very different physical signs from one with spastic cerebral palsy. In extrapyramidal cerebral palsy, the resistance to movement is called *lead pipe rigidity.* The limb may appear rigid but generally can be bent with persistent pressure. Also, in extrapyramidal cerebral palsy, changes in muscle tone vary from one time to another. Furthermore, tone may appear normal and involuntary movements are generally absent during sleep. In addition, a physician or therapist examining the child can "shake out," or briefly reduce, the increased tone by rapidly flexing and extending the child's arm or leg (Denhoff & Robinault, 1960).

Because of the variability in tone, muscle contractures are less likely to occur in this form of cerebral palsy than in spastic cerebral palsy. However, facial muscles more often are affected in choreoathetoid cerebral palsy than in the other types of cerebral palsy. Consequently, the child may have more sucking, swallowing, drooling, and speaking difficulties than the child with the spastic form of cerebral palsy (Platt, Andrews, & Howie, 1980). Also, because the muscle tone fluctuates and the child experiences involuntary movements, it is more difficult for him or her to develop the stability needed for sitting and walking.

Besides choreoathetoid cerebral palsy, the other forms of extrapyramidal cerebral palsy are called **rigid** and **atonic.** Neither of these disorders has choreoathetoid movements. Instead, lead pipe, or malleable, rigidity characterizes rigid cerebral palsy, and floppy muscle tone predominates in atonic cerebral palsy. Physicians must be careful when diagnosing atonic cerebral palsy in an infant because spastic cerebral palsy may present in the first months of life with symptoms of hypotonia, while choreoathetoid movements rarely are seen before 18 months of age.

Mixed-Type Cerebral Palsy

As the name implies, the mixed-type of cerebral palsy includes elements of both the pyramidal and extrapyramidal forms of this disorder. For example, in a child with mixed-type cerebral palsy, there may be a right-sided hemiplegia superimposed on generalized choreoathetosis. Since brain injury must be extensive to produce this combination, these children usually have mental retardation and other developmental disabilities.

EARLY DIAGNOSIS OF CEREBRAL PALSY

Certain groups of high-risk newborns, especially low birth-weight infants who weigh less than 1,500 grams, twins, and small for gestational age infants, have a higher than normal risk of cerebral palsy (Ellenberg & Nelson, 1981; Galjaard, 1987; Hagberg, berg, Hagberg, & Olow, 1982). The ability to identify infants who have the greatest risk of developing disabilities allows closer monitoring of their development and admission into early intervention programs. Tests such as the Denver Developmental Screening Test, which have traditionally been used by pediatricians to screen infants in developmental follow-up programs, often fail to detect cerebral palsy during the first 12 months of life (Nickel, Renken, & Gallenstein, 1989). For this reason, a large number of neuromotor tests have been developed to evaluate the quality of movement skills in young infants. Examples of such tests include the Movement Assessment of Infants, the Milani-Comparetti Motor Screening Test, the Primitive Reflex Profile, the Infant Motor Screen, and the Wolanski Motor Scale (Paban & Piper, 1987).

In addition to these formal tests, a group of behavioral symptoms may indicate cerebral palsy. Children with cerebral palsy may sleep excessively, be irritable when awake, have weak cries and poor sucks, and show little interest in their surroundings. The resting position is also different. Instead of lying in a semiflexed position, children with cerebral palsy may lie in a floppy, rag-doll way. Alternatively, they may have markedly increased tone and lie in an extended, arched position, called **opisthotonos.**

When examining such a child, a physician looks for abnormalities in muscle tone and deep tendon reflexes (DTR). Muscle tone may be increased, decreased, or variable. It also may be asymmetrical, since one side of the body may be more affected than the other side. Also, the deep tendon reflexes, such as the knee jerk, may be too brisk, or the child may have tremors, or *clonus*, in the arms and legs.

The persistence of primitive reflexes is also a sign of cerebral palsy. Primitive reflexes are seen normally only in the first 6–12 months of life. Their persistence beyond this time interferes with the expression of what are called **automatic,** or **protective movement reactions,** which are necessary for such motor skills as sitting, standing, and walking. As a result, the child with cerebral palsy does not attain motor skills at the appropriate age. Although motor development is significantly delayed in children with cerebral palsy, cognitive and language skills may progress at more normal rates. Thus, a discrepancy between the rates of motor and intellectual development is another clue to the existence of cerebral palsy.

As children with cerebral palsy grow from infancy to 2 years of age, other signs become evident. Normally, 3-month-old infants hold their hands open most of the time. In a child with cerebral palsy, the hands often remain clenched in fists. Also, a child does not typically become right-handed or left-handed until around 18 months of age, whereas a child with cerebral palsy may do so before 6 months of age. This suggests that one side of the child's body is weaker than the other. As the child grows, this may become more obvious because the spastic limb atrophies, becoming smaller both in circumference and in length.

Not all of these signs are found in every infant with cerebral palsy, and not all infants who have these signs develop cerebral palsy (Allen & Capute, 1989; Nelson & Ellenberg, 1982). Diagnostic errors are greatest in the group of children who exhibit mild abnormalities. For example, slightly more than half of high-risk infants suspected of having cerebral palsy at 12 months of age are considered neurologically normal by 2 years of age (Piper, Mazer, Silver, et al., 1988).

PRIMITIVE REFLEXES

One of the chief diagnostic signs of cerebral palsy is the persistence of primitive reflexes. These reflexes cause changes both in muscle tone and in movement of the limbs. They are called primitive because they are present in early life (in some cases during intrauterine development) and because they are controlled by the primitive regions of the nervous system: the spinal cord, the labyrinths of the inner ear, and the brain stem. As the cortex matures, these reflexes are gradually suppressed and integrated into voluntary movement patterns. During early infancy, such primitive reflexes as the **moro** and tonic neck reflex dominate movement; by 12 months of age, integration of the primitive reflexes should be complete (Capute, 1986).

This is not true of the child with cerebral palsy. In such a child, primitive reflexes are stronger than normal and often last into adult life. In a previously unaffected child, these primitive reflexes may reemerge following traumatic brain injury or during a coma.

Although there are many primitive reflexes, only three are considered in this section: the asymmetric tonic neck reflex (ATNR), the tonic labyrinthine reflex (TLR), and the positive support reflex (PSR). Each of these significantly affects posture and movement, and each has a different stimulus that elicits it (Illingworth, 1987).

The stimulus for the *asymmetric tonic neck reflex* is the active or passive rotation of the head. When the head is turned, the ATNR causes the arm and leg on the same side as the chin to extend further, while the opposite arm and leg become more flexed (Figure 24.3). Changes in muscle tone may occur in the trunk as well. Thus, the ATNR causes an increase in muscle tone and also frequently brings about a change in position.

Infants under 3 months of age normally show the ATNR. Yet, even in infancy, a child can overcome the reflex (i.e., flex and move the arm once it is extended). Some children with cerebral palsy cannot. They remain in the extended position until the

Full-Term Infant
Resting Position

Asymmetric Tonic
Neck Reflex

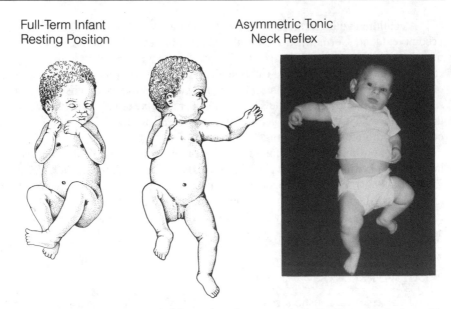

Figure 24.3. Asymmetric tonic neck reflex, or fencer's response. As the head is turned, the arm and leg on the same side as the chin extend, and the other arm and leg flex.

head turns and releases the reflex. This predicament illustrates the obligatory nature of the primitive reflexes.

For the *tonic labyrinthine reflex,* the stimulus is the position of the labyrinth inside the inner ear. When the neck is in an extended position or when the child is lying on his or her back, the labyrinth is tilted, and the reflex is elicited. The legs extend and the shoulders retract, or pull back (Figure 24.4). When the neck is flexed or the child is lying on the stomach, the hips and knees flex while the shoulders protract, or roll forward. When the reflex is present, but is not as strong, changes in muscle tone may occur without any change in the position of the limbs.

The third primitive reflex is the *positive support reflex.* When the balls of the feet come in contact with a firm surface, the child extends the legs (Figure 24.5). This reflex enables a normal child to support weight while standing. However, the increased response in a child with cerebral palsy leads to a rigid extension of the legs and feet. Rather than helping, this reflex then interferes with standing and walking.

Because these primitive reflexes result in changes in muscle tone and in position of the limbs, their persistence interferes with the normal development of voluntary motor activity. For example, to be able to roll over (normally accomplished at 4–5 months of age), a child must have an ATNR that is fairly well suppressed (see next section). If the ATNR persists, the infant has difficulty beginning this movement. As he or she turns the head, the extended arm and leg hinder the start of the roll. Once the roll is begun, the flexed arm of the strong ATNR prevents its completion.

A similar problem occurs with the TLR and sitting. To sit independently, equilibrium reactions must be present. These reactions require constant, fine changes

Tonic Labyrinthine Reflex

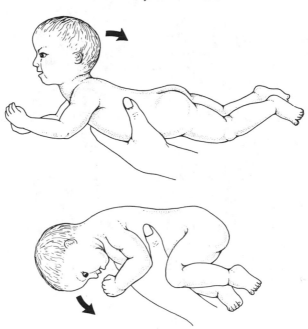

Figure 24.4.   Tonic labyrinthine reflex. Extension of the head backward leads to retraction of the shoulders and extension of the legs. The opposite occurs if the head is flexed forward.

in muscle tone to maintain balance. If a strong TLR is present, movement of the head causes patterns of flexion and extension throughout the body. These changes are incompatible with the equilibrium reactions needed to maintain balance in a sitting position, and the child falls over.

AUTOMATIC MOVEMENT REACTIONS

As primitive reflexes diminish in intensity, **postural reactions,** also known as *automatic movement reactions,* are developing (Figure 24.6). Some of the more important of these reactions include what are called righting, equilibrium, and protective reactions. These enable the child to have more complex voluntary movement and better control of posture.

Up to 2 months of age, a baby's head tilts passively in the same direction that the body is leaning. However, by 3 months of age, the baby should be able to compensate and hold the head upright even if the body is tilted. This is called *head righting*.

Before 5 months of age, if a child is placed in a sitting position and starts to fall forward, he or she will tumble over without trying to regain balance. At 5 months, when he or she begins to fall forward, he or she will push out the arms to prevent the fall. This is called the *anterior protective response*. By 7 months, a similar response,

Positive Support Reflex

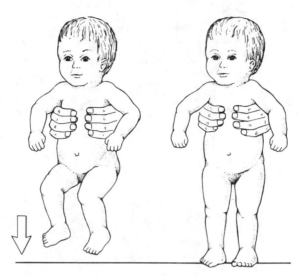

Figure 24.5. Positive support reflex. As the baby is bounced, the legs straighten to support the child's weight.

the *lateral protective response,* occurs when the child starts to fall sideways (Capute, Accardo, Vining, et al., 1977). Combined, these equilibrium reactions enable the child to sit and move comfortably by automatically compensating when the center of gravity is shifted. In children with cerebral palsy, not only do the primitive reflexes persist, but the development of the automatic movement reactions may lag behind or never occur.

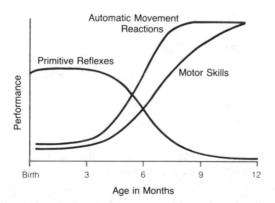

Figure 24.6. Relationship of primitive reflexes, automatic movement reactions, and motor skills. (From Capute, A., Accardo, P., Vining, E., et al. [1977]. *Primitive reflex profile.* Baltimore: University Park Press; reprinted by permission.)

WALKING

To walk, a child must be able to maintain upright posture and move forward in a smoothly coordinated manner at the same time. Even the child with mildest form of cerebral palsy has difficulty performing the continuous changes in muscle tone that are required for normal walking. The child's walk or gait is affected in many ways. *Scissoring,* the most common gait disturbance, occurs because of increased tone in the muscles that control adduction and internal rotation of the hips (Figure 24.7). *Toe walking* results from an **equinus** position of the feet (see Figure 24.7) and an increased **flexor** tone in the legs. These abnormalities may need to be treated using **orthoses** (see next section), walking aids such as **posterior walkers** (Logan, Byers-Hinkley, & Ciccone, 1990), or surgical intervention.

DISABILITIES ASSOCIATED WITH CEREBRAL PALSY

All children with cerebral palsy have problems with movement and posture. Many also have other disabilities associated with damage to the nervous system. The most common associated disabilities are mental retardation, visual deficits, hearing, speech-language disorders, and seizures (Table 24.2).

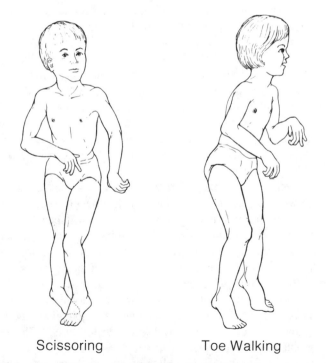

Scissoring   Toe Walking

Figure 24.7. Scissoring results from increased tone in the muscles that control adduction and internal rotation of the hip. Toe walking is due to an equinus position of the feet and increased flexor tone in the legs.

Table 24.2. Associated deficits in cerebral palsy

	Percentage with specific deficit				
Deficit	Quadriplegia	Hemiplegia	Diplegia	Extrapyramidal	Mixed
Visual impairment	55	23	38	50	64
Auditory impairment	22	8	17	17	21
Mental retardation	67	38	56	92	79
Seizure disorder	45	12	12	45	12

Source: Robinson (1973).

Assessment of intellectual function in children with cerebral palsy may be difficult, since the majority of IQ tests require motoric or verbal responses. Even taking this into account, approximately two-thirds of children with cerebral palsy have mental retardation, and many of those with normal intelligence exhibit some degree of perceptual impairment and learning disability. The particular type of cerebral palsy influences the incidence and degree of mental retardation. Hemiplegia, the most common type of cerebral palsy, is associated with the best intellectual outcome. Over 60% have normal intelligence. Spastic diplegia, the form of cerebral palsy typically associated with prematurity, also has a fairly good intellectual outcome (Crothers & Paine, 1959). Less than 30% of individuals with spastic quadriplegia, extrapyramidal, and mixed-type cerebral palsy have normal intelligence. Among those children with cerebral palsy *and* mental retardation, 15% have mild retardation, 35% have moderate retardation, and 50% have severe-to-profound retardation.

Visual problems are also common and diverse in children with cerebral palsy (Black, 1982). The premature infant may have blindness caused by retinopathy of prematurity (see Chapter 17). Nystagmus may be present in the child with ataxia. Children with hemiplegia frequently present with *homonymous hemianopsia,* a condition causing loss in one part of the visual field. Strabismus, or squint, is seen in a majority of children with cerebral palsy.

Hearing, speech, and language deficits are also common, occurring in about 30% of children with cerebral palsy. Children with congenital rubella or other viral syndromes often have a high-frequency hearing loss (see Chapter 18). Extrapyramidal cerebral palsy is associated with articulation problems, as choreoathetosis affects tongue and vocal cord movements. Expressive and/or receptive disorders of language also may result from the brain damage that caused the cerebral palsy (see Chapter 19).

Roughly 50% of children with cerebral palsy also have a seizure disorder (Aksu, 1990). Spastic forms of cerebral palsy carry the highest incidence of seizures. Tonic-clonic seizures occur frequently in individuals with hemiplegia, while minor motor seizures are common in those with quadriplegia and rigidity (see Chapter 26).

Feeding problems are often present in people with cerebral palsy and may be secondary to a variety of problems, including hypotonia, weak suck, poor coordination of the swallowing mechanism, tonic bite reflex, hyperactive gag reflex, and exaggerated tongue thrust (Jones, 1989). These problems may lead to poor nutrition and may require the use of alternative feeding methods, such as tube-feeding (Rempel, Colwell, & Nelson, 1988) (see Chapter 12).

Finally, behavior and emotional disorders play an important role in the lives of children with cerebral palsy and their families. Behavior disorders range from attention deficits and hyperactivity to self-injurious behavior. Early intervention programs and agencies, such as the United Cerebral Palsy Association, Incorporated, (UCPA), can provide invaluable support and training for preschool children and their families (see Resources for Children with Disabilities, Appendix C).

TREATMENT AND INTERVENTION

In developing a treatment and intervention program for a child with cerebral palsy, an interdisciplinary approach is important. Many disciplines are involved, including occupational therapy, physical therapy, biomedical engineering, special education, speech-language pathology, audiology, social services, psychology, nutrition, and developmental pediatrics. Each discipline addresses some aspect of the child's disability. For instance, the occupational therapist evaluates the motor development of the arms, oral motor functions, visual-perceptual problems, and the activities of daily living (Carrasco, 1989; Finnie, 1990). The physical therapist is involved in the development of posture and movement, including the use of adaptive devices and seating. The educator establishes an individualized education program (IEP) for the child (Palmer, Shapiro, Allen, et al., 1990). The speech-language pathologist evaluates the child's ability to communicate, and the audiologist identifies a hearing loss and recommends correction. The clinical psychologist evaluates the child's intellectual functioning and if necessary, the behavioral psychologist develops a behavior management program. The nutritionist recommends an appropriate diet and monitors growth (Fried & Pencharz, 1991). The social worker assesses family problems, coping mechanisms, and offers support and counseling. The developmental pediatrician provides medical care and coordinates the various disciplines, including medical subspecialties such as orthopedics, neurology, neurosurgery, and ophthalmology.

This multidisciplinary model is time-consuming and expensive, and it has proved difficult to assess the effectiveness of this approach to treatment (Ottenbacher, Biocca, DeCremer, et al., 1986; Palmer, et al., 1988; Tirosh & Rabino, 1989). Many studies, especially those attempting to measure the effects of neurodevelopmental approaches to therapy, fail to meet acceptable criteria for scientific research. Nevertheless, there is some evidence to suggest that early intervention has the potential to improve the rate and quality of motor development in children with cerebral palsy (Jenkins, Sells, Brady, et al., 1982; Kanda, Yuge, Yamori, et al., 1984).

Early Intervention

The key to success in any therapy program is the consistency of its delivery and the early involvement of parents so that they can learn to manage the child at home and to accept the child's disability (Schleichkorn, 1983). Recent amendments to the legislation governing public education for children with disabilities have provided guidelines and financial incentives for the development of statewide early intervention systems. This has led to a tremendous growth in the number of programs available as well as to changes in the model of service delivery. Federal guidelines support a family-centered approach to care that addresses not only the educational needs of the child, but also the broader based social, psychological, economic, and medical needs of the entire family system. Parents are encouraged to participate actively in planning and implementing services, and in developing competence in advocacy for their child. Programs are individualized according to the specific needs of the family and may include a combination of consultative, home-based, or center-based intervention.

Neurodevelopmental Therapy

The primary method of physical and occupational therapy for the young child with cerebral palsy is **neurodevelopmental therapy (NDT)**, an approach designed to provide the child with sensorimotor experiences that enhance the development of normal movement patterns (Bobath, 1980; Perin, 1989). Assessment begins with observation of the child's posture at rest and during transitions from one position to another. The therapist evalutes muscle tone, range of motion, and the presence and quality of primitive reflexes and automatic movement reactions. An individualized program of positioning, therapeutic handling, and play is then developed for the child. Program goals include the normalization of tone and control of movement during functional activities. Close consultation with family members and others who have daily contact with the child is essential to ensure that therapeutic techniques are integrated into the child's daily routine.

A controversial approach to treating children with cerebral palsy is called *patterning*. Patterning involves putting the child through a series of exercises designed to improve "neurological organization." Three to five volunteers simultaneously manipulate the child's limbs and head for hours daily in patterns that are supposed to simulate prenatal and infantile movement of normal children. Proponents believe that if a child makes certain motions enough times, undamaged brain cells will be reprogrammed to take over the functions of the damaged cells (Zigler, 1981). The American Academy of Pediatrics (1982) is on record as being opposed to this treatment, as it has found no evidence to support its effectiveness. In addition, the regimen prescribed is so demanding and restrictive that it places considerable stress on parents and siblings (Matthews, 1988).

Physical Activity

Physical exercise is important to strengthen muscles and bones, enhance motor skills, and prevent contractures. In addition, the social and recreational aspects of organized physical activities can be highly enjoyable (Humphrey, 1985). Many popular programs, including swimming, dancing, and horseback riding, can be modified so that people with cerebral palsy can participate successfully (Jones, 1987). The Special Olympics has enabled thousands of children with disabilities to participate in running, swimming, basketball, gymnastics, and other sporting events. The rewards of engaging in competitive sports are invaluable for enhancing self-esteem and providing a sense of belonging to a peer group. Parents and professionals should encourage all children to participate in whatever physical activities their interests, motivation, and capabilities allow.

Orthotics and Splints

Orthotic devices, including braces and splints, may be used along with physical and occupational therapy to maintain a range of motion, prevent contractures at specific joints, provide stability, or control involuntary movements that interfere with functioning (Nuzzo, 1980). Contractures may develop when muscles consistently have increased tone and remain in shortened positions for prolonged periods of time. Orthoses may be used to maintain a specific group of muscles in a lengthened or less contracted state so that the function of the joint is improved.

One of the most commonly prescribed orthotics is the short leg brace. It prevents permanent shortening of the heel cords, often avoiding the need for an operation to lengthen the Achilles or ankle tendon (see upcoming subsection on Orthopedic Surgery). This brace usually consists of a plastic splint worn inside the shoe, called a *molded ankle-foot orthosis* (MAFO) (Sankey, Anderson, & Young, 1989) (Figure 24.8). Decreasing the foot extension also may decrease the muscle tone in the hips,

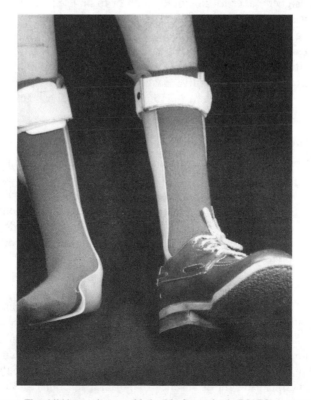

Figure 24.8.   Braces. The child is wearing a molded ankle-foot orthosis (MAFO) to counter toe walking.

allowing the child to sit in a more stable position. Also, the change in the position of the ankle allows the child to stand with the foot flat, improving the base of support and stability. Finally, correcting the child's abnormal foot posture may alter the position of the hips and knees when the child stands, thereby improving gait. For a child with choreoathetoid cerebral palsy, a similar brace may help to control involuntary movements at the ankle.

A variety of splints may be used to improve hand function. In the common resting hand splint, the thumb is held in an **abducted** position and the wrist in a neutral or slightly extended position (Figure 24.9A). This helps the child keep his or her hand open to prevent a deformity. Other splints are designed to position the arm and hand in such a way as to reduce tone and to allow greater functional gains during therapy (see Figure 24.9B).

Most pediatric braces and splints are custom-made of plastic materials that are molded directly on the child. They must be monitored closely and modified as the child grows or changes abilities.

The use of casts has become increasingly popular as an adjunct to more traditional methods of managing spasticity (Hanson & Jones, 1989; Smith & Harris, 1985). Tone-reducing, or "inhibitive," casts are made for upper or lower extremities and can be designed either for immobilization or to be used during weight-bearing activities. Casts position the extremities so that spastic muscles are in lengthened positions being gently stretched. Application of serial casts can allow the therapist to increase range of motion gradually when contractures are present. After maximal range and position have been achieved, the cast is worn intermittently to maintain the improvement. Benefits of inhibitive casting include improved gait and weight-bearing, increased range of motion, and improved functional hand use (Bertoti, 1986; Smelt, 1989; Yasukawa, 1990).

Positioning and Mobility Equipment

Adaptive equipment is often a necessary and useful adjunct to treatment of the child with cerebral palsy (Perin, 1989). Static positioning devices including sidelyers, prone boards, and supine standers, may be used to promote skeletal alignment, to compensate for abnormal postures, or to prepare the child for independent mobility. Other devices, including scooters, tricycles, and wheelchairs, provide the child with the means to move independently within the environment and to increase opportunities for exploratory play and social interaction.

Mobility Training and Equipment

One of the questions of greatest concern to parents of young children with cerebral palsy is, "Will my child ever walk?" Early factors that may predict prognosis for ambulation include type of cerebral palsy, age of independent sitting, and postural and tonic reflex activity. A diagnosis of hemiplegia or ataxia and attainment of independent sitting by 2 years of age generally predict community ambulation. A diagnosis of spastic quadriplegia or absence of postural reactions and obligatory persistence of primitive reflexes at 2 years of age carries a poor prognosis (Watt,

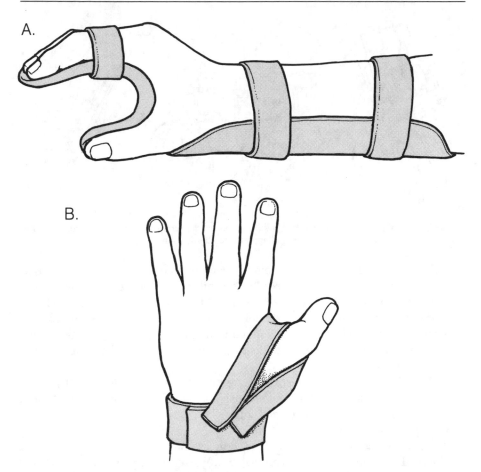

Figure 24.9. Splints. A) Resting hand splint. This may decrease the risk of contracture and increase the use of the hand. B) Thumb loop. This splint, which is made of soft material, inhibits tone in the hand and arm, yet keeps the hand free to engage in play.

Robertson, & Grace, 1989). Treatment interventions commonly used for ambulation training may include a combination of physical therapy, assistive devices, such as walkers or crutches, orthotics, and surgery.

For children with limited walking skills, wheelchairs are essential for maximizing mobility and function (Hulme, Shaver, Acher, et al., 1987; Schultz-Hurlburt & Tervo, 1982). A wheelchair with a solid seat and back is usually recommended. However, some children have difficulty using this type of chair unless modifications are made. The addition of head and trunk supports or a tray may be needed for the child who lacks postural control due to low tone. The child with limited head control or with feeding difficulties may benefit from a high-backed chair that can be tilted back 10°–15° (Figure 24.10A). This helps to maintain the child's body and head in proper alignment.

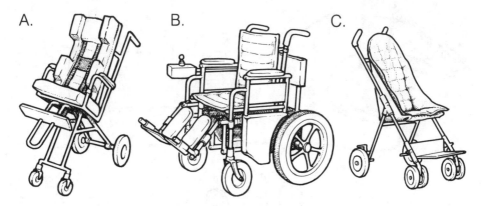

Figure 24.10.   Wheelchairs: A) High-backed, tilting chair with lateral inserts and head supports. B) Motorized wheelchair with joystick control. C) Supportive collapsible stroller.

Special seating cushions or custom-molded inserts that conform to the contours of the body can offer necessary support for the child with orthopedic deformities such as scoliosis (Katz, Liebertal, & Erken, 1988). Motorized wheelchairs can enhance the independence of children who are able to use them. Although these usually employ an easily manipulated joystick for controlling both speed and direction, other types of switches are available for children who cannot control their hand movements (see Figure 24.10B).

Special supportive strollers are an alternative to wheelchairs for mobility within the community or for the young child whose potential for ambulation has yet to be determined. These are light weight and collapsible, yet support the back and keep the hips properly aligned (see Figure 24.10C).

Ambulation aids, including walkers, crutches, and canes, may be appropriate for the child with milder forms of cerebral palsy. Walkers are available with or without wheels and offer a stable base of support to the child who can maintain correct positional alignment while in a standing position (Logan, Byers-Hinkley, & Ciccone, 1990). However, they are difficult to maneuver around obstacles or over rough terrain. Crutches and canes are easier to maneuver, but require considerable strength, endurance, and balance for functional use. They are recommended rarely.

Car seats are essential to the safety of all children who ride in automobiles. Several manufacturers offer adapted car seats that meet federal safety guidelines as well as provide proper support for the child with disabilities. Often these models include a base that allows the seat to be used as a stroller or positioning chair outside of the car.

Medication

Unfortunately, medications have limited usefulness in improving muscle tone in children with cerebral palsy. No drug has proved helpful for treating choreoathetosis. The medications most commonly used to control spasticity and rigidity are diazepam (Valium), baclofen (Lioresal) and dantrolene (Dantrium). Diazepam—and its derivative compounds, lorazepam and clonazepam—have been used most commonly.

They affect brain control of muscle tone, beginning within half an hour after ingestion and lasting about 4 hours. Withdrawal should be gradual, as physical dependency can develop. Side effects include drowsiness and excessive drooling that may interfere with feeding and speech.

Baclofen is also a central nervous system inhibitor. It has been most effective in treating adults with multiple sclerosis and traumatic damage to the spinal cord. Thus far, this drug has not been used very often for treating cerebral palsy in children. Drowsiness, nausea, headache, and low blood pressure are the most common side effects. About 10% of children treated with baclofen experience side effects unpleasant enough to discontinue treatment.

Finally, dantrolene works on muscle cells directly to inhibit their contraction. About half of the children who were tested with this drug showed modest improvement (Joynt & Leonard, 1980). It is usually given 2–3 times daily. Side effects include drowsiness, muscle weakness, and increased drooling. A rare side effect of this drug is severe liver damage.

Medication also has been used to treat two other complications of cerebral palsy, constipation and decubital ulcers. Constipation is a common problem in many children with developmental disabilities and may require both dietary and medical approaches. Medications include stool softeners and laxatives and are discussed in Chapter 12. Skin ulcers are a particular problem in children confined to wheelchairs or their beds. The best treatment is prevention by maintaining good nutrition and skin hygiene. Foam or sheepskin can be used to relieve pressure areas, and frequent changes of position can reduce prolonged pressure to one area. If a skin sore develops, the child should be positioned so that no weight is placed on the ulcer. The wound is treated with wet to dry dressings throughout the day. After the soaks, a dense ointment, such as Duoderm, should be applied. Antibiotics are infrequently needed and improvement should be evident in 2–3 weeks.

Orthopedic Surgery

Because of the abnormal or asymmetrical distribution of muscle tone, children who have cerebral palsy are susceptible to the development of joint deformities. The most common of these result from permanent shortening or contracture of one or more groups of muscles around a joint. This limits joint mobility. Orthopedic surgery is done to increase the range of motion through the release, lengthening, or transfer of affected muscles and tendons. For example, a partial release or transfer of the hip adductor muscles may improve the child's ability to sit and walk (Binder & Eng, 1989). A partial hamstring release, involving the lengthening or transfer of muscles around the knee, also may facilitate sitting and walking. A lengthening of the Achilles tendon at the ankle improves walking (Figure 24.11). All of these procedures require the use of a cast or splint for 6–8 weeks after surgery and a brace at night for at least several more months (Bleck, 1987).

A more complicated orthopedic procedure is the correction of a dislocated hip (Cooke, Cole, & Carey, 1989). If this is diagnosed when there is a partial dislocation (called **subluxation**), release of the hip adductor muscles can be effective. This oper-

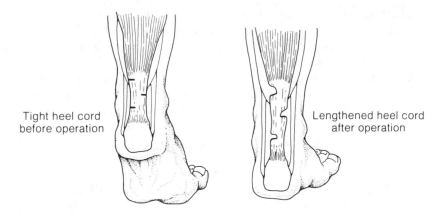

Tight heel cord
before operation

Lengthened heel cord
after operation

Figure 24.11.   Achilles tendon lengthening operation. When the heel cord is tight, the child walks on his or her toes. Surgery lengthens the heel cord and permits a more flat-footed gait.

ation, called an *adductor tenotomy and obturator neurectomy* (ATON), is usually adequate to decrease the abnormal pull and correct the dislocation (Moreau, Drummond, Rogala, et al., 1979) (Figure 24.12). If the head of the femur is dislocated more than one-third to one-half of the way out of a hip joint socket, a more complex procedure, a varus osteotomy, may be necessary. In this operation, the angle of the femur (the thigh bone) is changed surgically to place the head of the femur back into the hip socket (Figure 24.13). In some cases, the hip socket also must be reshaped to ensure that the hip joint remains functional.

Before performing surgery, the orthopedist is careful to evaluate and explain to the parents both the potential risks and benefits of an operation. Computerized gait analysis conducted prior to surgical intervention to improve ambulation has become increasingly common. Precise measurements obtained through motion analysis, force plates, and electromyography offer detailed information relating to specific abnormalities at each lower extremity joint as well as the muscle activity that controls motion through all phases of the gait cycle (Cahan, Adams, Perry, et al., 1990; Russman & Gage, 1989). Such precise definition is not possible through clinical observation alone. Pre-operative gait analysis helps to determine exactly which procedures are likely to be successful. Postoperative analysis can provide an objective measure of outcome.

Besides treating contractures and dislocations, orthopedic surgeons also are involved in the care of scoliosis, a complication of both spastic and extrapyramidal cerebral palsy. If untreated, a spinal curvature can interfere with sitting, walking, and self-care skills. If severe enough, it also can affect respiratory efforts. Treatment of significant scoliosis ranges from a molded plastic jacket or chair insert to surgery to straighten the spine as much as possible. The surgery involves using metal hooks, rods, and wires to hold the spine in an improved position while bone graft material fuses the spine in position (Figure 24.14). With an improved surgical technique called

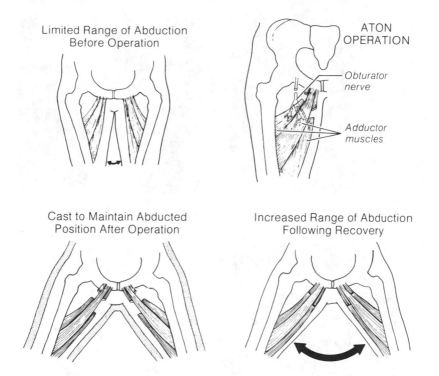

Figure 24.12.   Adductor tenotomy and obturator neurectomy. This operation is done to improve scissoring and to prevent hip dislocation caused by contractures of the adductor muscles in the thigh. Some of these muscles are cut, and the nerve fibers leading to them also are severed. The child is placed in a cast for 6–8 weeks to maintain a more open position. The muscles eventually grow together in a lengthened position, allowing improved sitting and/or walking.

a *Lucque procedure,* scoliosis surgery now is being pursued more aggressively (Ferguson & Allen, 1988).

Neurosurgery

A number of neurosurgical procedures have been used to treat cerebral palsy, including placement of cerebellar or dorsal column stimulators and performance of dorsal rhizotomy (Park & Owen, 1992). The stimulators (i.e., electrodes) are placed surgically in the cerebellum or outside the coverings of the cervical spinal cord. The electrodes are connected to an electrical stimulator that emits a very small current. These signals are thought to block some of the abnormal impulses and decrease choreoathetosis. Although some studies report improvement, the results have not been impressive, and these procedures carry a significant risk of infection (Davis, Schulman, Nanes, et al., 1987; Hugenholtz, Humphreys, McIntyre, et al., 1988).

A more promising operation is *selective posterior rhizotomy,* a relatively new neurosurgical procedure designed to reduce spasticity in children with severe lower extremity involvement, especially spastic diplegia. This procedure involves isolating

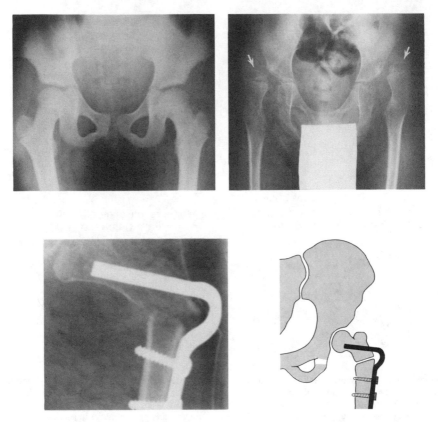

Figure 24.13.   Dislocation of the hip. The upper X rays show a normal hip to the left and a hip dislocated on both sides on the right. The arrows indicate the points of dislocation. The lower picture shows the results of a varus osteotomy to correct the left-side dislocation. The femur has been cut and realigned so that it now fits into the acetabulum. Pins, which are later removed, hold the bone in place until it heals.

the posterior roots of the second lumbar to first sacral spinal nerves and providing selective electrical stimulation to discover which **rootlets** make the greatest contribution to the spasticity. These rootlets are cut. Since only those rootlets with abnormal responses are cut, touch and position sense remain intact. Postoperative clinical findings include functional improvement in sitting, standing, and walking (Abbott, Forem, & Johann, 1989; Berman, Vaughan, & Peacock, 1990; Peacock & Staudt, 1990). Results have been long-lasting, and there have been progressive functional gains over time (Arens, Peacock, & Peter, 1989).

Computers

Computers are playing an increasingly important role in the habilitation of children with cerebral palsy. They can be used to control the environment, provide a lifeline with the outside world, enable a person to work at home, and give artificial speech, sight, and entertainment (Cole & Dehdashti, 1990; Levy, 1983; Treviranus & Tan-

Figure 24.14. Treatment of scoliosis may require a spinal fusion. This X ray shows improved scoliosis following a Lucque procedure. During this surgery the position of the spine is improved using metal hooks, rods, and wires while bone graft material fuses the spine in position.

nock, 1987). Control of the environment can include a system that operates lights, unlocks the front door, and turns on various appliances. The telephone also can be controlled and a message automatically sent in an emergency.

For individuals with severe speech deficits, the computer can provide synthesized speech (Newman, Sparrow, & Hospod, 1989). Individuals with visual impairment can use computers to receive spoken instructions and verify letters they have written. For those who are unable to use a keyboard because of poor fine motor coordination, alternate input devices are available. Since a home computer can be linked with other computers by modem, shopping, banking, and even employment from home is possible. In addition, the computer is a source of recreation with games and educational programs. The use of a computer is almost limitless and may enrich the lives of many individuals with disabilities (Harwin & Jackson, 1990).

CASE STUDIES OF CHILDREN WITH CEREBRAL PALSY

Tommy

Tommy's birth was traumatic. His mother had an abruptio placenta, and she required an emergency cesarean section. She lost a great deal of blood, and the physician could not detect a fetal heartbeat during the 3 minutes before birth. Tommy's Apgar scores were 1 at 1 minute and 2 at 5 minutes. An injection of adrenalin into his heart and artificial ventilation were required. The doctors were able to stabilize Tommy within the first day of life, but they were afraid that significant brain damage had already occurred.

Their concern was justified. Tommy fed poorly and slept most of the time. When he was awake, he was irritable and screamed. His muscle tone remained floppy. At 3 months of age, he still held his hands in fists and could not hold his head upright. He had intermittent minor-motor seizures. By 6 months of age, Tommy still made no attempt to roll over and was only beginning to make cooing sounds. When he was 12 months old, he started having choreoathetoid movements of his arms, and his muscle tone was variable (i.e., sometimes decreased and other times increased). At 2 years of age, he rolled over and reached for objects. Because of the choreoathetosis and severe mental retardation, Tommy could not grab objects but rather batted at them. He responded inconsistently to sounds and was later found to have severe sensorineural hearing loss.

Emotionally, things became progressively more difficult for Tommy's parents as they realized he had severe retardation and would never be self-sufficient. However, with the support of relatives and the use of special schools and respite care, they were able to cope over the years. Now, at 21 years of age, Tommy still lives at home and attends a cerebral palsy activity center. He is happy at the center and enjoys the company of others. His cerebral palsy continues to make it impossible for him to feed or dress himself. He functions mentally at around an 18-month level. He can now sit without support but remains in a wheelchair. His parents worry about his future when they are no longer able to care for him.

Tina

Tina, a premature infant, weighed less than 2 pounds when she was born in the seventh month. She had a rocky newborn period with hypoglycemia, respiratory distress syndrome, and a patent ductus arteriosus. When finally released from the hospital at 3 months of age, she was an alert, active, and happy baby. However, her legs were spastic and were held in a scissored position. She started to receive regular physical therapy at this age.

Apart from her motor development, many of her developmental milestones were normal, especially considering her prematurity. She said "mama" at 1 year of age to everyone and followed 1-step commands. She also could drink from a cup. She could roll over from stomach to back, but she could not sit or stand. Her primitive reflexes persisted, and the muscle tone, especially in her legs, was increased. Her hips were partially dislocated. Although her intellectual skills fell around the 9-month level, her gross motor skills were at a 4-month level.

By 2 years of age, the scissoring of her legs became more and more troublesome, and the problem with her hips was more prominent. Dressing and sitting were difficult. Orthopedic surgery successfully released the adductor muscles of her hips. After intensive physical therapy, she learned to roll over and sit. By 4 years of age, she was walking with short leg braces and canes. Her language development continued right on course, and IQ testing using the Wechsler Intelligence Scale for Children–Revised at 6 years of age showed a verbal score of 110 and a performance score of 82. In children with cerebral palsy, such a discrepancy is common. For Tina, it was the first clue to the presence of a learning disability that became more apparent in the first grade.

Another problem, a squint, also was corrected surgically, and Tina's appearance improved. She was a vibrant, pretty, and happy child. However, her problems were not over. In the second grade, she had a number of generalized tonic-clonic seizures. An EEG confirmed the diagnosis of a seizure disorder, and she was placed on car-bamazepine (Tegretol). Tina is now 9 years old and has had only one seizure in the last year.

Right now, Tina is doing well in a public school setting. She is in a regular class for most of her subjects and gets help in a resource room for her reading problems. She also continues to have physical and occupational therapy. Emotionally, both she and her parents have done well coping with her disabilities.

PROGNOSIS

Although most children with cerebral palsy will live to adulthood, their projected life expectancy is somewhat less than that of the normal population (O'Grady, Nishimura, Kohn, et al., 1985). The prognosis varies for each type of cerebral palsy. A child with a mild left hemiplegia probably will have a normal life expectancy, while a child with spastic quadriplegia may not live beyond age 40.

Although about 40% of the individuals who have cerebral palsy have normal intelligence, only a small number of them are able to lead normal lives (O'Grady et al., 1985). Studies suggest that employability is not related solely to the degree of disability, but to a variety of other factors including family support, quality of educational programs, and the availability of community-based training and technical support (Russman & Gage, 1989). As adults, only 10% are entirely self-supporting. Another 40% work in sheltered workshops or supported employment programs. An additional 35% have sufficient self-help skills to be partially independent at home. The remaining 15% are dependent on others; a few of these individuals are in institutions (O'Grady et al., 1985) (Table 24.3). It is hoped that these figures will improve as a result of the new federal mandates to provide employment for individuals with disabilities.

SUMMARY

Cerebral palsy refers to a group of disorders that cause brain damage in children. The disability is not progressive, nor does it have a cure. Certain types of cerebral palsy, such as hemiplegia and spastic diplegia, have a fairly good prognosis for independent functioning, while others, such as rigid and spastic quadriplegia, usually lead to a

Table 24.3. Outcome of cerebral palsy in adults

	Percentage with specific outcomes		
Outcome	Complete	Partial	Very little
Independence at home	55	28	17
Independence in community	48	23	29
Competitive employment	59	18	23
Use of hands	86	7	7
Speech	78	12	10

Adapted from O'Grady, R.S., Nishimura, D.M., Kohn, J.G., et al. (1985). Vocational predictions compared with present vocational status of 60 young adults with cerebral palsy. *Developmental Medicine & Child Neurology, 27,* 775–784.

future of dependence. In many cases, other problems besides motor abnormalities exist, including seizures and visual, auditory, and intellectual deficits.

The most effective treatment involves the use of an interdisciplinary approach. A number of children with good intellectual abilities and limited disabilities can lead normal lives. Others are capable of various degrees of independence.

REFERENCES

Abbott, R., Forem, S.L., & Johann, M. (1989). Selective posterior rhizotomy for the treatment of spasticity: A review. *Child's Nervous System, 5,* 337–346.

Aksu, F. (1990). Nature and prognosis of seizures in patients with cerebral palsy. *Developmental Medicine and Child Neurology, 32,* 661–668.

Allen, M.C., & Capute, A.J. (1989). Neonatal neurodevelopmental examination as a predictor of neuromotor outcome in premature infants. *Pediatrics, 83,* 498–506.

American Academy of Pediatrics. (1982). The Doman-Delacato treatment of neurologically handicapped children. *Pediatrics, 70,* 810–812.

Arens, L.J., Peacock, W.J., & Peter, J. (1989). Selective posterior rhizotomy: A long-term follow-up study. *Child's Nervous System, 5,* 148–152.

Berman, B., Vaughan, C.L., & Peacock, W.J. (1990). The effect of rhizotomy on movement in patients with cerebral palsy. *American Journal of Occupational Therapy, 44,* 511–516.

Bertoti, D.B. (1986). Effect of short-leg casting on ambulation in children with cerebral palsy. *Physical Therapy, 66,* 1522–1529.

Binder, H., & Eng, G.D. (1989). Rehabilitation management of children with spastic diplegic cerebral palsy. *Archives of Physical Medicine and Rehabilitation, 70,* 482–489.

Black, P. (1982). Visual disorders associated with cerebral palsy. *British Journal of Ophthamology, 66,* 46–52.

Bleck, E.E. (1987). *Orthopedic management of cerebral palsy.* Philadelphia: J.B. Lippincott.

Bobath, K. (1980). A neurophysiological basis for the treatment of cerebral palsy. *Clinics in Developmental Medicine (No. 75),* 77–87.

Cahan, L.D., Adams, J.M., Perry, J., et al. (1990). Instrumented gait analysis after selective dorsal rhizotomy. *Developmental Medicine and Child Neurology, 32,* 1037–1043.

Capute, A.J. (1986). Early neuromotor reflexes in infancy. *Pediatric Annals, 15,* 217–218, 221–223, 226.

Capute, A.J., & Accardo, P.J. (Eds.). (1991). *Developmental disabilities in infancy and childhood.* Baltimore: Paul H. Brookes Publishing Co.

Capute, A.J., Accardo, P.J., Vining, E.P.G., et al. (1977). *Primitive reflex profile*. Baltimore: University Park Press.

Carrasco, R.C. (1989). Children with cerebral palsy. In P.N. Pratt & A.S. Allen (Eds.), *Occupational therapy for children* (2nd ed.) (pp. 396–421). St. Louis: C.V. Mosby.

Cole, E., & Dehdashti, P. (1990). Interface design as a prosthesis for an individual with brain injury. *SIGCHI (Special Interest Group on Computer and Human Interaction) Bulletin, 22*, 28–32.

Cooke, P.H., Cole, W.G., & Carey, R.P. (1989). Dislocation of the hip in cerebral palsy: Natural history and predictability. *Journal of Bone and Joint Surgery (British Volume), 71*, 441–446.

Crothers, B., & Paine, R.S. (1959). *The natural history of cerebral palsy*. Cambridge, MA: Harvard University Press.

Davis, R., Schulman, J., Nanes, M., et al. (1987). Cerebellar stimulation for spastic cerebral palsy—Double-blind quantitative study. *Applied Neurophysiology, 50*, 451–452.

Denhoff, E., & Robinault, I.P. (1960). *Cerebral palsy and related disorders: A developmental approach to dysfunction*. New York: McGraw-Hill.

Eiben, R.M., & Crocker, A.C. (1983). Cerebral palsy within the spectrum of developmental disabilities. In G.H. Thompson, I.L. Rubin, & R.M. Bilenker (Eds.), *Comprehensive management of cerebral palsy* (pp. 19–23). New York: Grune & Stratton.

Ellenberg, J.H., & Nelson, K.B. (1981). Early recognition of infants at high risk for cerebral palsy: Examination at age four months. *Developmental Medicine and Child Neurology, 23*, 705–716.

Ferguson, R.L., & Allen, B.L., Jr. (1988). Considerations in the treatment of cerebral palsy patients with spinal deformities. *Orthopedic Clinics of North America, 19*, 419–425.

Finnie, N.R. (1990). *Handling the young cerebral palsied child at home* (3rd ed.). New York: E.P. Dutton.

Fried, M.D., & Pencharz, P.B. (1991). Energy and nutrient intakes of children with spastic quadriplegia. *Journal of Pediatrics, 119*, 947–949.

Galjaard, H. (1987). *Early detection and management of cerebral palsy*. Netherlands: Martins-Nijhoff Publisher, Kluwer.

Hagberg, B., & Hagberg, G. (1984). Prenatal and perinatal risk factors in a survey of 681 Swedish cases. In F. Stanley & E. Alberman (Eds.), *The epidemiology of the cerebral palsied* (pp. 116–134). Philadelphia: J.B. Lippincott.

Hagberg, B., Hagberg, G., & Olow, I. (1982). Gains and hazards of intensive neonatal care: An analysis from Swedish cerebral palsy epidemiology. *Developmental Medicine and Child Neurology, 24*, 13–19.

Hagberg, B., Hagberg, G., & Zetterstrom, R. (1989). Decreasing perinatal mortality—Increase in cerebral palsy morbidity. *Acta Paediatrica Scandinavica, 78*, 664–670.

Hanson, C.J., & Jones, L.J. (1989). Gait abnormalities and inhibitive casts in cerebral palsy. *Journal of the American Podiatric Medical Association, 79*, 53–59.

Harwin, W.S., & Jackson, R.D. (1990). Analysis of intentional head gestures to assist computer access by physically disabled people. *Journal of Biomedical Engineering, 12*, 193–198.

Hugenholtz, H., Humphreys, P., McIntyre, W.M., et al. (1988). Cervical spinal cord stimulation for spasticity in cerebral palsy. *Neurosurgery, 22*, 707–714.

Hulme, J.B., Shaver, J., Acher, S., et al. (1987). Effects of adaptive seating devices on the eating and drinking of children with multiple handicaps. *American Journal of Occupational Therapy, 41*, 81–89.

Humphrey, F. (1985). Therapeutic recreation. In D.A. Umphred (Ed.), *Neurological rehabilitation* (Vol. 3, pp. 653–662). St. Louis: C.V. Mosby.

Illingworth, R.S. (1987). *The development of the infant and young child: Normal and abnormal* (9th ed.). New York: Churchill Livingstone.

Jenkins, J.R., Sells, C.J., Brady, D., et al. (1982). Effects of developmental therapy on motor impaired children. *Physical and Occupational Therapy in Pediatrics, 2*, 19–28.

Jones, J.A. (Ed.). (1987). *Training guide to cerebral palsy sports* (3rd ed.). Champaign, IL: Human Kinetics Publishers.

Jones, M.H. (1975). Differential diagnosis and natural history of the cerebral palsied child. In R.L. Samilson (Ed.), *Orthopaedic aspects of cerebral palsy.* Philadelphia: J.B. Lippincott.

Jones, P.M. (1989). Feeding disorders in children with multiple handicaps. *Developmental Medicine and Child Neurology, 31,* 404–406.

Joynt, R.L., & Leonard, J.A., Jr. (1980). Dantrolene sodium suspension in treatment of spastic cerebral palsy. *Developmental Medicine and Child Neurology, 22,* 755–767.

Kanda, T., Yuge, M., Yamori, Y., et al. (1984). Early physiotherapy in the treatment of spastic diplegia. *Developmental Medicine and Child Neurology, 26,* 438–444.

Katz, K., Liebertal, M., & Erken, E.H.W. (1988). Seat insert for cerebral-palsied children with total body involvement. *Developmental Medicine and Child Neurology, 30,* 222–226.

Kudrjavcev, T., Schoenberg, B.S., Kurland, L.T., et al. (1985). Cerebral palsy: Survivor rates, associated handicaps, and distribution by clinical subtypes (Rochester, MN, 1950–1976). *Neurology, 35,* 900–903.

Levy, R. (1983). Interface modalities of technical aids used by people with disability. *American Journal of Occupational Therapy, 37,* 761–765.

Logan, L., Byers-Hinkley, K., & Ciccone, C.D. (1990). Anterior versus posterior walkers: A gait analysis study. *Developmental Medicine and Child Neurology, 32,* 1044–1048.

Matthews, D.J. (1988). Controversial therapies in the management of cerebral palsy. *Pediatric Annals, 17,* 762–764.

Moreau, M., Drummond, D.S., Rogala, E., et al. (1979). Natural history of the dislocated hip in spastic cerebral palsy. *Developmental Medicine and Child Neurology, 21,* 749–753.

Naeye, R.L., Peters, E.C., Bartholomew, M., & Landis, J.R. (1989). Origins of cerebral palsy. *American Journal of Diseases of Children, 143,* 1154–1161.

Nelson, K.B., & Ellenberg, J.H. (1982). Children who "outgrew" cerebral palsy. *Pediatrics, 69,* 529–536.

Nelson, K.B., & Ellenberg, J.H. (1986). Antecedents of cerebral palsy: Multivariate analysis of risk. *The New England Journal of Medicine, 315,* 81–86.

Newman, G.C., Sparrow, A.R., & Hospod, F.E. (1989). Two augmentative communication systems for speechless disabled patients. *American Journal of Occupational Therapy, 43,* 529–534.

Nickel, R.E., Renken, C.A., & Gallenstein, J.S. (1989). The infant motor screen. *Developmental Medicine and Child Neurology, 31,* 35–42.

Nuzzo, R.M. (1980). Dynamic bracing: Elastics for patients with cerebral palsy, muscular dystrophy and myelodysplasia. *Clinical Orthopaedics and Related Research, 148,* 263–273.

O'Grady, R.S., Nishimura, D.M., Kohn, J.G., et al. (1985). Vocational predictions compared with present vocational status of 60 young adults with cerebral palsy. *Developmental Medicine & Child Neurology, 27,* 775–784.

O'Reilly, D.E. (1975). Care of the cerebral palsied: Outcome of the past and needs for the future. *Developmental Medicine and Child Neurology, 17,* 141–149.

Ottenbacher, K.J., Biocca, Z., DeCremer, G., et al. (1986). Quantitative analysis of the effectiveness of pediatric therapy. Emphasis on the neurodevelopmental treatment approach. *Physical Therapy, 66,* 1095–1101.

Paban, M., & Piper, M.C. (1987). Early predictors of one-year neurodevelopmental outcome for "at risk" infants. *Physical and Occupational Therapy in Pediatrics, 7,* 17–34.

Palmer, F.B., Shapiro, B.K., Allen, M.C., et al. (1990). Infant stimulation curriculum for infants with cerebral palsy: Effects on infant temperament, parent-infant interaction, and home environment. *Pediatrics, 85,* 411–415.

Palmer, F.B., Shapiro, B.K., Wachtel, R.C., et al. (1988). The effects of phsyical therapy on cerebral palsy. A controlled trial in infants with spastic diplegia. *New England Journal of Medicine, 318,* 803–808.

Paneth, N. (1986). Etiologic factors in cerebral palsy. *Pediatric Annals, 15,* 191, 194–195, 197–201.

Paneth, N., & Kiely, J.L. (1984). The frequency of cerebral palsy: A review of population studies in industrialized nations since 1950. *Clinics in Developmental Medicine, 87,* 46–56.

Park, T.S., & Owen, J.H. (1992). Surgical management of spastic diplegia in cerebral palsy. *New England Journal of Medicine, 326,* 745–749.

Peacock, W.J., & Staudt, L.A. (1990). Spasticity in cerebral palsy and the selective posterior rhizotomy procedure. *Journal of Child Neurology, 5,* 179–185.

Perin, B. (1989). Physical therapy for the child with cerebral palsy. In J.S. Tecklin (Ed.), *Pediatric physical therapy* (pp. 68–105). Philadelphia: J.B. Lippincott.

Pharoah, P.O., Cooke, T., Rosenbloom, L., et al. (1987). Trends in birth prevalence of cerebral palsy. *Archives of Disease in Childhood, 62,* 379–384.

Pidcock, F.S., Graziani, L.J., Stanley, C., et al. (1990). Neurosonographic features of periventricular echodensities associated with cerebral palsy in preterm infants. *Journal of Pediatrics, 116,* 417–422.

Piper, M.C., Mazer, B., Silver, K.M., et al. (1988). Resolution of neurological symptoms in high-risk infants during the first two years of life. *Developmental Medicine and Child Neurology, 30,* 26–35.

Platt, L.J., Andrews, G., & Howie, P.M. (1980). Dysarthria of adult cerebral palsy II. Phonemic analysis of articulation errors. *Journal of Speech and Hearing Research, 23,* 41–55.

Rempel, G.R., Colwell, S.O., & Nelson, R.P. (1988). Growth in children with cerebral palsy fed via gastrostomy. *Pediatrics, 82,* 857–862.

Robinson, R.O. (1973). The frequency of other handicaps in children with cerebral palsy. *Developmental Medicine and Child Neurology, 15,* 305–312.

Russman, B.S., & Gage, J.R. (1989). Cerebral palsy. *Current Problems in Pediatrics, 19,* 65–111.

Sankey, R.J., Anderson, D.M., & Young, J.A. (1989). Characteristics of ankle-foot orthoses for management of the spastic lower limb. *Developmental Medicine and Child Neurology, 31,* 466–470.

Scher, M.S., Belfar, H., Martin, J., et al. (1991). Destructive brain lesions of presumed fetal onset: Antepartum causes of cerebral palsy. *Pediatrics, 88,* 898–906.

Schleichkorn, J. (1983). *Coping with cerebral palsy: Answers to questions parents often ask.* Austin, TX: PRO-ED.

Schultz-Hurlburt, B., & Tervo, R.C. (1982). Wheelchair users at a children's rehabilitation center: Attributes and management. *Developmental Medicine and Child Neurology, 24,* 54–60.

Smelt, H.R. (1989). Effect of an inhibitive weight-bearing mitt on tone reduction and functional performance in a child with cerebral palsy. *Physical and Occupational Therapy in Pediatrics, 9,* 53–80.

Smith, L.H., & Harris, S.R. (1985). Upper extremity inhibitive casting for a child with cerebral palsy. *Physical and Occupational Therapy in Pediatrics, 5,* 71–79.

Stanley, F., & Alberman, E. (1984). The epidemiology of the cerebral palsies. *Clinics in Developmental Medicine, 87,* 57–149.

Tirosh, E., & Rabino, S. (1989). Physiotherapy for children with cerebral palsy. Evidence for its efficacy. *American Journal of Diseases of Children, 143,* 552–555.

Treviranus, J., & Tannock, R. (1987). A scanning computer access system for children with severe physical disabilities. *American Journal of Occupational Therapy, 41,* 733–738.

Uvebrant, P. (1988). Hemiplegic cerebral palsy. Aetiology and outcome. *Acta Paediatrica Scandinavica, 345*(Suppl.), 1–100.

Watt, J.M., Robinson, C.M., & Grace, M.G. (1989). Early prognosis for ambulation of neonatal intensive care survivors with cerebral palsy. *Developmental Medicine and Child Neurology, 31,* 766–773.

Yasukawa, A. (1990). Upper extremity casting: Adjunct treatment for a child with cerebral palsy hemiplegia. *American Journal of Occupational Therapy, 44,* 840–846.

Zigler, E. (1981). A plea to end the use of the patterning treatment for retarded children. *American Journal of Orthopsychiatry, 51,* 388–390.

Chapter 25

Neural Tube Defects
Spina Bifida and Myelomeningocele

Edward B. Charney

Upon completion of this chapter, the reader will:
—be able to define spina bifida and myelomeningocele
—be able to discuss the incidence and multifactorial causes of myelomeningocele
—know the nature of myelomeningocele's effects on the spinal cord and brain
—appreciate the diversity of the myelomeningocele population
—recognize disabilities associated with neural tube defects
—become familiar with intervention strategies, the need for team management, and establishment of goals for independence

Neural tube defects refer to a group of congenital malformations of the vertebrae and spinal cord. The most common type of neural tube defect is the combination of spina bifida and myelomeningocele. The term *spina bifida* refers to a separation in the bones of the spinal column (the vertebral arches). Myelomeningocele describes a fluid-filled sac that protrudes from the defective spine and contains the malformed spinal cord. In spina bifida with myelomeningocele, a portion of the spinal cord is visible at birth. Typically, this exposed section would be contained within the vertebral column (Figure 25.1). The nerves below the opening fail to develop, leading to paralysis and loss of sensation. The other types of neural tube defects vary in severity, according to the extent of vertebral closure and spinal cord exposure. At the mild end is benign meningocele, in which a protruding sac surrounds a normal spinal cord, resulting in no neurological deficits. The most severe neural tube defect is the invariably fatal anencephaly, in which there is no development above the brain stem.

As a result of the paralysis and loss of sensation, the child with spina bifida and myelomeningocele usually has difficulty with ambulation and experiences impaired

Edward B. Charney, M.D., is Associate Professor of Pediatrics at The University of Pennsylvania School of Medicine in Philadelphia and is Director of the Spina Bifida Program for The Children's Hospital of Philadelphia and Children's Seashore House.

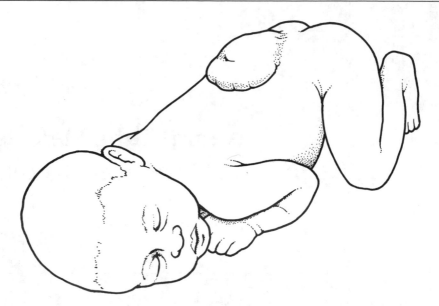

Figure 25.1.   A newborn with a neural tube defect. The sac (i.e., myelomeningocele) covers the malformed spinal cord and rests above the defect in the vertebral column (i.e., spina bifida).

bowel and bladder control. This chapter addresses not only these disabilities and approaches to their treatment, but also the resulting effects on the psychosocial and cognitive development of the child, and the severe psychological and economic stress that can affect the family of the child with a neural tube defect.

INCIDENCE AND CAUSES OF NEURAL TUBE DEFECTS

As a group, neural tube defects occur in approximately 1 in 1,000 births in the United States (Hobbins, 1991). The causes of these defects are unclear. It is known that the defect occurs approximately 28 days after the fertilization of the egg, when the neural tube fails to close (Figure 25.2). As a result, the vertebral arches also do not close completely. These disorders are believed to be multifactorial in origin, with both environmental and genetic influences. Many environmental causes have been proposed, including iodine deficiency, blighted potatoes, and folic acid deficiency. None of these has been proven (Mills, Rhoads, Simpson, et al., 1989). However, in women who have previously given birth to infants with neural tube defects, prenatal treatment with folic acid has been quite successful in preventing recurrences (MRC Vitamin Study Research Group, 1991). Furthermore, maternal alcoholism and treatment with certain antiepileptic drugs (e.g., valproic acid, carbamazepine) during the first trimester of pregnancy predispose the fetus to neural tube defects (Main & Mennuti, 1986; Rosa, 1991).

Regarding genetic influences, couples who have had one child with spina bifida have a recurrence risk about 50 times higher than the general population (Noetzel, 1989). Certain ethnic groups also have a higher incidence of neural tube defects. For

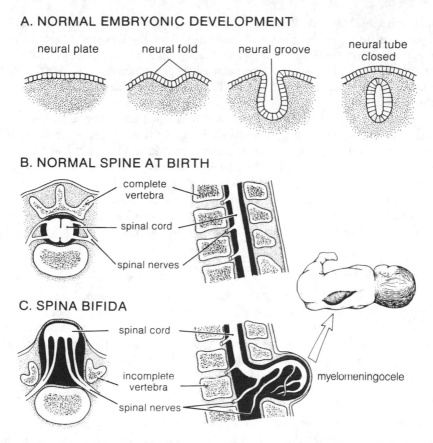

A. NORMAL EMBRYONIC DEVELOPMENT

neural plate   neural fold   neural groove   neural tube closed

B. NORMAL SPINE AT BIRTH

complete vertebra
spinal cord
spinal nerves

C. SPINA BIFIDA

spinal cord
incomplete vertebra
spinal nerves
myelomeningocele

Figure 25.2. Spina bifida with myelomeningocele: A) The normal formation of the neural tube (i.e., the precursor of the spinal column) during the first month of gestation. B) Complete closure of the neural groove has occurred, and the vertebral column and spinal cord appear normal in cross-section on the left and in the longitudinal section on the right. C) Incomplete closure of an area of the spine is called *spina bifida* and is usually accompanied by a sac-like abnormality of the spinal cord, the myelomeningocele. As no nerves form below this malformation, the child is paralyzed below that point.

example, the incidence of spina bifida in Ireland and in Americans of Irish descent is four times higher than that found in the general population of the United States (Noetzel, 1989). Finally, neural tube defects may occur as part of a complex genetic syndrome—for example, in the chromosomal disorders trisomy 13 and trisomy 18. It is encouraging to note that the incidence of spina bifida appears to be declining, although the reason for this remains unclear (Edmonds & James, 1990).

PRENATAL DIAGNOSIS

A neural tube defect can be diagnosed prenatally using several techniques (Main & Mennuti, 1986) (see Chapter 3). The classic approach has been to measure levels of alpha-fetoprotein (AFP) in the amniotic fluid of a mother who has previously had a child with spina bifida. AFP, which is synthesized by the yolk sac and fetal liver, is a major circulatory protein in the early months of fetal development. In fetuses with neural tube defects, AFP spills into the amniotic fluid from fetal blood vessels on the surface of the open neural tube. Amniocentesis is performed in the second trimester of pregnancy, at which time AFP levels will be significantly elevated in about 95% of fetuses with open neural tube defects.

More recently, the measurement of AFP in maternal serum during the 16th–18th week of pregnancy has been offered as a screening test to all pregnant women regardless of their risk of carrying a fetus with a neural tube defect (Committee on Genetics, 1991; Johnson, Palomaki, & Haddow, 1990). This test detects about 75%–80% of open neural tube defects. Amniocentesis can be augmented by other studies that aid in prenatal diagnosis, including high resolution ultrasonography to visualize the vertebral malformation (Nadel, Green, Holmes, et al., 1990) and enzyme analysis to detect elevation in the level of acetylcholinesterase (ACHE).

NEUROLOGICAL DEFICITS

Surgical closure of the myelomeningocele defect is usually performed within the first few days of life (Charney, Weller, Sutton, Bruce, & Schut, 1985; Rekate, 1991). Although this may prevent an infection of the spinal cord or brain, the surgery has no effect on the neurological function of the infant. The extent of motor paralysis and sensory loss depends on where the defect occurs in the spinal cord, with all sensory and motor function below that point being impaired.

Paralysis

The chest and back regions of the spinal cord contain twelve thoracic (T1–T12) and five lumbar (L1–L5) vertebrae, respectively (Figure 25.3). The lower back region contains five sacral vertebrae (S1–S5). Children with defects at the thoracic or high lumbar (L1 or L2) level are said to have high-level paralysis that affects the lower extremities and causes variable weakness in the lower body region (Figure 25.4). Children with defects at L3 have mid paralysis, which means they can flex at the hips and extend at the knees, but are paralyzed at the ankles and toes. Children with low lumbar lesions (L4 or L5) have low paralysis. They can flex the hips and extend the knees and ankles, but may often have weak or absent ankle/toe flexion, and hip extension. Children with sacral lesions usually have only mild weakness at the ankles or toes. The higher the lesion, the greater the impairment in ambulation.

Arnold-Chiari Malformation and Hydrocephalus

Children with myelomeningocele have not only a defect of the spinal cord, but also associated congenital malformations of the brain. Almost all of these children have what is called an *Arnold-Chiari type II malformation* of the hindbrain (Griebel, Oakes, & Worley, 1991). As part of this malformation, the brain stem and part of the cerebellum are displaced downward toward the neck, rather than remaining within the skull (Figure 25.5).

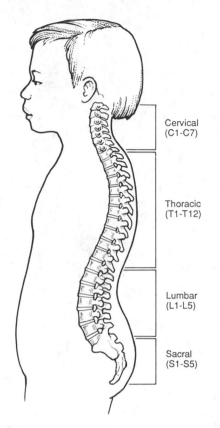

Cervical
(C1-C7)

Thoracic
(T1-T12)

Lumbar
(L1-L5)

Sacral
(S1-S5)

Figure 25.3. The vertebral column is divided into seven neck (cervical), twelve chest (thoracic), five back (lumbar), and five lower-back (sacral) vertebrae. Spina bifida most commonly affects the thoracolumbar region.

This malformation interferes with the normal flow of cerebrospinal fluid and results in enlargement of the ventricles (i.e., the fluid-filled spaces in the brain), a condition termed *hydrocephalus*. Hydrocephalus develops in 60%–95% of children with myelomeningocele and is more common in higher-level lesions (Griebel et al., 1991). A diagnosis of hydrocephalus can be made with ultrasound in the newborn period.

In general, infants with hydrocephalus require a shunting procedure several days after the spinal opening is surgically closed. In this procedure, cerebrospinal fluid (CSF) from the enlarged ventricular system is diverted to another place in the body where it can be better absorbed. Most frequently, a ventriculo-peritoneal (V-P) shunt is used, through which the fluid is drained into the infant's abdominal cavity (Figure 25.6). A small plastic catheter is inserted into one of the enlarged ventricles and connected to another catheter that is placed under the skin behind the child's ear. This catheter runs under the skin of the neck and chest and into the abdominal cavity. Extra

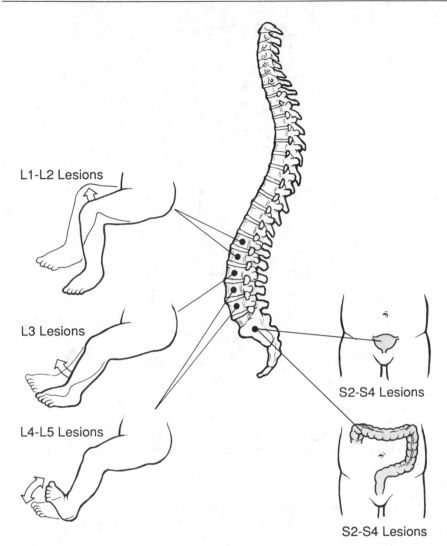

Figure 25.4.   The effects of various levels of spina bifida on the child's ability to move lower extremities and to control bowel and bladder function.

tubing is left in the abdomen so that as the child grows it can uncoil without getting clogged.

Once placed, the shunt may become blocked, especially during the first year of life. In infants, a blocked shunt results in excessive head growth and a tense "soft spot" on the forehead. By the second year of life, a blocked shunt results in symptoms of severe headache, vomiting, and irritability because the skull bones have fused and pressure builds inside the closed space. It is important to recognize this early, as a blocked shunt can be life-threatening. If there is concern about a blocked shunt, the child should be taken to a neurosurgeon, who will consider surgically revising the

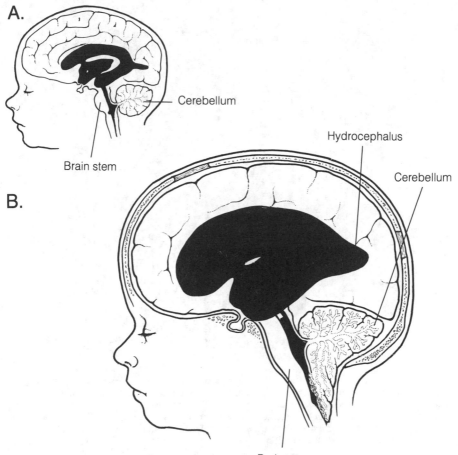

A.

Cerebellum

Brain stem

B.

Hydrocephalus

Cerebellum

Brain stem

Figure 25.5.   A) The normal brain. B) The Arnold-Chiari malformation, which predisposes a child with myelomeningocele to have hydrocephalus. The brain stem and part of the cerebellum are displaced downward toward the neck region, leading to blockage of cerebrospinal fluid flow.

shunt. The neurosurgeon may order a CT or MRI scan to determine if the ventricles have enlarged or may tap the shunt to detect increased intracranial pressure. If there is evidence of a blockage, the neurosurgeon removes the blocked part of the shunt and replaces it with a new catheter. As an interim measure the medications acetazolamide (Diamox), dexamethasone (Decadron) and/or furosemide (Lasix) may be given to decrease cerebrospinal fluid production and resultant increased intracranial pressure.

A second potential complication of a ventriculo-peritoneal shunt is infection. In this case, the child may become febrile and have clinical symptoms of vomiting or lethargy. The neurosurgeon again withdraws fluid through the tubing, this time in order to culture it for bacteria. If found to be infected, the child receives intravenous antibiotics. It also may be necessary to remove an infected shunt and, after antibiotic treatment, replace it with a new one.

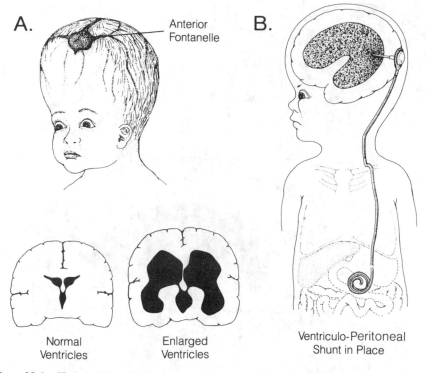

Figure 25.6. Hydrocephalus. A) The head is enlarged with fullness or bulging around the "soft spot," or anterior fontanelle. A cross-section of the brain shows markedly enlarged lateral ventricles. B) A ventriculo-peritoneal shunt has been placed. A plastic tube is inserted into one of the lateral ventricles. Another tube runs under the skin from the skull to the abdominal cavity. Enough extra tubing is left in the abdomen to uncoil as the child grows. The block is bypassed, and cerebrospinal fluid can then flow directly from the ventricles to the abdominal cavity.

In addition to hydrocephalus, the Arnold-Chiari malformation may lead to 6th cranial nerve palsy that may cause strabismus (see Chapter 17). Other cranial nerve involvement may cause vocal cord paralysis with breathing difficulties, swallowing difficulties, and/or periodic breathing (Charney, Rorke, Sutton, 1987) (see Chapter 7).

DISABILITIES ASSOCIATED WITH NEURAL TUBE DEFECTS

The combination of the neural tube defect, hydrocephalus, and other less well-defined neuropathological abnormalities of the brain contribute to deficits of mobility, musculoskeletal deformities, spinal malformations, bladder and bowel dysfunction, skin sores, obesity, seizure disorders, and visual and cognitive deficits.

Mobility

Depending on the level of the spinal cord lesion and the presence of hydrocephalus, there are varying degrees of compromise in early motor development and the subsequent ability to walk (Sousa, Telzrow, Holm, et al., 1983). Though the disabilities may be most marked among children with high-level paralysis (i.e., high lumbar and thoracic levels), there also may be significant delays among children with lower-level lesions.

Sensorimotor assessment during the child's first year should include evaluations of range of motion of joints, muscle tone, muscle strength, sensation, movement skills, postural control, and sensory integrative skills (Williamson, 1987). Because of the considerable diversity in the degree of delay among these children, individualized intervention plans must be developed. Overall, the goal should be to facilitate the child's development in a manner that will promote independence.

Many infants with myelomeningocele have delayed rolling and sitting skills. Typically, an infant learns to crawl on all fours at about 8–10 months of age. Most infants with myelomeningocele, regardless of their level of lesion, learn to belly crawl "commando style" as their first means of mobility. Infants with strong voluntary hip flexion and some knee movement may eventually assume the all-fours crawl, but often not until after 1 year of age.

Children with sacral (S1, S2) lesions generally learn to walk well by 2 or 3 years of age with bracing at the ankles or no bracing at all. Children with mid-lumbar (L3) paralysis often require crutches and bracing up to the hip (Table 25.1). Children with thoracic or high-lumbar paralysis may eventually walk, but require extensive bracing and crutches for independent ambulation. Those children with high-level paralysis who learn to walk are generally children who do not have mental retardation, who receive regular physical therapy for walking, and who have parents committed to carrying out walking therapy at home (Charney, Melchionni, & Smith, 1991). For those children with a combination of high-level paralysis and mental retardation, walking may not be a realistic goal. In these children, wheelchairs may be introduced at some time prior to 5 years of age to enhance mobility.

Table 25.1. Degree of paralysis and functional implications

Paralysis	Hydrocephalus (%)	Ambulation	Bowel/bladder incontinence (%)
Thoracic or high lumbar (L1, L2)	90	May walk with extensive braces and crutches	>90
Mid lumbar (L3)	85	Can walk with either extensive, moderate, or minimal braces, and usually with crutches	>90
Low lumbar (L4, L5)	70	Will walk with moderate, minimal, or no bracing with or without crutches	>90
Sacral (S1 to S4)	60	Will walk with minimal or no braces and usually without crutches	>90

From Charney, E.B. (1990). Myelomeningocele. In M.W. Schwartz (Ed.), *Pediatric primary care: A problem-oriented approach*, p. 663. Chicago: Mosby-Year Book; reprinted by permission.

Children should be encouraged to walk as early as possible. If ambulation is achieved by adolescence, the child will be much more independent both at home and in the community than if he or she is dependent on a wheelchair (Mazur, Shurtleff, Menelaus, et al., 1989). Adolescents who must rely on wheelchairs have an increased likelihood of developing fractures and skin pressure sores as well as a lack of independence.

Musculoskeletal Deformities

With partial or total paralysis, there may be muscle imbalances that lead to deformities around the joints. For example, club foot is often present in infants with mid-lumbar (L3) or higher-level paralysis. Treatment involves serial casting during the first 3–4 months of life to gradually straighten the deformity; corrective surgery follows at 4 months to 1 year of age. Other ankle and foot deformities also may require surgical intervention to facilitate proper foot placement in shoes. Another option is bracing, which helps to minimize the likelihood of skin breakdown over bony prominences (Figure 25.7).

Muscle imbalance also accounts for hip deformities. Children with high-lumbar or thoracic-level paralysis are vulnerable to developing hip muscle contractures that interfere with walking and lead to hip dislocation. Surgical correction may be appropriate only for those children with low lumbar level paralysis who have the potential for ambulation (Menelaus, 1980; Sherk, Uppal, Lane, & Melchionni, 1991).

Knee deformities are much less common than those involving the ankle and foot or hip. Surgical correction may be necessary only for those deformities that interfere with sitting or walking.

Spinal Curvatures and Humps

Spinal curvatures and humps occur in almost 90% of children with myelomeningocele (Mayfield, 1991). These deformities include scoliosis, a spinal curvature; **kyphosis**, a spinal hump; and **kyphoscoliosis**, a combination of both conditions (Figure 25.8). Scoliosis, the most common of these deformities, may be congenital or may develop in later childhood. Kyphosis is usually congenital.

Like club foot and hip dislocation, developmental scoliosis is a consequence of muscle imbalance. It is most often seen in children with high-lumbar or thoracic-level paralysis. Congenital scoliosis and kyphosis are usually associated with spine and rib malformations. The curve or hump associated with congenital spinal deformities is rigid, and usually gets worse early. In contrast to this, developmental curvatures are flexible until later in childhood and are more amenable to correction.

If untreated, spinal deformities may eventually interfere with sitting and walking. Developmental scoliosis equal to or greater than 30° requires an orthotic (molded plastic shieldlike jacket) support (see Chapter 24). Despite this, the curvature often progresses and surgery may be necessary (Mayfield, 1991). Surgical correction involves a spinal fusion, with the external fixation and stabilization of the spinal column (see Figure 24.14) (Ward, Wenger, & Roach, 1989). Children with congenital rather

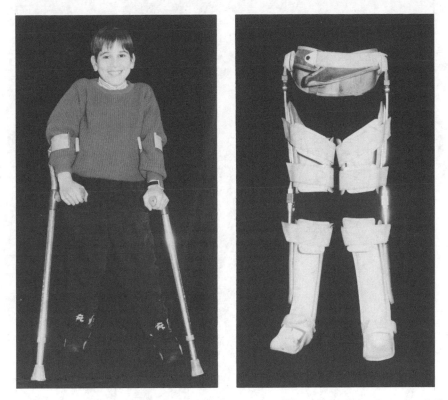

Figure 25.7. A child with a high-lumbar myelomeningocele walking with bracing and crutches (left). Long leg braces with pelvic band (right).

than developmental scoliosis generally respond poorly to orthotic treatment and may require spinal fusions at young ages.

Kyphosis is usually located in the lumbar spine and may measure 80°–90° at birth. The hump on the spine is rigid and may worsen during infancy. Surgical removal of the deformity, called a *kyphectomy*, is possible but controversial. A kyphectomy performed at the time of myelomeningocele back closure has not been universally successful and has had a high incidence of complications and recurrence (Mayfield, 1991).

Whenever surgery is being considered to correct a musculoskeletal deformity, it should be performed only if there will be some functional benefit to the child. It may be done to improve positioning in a brace, to minimize pressure sites, or to facilitate sitting. Surgery should not be performed solely to improve the child's appearance.

Bladder Dysfunction

Bladder and bowel dysfunction are present in virtually all children with myelomeningocele, regardless of their level of spinal cord lesion or paralysis. Messages from both motor and sensory nerves for bladder and bowel function are conveyed through the

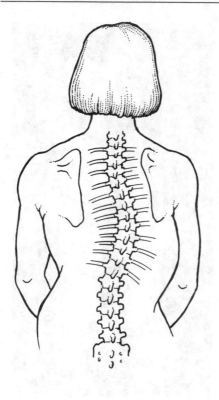

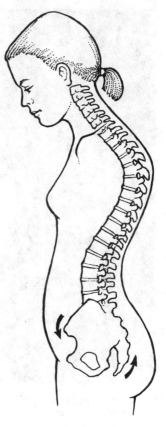

Scoliosis

Kyphosis

Figure 25.8.   Common spinal deformities associated with spina bifida: spinal curvature scoliosis (left) and spinal humping or kyphosis (right).

S2–S4 level of the spinal cord (see Figure 25.4). Therefore, even those children with sacral lesions and normal leg movement often have bladder and bowel problems.

The bladder has two major functions: to store urine that has been produced by the kidney, and to empty the urine when the bladder is full. Children with myelomeningocele may have difficulty with both functions. Problems with either storage or emptying can lead to incontinence (i.e., the inability for normal toileting with urinary control) and infection of the bladder and/or kidneys. These children also may be at risk for kidney damage because of the high pressure generated in the bladder and resultant back flow into the kidney.

In infancy, management of the bladder dysfunction is directed at minimizing bladder infections by giving daily oral antibiotics. The kidneys are also studied with ultrasound at 6- to 12-month intervals to ensure that they remain normal. Attempts to achieve urinary continence are generally begun at 3–4 years of age. This is done using a technique termed *clean intermittent bladder catheterization* (CIC). Parents are taught how to insert a clean, but not sterile, catheter (tube) through the urethra and into the bladder. This is done four times a day to drain urine. In this manner, urine does not accumulate, become infected, and flow back into the kidney. For a catheterization program to be successful, both the parents and child must comply. Medications may be necessary if CIC does not result in continence. Medications such as oxybutynin chloride (Ditropan) are often used to diminish bladder wall contractions, and ephedrine sulfate or imipramine chloride (Tofranil) may also be used to enhance storage of urine. Using a combination of CIC and medications, continence is achieved during the elementary school years in about 85% of children with bladder dysfunction due to myelomeningocele. A surgical intervention such as bladder augmentation, in which the bladder capacity is increased, is only considered for a well-motivated and mature child who has remained incontinent despite regular CIC and medication trials (Shurtleff, 1986).

Bowel Dysfunction

Bowel problems in children with myelomeningocele are related to either ineffective relaxation or contraction of the internal anal sphincter, combined with a lack of sensation in or around the anus. Inability to relax the sphincter results in a dilated large bowel and the infrequent passage of constipated hard stools, interspersed with periods of "overflow" diarrhea. In addition, lack of sensation leads to soiling. Attempts at bowel management are usually begun between 2½ and 4 years of age, before the trials of CIC for urinary continence. Some children achieve bowel continence with "timed" potty-sitting after every meal. At this time, they may be able to supplement the postfeeding gastrocolic reflex with abdominal straining. If, after several months, bowel control has not been achieved by this method, parents may be instructed in the administration of a nightly rectal suppository (e.g., bisacodyl, Dulcolax) that will facilitate more complete bowel emptying. Attention to diet is also important to maintain a stool consistency that is neither too hard nor too loose. This includes providing adequate fluids, bulking agents, and natural laxatives such as prunes.

Achievement of bladder and bowel continence is both a realistic and critical part of the child's development. Competence in toileting, as a very basic activity of daily living, is necessary for normal emotional and social growth toward independence. Prevention of soiling, wetness, and odor also enhances the child's self-esteem.

Skin Sores (Decubital Ulcers)

Skin sores or decubital ulcers often occur in children with myelomeningocele. For most of these children, the weight-bearing surface of their bodies (e.g., feet, buttocks) are not sensitive to pain. Sores thus become a problem when young children are mobile and sustain injuries that they do not feel. Inadequate circulation increases the problem, because the wounds do not heal properly. Management of this problem should be anticipatory—using sunscreen to prevent sunburn, replacing tight-fitting shoes or braces, and avoiding hot baths or crawling about on rough or hot surfaces. For children in wheelchairs, pressure sores on the buttock region can be prevented by modifying the wheelchair with adaptive seating cushions. Existing sores should be treated with specialized dressings. Additional pressure or trauma to the affected skin should be avoided.

Obesity

Children with myelomeningocele are at increased risk for obesity because their impaired mobility means they burn fewer calories. As a result, about two-thirds of these children are significantly overweight in spite of what appears to be a normal or even reduced-calorie diet. Attention should be directed at increasing involvement in regular physical activities and limiting sweets and fats in the diet.

Seizure Disorders

Approximately 15% of individuals with myelomeningocele have seizures at some time in their lives (Noetzel, 1989). Seizures most commonly occur during early childhood and may be associated with a blocked shunt. Usually these seizures are tonic-clonic and respond well to antiepileptic medication (see Chapter 26) or to the correction of the blocked shunt.

Visual Deficits

Strabismus, or squint, is present in about 20% of children with myelomeningocele. This may result from cranial nerve palsies associated with an Arnold-Chiari malformation of the brain stem. Strabismus also may result in association with hydrocephalus. The increased pressure on cranial nerve VI, which controls the sideways movement of the eye, can cause the eye to turn inward. Strabismus often requires surgical correction (see Chapter 17).

Cognitive Deficits

Approximately two-thirds of children with myelomeningocele and shunted hydrocephalus have intelligence that falls within the range of normal (Diller, Swinyard, & Epstein, 1978). The remaining one-third have mental retardation, usually in the mild range. The few children with myelomeningocele who have severe mental retardation often have a head circumference at birth well above the 95th percentile and/or a history of brain infection in the newborn period.

A communication disorder involving hyperverbal behavior also may be evident in children with myelomeningocele, mental retardation, and hydrocephalus (Tew, 1979). This term implies that the child will talk incessantly using sophisticated words but with poor understanding of meaning. The child may repeatedly use social phrases or greetings, such as "Oh, come on . . . ," or "Hi." In receptive language, these children have difficulty answering, "who," "what," "where," "when," and "why" questions. This hyperverbal behavior must be distinguished from what may at first appear to be normal or precocious language development (see Chapter 19).

Children who do not have mental retardation may still have difficulties in perceptual organizational abilities, attention, speed of motor response, memory, and hand function (Wills, Holmbeck, Dillon, et al., 1990). As a consequence, many of these children have learning problems in most subjects (Williamson, 1987) (see Chapter 20). It is critical that these children not be simply pushed along in a regular school placement. Realistic expectations must be established, individual strengths and weaknesses identified, and appropriate education programs developed.

PSYCHOSOCIAL ISSUES

Failure in the school setting may exacerbate a preexisting poor self-image that many of these children have as a result of their physical disability. This feeling of being different can contribute to problems in establishing peer relationships in both the school and the community (Hayden, 1985). School is but one of the many stresses that children with myelomeningocele and their families experience at various times in childhood and adolescence. During the preschool years, increased independence may be thwarted by problems with mobility and bladder or bowel control. The child's self-esteem also may be lowered if he or she must continue to wear diapers. As an older child, lowered self-esteem may also relate to a poor body image and difficulty with the normal sexual changes and feelings of emerging puberty (Blum, Resnick, Nelson, et al., 1991; Rinck, Berg, & Hafeman, 1989). This may include the presence of impotence because of the spinal cord lesion. The more physical disabilities the adolescent has, the more difficult it is to achieve independence in activities of daily living. There may also be ongoing bladder and bowel dysfunction and inadequately addressed educational and socialization needs.

MULTIDISCIPLINARY MANAGEMENT

Multidisciplinary team care of children with neural tube defects is of utmost importance. Because of the many associated disabilities, it is difficult, if not impossible, for one individual or discipline to be solely responsible for the child and family. Core team members should include a physician (e.g., developmental pediatrician, pediatric neurologist, physiatrist) with particular interest and expertise in care of myelomeningocele, a nurse coordinator, a physical and occupational therapist, a social worker, and consulting orthopedic, urological, and neurosurgical surgeons. Other team members or consultants may include an orthotist (who measures for braces and splints), a psychologist, a special educator, a speech-language therapist, a genetic counselor, and a financial counselor. Coordination of all these services should become the responsibility of a designated case manager. Efforts should be directed at developing a consensus of team management, whereby the child and family are presented with a management plan that is both appropriate and realistic for the child. The success of children with myelomeningocele is largely dependent on how well the team works and communicates with the child and family, and how well it coordinates services in the community.

BRIAN: A CHILD WITH MYELOMENINGOCELE

Brian was born at term to his 17-year-old mother. At the time of birth a thoracic-level spina bifida with myelomeningocele was evident. This was surgically closed at 2 days of age, and a ventriculo-peritoneal shunt was inserted at 7 days of age. Prior to Brian's discharge from the hospital, his mother was instructed in range of motion exercises and proper positioning. During his first year of life, Brian made good developmental progress so that by 1 year of age, he was sitting independently, crawling about "commando style" by propelling himself with his arms, and speaking several single words. By 13 months of age, he began to stand in a set of long leg braces with a pelvic support band and received weekly physical therapy for walking. By 3 years of age, Brian was walking independently in the community using braces and crutches (see Figure 25.7).

At 5 years, Brian was enrolled in a special school for children with orthopedic disabilities. He was found to have normal intelligence, but learning disabilities soon became evident. Brian did well in school and maintained close friendships with children from his neighborhood. Brian particularly enjoyed playing football and other sports with them. During this time, Brian also became independent in a CIC and bowel program. When he was 11 years old, Brian required a spinal fusion procedure for progressive scoliosis. The scoliosis has not progressed since that time.

Brian is now 20 years old and majoring in mental health counseling at a community college. He is still walking in the community and has an active social life.

PROGNOSIS

Great strides have been made in the survival rate of children with myelomeningocele over the past 40 years (Dunne & Shurtleff, 1986). In the 1950s, survival to adulthood occurred in less than 10% of children with spina bifida. At present, survival to adulthood stands at about 85% (McLone, 1989). The change in the survival rate is attributable to many factors including placing of ventriculo-peritoneal shunts and prevention of kidney damage.

Adult outcome data are thus far incomplete, and the population is quite heterogeneous. Most adults who are over 30 years of age are individuals without hydrocephalus who survived the preshunt era of the 1950s, while adults in their 20s now include individuals with more severe disabilities who benefited from the recent advances in medical and surgical management. According to several studies, these adults have experienced problems with unemployment and social isolation (Dunne & Shurtleff, 1986; Smith, 1983).

In a study conducted by Hunt (1990), half of the individuals with myelomeningocele were still able to walk 50 yards or more in adulthood. Half were also able to maintain urinary and bowel continence. Overall, 12% had minimal disabilities, implying normal intelligence, community ambulation, and well-managed continence. Fifty-two percent had moderate disability, defined as using a wheelchair with the ability to transfer, near-normal intelligence, and the ability to attend to toilet needs independently. Severe disability involving mental retardation, incontinence, and dependence for most self-help skills was found in 37%. Among the total group about one-quarter are employed.

SUMMARY

Neural tube defects most commonly involve an area of unclosed vertebral column (spina bifida) together with an overlying sac containing a malformed spinal cord (myelomeningocele). There is paralysis below the level of the spinal cord defect. There is a range of disabilities associated with this condition, including paralysis, musculoskeletal abnormalities, bowel and bladder incontinence, obesity, and learning disabilities. Recent advances in surgical and medical technology have enhanced the survival and physical well-being of these individuals, although not "cured" the associated deficits. The challenge now is to intervene effectively in the areas of education and psychosocial adjustment for these children and their families so that they can reach their potential.

REFERENCES

Blum, R.W., Resnick, M.D., Nelson, R., et al. (1991). Family and peer issues among adolescents with spina bifida and cerebral palsy. *Pediatrics, 88,* 280–285.

Charney, E.B. (1990). Myelomeningocele. In M.W. Schwartz, E.B. Charney, T.A. Curry, & S. Ludwig (Eds.), *Pediatric primary care: A problem-oriented approach* (2nd ed.). Chicago: Yearbook Medical Publishers.

Charney, E.B., Melchionni, J.B., & Smith, D.R. (1991). Community ambulation by children with myelomeningocele and high level paralysis. *Journal of Pediatric Orthopaedics, 11,* 579–582.

Charney, E.B., Rorke, L.B., Sutton, L.N., et al. (1987). Management of Chiari II complications in infants with myelomeningocele. *Journal of Pediatrics, 111,* 364–371.

Charney, E.B., Weller, S.C., Sutton, L.N., Bruce, B.A., & Schut, L. (1985). Management of the newborn with myelomeningocele. Time for a decision making process. *Pediatrics, 75,* 58–64.

Committee on Genetics. (1991). Maternal serum alpha-fetoprotein screening. *Pediatrics, 88,* 1, 282–283.

Diller, L., Swinyard, C.A., & Epstein, F.J. (1978). Cognitive function in children. In C.A. Swinyard, (Ed.), *Decision making and the defective newborn: Proceedings of a conference on spina bifida and ethics.* Springfield, IL: Charles C Thomas.

Dunne, K.B., & Shurtleff, D.B. (1986). The adult with myelomeningocele: A preliminary report. In R.L. McLaurin (Ed.), *Spina bifida* (pp. 38–51). New York: Praeger.

Edmonds, L.D., & James, L.M. (1990). Temporal trends in the prevalence of congenital malformations at birth based on the Birth Defects Monitoring Program, United States, 1979–1987. *Mortality and Morbidity Weekly Report, 39*(SS-4), 19–23.

Griebel, M.L., Oakes, W.J., & Worley, G. (1991). The Chiari malformation associated with myelomeningocele. In H.L. Rekate (Ed.), *Comprehensive management of spina bifida* (pp. 67–92). Boca Raton, FL: CRC Press.

Hayden, P.W. (1985). Adolescents with myelomeningocele. *Pediatrics in Review, 6,* 245–252.

Hobbins, J.C. (1991). Diagnosis and management of neural-tube defects today. *New England Journal of Medicine, 324,* 690–691.

Hunt, G.M. (1990). Open spina bifida: Outcome for a complete cohort treated unselectively and followed into adulthood. *Developmental Medicine and Child Neurology, 32,* 108–118.

Johnson, A.M., Palomaki, G.E., & Haddow, J.E. (1990). Maternal serum alpha-fetoprotein levels in pregnancies among black and white women with fetal open spina bifida: A United States collaborative study. *American Journal of Obstetrics and Gynecology, 162,* 328–331.

Main, D.M., & Mennuti, M.T. (1986). Neural tube defects: Issues in prenatal diagnosis and counselling. *Obstetrics and Gynecology, 67*(1), 1–16.

Mayfield, J.K. (1991). Comprehensive orthopedic management in myelomeningocele. In H.L. Rekate (Ed.), *Comprehensive management of spina bifida* (pp. 113–163), Boca Raton, FL: CRC Press.

Mazur, J.M., Shurtleff, D.B., Menelaus, M., et al. (1989). Orthopedic management of high-level spina bifida. Early walking compared with early use of wheel chair. *Journal of Bone and Joint Surgery, 71,* 56–61.

McLone, D.G. (1989). Spina bifida today: Problems adults face. *Seminars in Neurology, 9,* 169–175.

Menelaus, M.B. (1980). *The orthopedic management of spina bifida cystica.* New York: Churchhill Livingstone.

Mills, J.L., Rhoads, G.G., Simpson, J.L., et al. (1989). The absence of a relation between the periconceptional use of vitamins and neural-tube defects. *New England Journal of Medicine, 321,* 430–435.

MRC Vitamin Study Research Group. (1991). Prevention of neural tube defects: Results of the Medical Research Council Vitamin Study. *Lancet, 338,* 131–137.

Nadel, A.S., Green, J.K., Holmes, L.B., et al. (1990). Absence of need for amniocentesis in patients with elevated levels of maternal serum alpha-fetoprotein and normal ultrasonographic examinations. *New England Journal of Medicine, 323,* 557–561.

Noetzel, M.J. (1989). Myelomeningocele: Current concepts of management. *Clinics in Perinatology, 16,* 311–329.

Rekate, H.L. (1991). Neurosurgical management of the newborn with spina bifida. In H.L. Rekate (Ed.), *Comprehensive management of spina bifida* (pp. 1–28). Boca Raton, FL: CRC Press.

Rinck, C., Berg, J., & Hafeman, C. (1989). The adolescent with myelomeningocele: A review of parent experiences and expectations. *Adolescence, 24,* 699–710.

Rosa, F.W. (1991). Spina bifida in infants of women treated with carbamazepine during pregnancy. *New England Journal of Medicine, 324,* 674–677.

Sherk, H.H., Uppal, G.S., Lane, G., & Melchionni, J.B. (1991). Treatment versus non-treatment of hip dislocations in ambulatory patients with myelomeningocele. *Developmental Medicine and Child Neurology, 33,* 491–494.

Shurtleff, D.B. (1986). *Myelodysplasias and extrophies: Significance, prevention, and treatment.* New York: Grune & Stratton.

Smith, A.D. (1983). Adult spina bifida survey in Scotland: Educational attainment and employment. *Zeitschrift fur Kinderchirurgie (Journal for Pediatrics), 38*(Suppl. 2), 107–109.

Sousa, J.C., Telzrow, R.W., Holm, R.A., et al. (1983). Developmental guidelines for children with myelodysplasia. *Physical Therapy, 63*(1), 21–29.

Tew, B. (1979). The "cocktail party syndrome" in children with hydrocephalus and spina bifida. *British Journal of Disorders of Communication, 14,* 89–101.

Ward, W.T., Wenger, D.R., & Roach, J.W. (1989). Surgical correction of myelomeningocele scoliosis: A critical appraisal of various spinal instrumentation systems. *Journal of Pediatric Orthopedics, 9,* 262–268.

Williamson, G.G. (Ed.). (1987). *Children with spina bifida: Early intervention and preschool programming.* Baltimore: Paul H. Brookes Publishing Co.

Wills, K.E., Holmbeck, G.N., Dillon, K., et al. (1990). Intelligence and achievement in children with myelomeningocele. *Journal of Pediatric Psychology, 15,* 161–176.

Chapter 26

Seizure Disorders

Upon completion of this chapter, the reader will:
— understand what constitutes a seizure and how it happens
— know the various types of seizures
— be able to identify the various drugs used to treat seizures and know for which seizures they are effective
— realize what to do in case of a seizure
— be aware of the prognosis for children with seizure disorders

At some time during their lives, about 6% of the population in the United States will have a seizure (Aicardi, 1986). Over half of these seizures occur in early childhood, associated with a high fever or a head injury. Usually, these are single episodes that never recur and do not require medication. Even among children who have had non-**febrile** seizures only about 40% will have a second one within a subsequent 3-year period (Shinnar, Berg, Moshe, et al., 1990). These children do not have a seizure disorder. Recurrence of seizures is best predicted by abnormal electroencephalograms (EEGs) obtained shortly after the seizure episodes (Figure 26.1).

Individuals with repeated seizures have a seizure disorder, also called *epilepsy*. About 50% of all the children with a seizure disorder have normal intelligence; the other half have various degrees of mental retardation. Conversely, among children with developmental disabilities, the prevalence of seizure disorders is 16% in those with mental retardation, 25% in children with cerebral palsy, and 25% in children with spina bifida and hydrocephalus (Wallace, 1990). Children with learning disabilities do not have an increased risk of seizure disorders. However, children with seizure disorders do have a high incidence of learning disabilities and behavior and psychological problems (Aldenkamp, Alpherts, Dekker, et al., 1990).

Seizures in children without other developmental disabilities are generally well controlled with antiepileptic medication, and these drugs can usually be stopped if the child has no seizures for 2 years. However, children with multiple developmental disabilities in addition to seizure disorders often have more complex seizure patterns that are more difficult to control. They may require prolonged medication.

This chapter defines seizure disorders and describes various types of seizures, diagnostic tests, antiepileptic drugs and other forms of treatment, and prognosis.

WHAT IS A SEIZURE?

A seizure is a self-limited, repetitive, simultaneous electrical discharge from the neurons in the cortex of the brain (Clancy, 1990). A seizure begins in an area of the cortex called the *focus,* which contains neurons that are more apt to discharge electrically than normal cells. This discharge spreads and recruits the neurons that surround the seizure focus, causing them to discharge electrically. It is this excessive and periodic discharge that constitutes a seizure. Such a discharge, depending on its location in the brain, may lead to loss of consciousness, behavior changes, involuntary movements, altered muscle tone, or abnormal sensory phenomena.

The mechanism of seizure discharges is as follows: All nerve cells are enclosed by a membrane containing a pump that maintains a balance of mineral concentrations inside and outside of the cell. This balance is known as **polarization,** and neurons do not transmit impulses in this state. However, if there is a breakdown of the pump, **depolarization** occurs and the neurons fire off messages, lowering the **seizure threshold**. This is seen as the spike and wave pattern of seizure disorders on the electroencephalograph.

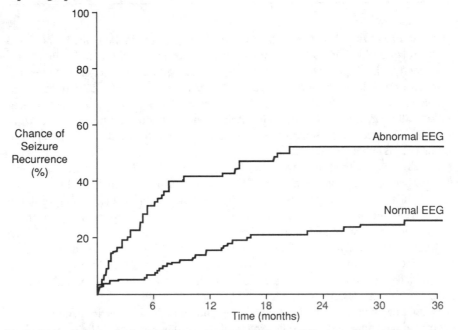

Figure 26.1. Percentage risk of seizure recurrence in the 3 years following a first nonfebrile seizure. Overall, about 40% of children had a second seizure. However, while those with normal EEGs had a 26% chance of recurrence, those with abnormal EEG patterns had a 56% chance of recurrence (From Shinnar, S., Berg, A.T., Moshe, S.L., et al. [1990]. Risk of seizure recurrence following a short unprovoked seizure in childhood: A prospective study. *Pediatrics, 85,* 1076; reprinted by permission. Copyright © 1990 *Pediatrics*).

This instability can occur if there is too much excitation or not enough inhibition of the neurons. As the central nervous system matures, a proper balance between excitatory and inhibitory neurotransmitters may be established. This new balance may explain why children may "grow out of" a seizure disorder.

OCCURRENCE OF SEIZURES

Seizures are often caused by developmental brain abnormalities, anoxia, hypoglycemia, inborn errors of metabolism, trauma, and infections. However, chromosomal disorders are less likely causes of seizures. Children with spastic cerebral palsy are more likely to have seizures than those with the extrapyramidal form. Children with severe mental retardation are more likely to have seizures than those with mild mental retardation (Goulden, Shinnar, Koller, et al., 1991). In general, males are at greater risk for seizures than females.

Once there is a seizure focus, the firing off of a seizure may occur at any time. However, certain circumstances make a seizure more likely. Fevers, sleep deprivation, head injury, and emotional excitement often prompt seizures. Actually, anyone can have a seizure, providing the fever is high enough or the head trauma severe enough to exceed the seizure threshold.

TYPES OF SEIZURES

There are two basic types of seizures, generalized and partial (Dreifuss, 1989). A generalized seizure involves the entire cortex, whereas a partial seizure is limited to a part of one hemisphere (Pellock, 1990). However, partial seizures may spread to become generalized, and an individual may have both generalized and partial seizures, which is called a *mixed seizure disorder*. A revised classification system was introduced in 1981 to describe types of seizures. New terms have replaced grand mal, petit mal, and temporal lobe seizures. The relationship between the old terms and their new equivalents is listed in Table 26.1. Generalized seizures include *tonic-clonic, absence, myoclonic,* and *atonic* forms. Partial seizures are divided into *simple* and *complex*, based on whether there is a change in consciousness. There is also a category of syndromes in which seizures play a principal role.

Some seizures that exist in early childhood (i.e., neonatal seizures and febrile convulsions) are somewhat unique and do not constitute a seizure disorder. They are discussed separately. Finally, the habits and conditions that simulate epilepsy but are not seizures are also discussed.

Generalized Seizures

Generalized seizures affect both hemispheres of the brain. They account for about 40% of all cases of epilepsy (Niedermeyer, 1990).

Tonic-Clonic Seizures   Of the generalized seizures, tonic-clonic is the most common type and is the prototype of an epileptic seizure. It involves excessive firing of neurons from both hemispheres in a symmetrical and simultaneous manner. This type of seizure can occur at any age (Figure 26.2). When a person has a tonic-clonic

Table 26.1.   Seizure classification system

International classification	Previous label
Generalized seizures	**Generalized seizures**
Absence	Petit mal
Myoclonic	Minor motor
Tonic-clonic	Grand mal
Atonic	Akinetic, drop attacks
Partial seizures	**Focal seizures**
Simple partial with motor symptoms	Jacksonian seizures
Complex partial seizures	Psychomotor seizures
	Temporal lobe seizures

Source: Commission on Classification and Terminology of the International League Against Epilepsy (1981).

seizure, there sometimes is an **aura** that precedes the major seizure and is actually a form of a simple partial seizure (see discussion of Simple Partial Seizures in this chapter). The major seizure starts with the person losing consciousness and falling to the floor. The individual initially becomes rigid for about 30 seconds to 1 minute during the tonic stage. During this period, the person may stop breathing or bite the tongue. Next is a clonic phase with rhythmic jerking of the body, sweating, and incontinence (Figure 26.3). This phase may last several minutes and may be followed by lethargy or sleep. This is called the *postictal* period and represents a period of cortical inhibition following the massive seizure discharge. Upon recovery, the person has no memory of the seizure itself. Some individuals have only tonic seizures or only clonic seizures.

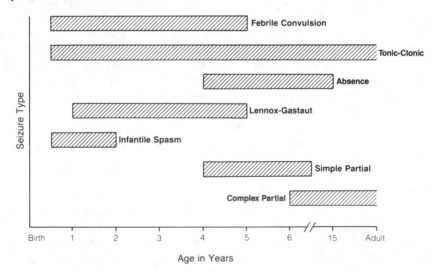

Figure 26.2.   Ages of occurrence of various types of seizures.

Tonic-Clonic

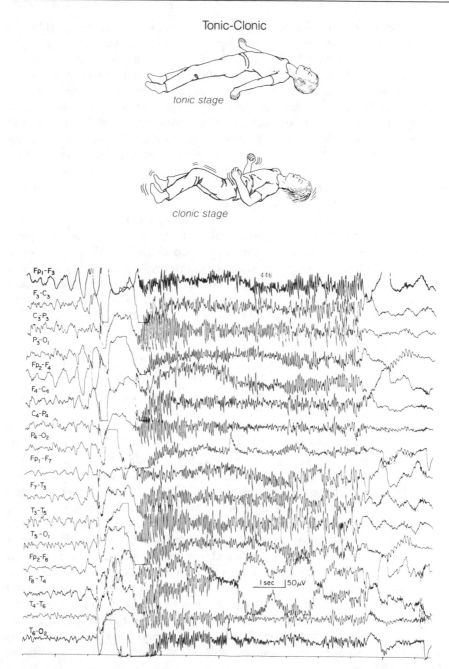

Figure 26.3. EEG pattern of a child with tonic-clonic seizures. There is a burst of spike activity over the entire cortex during the course of the seizure. (EEG from Neidermeyer, E., & Lopes da Silva, F. [1987]. *Electroencephalography: Basic principles, clinical applications, and related fields* [2nd ed]. Baltimore: Urban & Schwarzenberg; reprinted by permission of Williams & Wilkins.)

Tonic-clonic seizures can occur as often as several times a day or as seldom as once a year. A child with this form of epilepsy is typically treated with antiepileptic drugs until free of seizures for 2 years. Stopping the medication after this time is successful in about 80% of these children (Thurston, Thurston, Hixon, et al., 1982).

While these seizures are not usually dangerous, they may become life-threatening in the case of *status epilepticus*. This is defined as a seizure or group of seizures that lasts more than 30 minutes, during which time the child never regains consciousness (Brown & Hussain, 1991). Status epilepticus occurs most often during the first 3 years of life. Common causes include birth injury, traumatic brain injury (see Chapter 27), fever, meningitis, and inborn errors of metabolism. However, perhaps the most common cause of a tonic-clonic seizure is a subtherapeutic antiepileptic drug level in a child known to have epilepsy.

Status epilepticus is a medical emergency requiring rapid and effective management. For anyone working with a young child with epilepsy, this means that paramedics should be called if a seizure lasts more than 15 minutes. If the child is still seizing on arrival in the emergency room, an intravenous injection of lorazepam is likely to be given (see the discussion of Antiepileptic Drugs in this chapter) (Lockman, 1990). This medication usually stops the seizure within 2–3 minutes. If these and other drugs are ineffective, the child may be placed in a drug-induced coma using a barbiturate to protect the brain from the prolonged seizure. Outcome seems to depend most on the underlying cause of the seizure (Dunn, 1990). With rapid treatment, the child should not sustain additional brain injury (Dodrill & Wilensky, 1990; Maytal, Shinnar, Moshe, et al., 1989). Of children who have had one episode of status epilepticus, 70% will never have a second one (Freeman, Vining, & Pillas, 1990).

Absence Seizures   Absence seizures are much less common than tonic-clonic seizures and account for less than 5% of all seizure disorders. These start most often in children who are between 4 and 15 years old (Holmes, 1987). In this type of seizure, the child suddenly assumes a glazed look, blinks, and is unaware of surroundings (Figure 26.4). The child's muscle tone remains fairly normal, so the child does not fall. However, there may be brief arm jerking. Unlike daydreaming, absence seizures cannot be interrupted by talking to or touching the child. Following the seizure, there is rapid and complete recovery and the child is unaware of the episode. The child may well continue a conversation begun just prior to the seizure. This type of seizure usually lasts less than 10 seconds and may occur hundreds of times a day. If the seizures remain undetected and untreated, a child may do poorly at school because of missing pieces of instructions due to these frequent seizures. Children who experience frequent absence seizures describe their lives as being like movies where certain scenes have been cut out (Freeman et al., 1990). These children usually have normal intelligence. Ethosuximide is the antiepileptic drug of choice; valproic acid is also effective. Using these medications, 80% of these seizures go into remission (Holmes, 1987).

Atypical Absence, Myoclonic, and Atonic Seizures   A variant form of absence seizure is called *atypical absence* because its EEG pattern has certain similarities to

Absence

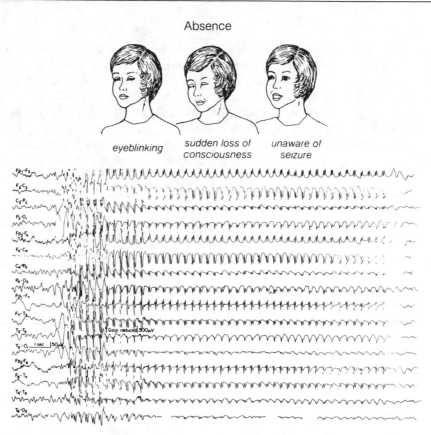

eyeblinking | sudden loss of consciousness | unaware of seizure

Figure 26.4. EEG pattern in absence seizures shows a regular, slow spike and wave pattern that lasts less than 30 seconds. (EEG from Neidermeyer, E., & Lopes da Silva, F. [1987]. *Electroencephalography: Basic principles, clinical applications, and related fields* [2nd ed.]. Baltimore: Urban & Schwarzenberg; reprinted by permission of Williams & Wilkins.)

that seen in absence seizures (Holmes, 1987). In atypical absence seizures, the onset of the seizure is more gradual than in typical absence seizures and atypical absence seizures last longer; confusion may persist after the seizure stops. This seizure type carries a more ominous prognosis than absence seizures. Usually, atypical absence seizures are associated with mixed seizure patterns in which the child will also have tonic-clonic, myoclonic, and atonic seizures. Together these form the Lennox-Gastaut syndrome. Children with Lennox-Gastaut syndrome tend to have multiple disabilities (see the discussion of Lennox-Gastaut Syndrome in this chapter).

In myoclonic seizures, there is an abrupt jerking of muscles—for example, a hand may fling out or the entire body startle. The classic example of a myoclonic seizure is infantile spasms (see the discussion of Infantile Spasms in this chapter). Atonic seizures are the opposite of myoclonic seizures. There is sudden loss of muscle tone, followed by a fall and loss of consciousness (Lockman, 1989).

Partial Seizures

In partial seizures, discharges are limited to one hemisphere of the brain. When consciousness is not lost, they are called *simple partial seizures*; when consciousness is impaired, they are termed *complex partial seizures* (Alvarez, 1989). Partial seizures are the most common type of seizure disorder, accounting for almost 60% of all cases (Wallace, 1990). About three-quarters of affected children can be found to have structural brain lesion, most of congenital origin.

Simple Partial Seizures   Simple partial seizures commonly begin between 4 and 12 years of age. The clinical symptoms depend on which area of the brain is the focus of the seizure. A common example of a simple partial seizure is an aura that may arise from the frontal, parietal, temporal, or occipital lobes of one hemisphere. The aura often has associated psychic symptoms if the temporal lobe is involved. The individual may become fearful or have feelings of déjà vu. He or she can remember these sensations because consciousness is not lost. However, this aura may ultimately spread, causing a generalized seizure (Figure 26.5).

Another example of a simple partial seizure is one involving twitching of one arm or leg. This is called a *focal-motor seizure*. The seizure may start in one limb and then move upward to gradually involve other parts of the body, previously called a "jacksonian march" (Wyllie, Rothner, & Luders, 1989). In this case, the focus is in the motor strip of the frontal lobe.

A final type of simple partial seizures is associated with autonomic symptoms and involves areas of the brain controlling involuntary functions. The child's face may

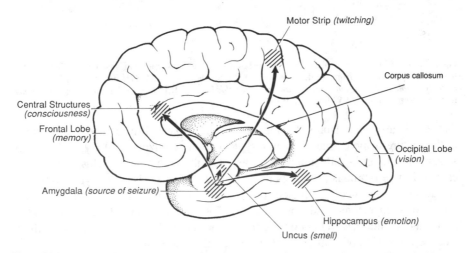

Figure 26.5.   Spread of a simple partial seizure. A simple partial seizure may begin anywhere, in this case in the amygdala of the temporal lobe. The initial feature may be the child smelling an unusual odor. The seizure may stop there or project out to the hippocampus, which might trigger feelings of fearfulness or abdominal queasiness. Memory and visual perception may be affected if the frontal or occipital lobes are involved. It might ultimately extend to the motor strip, resulting in twitching of a limb, which may spread to other limbs or to central structures causing loss of consciousness, converting it into a complex partial seizure. Finally, it may cross the corpus callosum to the other cerebral hemisphere, converting the partial into a generalized seizure.

become pale or flushed, the pulse races, and there may be a feeling of discomfort in the chest or abdomen. The EEG often identifies the specific area of the brain in which the seizure focus rests. Approximately 70% of these simple partial seizures can be controlled with antiepileptic drugs, most commonly phenytoin, carbamazepine, or phenobarbital (Holmes, 1987).

Complex Partial Seizures Complex partial seizures were once called *psychomotor* or *temporal lobe seizures*. Clinically, it is important to distinguish these seizures from absence seizures, which they resemble. About half of all persons with this type of seizure have an aura (simple partial seizure) preceding the onset of the main seizure. This compares to an incidence of aura in 15% of individuals with tonic-clonic seizures (Alvarez, 1989).

Most complex partial seizures emanate from the temporal lobe of the brain. Because the temporal lobe controls such senses as smell, sound, and taste, the individual may experience a variety of psychic phenomena during a partial complex seizure. The person may smell acrid or sweet odors, have a funny taste in the mouth, or hallucinate (Figure 26.6). There also may be emotional expressions, such as anger, laughter, or fear.

The seizure itself often includes blinking, lip smacking, facial grimacing, groaning, chewing, unbuttoning and buttoning clothing, or other automatic actions. The child may even walk around aimlessly. Although less common, these automatisms can also occur with absence seizures. However, unlike absence seizures that last about 10 seconds, partial complex seizures continue from 30 seconds to 5 minutes. Also, unlike absence seizures, they occur infrequently, rarely more than a few times a day. There is partial amnesia and confusion after the episode. The seizure activity shown on EEG is restricted to one temporal lobe rather than being generalized, as it is with an absence seizure. About half of the individuals with this type of seizure have progressed to a tonic-clonic seizure at one time or another (Gomez & Klass, 1983).

Most children with partial complex seizures respond to anticpileptic drugs. In addition, spontaneous remission occurs in about 20% of cases (Kotagal, Rothner, Erenberg, et al., 1987). However, in rare instances, antiepileptic drugs are unsuccessful, and surgery should be considered (see discussion of Surgical Treatment of Seizure Disorders in this chapter).

EPILEPTIC SYNDROMES

Epilepsy plays an important role in a group of syndromes (Aicardi, 1988b). These include infantile spasms, Lennox-Gastaut syndrome, the neurocutaneous syndromes, and Aicardi syndrome. All of these disorders are associated with mental retardation as well as seizures that are difficult to control.

Infantile Spasms

Infantile spasms commonly start at around 6 months of age and disappear by 24 months (Bobele & Bodensteiner, 1990). When the spasms begin, neurodevelopment appears to stop. There actually may be a loss in skills. After the infantile spasms stop,

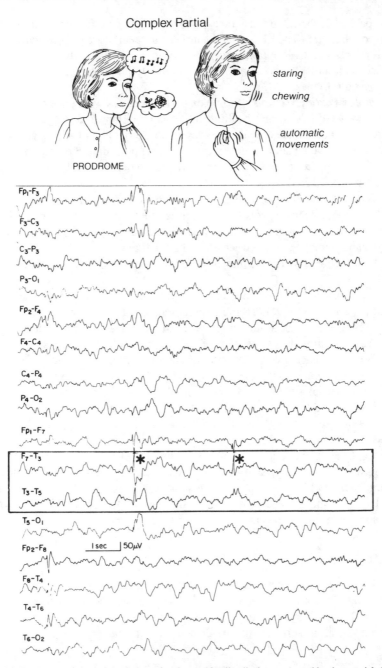

Figure 26.6. In complex partial seizures, the abnormal spike discharges (noted by the asterisks) are confined to the temporal lobe of the brain, leads F_7-T_3 and T_3-T_5. The remainder of the EEG record appears normal. (EEG from Neidermeyer, E., & Lopes da Silva, F. [1987]. *Electroencephalography: Basic principles, clinical applications, and related fields* [2nd ed.]. Baltimore: Urban & Schwarzenberg; reprinted by permission of Williams & Wilkins.)

a common aftermath is the development of Lennox-Gastaut syndrome associated with severe mental retardation. The incidence of infantile spasms is about 1 in 6,000 children (Bobele & Bodensteiner, 1990). The spasm usually takes the form of a myoclonic seizure with a sudden jackknifing, forward or backward extension of the body occurring 5–10 times in a row and lasting about 30 seconds; this recurs as often as every 10 minutes and may occur frequently throughout the day. A specific EEG pattern of chaotic spike and wave activity called **hypsarrhythmia** is usually found (Figure 26.7). A number of disorders including tuberous sclerosis, Tay-Sachs disease, phenylketonuria, and Down syndrome are associated with an increased incidence of infantile spasms. Birth asphyxia, developmental brain abnormalities, and congenital infections also play a role. However, in about half of the cases, the cause of the sei-

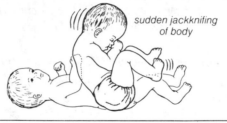

Infantile Spasm

sudden jackknifing
of body

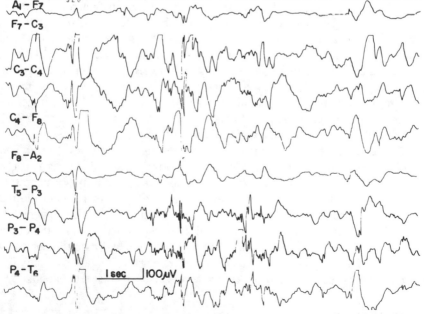

Figure 26.7. EEG pattern of a child with infantile spasms. Note the irregular high-voltage activity. This pattern is called hypsarrhythmia. (EEG from Neidermeyer, E., & Lopes da Silva, F. [1987]. *Electroencephalography: Basic principles, clinical applications, and related fields* (2nd ed.). Baltimore: Urban & Schwarzenberg; reprinted by permission of Williams & Wilkins.)

zures is unknown. Early treatment with adrenocorticotropic hormone (ACTH) usually stops the spasms. However, even with treatment, over 90% of children who have a known cause for their seizures have mental retardation. About two-thirds of the group with unknown causes also have retardation (Glaze, Hrachovy, Frost, et al., 1988).

Lennox-Gastaut Syndrome

Lennox-Gastaut syndrome is the term used to describe a mixed seizure pattern including atypical absence, tonic-clonic, myoclonic, and atonic seizures. It generally begins between 1 and 8 years of age, often in children who previously had infantile spasms. These seizures are difficult to control with medications and are associated with mental retardation in 80% of cases. Valproic acid is the antiepileptic drug of choice, with the benzodiazepines as secondary medications. The ketogenic diet, which is high in fats and low in carbohydrates, has also been found to be successful in some cases (Freeman et al., 1990). (This diet is discussed in a later section of this chapter.)

Neurocutaneous Syndromes: Tuberous Sclerosis and Sturge-Weber

Neurocutaneous syndromes refer to disorders in which there is a combination of skin abnormalities, seizures, and cognitive deficits. One example, *tuberous sclerosis,* consists of **adenoma sebaceum** (which looks like a bad case of acne but is present before 5 years of age), infantile spasms, and severe mental retardation (Pinto & Bolognia, 1991). The skin abnormalties also include cafe au lait spots, which are white birthmarks and round beige-colored areas on the torso. The seizures are both myoclonic and tonic-clonic in nature with a hypsarrhythmic pattern on EEG. On the CT scan, calcified areas are visible around the ventricles and basal ganglia, probably representing small calcified tumors. There are often abnormalities in the retina as well. Treatment approaches are similar to those used in infantile spasms. Inheritance is autosomal dominant or sporadic. Tuberous sclerosis accounts for about 0.5% of all children with severe mental retardation (Pinto & Bolognia, 1991).

Sturge-Weber syndrome, another neurocutaneous disorder, involves an abnormality of blood vessels and is not inherited. The principal skin finding is a port wine stain birthmark on one side of the face. The blood vessel malformation is present in the brain as well as the skin, leading to cortical atrophy of that side of the brain. Calcifications are visible by CT scan in the temporal and occipital regions of the brain. Neurological findings include partial seizures and paralysis on the opposite side of the body from the birthmark. The seizures are often difficult to control with antiepileptic drugs. They may require surgical removal of the affected area of the brain. Most children with Sturge-Weber syndrome have mental retardation.

Aicardi Syndrome

Aicardi syndrome occurs only in girls. It involves infantile spasms associated with congenital absence of the corpus callosum and abnormalities of the eye (Neidich, Nussbaum, Packer, et al., 1990). These children have severe mental retardation.

SELF-LIMITED AND EPILEPTIC-LIKE DISORDERS

Not all disorders that look like seizures are epileptic seizures, and not all seizures represent epilepsy. Infants may have seizures in the newborn period related to a difficult delivery, but may never again experience seizure activity. Young children may have febrile convulsions that they eventually outgrow. Neither of these conditions is epilepsy. Furthermore, some children have habits or paroxysmal disorders that superficially resemble seizures. These include fainting, breathholding, and tantrums. These conditions must be distinguished from epilepsy so that antiepileptic drugs are not prescribed indiscriminately.

Febrile Convulsions

Between 6 months and 5 years of age, about 1 in 200 children have at least one convulsion associated with high fever (Nelson & Ellenberg, 1990) (see Figure 26.2). In this age group, there is a low seizure threshold. The peak age for having this type of seizure is 8–24 months. Upper respiratory illnesses, ear infections, stomach flu, and rashes (roseola) often precede these convulsions. These are mostly viral infections. Bacteria have been cultured in about 5% of cases and have included urinary tract infections and **Shigella diarrhea** (Ferry, Banner, & Wolf, 1986). Occasionally, children have febrile convulsions after they have received DPT (diphtheria, pertussis, tetanus) or measles shots. Only the pertussis (whooping cough) immunization should be deferred in children who have had febrile convulsions.

Why some children are more likely to have febrile convulsions than others is unclear. However, about 6% of families have more than one member who has experienced a febrile convulsion in childhood. This suggests a possible genetic factor (Wallace, 1988).

The most likely time for a febrile convulsion to occur is when a fever is rising, usually above 102° F (39° C). The seizure is tonic-clonic in type, generally lasting less than 5 minutes. By the time the child is brought to the emergency room, the seizure usually has stopped, and the child is lethargic or sleeping. The child returns to normal in 1–4 hours. The seizure should not recur within the same day, and by the next day, the illness causing the fever is usually controlled. Following the seizure, the physician finds no abnormalities other than the infection that led to the seizure. A spinal tap, or **lumbar puncture**, is often done the first time such a seizure occurs, especially in children younger than 1 year of age, to be certain the child does not have meningitis (Hirtz, 1989). This spinal fluid should be normal. The child is not hospitalized, nor does he or she need antiepileptic medication. Brain imaging studies and EEGs are also not needed; if done they will be normal. No evidence indicates that these seizures increase the risk for subsequent development of mental retardation, cerebral palsy, or learning disabilities.

A child who has already had one febrile convulsion runs an increased risk of having another febrile seizure before 4 years of age (Berg, Shinnar, Hauser, et al., 1990). The risk depends on the age at occurrence of the first seizure. If the first seizure happened in the first year of life, the recurrence risk is about 50%. If the seizure occurred after 1 year of age, the risk of recurrence drops to 11% (Berg et al., 1990).

Overall, about 2% of children who have febrile convulsions go on to develop seizure disorders in later childhood. However, children who have family histories of seizure disorders, abnormal neurological development before their first febrile convulsions, or atypical febrile convulsions that last longer than 15 minutes or are focal have about a 10% risk of subsequently developing a seizure disorder.

After a child has had two febrile convulsions, prophylactic treatment with anticonvulsants is sometimes considered (Consensus Development Conference, 1980). The most commonly used drug is phenobarbital. For this drug to be effective, it must be taken daily. Studies have shown that it reduces the risk of febrile convulsion recurrence from 30% to 2%. Unfortunately, side effects, including fatigue or hyperactivity, and other behavior and cognitive problems, are common (Farwell, Lee, Hirtz, et al., 1990). Because of these side effects and the apparent benign nature of febrile seizures, most neurologists do not suggest treatment unless there have been many recurrences, the child has a developmental disability, or the parents are very anxious about the threat of future seizures (Berg et al., 1990).

Neonatal Seizures

Seizures in the newborn period are most often the result of metabolic abnormalities, birth trauma, hypoxia, or developmental brain abnormalities. These may be isolated seizures and often do not require long-term antiepileptic therapy (see Chapter 6).

Conditions that Mimic Seizures

A number of conditions can mimic seizures. These conditions occur in nondisabled children and in children with disabilities. They include breathholding spells, fainting, migraine headaches, drug reactions, tics, night terrors, gastroesophageal reflux, rage reactions, and masturbation.

Breathholding Breathholding is the most common habit confused with seizures. It occurs in about 4% of children between the ages of 6 and 18 months (Barron, 1991). Episodes begin with prolonged crying, followed by the arrest of breathing in expiration. This may last close to a minute with associated blue tinging of the lip, arching of the back, and unconsciousness. It ends with the sudden gulping in of air and neurological recovery. Breathholding can be distinguished from a seizure by a normal EEG. These episodes are often precipitated by pain from a fall or anger from frustration and can often be controlled by behavior management techniques.

Sleep Disorders Sleep disorders may also resemble seizures. *Narcolepsy*, which occurs more commonly in teenagers and adults, is one example. In this condition, there are daytime sleep attacks, sleep paralysis, and abrupt loss of postural tone. The sudden nodding off to sleep may resemble an atonic seizure, or if it is a brief episode, an absence seizure. The diagnosis is made with an abnormal sleep pattern on an EEG but no seizure activity. A related phenomenon occurring in children 2–5 years old is *night terrors*. The child awakens suddenly in the middle of the night, cries out inconsolably as if in terror, and appears disoriented. The episode ends in about 10–15 minutes with the child falling back to sleep. This occurs during deepest sleep, usually within 2 hours of bedtime. There is no sign of a seizure focus on EEG.

Tics   Tics are repetitive, brief, stereotypic movements or vocalizations (Tardo, 1988). These may include facial twitches, head shaking, eye blinking, and other mannerisms. They often begin in school-age children and can be intensified by anxiety, fatigue, or excitement. When combined with simple vocal tics, cursing (coprolalia), attention deficit hyperactivity disorder, and obsessive-compulsive disorder, they form Tourette syndrome. Repeated tics may resemble partial or myoclonic seizures. The differences are that tics are not associated with a loss of consciousness; they can come under some voluntary control; and they tend to improve with the medication clonidine. The EEG does not show spike and wave activity.

Migraine Headaches   Complex migraine headaches can occur with visual phenomena, hemiplegia, speech impairment, and mood changes. These can be confused with seizure auras (Hockaday, 1990). Vomiting and lethargy may be followed by sleep and the resolution of the headache within about 6 hours. An EEG does not usually show seizure activity, but there is some overlap of migraines and seizures. The diagnosis of a migraine is made by the history of a pounding, one-sided headache and nausea; there is often a family history.

Fainting   Fainting, or *syncope*, is caused by a decreased blood supply to the brain. It can be the result of many problems, mostly benign. These include blood drawing, a viral illness, standing in a long line on a hot day, maintaining a starvation diet, hyperventilating, or attending a highly exciting event (e.g., a rock concert). It occurs most commonly in adolescent girls. Fainting may appear to be an atonic seizure but has a somewhat different clinical picture. The child feels dizzy and becomes pale and sweaty; vision is impaired, and the room seems to spin; then the child gradually slips to the floor, but not forcefully as in a seizure. Recovery is within seconds and without amnesia. An EEG is normal.

Gastroesophageal Reflux   Gastroesophageal reflux results from an incompetent muscular valve at the junction of the stomach and esophagus (see Chapter 12). This leads to backward flow of stomach acid into the esophagus. In children, especially those with cerebral palsy, this may result in the child assuming a back-arched position that may resemble a tonic seizure. This position appears to decrease the reflux and relieve the associated pain. After a correct diagnosis is made and treatment is started, the episodes usually stop.

Behavior Disturbances   Finally, certain behaviors may resemble seizures. A rage reaction, for example, is most common in teenagers with ADHD (see Chapter 21). They may have episodes of abrupt mood changes and uncontrollable violent behavior that resemble a partial complex seizure. However, intentional violence almost never occurs as part of a seizure. Also, there is no loss of consciousness or amnesia in a rage reaction. The episodes are usually precipitated by frustration and can often be controlled using behavior management techniques.

In children with severe mental retardation, certain self-stimulatory or self-injurious behavior may also resemble complex partial seizures. Lastly, masturbation, especially with its shuddering climax and subsequent sleepiness, may resemble a seizure in infant girls or children with developmental disabilities in whom it may not be expected.

DIAGNOSING EPILEPSY

A diagnosis of epilepsy is based on a history of recurrent seizures. The EEG helps to localize the area in the brain where the focus of the seizure exists and to determine the type of epilepsy (Figure 26.8). More recently, brain imaging techniques have also been used to evaluate seizure disorders.

The Electroencephalogram

An EEG should be performed on all children who are suspected to have a seizure disorder as soon after a seizure as possible. Approximately 80% of all children with seizure disorders have abnormal EEG patterns (Holmes, 1989). In tonic-clonic seizures (see Figure 26.3), a normal EEG pattern is interrupted by bursts of spike and wave activity throughout the whole brain. Figure 26.9 is provided for comparison. In typical absence seizures, the epileptic pattern has spikes and slow waves repeating at a frequency of 2.5–3.0 per second and lasts only a few seconds. These may recur throughout the EEG (see Figure 26.4). The abnormality may disappear with ethosuximide treatment. As partial seizures are typified by seizure activity that occurs only in one part of a hemisphere, most commonly the temporal lobe, seizure spikes are restricted to the affected region (see Figure 26.6). Finally, in infantile spasms (see Figure 26.7), the EEG shows chaotic bursts of seizure activity throughout the brain.

However, some individuals have abnormal EEGs but never have seizures. For this reason, neurologists are not apt to treat an abnormal EEG in the absence of clinically obvious seizures. Conversely, in some cases, even though a child has a seizure disorder, the EEG may appear normal at the time it is done. Under these circumstances, a few other approaches can be used to discover seizure activity. Sleep is a powerful force in increasing seizure activity. In some children, seizures occur when coming out of sleep. Therefore, a portion of the EEG should be done while the child is sleeping, using a sedative, such as chloral hydrate, to induce sleep. Because sleep deprivation may also induce seizure activity, the child may be kept awake late the night before the EEG. Placing a child before a strobe light (photic stimulation) may induce seizure discharges in children with photosensitive epilepsy. Hyperventilation

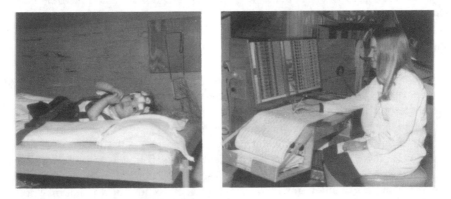

Figure 26.8.   The taking of an electroencephalogram.

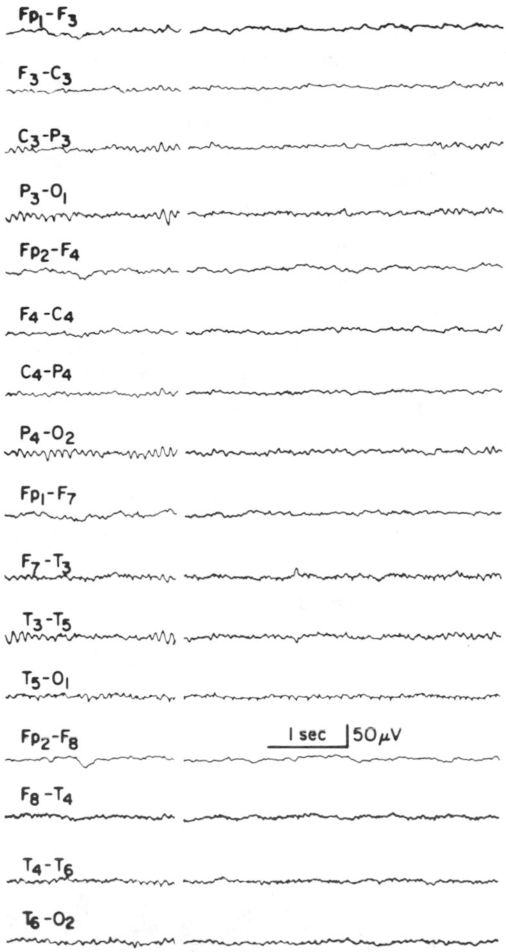

Figure 26.9.   Appearance of a normal electroencephalogram (EEG). Note the relatively regular, undulating brain wave pattern. (From Neidermeyer, E., & Lopes da Silva, F. [1987]. *Electroencephalography: Basic principles, clinical applications, and related fields* [2nd ed.]. Baltimore: Urban & Schwarzenberg; reprinted by permission of Williams & Wilkins.)

can increase seizure activity in a person with absence seizures. Finally, long-term ambulatory monitoring can be done in a child wearing a small tape recorder attached to EEG electrodes on the scalp. This records the EEG continuously over 24 hours. This record can then be analyzed for more intermittent signs of seizure activity.

In some cases, it may not be clear if the child is actually having a seizure. **Radio-telemetry** combined with video recording (video-EEG) may prove helpful in these cases, by permitting the simultaneous observation of individual's behavior and EEG. If the child is observed to have a seizure-like episode, such as staring spells or loss of consciousness, but the EEG remains normal during the episode, it is probably not a seizure.

Brain Imaging Techniques

Besides EEGs, brain imaging techniques can help to identify discrete areas of brain abnormality in about 5% of children with seizure disorders (Holmes, 1987). Findings include tumors, aneurisms, calcifications, atrophy, or developmental brain lesions. These techniques are most useful in children who have more than one type of seizure and for those who have other developmental disabilities. One such technique is the computed tomography (CT) scan. Here a series of X rays of sections of the brain are synthesized by a computer to form an image at various levels of the brain. A similar image is obtained using magnetic resonance imaging (MRI). Rather than using X rays, this technique makes use of the natural magnetic characteristics of the molecules in the brain. It is even better than the CT scan in identifying structural abnormalities and differentiating gray and white matter. Lastly, positron emission tomography (PET) scans highlight the metabolic activity of the brain rather than its physical structure (Chugani, Shields, Shewmon, et al., 1990). Between seizures, an epileptic region appears different because it uses less glucose than a normal area; this can be visualized by PET (Figure 26.10) or the related **single photon emission computed tomography** (**SPECT**) scan. Doing a PET or SPECT scan requires the injection of small amounts of radioactive material. PET and SPECT scans are not now widely available, but are likely to become more so in the future.

TREATMENT OF SEIZURE DISORDERS

Seizure disorders can be treated with medications, a special diet, or surgery. The options are discussed here in more detail.

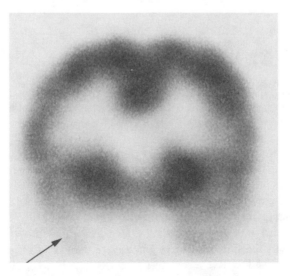

Figure 26.10.   A PET scan shows decreased metabolic activity in the seizure focus of this adult with tonic-clonic seizures.

Antiepileptic Drugs

Once epilepsy is diagnosed, appropriate medications, usually anticonvulsants, are started to control the seizures. The most commonly used antiepileptic drugs, dosages, and side effects are listed in Table 26.2. Interestingly, there is no significant difference in effectiveness among a number of drugs used to treat specific seizure types (Table 26.3). For example, carbamazepine, phenobarbital, phenytoin, primidone, and valproic acid are equally effective in treating tonic-clonic seizures. As a result, the reason for choosing a specific antiepileptic drug for a specific type of seizure is based more on side effects, cost, and the doctor's experience than anything else. In terms of cost, phenobarbital and phenytoin are the least expensive, and carbamazepine and valproic acid are the most expensive. However, in terms of side ef-

Table 26.2.   Antiepileptic drugs

Drug	How supplied (mg)	Tablet/capsule/ liquid (T/C/L)	Dosage (mg/kg/d)	Side effects
Phenytoin (Dilantin)	50, 100	T/C/L	4–12	Ataxia, nystagmus, gum swelling, acne, hairiness, coarsened features
Phenobarbital	15, 60	T/L	1–5	Lethargy, rash, hyperactivity, decreased cognitive performance
Primidone (Mysoline)	50, 200	T/L	10–20	Lethargy, rash, hyperactivity, decreased cognitive performance
Ethosuximide (Zarontin)	250	T/L	10–70	Vomiting, sedation, dizziness, liver damage
Carbamazepine (Tegretol)	200	T	15–25	Lethargy, ataxia, rash, aplastic anemia
Clonazepine (Klonopin)	0.5, 2.0	T	0.03–0.1	Ataxia, sedation, anemia, salivation, personality changes
Valproic acid (Depakene)	250, 500	C/L	10–70	Lethargy, hair loss, stomach upset
ACTH	40, 80	Injection	20–80 units/day	Cataracts, brittle bones, diabetes, hypertension

Sources: Dobson (1989); *Physicians' Desk Reference* (1992).

Table 26.3. Efficacy of antiepileptic drugs

Drug	Absence	Generalized tonic-clonic	Lennox-Gastaut	Infantile spasm	Simple/Complex partial
Carbamazepine	0	+ +	0	0	+ +
Clonazepam	+ +	+	+ +	+	+
Ethosuximide	+ +	0	0	0	0
Phenobarbital	0	+ +	0	0	+ +
Phenytoin	0	+ +	0	0	+ +
Primidone	0	+ +	0	0	+ +
Valproic acid	+ +	+ +	+ +	+	+
ACTH	0	0	+ +	+ +	0
Ketogenic diet	0	+ +	+	+	0

0 = ineffective, + = partial, + + = effective.

fects, phenobarbital and phenytoin have the most side effects and valproic acid and carbamazepine the least (Collaborative Group for the Epidemiology of Epilepsy, 1988; Herranz, Armijo, & Arteaga, 1988).

In a child with a single type of seizure, there is a 90% success rate in controlling the seizures using a single antiepileptic drug (Herranz et al., 1988). To begin therapy, a drug is chosen, and the dosage adjusted so that seizures are controlled and side effects are minimized (Dodson, 1989; Pellock, 1989). Ordinarily, drug levels in the blood are monitored a few times a year. However, if significant side effects develop, a blood level is taken immediately to make sure the dosage is not toxic. Also, the person may be asked to keep a record of seizures in order to document the frequency and determine the effectiveness of the medication.

As noted previously, the majority of children with seizure disorders are controlled with one drug; for the remainder, two or more drugs are required. The child who has mixed (i.e., both generalized and partial) seizures or infantile spasms is the most likely to require two or more medications to achieve seizure control.

When a child is initially placed on a medication, he or she is not protected for a number of days because it takes 4–5 half-lives for a steady state blood level to be achieved (Figure 26.11). A half-life is defined as the time it takes for half of the drug dose to be eliminated from the body. A steady state exists when the rate of elimination equals the rate of input. Antiepileptic drugs have half-lives that vary from 6 to 48 hours. Therefore, it may be 1–2 weeks before the child is in a steady state. For this reason, the child may receive a single large "loading dose" of medication after a seizure to achieve a steady state more rapidly. The child would also be placed on a long-term daily dose.

Drug levels are measured 4–5 half-lives after a drug has been started or the dose changed. Periodic levels should be measured a few times a year. They should be drawn at the same time relative to a dose. Usually this is done just prior to a dose to measure the "trough" or lowest level. A peak level can be obtained about 2 hours after the drug has been taken. If the physician is worried that the drug levels are too low, a trough level is needed. If there is concern about drug toxicity, a peak level is more helpful.

Phenytoin (Dilantin) Phenytoin appears to control seizures by inactivating the calcium channel that normally permits depolarization of the neuron. It also prevents the release of excitatory neurotransmitters from the synapse so that the impulse cannot pass from one neuron to another. This prevents the recruitment of nerve cells that surround the focus of the seizure, thereby stopping the seizure's progress (Matsuda, Higashi, & Inotsume, 1989). Thus, phenytoin controls the spread rather than prevents the initiation of a seizure.

Phenytoin can be used to control both tonic-clonic and partial seizures. Young children usually take it twice a day, while older children can receive it as a single daily dose. Among the common side effects are swelling of the gums, excessive hairiness, worsening of acne, and coarsening of facial features. Signs of acute toxicity include vomiting, lethargy, and an unsteady gait (ataxia). Nonambulatory individuals are at risk of developing osteoporosis related to folic acid and vitamin D deficiency. Phenytoin also can have an adverse effect on learning and behavior. All of these symptoms disappear when the dosage is lowered or stopped. Generally, phenytoin is considered to be safe and effective, but it does have a relatively high incidence of bothersome side effects. Also, it may damage the developing fetus of a pregnant woman with a seizure disorder (see Chapter 4).

Phenobarbital Similar to phenytoin, phenobarbital is used to treat tonic-

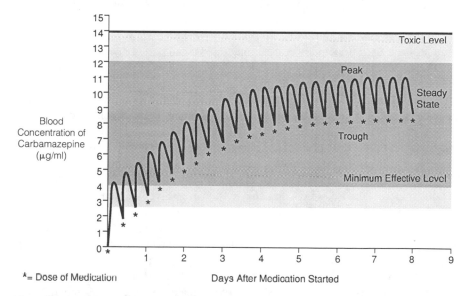

A= Dose of Medication   Days After Medication Started

Figure 26.11. Achieving a steady-state of the antiepileptic drug carbamazepine (Tegretol), which is given three times a day. The medication has been started on day 0. Approximately 1 hour after each dose, the peak level is achieved and it declines over the next 8 hours, at which time the second of three daily doses is given. After each successive dose, the peak level gets higher until after about 7 days, it reaches a steady state, and the child should be well protected against seizures. For a drug with a shorter half-life, it takes less time to achieve a steady state, and for one with a longer half-life (e.g., phenobarbital), it takes longer.

clonic and partial seizures. It can be given in one dose a day. Yet, phenobarbital works quite differently from phenytoin. It prevents the onset of a seizure by raising the intensity of the stimulus needed to trigger the seizure. Side effects include drowsiness or sleep disturbance, irritability, and skin rash. About 20%–40% of the children who take phenobarbital become hyperactive and experience other behavior and learning problems; eventually, they have to stop taking the medication (Vining, Mellits, Dorsen, et al., 1987). Side effects may improve over time and are less apparent if the drug is started at a low dose and gradually increased.

As with phenytoin, the risk of osteoporosis and related pathological fractures is increased in nonambulatory persons who do not get enough folic acid or exposure to sunlight to promote vitamin D activation. Treatment with activated vitamin D has been suggested. An overdose of phenobarbital leads to severe lethargy but this generally improves within 24 hours of stopping the medication (Dodson, 1989). Phenobarbital may interact with other antiepileptic drugs affecting the blood levels. This most commonly occurs with phenytoin, carbamazepine, and valproic acid. Dosages of these medications may need to be adjusted to maintain seizure control while minimizing side effects.

Primidone (Mysoline) Primidone is similar in chemical structure to phenobarbital. It is primarily used to treat tonic-clonic seizures, but it is also useful in treating partial seizures. Drowsiness and ataxia are the most common side effects. These side effects disappear when the drug is discontinued (Aicardi, 1986). It is not a commonly used antiepileptic drug, as it is no more effective than phenobarbital and tends to have more frequent and severe side effects.

Carbamazepine (Tegretol) Similar to phenytoin and phenobarbital, carbamazepine is used principally to treat tonic-clonic and partial seizures. It may actually worsen absence seizure activity (Snead & Hosey, 1985). Its mechanism of action is thought to be similar to that of phenytoin. Side effects are generally milder and less frequent than phenytoin or phenobarbital, making it the drug many neurologists choose. Side effects, although numerous, are uncommon. They include ataxia, double vision, drowsiness, slurred speech, tremor, headache, and nausea. They occur less frequently if the drug is started at a low dosage and gradually increased to therapeutic levels. It can be given twice a day. On rare occasions, a person may develop bone marrow suppression that leads to anemia (*Physicians' Desk Reference*, 1992). It has only modest adverse effects on behavior and cognitive function.

Ethosuximide (Zarontin) Unlike the drugs mentioned previously, ethosuximide is used exclusively for treating absence seizures. It remains the drug of choice for treating this form of seizure disorder. Side effects include drowsiness, dizziness, gastric distress, insomnia, rash, headache, and depression.

Benzodiazepines The benzodiazepines include diazepam (Valium), clonazepam (Klonopin), lorazepam (Ativan), and clorazepate (Tranxene). Diazepam is not used in the chronic treatment of seizures because clonazepam and clorazepate are more effective for the long-term management of seizures, and lorazepam is better for treating status epilepticus (Lockman, 1990). Clonazepam and clorazepate have been used to treat multiple types of seizures. However, they are most often used to treat infantile spasms, Lennox-Gastaut syndrome, and absence seizures. Drowsiness and irritability are common when the medication is first started but usually subside after a few weeks. In children with cerebral palsy, other side effects include decreased muscle tone, excessive drooling, and increased swallowing difficulties (Eadie, 1984).

Valproic Acid (Depakene) Valproic acid is the most recently approved antiepileptic drug (1978). Like clonazepam, it has been used to treat all types of seizures. However, it is most effective as a drug to treat tonic-clonic seizures, Lennox-Gastaut syndrome, and absence seizures. It works in part by inhibiting the breakdown of the neurotransmitter gamma-aminobutyric acid (GABA) to suppress seizure activity. Side effects are seen in about 12% of treated children and include nausea, drowsiness, excessive weight gain, and hair loss (Vining et al., 1987). These problems usually improve over time and stop if the drug is discontinued. Certain metabolic abnormalities, including elevated levels of ammonia and glycine, also may develop. However, these do not appear to be associated with clinical symptoms in most cases. Supplements of carnitine are sometimes used to correct these alterations. A more severe, but very rare complication, is liver and pancreas damage. Fewer than 1 in 50,000 individuals who take this drug develop severe, irreversible liver failure or pancreatitis (Dreifuss, Langer, Moline, et al., 1989). However, these complications are more common in children under 2 years of age and in those with multiple disabilities. In these children, valproic acid should be used with care and preferably as the sole antiepileptic drug. Despite these potential hazards, valproic acid is considered to be an excellent and quite safe antiepileptic drug.

New Antiepileptic Drugs A number of novel medications are being considered by the Food and Drug Administration (FDA) and may be released within the next 5 years. These drugs include tamotrigine (Sander, Trevisol-Bittencourt, Hart, et al., 1990), tiagabine (Nielsen, Suzdak, Andersen, et al., 1991), gabapentin (Sivenius, Kalviainen, Ylinen, et al., 1991), vigabatrin (Grant & Heel, 1991), and felbamate (Theodore, Raubertas, Porter, et al., 1991). While most of these drugs act in similar ways as the antiepileptic drugs described previously, they may be more powerful and have fewer side effects. They also increase the armentarium for drug-resistant seizures.

Adrenocorticotropic Hormone (ACTH) ACTH, a steroid-releasing hormone, is used only to treat infantile spasms and Lennox-Gastaut syndrome. This drug must be injected into muscle tissue. Treatment is sometimes stopped after a few months or may be continued on a long-term basis; it is effective in stopping about 80% of infantile spasms with unknown causes if it is started within 1 month of the onset of the seizures (Bobele & Bodensteiner, 1990). It is less effective in controlling infantile spasms of known causes and Lennox-Gastaut syndrome. The problem with this form of therapy is that steroids have severe side effects, including osteoporosis, high blood pressure, diabetes, cataracts, and an increased risk of infection. Thus, it is used with extreme care. It is also unclear whether stopping the seizures has a beneficial effect on neurodevelopmental outcome.

Maintaining Drug Control

The most common cause of poorly controlled seizures is noncompliance. This may range from a teenager's acting out behavior to an overstressed parent who tends to forget the occasional dose of medication. Thus, if seizure activity increases, the physician's first thought is not to increase the dosage or to change the medication, but rather to make sure the child is receiving the proper dosage. A blood level is obtained, and if it is subtherapeutic, the possibility of noncompliance is explored. Compliance may improve with the use of a weekly pill box. There are even containers with built in alarms that ring each day at the proper time for the medication.

Administering the proper dosage may be a problem even if the parent is compliant. The child may spit out or throw up the medication. The parent may then be concerned about overdosing the child by repeating the medication. In general, if the child spits out or vomits most of the medication, the dose should be repeated. Low blood level also may be the result of a change in the brand of medication. Generic brands are available for most antiepileptic drugs. Although nominally equivalent in strength, they may vary in absorption rate, leading to variable drug levels.

If compliance appears to be good and the seizures are still poorly controlled, the physician may decide to increase the dosage of the medication. The medication can be increased until the child develops side effects or there are significant biochemical abnormalities found on blood tests. Because of drug interactions, it is always preferable to use a single antiepileptic drug rather than two or more.

When To Stop Antiepileptic Drugs

In the past, after an individual was placed on antiepileptic drugs, it was assumed he or she would require them for life, similar to the insulin needs of a person with diabetes. However, in most cases, this does not seem to be true. Recently, a number of studies have reported the effects of stopping antiepileptic drug therapy in children who have been seizure-free for 2–4 years. In one study, Shinnar, Vining, Mellits, et al. (1985) followed children for 4 years after they stopped treatment and found that 69% remained free of seizures (Figure 26.12). In the children who had seizures after stopping treatment, these tended to occur within a year after stopping therapy, most often while the medication was being withdrawn. The risk of recurrence was higher in children with mental retardation, in children who started having seizures before they were 2 years old, in individuals who had experienced more than 30 seizures (Figure 26.13) and in those who had abnormal EEG patterns when they stopped treatment (see Figure 26.1).

In a second study, individuals were followed for 15–23 years after termination of treatment (Thurston, Thurston, Hixon, et al., 1982). They found a 72% chance of remaining seizure-free in general and virtually a 100% chance if no seizure occurred within 5 years after stopping the medication. Overall, about 50% of children with mental retardation and seizures remain seizure-free without medication. It has also been shown that the removal of medication has led to some improvement in cognitive function (Siemes, Spohr, Michael, et al., 1988). Therefore, even for a child with a

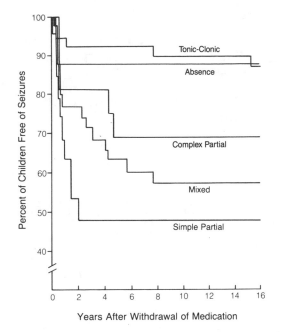

Figure 26.12. Percentage of children who remained seizure-free after withdrawal of antiepileptic drugs. Over 80% of children with tonic-clonic seizures or absence seizures remained seizure-free compared to 50%–70% of children with other types of seizures. All children had been free of seizures for at least 4 years before stopping the medication. (From Thurston, J.H., Thurston, D.L., Hixon, B.B., et al. [1982]. Prognosis in childhood epilepsy. Additional follow-up of 148 children 15 - 23 years after withdrawal of anticonvulsant therapy. *New England Journal of Medicine, 306*, 831–836; reprinted by permission of *The New England Journal of Medicine*.)

seizure disorder, mental retardation, and an abnormal EEG, stopping medication after 2 seizure-free years may be considered.

The Ketogenic Diet

Besides antiepileptic drugs, another approach to treating seizures is the ketogenic diet. This diet is high in fats and low in carbohydrates. To compensate for the deficiency in carbohydrates, the body breaks down the fats, leading to a condition called **ketosis**. This is associated with a decrease in seizure activity in about half of the children treated, and antiepileptic drugs may be able to be reduced or eliminated with this diet (Schwartz, Eaton, Bower, et al., 1989).

The diet regimen starts with 2–3 days of starvation and limited fluid intake. The high-fat diet is then gradually started. The fats are largely provided as butter and heavy cream. This diet is quite unpalatable and difficult to administer, especially for older children, who have access to candy and other carbohydrate treats. If ketosis is not maintained, seizures return. During therapy, supplemental vitamins and minerals must be provided. The child will not gain much weight or height. As a result, the diet is rarely continued for more than 2 years.

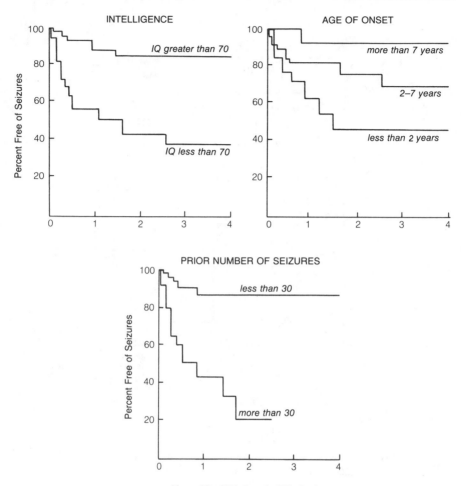

Figure 26.13.   Percentage of children who remained free of seizures for 4 years after withdrawal of anti-epileptic drugs. The risk of recurrence of seizures was higher in children with mental retardation, in those with onset of seizures before 2 years of age, and in those with histories of many seizures. All children had been free of seizures for 4 years before stopping medications. (From Emerson, R.D., D'Sonza, B.J., Vining, E.P., et al. [1981]. Stopping medication in children with epilepsy: Predictors of outcome. *New England Journal of Medicine, 304*, 1125–1129; reprinted by permission of *The New England Journal of Medicine*.)

The ketogenic diet is rarely utilized these days. However, it has been effective in treating infantile spasms, and tonic-clonic and Lennox-Gastaut seizures.

Surgical Treatment of Seizure Disorders

Although used infrequently, surgery is another treatment for some seizure disorders (Aicardi, 1988a). It should only be considered if the seizures have proved resistant to antiepileptic drugs and are interfering with the child's life. However, in appropriate cases, surgery should be considered sooner rather than later. Three types of procedures have been used: focal excision, hemispherectomy, and corpus callosotomy.

Focal Excision Focal excision, the removal of a seizure focus, is performed when there are partial seizures that can be localized to one brain region. The most commonly performed surgery is the excision of an abnormal region of one temporal lobe of the brain (Duchowny, 1989; Hopkins & Klug, 1991). Identification of this region is facilitated by the use of EEG, MRI scan, and/or PET scan.

Appropriate candidates for focal excision are children who have had uncontrolled partial complex seizures for at least 2 years, associated with behavioral and academic deterioration (Mizrahi, Kellaway, Grossman, et al., 1990). Once the affected area is removed, almost 80% of previously uncontrollable partial complex seizures are improved or go into remission (Walczak, Radtke, McNamara, et al., 1990). There is also marked improvement in psychosocial and school function, but no change in IQ. Risks of the procedure include some memory deficits, visual field loss, and speech impairment. These occur most commonly if the temporal lobe in the dominant hemisphere has been removed. The Wada test can be performed before surgery to determine which is the dominant hemisphere. In 90% of people, it is the left hemisphere. There is also the risk of surgery itself that includes the possibilities of infection or stroke. The mortality rate is less than 1 in 1,000 (Walczak et al., 1990).

Focal excisions have also been used to control partial seizures in other areas of the brain (Adler, Erba, Winston, et al., 1991). The best candidates are children with normal intelligence and a single type of seizure that can be localized to a region that is not critical to brain function. Approximately 70% of children have improvement following surgery, but complete cessation of seizure activity is less likely to occur than with temporal lobe excision (Wyllie, 1991).

Corpus Callosotomy The corpus callosum is the band of tissue that connects the two hemispheres. It is the bundle that permits the transmission of messages between the two sides of the brain (Sass, Spencer, Spencer, et al., 1988). However, it also transmits seizure discharges and participates in the extension of a partial seizure to a generalized seizure. Cutting this tissue, an operation termed *callosotomy*, has been effective in preventing spread of seizure discharge in certain individuals with poorly controlled generalized seizures and partial seizures with secondary generalization. It has also been used to treat Lennox-Gastaut syndrome (Green, Adler, & Erba, 1988).

Side effects are not uncommon. Such surgery can lead to mutism and behavioral depression for a number of weeks after surgery. However, this usually resolves. Manual dexterity may be impaired on a permanent basis. However, attention, behavior, and performance of cognitive tasks have usually improved (Mizrahi et al., 1990). Overall, between 25% and 75% of treated persons show significant improvement in seizure control (Wyllie, 1988).

Hemispherectomy A hemispherectomy is the removal of most of one of the cerebral hemispheres (Lindsay, Ounsted, & Richards, 1987). This is a radical solution and is considered only in children with the most severe uncontrolled seizure disorders. It is most commonly used in children who have partial seizures with hemiplegia, suggesting that the hemisphere is already severely impaired. These children also have significant behavior problems and cognitive deficits.

About 85% of children treated with this surgery become seizure-free, with associated improvement in behavior and cognitive function (Wyllie, 1991). However, it is not accomplished without considerable risk. The hemiplegia may become worse, and hydrocephalus may develop. In addition, a rare condition termed **hemosiderosis** may occur. Hemosiderosis results from the breakdown of blood cells and release of hemosiderin, a toxin. This can be life-threatening. A recent modification of the surgical procedure has greatly reduced this risk (Lindsey et al., 1987).

WHAT TO DO IN THE EVENT OF A SEIZURE

Even though antiepileptic drugs and surgery generally improve the frequency of seizures, some individuals will not be entirely seizure-free. Seizures may be as infrequent as once a year or as often as 50 times a day. The role of a professional or a parent who has to deal with the seizure depends on its type and duration. Repeated absence seizures require no immediate action, provided they stop within 15 minutes. An increased frequency, however, signals the possible need for an increase or change in medication.

A more difficult problem is a tonic-clonic seizure. With this seizure the child may fall and sustain an injury. The appropriate first aid procedure is as follows: The child should be laid on the floor or a bed with a soft pillow under the head. The child should be turned to one side to prevent choking or aspirating if vomiting occurs. The child should not, however, be restrained. Clothing should be loosened around the neck. A spoon or finger should not be inserted between the child's teeth to prevent swallowing of the tongue, which is physically impossible. The most common result of trying to insert a spoon is a bitten finger or a broken tooth. An ambulance should be called only if the seizure lasts more than 10–15 minutes, which is very uncommon. The child should be attended until awake and alert. Reassurance and comforting is often needed, and the child should be encouraged to resume normal activities once fully recovered.

MULTIDISCIPLINARY MANAGEMENT

Caring for the child with a seizure disorder does not just involve medical and surgical management of seizures. One must also consider educational and psychosocial issues (Hermann & Seidenberg, 1989).

Educational Setting

From an educational perspective, the student's basic needs are dictated by his or her cognitive and learning abilities. In addition, teachers must be alert for signs of difficulty attributable to seizures or their treatment. The child who is known to have absence seizures and suddenly begins to do poorly in class may be having increased seizure activity. Alternatively, new school problems may be attributable to the physician having increased the drug dosage or changed to a new medication. New side effects may include fatigue, inattention, or altered behavior. Teachers must be alert to these signs for they may indicate that the drug level is too high and should be checked.

There is also the psychological side of a child having a seizure in class. If it is a tonic-clonic seizure, the child may make quite a spectacle, including being incontinent of bowel and bladder during the seizure. The best approach is to teach the classmates about seizures before they occur so they know what to expect and do not ostracize the child with the seizure disorder. A fresh change of clothing should also be kept in the classroom.

Psychosocial Issues

The child with a seizure disorder must be educated about the cause of the seizures. The more matter of fact one can be, the better it is for everyone. In many cases, seizures are rare after the proper dosage of medication has been achieved. It is fine if everyone eventually forgets that the child has a problem.

The issue of sports has been a controversial one. At one point, children with epilepsy were precluded from participation in many sports. Now it is felt that virtually all sports are permissible. Of course, some precautions should be taken. For example, the child with tonic-clonic seizures should not swim or dive without the presence of an experienced lifeguard. Bicycling should only be done wearing a helmet. (However, these safeguards should be employed for everyone.)

Like sports, family vacations and camping trips do not need to be curtailed. If possible, excessive fatigue should be avoided and an ample supply of medication should be kept in the luggage. Ideally, the decision to wear a medical identification bracelet should be made with the assent of the child. If it is felt to be stigmatizing, its value is considerably diminished.

The family structure should be disrupted as little as possible, and it is important not to overprotect the child (Lechtenberg, 1984). As the child moves toward adulthood, independence should not be affected. This includes living independently, driving a car (if seizure-free for a suitable time period), and engaging in almost any job. Some types of seizures may increase transiently during adolescence, but most do not (Niijima & Wallace, 1989).

However, a few concerns should be addressed as the child approaches adulthood. Alcohol and drugs should be avoided because of their effect on lowering the seizure threshold and interacting with the antiepileptic medications. Some antiepileptic medications may break down birth control pills, resulting in contraceptive failure. There is also concern over pregnancy because most antiepileptic drugs have been associated with an increased risk of malformations in the fetus. Yet, these risks are low, with 80%–90% of children being born healthy (see Chapter 4).

Because of the many psychosocial issues, it is wise to have a child with difficult seizures followed at a comprehensive epilepsy program. These are multidisciplinary clinics staffed with an interdisciplinary team of neurologists, nurses, social workers, and other therapists working together (Vining, 1989). They are found at children's hospitals and university medical centers.

CASE HISTORIES OF CHILDREN WITH EPILEPSY

The stories of Tiffany, Melissa, and Jason help to illustrate the range of seizure disorders and their treatment.

Tiffany

Tiffany was 1 year old when she had her first seizure during a high fever. Her mother was giving her a sponge bath, trying to bring down her fever, when she began having tonic-clonic convulsive movements. Her parents rushed her to a nearby hospital. When she arrived there 15 minutes later, she was no longer convulsing. Within 2 hours she was back to normal. Blood tests were done, and she underwent a spinal tap. Neither meningitis nor a chemical imbalance was found. An EEG was normal. The physician told Tiffany's parents that she had a febrile convulsion. He indicated that this was not dangerous but might recur before she was 4 years old. He reassured Tiffany's parents that she was fine and had not sustained brain damage. The parents were also instructed that the best prevention of future seizures was to keep her fever from going above 102° F by using acetaminophen plus sponge baths.

By the next day, Tiffany was quite normal. She did have two more febrile convulsions in the next year, but her parents were better prepared, and the seizures were not as traumatic for them. She has been well since then and is now an "A" student in the second grade.

Melissa

Like Tiffany, Melissa's first seizure was tonic-clonic. However, it was not associated with fever and occurred when she was 5 years old. There was no infection or injury to explain the seizure. Unlike Tiffany's normal EEG, Melissa's EEG showed a seizure pattern. She was placed on carbamazepine to control the seizures. Despite the medication, Melissa's seizures continued. The family had difficulty coping with the illness, and they found it hard to give her the support and encouragement they knew she needed. Melissa felt ostracized in school; she was self-conscious about her disability, and she developed few friendships. Melissa was very sad and forlorn. Phenytoin was soon added to the carbamazepine, and her seizures became less frequent. However, the physician had difficulty reaching an appropriate dose for Melissa. Sometimes it was too high, and she was lethargic and irritable. Other times, it was too low, and she had seizures. Finally, the right dose was determined, and her seizures came under control.

Unfortunately, the emotional problems for Melissa and her family persisted. Eventually, they were referred to a social worker for counseling. Melissa began to feel better about herself and gained self-esteem. Her parents developed ways of coping with her illness and began to handle the situation more effectively. Now, at 8 years of age, Melissa is doing well in class and is making more friends. Although still shy,

Melissa has made progress. Her prognosis depends, to a great extent, on those around her and how much support and encouragement she receives from them.

Jason

The least encouraging of the cases is the story of Jason. For him, seizures are but one part of a more complicated and serious condition. Jason was born prematurely and had sepsis as a newborn. He developed infantile spasms when he was 2 months old; he also had microcephaly. By 6 months, it was clear Jason had spastic cerebral palsy and severe mental retardation. His seizures were poorly controlled, even though he took valproic acid. By 16 months of age, he averaged 20–30 seizures of various types a day. His mother preferred not to administer additional medication because she found doing so made him lethargic and uninterested in his environment.

His parents know Jason has severe mental retardation, and they worry about his future. He is now in a preschool program for children with cerebral palsy, and his parents are strengthened by the support of the physical therapist and teacher who work with Jason. For now, both Jason and his family are coping. Yet, his seizures continue.

PROGNOSIS

Most individuals with seizure disorders have normal intelligence. Yet, according to a controversial view, seizures themselves may cause subtle brain injury, causing the potential of children with seizure disorders to be limited over time (Ellenberg, Hirtz, & Nelson, 1986). However, repeated IQ tests do not show a decline in intellectual abilities unless the child is being overmedicated or has had a prolonged episode of status epilepticus.

Prognosis most depends on the seizure type and the underlying brain pathology. Virtually all children with absence seizures have normal intelligence, while those with Lennox-Gastaut syndrome have mental retardation (Holmes, 1987). Yet, prognosis does not depend solely on intelligence. It also depends on how the child and family handle this chronic illness. If the seizures come under control easily and drug reactions are few, the family is likely to cope well. If the seizures prove resistant to treatment and drug effects are many, additional stresses may interfere with the child's functioning.

Finally, there are emotional issues. Some children with seizure disorders have low self-esteem and depression leading to absenteeism in school and overdependence on their parents. When combined with subtle deficits in memory or learning, school failure may result. Yet, if these issues can be approached in an effective manner, the prognosis is generally positive. Because a majority of seizures go into remission by young adulthood, the child who has made it through school psychologically intact is likely to do well in life. For those who have seizure disorders as one part of a multiple disability disorder, the eventual outcome is more likely to be a function of the other disabilities than the seizures.

SUMMARY

Seizure disorders are conditions in which there are abnormally functioning neurons that discharge at the least provocation and cause seizures. Generalized seizures include those classified tonic-clonic, absence, myoclonic, and atonic. Partial seizures may be simple or complex, depending on the level of consciousness. Seizures may occur singly or in combination and may start in the newborn period, in infancy, or in later childhood. For about half of children, the seizures are an isolated disability. These children lead almost normal lives. For a child with multiple disabilities, the prognosis is generally a function of the other disabilities.

REFERENCES

Adler, J., Erba, G., Winston, K.R., et al. (1991). Results of surgery for extratemporal partial epilepsy that began in childhood. *Archives of Neurology, 48*, 133–140.

Aicardi, J. (1986). *Epilepsy in children*. New York: Raven Press.

Aicardi, J. (1988a). Clinical approach to the management of intractable epilepsy. *Developmental Medicine and Child Neurology, 30*, 429–440.

Aicardi, J. (1988b). Epileptic syndromes in childhood. *Epilepsia, 29*(Suppl. 3), S1–S5.

Aldenkamp, A.P., Alpherts, W.C., Dekker, M.J., et al. (1990). Neuropsychological aspects of learning disabilities in epilepsy. *Epilepsia, 31*(Supp. 4), S9–S20.

Alvarez, N. (1989). Epilepsy. In L.L. Rubin & A.C. Crocker (Eds.), *Developmental disabilities: Delivery of medical care for children and adults* (pp. 130–147). Philadelphia: Lea & Febiger.

Barron, T. (1991). The child with spells. *Pediatric Clinics of North America, 38*, 711–724.

Berg, A.T., Shinnar, S., Hauser, W.A., et al. (1990). Predictors of recurrent febrile seizures: A metaanalytic review. *Journal of Pediatrics, 116*, 329–337.

Blennow, G., Heijbel, J., Sandstedt, P., et al. (1990). Discontinuation of antiepileptic drugs in children who have outgrown epilepsy: Effects on cognitive function. *Epilepsia, 31*(Suppl. 4), S50–S53.

Bobele, G.B., & Bodensteiner, J.B. (1990). Infantile spasms. *Neurologic Clinics, 8*, 633–645.

Brown, J.K., & Hussain, I.H. (1991). Status epilepticus: I: Pathogenesis. *Developmental Medicine and Child Neurology, 33*, 3–17.

Brown, J.K., & Hussain, J.H. (1991). Status epilepticus. II. Treatment. *Developmental Medicine and Child Neurology, 33*, 97–109.

Chugani, H.T., Shields, W.D., Shewmon, D.A., et al. (1990). Infantile spasms I: PET identifies focal cortical dysgenesis in cryptogenic cases for surgical treatment. *Annals of Neurology, 27*, 406–413.

Clancy, R.R. (1990). Valproate: An update—The challenge of modern pediatric seizure management. *Current Problems in Pediatrics, 20*, 161–233.

Collaborative Group for Epidemiology of Epilepsy. (1988). Adverse reactions to antiepileptic drugs: A follow-up study of 355 patients with chronic antiepileptic drug treatment. *Epilepsia, 29*, 787–793.

Commission on Classification and Terminology of the International League Against Epilepsy. (1981). Proposal for revised clinical and electroencephalographic classification of epileptic seizures. *Epilepsia, 22*, 489–501.

Consensus Development Conference. (1980). Febrile seizures: Long-term management of children with fever—associated seizures. *Pediatrics, 66*, 1009–1012.

Dam, M. (1990). Children with epilepsy: The effect of seizures, syndromes, and etiological factors on cognitive functioning. *Epilepsia, 31*(Suppl. 4), S26–S29.

Dodrill, C.B., & Wilensky, A.J. (1990). Intellectual impairment as an outcome of status epilepticus. *Neurology, 40*(Suppl. 2), 23–27.

Dodson, W.E. (1989). Medical treatment and pharmacology of antiepileptic drugs. *Pediatric Clinics of North America, 36*, 421–433.

Dreifuss, F.E. (1989). Classification of epileptic seizures and the epilepsies. *Pediatric Clinics of North America, 36*, 265–278.

Dreifuss, F.E., Langer, D.H., Moline, K.A., et al. (1989). Valproic acid hepatic fatalities. II. US experience since 1984. *Neurology, 39*, 201–207.

Duchowny, M.S. (1989). Surgery for intractable epilepsy: Issues and outcome. *Pediatrics, 84*, 886–894.

Dunn, D.W. (1990). Status epilepticus in infancy and childhood. *Neurologic Clinics, 8*, 647–657.

Eadie, M.J. (1984). Anticonvulsant drugs. An update. *Drugs, 27*, 328–363.

Ellenberg, J.H., Hirtz, D.G., & Nelson, K.B. (1986). Do seizures in children cause intellectual deterioration? *New England Journal of Medicine, 314*, 1085–1088.

Emerson, R., D'Souza, B.J., Vining, E.P., et al. (1981). Stopping medication in children with epilepsy: Predictors of outcome. *New England Journal of Medicine, 304*, 1125–1129.

Farwell, J.R., Lee, Y.J., Hirtz, D.G., et al. (1990). Phenobarbital for febrile seizures: Effects on intelligence and on seizure recurrence. *New England Journal of Medicine, 322*, 364–369.

Ferry, P.C., Banner, W., Jr., & Wolf, R.A. (Eds.) (1986). *Seizure disorders in children*. Philadelphia: J.B. Lippincott.

Freeman, J.M., Vining, E.P.G., & Pillas, D.J. (1990). *Seizures and epilepsy in childhood: A guide for parents*. Baltimore: The Johns Hopkins University Press.

Glaze, D.G., Hrachovy, R.A., Frost, J.D., Jr., et al. (1988). Prospective study of outcome of infants with infantile spasms treated during controlled studies of ACTH and prednisone. *Journal of Pediatrics, 112*, 389–396.

Gomez, M.R., & Klass, D.W. (1983). Epilepsies of infancy and childhood. *Annals of Neurology, 13*, 113–124.

Goulden, K.J., Shinnar, S., Koller, H., et al. (1990). Epilepsy in children with mental retardation: A cohort study. *Epilepsia, 32*, 690–697.

Grant, S.M., & Heel, R.C. (1991). Vigabatrim. A review of its pharmacodynamic and pharmacokinetic properties and therapeutic potential in epilepsy and disorders of motor control. *Drugs, 41*, 889–926.

Green, R.C., Adler, J.R., & Erba, G. (1988). Epilepsy surgery in children. *Journal of Child Neurology, 3*, 155–166.

Hermann, B.P., & Seidenberg, M. (Eds.). (1989). *Childhood epilepsies: Neuropsychological, psychosocial and intervention aspects*. New York: John Wiley & Sons.

Herranz, J.L., Armijo, J.A., & Arteaga, R. (1988). Clinical side effects of phenobarbital, primidone, phenytoin, carbamazepine, and valproate during monotherapy in children. *Epilepsia, 29*, 794–804.

Hirtz, D.G. (1989). Generalized tonic-clonic and febrile seizures. *Pediatric Clinics of North America, 36*, 365–382.

Hockaday, J.M. (1990). Management of migraine. *Archives of Diseases in Childhood, 65*, 1174–1176.

Holmes, G.L. (1987). *Diagnosis and management of seizures in children*. Philadelphia: W.B. Saunders.

Holmes, G.L. (1989). Electroencephalographic and neuroradiologic evaluation of children with epilepsy. *Pediatric Clinics of North America, 36*, 395–420.

Hopkins, I.J., & Klug, G.L. (1991). Temporal lobectomy for the treatment of intractable complex partial seizures of temporal lobe origin in early childhood. *Developmental Medicine and Child Neurology, 33*, 26–31.

Kotagal, P., Rothner, A.D., Erenberg, G., et al. (1987). Complex partial seizures of childhood onset: A five-year follow-up study. *Archives of Neurology, 44*, 1177–1180.

Lechtenberg, R. (1984). *Epilepsy and the family*. Boston: Harvard University Press.

Lindsay, J., Ounsted, C., & Richards, P. (1987). Hemispherectomy for childhood epilepsy: A 36-year study. *Developmental Medicine and Child Neurology, 29*, 592–600.

Lockman, L.A. (1989). Absence, myoclonic, and atonic seizures. *Pediatric Clinics of North America, 36*, 331–341.

Lockman, L.A. (1990). Treatment of status epilepticus in children. *Neurology, 40*(Suppl. 2), 43–46.

Matsuda, I., Higashi, A., & Inotsume, N. (1989). Physiologic and metabolic aspects of anticonvulsants. *Pediatric Clinics of North America, 36*, 1099–1111.

Maytal, J., Shinnar, S., Moshe, S.L., et al. (1989). Low morbidity and mortality of status epilepticus in children. *Pediatrics, 83*, 323–331.

Mizrahi, E.M., Kellaway, P., Grossman, R.G., et al. (1990). Anterior temporal lobectomy and medically refractory temporal lobe epilepsy of childhood. *Epilepsy, 31*, 302–312.

Neidich, J.A., Nussbaum, R.L., Packer, R.J., et al. (1990). Heterogeneity of clinical severity and molecular lesions in Aicardi syndrome. *Journal of Pediatrics, 116*, 911–917.

Nelson, K.B., & Ellenberg, J.H. (1990). Prenatal and perinatal antecedents of febrile seizures. *Annals of Neurology, 27*, 127–131.

Niedermeyer, E. (1990). *The epilepsias*. Baltimore: Urban & Schwarzenberg.

Niedermeyer, E., & Lopes da Silva. (1981). *Electroencephalography: Basic principles, clinical applications, and related fields*. Baltimore: Urban & Schwarzenberg.

Nielsen, E.B., Suzdak, P.D., Andersen, K.E., et al. (1991). Characterization of tiagabine (NO-328), a new potent and selective GABA uptake inhibitor. *European Journal of Pharmacology, 196*, 257–266.

Niijima, S., & Wallace, S.J. (1989). Effects of puberty on seizure frequency. *Developmental Medicine and Child Neurology, 31*, 174–180.

Pellock, J.M. (1989). Efficacy and adverse effects of antiepileptic drugs. *Pediatric Clinics of North America, 36*, 435–448.

Pellock, J.M. (1990). The classification of childhood seizures and epilepsy syndromes. *Neurologic Clinics, 8*, 619–632.

Physicians' Desk Reference (46th ed.). (1992). Montvale, NJ: Medical Economics Data.

Pinto, F.J., & Bolognia, J.L. (1991). Disorders of hypopigmentation in children. *Pediatric Clinics of North America, 38*, 991–1017.

Reisner, H. (Ed.). (1988). *Children with epilepsy: A parent's guide*. Kensington, MD: Woodbine House.

Ross, E., Chadwick, D., & Crawford, R. (Eds.). (1987). *Epilepsy in young people*. New York: John Wiley & Sons.

Sander, J.W., Trevisol-Bittencourt, P.C., Hart, Y.M., et al. (1990). The efficacy and long-term tolerability of lamotrigine in the treatment of severe epilepsy. *Epilepsy Research, 7*, 226–229.

Sander, L., & Thompson, P. (1990). *Epilepsy: A partial guide to coping*. North Pomfret, UT: Cromwood.

Sass, K.J., Spencer, D.D., Spencer, S.S., et al. (1988). Corpus callosotomy for epilepsy. II. Neurologic and neuropsychological outcome. *Neurology, 38*, 24–28.

Schwartz, R.H., Eaton, J., Bower, B.D., et al. (1989). Ketogenic diets in the treatment of epilepsy: Short-term clinical effects. *Developmental Medicine and Child Neurology, 31*, 145–151.

Shinnar, S., Berg, A.T., Moshe, S.L., et al. (1990). Risk of seizure recurrence following a short unprovoked seizure in childhood: A prospective study. *Pediatrics, 85*, 1076–1085.

Shinnar, S., Vining, E.P., Mellits, E.D., et al. (1985). Discontinuing antiepileptic medication in children with epilepsy after two years without seizures: A prospective study. *New England Journal of Medicine, 313*, 976–980.

Siemes, H., Spohr, H.L., Michael, T., et al. (1988). Therapy of infantile spasms with valproate: Results of a prospective study. *Epilepsia, 29*, 553–560.

Sivenius, J., Kalviainen, R., Ylinen, A., et al. (1991). Double-blind study of Gabapontin in the treatment of partial seizures. *Epilepsia, 32*, 539–542.

Snead, O.C., III, & Hosey, L.C. (1985). Exacerbation of seizures in children by carbamazepine. *New England Journal of Medicine, 313*, 916–921.

Tardo, C. (1988). Tics and Tourette syndrome. *Seminars in Neurology, 8*, 78–82.

Theodore, W.H., Raubertas, R.F., Porter, R.J., et al. (1991). Felbamate: A clinical trial for complex partial seizures. *Epilepsia, 32*, 392–397.

Thurston, J.H., Thurston, D.L., Hixon, B.B., et al. (1982). Prognosis in childhood epilepsy: Additional follow-up of 148 children 15 to 23 years after withdrawal of anticonvulsant therapy. *New England Journal of Medicine, 306*, 831–836.

Vining, E.P. (1989). Educational, social, and life-long effects of epilepsy. *Pediatric Clinics of North America, 36*, 449–461.

Vining, E.P., Mellits, E.D., Dorsen, M.M., et al. (1987). Psychologic and behavioral effects of antiepileptic drugs in children: A double-blind comparison between phenobarbital and valproic acid. *Pediatrics, 80*, 165–174.

Walczak, T.S., Radtke, R.A., McNamara, J.O., et al. (1990). Anterior temporary lobectomy for complex partial seizures. Evaluation, results, and long-term follow-up in 100 cases. *Neurology, 40*, 413–418.

Wallace, S.J. (1990). Risk of seizures (Annotation). *Developmental Medicine and Child Neurology, 32*, 645–649.

Wallace, S.T. (1988). *The child with febrile seizures*. Stoneham, VT: Butterworth-Heinlein.

Wyllie, E. (1988). Corpus callosotomy for intractable generalized epilepsy. *Journal of Pediatrics, 113*, 255–261.

Wyllie, E. (1991). Cortical resection for children with epilepsy. Perspectives in pediatrics. *American Journal of Diseases of Children, 145*, 314–320.

Wyllie, E., Rothner, A.D., & Luders, H. (1989). Partial seizures in children: Clinical features, medical treatment, and surgical considerations. *Pediatric Clinics of North America, 36*, 343–364.

Chapter 27

Traumatic Brain Injury

Linda J. Michaud and Ann-Christine Duhaime

Upon completion of this chapter, the reader will:
—know the definition and major causes of traumatic brain injury in children
—be aware of the major types of brain injuries
—understand some of the problems that result from head trauma of varying severity
—be able to discuss the components of management of a child with head injury
—be able to identify prognostic factors

Most head trauma in children is minor and not associated with persisting deficits. However, severe head injury occurs with sufficient frequency to make it the most common cause of acquired disability in childhood (Kraus, Rock, & Hemyari, 1990). Even when obvious physical problems are minimal, neuropsychological deficits may lead to chronic academic, behavioral, and interpersonal difficulties that place an enormous burden on the child, family, and society. Disabilities caused by severe head injury may prevent a child from ever fulfilling his or her potential as a productive member of society. Effective acute management and long-term rehabilitation are vital after head injury in order to optimize the child's outcome.

INCIDENCE OF HEAD INJURIES

Each year approximately 1 in 25 children receives medical attention because of a head injury (Brookes, MacMillan, Cully, et al., 1990). These injuries range from confined areas of scalp or skull trauma to more diffuse and severe brain damage. Brain injury, defined as trauma sufficient to result in a change in level of consciousness and/or an

Linda J. Michaud, M.D., is Assistant Professor of Rehabilitation Medicine and Pediatrics at The University of Pennsylvania School of Medicine in Philadelphia and is Director of Rehabilitation at Children's Seashore House.

Ann-Christine Duhaime, M.D., is Assistant Professor of Neurosurgery at The University of Pennsylvania School of Medicine and Associate Neurosurgeon in the Division of Neurosurgery at The Children's Hospital of Philadelphia.

anatomical abnormality of the brain, occurs in approximately 1 in 500 children per year (Baker, O'Neill, & Karpf, 1984). Approximately 150,000 children sustained a traumatic brain injury in 1986, with the rate for boys being twice that for girls (Centers for Disease Control, 1990). Head injuries most commonly occur in the spring and summer, on weekends, and in the afternoons, when children are most likely to be outside playing or riding in cars.

CAUSES OF TRAUMATIC BRAIN INJURY

Common causes of head injury include falls from heights, sports and recreation-related injuries, motor vehicle accidents, and assaults, including child abuse. The incidence of these types of brain injury varies with age (Figure 27.1). Young children are more likely to sustain head injuries as a result of falls, while teenagers are more often involved in motor vehicle accidents (Agran, Castillo, & Winn, 1990; Centers for Disease Control, 1990).

Certain psychosocial factors may increase the risk of childhood head trauma (Craft, Shaw, & Cartlidge, 1972). Children with hyperactive or impulsive behavior (as seen in attention deficit hyperactivity disorder) may act in a dangerous manner, although overactive behavior does not necessarily increase the risk of injury (Davidson, Hughes, & O'Connor, 1988). Severely depressed adolescents may attempt sui-

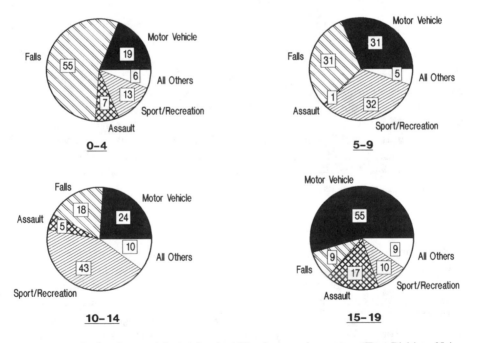

Figure 27.1. Causes of traumatic brain injury in children by age and percentage. (From Division of Injury Control, Center for Environmental Health and Injury Control, Centers for Disease Control [1990]. *American Journal of Diseases of Children, 144,* 627–646).

cide (Holinger, 1990). Social factors, such as poverty, living in congested residential areas, and marital instability, have been associated with an increased risk of head injury in children as a result of physical abuse or neglect (Alexander, Sato, Smith, et al., 1990; Braddock, Lapidus, Gregorio, et al., 1991; Klonoff, 1971).

TYPES OF BRAIN INJURIES

The type of brain injury that a child sustains depends in large part on the nature of the force that caused the injury and the severity of the injury. The gradations of severity are discussed later in the chapter.

Head trauma can be caused by **impact**, or **inertial**, forces. Impact, or contact, forces are those that occur when the head strikes a surface or is struck by a moving object. Impact forces can result in scalp injuries, skull fractures, focal brain bruises (**contusions**), or blood clots beneath the skull (i.e., **epidural hematomas**). Inertial forces are those that occur when the brain undergoes violent motion inside the skull, which tears the nerve fibers and blood vessels. The severity of injuries caused by inertial forces depends on the magnitude and the direction of the motion. Angular acceleration-deceleration forces, such as those that might occur in a high-speed motor vehicle accident, cause much more serious damage than do straight-line forces, such as those that might occur in a fall. Injuries caused by inertial forces range from relatively mild **concussions** to more serious injuries, such as **subdural hematomas** and **diffuse axonal injury** (DAI) (see subsections on these injuries in this chapter).

Most clinical head injuries include both impact and inertial components, with several injury types occurring simultaneously. Thus, the individual injuries discussed in the following sections do not usually occur singly.

Scalp and Skull Injury

Scalp and skull injuries result from impact forces applied to these areas. Although scalp injuries sometimes cause considerable blood loss, they have no neurological consequence. Skull fractures can be either benign or serious. A **linear fracture**, in which there is no visible injury, but a crack in the skull bones is visible on an X ray, is often seen in young children who have fallen from low heights. These fractures usually are not associated with significant neurological damage. A **depressed fracture**, in which the skull bone is broken and presses against the underlying brain tissue, however, may be associated with significant brain injury and associated disabilities. For example, a depressed fracture directly over the motor cortex (that part of the brain controlling movement) will result in weakness of the opposite side of the body.

Brain Contusion

Brain contusions, or bruises of the brain, most often result from direct impact to the head. As is true of bruises in other areas of the body, brain contusions often evolve during the first few days after the injury, such that clinical symptoms may worsen, occasionally requiring surgical removal. Deficits depend on the extent of the bruise and resultant damage to the brain.

Epidural Hematoma

Though epidural hematomas are one of the most lethal types of head injury, they are also one of the most treatable. The hematoma, or blood clot, forms between the skull and the coverings of the brain (i.e., dura), and it may originate in either an artery or a vein (Figure 27.2). The former occurs when an artery in the brain's covering, most often the middle meningeal artery, ruptures due to impact. This is usually associated with a skull fracture and is the only life-threatening head injury to occur in young children from a low-height fall. In older children, epidural hematomas may occur from falls and other contact injuries, such as those that occur in sports. Venous epidural hematomas occur when there is bleeding from a fractured bone, or from a tear in a large vein in the dura. Because veins generally bleed more slowly than arteries, venous epidural hematomas are usually self-limited and less serious than the arterial type.

The classic clinical hallmark of an epidural hematoma is delayed onset of symptoms. Thus, when a child sustains the injury, neurological symptoms may be minimal or absent. However, as the hematoma enlarges, secondary injury, caused by increased pressure on the brain, may occur. This leads to symptoms of headache, confusion, vomiting, focal neurological deficit (e.g., one-sided weakness), and agitation. These

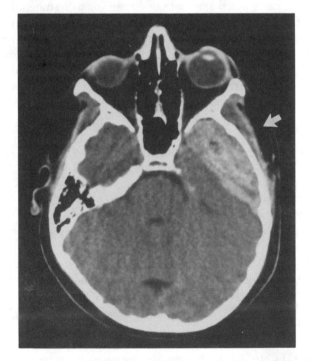

Figure 27.2.   Epidural hematoma in the right temporal region of an 8-year-old boy who fell from his bicycle (see arrow). He was initially dazed but awake and conversant. He became progressively less responsive during the subsequent few hours. Upon arrival at the hospital, he was comatose with a dilated right pupil. He made a complete recovery after removal of the clot.

symptoms may progress to lethargy, coma, and even death if left untreated. If surgery is performed before secondary injury becomes irreversible, outcome is remarkably favorable (Dhellemmes, Lejune, Christiaens, et al., 1985) and these children quickly return to normal function. If surgery is delayed, various physical and cognitive deficits are likely to persist.

Concussion

Concussion is defined as head injury sufficient to cause a brief loss of consciousness or amnesia for the event. Physiologically, a concussion indicates a relatively mild injury to the nerve fibers in the brain. In children, concussions occur most commonly from falls and represent one of the most frequent reasons for trauma admissions to the hospital (Kraus, Fife, & Conroy, 1987). Usually, a brief loss of consciousness is followed in minutes by a complete return to a normal mental status and behavior. However, in some children, a period of headache, drowsiness, confusion, or irritability will occur, often several hours after the injury, and these symptoms may last for a few days. The CT scan will be normal, differentiating these children from those whose deterioration is caused by a blood clot requiring surgery.

Diffuse Axonal Injury

While concussion falls at the mild end of the spectrum of diffuse injuries, persons with more severe symptoms are classified as having sustained diffuse axonal injury. This indicates that nerve fibers (i.e., axons) throughout the brain have been damaged or torn, usually by violent motion, such as that which occurs in motor vehicle accidents. The individual may have been a passenger, pedestrian, or bicycle rider. Persons who have sustained DAI lapse into immediate unconsciousness. For practical purposes, a diagnosis of DAI is given if unconsciousness lasts at least 6 hours without other causes, such as seizures or pressure from a hematoma. Depending on the severity of the injury, persons also may exhibit abnormal movements (i.e., posturing), abnormal reactions of the pupils, and difficulty regulating breathing and blood pressure. CT and MRI scans reveal small, scattered brain tissue tears and hemorrhages (Figure 27.3). In more mild cases, the CT scan may appear essentially normal. Because of the large mechanical forces involved in this type of injury, trauma to other organ systems or to the spine is not uncommon, and lack of oxygen or blood loss may exacerbate the primary insult to the nervous system.

Recovery from DAI occurs over weeks to years, depending on the severity of injury. Long-lasting deficits may include motor, communicative, cognitive, and behavior problems, ranging from mild to severe. A few severely injured individuals may remain unresponsive, but the majority regain consciousness.

Subdural Hematoma

Acute subdural hematomas are blood clots that form beneath the dura, over the surface of the brain itself (Figure 27.4). Unlike an epidural hematoma, hemorrhages in the subdural compartment occur not from impact, but from shear forces applied to the veins that course between the brain surface and the large, draining dural veins. Tre-

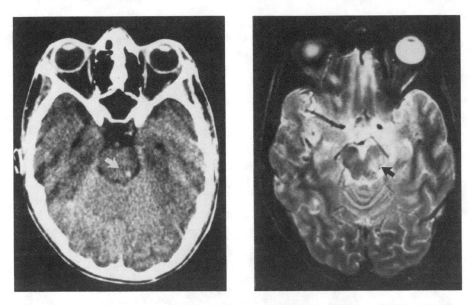

Figure 27.3. Computed tomography (CT) scan (left) and magnetic resonance image (MRI) (right) of the brain of a 9-year-old boy who was struck by a car. He was immediately unresponsive with abnormal posturing movements. Both the CT and MRI studies show changes typical of diffuse axonal injury (DAI). The MRI is much more sensitive, displaying the extent and degree of damage. In these images, the small white dot in the center of the CT scan is a brain stem hemorrhage. This area appears as a more extensive white region on MRI, which also shows the surrounding tissue disruption and swelling (see arrow).

mendous angular acceleration-deceleration forces are required to displace the brain from the dura sufficiently to rupture these bridging veins. As a result, an acute subdural hematoma usually accompanies a major generalized injury to the brain itself, which occurs in addition to the damage done by direct pressure from the overlying blood clot. This explains why morbidity and mortality are so high in this particular injury type and why surgical removal of the clot often appears to make only a small difference in the clinical status of the individual. This contrasts with the epidural hematoma, for which prompt surgery markedly improves the prognosis.

Recovery from subdural hematoma has many features similar to that of recovery from DAI, and in fact, the two injuries often occur simultaneously. A subdural hematoma may cause major brain swelling and stroke. It is almost always unilateral (i.e., on one side of the brain) and there may be a large area of brain damage on the affected side, in addition to the diffuse injury throughout the brain.

DETECTING SIGNIFICANT BRAIN INJURY

As noted previously, most head trauma is minor and does not require treatment or result in significant consequences. But how does a parent or teacher know whether a head injury warrants treatment? Generally speaking, if a child hits his or her head and does not become unconscious, no treatment is necessary unless the child develops

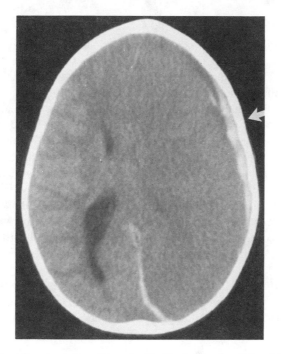

Figure 27.4. Subdural hematoma in an 11-month-old girl who was the victim of inflicted injury (see arrow). She was comatose upon hospital admission and remained so after surgery to remove the clot. The right hemisphere of the brain was extremely swollen. Follow-up studies show massive brain damage on the right side, and the child has severe deficits.

symptoms suggestive of an epidural hematoma. Medical evaluation is needed if the child becomes lethargic, confused, or irritable; has a severe headache; demonstrates changes in speech, vision, or movements of the arms or legs; has significant bleeding from the wound; or starts vomiting 1–2 hours later. Then a visit to the emergency room for examination is warranted.

If the child is momentarily unconscious and then resumes activities, he or she may have a mild concussion. If there has been more than a momentary loss of consciousness, the child should be taken to the emergency room, where a neurological examination will be performed. A skull X ray may be taken to rule out a fracture, or a CT scan may be performed to be certain there is no brain injury. If there are no abnormal neurological or radiologic findings, the child may be sent home. Parents will be given instructions to make sure the child can be roused from sleep, is not confused, and develops no new neurological symptoms.

If the child remains unconscious for more than a few minutes, the paramedics should be called. If, upon arrival at the hospital, the child is still unconscious, he or she will be stabilized in the emergency room and then usually transferred to the intensive care unit. Immediate coma after head trauma is the result of primary injury to neural pathways. There may be worsening in the subsequent 24 hours, as a consequence of secondary hemorrhaging or brain swelling.

SEVERITY OF BRAIN INJURY

The duration and severity of coma indicate the seriousness of a brain injury. The most frequently used scale for coma severity is the Glasgow Coma Score (GCS) (Jennett & Teasdale, 1981). This scale was devised for use in adults and can be difficult to apply to very young children; however, it remains the most useful means available for classifying severe injuries in the early phase after trauma. Using this scale within the first 6 hours after injury, the trauma team assigns the child a score based on the degree and quality of movement, vocalization, and eye opening (Table 27.1).

The lowest score on each of the three subscales is 1, so that the worst Glasgow Coma Score obtainable is 3. The best score is 15, representing the least severe head injury. An individual with a score of 3 would have no eye opening, no movement, and no verbal response, and would be in deep coma. An individual who looks about, moves limbs in response to requests, and is oriented to the environment receives a score of 15. Someone who opens his or her eyes when physically prodded, who withdraws a limb that is touched, and who makes only incomprehensible sounds receives a score of 8.

Severe head injury is defined as a score of 8 or less (Langfitt & Gennarelli, 1982). Scores of 9–12 reflect moderate head injury, and scores of 13–15, minor head injury. Fatality rates in these latter groups is about one-third (Berger, Pitts, Lovely, et al., 1985).

Table 27.1. Glasgow Coma Scale

Response	Score
Eye opening:	
Spontaneous	4
To speech	3
To pain	2
Nil	1
Best motor response	
Obeys	6
Localizes	5
Withdraws	4
Abnormal flexion	3
Extensor response	2
Nil	1
Verbal response	
Oriented	5
Confused conversation	4
Inappropriate words	3
Incomprehensible sounds	2
Nil	1

From Jennett, B., Teasdale, G., Galbraith, S., et al. (1987). Severe head injuries in three countries. *Journal of Neurology, Neurosurgery, and Psychiatry, 40,* 293; reprinted with permission.

STAGES OF RECOVERY FROM COMA

Recovery from severe injury may be divided into early, middle, and late stages. Not all children complete all three stages; instead, they may plateau at a certain level. Furthermore, the timetable over which individuals progress is quite variable, ranging from days to years.

In the early stage, there is some spontaneous limb movement and absent or minimal response to a voice command, such as "open your eyes." There may be some recognition of parents and an attempt at vocalization. Toward the end of this stage, the child may become agitated and combative, pulling at tubes and clothes. In the middle stage, there is clear recognition and memory of familiar objects and people. Speech begins, but verbal responses are delayed and often tangential. The child can perform some simple self-care skills, such as brushing hair. However, there continues to be some confusion of time, place, and person. Behavior is impulsive and agitated, and social interactions are strained. By the late stage, the child appears to be close to normal. However, there is often a decreased attention span, poor organizational abilities, subtle visual-perceptual problems, and deficits in memory and abstract reasoning. There also may be poor social interactions and judgment.

TREATMENT APPROACHES

Approaches to therapy depend on the stage of recovery from coma and the associated medical and physical problems. Treatment can be divided into an acute medical phase and a later rehabilitative phase. Initial rehabilitation, which may last for weeks to months, is generally provided in an inpatient setting. Subsequent outpatient rehabilitation can be provided in a hospital, rehabilitation center, or school.

Acute Medical Management

The first priority in the emergency room is to stop hemorrhaging, aid respiration, and support blood pressure. Once these vital signs are stable, the medical examination identifies fractures and damage to various internal body organs. A neurological examination is also performed. As part of this examination, the child's level of consciousness is assessed. Also, a light is shined into the child's eyes. The pupils of the eye normally constrict equally in bright light and dilate equally in the dark. If these responses are absent, delayed, or asymmetrical, brain swelling or damage is likely. Movement of limbs and reflexes are also tested to see if there are tone changes or asymmetry. For example, left-sided weakness indicates damage to the right side of the brain.

Certain physical findings suggest damage to a specific region of the skull or brain. Blood behind the eardrum, cerebrospinal fluid drainage from the nose or ear, and bruising around the orbits of the eye suggest the presence of a fracture at the base of the skull. Hemorrhages in the retina of the eye may be associated with subdural hematoma (Raimondi & Hirschauer, 1984).

Neurosurgical consultation is recommended for all children who have sustained severe head trauma. An open skull fracture may warrant surgery to prevent infection of the brain. An epidural or subdural hematoma also may require surgery to prevent or treat potentially life-threatening increased intracranial pressure (Dhellemmes et al., 1985). Concern over increased intracranial pressure also may lead the neurosurgeon to insert a pressure transducer to monitor intracranial pressure.

The cranial CT scan is used routinely following significant head trauma to diagnose skull fracture, intracranial hemorrhage, swelling, or DAI. MRI scans are being used during the recovery stage to determine more clearly the extent of residual brain damage (Gentry, Godersky, & Thompson, 1988).

The main goal of medical management of coma is to prevent or limit secondary brain damage, which can result from a buildup of pressure, a lack of oxygen, a lack of sufficient energy supply, or an accumulation of neurotoxins. Pressure often builds as a result of brain swelling. If this is found, hyperventilation or medications, such as mannitol or barbiturates, may be used to shrink brain tissue. Blood flow to the brain affects both pressure within the brain and the supply of nutrients and oxygen. Thus, blood supply must be carefully controlled (Pfenninger, Kaiser, Lütschg, et al., 1983).

The occurrence of seizures immediately after the injury or within the first few days after a head injury is rather common, even in children with only mild concussions. However, less than 2% of persons develop persistent seizure disorders (Ylvisaker, 1985). Factors that increase the risk of later seizure disorders include bleeding into the brain and penetrating injury that may cause the formation of scar tissue. Antiepileptic medication may be given preventively for a week after the injury, but prolonged treatment should be used only if the child develops a persistent seizure disorder (see Chapter 26).

Recent research suggests that brain damage following head injury is, at least in part, intensified by excitatory neurotransmitters that are released in toxic amounts at the time of injury. These neurotoxins lead to swelling and death of nerve cells. Experimental trials with drugs that block receptors for these chemicals have shown some promise in protecting the brain. Interestingly, one potentially helpful drug is dextromethorphan, the active ingredient in commonly used cough medicines (Steinberg, George, DeLaPaz, et al., 1988).

Rehabilitation

The goals of rehabilitation are to limit secondary damage, relearn lost skills, and learn new skills that will be needed to compensate for disabilities. Rehabilitation begins almost immediately after vital signs are stabilized, often while the child is still in a coma.

Acute rehabilitative care following head injury aims to limit secondary musculoskeletal damage by passive range of motion exercises, positioning, and splinting of limbs. These efforts can help to prevent the later development of contractures, which could interfere with seating, ambulation, and participation in daily activities (Blasier & Letts, 1989). Other important acute rehabilitative measures include changing body position and caring for the skin in order to prevent the development of pressure sores (Jaffe & Hays, 1986). Provision of adequate nutrition promotes wound healing. These measures, taken together, appear to shorten hospitalization and improve outcome.

As the child begins to recover from coma, multiple neurological problems may be evident, including motor, communication, cognitive, behavioral, and sensory deficits (Hall, Johnson, & Middleton, 1990). Rehabilitation aims to: 1) avert complications that arise from immobilization, disuse, and neurological dysfunction; 2) augment the use of abilities regained as a result of recovery from coma; 3) teach adaptive compensation for impaired or lost function; and 4) alleviate the effect of chronic disability on the process of growth and development (Molnar & Perrin, 1983).

The severity of the head injury will determine the rehabilitative strategy (Filley, Cranberg, Alexander, et al., 1987). Severe diffuse brain injury is likely to result in impairment in all areas of function, while focal damage may result in more localized abnormalities. Interdisciplinary therapy may involve physical, occupational, and speech-language therapy (Ylvisaker, 1985). Additional services may include neuropsychological and academic assessments, psychological counseling, special education, and recreational therapy (Jaffe & Hays, 1986). Each is discussed in relation to the specific deficits it is intended to remediate.

Motor Deficits The site(s) of brain injury determines the type of motor dysfunction that occurs. Spasticity, ataxia, and tremor are the most common motor abnormalities, indicating damage to the corticospinal tract, basal ganglia, and cerebellum (Brink, Garrett, Hale, et al., 1970; Mysiw, Corrigan, & Gribble, 1990) (see Chapter 14).

Medication and surgery have had varying success in treating motor deficits. At this time, there are no effective medical or surgical approaches to ataxia. However, there have been some promising results from the use of the medication propranolol to treat posttraumatic tremor (Biary, Cleeves, Findley, et al., 1989). Both medical and neurosurgical approaches have proven somewhat helpful in controlling spasticity. Medications include those that are used to treat spastic cerebral palsy: diazepam (Valium), baclofen (Lioresal), and dantrolene (Dantrium) (see Chapter 24).

Neurosurgical approaches to spasticity include nerve blocks—injecting anesthetic agents into specific nerve roots—and dorsal rhizotomy (see Chapter 24). The effects of nerve blocks last for a number of weeks or months, but repeated injections are required if spasticity persists.

Orthopedic surgery also may be required. Long-term contractures or dislocations may need to be treated by performing tendon releases, femoral osteotomies, or scoliosis surgery (see Chapter 24). Surgery is more likely to be undertaken with spasticity than with ataxia. Serial casting may be used to correct a deformity in some cases of spasticity.

Medical and surgical approaches may be helpful, but they offer no cure. The child may continue to have motor deficits that impair the ability to move around and to participate in adaptive skills. Furthermore, cognitive and visual-perceptual deficits may exacerbate motor difficulties. Active physical and occupational therapy is needed to assist the child in regaining motor function. Exercises and activities are designed to increase strength, balance, and coordination, to reduce spasticity, and to prevent contractures and dislocations. The child may need to relearn ambulation. Crutches, walkers, or wheelchair training may be needed (see Chapter 24).

Feeding Disorders Feeding disorders often accompany motor deficits (Ylvisaker & Weinstein, 1989). Food intake may decrease if the child is unable to communicate when hungry; if the ability to obtain food or to eat is compromised because of impaired motor skills; or if there are problems with swallowing or gastroesophageal reflux.

Nutritional treatment during coma may involve hyperalimentation, in which a solution containing protein, carbohydrate, and fat is given intravenously. Nasogastric or gastrostomy tube-feedings with high-caloric formulas may be used as part of long-term therapy if the child remains unable to take in sufficient sustenance by mouth (see Chapter 12).

A number of rehabilitation therapies also are involved in treating feeding disorders. An occupational therapist may work on proper positioning for feeding. A speech therapist may use desensitization techniques, stimulation of the swallowing reflex, and facilitation of tongue, lip, and jaw control to improve swallowing. Nutritionists provide advice concerning the textures, taste, temperature, and caloric density of the food. Finally, medication to control reflux may improve the child's ability to eat and gain weight (see Chapter 12).

Sensory Deficits Vision and hearing can be affected by traumatic brain injury. The most common vision problem is diplopia (i.e., double vision), caused by eye muscle palsy. Another problem is nystagmus, caused by injury to the cerebellum. Less commonly, a crush injury can damage an eye; a missile injury can sever a portion of the visual pathway; both cause irreversible damage. Rarely, a head injury accompanied by severe brain swelling can result in a stroke or cortical blindness. Cortical blindness involves an abnormality in the visual cortex and partial or complete recovery can occur (see Chapter 17). As a result of these problems, vision testing should be included in the evaluation after recovery from coma, and glasses may be needed.

Hearing loss is a less common problem following head injury. If present, it is usually unilateral and caused by direct physical trauma to the temporal bone. Deafness does not generally result. However, a formal hearing test should be conducted following recovery from coma because the child will need all of the senses to work toward optimal recovery. Even a mild hearing loss should be identified and corrected with amplification (see Chapter 18).

Communication Deficits If the left hemisphere of the brain is damaged, speech and language deficits are likely. Language disorders may be expressive, receptive, or mixed. Dysarthria and **dysphasia** are the most common expressive language problems in children with head injury (see Chapter 19). Receptive language deficits most commonly involve auditory perceptual problems. In terms of recovery, speech has been observed to be relearned parallel to motor function. Recovery of speech motor function often is more complete than recovery of receptive language abilities (Brink, Garnett, Hale, et al., 1970). Usually when language is disordered, cognition also is affected. Intervention by a speech-language pathologist is directed at improving both the speech disorder and the cognitive deficits. Initially, this involves teaching simple commands and discussing uncomplicated topics related to the surroundings. The speech-language pathologist will also help to train the nursing staff and parents to use simple commands and alternate means of communication (see Chapter 19).

Cognitive Deficits Even after severe head injury, significant recovery of intellectual function often occurs (Figure 27.5). Recovery of intellectual function is generally not as complete as recovery of motor function (Brink et al., 1970). Performance on an IQ test may be low and the subscale scores variable (Chadwick, Rutter, Brown, et al., 1981).

There may be subtle cognitive deficits even following less severe head trauma. Here, the IQ score and the neurological examination may be normal (Raimondi & Hirschauer, 1984), yet, there may be deficits in attention, concentration, memory, information processing, performance speed, cognitive flexibility, abstract problem-solving, and judgment.

Neuropsychological assessment is useful in identifying many of these more subtle deficits and in planning appropriate rehabilitation programs and educational curricula (Goldstein & Levin, 1985). This assessment involves a series of tests that measure concept formation, reasoning, adaptive problem-solving skills, language, memory, concentration, visual-spatial abilities, sensory-perceptual/sensory-motor abilities, and academic performance (Fay & Janesheski, 1986). Performance on cognitive tasks varies in different settings (Cohen, 1986). The test setting for the assess-

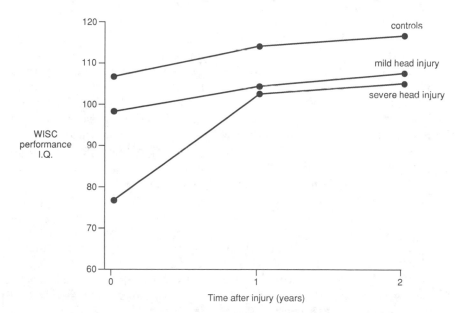

Figure 27.5. Recovery of cognitive function following head injuries of variable degrees of severity in children. (From Chadwick, O., Rutter, M., Brown, G., et al. [1981]. A prospective study of children with head injuries: II. Cognitive sequelae. *Psychological Medicine, 11*, 53; reprinted by permission.)

ment is idealized and nondistracting, unlike the normal classroom with its many distractions. For this reason, neuropsychological tests may overestimate the child's ability to function in a normal classroom setting (Ewing-Cobbs, Fletcher, & Levin, 1986).

Intervention for cognitive deficits may be useful even during the inpatient phase of management. Cognitive remediation may use a combination of memory training exercises (psychology), language therapy (speech-language pathology), and educational programming (special education). The strategy is to improve areas of disability and to encourage the development of compensatory techniques (Volpe & McDowell, 1990). One example of a compensatory technique is the use of computer-assisted learning to help memory and writing in a child with persisting visual-motor deficits (Fay & Janesheski, 1986). The impairments in communication and cognition often are the main deterrents to successful reintegration into home, school, and community following traumatic brain injury.

Academic Deficits Much remains to be learned about the optimal educational management of children with head injury. Traumatic brain injury is now recognized as a specific category of disability within special education, with the passage of PL 101-476, the Individuals with Disabilities Education Act Amendments (IDEA), in 1990. This law represents the reauthorization and retitling of PL 94-142, the Education for All Handicapped Children Act of 1975. Depending on the severity of deficits, these children may be placed in self-contained, special education classes or receive resource help. Additionally, physical, occupational, and/or speech-language therapies may be provided as part of the child's individualized education program (IEP).

Patterns of cognitive deficits in children with brain injury are different from those seen in children with learning or behavior disorders related to other causes. Two hallmarks of brain injury are extreme variability in function and rapid change over time. For example, a child with learning disabilities as a result of a head injury may do well in some subjects, such as reading, but poorly in subjects that emphasize memory and abstract reasoning (Ewing-Cobbs et al., 1986). Furthermore, depending on the time since the injury, recovery may still be proceeding rapidly, with abilities changing from month to month. As a result, an appropriate educational approach in September may be outdated by November. Thus, flexibility and innovative approaches are needed to teach the child recovering from brain injury (Telzrow, 1987).

Psychobehavioral Deficits Changes in personality and behavior also may follow brain injury (Filley et al., 1987). Fortunately, these changes usually improve over time. Overarousal or underarousal may occur. The overaroused child may be inattentive, irritable, hyperactive, impulsive, and aggressive, while the underaroused child may be apathetic, poorly motivated, and socially withdrawn (Filley et al., 1987). There also may be depression, especially in teenagers. The child may realize that he or she no longer has the same physical or mental capabilities as before the accident. If the injury was the child's fault, it may lead to self-directed anger or suicidal thoughts. Treatment must involve a combination of behavior management, counseling, and sometimes antidepressant medication (Deaton, 1987).

Social and Family Problems The effects of a severe head injury on the family are enormous (Jacobson, Rubenstein, Bohannon, et al., 1986; Urbach & Culbert,

1991). In many ways, they are similar to the problems any family faces having a child with a disability (see Chapter 29). However, parents may face overwhelming feelings of guilt and remorse, particularly if the child was in the parent's care when the injury occurred or if the parent feels otherwise responsible. Siblings also may feel guilty that they were left unharmed or did not protect their brother or sister (Florian, Katz, & Lahav, 1989). In addition, prolonged hospitalization and rehabilitation can place heavy financial demands on the family. One parent may be forced to take a leave of absence from work to be with the child. This loss of income combined with the additional costs of modifying a home or providing outpatient rehabilitation can have a devastating effect on family finances (McMordie & Barker, 1988).

Even after a less severe brain injury, psychosocial problems may develop. The family may rush to put the experience behind them, and thus deny or ignore residual deficits, especially if the child appears to have recovered completely. This can lead parents and teachers to expect normal achievement by the child, even if subtle intellectual deficits persist. If these deficits go undetected, they can lead to frustration, behavior problems, and poor learning.

As a result of these concerns, counseling is often indicated for both the child and family. It can be provided by a psychologist, psychiatrist, or social worker (McGuire & Rothenberg, 1986). Counseling should begin the day of admission and may need to continue through outpatient rehabilitation. It is often a year or more before the family has adjusted and is able to function effectively.

PREVENTION

Most head trauma to children is preventable (American Academy of Pediatrics, Committee on Accident and Poison Prevention, 1987; Rivara, 1984). However, because a number of factors contribute to the risk of injury, no single intervention will be completely effective. Rather, specific preventive strategies must be employed for each major category of head injury (i.e., motor vehicle accidents, including those associated with pedestrian and bicycle injuries; assaults and abuse; household incidents, including falls and drownings; sports and recreation-related injuries; and suicide attempts). Prevention also is important in children who have already sustained brain injury, as the effect of subsequent injury is cumulative. Persistent neurological deficits that result in impulsivity or overactivity place these children at high risk for additional injury.

For motor vehicle accidents, infant restraints and seat belts have been found to be highly (but not completely) effective in averting serious head injury following an impact (Greensher, 1988). Their use is mandated by law in most states. Improvements in car construction, including antilock brakes and air bags, also have helped. Nevertheless, the number of motor vehicle accidents in which teenagers sustain head injuries continues to rise. Education about the risks of drinking and driving has had some impact, but many experts believe that effective prevention must include nighttime curfews, increased punishment for drunk driving, and delaying licensure to 17 years of age. It even has been recommended that driver training courses in schools be stopped because it has been shown that without these courses teenagers obtain their licenses at older ages (Agran et al., 1990).

Efforts also should be supported to improve pedestrian safety, including programs to increase young children's street-crossing skills (Yeaton & Bailey, 1978). Walkways, crosswalks, and traffic controls (i.e., converting two-way streets to one-way) also appear to improve pedestrian safety (Centers for Disease Control, 1990).

In bicycle accidents involving motor vehicles, safety helmets have been found to reduce the risk of brain injury by 88%, and their use should be strongly promoted (Thompson, Rivara, & Thompson, 1989). Helmets also should be worn by individuals riding on motorcycles, scooters, and skateboards.

Assaults and physical abuse theoretically represent entirely preventable causes of childhood head injury. Yet, it is here that society is making the least progress (Christoffel, 1990). Gun control legislation represents one important attempt to limit access to lethal weapons, but enactment has proven a political minefield. Schools have started to teach conflict resolution skills where words rather than violence win arguments. Programs that provide "in-home" support and teaching of parenting skills to young mothers also have been used in an attempt to decrease the risk of child abuse (Olds, Henderson, Chamberlin, et al., 1986).

Most suicides in children also should be preventable. A suicide attempt in a child is usually an impulsive act, a cry for help. Therefore, if depression, drug abuse, or other problems leading to this gesture were recognized early, many suicide attempts could be prevented. Parent and teacher awareness needs to improve in this area. Finally, parents, teachers, and community groups need to be educated in prevention of falls from heights, playground injuries, pool drownings, and sports injuries (Rivara, 1984).

CASE STUDIES OF CHILDREN WITH TRAUMATIC BRAIN INJURIES

Heather

Heather was 9 years old and on her summer vacation when she fell from the top of a 6-foot ladder and hit her head on the concrete pavement. She immediately lost consciousness and was taken to the hospital by paramedics. At the hospital, she opened her eyes on command, withdrew her feet to pain, and spoke some garbled words. Her score was 10 on the Glasgow Coma Scale (see Table 27.1). Her neurological examination and cranial CT scan were normal. There was no evidence of hemorrhage or edema. Heather improved so rapidly that in one week she seemed back to "normal" and was discharged.

Yet, after returning home, Heather's parents noticed that she was very irritable, which was not typical for her. They initially attributed this to her stay in the hospital. They became concerned when the irritability persisted for the next 2 months. They also noticed that Heather was becoming quite aggressive toward her brother, her friends, and her dog.

When Heather returned to school in the fall, her teachers also noticed these changes in her behavior. In addition, they were concerned by changes in her school performance. She had previously been a straight "A" student, but was now receiving "C"s or "D"s in most subjects. Heather's teachers requested a conference with her parents to discuss these changes.

Heather's parents wondered whether the changes in her personality, behavior, and school performance could be attributed to her head injury and took her to a pediatrician. Yet, Heather's doctor was unable to detect any neurological abnormalities.

The pediatrician referred Heather for a neuropsychological assessment. A Weschler Intelligence Scale for Children (WISC-R) indicated normal intellectual functioning with no significant verbal-performance discrepancy. Her scores were also normal in arithmetic, spelling, and reading achievement tests. However, the tests indicated deficits in auditory memory, abstract problem-solving abilities, and attention span.

As a result of this evaluation, Heather was provided special educational support in math and social studies, the subjects that were most difficult for her. Her behavior and school performance gradually improved over the next few months, and it was expected that resource help would not be required during the next school year. Also, Heather's parents thought that her personality was gradually returning to normal.

Ethan

Ethan was 7 years old when he was hit by a car while riding his bicycle without a helmet. Minutes after the accident, medics arrived and found Ethan with an abnormal flexion motor response and no verbal or eye opening responses. A cranial CT scan showed a large subdural hematoma over the left frontal, temporal, and parietal lobes. There were no other injuries. Ethan was taken to the operating room for removal of the hematoma and placement of an intracranial pressure monitor. He was found to have elevated intracranial pressure that was eventually controlled with mannitol and hyperventilation.

Ethan remained in coma for 10 weeks. He then began to respond to the command "move your hand" by moving his left hand. He also followed objects placed in his field of vision, but did not speak. He was transferred to the neurorehabilitation service, where he received physical, occupational, and speech therapy twice daily. Gradually, over the next 12 weeks, his motor control improved, although he had spasticity on the right side of his body. He began to walk with a leg brace and was able to complete self-care activities independently, primarily using his left arm, with some assistance from the right. Communication remained a major problem, as both expressive and receptive deficits were evident. Cognitive testing revealed persisting deficits, with scores on both verbal and performance subtests more than two standard deviations below the norms.

He was discharged and enrolled in an outpatient rehabilitation program, where he received physical and occupational therapy weekly, and speech-language therapy three times weekly. Three months later he returned to school in a self-contained communication disorder class with added physical and occupational therapy.

At a 1-year follow-up, Ethan's right hand function had gradually improved, but he continued to prefer using his left hand. Both expressive and receptive language skills had significantly improved. His IEP for the next school year included continued communication disorder class placement with mainstreaming in a third-grade class for 20% of the day and continued physical and occupational therapies. Ethan has not been able to keep up with his old friends but is making new ones. It is likely that he will continue to have disabilities, but he will also continue to gain new skills and knowledge that should help him cope with the disabilities.

PROGNOSIS

Almost 95% of children admitted to a hospital following traumatic brain injury survive. For these children, a number of factors have been identified as predictors of good or bad outcome. Lower Glasgow Coma Scale scores generally indicate greater severity of brain injury and a more negative outcome (Luerssen, Klauber, & Marshall, 1988; Walker et al., 1985). As in the cases of Heather and Ethan, the duration of coma is a major index of the severity of the brain injury (Filley et al., 1987). Children who come out of coma within 6 weeks have a good prognosis. When coma duration is between 6 weeks and 3 months, outcome is variable (Brink & Hoffer, 1978). When the duration of coma is longer than 3 months, prognosis for recovery of function is poor (Kraus, Rock, & Hemyari, 1990). In those children who do recover motor function after prolonged coma, there are usually deficits in intellectual function and changes in personality (Brink & Hoffer, 1978).

The type of brain injury also is important in determining prognosis. Children with focal lesions in addition to DAI have been observed to have worse outcomes than those with only DAI (Filley et al., 1987). Outcomes are usually good for children who have epidural hematomas but poor for those with subdural hematomas (Raimondi & Hirschauer, 1984). Injuries resulting in multiple organ damage also carry a poor prognosis, as the associated oxygen deprivation and low blood pressure cause secondary injury to the brain (Walker, Mayer, Storrs, et al., 1985).

The impact of age is complex, and the results of different studies have been inconsistent. In some studies, the worst outcomes have been observed in children of younger ages at the time of injury (Luerssen et al., 1988; Mahoney, D'Souza, Haller, et al., 1983). In other studies, outcome has not been found to be related to age (Berger et al., 1985; Zuccarello, Facco, Zampieri, et al., 1985). These contrasting findings may reflect the fact that different areas of functional outcome were being assessed. The brain of the young child may have a greater degree of plasticity than that of the older child or adult. Yet, this advantage may be offset by the fact that brain injury impairs new learning more than the retention of prior information. The young child has had less time to build up knowledge before the injury and therefore may experience more loss in cognition.

Finally, one must consider any preexisting developmental disability in predicting outcome. If attention deficit hyperactivity disorder is evident in a child after recovery from head injury, it is important to know whether this predated the incident. Children with mental retardation will have immature judgment for age and are more likely to run into the street. Thus, intellectual deficits following an accident should be contrasted with any preexisting deficits.

SUMMARY

Head trauma is a common childhood event and the spectrum of consequences is broad. Depending on the severity, type, and location of traumatic brain injury, outcome may range from complete recovery to severe functional disability. Persistent motor, communication, cognitive, behavioral, and sensory deficits may result. Restoration of function in affected areas is the goal of rehabilitation, and requires the participation of multiple medical specialists, allied health professionals, and educators. While treatment is important, most head injuries in children are preventable. Injury prevention programs must be supported if there is to be a decrease in traumatic brain injury in the future.

REFERENCES

Agran, P., Castillo, D., & Winn, D. (1990). Childhood motor vehicle occupant injuries. *American Journal of Diseases of Children, 144*, 653–662.

Alexander, R., Sato, Y., Smith, W., et al. (1990). Incidence of impact trauma with cranial injuries ascribed to shaking. *American Journal of Diseases of Children, 144*, 724–726.

American Academy of Pediatrics, Committee on Accident and Poison Prevention. (1987). *Injury control for children and youth.* Elk Grove Village, IL: American Academy of Pediatrics.

Baker, S.P., O'Neill, B., & Karpf, R.S. (1984). *The injury fact book.* Lexington, MA: Lexington Books.

Berger, M.S., Pitts, L.H., Lovely, M., et al. (1985). Outcome from severe head injury in children and adolescents. *Journal of Neurosurgery, 62*, 194–199.

Biary, N., Cleeves, L., Findley, L., et al. (1989). Post-traumatic tremor. *Neurology, 39*, 103–106.

Bijur, P.E., Haslum, M., & Golding, J. (1990). Cognitive and behavioral sequelae of mild head injury in children. *Pediatrics, 86*, 337–344.

Blasier, D., & Letts, R.M. (1989). The orthopaedic manifestations of head injury in children. *Orthopaedic Review, 18*, 350–358.

Braddock, M., Lapidus, G., Gregorio, D., et al. (1991). Population, income, and ecological correlates of child pedestrian injury. *Pediatrics, 88*, 1242–1247.

Brink, J.D., & Hoffer, M.M. (1978). Rehabilitation of brain injured children. *Orthopedic Clinics of North America, 9*, 451–454.

Brink, J.D., Garrett, A.L., Hale, W.R., et al. (1970). Recovery of motor and intellectual function in children sustaining severe head injuries. *Developmental Medicine and Child Neurology, 12*, 565–571.

Brookes, M., MacMillan, R., Cully, S., et al. (1990). Head injuries in accident and emergency departments: How different are children from adults? *Journal of Epidemiology and Community Life, 44*, 147–151.

Bruce, D.A. (1990). Head injury in the pediatric population. *Current Problems in Pediatrics, 20*, 61–107.

Butterworth, J.F., & DeWitt, D.S. (1989). Severe head trauma: Pathophysiology and management. *Critical Care Clinics, 5*, 807–820.

Carney, J., & Gerring, J. (1990). Return to school following severe closed head injury: A critical phase in pediatric rehabilitation. *Pediatrician, 17*, 222–229.

Centers for Disease Control. (1990). Childhood injuries in the United States. *American Journal of Diseases of Children, 144*, 627–646.

Chadwick, O., Rutter, M., Brown, G., et al. (1981). A prospective study of children with head injuries: II. Cognitive sequelae. *Psychological Medicine, 11*, 49–61.

Chadwick, O., Rutter, M., Shaffer, D., et al. (1981). A prospective study of children with head injuries: IV. Specific cognitive deficits. *Journal of Clinical Neuropsychology, 3*, 101–120.

Chadwick, O., Rutter, M., Thompson, J., et al. (1981). Intellectual performance and reading skills after localized head injury in childhood. *Journal of Child Psychology and Psychiatry and Allied Disciplines, 22*, 117–139.

Christoffel, K.K. (1990). Violent death and injury in U.S. children and adolescents. *American Journal of Diseases of Children, 144*, 697–706.

Cohen, S.B. (1986). Educational reintegration and programming for children with head injuries. *Journal of Head Trauma Rehabilitation, 1*, 22–29.

Costeff, H., Groswasser, Z., & Goldstein, R. (1990). Long-term follow-up of 31 children with severe closed head trauma. *Journal of Neurosurgery, 73*, 684–687.

Craft, A.W., Shaw, D.A., & Cartlidge, N.E. (1972). Head injuries in children. *British Medical Journal, 4*, 200–203.

Davidson, L.L., Hughes, S.J., & O'Connor, P.A. (1988). Preschool behavior problems and subsequent risk of injury. *Pediatrics, 82*, 644–651.

Deaton, A.V. (1987). Behavioral change strategies for children and adolescents with severe brain injury. *Journal of Learning Disabilities, 20*, 581–589.

Dhellemmes, P., Lejeune, J.P., Christiaens, J.L., et al. (1985). Traumatic extradural hematomas in infancy and childhood: Experience with 144 cases. *Journal of Neurosurgery, 62*, 861–864.

Ewing-Cobbs, L., Fletcher, J.M., & Levin, H.S. (1986). Neurobehavioral sequelae following head injury in children: Educational implications. *Journal of Head Trauma Rehabilitation, 1*, 57–65.

Fay, G., & Janesheski, J. (1986). Neuropsychological assessment of head-injured children. *Journal of Head Trauma Rehabilitation 1*, 16–21.

Filley, C.M., Cranberg, L.D., Alexander, M.P., et al. (1987). Neurobehavioral outcome after closed head injury in childhood and adolescence. *Archives of Neurology, 44*, 194–198.

Florian, V., Katz, S., & Lahav, V. (1989). Impact of traumatic brain damage on family dynamics and functioning: A review. *Brain Injury, 3*, 219–233.

Gentry, L.R., Godersky, J.C., & Thompson, B. (1988). MR imaging of head trauma: Review of the distribution and radiopathologic features of traumatic lesions. *American Journal of Roentgenology, 150*, 663–672.

Gerring, J.P. (1986). Psychiatric sequelae of severe closed head injury. *Pediatrics in Review, 8*, 115–121.

Goldstein, F.C., & Levin, H.S. (1985). Intellectual and academic outcome following closed head injury in children and adolescents: Research strategies and empirical findings. *Developmental Neuropsychology, 1*, 195–214.

Greensher, J. (1988). Recent advances in injury prevention. *Pediatrics in Review, 10*, 171–177.

Gualtieri, C.T. (1988). Pharmacotherapy and the neurobehavioral sequelae of traumatic brain injury. *Brain Injury, 2*, 101–129.

Hall, D.M., Johnson, S.L., & Middleton, J. (1990). Rehabilitation of head injured children. *Archives of Disease in Childhood, 65*, 553–556.

Holinger, P.C. (1990). The causes, impact, and preventability of childhood injuries in the United States: Childhood suicide in the United States. *American Journal of Diseases of Children, 144*, 670–676.

Jacobson, M.S., Rubenstein, E.M., Bohannon, W.E., et al. (1986). Follow-up of adolescent trauma victims: A new model of care. *Pediatrics, 77*, 236–241.

Jaffe, K.M., & Hays, R.M. (1986). Pediatric head injury: Rehabilitative medical management. *Journal of Head Trauma Rehabilitation, 1*, 30–40.

Jennett, B., & Teasdale, G. (1981). *Management of head injuries*. Philadelphia: F.A. Davis.

Jennett, B., Teasdale, G., Galbraith, S., et al. (1987). Severe head injuries in three countries. *Journal of Neurology, Neurosurgery, and Psychiatry, 40*, 291–298.

Klonoff, H. (1971). Head injuries in children: Predisposing factors, accident conditions, accident proneness, and sequelae. *American Journal of Public Health, 61*, 2405–2417.

Kraus, J.F., Fife, D., & Conroy, C. (1987). Pediatric brain injuries: The nature, clinical course, and early outcomes in a defined United States' population. *Pediatrics, 79*, 501–507.

Kraus, J.F., Rock, A., & Hemyari, P. (1990). Brain injuries among infants, children, adolescents, and young adults. *American Journal of Diseases of Children, 144*, 684–691.

Kriel, R.L., Krach, L.E., & Sheehan, M. (1988). Pediatric closed head injury: Outcome following prolonged unconsciousness. *Archives of Physical Medicine and Rehabilitation, 69*, 678–681.

Langfitt, T.W., & Gennarelli, T.A. (1982). Can the outcome from head injury be improved? *Journal of Neurosurgery, 56*, 19–25.

Luerssen, T.G., Klauber, M.R., & Marshall, L.F. (1988). Outcome from head injury related to patient's age: A longitudinal prospective study of adult and pediatric head injury. *Journal of Neurosurgery, 68*, 409–416.

Mahoney, W.J., D'Souza, B.J., Haller, J.A., et al. (1983). Long-term outcome of children with severe head trauma and prolonged coma. *Pediatrics, 71*, 756–762.

Masters, S.J., McClean, P.M., Arcarese, J.S., et al. (1987). Skull X-ray examinations after head trauma. Recommendations by a multidisciplinary panel and validation study. *New England Journal of Medicine, 316*, 84–91.

Mayes, S.D., Pelco, L.E., & Campbell, C.J. (1989). Relationships among pre- and post-injury intelligence, length of coma and age in individuals with severe closed-head injuries. *Brain Injury, 3*, 301–313.

McGuire, T.L., & Rothenberg, M.B. (1986). Behavioral and psychosocial sequelae of pediatric head injury. *Journal of Head Trauma Rehabilitation, 1*, 1–6.

McMordie, W.R., & Barker, S.L. (1988). The financial trauma of head injury. *Brain Injury, 2*, 357–364.

Molnar, G.E., & Perrin, J.C.S. (1983). Rehabilitation of the child with head injury. In K. Shapiro (Ed.), *Pediatric head trauma* (pp. 241–269). Mt. Kisco, NY: Futura Publishing.

Mysiw, W.J., Corrigan, J.D., & Gribble, M.W. (1990). The ataxic subgroup: A discrete outcome after traumatic brain injury. *Brain Injury, 4*, 247–255.

Olds, D.L., Henderson, C.R., Jr., Chamberlin, R., et al. (1986). Preventing child abuse and neglect: A randomized trial of nurse home visitation. *Pediatrics, 78*, 65–78.

Oppenheimer, D.R. (1968). Microscopic lesions in the brain following head injury. *Journal of Neurology, Neurosurgery, and Psychiatry, 31*, 299–306.

Parmelee, D.X. (1989). Neuropsychiatric sequellae of traumatic brain injury in children and adolescents. *Psychiatric Medicine, 7*, 11–16.

Pfenninger, J., Kaiser, G., Lütschg, J., et al. (1983). Treatment and outcome of the severely head injured child. *Intensive Care Medicine, 9*, 13–16.

Pittman, T., Bucholz, R., & Williams, D. (1989). Efficacy of barbiturates in the treatment of resistant intracranial hypertension in severely head-injured children. *Pediatric Neuroscience, 15*, 13–17.

Raimondi, A.J., & Hirschauer, J. (1984). Head injury in the infant and toddler: Coma scoring and outcome scale. *Child's Brain, 11*, 12–35.

Rivara, F.P. (1984). Childhood injuries. III: Epidemiology of non-motor vehicle head trauma. *Developmental Medicine and Child Neurology, 26*, 81–87.

Steinberg, G.K., George, C.P., DeLaPaz, R., et al. (1988). Dextromethorphan protects against cerebral injury following transient focal ischemia in rabbits. *Stroke, 19*, 1112–1118.

Telzrow, C.F. (1987). Management of academic and educational problems in head injury. *Jour-*

nal of Learning Disabilities, 20, 536–545.

Thompson, R.S., Rivara, F.P., & Thompson, D.C. (1989). A case-control study of the effectiveness of bicycle safety helmets. *New England Journal of Medicine, 320*, 1361–1367.

Urbach, J.R., & Culbert, J.P. (1991). Head-injured parents and their children. Psychosocial consequences of a traumatic syndrome. *Psychosomatics, 32*, 24–33.

Volpe, B.T., & McDowell, F.H. (1990). The efficacy of cognitive rehabilitation in patients with traumatic brain injury. *Archives of Neurology, 47*, 220–222.

Walker, M.L., Mayer, T.A., Storrs, B.B., et al. (1985). Pediatric head injury—factors which influence outcome. *Concepts in Pediatric Neurosurgery, 6*, 84–97.

Winn, D.G., Agran, P.F., & Castillo, D.N. (1991). Pedestrian injuries to children younger than 5 years of age. *Pediatrics, 88*, 776–782.

Yeaton, W.H., & Bailey, J.S. (1978). Teaching pedestrian safety skills to young children: An analysis and one-year followup. *Journal of Applied Behavior Analysis, 11*, 315–329.

Ylvisaker, M. (Ed.). (1985). *Head injury rehabilitation: Children and adolescents.* San Diego: College-Hill Press.

Ylvisaker, M., & Weinstein, M. (1989). Recovery of oral feeding after pediatric head injury. *Journal of Head Trauma Rehabilitation, 4*, 51–63.

Zuccarello, M., Facco, E., Zampieri, P., et al. (1985). Severe head injury in children: Early prognosis and outcome. *Child's Nervous System, 1*, 158–162.

Chapter 28

Some Ethical Dilemmas

Upon completion of this chapter, the reader will:

—understand a number of ethical issues concerning persons with disabilities, including genetic screening, prenatal diagnosis, therapeutic abortion, treatment issues, human experimentation, and sexual rights

---

Advances in complex technology and the resulting options now available regarding the care of children with disabilities have led to numerous difficult ethical questions. Should screening and prenatal diagnosis be performed on women who are genetically at risk of having children with severe disabilities? If so, should their fetuses be aborted? Are there instances in which medical care can ethically be withheld from a newborn infant with a disability? Is it ethical to perform experimental research on children with disabilities? Is it ethical to use infants who have ultimately fatal birth defects as organ donors? Should young adults with mental retardation have full "sexual rights"? In this chapter, these ethical questions are examined from various perspectives.

ETHICAL CHOICES

An ethical problem exists when, given the facts of a situation, the "right" thing to do is unclear (Weil, 1989). Inherent in ethics, then, are choices. In most cases, ethical decisions result from moral values. For example, an individual who believes in the sanctity of life above all else will judge that abortion is wrong for virtually any reason and that "do not resuscitate" orders should never be logged in medical charts. The opposite side of this view might be considered *objectivism*. Here, decisions about treatment are made for entire populations using statistical methods and attempts are made to allocate resources by determining who will benefit most from a treatment rather than by an individual's right to life. Decisions about treatment of infants with spina bifida were made in this manner some years ago. Children who had high-level lesions—and therefore the greatest physical disability—did not receive surgery to close the defects (Lorber, 1974) (see Chapter 25).

In the middle rest the majority of people, practicing what may be called *util-*

itarianism (Rostain & Bhutani, 1989). Here, there are no absolutes, and separate decisions are considered for each individual. An attempt is made to determine what treatment is in the best interest of the individual, given a specific set of circumstances (Coulter, Murray, & Cerreto, 1988).

SCREENING PROGRAMS

One area where ethical questions have arisen is screening programs. By using screening tests, many conditions can now be diagnosed before they become clinically apparent. This is beneficial because it permits early institution of therapy to prevent or lessen the impact of a disease. Common examples are blood pressure and cholesterol screening programs. If an individual is identified as having an abnormality, after further testing he or she may receive medications or be placed on a special diet to control the blood pressure or reduce the cholesterol level. This, in turn, decreases the risk of developing heart disease or having a stroke. Most people probably agree that these screening programs are in the best interest of the individual and do not represent ethical dilemmas. But what if these tests were obligatory, rather than voluntary, and had to be taken prior to being hired for a job? Abnormal test results might then be used to prevent an individual from obtaining the job or medical insurance; then there would be a problem.

Screening tests also present ethical dilemmas in the care of children with disabilities. One example of compulsory testing is newborn screening for phenylketonuria (PKU). Virtually all newborns have blood drawn before they are discharged from the hospital to test for PKU and other inborn errors of metabolism (see Chapter 10). The rationale is that early identification of PKU permits treatment that prevents mental retardation. If therapy is delayed, brain damage invariably occurs. Most states have passed laws requiring this test for all newborns. Yet, even considering its worthwhile nature, is it ethical to mandate this test? Some parents may object to the requirement on the grounds that it violates their right to give **informed consent.** Maryland was the first state to repeal the law requiring this test and to offer it on a voluntary basis. Over 95% of parents agreed to have the test performed (Culliton, 1976). The end result, therefore, was close to what had been previously legislated, and the rights of both the state and the individual were protected. Other states have followed Maryland's lead.

PRENATAL DIAGNOSIS, THERAPEUTIC ABORTION, AND FETAL THERAPY

Closely linked to the question of genetic screening are the issues surrounding prenatal diagnosis and therapeutic abortion.

Susan is 38 years old and is pregnant for the first time. There is no family history of genetic disease. However, her obstetrician has advised her to have prenatal diagnosis performed because of her age. Susan is unsure. She knows the procedure carries only a slight risk to her and her fetus (see Chapter 3). Nonetheless, she is hesitant, primarily because she wants to avoid the possible decision about abortion should the fetus be found to have Down syndrome or spina bifida. After much thought and a few contacts with a genetic counselor, Susan decides not to have the prenatal diagnosis.

In recognition of some of the concerns individuals have about prenatal diagnosis and the difficulties they face in deciding whether to have such diagnosis performed, the Hastings Center has suggested certain criteria that prenatal diagnostic programs should follow. These include: 1) a woman at risk should not be denied prenatal diagnosis simply because she has decided against having an abortion; 2) counseling must be noncoercive and respectful of the various opinions about abortion; 3) physicians must inform parents about possible postnatal treatment, if it exists; and 4) all results of the prenatal diagnosis should be shared with parents. In addition, these guidelines express opposition to the use of amniocentesis for sex choice alone, but also oppose any restriction on this option, to protect parents' right to choose (Fletcher, 1981; Powledge & Fletcher, 1979). While the use of prenatal diagnosis often leads to the therapeutic abortion of an affected fetus, parents who are opposed to abortion might use this information to prepare themselves and their families psychologically for the birth of a child with a disability and for the care of that child. It might also lead them to have the child delivered at a tertiary care hospital that has a newborn intensive care unit needed in the early treatment of certain disabilities.

When making her decision, Susan's opposition to abortion was the key factor, and many other individuals who oppose prenatal diagnosis share her view. It is not the prenatal diagnostic techniques that are the problem, they would argue, but rather that these techniques often lead to abortion (Fletcher, 1981). There is a range of positions on whether abortion is morally justifiable (Weber, 1976). At one extreme are those who believe that abortion is never acceptable. They say the unborn fetus is a human being from the moment of conception and that its life must be protected under all circumstances (Churchill & Siman, 1982; Drinan, 1970). And, they would say, once abortion is allowed, this may lead to infanticide and then genocide. They would argue that once one takes the first step on the "slippery slope" of allowing some destruction of life, it is difficult, if not impossible, to control the rest of the steps (Horan & Dela-hoyde, 1982).

A slightly less extreme viewpoint is that abortion is acceptable only if the mother's life is in danger. Those who advocate this position also believe that the fetus is a human being from the time of conception. Nevertheless, they argue that the life of the mother must be considered before that of the fetus.

Those in the middle might argue that abortion is morally acceptable in certain defined conditions, but not in others. For example, members of this group would allow abortion following rape or incest or when the fetus is malformed or has a severe genetic disorder. The difficulty with this position is drawing the line as to which conditions are serious enough to justify abortion (Veatch, 1977). Those who reject this position fear that as prenatal diagnoses become more widespread, women will be pressured to undergo abortions of any damaged or potentially damaged fetus. Combined with this pressure may be society's unwillingness to continue to pay for care of persons with disabilities (Kolata, 1980).

Finally, at the other extreme are those who believe that abortion is acceptable whenever a woman wants it. Those who advocate this position argue that a woman has a right to privacy and that part of exercising that right means being able to choose to have an abortion and having access to a safe abortion if she determines it is needed (Churchill & Siman, 1982). Such advocates believe that the fetus is not human until it is able to live independently outside the mother's womb, generally considered to be after the 24th week of gestation. Prior to that time, a woman should have the right to make a choice as she sees fit.

Recently, the possibility of fetal therapy has added dimensions to the prenatal diagnosis/therapeutic abortion debate (Johnson & Elias, 1988). As treatment of the fetus for certain congenital disorders becomes more common (see Chapter 3), important questions will be raised about the rights of the mother as a patient and the rights of the fetus as a patient. How to weigh the risks and benefits to the fetus and the mother is difficult to determine (Ruddick & Wilcox, 1982). Some court cases have granted certain rights to the fetus—for example, forcing a mother to undergo treatment to protect the fetus (Bainbridge, 1983). As the fetus is assigned more rights, one of the results may be an impact on the availability of, legality of, and access to abortion.

In the future, the resolution of the abortion issue will depend on defining the moral and legal status of the fetus. What is likely to happen in the United States is that the Supreme Court will decide much of this essentially ethical question as it considers and reviews *Roe v. Wade,* the landmark 1973 abortion case, and other related cases. Some modifications have already been made in the area of abortion counseling (Anonymous, 1991) and challenges to overturn or limit *Roe v. Wade* are before the courts as this book goes to press in 1992. The other "wild card" is RU 486, the medication that can be used to precipitate abortion in the first trimester (Heikinheimo, Ylikorkala, & Lahteenmaki, 1990). This drug is already in use in Europe and may take the issue of abortion out of the doctor's office and into the privacy of the home.

WITHHOLDING TREATMENT

Many children with disabilities are born with medical problems that are life-threatening in the newborn period. For example, approximately 10% of children with Down syndrome have a narrowing of the small intestine called **duodenal atresia** (Penrose & Smith, 1966). This condition leads to vomiting and dehydration. If untreated, these infants starve to death during the first weeks of life. As a different example, approximately 1 in 1,000 infants is born with spina bifida (Gallo, 1984). The exposed spinal cord that is part of this condition places these infants at great risk for developing meningitis, an infection of the spinal cord that carries a mortality rate of over 50% (Lorber, 1974). Most of these infants also have hydrocephalus, which requires the placement of a ventricular-peritoneal shunt (see Chapter 25).

For both of these disorders, surgical treatment is not difficult. In the child with Down syndrome, the damaged portion of the small intestine can be removed surgically, and the child can then eat and drink normally. Likewise, the spinal opening in the child with spina bifida can be closed and the shunt placed. The catch is that these children often have remaining disabilities for their entire lives. The ethical question raised is whether parents or others have the right to withhold treatment from these infants (Reich, 1987).

Who should decide whether surgery takes place? Traditionally, the individual, if able, or parents of the individual have made the decision. For parents to be able to give informed consent, they must receive information from the physician as to the risks of the procedure, the possible benefits, and the long-term prognosis for their child. In giving information, physicians may be influenced by their own biases concerning a particular infant and his or her disability (Bridge & Bridge, 1981). When describing an operation, a physician, consciously or unconsciously, may accentuate certain risks or benefits (Duff & Campbell, 1973; Shaw, 1973) and influence the parents' decision. An awareness of these factors is important in the decision-making process.

Once the parents have received the information, the question is whether they can really give informed consent. Some argue that parents faced with the birth of a child with disabilities are in a state of shock, overwhelmed by fear, guilt, and horror (Johnson, 1980; Shaw, 1973). These feelings, then, may keep them from making a reasonable decision (Ellis, 1982). The parents may feel they have no alternative but surgery. Others argue that even though parents have these feelings, it does not mean that their right to decide and their wishes should be overridden (Strong, 1984). Generally, studies have found that parents' decisions in these situations are thoughtful, reasonable, and responsible, especially if they are given sufficient time to consider the choices (Strong, 1984). In most instances, delays of a few days will not affect the infant's outcome adversely and will lead to more informed decision-making (Charney, Weller, Sutton, et al., 1985).

The issue of "quality of life" in making medical decisions about withholding therapy came to the forefront as a result of the "Baby Doe" cases in the early 1980s (Fost, 1985). The first case was that of an infant with Down syndrome who had a blockage in the gastrointestinal tract that precluded oral feeding. The baby's parents decided not to give permission for their child to have corrective surgery. The infant was then denied food and water. An attempt was made by a consulting physician to force treatment. However, the courts let the parents' decision stand and the infant died (Fost, 1982). A public outcry ensued.

The second case was that of Baby Jane Doe, who was born with myelomeningocele and hydrocephalus. Her prognosis, according to her doctors, was severe mental retardation, a seizure disorder, and paralysis. After consultation with physicians, nurses, religious counselors, and a social worker, her parents initially decided not to consent to surgery in which a ventricular-peritoneal shunt would be placed (Steinbock, 1984).

At this point, a local lawyer heard of the case and filed a suit seeking the appointment of a guardian and additional treatment for the child. The judge appointed a guardian, ruled that the infant was in need of immediate surgery, and authorized the guardian's consent to surgery. The case was appealed, and the appellate court reversed the judge's order, saying that the parents' decision was in the best interests of the infant, and the courts had no basis for intervention. The highest court in the state upheld this appellate decision. The parents subsequently changed their decision and permitted their child to receive a shunt. They have cared for their child at home.

This was not the end of the story. In June 1982, the federal government notified all hospitals that it was unlawful to withhold treatment from a baby born with a disability. Nine months later, the government issued another order requiring that signs be placed in public areas of nurseries and delivery rooms stating that discrimination against children with disabilities is prohibited and that federal funds could be withdrawn from hospitals violating this order.

This rule created more furor, which was finally settled in 1985 with compromise legislation contained as an amendment to the Child Abuse and Neglect Prevention and Treatment Act. This amendment stated that therapy should not be withheld unless:

> the infant is chronically and irreversibly comatose; the provision of such treatment would merely prolong dying, not be effective in ameliorating or correcting all of the infant's life-threatening conditions, or otherwise be futile in terms of the survival of the infant; or the provision of such treatment would be virtually futile in terms of the survival of the infant and the treatment itself under such circumstances would be inhumane. (U.S. Department of Health and Human Services, 1985, p. 1111)

Using these guidelines, both of the Baby Does would have received corrective surgery (Pueschel, 1989). It is now generally accepted by the medical community that the benefit of life as a person with Down syndrome or myelomeningocele exceeds the burden of surgery and the burden of having these disorders. In other words, this legislation requires that when treatment of an ill infant has a reasonable chance of being successful, and the infant is likely to survive and be able to interact with the environment, even with a serious disability, the best interests of that infant are served by treatment.

Interestingly, violation of this rule carries fairly minor penalties. The maximum sanction is a loss of a limited amount of federal money. Neither criminal nor civil actions are authorized or threatened by the legislation. Despite this, evidence suggests that care of neonates with disabilities has been altered significantly by these rules (Lantos, 1987). One study done in the early 1970s found that, of 299 deaths in an intensive care nursery, 43 (14%) were related to the withholding of treatment (Duff & Campbell, 1973). In a survey of pediatricians taken 3 years after the Baby Doe regulations were instituted, the majority of respondents indicated that it had significantly affected their care of infants with severe disabilities, making it much more likely for them to give maximal life-prolonging treatment. One-third of respondents questioned whether this increased care was in fact in the best interest of the child (Kopelman, Irons, & Kopelman, 1988).

However, despite these regulations, a commission appointed by Ronald Reagan when he was president acknowledged the importance of parents' involvement in decision-making for infants with disabilities. "In nearly all cases, parents are best suited to collaborate with practitioners in making decisions about an infant's care, and the range of choices practitioners offer should normally reflect the parents' preferences regarding treatment" (President's Commission for the study of Ethical Problems in Medicine and Biomedical and Behavioral Research, 1983).

Yet, this report does indicate that outside intervention (i.e., court action) will be necessary when parents make choices that are not in the best interests of their child. In the rare instances in which the courts have overruled the parents' decision to withhold therapy, a new issue arises—whether it remains the parents' responsibility to care for the child they did not want to have treated. One might argue that if the state decides to save a child's life, then it, and not the parents, should be responsible for the child's future care (Shaw, 1973).

DO NOT RESUSCITATE ORDERS
AND TERMINATING LIFE SUPPORT SYSTEMS

Another example of withholding therapy is the "do not resuscitate" order, which refers to a physician's order in an individual's medical chart to prospectively limit the amount of intervention that should occur in the event of a medical emergency. Such an order might indicate that, in the event of a cardiopulmonary arrest, no resuscitative actions should be taken. Alternatively, it might limit, rather than exclude, intervention—for example, in the event of a cardiopulmonary arrest, resuscitation should be undertaken but the child should not be intubated. "Do not resuscitate" orders have been used with children with disabilities who are neurologically devastated and have no hope of improvement. In this case and according to the Baby Doe rules, normal care is provided, but extraordinary measures are not taken simply to prolong life. A "do not resuscitate" order is written by the attending physician after discussion with and assent of the parents. This order can be rescinded at any time during the hospitalization at the parent's request.

An even more difficult problem is whether to withdraw life support systems (Farrell & Fost, 1989). A critical case in the legal literature is that of Nancy Beth Cruzan, a 32-year-old woman who had been in a persistent vegetative state for almost 8 years following a motor vehicle accident (Meisel, 1990). Her parents wished to have her removed from life support, which in her case consisted of gastrostomy tube-feedings. Her parents believed that they were carrying out wishes she had expressed to them prior to the accident—that her life not be prolonged if she were unable to appreciate it. The Cruzan case was the first in which the Supreme Court addressed the "right to die" issue (*Cruzan v. Director, Missouri Department of Health*). The Court decided in favor of the State, noting that there needed to be "clear and convincing" evidence that a presently noncompetent person previously expressed specific wishes about medical care. The case subsequently went back to a Missouri county probate judge, who, after presentation of additional evidence, ruled that clear and convincing evidence did exist. The parents were permitted to discontinue nutrition and hydration and Nancy Beth Cruzan died. These treatment issues remain thorny, especially for noncompetent individuals with mental retardation (Sprung, 1991). One advance has been the presence of medical ethics committees to advise in these and other ethically difficult matters.

MEDICAL ETHICS COMMITTEES

A direct and generally considered positive outcome of the Baby Doe rules has been the development of medical ethics committees in most hospitals. These consist of multidisciplinary teams that meet to consider issues of medical treatment and advise physicians and other caregivers about how to approach ethical dilemmas (Kliegman, Mahowald, & Youngner, 1986). A typical committee consists of a physician, nurse, clergy member, community members, social worker, lawyer, and possibly a medical ethicist. Typical functions include advising parents about a suggested treatment's degree of benefit, mediating between parents and caregivers or between members of the caregiving team in situations in which there are irreconcilable differences of opinion, reviewing the ethical reasoning in decisions to withhold or withdraw life support systems, ensuring that the best interests of the child are being considered in treatment decisions, helping to formulate hospital policies that promote ethical practices, and educating hospital staff about ethical issues (American Academy of Pediatrics, 1984). These are consultative, not regulatory, committees. They do not have the authority to enforce rules. However, their presence has proved very helpful in leading to consensus and providing guidance in a number of ethically difficult hospital situations.

RESEARCH ON CHILDREN WITH DISABILITIES

Research on children revolves around two central points: informed consent and benefit to the individual (Baudouin, 1990). Some persons argue that any research that does not directly benefit a child or person with mental retardation is unethical. Thus, a parent or guardian should have no legal right to consent to such studies. While an adult may choose for altruistic reasons to engage in research that would benefit society, a child or person with mental retardation is neither given that choice nor is rationally able to make that decision. Others argue that even children and individuals with mental retardation have an obligation to benefit society and that their consent may be presumed (as long as their parents or guardian give their consent) in experiments of minimal risk to them (Capron, 1985). Of additional concern is research that may benefit the individual but may also involve significant risks (Gaylin, 1982). In these instances, the risks versus the benefits must be weighed, and both the consent of the participant, if possible, and that of the parent(s) should be obtained.

Unfortunately, procedures to safeguard children and people with mental retardation from nonbeneficial research have not always been followed. In the early 1950s and 1960s, research was conducted on healthy children with mental retardation in a state institution in New York. These children were infected with the hepatitis virus to study the natural course of this disease (Krugman, 1986). When this information became public, there was a great uproar. Subsequently, the National Commission for the Protection of Human Subjects formulated guidelines for research on children and individuals with mental retardation (Jonsen, 1978). These rules require that research must first be scientifically sound and significant. Second, if at all possible, the research should be done first on animals, followed by adults and older children, before using young children. Third, informed consent must be obtained from the participant if he or she is able to give consent and from at least one parent. Finally, the risks must be minimized. Once these criteria are met, research may be performed as long as the risk does not exceed that encountered normally in the children's daily lives. If the risk is greater than that, the research may be done only if the expected benefits to the individual outweigh the possible risks. When there is no direct benefit to the participant, the research is acceptable only if the risk is minimal and the research is likely to yield knowledge that is vital to the understanding and treatment of the individual's disability (Jonsen, 1978).

ORGAN DONATION

There is a significant need for hearts and kidneys to be transplanted in infants who have been born with life-threatening malformations of these organs. Yet, few organ donors of a size required for the operations are available. One potential source of organs is infants with anencephaly. These infants are born with an open skull that contains very little or no brain tissue above the level of the brain stem (see Chapter 25). This is a universally fatal disease during the first months of life and occurs in about 1 in 3,000 births (Shewmon, 1988).

Paradoxically, although these infants have severe brain malformations, their other body organs are normally formed. Initially, they would seem to be ideal candidates as organ donors, and they have been used as such. However, an ethical problem exists. In order to be useful, the organs must be "fresh," and the only way to accomplish this is to obtain them prior to "brain death" in the infant with anencephaly. In a sense, these transplants require practicing euthanasia. After much soul searching, there is now agreement in the medical community that it is not morally justified to use these infants as organ donors, and this practice is being abandoned. At present there are very few substitute infant organs available. Research is now focusing on the use of organs of nonhuman primates and artificial organs (Shewmon, Capron, Peacock, et al., 1989).

SEXUAL AND REPRODUCTIVE
RIGHTS OF INDIVIDUALS WITH MENTAL RETARDATION

Another issue involving consent is the sexual rights of persons with mental retardation, including sexual relations, marriage, and procreation. Sexual drive is presumed to be as strong in individuals with mental retardation as it is in the rest of the population (Monat-Haller, 1992). It may be somewhat delayed in people with mild-to-moderate mental retardation, and it may be less evident in individuals with severe-to-profound mental retardation. In any case, the attitude that previously ignored sexual drive in individuals with mental retardation is unacceptable.

This paternalistic attitude toward individuals with mental retardation included separating the sexes in institutions and in special education classes and punishing sexual "acting out" behavior. Segregation and punishment were generally ineffective and are considered ethically suspect. Sexual activity can be highly pleasurable and it is not clear why one would wish to exclude others from this enjoyment. Obviously, there are appropriate and inappropriate times and places to engage in sexual behavior, and those guidelines can be taught. For example, persons with mental retardation can learn how to engage in masturbation in private. Similarly, sexual relations among consenting adults are considered permissible in the general population provided certain precautions are taken. Most individuals with mental retardation can learn what those precautions are and how to take them or how to decline sexual opportunities.

The rights to marry and to bear children are protected under the Fourteenth Amendment to the Constitution. Some states have laws about marriage and sexual relations among individuals with mental retardation, but these have not been enforced and may be unconstitutional. Given this information, do parents have the right to prevent their adult children with mental retardation from marrying and/or having children? Some would say that this is an ethically sound position. Some research indicates that the incidence of failed marriages and of child abuse is higher among individuals with mental retardation (Feldman, 1986). However, opponents of this view contend that singling out people with mental retardation is discriminatory. For this selection of whom may marry and/or have children to be just, all nonretarded individuals with histories of behavior that would place a child at risk for abuse or abandonment (e.g., drug abuse or alcoholism) would also be prevented from marrying and/or having children (Blank, 1984; Whitman & Accardo, 1990).

A middle position might be to provide support to individuals considering marriage, and to continue that support if they decide to marry. Support could take the form of counseling, in which the couple is advised of their options. Depending on the couple's circumstances and wishes, options might include an engagement period or living together. Also, new options and strategies in supported living provide further opportunities for couples who wish to build a life together.

A final issue is sterilization, primarily of women with moderate-to-severe mental retardation. Proponents of sterilization state that it may decrease the incidence of mental retardation in the general population; that it avoids the stress of parenthood for individuals unable to cope with the normal pressures of living independently; and that it may improve personal hygiene by stopping menstruation, which may be frightening to young women and difficult for their families to manage (Bayles, 1981).

An opposing view stresses that while the risk of having children with mental retardation is higher among individuals with mental retardation (Blank, 1984), at least 80% of children with mental retardation are born to parents of normal intelligence (American Academy of Pediatrics Committee on Bioethics, 1990; Macklin & Gaylin,

1981). In terms of the difficulty of menstruation, they counter that the majority of women can be taught menstrual hygiene.

Even if all agreed that it is wise to sterilize individuals with mental retardation, the question of consent must be addressed. A major stumbling block is the definition of *consent:* It must be voluntary, informed, and the person involved must be capable of making a decision (Rivet, 1990). This may be a catch-22 situation. If an individual is capable of giving consent, might not that individual also be competent to raise children?

Perhaps the most easily defended position concerning sterilization is one that takes the child's best interests as the basis for decision-making (Cooke, 1991). According to this view, sterilization should be considered only if it is best for the child, not for the convenience of the parents, school, institution, or society. The individual with mental retardation should be permitted to give informed consent to whatever extent possible. This involves understanding the alternatives, risks, and benefits of the procedures and being able to express a choice. This may require multiple interviews and simplification of information. Because sterilization involves an operation and a loss of reproductive capacity, whenever possible, alterative approaches should be used. These could include family counseling, menstrual hygiene training, and contraceptive pills or devices.

The point that is often missed in this controversy is that sterilization does not solve a number of the most important issues of sexual relations. It can prevent pregnancy and menstruation, but it does not prevent sexual abuse or the contraction of sexually transmitted diseases. These issues can only be addressed by socialization training and sex education.

CASE STUDIES

George: A Newborn with Trisomy 18

George was born at term but was noted to have multiple congenital anomalies while still in the delivery room. He was small for gestational age, weighing only 4 pounds, with microcephaly, and unusual in appearance with low-set ears, and clenched hands with overriding fingers. A tentative diagnosis of trisomy 18 was made, and this was confirmed at 4 days of age when a chromosome analysis revealed an extra #18 chromosome. By this time George was also diagnosed as having a complex heart malformation that often accompanies this disorder. He was experiencing heart failure and the cardiologists felt that the only hope for survival was a complicated, multistep, open heart surgical procedure.

George's parents and doctors discussed the options. The life span of children with trisomy 18 is usually limited; many die in the first year of life. While this operation might prolong George's life to some extent, it would not alter the severe mental retardation and cerebral palsy that usually accompany this disorder. Both George's parents and doctors leaned toward not performing the operation, but they decided to seek the advice of the hospital ethics committee.

After considering George's case, the ethics committee concluded that it was ethical and consistent with federal guidelines to withhold cardiac surgery. They made this recommendation using the federal guidelines that surgery is not warranted in patients where it would be "virtually futile in terms of the long-term survival of the infant" (U.S. Department of Health and Human Services, 1985).

With the ethics committee's confirmation of their initial judgment, George's parents and doctors elected to treat him conservatively with heart medications. These were unsuccessful in controlling the heart failure and George died 3 days later.

Emily: A Young Adult with Down Syndrome

Emily has Down syndrome. She is an active, friendly 20-year-old whose intellectual function is in the range of moderate mental retardation. Emily wants to marry her boyfriend, Fred, who also has Down syndrome and is 25 years old. They met in a social group and have been going together for a year. Emily lives with her parents and commutes daily to her job at a McDonald's restaurant.

Emily's parents don't know what to do. They are worried she will become pregnant and have a child with Down syndrome. They are concerned that Emily and Fred cannot live independently. Yet, they have always tried to practice normalization as much as possible. Emily attended a public school and was mainstreamed for certain subjects. She has always been an active participant in family activities. They chastised themselves that it was they who had encouraged her participation in the social club where she met Fred.

They sought counseling from a social worker in a developmental disabilities center. Subsequently, discussions were held with Emily and Fred and in the end, everyone agreed they were in love and were serious about the commitments of marriage. As part of the discussions, they were counseled about birth control and Emily elected to take contraceptive pills. She is proud to say that she takes them each day after she brushes her teeth.

Emily and Fred have decided to live together until they are ready to marry. An apartment in a group home has been located, and they are very excited about starting their new life together.

SUMMARY

All of us must struggle with the ethical issues raised in this chapter. It is very difficult to make decisions on issues such as genetic screening and treatment, prenatal diagnosis, abortion, withholding treatment, organ donation, sterilization, and research on children with developmental disabilities. Yet, these issues must be discussed in an open and frank manner. Society must make choices on what should be funded and what should not. Without a public discussion, ethical decisions are made by a select few. With discussion, more of us may have a chance to influence this decision-making process. Only in this way will we all be better served.

REFERENCES

American Academy of Pediatrics Committee on Bioethics. (1990). Sterilization of women who are mentally handicapped. *Pediatrics, 85,* 868–871.

American Academy of Pediatrics, Infant Bioethics Task Force and Consultants. (1984). Guidelines for infant bioethics committees. *Pediatrics, 74,* 306–310.

Anonymous. (1991). Court upholds Title X ban on abortion information. *Family Planning Perspectives, 23,* 178–181.

Bainbridge, J.S., Jr. (1983, May 29). More and more, courts grant fetuses legal rights. *The Baltimore Sun,* pp. K1, K3.

Baudouin, J.L. (1990). Biomedical experimentation on the mentally handicapped: ethical and legal dilemmas. *Medicine and Law, 9,* 1052–1061.

Bayles, M.D. (1981). Voluntary and involuntary sterilization: the legal precedents. In R. Macklin & W. Gaylin (Eds.), *Mental retardation and sterilization: A problem of competency and paternalism* (pp. 742–775). New York: Plenum.

Blank, R.H. (1984). Human sterilization: Emerging technologies and reemerging social issues. *Science, Technology & Human Values, 9,* 8–20.

Bridge, P., & Bridge, M. (1981). The brief life and death of Christopher Bridge. *Hastings Center Report, 11,* 17–19.

Capron, A.M. (1985). When well-meaning science goes too far. *Hastings Center Report, 15,* 8–9.

Charney, E.B., Weller, S.C., Sutton, L.N., et al. (1985). Management of the newborn with myelomeningocele: Time for a decision-making process. *Pediatrics, 75,* 58–64.

Churchill, L.R., & Siman, J.J. (1982). Abortion and the rhetoric of individual rights. *Hastings Center Report, 12,* 9–12.

Cooke, R.E. (1991). Ethics and developmental disabilities. In A.J. Capute & P.J. Accardo (Eds.), *Developmental disabilities in infancy and childhood* (pp. 251–259). Baltimore: Paul H. Brookes Publishing Co.

Coulter, D.L., Murray, T.H., & Cerreto, M.C. (1988). Practical ethics in pediatrics. *Current Problems in Pediatrics, 18,* 137–195.

Cruzan v. Director, Missouri Department of Health, 100S Ct 2841 (1990).

Culliton, B.J. (1976). Genetic screening: States may be writing the wrong kinds of laws. *Science, 191,* 926–929.

Duff, R.S., & Campbell, A.G.M. (1973). Moral and ethical dilemmas in the special care nursery. *New England Journal of Medicine, 289,* 890–894.

Drinan, R.J. (1970). Abortion and the law. In K. Vaux (Ed.), *Who shall live? Medicine, technology, ethics.* Philadelphia: Fortress Press.

Ellis, T.S., III. (1982). Letting defective babies die: Who decides? *American Journal of Law and Medicine, 7,* 393–423.

Farrell, P.M., & Fost, N.C. (1989). Long-term mechanical ventilation in pediatric respiratory failure: Medical and ethical considerations. *American Review of Respiratory Disease, 140,* S36–S40.

Feldman, M.A. (1986). Research on parenting by mentally retarded persons. *Psychiatric Clinics of North America, 9,* 777–796.

Fletcher, J.C. (1981). Ethical issues in genetic screening and antenatal diagnosis. *Clinical Obstetrics and Gynecology, 24,* 1151–1168.

Fost, N. (1982). Putting hospitals on notice. *Hastings Center Report, 12,* 5–8.

Fost, N.C. (1985). Ethical issues in the care of handicapped, chronically ill, and dying children. *Pediatrics in Review, 6,* 291–296.

Gallo, A. (1984). The case of Baby Jane Doe. 1. Spina bifida: The state of the art of medical management. *Hastings Center Report, 14,* 10–13.

Gaylin, W. (1982). The competence of children: No longer all or none. *Hastings Center Report, 12,* 33–38.

Heikinheimo, O., Ylikorkala, O., & Lahteenmaki, P. (1990). Antiprogesterone RU 486-a drug for non-surgical abortion. *Annals of Medicine, 22,* 75–84.

Horan, D.J., & Delahoyde, M. (Eds.). (1982). *Infanticide and the handicapped newborn.* Provo, UT: Brigham Young University Press.

Johnson, J.M., & Elias, S. (1988). Prenatal treatment: Medical and gene therapy in the fetus. *Clinical Obstetrics and Gynecology, 31,* 390–407.

Johnson, P.R. (1980). Selective nontreatment of defective newborns: An ethical analysis. *Linacre Quarterly, 47,* 39–53.

Jonsen, A.R. (1978). Research involving children: Recommendations of the National Commission for the Protection of Human Subjects of Biomedical and Behavioral Research. *Pediatrics, 62,* 131–136.

Kliegman, R.M., Mahowald, M.B., & Youngner, S.J. (1986). In our best interests: Experience and working of an ethics review committee. *Journal of Pediatrics, 108,* 178–188.

Kolata, G.B. (1980). Mass screening for neural tube defects. *Hastings Center Report, 10,* 8–10.

Kopelman, L.M., Irons, T.G., & Kopelman, A.E. (1988). Neonatologists judge the "Baby Doe" regulations. *New England Journal of Medicine, 318,* 677–683.

Krugman, S. (1986). The Willowbrook hepatitis studies revisisted: Ethical aspects. *Reviews of Infectious Diseases, 8,* 157–162.

Lantos, J. (1987). Baby Doe five years later: Implications for child health. *New England Journal of Medicine, 317,* 444–447.

Lorber, J. (1974). Selective treatment of myelomeningocele: To treat or not to treat? *Pediatrics, 53,* 307–308.

Macklin, R., & Gaylin, W. (Eds.). (1981). *Mental retardation and sterilization: A problem of competency and paternalism.* New York: Plenum.

Meisel, A. (1990). Lessons from Cruzan. *Journal of Clinical Ethics, 1,* 245–250.

Monat-Haller, R.K. (1992). *Understanding and expressing sexuality: Responsible choices for individuals with developmental disabilities.* Baltimore: Paul H. Brookes Publishing Co.

Penrose, L.S., & Smith, G.F. (1966). *Down's anomaly.* London: J. & A. Churchill.

Powledge, T.M., & Fletcher, J. (1979). Guidelines for the ethical, social, and legal issues in prenatal diagnosis: A report from the Genetics Research Group of the Hastings Center, Institute of Society, Ethics and the Life Sciences. *New England Journal of Medicine, 300,* 168–172.

President's Commission for the study of Ethical Problems in Medicine and Biomedical and Behavioral Research. (1983). Seriously ill newborns. In *Deciding to forego life-sustaining treatment* (pp. 197–229). Washington, DC: U.S. Government Printing Office.

Pueschel, S.M. (1989). Ethical considerations in the life of a child with Down syndrome. *Issues in Law and Medicine, 5,* 87–99.

Reich, W.T. (1987). Caring for life in the first of it: Moral paradigms for perinatal and neonatal ethics. *Seminars in Perinatology, 11,* 279–287.

Rivet, M. (1990). Sterilization and medical treatment of the mentally disabled: Some legal and ethical reflections. *Medicine and Law, 9,* 1150–1171.

Rostain, A.L., & Bhutani, V.K. (1989). Ethical dilemmas of neonatal-perinatal surgery. *Clinics in Perinatology, 16,* 275–302.

Ruddick, W., & Wilcox, W. (1982). Operating on the fetus. *Hastings Center Report, 12,* 10–14.

Shaw, A. (1973). Dilemmas of "informed consent" in children. *New England Journal of Medicine, 289,* 885–890.

Shewmon, D.A. (1988). Anencephaly: Selected medical aspects. *Hastings Center Report, 18,* 11–19.

Shewmon, D.A., Capron, A.M., Peacock, W.J., et al. (1989). The use of anencephalic infants as organ sources. A critique. *Journal of the American Medical Association, 261,* 1773–1781.

Sprung, C.L. (1991). Changing attitudes and practices in foregoing life-sustaining treatments. *Journal of the American Medical Association, 263,* 2211–2215.

Steinbock, B. (1984). The case of Baby Jane Doe. 2. Baby Jane Doe in the courts. *Hastings Center Report, 14,* 13–19.

Strong, C. (1984). The neonatologist's duty to patient and parents. *Hastings Center Report, 14,* 10–16.

U.S. Department of Health and Human Services. (1985, April 15). Child abuse and neglect prevention and treatment program: Final rules. 45 CFR, Part 1340. *Federal Register, 50*(72), 14,878–14,901.

Veatch, R.M. (1977). *Case studies in medical ethics.* Cambridge, MA: Harvard University Press.

Weber, L.F. (1976). *Who shall live? The dilemma of severely handicapped children and its meaning for other moral questions.* New York: Paulist Press.

Weil, W.B., Jr. (1989). Ethical issues in pediatrics. *Current Problems in Pediatrics, 19,* 617–698.

Whitman, B.Y., & Accardo, P.J. (Eds.). (1990). *When a parent is mentally retarded.* Baltimore: Paul H. Brookes Publishing Co.

Chapter 29

Caring and Coping
The Family of a
Child with Disabilities

with Symme W. Trachtenberg

Upon completion of this chapter, the reader will:
—understand the various stages of the development of the family over the life cycle
—be aware of the impact a child's disability has upon family and friends
—recognize strategies and resources available to the child and family
—be alert to how societal attitudes influence the outcome of children with disabilities
—understand some of the ways in which professionals can best help the families of children with disabilities

---

Until now, this book has focused on the medical, physical, and ethical aspects of various developmental disabilities. Equally important is the emotional impact that these disabilities have on the child and the members of the child's family. How the family handles the day-to-day stresses, concerns, and needs of its members influences, to a great extent, the outcome of the child with developmental disabilities (Cobb & Hancock, 1984). To be effective in working with these families, professionals must give sound therapeutic advice that takes into account the family's coping abilities, their financial and practical resources, and their support systems. This means seeing the entire family as being in need of assistance and not solely addressing the physical needs of the child with disabilities.

This chapter examines some of the issues that families face throughout the life of a child with a severe disability, such as mental retardation, cerebral palsy, or a sensory loss. The psychosocial issues of milder disabilities, such as specific learning disabili-

Symme W. Trachtenberg, M.S.W., A.C.S.W., is a Clinical Associate of Social Work in Pediatrics at The University of Pennsylvania School of Medicine in Philadelphia and Director of Social Work at Children's Seashore House.

ties (e.g., dyslexia) and attention deficit hyperactivity disorder, have been discussed in earlier chapters (see Chapters 20 and 21).

THE LIFE CYCLE OF THE FAMILY

Analogous to the developmental stages of an individual are the stages a family experiences as it progresses through life. For the purposes of this book, the 6-stage life cycle model is used in traditional families (Carter & McGoldrick, 1980). In the first stage, an unattached young adult separates from his or her original family, moves out of the house, and gets a job. Relationships with parents change from that of child-adult to adult-adult. In the second stage, the individual develops an intimate relationship with another independent person and they marry, joining together two families. The newly married couple commits themselves to their new **nuclear family.** In the third stage, the couple has children and the marital relationship adjusts to make space, both emotional and physical, for new members. The relationships with the families of origin are adjusted to the new role of grandparents.

In the fourth stage, the couple's children become adolescents and begin to test the waters of independence. The relationship between parents and children shift to allow the children to broaden their horizons and to branch out more into the world. In the fifth stage, this next generation of children moves out and the marital relationship has to readjust to having only two people in the home. It is at this point that parents may also deal with ill health or dependency of grandparents, reversing the adult-child role. In the final stage, the parents, in their older years, engage in some sort of review of their lives or may look at integrating their failures and successes.

For all families, the adjustments and realignments each member must make during the various times of change are stressful. When a family has a child with a disability, the stress is amplified, especially if the life cycle remains incomplete. For example, the individual with a disability may remain in one stage, that of the dependent child, for the rest of his or her life. In this case, on each occasion that a life cycle change should occur and does not, the difference between the family of a child with a disability and one without is accentuated, often leading to reemergence of sorrow.

FAMILY REACTIONS AND ADAPTATIONS
TO HAVING A CHILD WITH A DISABILITY

It is natural for parents to want their children to be smarter, more accomplished, and happier than they, the parents, are. When parents first learn that their child has a severe disability, these hopes are dashed. However, initial feelings may differ, depending on the parents' religious and cultural backgrounds and whether the disability is identified prenatally, shortly after birth, or later in the child's life (Davis, 1987). For example, some very religious parents may feel "blessed" in having been chosen to care for a "special" child, while some secular parents initially may not accept this child with an unanticipated disability. If the diagnosis of the disability is delayed, parents may experience a feeling of relief at finally getting answers to long-held questions and finding clearer paths to follow in getting help for the child. However, there may be feelings of anger because of the delay in starting therapy resulting from the physician's reassurance that their child would "grow out of it."

The most common response to being told that a child has a severe disability is some combination of shock, disbelief, guilt, and an overwhelming feeling of loss (Singer & Irvin, 1989). Families must have time to grieve for the loss of their "normal" child. Kubler-Ross (1969) described the stages of grieving, including denial, depression, anger and guilt, bargaining, and acceptance. These stages are neither time bound nor orderly in their progression, and some elements of the various stages may be combined (Schleifer & Klein, 1985). Furthermore, not all people will experience or complete all the stages, and, as noted above, the sense of loss and grieving may reemerge at critical points in the family's life cycle (Shonkoff, Jarman, & Kohlenberg, 1987).

Denial

It is not uncommon for parents to initially deny their child's diagnosis. They may think that the doctors have made a mistake. As a consequence, the family may visit many medical centers looking for a more optimistic diagnosis or prognosis. This approach may help parents to come to a more complete understanding of their child's disability and needs and to feel more in control because they are able to influence the diagnostic testing. However, multiple consultations may lead to confusion and a delay in the institution of appropriate therapy. It may also waste time, money, and physical and emotional energy. Generally, if two consultations at reputable institutions have yielded similar diagnoses and approaches toward therapy, it is unlikely that further "shopping" will be beneficial. Yet some parents need to do this and their desires must be respected. Physicians should not "shove" a diagnosis down the parents' throats, but they should encourage parents to start their child's rehabilitative and educational programs.

Depression

After the initial shock and denial have worn off, family members typically go through a period of depression. Symptoms include extreme fatigue, insomnia, loss of appetite, or overeating, restlessness, and irritability. Depression may also interfere with the couple's sexual relationship.

Social isolation in the months following the diagnosis may add to the depression. At a time when the parents are most in need of support, their extended family and friends may be least able to provide it. Grandparents may be unaccepting of the diagnosis or assign blame to one of the parents, most commonly to the one unrelated to them. Friends may be uncomfortable in the presence of the child with a disability or not know what to say in consolation; as a result, they often stay away. The parents themselves may be embarrassed by the child's disability and rarely venture from the house, or the child's needs may be so complex that simply going shopping becomes a major production. Going to the movies or to dinner alone may also be a problem for parents because of the need to find a babysitter who is capable of caring for the child.

Furthermore, because the parents feel depressed, they tend to stay at home rather than face the requirements of social interactions.

Fortunately, the initial depression usually improves over time; but episodes of depression may recur. Life cycle events may trigger these feelings. These events may include the first birthday party if the child's developmental delay is obvious compared to other infants; entry into a special education program; adolescence, when anticipated independence does not develop; and young adulthood, when going to college or getting married may not occur. As the child gets older, depression can also be brought on by the child's increasing behavior problems or health care needs, inadequate family finances, or feelings of inadequacy in meeting the needs of other family members.

In some instances, depression may become chronic sorrow with frequently recurring periods of sadness (Copley & Bodensteiner, 1987). In these situations, the parents are not only burdened by what seems to them to be neverending sadness, but they also must contend with the feeling that something is wrong with them for feeling this way. Psychotherapy is often helpful in these instances.

Anger and Guilt

At some point, many parents feel angry and search for someone or something to blame. Often the anger is directed at God or at the whole world. They may ask, "Why did this happen to me and my child?" Anger also may be self-directed, such as when a parent asks, "What did I do or not do that contributed to or caused the disability?" Or, anger may be directed at the other parent or at one of the children, perhaps even the child with the disability.

It is not uncommon for anger to be directed at the professionals caring for the child. This anger may be appropriate if a physician has presented the diagnosis in an insensitive manner. However, anger directed at the physician may represent a "kill the messenger" response.

Regardless of where the anger is directed, it is important to recognize that such expressions are part of a normal coping strategy. Parents may need to express anger until they are able to deal with their underlying feelings of pain and lack of control.

Bargaining

Some parents experience a bargaining stage, during which they may turn to nonconventional forms of therapy in hopes of finding a cure for their children. This stage is often filled with frustration and a sense of failure.

Acceptance

How well individuals ultimately adjust to their child's disability depends on many factors, including marital status, support systems, and previous life experiences (Crnic, Friedrich, & Greenberg, 1983). In general, couples with strong marital relationships and supportive social networks do well, especially if the parents have the same view of their child's disability (Bristol, 1987; Brown & Pacini, 1989; Friedrich, Wilturner, & Cohen, 1985). Strong religious affiliation and effective behavior interventions in the home are also associated with early acceptance (Baker & Brightman,

1984; Leyser & Dekel, 1991). Interestingly, related life experiences may have different effects. For example, a parent who has experienced the challenge of dealing with a chronic illness or disability with another family member may feel more competent in handling this new disability. Alternately, a previous caregiving experience may have left the parent "burned out," and the child's needs may seem insurmountable.

Fortunately, after a period of time, most parents feel more accepting of their child's situation (Blacher, 1984; Bogdan & Taylor, 1987; Moen & Howery, 1988). They then are able to redirect their energies toward handling the problems (Trute & Hauch, 1988). However, as Helen Featherstone (1980), the mother of a child with severe disabilities, has written, "Few parents, even though they are coping effectively, ever reach an 'emotional promised land'" (p. 232).

EFFECTS ON PARTNERS

Even in a well-functioning family, partners may react to having a child with a disability differently (Glendenning, 1983). It is important to recognize that mothers and fathers deal with their child's disability differently. Not understanding this can lead to discord. For example, if the child is unresponsive, the mother may have difficulty bonding with him or her, or the mother may become overly bonded and unable to give to her partner, the other children, or herself. The father may avoid the reality of the child's disability by spending excessive amounts of time at work or not participating in child care responsibilities (Cobb & Hancock, 1984). When the father does get involved, he may focus more on long-term problems, especially financial and treatment issues, than on daily needs. However, there is a trend toward a generation of new parents of the late 1980s, in which fathers assume greater child care responsibilities and, at times, reverse roles with the mother. Some marriages are able to meet and even be strengthened by these challenges, but others deteriorate. This is particularly true if the couple did not have a strong relationship to begin with or does not have a supportive network of family, friends, and community services (Goldfarb, Brotherson, Summers, & Turnbull, 1986). Counseling is often helpful in getting partners to recognize the differences in their coping abilities and to accommodate them.

EFFECTS ON THE CHILD WITH A DISABILITY

Prior to school age, the child with a disability may not realize he or she is different from other children. This is especially true if the child has been in an early intervention program with other children with disabilities (Harvey & Greenway, 1982). By school age, most children with disabilities are aware of their abilities and disabilities and may need help in dealing with feelings of sadness and of being different (Kaufman, 1988).

The first step is acceptance in the home. If the child is seen as being worthwhile by parents and siblings, self-image is usually good. This acceptance includes being part of family activities, accepting appropriate responsibilities, and being able to discuss the disability openly.

Acceptance outside of the home can be more difficult to attain. Classmates may tease the child with a disability and school work may be difficult, especially in a mainstreamed classroom. Communication and social skills may be limited, further interfering with normal interpersonal interactions. If the child is not accepted by others, he or she may not be self-accepting, exhibiting depression or other behavior problems. The transition may be eased by preparing the class for the entrance of a child with disabilities. This may be accomplished by explaining the disorder and necessary adaptations to the other students. The child with disabilities may also gain self-confidence through activities and friendships with children who have similar disabilities. The Special Olympics provides one venue for this.

EFFECTS ON SIBLINGS

The siblings of a child with a disability have special needs and concerns that vary according to age, birth order, and temperament (Breslau & Prabueki, 1987; Simeonsson & McHale, 1981). Their concerns are also affected by situational variables, such as whether their own needs are being met, how the parents are handling the diagnosis emotionally, what they are told, and how much they understand.

Having a child with a disability in a family does not necessarily adversely affect the development of the siblings. In fact, there is some evidence that siblings may have increased maturity, a sense of responsibility, a tolerance for "being different," a sense of closeness in the family, and enhanced feelings of self-confidence and independence. Many siblings of individuals with disabilities ultimately enter helping professions (Lobato, 1990).

In working to achieve this outcome, the first point to remember is that children take their parents' lead. If the parents are upset, so too will be the children, even if they don't understand why. If the parents see their child who has a disability as being of little value, the siblings will follow suit. Yet, if the parents can acknowledge their pain while being proud of the accomplishments of the child with disabilities and accepting of this child as a part of the family, so too will the siblings.

It is important to acknowledge that children may have mixed feelings toward their sibling with a disability (Ellifritt, 1984). They may be glad that they are "normal," while at the same time feel guilty that they do not have disabilities. They may worry that they will "catch" the disability or that they actually caused it by having bad thoughts about their sibling. Adolescents may question if they will pass a similar disability to their own children. Because of the extra care and time required by the child with a disability, the unaffected children may think that their parents love their brother or sister more than them. They may act out or get in trouble in order to get attention. Alternately they may withdraw, not wanting to ask for attention from their overly stressed parents (Powell & Ogle, 1985).

At some time, all children who have siblings with disabilities must be able to ask questions, to sort out their feelings, and to have time alone with their parents. Parents must recognize and accept that their other children often feel torn between protecting their brother or sister with a disability, whom they love, and being accepted by children outside the family, who may tease them and their sibling. Siblings do best psychologically when their parents' marriage is stable and supportive, when feelings are discussed openly, when the disability is explained honestly, and when the children are not burdened with excessive child care responsibilities (Lobato, 1990; Schleifer, 1987).

EFFECTS ON GRANDPARENTS, EXTENDED FAMILY, AND FRIENDS

Grandparents are also affected by the presence of a child with disabilities in the family. Normally, grandchildren are a source of joy, comfort, and satisfaction (Schleifer, 1988). When a child is born with a disability, grandparents grieve for their own loss and for the pain their child is experiencing (George, 1988). Yet, grandparents can be of great help to the nuclear family as a strong source of emotional and financial support. They can provide respite care and financial assistance that may be crucial to the parents' ability to maintain a child with a severe disability at home. Unfortunately, they may also interfere with the parents' adaptation to the disability as their denial of the disability may last longer. In some cases, grandparents may discourage the parents from participation in programs for the child because they believe that "special" help is not necessary (Gabel & Kotsch, 1981). Counseling can often help grandparents to accept the reality of the child's disability and lead them to become more involved in supporting the family.

Extended family members and friends can also help or hinder the parents' ability to cope. Some family members may have their own issues that will interfere with their ability to be supportive. For example, if the child's condition is genetically based, siblings of the parents may be concerned about their own risk of having a child with the same disability. Some friends or family members may be saddened or uncomfortable with the child's diagnosis and may not know what to say or do for the child and family. This discomfort may lead to a withdrawal of much needed support.

Families tend to get closer to those relatives and friends who are the most accepting of the child's disability. Professionals can suggest ways to discuss the issue with friends and family and help parents to feel comfortable in explaining the diagnosis or asking for help. Parents should be encouraged to assess their support systems so they can fill in the gaps with support groups, other parents of children with disabilities, and available community service agencies.

PSYCHOSOCIAL AND EDUCATIONAL NEEDS OF THE FAMILY AND CHILD

The psychosocial and educational needs of the family of a child with a disability change over time (Thompson, 1986). Some of the age-specific issues are addressed here (Figure 29.1).

Preschool Years

After a diagnosis has been made, the most important issue for many parents is getting the child into a therapy or an early intervention program as soon as possible (Dunst & Leet, 1987). Fortunately, these programs are now mandated by law (PL 99-457, The

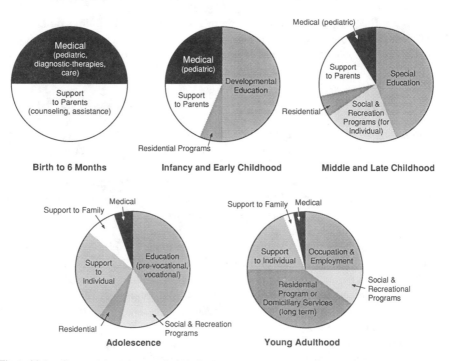

Birth to 6 Months   Infancy and Early Childhood   Middle and Late Childhood

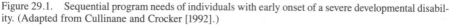

Adolescence   Young Adulthood

Figure 29.1.   Sequential program needs of individuals with early onset of a severe developmental disability. (Adapted from Cullinane and Crocker [1992].)

Education of the Handicapped Act Amendments of 1986 and PL 102-119, the 1991 Amendments to the Individuals with Disabilities Education Act) for preschool-age children. However, there are not enough programs to meet the needs, and not all states have been quick to implement the provisions of this law. Parents can arrange for early intervention programs through the local health care systems, school systems, or "child find" services. A social worker specializing in developmental disabilities also can be helpful in identifying appropriate programs and advocating for entrance (Singer & Irvin, 1989).

Early intervention can start before 6 months of age and generally involves home visits by an early childhood educator, a physical therapist, occupational therapist, or speech-language therapist, depending on the child's needs. Language and motor skills are promoted by various exercises and child-specific programs. The therapist also observes the quality of interaction between the child and parents and models ways for the parents to best handle their child.

Once the child is in therapy, the parents generally relax to some extent (Shonkoff & Hauser-Cram, 1987). They may feel more confident that everything possible is being done for their child. Once taught how to follow through on the therapeutic and play recommendations, they will get satisfaction from helping their child and enjoyment from their child's progress.

Support groups are often most effective during this time. These groups are usually established at the child's early intervention program. Although many parents do not follow through on recommendations to attend community support groups or to call parent telephone networks, they are more likely to view support groups as helpful when they are part of their child's therapy or education program or are diagnostic specific.

Although the family may adjust to the diagnosis and engage in an early intervention program and support group, certain financial and personal issues also may crop up. If the child has a physical disability, is medically fragile, and/or requires technology assistance (see Chapter 9), the financial burden can be enormous. Even with insurance, there may be uncovered costs, such as medications, house alterations, a wheelchair-accessible van, and so on. Insurance itself may require the expenditure of significant time and energy in maneuvering through bureaucratic red tape. Furthermore, if the medical insurance is provided through the parent's place of employment, the ability to change jobs may be limited. The family's choice of housing and location also may be affected by physical barriers or the need to be close to the child's school, doctors, or a hospital.

School Age

By 6 years of age, there are the new challenges of entering the public school system (Forness & Hecht, 1988). To qualify for special education, the child must be tested and classified (see Chapter 16). Elementary school is a time when parents should start to allow their child more autonomy in learning to live with the disability. Summer day and overnight camps for children with special needs enable children to develop important independence skills. At home, children should be expected to perform chores and adhere to behaviors that are appropriate for their development and abilities.

After their child's educational services have been ensured, parents often turn their energies toward advocacy and fundraising projects that will benefit other children with similar disabilities (Callanan, 1990). These projects are a productive and adaptive way for parents to mobilize their frustration, anger, and disappointment toward a positive end. Meaningful friendships may also develop with others who are pursuing a similar cause.

Adolescence

Adolescence can be difficult for any child, and, in children with disabilities, the problems are often magnified (Anderson & Clarke, 1982). Like other adolescents, these children may become preoccupied with how they compare to their peers. The desire for sameness and peer approval in areas of physical development and self-image may be unattainable because of a physical or intellectual disability (Dossetor & Nicol, 1989). This will be less of an issue if the adolescent with a disability has already come to terms with being "different" and has moved on to reach his or her potential. If he or she has not come to terms with the disability or has just acquired the disability (e.g., from a car accident), the adolescent may need counseling and more time and understanding to work through concerns.

It is during adolescence that the issue of sexuality is also confronted. Adolescents should be recognized as sexual beings and encouraged to talk about their sexuality (Rousso, 1985). If capable of understanding, adolescents should be given the opportunity to be exposed to appropriate material about intimate relationships and safe sex and to discuss these issues with peers.

Although sexual liaisons are sometimes an issue, a more common problem is social isolation. Because of the limitations imposed by their disabilities and the attitudes and reactions of those around them, adolescents with disabilities may feel socially isolated (Fraser, 1980). As a result, they may have less developed social skills and may feel awkward in social interactions. They may appear to be uncomfortable around other people, who may feel equally uncomfortable. In order to correct this, many schools incorporate social skills training into the curriculum for adolescent students with disabilities.

Adolescence is also a critical time for predicting the person's ability to function as an adult; those who are dependent through adolescence tend to remain dependent as adults (Ludlow, Turnbull, & Luckasson, 1988). Therefore, adolescents with disabilities who have difficulty with issues of independence, separation, and individuation need assistance with these developmental tasks. Parents should be encouraged to give their children the necessary freedom to become independent. When parents persist in managing their child's life or the way he or she deals with the disability (e.g., speaking for the child at the doctor's office, taking over responsibilities that the child is capable of handling alone), the parents give the adolescent the message that he or she is incompetent. For those adolescents who appear dependent, it may be difficult for the professional to determine whether the dependency is the result of the disability itself or of the family's fostering of dependency.

Young Adulthood

In the past, the transition to adulthood was very difficult both for the person with disabilities and the family. Up to age 21, the individual generally was in a community school. However, after this age, very limited services were available. With the passage of PL 98-199, The Education of the Handicapped Act Amendments of 1983, and other legislation, educational agencies have been provided with incentives to provide transitional services. These services involve teaching skills necessary for competitive or supported employment and living independently in the community. The goal is a quality life that provides the opportunity to live, work, and play in the community, and to have meaningful personal relationships (Hayes, 1991).

Besides job training, the issue of "competence" must be addressed. Often, this is not an all or none situation. A person may be capable of making day-to-day decisions (e.g., whether to go to a movie or buy a hat), but unable to make life decisions (e.g., where to live, what job to take). Individuals are assumed to be competent at the age of majority (i.e., 18 years in most states); after this time parents cannot make life decisions for their child without being given guardianship in a court proceeding.

The issue of where the young adult should live must also be faced. More families are choosing small group homes for their grown children (Schulman, 1990). Unfortunately, the demand has exceeded the supply so that there are long waiting lists. Partial payment for this placement can be made by Supplemental Security Income (SSI). This income is available to every individual with a disability over 18 years of age. Other entitlements that help fund the living situation and associated health care needs include food stamps and Medicaid. However, many of these services are private, and the expense is not completely covered by the entitlement programs.

Options for occupations range from day care to independent jobs, depending on the abilities of the individual. The lowest functional placement is the adult day care center, which combines skill development with recreational activities. These programs are rarely mandated by the government and vary significantly in quantity and quality from one location to another (Hayes, 1991). The next step up is the sheltered workshop, which teaches both prevocational activities (e.g., sorting) and simple work station activities (e.g., packaging). A higher level placement is supported employment in which the individual holds a regular job, such as doing janitorial work, but is closely supervised by a job coach. The highest level is integrated competitive employment, which is often appropriate for individuals with severe physical disabilities but normal intellectual function. This involves winning a job by competition with nondisabled individuals. However, once hired, the job may be adapted as needed by the physical disability.

An important adjunct to work is leisure time activity. This is a good source of enjoyment, socialization, and skill development, and may include watching television, playing sports or games, participating in hobbies, attending social and religious activities, and taking trips. Leisure time presents an opportunity for the individual to remain an active participant in the family and be included in family outings and trips.

THE ROLE OF SOCIETY AND COMMUNITY

So far, the focus of this chapter has been the internal dynamics of the family. However, the family's social context plays an important role in determining the outcome of its members. In many ways, modern circumstances make this the best of times for people with disabilities. There is less public stigma and more educational, vocational, and housing services and entitlements are available. PL 101-476, the Individuals with Disabilities Education Act of 1990 reauthorized, retitled, and expanded PL 94-142, the initial Education for All Handicapped Children Act of 1975. This law provides free educational and rehabilitative services for school-age children. As noted previously, PL 99-457 mandates early intervention programs for preschoolers with developmental disabilities. At the other end of the age continuum is PL 101-336, the 1990 Americans with Disabilities Act, which focuses on the establishment of rights regarding access to employment, transportation, and public accommodations for individuals with disabilities.

The effects of these mandated programs are visible already. Sidewalks now have direct curb access so that wheelchairs can be used. Many buses are equipped with wheelchair lifts. Buildings must have wheelchair access, and theater and sporting events must be able to accommodate individuals with disabilities.

While laws are important, they must be combined with a change in the public's perception of individuals with disabilities. This too seems to be happening, perhaps as a consequence of mainstreaming, which began in the mid 1970s. Young adults who have grown up in schools with children with disabilities are more sensitive to their needs and more cognizant of their abilities (Fortini, 1987). Individuals with disabilities are being portrayed in movies and television in a positive, if not idealized, light. Finally, there has been an increase in "volunteerism," with religious organizations, civic groups, and social-recreational groups championing the cause of individuals with disabilities (Schalock & Kiernan, 1990).

Although society has made itself more accessible, much more needs to be done. Furthermore, not all of the problems are external to the individual with a disability. Evidence suggests that relatively few adults with disabilities are taking full advantage of their new opportunities (Schalock & Kiernan, 1990). Clearly, additional educational programs and skills training are needed. It also indicates the need for counseling of these individuals to empower them for improved self-confidence so they can be integrated into society more effectively.

THE ROLE OF THE PROFESSIONAL

Families of children with disabilities come into contact with a bevy of professionals (e.g., physicians, nurses, teachers, therapists, psychologists, social workers). Individually, and as a group, professionals can do much to lighten the burden on these families. However, in beginning to work with them, each professional must first come to terms with his or her own attitudes toward individuals with disabilities (Cobb & Hancock, 1984). As members of a society that has a history of stigmatizing these persons, professionals are not immune to adopting some of the stereotypes. They must also recognize that in working with these families, they will experience frustration and feelings of helplessness. Knowing that this will happen may prepare professionals to better handle these feelings when they occur.

Another important consideration for professionals is the nature of their relationships with families (Mori, 1983). In the past this has been an unequal "parent-child" relationship, with professionals assuming the role of the parent. This is now changing, with the responsibility of the professional focusing on empowering the parents to meet the care needs of their children. A consequence of this empowerment is that families are more likely to challenge or reject the advice of professionals (Buscaglia, 1983). It is, in fact, their right to choose what help they do and do not want. For example, parents must be partners in the development of individualized family services plans (IFSPs) for children in early intervention programs. While this change may require an adjustment in thinking, it ultimately leads to a true partnership of parents and professionals (Turnbull, Turnbull, Bronicki, Summers, & Roeder-Gordon, 1988). Parents who help to develop a program that is consistent with their personal needs and desires are much more likely to follow it to their child's advantage.

If, however, the parents are resistant to professionals' suggestions, the professionals should try to understand the reasons in order to better serve them. Perhaps what has been suggested goes against their cultural or ethnic values or traditions.

Alternatively, compliance with the suggestion may have been beyond their emotional, physical, or financial capacity. After all, these parents are expected to care for the needs of their child, but not overprotect; to grieve, but not reject their child; and to treat the child as normal, but not deny the disability. Professionals must acknowledge, and not be offended by, negative feelings that may result from these paradoxes.

Professionals should exhibit this supportive attitude from the time the family first hears the child's diagnosis. The response the family receives at this time sets a tone for future contacts with professionals (Hasenfeld & Chesler, 1989). Many professionals find that the most progress is made during this time of crisis. This progress may result from the fact that during a crisis, people are willing to do almost anything to decrease the stress and anxiety they are feeling. If they are aware of this, professionals can help families to examine and alleviate the symptoms of the crisis. However, the professionals must be willing to listen as well as dispense advice. Any plans that are developed for the family should be reviewed as frequently as every 3 months for young children and at 6- to 12-month intervals for older children.

JIMMY: A CHILD WITH A DEVELOPMENTAL DISABILITY

Jimmy had always been slower in his development than his brother David. He didn't walk until 20 months and wasn't talking until 3 years of age. Throughout this time, his parents would ask their pediatrician how Jimmy was doing. They were comforted by his reassurances that their son would catch up, but some of their doubts lingered.

By the time Jimmy was 4 years old and had made little additional progress, his parents could no longer believe he was doing fine. They began to look for an answer, a reason for his delay in development. They located a developmental pediatrician who spent time with them and Jimmy. In meetings with her and the multidisciplinary team at the center where she worked, Jimmy's parents learned that Jimmy had moderate mental retardation. Even though they had suspected this, they still felt numb and shocked. The members of the team advised them of ways to help Jimmy. They reassured them that Jimmy's disability was not their fault.

Gradually, with the support and assistance of this professional team and the encouragement of their own parents, Jimmy's parents began to adjust to the reality of Jimmy's condition. They became involved with a group of parents of children with mental retardation and learned they were not alone in experiencing ambivalent feelings about their child. This helped them a great deal.

When Jimmy was 5 years old, his parents entered him in a special education program. He was happy there and made progress. Jimmy's mother became active in his school, volunteering her services there once a week. Jimmy's achievements pleased her.

For Jimmy's father, however, the situation was more difficult. He was not involved in Jimmy's schooling and found Jimmy's slow progress to be disconcerting. In the support group, Jimmy's father was able to express these feelings. This helped him and provided his wife with a better understanding of these feelings.

The family remained in contact with the treatment center. Through the center, they found out about respite care, and the parents were able to go on some weekend vacations. This was rejuvenating for them. They also learned about special community programs that were available.

Jimmy is now 8 years old and remains in a special education program. He continues to make slow but steady progress. Although his parents continue to have their ups and downs, the bad times are less frequent and are weathered more easily. Jimmy's brother has also been getting more attention from his parents and feels better about himself and his brother. Through the help and guidance of people who cared for them and through their own hard work, this family has survived and is functioning well.

SUMMARY

As a family progresses through life, its members face various changes and adjustments. These are magnified for the family with a child who has a disability. Parents, siblings, and extended family members are all affected. The child with a disability has a particularly difficult time during adolescence, when acceptance by peers and one's body image become more important. Even though the family has to cope with extra burdens, many develop positive relationships and manage to cope effectively with their extra cares. The social worker, therapist, and physician can all play a critical role in helping these families, and may be instrumental in determining the prognosis for the child and the outcome for the entire family.

REFERENCES

Anderson, E.M., & Clarke, L. (1982). *Disability in adolescence*. London: Methuen.

Baker, B.L., & Brightman, R.P. (1984). Training parents of retarded children: Program-specific outcomes. *Journal of Behavioral Therapy and Experimental Psychiatry, 15,* 255–260.

Blacher, J. (1984). Sequential stages of parental adjustment to the birth of a child with handicaps: Fact or artifact? *Mental Retardation, 22,* 55–68.

Bogdan, R., & Taylor, S. (1987). Toward a sociology of acceptance: The other side of the study of deviance. *Social Policy 18,* 34–39.

Breslau, N., & Prabueki, K. (1987). Siblings of disabled children. Effects of chronic stress in the family. *Archives of General Psychiatry, 44,* 1040–1047.

Bristol, M.M. (1987). Mothers of children with autism or communication disorders: Successful adaptation and the double ABCX model. *Journal of Autism and Developmental Disorders, 17,* 469–486.

Brown, R.T., & Pacini, J.N. (1989). Perceived family functioning, marital status, and depression in parents of boys with attention deficit disorder. *Journal of Learning Disabilities, 22,* 581–587.

Buscaglia, L. (1983). *The disabled and their parents: A counseling challenge*. Thorofare, NJ: Slack.

Callanan, C.R. (1990). *Since Owen*. Baltimore: John Hopkins University Press.

Carter, E.A., & McGoldrick, M. (Eds.). (1980). *The family life cycle: A framework for family therapy*. New York: Gardner Press.

Cobb, L.S., & Hancock, K.A. (1984). Development of the child with a physical disability. *Advances in Developmental and Behavioral Pediatrics, 5,* 75–107.

Copley, M.F., & Bodensteiner, J.B. (1987). Chronic sorrow in families of disabled children. *Journal of Child Neurology, 2,* 67–70.

Crnic, K.A., Friedrich, W.N., & Greenberg, M.T. (1983). Adaptation of families with mentally retarded children: A model of stress, coping, and family ecology. *The American Journal of Mental Deficiency, 88,* 125–138.

Cullinane, M.M., & Crocker, A.C. (1992). Service coordination. In M.D. Levine, W.B. Carey, & A.C. Crocker (Eds.), *Developmental-behavioral pediatrics* (2nd ed.) (pp. 737–739). Philadelphia: W.B. Saunders.

Davis, B.D. (1987). Disability and grief. *Social Casework, 6,* 352–357.

Dossetor, D.R., & Nicol, A.R. (1989). Dilemmas of adolescents with developmental retardation: A review. *Journal of Adolescence, 12,* 167–185.

Dunst, C.J., & Leet, H.E. (1987). Measuring the adequacy of resources in households with young children. *Child: Care, Health and Development, 13,* 111–125.

Ellifritt, J. (1984). Life with my sister—guilty no more. *The Exceptional Parent, 14,* 16–21.

Featherstone, H. (1980). *A difference in the family: Life with a disabled child.* New York: Basic Books.

Forness, S.R., & Hecht, B. (1988). Special education for handicapped and disabled children: Classification, programs, and trends. *Journal of Pediatric Nursing, 3,* 75–88.

Fortini, M.E. (1987). Attitudes and behavior toward students with handicaps by their non-handicapped peers. *American Journal of Mental Deficiency, 92,* 78–84.

Fraser, B.C. (1980). The meaning of handicap in children. *Child: Care, Health and Development, 6,* 83–91.

Friedrich, W.N., Wilturner, L.T., & Cohen, D.S. (1985). Coping resources and parenting mentally retarded children. *American Journal of Mental Deficiency, 90,* 130–139.

Gabel, H., & Kotsch, L. (1981). Extended families and young handicapped children. *Topics in Early Childhood Special Education, 1,* 29–35.

Gath, A., & Grumley, D. (1984). Down's syndrome and the family: Follow-up of children first seen in infancy. *Developmental Medicine and Child Neurology, 26,* 500–508.

George, J.D. (1988). Therapeutic intervention for grandparents and extended family of children with developmental delays. *Mental Retardation, 26,* 369–375.

Glendenning, C. (1983). *Unshared care: Parents and their disabled children.* London: Routledge & Kegan Paul.

Goldfarb, L.A., Brotherson, M.J., Summers, J.A., & Turnbull, A.P. (1986). *Meeting the challenge of disability or chronic illness: A family guide.* Baltimore: Paul H. Brookes Publishing Co.

Harvey, D., & Greenway, P. (1982). How parent attitudes and emotional reactions affect their handicapped child's self-concept. *Psychological Medicine, 12,* 357–370.

Hasenfeld, Y., & Chesler, M.A. (1989). Client empowerment in the human services: Personal and professional agenda. *The Journal of Applied Behavioral Science, 25*(4), 499–521.

Hayes, A. (1991). What the future holds. In M.L. Batshaw, *Your child has a disability* (pp. 308–321). Boston: Little, Brown.

Kaufman, S.Z. (1988). *Retarded isn't stupid, Mom!* Baltimore: Paul H. Brookes Publishing Co.

Kubler-Ross, E. (1969). *On death and dying.* New York: Macmillan.

Leyser, Y., & Dekel, G. (1991). Perceived stress and adjustment in religions Jewish families with a child who is disabled. *Journal of Psychology, 125,* 427–438.

Lobato, D.J. (1990). *Brothers, sisters and special needs: Information and activities for helping young siblings of children with chronic illnesses and developmental disabilities.* Baltimore: Paul H. Brookes Publishing Co.

Ludlow, B.L., Turnbull, A.P., & Luckasson, R. (Eds.). (1988). *Transitions to adult life for people with mental retardation: Principles and practices.* Baltimore: Paul H. Brookes Publishing Co.

Moen, P., & Howery, C.B. (1988). The significance of time in the study of families under stress. In D.M. Klein & J. Aldous (Eds.), *Social stress and family development* (pp. 131–152). New York: Guilford Press.

Mori, A.A. (1983). *Families of children with special needs: Early intervention techniques for the practitioner.* Rockville, MD: Aspen Systems Corporation.

Powell, T.H., & Ogle, P.A. (1985). *Brothers and sisters: A special part of exceptional families.* Baltimore: Paul H. Brookes Publishing Co.

Rousso, H. (1985). Fostering self-esteem. Part two. What parents and professionals can do. *The Exceptional Parent, 15,* 9–12.

Schalock, R., & Kiernan, W. (1990). *Habilitation planning for adults with disabilities.* New York: Springer-Verlag.

Schleifer, M.J. (1987). I'm not going to be John's baby sitter forever: Siblings, planning and the disabled child. *Exceptional Parent, 17,* 60–64.

Schleifer, M.J. (1988). I wish our parents would help us more. Understanding grandparents of children with disabilities. *Exceptional Parent, 18,* 62–68.

Schleifer, M.J., & Klein, S.D. (Eds.). (1985). *The disabled child and the family: Understanding and treatment.* Boston: The Exceptional Parent Press.

Schulman, E.D. (1990). *Focus on the retarded adult, programs, and services.* St. Louis: C.V. Mosby.

Shonkoff, J.P., & Hauser-Cram, P. (1987). Early intervention for disabled infants and their families: A quantitative analysis. *Pediatrics, 80,* 650–658.

Shonkoff, J.P., Jarman, F.C., & Kohlenberg, T.M. (1987). Family transitions, crises, and adaptations. *Current Problems in Pediatrics, 17,* 503–553.

Simeonsson, R.J., & McHale, S.M. (1981). Review: Research on handicapped children: Sibling relationships. *Child: Care, Health and Development, 7,* 153–171.

Singer, G.H.S., & Irvin, L.K. (Eds.). (1989). *Support for caregiving families: Enabling positive adaptation to disability.* Baltimore: Paul H. Brookes Publishing Co.

Thompson, C.E. (1986). *Raising handicapped children.* New York: William Morrow.

Trute, B., & Hauch, C. (1988). Building on family strength: A study of families with positive adjustment to the birth of a developmentally disabled child. *Journal of Marital and Family Therapy, 14,* 185–193.

Turnbull, H.R., Turnbull, A.P., Bronicki, G.J., Summers, J.A., & Roeder-Gordon, C. (1988). *Disability and the family: A guide to decisions for adulthood.* Baltimore: Paul H. Brookes Publishing Co.

Abducted Having part of the body moved away from the body's midline.

Abruptio placenta Premature detachment of a normally situated placenta.

Abscesses Localized collections of pus in cavities caused by the disintegration of tissue. They are usually the consequence of bacterial infections.

Acetabulum The cup-shaped cavity of the hip bone that holds the head of the femur.

Acetaminophen A medication used to control fever and pain. It has a different chemical structure than aspirin and fewer side effects.

Achondroplasia *See* Syndromes and Inborn Errors of Metabolism, Appendix B.

Acid-base balance In metabolism, the balance of acid to base necessary to keep the pH of the blood neutral.

Acidotic Having too much acid in the bloodstream. The normal pH is 7.42; acidosis is generally less than 7.30.

Acquired immunodeficiency syndrome (AIDS) *See* Syndromes and Inborn Errors of Metabolism, Appendix B.

Actin Protein involved in muscle contraction.

Acute polyneuropathy Short-term ascending paralysis following a viral illness. The most common example is Guillain-Barré syndrome.

ADA deficiency Adenosine deaminase deficiency. An inborn error of metabolism, inherited as an autosomal recessive disorder, which causes severe combined immunodeficiency (*see* Syndromes and Inborn Errors of Metabolism, Appendix B).

Adenoids Lymphatic tissue in nasopharynx.

Adenoma sebaceum Benign cutaneous growths usually seen around the nose; occurs in persons with tuberous sclerosis. They resemble acne.

Adrenalin A potent stimulant of the autonomic nervous system. It increases blood pressure, heart rate, and other physiological changes needed for a "fight or flight" response.

Afferent In the nervous system, *afferent* refers to the signals sent from the periphery to the brain.

Alleles Alternate forms of a gene that may exist at the same site on the chromosome.

Alopecia Hair loss.

Alpha-fetoprotein (AFP) Fetal protein found in amniotic fluid and serum of pregnant women. It is used to test for meningomyelocele and Down syndrome in the fetus.

Alveoli Small air sacs in the lungs. Carbon dioxide and oxygen are exchanged through their walls.

Amblyopia Dimness of vision with no detectable organic cause.

Ambulatory Able to walk.

Amniotic fluid Fluid that surrounds and protects the developing fetus. This fluid is sampled through amniocentesis.

Anemia Disorder in which the blood has either too few red blood cells or too little hemoglobin; adjective: anemic.

Anencephaly Birth defect in which either the whole brain or all but the most primitive regions of the brain are missing.

Anorexia A severe loss of appetite.

Anterior fontanel The membrane-covered area on the top of the head; also called the *soft spot*. It generally closes by 18 months of age.

Anterior horn cells Cells in the spinal column that transmit impulses from the pyramidal tract to the peripheral nervous system.

Antibodies Proteins formed in the bloodstream to fight infection.

Antihistamine A drug that counteracts the effects of histamines, substances involved in allergic reactions.

Anxiety disorders A group of emotional disorders characterized by feelings of anxiety. These include panic attacks, separation anxiety, obsessive-compulsive disorder, and posttraumatic stress disorder.

Aorta The major artery of the body. It originates in the left ventricle of the heart and carries oxygenated blood to the rest of the body.

Apgar score A scoring system used to assess neurological status in the newborn infant. Scores range from 0 to 10.

Aphasia Markedly decreased expressive or receptive language, often due to traumatic injury or stroke; adjective: aphasic.

Apnea Episodic arrest of breathing.

Aqueous humor The fluid in the eyeball that fills the space between the lens and the cornea.

Arcuate fasciculus A nerve tract that connects Wernicke's and Broca's areas of the brain. It is involved in the control of language.

Asphyxia Interference with oxygenation of the blood that leads to loss of consciousness and possible brain damage.

Aspirated Inhaled.

Aspiration pneumonia Inflammation of the lung(s) caused by inhaling a foreign body, such as food, into the lungs.

Ataxic Having an unbalanced gait caused by loss of cerebellar control; noun: ataxia.

Atonic Absence of normal muscle tone.

Atresia Congenital absence of a body part or failure of closure of a body orifice.

Atria Upper two chambers of the heart.

Atrophy A wasting away.

Audiometry The testing of hearing.

Auditory brain stem response (ABR) A test to evaluate the processing of sound by the brain stem; also called brainstem auditory evoked response (BAER). It is primarily used to test hearing in infants.

Aura Visual changes or alterations of sensations that represent a simple partial seizure and often precede a complex partial or generalized seizure.

Autoimmune Reaction in which one's immune system attacks other parts of the body.

Automatic (protective) movement reactions Motor responses that become evident in the first year of life, permitting normal motor developmental progression. Examples include neck righting and propping responses.

Autonomic nervous system The part of the nervous system that regulates certain automatic functions of the body—for example, heart rate, sweating, and bowel movement.

Autosomal dominant (trait) A genetic trait carried on the autosomes. The disorder appears when one of a pair of chromosomes contains the abnormal gene. Statistically, it is passed on from the affected parent to half of the children.

Autosomal recessive (trait) A genetic trait carried on the autosomes. Both asymptomatic parents must carry the trait to produce an affected child. This child has two abnormal genes. The risk of recurrence in subsequent children is 25%.

Autosomes The first 22 pairs of chromosomes. All chromosomes are autosomes except for the two sex chromosomes.

Banding pattern A series of dark and light bars that appear on chromosomes after they are stained. Each chromosome has a distinct banding pattern.

Barotrauma Injury related to excess pressure, especially to the lungs or ears.

Beri-beri Disease caused by thiamine deficiency.

Binocular vision The focusing of both eyes on an object to provide a stereoscopic image.

Biotin A B-group vitamin.

Biotinidase deficiency Inborn error of organic acid metabolism that results in the body's inability to recycle the vitamin biotin; can be fatal if untreated, but patients respond well to oral biotin supplementation.

Blastocyst The embryonic group of cells that exists at the time of implantation.

Bolus A small rounded mass of food made ready by tongue and jaw movement for swallowing.

Bradycardia Slowing of the heart rate, usually to fewer than 60 beats per minute.

Brain stem The primitive portion of the brain that lies between the cerebrum and the spinal cord.

Braxton-Hicks Usually painless, irregular contractions that occur intermittently throughout pregnancy.

Bronchopulmonary dysplasia (BPD) A chronic lung disorder that occurs in about 7% of premature infants with respiratory distress syndrome. It is associated with "stiff" lungs that do not permit adequate gas exchange and frequently leads to dependence on ventilator assistance for extended periods of time.

Bronchospasm Acute constriction of the bronchial tubes, most commonly associated with asthma.

Bruxism Repetitive grinding of the teeth.

Bulk Material to increase quantity of intestinal contents and stimulate regular bowel movements. Fruits, vegetables, and fiber provide bulk in the diet.

Butyrophenones Drugs that inhibit the neurochemical dopamine in the brain and are used to control Tourette syndrome, psychosis, and self-injurious behavior. An example is haloperidol (Haldol).

Caffeine A central nervous system stimulant found in coffee, tea, and cola.

Calcified Hardened through the laying down of calcium salts.

Callus A disorganized network of bone tissue formed around the edges of a fracture.

Cataracts Clouding of the lenses of the eyes.

Celiac disease Congenital malabsorption syndrome that leads to failure to gain weight and passage of loose, foul-smelling stools. It is caused by an intolerance of cereal products that contain gluten.

Central nervous system (CNS) The portion of the nervous system that consists of the brain and spinal cord. It is primarily involved in voluntary movement and thought processes.

Central venous line A catheter that is advanced through a neck vein to a position directly above the opening to the right atrium of the heart. It is used to provide long-term medication or nutrition.

Centrioles Tiny organelles that migrate to the opposite poles of a cell during cell division and align the spindles.

Cephalocaudal From head to tail; refers to neurological development that proceeds from the head downward.

Cephalohematoma A swelling of the scalp containing blood; often found in newborn infants. It is usually not harmful.

Cerebral palsy A disorder of movement and posture due to a nonprogressive defect of the immature brain (see Chapter 24).

Cervical Pertaining to the neck.

Cervical cerclage Surgical procedure done to prevent the cervix from opening prematurely.

CHARGE association *See* Syndromes and Inborn Errors of Metabolism, Appendix B.

Cholesteatoma A cyst-like mass lined with skin cells and filled with debris, including cholesterol. It is a complication of otitis media, in which skin cells from the ear canal migrate through the perforated ear drum into the middle ear, or mastoid region, forming a mass that must be removed surgically.

Choreoathetosis A form of extrapyramidal cerebral palsy marked by variable muscle tone and involuntary movements of the arms and legs.

Chorioamnionitis Infection of the amniotic sac, which surrounds and contains the fetus and amniotic fluid.

Chorion The outermost covering of the fetus.

Chorionic gonadotrophin The hormone secreted by the embryo that prevents its expulsion from the uterus. A pregnancy test measures the presence of this hormone in the urine.

Chorionic villus sampling A prenatal diagnostic procedure done in first trimester of pregnancy to obtain fetal cells for genetic analysis.

Chorioretinitis An inflammation of the retina and choroid that produces severe visual loss.

Choroid The middle layer of the eyeball between the sclera and the retina.

Choroid plexus Cells that line the ventricles of the brain and produce cerebrospinal fluid.

Chromatid Term given to chromosomes during cell division.

Cilia Hairlike projections attached to the surface of a cell. They beat rhythmically to move the cell.

Ciliary muscles Small muscles that affect the shape of the lens of the eye, permitting accommodation.

Clonus Alternate muscle contraction and relaxation in rapid succession.

Cochlea The snail-shaped structure in the inner ear containing the organ of hearing.

Computed tomography (CT) An imaging technique in which X ray "slices" of a structure are taken and synthesized by a computer, forming an image. It is most commonly used to visualize the brain. CT scans are less clear than magnetic resonance imaging (MRI) scans, but are better at localizing certain tumors and areas of calcification.

Concave Having a curved, indented surface.

Concussion   A clinical syndrome, caused by a blow to the head, characterized by transient loss of consciousness.

Cone cells   Photoreceptor cells of the eyes associated with color vision.

Congenital   Originating prior to birth.

Congenital hyperammonemias   *See* Syndromes and Inborn Errors of Metabolism, Appendix B.

Contractures   Irreversible shortening of muscle fibers that causes decreased joint mobility.

Contusion (of brain)   Structural damage limited to the surface layer of the brain, caused by a blow to the head.

Convex   Having a curved, elevated surface, such as a dome.

Cornea   The transparent, dome-like covering of the iris.

Corpus callosotomy   Surgical procedure in which the corpus callosum is cut to prevent the spread of seizures from one hemisphere to the other.

Corpus callosum   The bridge of white matter connecting the two cerebral hemispheres.

Cortical mapping   The placement of electrodes over the cortex during a neurosurgical operation. Stimulation of the electrodes results in motor or sensory activity that allows "mapping" of cortical control or body actions.

Craniofacial   Relating to the skull and the bones of the face.

Creatine kinase (CK)   An enzyme released by damaged muscle cells. Its level is elevated in muscular dystrophy.

Cretinism   *See* Syndromes and Inborn Errors of Metabolism, Appendix B.

Cri-du-chat syndrome   *See* Syndromes and Inborn Errors of Metabolism, Appendix B.

Crossing over   The exchange of genetic material between two closely aligned chromosomes during the first meiotic division.

Cry analysis   A research test in which acoustic measurements of the infant's cry are taken. Infants who have hypoxic brain damage tend to have an abnormal pattern.

Cryotherapy   The use of freezing temperatures to destroy tissue. A cryotherapy probe has been used to treat retinoblastoma and retinopathy of prematurity.

Cystic fibrosis   An autosomal, recessively inherited disorder of the secretory glands leading to malabsorption and lung disease.

Cytomegalovirus (CMV)   A virus causing symptoms that may mimic mononucleosis, or it may be asymptomatic. It can also lead to severe fetal malformations similar to congenital rubella.

Deciduous   Describes baby teeth, which are shed.

Deletion   Loss of genetic material from a chromosome.

Delirium   An organically based psychosis characterized by impaired attention, disorganized thinking, altered and fluctuating levels of consciousness, perceptual disturbances, changes in sleep-wake cycle, agitation or slowing of movements, and memory impairment. It may be caused by encephalitis, diabetes, or intoxication and is usually reversed by treating the underlying medical problem.

Delusions   False beliefs, often quite bizarre, that are symptoms of psychoses or drug intoxication.

Dementia   A progressive neurological disorder marked by loss of memory, decreased speech, impairment in abstract thinking and judgment, other disturbances of higher cortical function, and personality change. One example is Alzheimer disease.

Dentin   The principal substance of the tooth surrounding the tooth pulp and covered by the enamel.

Deoxyribonucleic acid (DNA)   The fundamental component of living tissue. It contains the genetic code.

Depolarization   Changing the electrical charge of a cell.

Depressed fracture   Fracture of bone, usually skull, that results in inward displacement of the bone at the point of impact. It requires surgical intervention to prevent damage to underlying tissue.

Detoxification   The conversion of a toxic compound to a nontoxic material.

Dialysis   Detoxification procedure. Can be hemodialysis (blood) or peritoneal dialysis (through abdominal wall); used to treat kidney failure.

Diffuse axonal injury   Diffuse injury to nerve cell components, usually resulting from shearing forces. This is the type of traumatic brain injury associated with motor vehicle accidents.

Diopters   The units of refractive power of a lens.

Diuretics   Medications used to reduce intercellular fluid buildup in the body (edema), especially in the lungs.

Duodenal atresia   Congenital absence of a portion of the first section of the small intestine; often seen in individuals with Down syndrome.

Duodenum   First part of the small intestine.

Dysarthria   Improper articulation of speech, resulting from problems in muscle control caused by damage to the central or peripheral nervous system.

Dyscalculic   Having a learning disability affecting arithmetic skills.

Dysgraphia   Learning disability in areas of processing and reporting information in written form.

Dyslexia   Learning disability affecting reading skills.

Dysphasia   Impairment of speech consisting of lack of coordination and failure to arrange words in proper order; due to a central brain lesion.

Dyspraxia   Inability to perform coordinated movements despite normal function of the central and peripheral nervous system and muscles.

Dysthymia   A mild form of depression characterized by a mood disturbance that is present most of the time and is associated with feelings of low self-esteem, hopelessness, poor concentration, low energy, and changes in sleep and appetite.

Dystocia   Structural abnormalities of the uterus that may cause premature or prolonged labor.

E. coli   Bacteria that can cause infections ranging from diarrhea and urinary tract infection to sepsis.

Echocardiography   An ultrasonic method of imaging the heart. It can be used to detect congenital heart defects.

Echodensities   Changes on ultrasound that reflect damage to brain tissue, seen in periventricular leukomalacia in premature infants.

Echolalia   Echoing words that have been heard without understanding their meaning.

Edema   An abnormal accumulation of fluid in the tissues of the body.

Edetate calcium disodium (EDTA)   A drug used to bind ingested heavy metals, especially lead. EDTA must be given by injection.

Efferent   Impulse that goes to a nerve or muscle from the central nervous system.

Electrolarynx   A vibrator/amplifier that permits the production of artificial speech sounds in an individual whose larynx is blocked by a tracheostomy tube or has been removed because of cancer.

Electrolyte   Mineral contained in the blood.

Ellis-van Creveld syndrome   *See* Syndromes and Inborn Errors of Metabolism, Appendix B.

Encephalitis   Inflammation or infection of the brain, usually viral in origin.

Encephalopathy   An acute or chronic disturbance of brain function. If caused by an infection, it is called *encephalitis.*

Enchondral ossification   Formation of bone from cartilage.

Endocarditis   Inflammation of the lining of the heart.

Endorphins   The body's natural opiates, probably involved in the perception of pain and pleasure.

Enterovirus   Virus that causes gastroenteritis (i.e., infection of stomach and small intestine).

Enzyme-multiplied immunoassay technique (EMIT)   A laboratory test performed on blood or urine to detect the recent use of cocaine or other abused substances.

Epidemiological   Pertaining to the study of factors determining the frequency and distribution of diseases—for example, an outbreak of food poisoning.

Epidural anesthesia   Pain relief by a spinal nerve block, used during childbirth. Mother is conscious during delivery.

Epidural hematomas   Localized collections of clotted blood lying between the skull and the outer (dural) membrane of the brain, resulting from the hemorrhage of a blood vessel resting in the dura. This most commonly results from a traumatic brain injury.

Epiglottis   A lidlike structure that hangs over the entrance to the windpipe and prevents aspiration of food or liquid into the lungs during swallowing.

Epithelial   Pertaining to the skin.

Equinus   Involuntary extension of the foot. This position is often found in spastic cerebral palsy.

Esophagus   Tube through which food passes from the pharynx to the stomach.

Estimated date of confinement (EDC)   Expected date of delivery.

Eustachian tube   Connection between oral cavity and middle ear, allowing equilibration of pressure and drainage of fluid.

Excitotoxic receptors   Receptors in the brain for excitotoxins, chemicals that can cause neuronal cell death and have been implicated in hypoxic brain damage and AIDS encephalopathy.

Expressive language   Communication by spoken language, gesture, signing, or "body" language.

Extract   A concentrated preparation.

Febrile   Term referring to an individual who has an elevated body temperature. Normal temperature is 98.6°F (37°C). A child is considered febrile when the fever is above 100.4°F (38°C).

Fetal alcohol syndrome   *See* Syndromes and Inborn Errors of Metabolism, Appendix B and Chapter 8.

Flagellum   Whiplike projection of a cell that gives it mobility. The sperm is one example of a cell having a flagellum; plural: flagella.

Flexor   A muscle with the primary function of flexion at a joint.

Flora   Bacteria normally residing within the intestine, such as *E. coli.*

Forebrain   The front portion of the brain during fetal development.

Fovea centralis   The small pit in the center of the macula; the area of clearest vision, containing only cones.

Fragile X syndrome   *See* Syndromes and Inborn Errors of Metabolism, Appendix B.

Fundal plication   An operation in which the top of the stomach is wrapped around the opening of the esophagus to prevent gastroesophageal reflux.

Fundus uteri   The upper portion of the uterus where the fallopian tubes attach.

Galactosemia   *See* Syndromes and Inborn Errors of Metabolism, Appendix B.

Gastroenteritis   Stomach flu.

Gastroesophageal reflux   The backward flow of food into the esophagus after it has entered the stomach.

Gastrostomy   An operation in which an artificial opening is made into the stomach through the wall of the abdomen.

Genotype   The genetic composition of an individual.

Germ cells   The cells involved in reproduction (i.e., the sperm and the egg).

Glaucoma   A disease of the eye caused by increased intraocular pressure.

Glucose   A sugar, also called sucrose, contained in fruits and other carbohydrates.

Glycogen   The chief carbohydrate stored in the body, primarily in the liver and muscle.

Goiter   Enlargement of the thyroid gland.

Goniotomy   An operation to treat glaucoma that decreases pressure by providing an opening for the release of fluid from the anterior chamber of the eye.

Graft versus host disease   A mechanism of the body's immune system that destroys foreign proteins. When it occurs in an immunosuppressed child who has received a bone marrow or other organ transplant, it can be life-threatening (10%–20% mortality). Symptoms include diarrhea, skin breakdown, and shock.

Grapheme   A unit, such as a letter, of a writing system.

Gyri   Convolutions of the surface of the brain; singular: gyrus.

Habilitation   The teaching of new skills to children with developmental disabilities. It is called *habilitation,* rather than rehabilitation, because these children did not possess these skills previously.

Hallermann-Streiff syndrome   *See* Syndromes and Inborn Errors of Metabolism, Appendix B.

Hallucinations   Sense perceptions without a source in the external world. These most commonly occur as symptoms of psychoses or drug intoxication.

Helix   The coiled structure of DNA.

Hematocrit   Percentage of red blood cells in whole blood, normally about 35%–40%.

Hemiplegia   Paralysis of one side of the body.

Hemodialysis   A procedure in which blood is pumped through a dialysis chamber that cleanses it of toxins. It serves as an artificial kidney.

Hemophilia   Hereditary (X-linked) recessive disease characterized by faulty blood clotting.

Hemosiderosis   Dangerous increase in tissue iron stores, which can lead to respiratory failure and death.

Hemostat   A small surgical clamp used to constrict a tube or blood vessel.

Herpesvirus   A virus leading to symptoms that range from cold sores to vaginal infections to encephalitis; also a cause of fetal malformations and sepsis in early infancy.

Heterozygote   A carrier of a recessive genetic disorder.

Holoprosencephaly   A brain malformation in which there is a single ventricle and/or incomplete development of the cerebral lobes. Children with this disorder have mental retardation.

Homeostasis   Equilibrium of fluid, chemical, and temperature regulation in the body.

Homocystinuria   *See* Syndromes and Inborn Errors of Metabolism, Appendix B.

Huntington disease   *See* Syndromes and Inborn Errors of Metabolism, Appendix B.

Hybrid   Offspring of parents of dissimilar species.

Hydrocephalus   A condition characterized by the abnormal accumulation of cerebrospinal fluid within the ventricles of the brain. This leads to enlargement of the head.

Hyperalimentation   Intravenous provision of high-quality nutrition (i.e., carbohydrates, protein, fat). This is also called *parenteral nutrition.* It is used in children with malabsorption, malnutrition, and short gut syndrome.

Hyperbilirubinemia   Excess of bilirubin in the blood.

Hyperimmune serum   Blood that is especially rich in antibodies against a virus.

Hypertelorism Widely spaced eyes.

Hyperthyroidism Overactivity of the thyroid gland characterized by increased metabolism. An example is Graves' disease.

Hypocalcemia Abnormally low levels of calcium in the blood.

Hypoglycemia Low blood sugar; often found in premature infants and infants of mothers with diabetes.

Hypothermia Low body temperature; especially a risk in the premature infant.

Hypothyroidism Deficiency of thyroid hormone. *See* Syndromes and Inborn Errors of Metabolism, Appendix B.

Hypotonic Having decreased muscle tone; noun: hypotonia.

Hypoxic Reduction of oxygen content in body tissues.

Hypsarrhythmia Electroencephalographic (EEG) abnormality seen in infants with infantile spasms. It is marked by chaotic spike and wave activity.

Ileum Lower portion of the small intestine.

Immunoglobulin An antibody.

Impact In references to traumatic brain injury, the forcible striking of the head against an object, such as a motor vehicle.

Impedance audiometry Test to detect the presence of middle ear fluid, commonly seen in otitis media. It also detects conductive hearing loss.

Imperforate The lack of a normal opening in a body organ. The most common example in childhood is an absent or closed anus.

Implantation The attachment and embedding of the fertilized egg into the mucus lining of the uterus.

Indomethacin Drug used to close a patent ductus arteriosus in premature infants. It is also used as an antiinflammatory drug.

Inertial Pertaining to inertia; the tendency to keep moving in the same direction as the force that produced the movement.

Influenza An acute illness caused by a virus; attacks respiratory and gastrointestinal tracts; often seen in epidemics.

Informed consent The written consent of a child or guardian to undergo a procedure or treatment after its risks and benefits have been explained in easily understood language.

Insufflation In this context, the "snorting" of cocaine into the nose.

Insult An attack on a body organ causing damage to it. This may be physical, metabolic, immunological, or infectious.

Intercurrent An illness occurring in the midst of a chronic disease process, often modifying the outcome.

Intracranial Within the skull.

Intubation The insertion of a tube through the nose or mouth into the trachea to permit mechanical ventilation.

In utero Occurring during fetal development.

Ionization The separation of a substance in solution into its component atoms.

Iris The circular, colored membrane behind the cornea, perforated by the pupil.

Ischemia Decreased blood flow to an area of the body; leads to tissue death.

Islet cells Cells in the pancreas that produce insulin and control blood sugar levels.

Jaundice Yellowing of the skin and whites of the eyes caused by an accumulation of bilirubin. This often is found in liver disease and Rh incompatibility; also called *icterus*.

Jejunum Second portion of small intestine.

Karyotyping Photographing the chromosomal makeup of a cell. In a human, there are 23 pairs of chromosomes in a normal karyotype.

Kernicterus *See* Syndromes and Inborn Errors of Metabolism, Appendix B.

Ketosis The buildup of acid in the body, most often associated with starvation, inborn errors of metabolism, and diabetes.

Kyphoscoliosis Spinal deformity including both curvature and humping of the spine.

Kyphosis Humping deformity of the spine; "hunchback."

Labyrinth The inner ear, made up of the vestibular apparatus and the cochlea.

Lacrimal Pertaining to tears.

Lactase Enzyme necessary to digest the milk sugar lactose.

Lactose Milk sugar composed of glucose and galactose.

Lateral ventricles Cavities in the interior of the cerebral hemispheres containing cerebrospinal fluid. They are enlarged with hydrocephalus or with brain atrophy.

Lens The biconvex, translucent body that rests in front of the vitreous humor and refracts light.

Lesch-Nyhan disease *See* Syndromes and Inborn Errors of Metabolism, Appendix B.

Lesions Injuries or loss of function.

Linear fracture Break in a long bone; occurs in a straight line.

Lissencephaly An abnormality of the brain in which few gyri are formed. This is associated with some forms of mental retardation.

Locus ceruleus An area of the brain involved in attention.

Lumbar Pertaining to the lower back.

Lumbar puncture The tapping of the subarachnoid space to obtain cerebrospinal fluid from the lower back region. This procedure is used to diagnose meningitis and to measure chemicals in the spinal fluid. It is also called *spinal tap*.

Lymphocyte A type of white blood cell.

Lymphomas Cancerous growths of lymphoid tissue. They are one of the complications of acquired immunodeficiency syndrome (AIDS).

Macula The area of the retina that contains the greatest concentration of cones and the fovea centralis.

Magnetic resonance imaging (MRI) Imaging procedure that uses the magnetic resonance of atoms to provide clear images of interior parts of the body. It is particularly useful in diagnosing structural abnormalities of the brain.

Mainstreamed The educational concept that a child with disabilities be placed in a normal classroom setting either for part or all of the school day.

Malaria An infectious, febrile illness caused by a protozoa; transmitted by mosquitos; tends to become chronic.

Malocclusion The improper fitting together of the upper and lower teeth.

Mandible Lower jaw bone.

Mania A distinct period of abnormally and persistently elevated, expansive, or irritable mood. The mood disturbance is sufficiently severe to cause impairment in function.

Manic-depressive Pertaining to a psychiatric disorder consisting of distinct periods of elevated mood and depressed mood. This is a type of psychosis and is associated with disorganization of personality and distortion of reality.

Maple syrup urine disease *See* Syndromes and Inborn Errors of Metabolism, Appendix B.

Mastoiditis Infection of the mastoid air cells that rest in the temporal bone behind the ear. This is an infrequent complication of a chronic middle ear infection.

Maxilla The bony region of the upper jaw.

Meconium aspiration Potentially severe illness due to infant inhaling meconium (i.e., feces) into lung passages with first respiratory efforts. Can cause aspiration pneumonia and inadequate ventilation of infant.

Medium chain triglycerides (MCT) Fatty food source that can bypass normal uptake process and go directly to the liver.

Megavitamin therapies *See* **Orthomolecular therapy.**

Meiosis Reductive cell division occurring only in eggs and sperm in which the daughter cells receive half (23) the number of chromosomes of the parent cells (46).

Meninges The three membranes covering the brain and spinal cord.

Meningitis Infection of the meninges.

Menses The menstrual flow.

Mental retardation Intellectual functioning at least two standard deviations below the mean.

Metachromatic leukodystrophy *See* Syndromes and Inborn Errors of Metabolism, Appendix B.

Methylmalonic acidemia *See* Syndromes and Inborn Errors of Metabolism, Appendix B.

Methylmalonic aciduria *See* Syndromes and Inborn Errors of Metabolism, Appendix B.

Microcephaly Head circumference more than two standard deviations below the average size.

Microswitch A switch, usually used to control a computer, environmental control system, or power wheelchair, that has been adapted so that less pressure than normal is required to activate it.

Milligram One-thousandth of a gram.

Milliliter One-thousandth of a liter; equal to about 15 drops.

Mitosis Cell division in which two daughter cells of identical chromosomal composition to the parent cell are formed; each contains 46 chromosomes.

Mononucleosis A viral illness whose symptoms include fever, malaise, sore throat, swollen lymph nodes, and an enlarged spleen.

Morbidity Medical complication of an illness, procedure, or operation.

Moro Primitive reflex present in the newborn in which the infant throws the arms out in an "embrace" attitude.

Morphemes The smallest linguistic units of meaning.

Morula The group of cells formed by the first divisions of a fertilized egg.

Mosaicism The presence of two genetically distinct types of cells in one individual—for example, a child with Down syndrome who has some cells containing 46 chromosomes and some cells containing 47 chromosomes.

Mucopolysaccharidoses Product of metabolism that may accumulate in cells and cause a progressive neurological disorder. One example is Hurler disease.

Mucosal Pertaining to the mucus membrane lining organs, such as the mouth, stomach, and vagina.

Multiple carboxylase deficiency Inborn error of metabolism (organic acidemia) presenting in the newborn period; results in severe illness due to the inability to couple the vitamin biotin to certain enzymes that need it; fatal if untreated, but response to biotin supplementation is usually excellent.

Mutation A change in a gene that occurs by chance.

Myelination The production of a coating called *myelin* around an axon. This quickens neurotransmission.

Myosin Protein necessary for muscle contraction.

Myringotomy The surgical incision of the eardrum. It is usually accompanied by the placement of pressure equalizing tubes to drain fluid from the middle ear.

Nasal pillows A prop attached to an oxygen line to permit the flow of oxygen directly into the nose.

Nasogastric feeding-tube A plastic feeding-tube placed in the nose and extended into the stomach.

Nasopharynx Posterior portion of the oral cavity above the palate.

Necrosis Death of tissue.

Necrotizing enterocolitis (NEC) Severe inflammation of the small intestine and colon, more common among premature infants.

Neural tube The precursor of the spinal column.

Neurodevelopmental therapy (NDT) Therapy that includes an understanding and utilization of normal developmental stages in working with children; commonly used theory underlying physical and occupational therapy.

Neuroectoderm Fetal skin cells that differentiate to form the retina and central nervous system.

Neurofibromatosis *See* Syndromes and Inborn Errors of Metabolism, Appendix B.

Neuroses Psychiatric disorders associated with unresolved conflicts and characterized by anxiety, but without the disorganization of personality and distortion of reality that occur in psychoses. Examples of neuroses include panic disorder, conversion hysteria, obsessive compulsive disorder, and phobias.

Neurotoxin A chemical that damages the central nervous system.

Neurotransmitter A chemical released at the synapse that permits transmission of an impulse from one nerve to another.

Nondisjunction Failure of a pair of chromosomes to separate during mitosis or meiosis, resulting in an unequal number of chromosomes in the daughter cells.

Nuclear family Parents and their children.

Nucleotides The four base compounds that form DNA—adenine, guanine, cytosine, and thymine.

Nystagmus Involuntary rapid movements of the eyes.

Obsessive-compulsive disorder A psychiatric disorder in which recurrent and persistent thoughts and ideas that cannot be suppressed are associated with repetitive behaviors, such as handwashing.

Ocular Pertaining to the eye.

Oligohydramnios The presence of too little amniotic fluid. It may result in fetal deformities including club foot and atretic lungs.

Ophthalmologist Physician specializing in treatment of diseases of the eye.

Ophthalmoscope An instrument containing a mirror and a series of magnifying lenses used to examine the interior of the eye.

Opisthotonos A spasm in which the head and heels are bent backward and body bowed forward.

Opsin The protein in rods and cones necessary for vision.

Opticokinetic Pertaining to movement of the eyes.

Organic acidemias Class of inborn errors of metabolism affecting organic acid metabolism. These include propionic acidemia, methylmalonic acidemia, isovaleric acidemia, and multiple carboxylase deficiency.

Organ of Corti A series of hair cells in the cochlea that form the beginning of the auditory nerve.

Orthodontist Dentist who specializes in the correction of irregularities of the teeth or the improper alignment of the jaw.

Orthomolecular therapy The use of at least 10 times the required amount of vitamins; also called *megavitamin therapy.*

Orthopedic   Relating to bones or joints.

Orthoses   Orthopedic devices, most commonly splints or braces, used to support, align, or correct deformities or to improve the function of limbs.

Ossicles   The three small bones in the middle ear: the stapes, incus, and malleus.

Osteoarthritis   Degenerative joint disease.

Osteoblast   Cell type that produces bony tissue.

Osteoclast   Cell type that absorbs and removes bone.

Osteogenesis imperfecta   *See* Syndromes and Inborn Errors of Metabolism, Appendix B.

Osteopetrosis   A genetic disorder marked by deficient osteoclastic activity. A buildup of bone encroaches on the eye, brain, and other body organs, leading to early death. Treatment with bone marrow transplantation has been successful in some cases.

Ostomies   Artificial openings in the abdominal region for discharge of stool or urine.

Oxygenation   The provision of sufficient oxygen for bodily needs.

Palatal   Relating to the palate, the back portion of the roof of the mouth.

Parenteral   Providing nutrition or medication by vein rather than by oral route.

Parkinson disease   A progressive neurological disease usually occurring in older people; associated with tremor, slowed movements, and muscular rigidity.

Parvovirus   A group of extremely small DNA viruses. Intrauterine infection with this virus increases the risk of miscarriage but has not been shown to result in fetal malformations.

Patterning   Controversial therapy program that involves repetition of movements in order to facilitate developmental progress.

Pavlik harness   A device used to correct congenital hip dislocation.

Penicillamine   A drug used to bind ingested heavy metals, particularly lead and copper. This drug may be given orally.

Periodontal   Pertaining to the gums and bony structures that surround the teeth.

Periosteum   Fibrous tissue covering and protecting all bones.

Peripheral nervous system   The parts of the nervous system that are outside the brain and spinal cord.

Peripheral venous lines   Catheters that are placed in a superficial vein of the arm or leg to provide medication.

Peritoneal   Referring to the membrane surrounding the abdominal organs. In kidney failure, dialysis can be performed by perforating the peritoneum and "washing out" the abdominal cavity.

Periventricular-intraventricular   Around or within the ventricles of the brain.

Periventricular leukomalacia (PVL)   Injury to part of the brain near the ventricles; caused by lack of oxygen; occurs principally in premature infants.

Persistent fetal circulation   Failure of closure of the fetal circulatory bypasses, the foramen ovale and ductus arteriosus, after birth that interferes with oxygenation of the lungs. This can lead to respiratory failure and death and may require treatment with extracorporeal membrane oxygenation (ECMO).

Phagocytes   Cells that ingest microorganisms or other foreign particles.

Phalanges   Bones of the fingers and toes.

Pharyngeal   *See* **Pharynx.**

Pharynx   The back of the throat; adjective: pharyngeal.

Phenothiazines   Drugs that affect neurochemicals in the brain and are used to control behavior.

Phenylketonuria   *See* Syndromes and Inborn Errors of Metabolism, Appendix B.

Phocomelia   Developmental anomaly characterized by extremely short and irregularly shaped arms and/ or legs. The classic example is the thalidomide-exposed baby.

Phoneme   The smallest units of sounds in speech.

Phonetic   Pertaining to articulate sound.

Phonics   The sounding out of words.

Pica   The hunger for nonfood items.

Pitch   The frequency of sounds, measured in cycles per seconds or Hertz (Hz). Low-pitched sounds have a frequency less than 500 Hz and a bass quality. High-pitched sounds have a frequency above 2,000 Hz and a tenor quality.

Placenta   The organ of nutritional interchange between the mother and the embryo. It has both maternal and embryonic portions and is disc-shaped and about 7 inches in diameter. The umbilical cord attaches in the center of the placenta. The placenta is also called the *afterbirth*; adjective: placental.

Placenta previa   Condition in which the placenta is implanted in the lower segment of the uterus extending over the cervical opening. This often leads to bleeding during labor.

Plasticity   The ability of an organ or part of an organ to take over the function of another damaged organ.

Pneumocystis carinii pneumonia   Lung infection caused by a virus or bacteria; often seen in immuno-compromised individuals, such as individuals with acquired immunodeficiency syndrome (AIDS).

Polarization   Separation of electrical charge between outside and inside the cells.

Porencephalic cysts   Fluid-filled sacs attached to the lateral ventricle of the brain; usually the consequence of liquifaction of brain tissue due to an *in utero* injury or infection.

Positron emission tomography (PET)   Imaging study utilizing radioactive labeled chemical compounds to study the metabolism of an organ, most commonly the brain.

Posterior walkers   Walkers with supports and wheels placed behind, rather than in front of, the child.

Postural reactions   Normal reflex-like protective responses of infant to changes in position.

Prader-Willi syndrome   *See* Syndromes and Inborn Errors of Metabolism, Appendix B.

Preeclampsia   Illness of late pregnancy characterized by high blood pressure, swelling, and protein in the mother's urine.

Presbyopia   A decrease in the accommodation of the lens of the eye that occurs with aging.

Prophylaxis   Preventive agent.

Psychosis   A psychiatric disorder characterized by hallucinations, delusions, loss of contact with reality, and unclear thinking; adjective: psychotic.

Psychotherapy   Providing treatment for an individual with an emotional disorder. There are varying types of psychotherapy ranging from supportive counseling to psychoanalysis. These services are usually provided by a psychologist, psychiatrist, or social worker.

Pulmonary   Pertaining to the lungs.

Pupil   The aperture in the center of the iris.

Purine   A type of organic molecule found in RNA and DNA.

Pylorus   The valve separating the stomach from the first section of the small intestine, the duodenum.

Quadriparesis   Weakness of all four extremities.

Quickening   The first signs of life felt by the mother as a result of fetal movements in the fourth or fifth month of pregnancy.

Rachitic rosary   Bead-like processes along the ribs that are associated with rickets.

Rad   A measure of radioactivity.

Radiotelemetry   Signals that permit the transmission of EEG recordings from a child to a distant machine by radio waves.

Rebus symbols   An educational system using pictured symbols in place of words. An example is using a picture of a tied knot to convey the word "not." This is one approach to teaching children with learning disabilities how to read.

Receptive aphasia   Impairment of receptive language due to a disorder of the central nervous system.

Receptive language   The understanding of language.

Refracted   Deflected.

Restriction fragment length polymorphism (RFLP)   The use of an enzyme to split DNA into fragments that can be analysed for genetic counseling.

Retina   The photosensitive nerve layer of the eye.

Retinitis pigmentosa   *See* Syndromes and Inborn Errors of Metabolism, Appendix B.

Retinoscope   An instrument used to detect errors of refraction in the eye.

Retrovirus   A DNA virus involved in gene transfer therapy. This is also the class of viruses in which HIV, the causative agent of acquired immunodeficiency syndrome (AIDS), belongs.

Rh sensitization   Changes that occur when an Rh+ baby's blood enters an Rh− mother's bloodstream. This predisposes subsequent Rh+ babies to kernicterus. Sensitization is prevented by the use of the drug Rhogam.

Ribonucleic acid   A molecule essential for protein synthesis within the cell.

Ribosome   Intracellular structure concerned with protein synthesis.

Rigid   Increased tone marked by stiffness; seen in extrapyramidal cerebral palsy.

Robin sequence   A small jaw with associated cleft palate and posterior placement of the tongue.

Rods   Photoreceptor cells of the eye associated with low light vision.

Rooting   A reflex in newborns that makes them turn their mouths toward the breast or bottle to feed.

Rootlets   Small branches of nerve roots.

Rubella   German measles.

Rumination   After swallowing, the regurgitation of food followed by chewing another time.

Salicylates   Chemicals found in many food substances and in aspirin.

Sarcomeres The contractile units of the myofibril.

Saturated In this context, a type of fatty acid in the diet that has been linked to heart disease less frequently than unsaturated fatty acids.

Schizophrenia A psychiatric disorder with characteristic psychotic symptoms including prominent delusions, hallucinations, loose associations, catatonic behavior, and/or flat emotions.

Sclera The white, outer lining of the eyeball.

Scoliosis Curvature of the spine.

Seizure threshold Tolerance level of brain for electrical activity. If level of tolerance is exceeded, a seizure occurs.

Sepsis Bacterial infection spread throughout the bloodstream; also called *blood poisoning*.

Sex chromosomes Those chromosomes that determine gender, the X and Y chromosomes.

Shigella diarrhea An infection of the gastrointestinal tract due to a bacterium called *Shigella;* causes bloody diarrhea and can be associated with febrile seizures.

Siblings Brothers and sisters.

Single photon emission computed tomography (SPECT) An imaging technique that permits the study of the metabolism of a body organ, most commonly the brain.

Soft signs Group of neurological findings found in children older than 7 years of age that are suggestive of an immature or disordered central nervous system; often found in children with ADHD. Examples include the inability to stand on one foot without support and difficulty performing rapid alternating movements.

Somatoform (disorder) An emotional disturbance expressed as feelings of physical illness (e.g., hypochondria, conversion reactions, phobias).

Spastic Increased muscle tone so that muscles are stiff and movements are difficult. Caused by damage to the pyramidal track in the brain; noun: spasticity.

Spastic quadriplegia A form of cerebral palsy in which all four limbs are affected. Increased muscle tone (i.e., spasticity) is caused by damage to the pyramidal track in the brain.

Speaking valve A valve that can be used in children who have tracheostomy tubes in place to permit vocalizations.

Spherical convex The type of optical lens used to correct farsightedness. It can be incorporated into eyeglasses or contacts. The lens has a dome shape.

Spica cast A cast that covers much of the lower body and is used following hip surgery.

Spina bifida A developmental defect of the spine. *See* Syndromes and Inborn Errors of Metabolism, Appendix B and Chapter 25.

Sporadic In the context of this book, a disease that occurs by chance and carries little risk of recurrence.

Status marmoratus Condition caused by excessive myelinization of nerve fibers of the corpus striatum; a cause of brain damage in premature infants.

Stereoscopic The blending together of two images of the same object from two slightly different viewpoints.

Steroids Medications used to treat severe inflammatory diseases and infantile spasms; also refers to certain natural hormones in the body.

Strabismus Squint; deviation of the eye inward or outward.

Subarachnoid Beneath the arachnoid membrane, or middle layer, of the meninges.

Subdural Resting between the outer (dural) and middle (arachnoid) layers of the meninges.

Subdural hematomas Localized collections of clotted blood lying in the space between the dura and arachnoid membranes that surround the brain. This results from bleeding of the cerebral blood vessels that rest between these two membranes and most often results from traumatic brain injury.

Subluxation Partial dislocation.

Suctioning The advancing of a catheter through the nose or throat and into the trachea for the purposes of removing secretions by suction.

Sudden infant death syndrome (SIDS) Diagnosis given to a previously well 2–6-month-old infant (often a former premature baby) who is found lifeless in bed without apparent cause; also called *crib death. See* Syndromes and Inborn Errors of Metabolism, Appendix B.

Sulci Furrow of the brain; singular: sulcus.

Surfactant Substance that coats the alveoli in the lungs, keeping them open. A deficiency of it leads to respiratory distress syndrome in premature infants.

Synapse The minute space separating one neuron from another. Neurochemicals breach this gap.

Syntax The way in which words are combined to produce meaning.

Syphilis A venereal disease.

Systemic Pertaining to the whole body.

Teratogens Agents that cause malformations in a developing embryo.

Tetralogy of Fallot A complex congenital heart defect, consisting of pulmonary stenosis, ventricular septal defect, and an overriding aorta. It is one cause of "blue babies."

Thrush Monilial yeast infection of the oral cavity in infants.

Tocolytic agents Medications used to stop premature labor. The most common example is ritodrine.

Tonic-clonic Spasmodic alteration of muscle contraction and relaxation.

Tonometer An instrument for measuring intraocular pressure and detecting glaucoma.

Torsion dystonia *See* Syndromes and Inborn Errors of Metabolism, Appendix B.

Toxemia Also called preeclampsia; the combination of high blood pressure, protein in the urine, and edema that may occur in the third trimester of pregnancy, especially in teenagers and women over 35 years of age.

Toxoplasmosis An infectious disease caused by a microorganism. It may be asymptomatic in adults, but can lead to severe fetal malformations.

Trabeculotomy A microsurgical ophthalmologic operation to relieve glaucoma.

Trachea Windpipe.

Tracheostomy The surgical creation of an opening into the trachea (windpipe) to permit insertion of a tube to facilitate mechanical ventilation.

Trachoma Parasitic infection of the eye that causes blindness in children. This is only seen in developing countries.

Transient situational disorders Psychiatric disturbances linked to environmental events. An example is posttraumatic stress disorder that is precipitated by an unanticipated, psychologically devastating event, such as a physical attack and/or sexual abuse, a car accident, or the sudden loss of a close family member.

Translocation The transfer of a fragment of one chromosome to another chromosome.

Trauma A wound or injury.

Turner syndrome *See* Syndromes and Inborn Errors of Metabolism, Appendix B.

Twinning The production of twins.

Unsaturated In this context, a type of fatty acid in the diet that has been linked to heart disease in susceptible individuals.

Urea End product of protein metabolism.

Varicella The virus that causes chickenpox and herpes.

Vasoconstrictor Chemical that causes blood vessels to decrease in diameter.

Ventilator A machine that provides a mixture of air and oxygen to an individual in respiratory failure. The oxygen content, pressure, volume, and frequency of respirators can be adjusted.

Ventricles Small cavities, especially in the heart or the brain.

Ventriculo-peritoneal shunt Plastic tube connecting a cerebral ventricle with the abdominal cavity; used to treat hydrocephalus.

Vertex presentation Downward position of infant's head during vaginal delivery.

Vesicles Small fluid-containing elevations in upper layer of skin.

Vestibular apparatus Three ring-shaped bodies located in the labyrinth of the ear that are involved in maintenance of balance.

Villi Tiny vascular projections coming from the embryo that become part of the placenta; singular: villus.

Vitreous humor The gelatinous content of the eye located between the lens and the retina.

Watershed infarct Injury to brain due to lack of blood flow in brain tissues between interfacing blood vessels.

X-linked recessive (trait) A trait transmitted by a gene located on the X chromosome; also called *sex-linked*. It is passed on by a carrier mother to an affected son.

REFERENCES

Chapman medical dictionary for the non-professional. (1984). Woodbury, NY: Barron's Educational Series.

Dorland's pocket medical dictionary (24th ed.). (1989). Philadelphia: W.B. Saunders.

Stedman, T.L. (1990). *Illustrated Stedman's medical dictionary* (25th ed.). Baltimore: Williams & Wilkins.

Taber's cyclopedic medical dictionary (16th ed.). (1991). Philadelphia: F.A. Davis Co.

Syndromes and Inborn Errors of Metabolism

Children with certain rare disorders look alike. For example, children with Down syndrome share common features that doctors recognize as a pattern of malformation. These children often look like brothers and sisters. When a combination of physical traits or malformations has the same cause, the condition is called a *syndrome*. Many, but not all, syndromes are inherited as a result of a gene or chromosome defect. Although many genetic defects cause syndromes, some genetic defects cause only one abnormality rather than a group of abnormalities. These conditions are called *inherited disorders* or *inborn errors*.

This appendix lists a number of syndromes and inborn errors that often are associated with developmental disabilities. Their principal characteristics, causes, patterns of inheritance, frequency of occurrence, risk of recurrence, availability of prenatal diagnosis, associated complications, and some common developmental abnormalities are noted. Inheritance is described as being autosomal recessive (AR), autosomal dominant (AD), X-linked recessive (XLR), X-linked dominant (XLD), multifactorial (MF), or **sporadic** (SP) (i.e., not known to be inherited). In most cases, no specific treatment is available to correct these abnormalities. However, in those cases where treatment is available, it, too, is included in the description.

Achondroplasia   Disproportionately short stature, relatively large head, prominent forehead, depressed nasal bridge, disproportionately short limbs, trident-shaped hand, normal intelligence. *Cause:* Defect in endochondral bone formation, possibly due to a defect in cellular energy production. *Inheritance:* AD. *Incidence:* 5/100,000–15/100,000; recurrence risk for patient's child, 50%. *Prenatal diagnosis:* Available. (*See* Chapter 15, p. 247–248.) *Associated complications:* Spinal cord compression, apnea. *Developmental abnormalities:* Delays in motor milestones, occasional deafness.
References: Elejalde, B.R., deElejalde, M.M., Hamilton, P.R., et al. (1983). Prenatal diagnosis in two pregnancies of an achondroplastic woman. *American Journal of Medical Genetics, 15,* 437–439. Mackler, B., & Shepard, T.H. (1989). Human achondroplasia: Defective mitochondrial oxidative energy metabolism may produce the pathophysiology. *Teratology, 40,* 571–582.
Acquired immunodeficiency syndrome (AIDS)   *See* Chapter 8, pp. 111–136.
ADA deficiency (adenosine deaminase deficiency)   Inherited combined immunodeficiency syndrome in which children have repeated severe infections. *Cause:* Deficiency of the enzyme adenosine deaminase (ADA). *Inheritance:* AR. *Incidence:* Rare; recurrence risk for siblings, 25%. *Prenatal diagnosis:* Available. *Treatment:* ADA enzyme injection. *Associated complications:* Early death from recurrent severe infections; 10% have neurological deficits; failure to thrive, bone abnormalities. *Developmental abnormalities:* Intelligence usually normal.
Reference: Levy, Y., Hershfield, M.S., Fernandez-Mejia, C., et al. (1988). Adenosine deaminase deficiency with late onset of recurrent infections: Response to treatment with polyethylene glycol-modified adenosine deaminase. *Journal of Pediatrics, 113,* 312–317.
Aicardi syndrome   Infantile spasms associated with congenital absence of the corpus callosum and ab-

---

This appendix was revised by Carolyn Bay, M.D., who is in a combined fellowship in Developmental Pediatrics and Genetics at Children's Seashore House and The Children's Hospital of Philadelphia.

normalities of the eyes. *Cause:* Unknown. *Inheritance:* SP. *Incidence:* Rare, occurring only in females; recurrence risk, rare in families. *Prenatal diagnosis:* Not available. *Associated complications:* Poorly controlled seizures. *Developmental abnormalities:* Severe mental retardation, visual impairment.
Reference: Neidich, J.A., Nussbaum, R.L., Packer, R.J., et al. (1990). Heterogeneity of clinical severity and molecular lesions in Aicardi syndrome. *Journal of Pediatrics, 116,* 911–917.

Anencephaly Malformation of the brain due to a defect in the closure of the head portion of the embryonic neural tube. The area above the brain stem is severely malformed; incompatible with prolonged survival. *Cause:* Unknown. *Inheritance:* MF. *Incidence:* 0.5/1,000–10/1,000; recurrence risk for siblings, 2%–5%. *Prenatal diagnosis:* Ultrasound, amniocentesis, measurement of alpha-fetoprotein in amniotic fluid. (*See* Chapter 25, p. 471.) *Associated complications:* Diaphragmatic defects, hypoplasia of lungs and heart. *Developmental abnormalities:* Not compatible with life.
References: Ferguson-Smith, M.A. (1983). The reduction of anencephalic and spina bifida births by maternal serum alphafetoprotein screening. *British Medical Bulletin, 39,* 365–372.
Medical Task Force on Anencephaly. (1990). The infant with anencephaly. *New England Journal of Medicine, 322,* 669–674.

Apert syndrome (Acrocephalosyndactyly, type I) Premature fusion of the sutures of the head so head appears misshapen, often with a high forehead, and flat occiput (back of head); widely spaced, downwardly slanting eyes; flattened nasal bridge and mid facial area; severe syndactyly (webbed hands and feet); 30% have a cleft of the soft palate; crowding of the teeth. *Cause:* Mutation in genes. *Inheritance:* AD. *Incidence:* 1/100,000–1/160,000; recurrence risk to patient's children, 50%. *Prenatal diagnosis:* Fetoscopy. *Treatment:* Surgical correction of sutures may reduce the risk of mental retardation. *Associated complications:* Hydrocephalus, developmental delays, hearing loss. *Developmental abnormalities:* Has been associated with mental retardation, but frequency is unknown.
References: Cohen, M.M., Jr., & Kreiborg, S. (1990). The central nervous system in the Apert syndrome. *American Journal of Medical Genetics, 35,* 36–45.
Leonard, C.O., Daikoku, N.H., & Winn, K. (1982). Prenatal fetoscopic diagnosis of the Apert syndrome. *American Journal of Medical Genetics, 11,* 5–9.

Arthrogryposis multiplex congenita Multiple joint contractures beginning prenatally. *Cause:* Multiple. Most frequently related to an underlying neurological abnormality, but can be caused by abnormalities of muscle or connective tissue, or *in utero* crowding due to the lack of the amniotic fluid or twinning. The limitation in fetal joint mobility results in contractures. *Inheritance:* Depends upon cause. *Incidence:* Unknown. *Prenatal diagnosis:* Unavailable. *Treatment:* Casting of affected joints. *Associated abnormalities:* Cleft palate, ptosis, decreased range of ocular motion, small chin, hernias, scoliosis, defects of abdominal wall. *Developmental abnormalities:* Occasional developmental delay.
Reference: Symposium: Arthrogryposis multiplex congenita. (1985). *Clinical Orthopedics, 194,* 1–123.

Batten disease (Neuronal ceroid lipofuscinosis) Progressive neurodegenerative disease. Child develops normally until 6–18 months of age and then starts to lose motor and cognitive skills. Eventually seizures, mental retardation, and severe visual impairment occur. Fatal outcome. *Cause:* Unknown. *Inheritance:* AR. *Incidence:* 1/100,000; recurrence risk for siblings, 25%. *Prenatal diagnosis:* Available by demonstrating inclusions in the chorionic villi. *Associated complications:* Microcephaly, seizures, behavior problems. *Developmental abnormalities:* Progressive neurological deterioration.
References: Boustany, R.M., Alroy, J., & Kolodny, E.H. (1988). Clinical classification of neuronal ceroid lipofuscinosis subtypes. *American Journal of Medical Genetics, 5,* 47–58.
Dyken, P.R. (1989). The neuronal ceroid lipofuscinoses. *Journal of Child Neurology, 4,* 165–174.

Brachmann-de Lange syndrome *See* Cornelia de Lange syndrome.

Cat cry syndrome *See* Cri-du-chat syndrome.

CHARGE association Coloboma (i.e., failure of normal fusion of ocular structures), Heart defect, Atresia choanae (i.e., membranous or bony blockage of nasal passage), Retarded growth and development, Genital anomalies, and Ear anomalies and/or deafness. *Cause:* Unknown. *Inheritance:* Usually SP. *Incidence:* Unknown; recurrence risk in families, rare. *Prenatal diagnosis:* Unavailable. (*See* Chapter 17, p. 293–294.) *Treatment:* Supportive. *Associated complications:* Hypoplastic genitalia, crypt-orchidism, cleft lip/palate, facial asymetry. *Developmental abnormalities:* Variable degrees of mental retardation, potentially severe visual and auditory impairments.
References: Goldson, E., Smith, A.C., & Stewart, J.M. (1986). The CHARGE association: How well can they do? *American Journal of Diseases of Children, 140,* 918–921.
Metlay, L.A., Smythe, P.S., & Miller, M.E. (1987). Familial CHARGE syndrome: Clinical report with autopsy findings. *American Journal of Medical Genetics, 26,* 577–581.

Cornelia de Lange syndrome (Brachmann-de Lange syndrome) Short stature, microcephaly, characteristic facial appearance including long eyelashes, rounded eyebrows, short nose with triangular shape, long philtrum, thin upper lip, small hands and feet, occasionally phocomelia. *Cause:* Unknown. *Inheritance:* Probable AD. *Incidence:* Approximately 1/10,000; recurrence risk for patient's siblings less than 1% if parents unaffected, 50% for affected patient's children. *Prenatal diagnosis:* Ultrasound. *Associated complications:* Autistic-like behaviors, language delays, gastroesophageal reflux, feeding abnormalities. *Developmental abnormalities:* Speech-language delays, global developmental delays, hearing abnormalities, self-injurious behaviors.

References: Hawley, P.P., Jackson, L.G., & Kurnit, D.M. (1985). Sixty-four patients with Brachmann-deLange syndrome: A survey. *American Journal of Medical Genetics, 20,* 453–459.

Robinson, L.K., Wolfsberg, E., & Jones, K.L. (1985). Brachmann-deLange syndrome: Evidence for autosomal dominant inheritance. *American Journal of Medical Genetics, 22,* 109–115.

Cretinism *See* (Congenital) Hypothyroidism.

Cri-du-chat syndrome Pre- and postnatal growth retardation, cat-like cry in infancy, widely spaced eyes with downward slant, mental retardation, congenital heart defects, microcephaly, simian creases. *Cause:* Partial deletion of short arm of chromosome #5. *Inheritance:* If mother carries a chromosomal abnormality, risk to patient's siblings is 15%–25%; if father carries the translocation, 8%. If parents' chromosomes appear normal, actual risk is unknown, but low. *Incidence:* 1/20,000; recurrence risk, low, unless parent carries a chromosomal translocation or other chromosomal abnormality. *Prenatal diagnosis:* Amniocentesis and chromosome analysis. (*See* Chapter 1, p. 7–8.) *Associated complications:* Severe respiratory and feeding abnormalities in infancy, hypotonia, inguinal hernias. *Developmental abnormalities:* Severe-to-profound mental retardation.

Reference: Wilkins, L.E., Brown, J.A., Nance, W.E., et al. (1983). Clinical heterogeneity in 80 home-reared children with cri-du-chat syndrome. *Journal of Pediatrics, 102,* 528–533.

Down syndrome Hypotonia, flat facial profile, upwardly slanted eyes, small ears, short stature, mental retardation, small nose with low nasal bridge, simian creases, congenital heart disease. *Cause:* Trisomy 21 (94%), mosaicism (2.4%), and translocation (3.6%). *Inheritance:* SP, age-related. *Incidence: See* Chapter 3, Figure 3.1, p. 24. Recurrence risk: in simple trisomy 21, risk to patient's siblings is related to maternal age. If mother is young, 1%–2%; if mother is older, risk is variable. If cause is translocation, risk is higher. *Prenatal diagnosis:* Amniocentesis or chorionic villus sampling and chromosome analysis. (Also, *see* Chapter 3, p. 24–25, 31.) *Associated complications:* Atlantoaxial instability, ligamentous laxity, strabismus, nystagmus, cataracts, glaucoma, seizures, leukemia, thyroid abnormalities, recurrent respiratory tract infections, obesity, depression, inappropriate behavior, premature senility. *Developmental abnormalities:* Mental retardation. Decreased muscle tone tends to improve with age, however ligamentous laxity results in increased range of joint movement. Expressive language delay. Rate of developmental progress slows with age. (*See* Chapter 16, p. 271–278.)

References: Cooley, W.C., & Graham, J.M., Jr. (1991). Common syndromes and management issues for primary care physicians: Down syndrome—An update and review for the primary pediatrician. *Clinical Pediatrics, 30,* 233–253.

Pueschel, S.M. (1990). Clinical aspects of Down syndrome from infancy to adulthood. *American Journal of Medical Genetics, 7*(Suppl.), 52–56.

Duchenne muscular dystrophy (DMD) Progressive pelvic muscle weakness and atrophy, enlargement of thigh muscles, tight heel cords. Patients develop progressive respiratory difficulty, heart failure; often mild mental retardation. Elevated serum creatine kinase. Survival beyond young adulthood is unusual. *Cause:* Mutation in dystrophin gene located on the short arm of X chromosome. *Inheritance:* Usually XLR, rare AR form. *Incidence:* 1/3,300 in United States; recurrence risk, male offspring of XLR carrier mother, 50%. *Prenatal diagnosis:* Following determination of sex of the child by amniocentesis, use of dystrophin cDNA probes for deletion identification and linkage of DMD markers and DMD gene. *Associated complications:* Contractures, scoliosis, wheelchair dependence (usually by age 10–12 years), progressive weakness, pneumonia, EKG abnormalities. *Developmental abnormalities:* Mild mental retardation or learning disabilities, hypotonia, delays in motor milestone achievement. (*See* Chapter 15, pp. 254–256.)

References: Darras, B.T., Koenig, M., Kunkel, L.M., et al. (1988). Direct method for prenatal diagnosis and carrier detection in Duchenne/Becker muscular dystrophy using the entire dystrophin cDNA. *American Journal of Medical Genetics, 29,* 713–726.

Francke, U., Darras, B.T., Hersh, J.H., et al. (1989). Brother/sister pairs affected with early onset, progressive muscular dystrophy: Molecular studies reveal etiologic heterogeneity. *American Journal of Human Genetics, 45,* 63–72.

Hyser, C.L., & Mendell, J.R. (1988). Recent advances in Duchenne and Becker muscular dystrophy. *Neurologic Clinics, 6,* 429–453.

Edwards syndrome *See* Trisomy 18.

Ellis-van Creveld syndrome (Chondroectodermal dysplasia) Disproportionately short stature (final height 43–60 inches), small thorax, extra fingers, neonatal teeth, missing teeth, delayed eruption of teeth, underdeveloped finger nails, heart defect, occasional mental retardation. *Cause:* Unknown. *Inheritance:* AR. *Incidence:* rare; recurrence risk to patient's siblings, 25%. *Prenatal diagnosis:* Possible with ultrasound and/or fetoscopy. *Associated complications:* Severe cardiorespiratory problems in infancy, which can be fatal; hydrocephalus; severe leg deformities. *Developmental abnormalities:* In the 66% that survive the first 6 months of life, mental retardation has been seen occasionally. The majority are of normal intelligence.

Reference: Preti, P., Stilli, S., Donzelli, O., et al. (1991). Ellis Van Creveld syndrome or chondroectodermic dysplasia. *Chirurgia Degli Organi Di Movimento (Surgery on the Organs of Movement), 76,* 87–91.

Fetal alcohol syndrome (Fetal alcohol effects) Pre- and postnatal growth retardation, mild-to-moderate mental retardation, microcephaly, small eyes with droopy eyelids, maxillary hypoplasia, long philtrum, joint abnormalities, congenital heart disease. *Cause:* Maternal ingestion of alcohol during pregnancy, particularly during first trimester. *Inheritance:* Not inherited, but can occur in siblings when mother ingests alcohol during successive pregnancies. *Incidence:* 1% of newborns in western countries. Approximately one-third of infants exposed to chronic alcohol intake prenatally have the disorder. Recurrence risk depends upon maternal ingestion of alcohol during subsequent pregnancies. *Prenatal diagnosis:* Unavailable. (*See* Chapter 8, p. 112–116.) *Associated complications:* Joint contractures, cardiac abnormalities, myopia, strabismus, hearing loss, dental malocclusion, eustachian tube dysfunction. *Developmental abnormalities:* Mental retardation, fine motor dysfunction, poor eye-hand coordination, hyperactivity, distractibility, short attention span, speech delays.

References: Graham, J.M., Jr., Hanson, J.W., Darby, B.L., et al. (1988). Independent dysmorphology evaluations at birth and four years of age for children exposed to varying amounts of alcohol *in utero*. *Pediatrics, 81,* 772–778.

Jones, K.L. (1988). The fetal alcohol syndrome. *Growth Genetics and Hormones, 4*(1) 1–3.

Fetal aminopterin syndrome (Fetal methotrexate syndrome) Prenatal growth deficiency, cranial dysplasia, broad nasal bridge, low-set ears, cleft palate, mental retardation. *Cause:* Maternal ingestion of the chemotherapeutic drug aminopterin or methotrexate during pregnancy. *Inheritance:* Not inherited. *Incidence:* Related to maternal exposure; recurrence risk, related to maternal ingestion of aminopterin. *Prenatal diagnosis:* Unavailable. (*See* Chapter 4, p. 42–44.) *Associated complications:* Hydrocephalus, myelomeningocele, cleft lip and palate, club hands and feet. *Developmental abnormalities:* Mental retardation possible.

References: Aviles, A., Diaz-Maqueo, J.C., Talavera, A., et al. (1991). Growth and development of children of mothers treated with chemotherapy during pregnancy: Current status of 43 children. *American Journal of Hematology, 36,* 243–248.

Kozlowski, R.D., Steinbrunner, J.V., MacKenzie, A.H., et al. (1990). Outcome of first-trimester exposure to low-dose methotrexate in eight patients with rheumatic disease. *American Journal of Medicine, 88,* 589–592.

Fetal Dilantin syndrome Growth deficiency, microcephaly, borderline-to-mild mental retardation, widely spaced eyes, depressed nasal bridge, cleft lip/palate, small or missing fingernails and/or toenails; rib anomalies, congenital heart disease. *Cause:* Maternal ingestion of the antiepileptic drug phenytoin (Dilantin) during pregnancy. *Inheritance:* Not inherited. Evidence suggests a genetic predisposition to teratogenic effects of the drug. *Incidence:* Full expression of syndrome: 10% of exposed infants; partial expression of syndrome: 33% of exposed infants; recurrence risk, related to maternal ingestion. *Prenatal diagnosis:* Unavailable. (*See* Chapter 4, p. 42–44.) *Associated complications:* Cardiac abnormalities, abnormalities of genito-urinary tract and central nervous system. *Developmental abnormalities:* Of children with full fetal effects, average IQ is 71.

References: Buehler, B.A., Delimont, D., van Waes, M., et al. (1990). Prenatal prediction of risk of the fetal hydantoin syndrome. *New England Journal of Medicine, 322,* 1567–1572.

Hansen, D.K. (1991). The embryotoxicity of phenytoin: An update on possible mechanisms. *Proceedings of the Society for Experimental Biology and Medicine, 197,* 361–368.

Fragile X syndrome Hereditary form of mental retardation, most apparent in males, that has been associated with an unusual "fragile" site on the X chromosome. It is thought to be the most common hereditary form of mental retardation in males. Associated physical features include prominent jaw, large ears, large testes, and mild connective tissue abnormalities. (*See* Chapter 16, p. 278–281.) *Cause:* Defect in X chromosome. *Inheritance:* XL. *Incidence:* 1/2,000 male births; slightly less common in females; recurrence risk, depends upon specific family tree. *Prenatal diagnosis:* Analysis of amniotic fluid cells for demonstration of fragile X site. Molecular methods are being researched.

Associated complications: Mental retardation, behavior problems, hyperactivity, autistic features. *Developmental abnormalities:* Mental retardation, pervasive developmental disorder, communication disorder.
References: Reiss, A.L., & Freund, L. (1990). Fragile-X syndrome. *Biological Psychiatry, 27,* 223–240.
Verkerk, A.J., Pieretti, M., Sutcliffe, J.S., et al. (1991). Identification of a gene (FMR-1) containing a CGG repeat coincident with a breakpoint cluster region exhibiting length variation in fragile-X syndrome. *Cell, 65,* 905–914.

Galactosemia Inborn error of metabolism. Children become ill when galactose (i.e., a natural sugar found in milk) is introduced into the diet. Jaundice in newborn period, enlarged liver, vomiting, lethargy, and increased risk of serious infection. Untreated, mortality is high. With dietary treatment, significantly reduced effects. *Cause:* Usually, a deficiency of galactose-1-phosphate uridyl transferase. *Inheritance:* AR. *Incidence:* 1/50,000–1/70,000; recurrence risk to patient's siblings, 25%. *Prenatal diagnosis:* Enzyme analysis of amniotic fluid and newborn screening available. *Treatment:* Galactose-free diet. *Associated complications: E. coli* sepsis, cataracts, failure to thrive, ovarian dysfunction. *Developmental abnormalities:* Difficult psychological adaptation to dietary limitations. In treated cases, IQ can be in normal range; however, IQ of patients is less than unaffected siblings. In patients whose dietary treatment compliance is less, IQs are lower. Abnormal visual perception, cerebellar ataxia, tremors, choreoathetosis.
Reference: Segal, S. (1989). Disorders of galactose metabolism. In C.R. Scriver, A.L. Beaudet, W.S. Sly, & D. Valle (Eds.), *The metabolic basis of inherited disease* (6th ed.) (pp. 453–480). New York: McGraw-Hill.

Hallermann-Streiff syndrome Proportionate short stature, unusual facial appearance with small eyes; cataracts; narrow beaked nose; undeveloped or missing teeth; small mouth; thin hair. *Cause:* Unknown. *Inheritance:* Possibly AD. *Incidence:* Unknown; recurrence risk, depends on genetic form. *Associated complications:* Feeding and respiratory problems, dental abnormalities. *Developmental abnormalities:* Decreased visual acuity, motor deficits, mental retardation.
Reference: Ryan, C.F., Lowe, A.A., & Fleetham, J.A. (1990). Nasal continuous positive airway pressure (CPAP) therapy for obstructive sleep apnea in Hallermann-Streiff syndrome. *Clinical Pediatrics, 29,* 122–124.

Homocystinuria Inborn error of metabolism associated with mental retardation, dislocated lenses, and increased risk of stroke. *Cause:* Deficiency of the enzyme Cystathionine beta-synthase. *Inheritance:* AR. *Incidence:* Less than 1/100,000; recurrence risk to patient's siblings, 25%. *Prenatal diagnosis:* Amniocentesis or chorionic villus sampling and enzyme analysis. *Treatment:* Pyridoxine (Vitamin B_6) and betaine. *Associated complications:* Skeletal abnormalities, osteoporosis, dislocation of optic lens, intravascular blood clots. *Developmental abnormalities:* One-third to three-fourths of untreated patients have mild or moderate mental retardation. Intelligence in treated individuals is markedly better, especially in those who respond to vitamin B_6.
References: Cacciari, E., & Salardi, S. (1989). Clinical and laboratory features of homocystinuria. *Haemeostasis, 19*(Suppl. 1), 10–13.
Mudd, S.H., Levy, H.L., & Skovby, F. (1989). Disorders of transsulfuration. In C.R. Scriver, A.L. Beaudet, W.S. Sly, & D. Valle (Eds.), *The metabolic basis of inherited disease* (6th ed.) (pp. 698–699). New York: McGraw-Hill.

Huntington disease (Huntington chorea) Choreic movement disorder and progressive neurological disease with dementia. Usual age of onset is 35–40 years, but it can present in juvenile onset form or as late as 60–65 years. Juvenile onset form is 3–5 times as likely to occur when gene is passed from father to child, and more likely to involve rigidity. *Cause:* Unknown. *Inheritance:* AD. *Incidence:* 1/18,000; recurrence risk to patient's child, 50%. *Prenatal diagnosis:* Unavailable. *Associated complications:* Joint contractures, swallowing dysfunction, depression. *Developmental abnormalities:* Patients with juvenile onset may have progressive neurological deterioration, seizures, speech abnormalities
References: Clarke, D.J., & Bundey, S. (1990). Very early onset Huntington's disease: Genetic mechanism and risk to siblings. *Clinical Genetics, 38,* 180–186.
Morris, M.J., Tyler, A., Lazarou, L., et al. (1989). Problems in genetic prediction for Huntington's disease. *Lancet, 2,* 601–603.

Hurler syndrome (Mucopolysaccharidosis I-H) Inborn error of mucopolysaccharide metabolism. Short stature, progressive mental retardation, coarse facial appearance, full lips, flat nasal bridge, clouded corneas, liver and spleen enlargement, bony abnormalities of spine and limbs. Cell, tissue, and organ dysfunction. Life span usually does not exceed 10 years. *Cause:* Deficiency of enzyme alpha iduronidase. *Inheritance:* AR. *Incidence:* 1/100,000; recurrence risk to patient's siblings, 25%. *Prenatal diagnosis:* Amniocentesis or chorionic villus sampling and enzyme analysis. *Associated complications:* Visual and hearing deficits, progressive joint limitation, kyphosis, hernias, progressive cardiac failure. *Developmental abnormalities:* Motor and mental development usually peak at 2 years of age and then deteriorate.

References: Kleijer, W.J., Thompson, E.J., & Niermeijer, M.F. (1983). Prenatal diagnosis of the Hurler syndrome: Report on 40 pregnancies at risk. *Prenatal Diagnosis, 3,* 179–186.

Neufeld, E.F., & Muenzer, J. (1989). The mucopolysaccharidoses. In C.R. Scriver, A.L. Beaudet, W.S. Sly, & D. Valle (Eds.), *The metabolic basis of inherited disease* (6th ed.) (pp. 1565–1588). New York: McGraw-Hill.

(Congenital) Hyperammonemia   Group of inborn errors of metabolism presenting with vomiting, lethargy, and coma in newborn period or early childhood. If untreated, infants die or have mental retardation. *Cause:* Defect in one of the five urea cycle enzymes, leading to buildup of ammonia. *Inheritance:* AR (except ornithine transcarbamylase enzyme deficiency (OTC), which is XLR). *Incidence:* 1/30,000; recurrence risk to patient's siblings, 25%, except OTC, which is 50% for patient's male siblings and 50% risk of female siblings being carriers of the gene. *Prenatal diagnosis:* Enzyme analysis of cells from amniotic fluid or DNA studies. (*See* Chapter 10, pp. 164–165.) *Treatment:* Protein restriction and arginine supplements with sodium benzoate/sodium phenylacetate therapy. *Associated complications:* Coma and death. *Developmental abnormalities:* Mental retardation, cerebral palsy.

References: Batshaw, M.L. (1984). Hyperammonemia. *Current Problems in Pediatrics, 14*(11), 1–69.

Msall, M., Batshaw, M.L., Suss, R., et al. (1984). Neurologic outcome of children with inborn errors of urea synthesis. *New England Journal of Medicine, 310,* 1500–1505.

(Congenital) Hypothyroidism (Cretinism)   Hoarse cry, large for gestational age, large tongue, umbilical hernia, floppy tone, mental retardation. *Causes:* Can be a primary defect in development of thyroid gland, an inborn error of metabolism, or an abnormality of the pituitary gland or hypothalamus. *Incidence:* 1/4,000; recurrence risk, depends on cause. *Prenatal diagnosis:* Unavailable, but newborn screening is available. (*See* Chapter 10, p. 161.) *Treatment:* Thyroid hormone supplementation. *Associated complications:* Mental retardation, growth retardation, delayed bone and dental maturation. *Developmental abnormalities:* If treatment is initiated prior to 6 weeks of age, intellect is normal in 95% of cases. If treatment is delayed beyond 1 year, 10% or less will have normal intelligence.

References: Dumont, J.E., Vassart, G., & Refetoff, S. (1989). Thyroid disorders. In C.R. Scriver, A.L. Beaudet, W.S. Sly, & D. Valle (Eds.), *The metabolic basis of inherited disease* (6th ed.) (pp. 1843–1879). New York: McGraw-Hill.

New England Congenital Hypothyroidism Collaborative. (1990). Elementary school performance of children with congenital hypothyroidism. *Journal of Pediatrics, 116,* 27–32.

Kernicterus   Mental retardation, choreoathetoid cerebral palsy, staining of secondary teeth, upward gaze paralysis, high-frequency hearing loss. *Cause:* Excessive levels of bilirubin in infant's blood that pass to the central nervous system; underlying problem is usually Rh incompatibility. *Inheritance:* Depends upon cause. *Incidence:* Since the initiation of Rho GAM therapy and medical management of hyperbilirubinemia, extremely low; recurrence risk depends on cause and management. *Prenatal diagnosis:* Measurement of level of bilirubin in amniotic fluid. (*See* Chapter 6, p. 83–84.) *Associated complications:* Spastic quadriplegia, deafness. *Developmental abnormalities:* Severe mental retardation, cerebral palsy, hearing impairment.

References: Chowdhury, R.J., & Arias, I.M. (1986). Disorders of bilirubin conjugation. In J.D. Ostrow (Ed.), *Bile pigments and jaundice* (pp. 317–332). New York: Marcel Dekker.

Connolly, A.M., & Volpe, J.J. (1990). Clinical features of bilirubin encephalopathy. *Clinics in Perinatology, 17,* 371–379.

Ketotic hyperglycinemia   *See* Methylmalonic aciduria, propionic acidemia.

Klinefelter syndrome (XXY syndrome)   Low-to-normal intelligence, long limbs, thin appearance, small penis and testes, gynecomastia, infertility, behavior problems. *Cause:* Chromosomal nondisjunction, resulting in 47,XXY constitution. *Inheritance:* Due to nondisjunction. *Incidence:* 1/500 liveborn males; recurrence risk to patient's siblings, ≤ 1%. *Prenatal diagnosis:* Amniocentesis or chorionic villus sampling and chromosome analysis. (*See* Chapter 2, p. 20.) *Associated complications:* Inadequate testosterone production, diabetes mellitus, scoliosis, infertility, behavior problems. *Developmental abnormalities:* Psychological and psychiatric abnormalities, 15%–20% of patients have IQs below 80, delays in language acquisition and articulation.

References: Stewart, D.A., Netley, C.T., & Park, E. (1982). Summary of clinical findings of children with 47,XXY, 47,XYY, and 47,XXX karyotypes. *Birth Defects, 18,* 1–5.

Theilgaard, A. (1984). A psychological study of the personalities of XYY- and XXY-men. *Acta Psychiatrica Scandinavica, 315*(Suppl.), 1–133.

Laurence-Moon-Biedl syndrome   Retinitis pigmentosa, hypogenitalism, obesity, and extra fingers and toes. *Cause:* Inherited failure of normal embryonic development. *Incidence:* Rare; recurrence risk to siblings, 25%. *Associated complications:* Ataxic gait. *Developmental abnormalities:* Mental retardation, night blindness, spastic paraplegia.

References: Green, J.S., Parfrey, P.S., Harnett, J.D., et al. (1989). The cardinal manifestations of Bardet-Biedl syndrome, a form of Laurence-Moon-Biedl syndrome. *New England Journal of Medicine, 321,* 1002–1009.

Leber congenital amaurosis   Congenital nystagmus and severely impaired vision detected in infancy. Ophthalmologic exam reveals optic atrophy with progressive pigmentary changes of the retina. *Cause:* Abnormality of rod and cone receptors in the retina, probably resulting from a defect in mitochondrial DNA. *Inheritance:* Mitochondrial. *Incidence:* Rare, but represents about 10%–15% of children in institutions for the blind; recurrence risk, all siblings may be affected. *Prenatal diagnosis:* May be possible by detecting abnormalities in mitochondrial DNA. *Treatment:* Rehabilitation for visual impairment and other developmental disabilities. *Associated complications:* Visual acuity ranging from finger counting at a few feet to no light perception. There may be progressive worsening of vision. Cataracts may develop. Microphthalmia is common, and MRI scan often shows cerebral atrophy. *Developmental abnormalities:* Blindness. Mental retardation and muscular hypotonia also have been found in one-fourth to one-half of cases. Self-injurious behavior in the form of eye gouging may be present.

References: Schroeder, R., Mets, M.B., & Maumenee, I.H. (1987). Leber's congenital amaurosis: Retrospective review of 43 cases and a new fundus finding in two cases. *Archives of Ophthalmology, 105,* 356–359.

Brown, M.D., Voljavec, A.S., Lott, M.T., et al. (1992). Mitochondrial DNA complex I and III mutation associated with Leber's hereditary optic neuropathy. *Genetics, 130,* 163–173.

Lesch-Nyhan syndrome (Lesch-Nyhan disease)   Progressive neurological disorder, self-injurious behavior, mental retardation, progressive choreoathetoid cerebral palsy, hyperuricemia (i.e., excessive uric acid in blood). *Cause:* Deficiency of enzyme HGPRT necessary for **purine** metabolism. *Inheritance:* XLR. *Incidence:* 1/100,000; recurrence risk to siblings, 50% for males. *Prenatal diagnosis:* Amniocentesis or chorionic villus sampling and enzyme analysis. *Associated complications:* Urinary uric acid stones, kidney disease, mild anemia, arthritis, dysphasia, vomiting. *Developmental abnormalities:* Cerebral palsy, mental retardation, self-mutilation.

References: Christie, R., Bay, C., Kaufman, I.A., et al. (1982). Lesch-Nyhan disease: Clinical experience with 19 patients. *Developmental Medicine and Child Neurology, 24,* 293–306.

Gibbs, D.A., McFadyen, I.R., Crawford, M.D., et al. (1984). First trimester diagnosis of Lesch-Nyhan syndrome. *Lancet, 2,* 1180–1183.

Lowe syndrome (Oculo-cerebro-renal syndrome)   Boys with bilateral cataracts at birth, physical and mental retardation, and hypotonia. Biochemical findings include renal tubular dysfunction with proteinuria, glucosuria, metabolic acidosis, aminoaciduria. *Cause:* Unknown. *Inheritance:* XLR. *Incidence:* Undetermined; recurrence risk in siblings, 50% for males. *Prenatal diagnosis:* Possible with DNA analysis. *Associated complications:* Kidney stones, glaucoma, growth failure, rickets. *Developmental abnormalities:* Visual impairment, mental retardation, hypotonia.

Reference: Tripathi, R.C. (1986). Lowe's syndrome. *Birth Defects: Original Articles Series, 18,* 629–644.

Maple syrup urine disease   An inborn error of amino acid metabolism presenting with vomiting, lethargy, and coma in the first week of life. Urine smells like maple syrup. If untreated, leads to mental retardation or death. *Cause:* Enzyme deficiency affecting branched chain amino acids. *Inheritance:* AR. *Incidence:* 1/125,000; recurrence risk to patient's siblings, 25%. *Prenatal diagnosis:* Amniocentesis or chorionic villus sampling and enzyme analysis. (*See* Chapter 10, p. 163–164.) *Treatment:* Diet low in branched chain amino acids. *Associated complications:* Acidosis, low blood sugar. *Developmental abnormalities:* With early diagnosis and meticulous medical management, intellectual outcome can be normal. Degree of mental retardation depends upon onset of dietary therapy.

References: Clow, C.L., Reade, T.M., & Scriver, C.R. (1981). Outcome of early and long-term management of classical maple syrup urine disease. *Pediatrics, 68,* 856–862.

Kaplan, P., Mazur, A., Field, M., et al. (1991). Intellectual outcome in children with maple syrup urine disease. *Journal of Pediatrics, 119,* 46–50.

Marfan syndrome   Tall, thin stature, spider-like limbs, hypermobile joints, dislocation of lens, aortic aneurysm, usually normal intelligence. *Cause:* Possibly an abnormality in the fibrillin gene. *Inheri-*

tance: AD. *Incidence:* 1/10,000; recurrence risk to patient's children, 50%. *Prenatal diagnosis:* Currently unavailable, but molecular studies in progress. *Associated complications:* Joint instability, thoracic deformities, loss of vision. *Developmental abnormalities:* Attention deficit hyperactivity disorder, learning disabilities.

References: Lee, B., Godfrey, M., Vitale, E., et al. (1991). Linkage or Marfan syndrome and a phenotypically related disorder to two different fibrillin genes. *Nature, 353,* 330–334.

Sun, Q.B., Zhang, K.Z., Cheng, T.O., et al. (1990). Marfan syndrome in China: A collective review of 564 cases among 98 families. *American Heart Journal, 120,* 934–948.

Meningomyelocele *See* Spina bifida; Chapter 25, pp. 471–488.

Menkes syndrome Small for gestational age; progressive neurological disorder; sparse, abnormal hair; profound mental retardation; bony abnormalities with tendency to fracture easily. *Cause:* Defective uptake or transport of copper that may be due to an abnormality of cytochrome c oxidase. *Inheritance:* XLR. *Incidence:* 3/100,000; recurrence risk to patient's siblings, 50% of males. *Prenatal diagnosis:* Possible. *Associated complications:* Developmental regression, severe visual abnormalities, 12% live to 2 years of age. *Developmental abnormalities:* Progressive neurological deterioration, severe mental retardation.

References: Horn, N. (1983). Menkes' X-linked disease: Prenatal diagnosis and carrier detection. *Journal of Inherited Metabolic Disease, 6*(Suppl. 1), 59–62.

DiMauro, S., Lombes, A., Nakase, H., et al. (1990). Cytochrome c oxidase deficiency. *Pediatric Research, 28,* 536–541.

Metachromatic leukodystrophy Progressive neurological disorder, profound mental retardation, loss of reflexes. Rapidly fatal. *Cause:* Deficiency of enzyme: arylsulfatase A. (*See* Chapter 10.) *Inheritance:* Usually AR. *Incidence:* 1/40,000; recurrence risk to patient's siblings, 25%. *Prenatal diagnosis:* Amniocentesis or chorionic villus sampling and enzyme analysis. *Associated complications:* Progressive loss of motor function, urinary tract infections, pneumonia. *Developmental abnormalities:* Progressive neurological degeneration, mental retardation.

Reference: Kolodny, E.H. (1989). Metachromatic leukodystrophy and mutiple sulfatase deficiency: Sulfatide lipidosis. In C.R. Scriver, A.L. Beaudet, W.S. Sly, & D. Valle (Eds.), *The metabolic basis of inherited disease* (6th ed.) (pp. 1721–1750). New York: McGraw-Hill.

Methylmalonic aciduria Inborn error of organic acid metabolism leading to an abnormal accumulation of methylmalonic acid. If untreated, results in repeated episodes of vomiting, lethargy, and coma associated with acidosis. *Cause:* Deficiency of enzyme methymalonyl CoA mutase, or defect in cobalamin metabolism. *Inheritance:* AR. *Incidence:* Unknown, over 100 known cases; recurrence risk to patient's siblings, 25%. *Prenatal diagnosis:* Amniocentesis or chorionic villus sampling and enzyme analysis. *Treatment:* Protein-restricted special diet. Some patients have an enzyme defect which responds to vitamin B_{12}. In these families, prenatal treatment of mother also has been useful. Prompt treatment of infections is important. *Associated complications:* Neutropenia, osteoporosis, infections, feeding abnormalities. *Developmental abnormalities:* Mental retardation, particularly in persons with poor dietary control or frequent episodes of ketoacidosis; feeding problems.

References: Nyhan, W.L. (1987). *Diagnostic recognition of genetic disease.* Philadelphia: Lea & Febiger.

Rosenberg, L.E., & Fenton, W.A. (1989). Disorders of propionate and methylmalonate metabolism. In C.R. Scriver, A.L. Beaudet, W.S. Sly, & D. Valle (Eds.), *The metabolic basis of inherited disease* (6th ed.) (pp. 821–844). New York: McGraw-Hill.

Muscular dystrophy *See* Duchenne muscular dystrophy.

Neurofibromatosis (type I) (Von Recklinghausen disease) Multiple "cafe-au-lait" spots on body; nerve tumors (neurofibromas) in body and on skin. If these tumors form in critical areas, they can cause serious disability or death. There is considerable variation in the expression of the gene. Some family members are significantly disfigured, others may have only spots. Intelligence is usually normal. (Note: Type II is associated with tumors of only the auditory nerve.) *Cause:* Mutation. *Inheritance:* AD, now linked to chromosome #17. *Incidence:* 1/3,000; recurrence risk to patient's children, 50%. *Prenatal diagnosis:* Unavailable. *Associated complications:* Optic gliomas, glaucoma, macrocephaly, hypertension. *Developmental abnormalities:* Slight increase in mental retardation, learning disabilities.

References: Fountain, J.W., Wallace, M.R., Bruce, M.A., et al. (1989). Physical mapping of a translocation breakpoint in neurofibromatosis. *Science, 244,* 1085–1087.

Riccardi, V.M., & Eichner, M.E. (1986). *Neurofibromatosis: Phenotype, natural history and pathogenesis.* Baltimore: Johns Hopkins University Press.

Noonan syndrome Short stature, congenital heart defects, webbed neck, widely spaced downwardly

slanting eyes, low-set ears, chest deformity. Predictable changes in appearance with age. Females resemble individuals with Turner syndrome. *Cause:* Unknown. *Inheritance:* AD. *Incidence:* 1/1,000– 1/2,500; recurrence risk to patient's children, 50%. *Prenatal diagnosis:* Unavailable. *Associated complications:* Coagulation defects, cryptorchidism. *Developmental abnormalities:* Mild mental retardation, motor delays, perceptual motor abnormalities, hearing loss, articulation defects.
Reference: Allanson, J.E., Hall, J.G., Hughes, H.E., et al. (1985). Noonan syndrome: The changing phenotype. *American Journal of Medical Genetics, 21,* 507–514.

Osteogenesis imperfecta   Increased susceptibility to fractures that result in bony deformities, blue-colored sclera, and translucent skin; normal intelligence; possible hearing impairment. X rays show thin bones. Four distinct types. *Cause:* Underlying abnormality in the formation of collagen. (*See* Chapter 15.) *Inheritance:* Usually AD, some AR families. *Incidence:* 1/30,000; recurrence risk to patient's children in AD type, 50%. *Prenatal diagnosis:* In congenital onset, X rays of the fetus show multiple fractures; research using molecular analyses of collagen DNA underway. *Associated complications:* Multiple bone fractures, tendon abnormalities, increased capillary fragility, neurological dysfunction, short stature. *Developmental abnormalities:* Deafness.
References: Marini, J.C. (1988). Osteogenesis imperfecta: Comprehensive management. *Advances in Pediatrics, 35,* 391–426.
Sillence, D.O. (1988). Osteogenesis imperfecta: Nosology and genetics. *Annals of the New York Academy of Sciences, 543,* 1–15.
Tsipouras, P., Schwartz, R.C., Goldberg, J.D., et al. (1987). Prenatal prediction of osteogenesis imperfecta type IV: Exclusion of inheritance using a collagen gene probe. *American Journal of Medical Genetics, 24,* 406–409.

Osteopetrosis   Bone becomes dense and sclerotic, leading to thickening of skull and long bones. The head enlarges. Bone marrow is encroached upon, resulting in anemia. Most children have died young. *Cause:* Congenital abnormality of osteoclast cells and therefore failure of resorption of bone. *Inheritance:* AR. *Incidence:* Very rare. Less than 100 cases have been reported; recurrence risk to patient's siblings, 25%. *Prenatal diagnosis:* X rays reveal sclerotic skeletal system. *Treatment:* Bone marrow transplantation has improved prognosis. *Associated complications:* Entrapment of cranial nerves, anemia, growth delay. *Developmental abnormalities:* Blindness, deafness, mental retardation.
Reference: Bollerslev, J. (1987). Osteopetrosis: A genetic and epidemiologic study. *Clinical Genetics, 31,* 86–90.

Pendred syndrome   The combination of thyroid goiter and moderate-to-profound sensorineural hearing loss. *Cause:* Inherited. *Inheritance:* AR. *Incidence:* 0.07/1,000; recurrence risk to siblings, 25%. *Treatment:* Thyroid hormone, possible surgery to remove goiter. *Associated complications:* Hypothyroidism. *Developmental abnormalities:* Congenital deafness, developmental delay.
Reference: Johnsen, T., Larsen, C., Friis, J., et al. (1987). Pendred's syndrome. Acoustic, vestibular and radiological findings in 17 unrelated patients. *Journal of Laryngology and Otology, 101,* 1187– 1192.

Phenylketonuria (PKU)   Inborn error of amino acid metabolism presenting with mental retardation. Untreated patients often have blond hair and blue eyes; hyperactivity. *Cause:* Deficiency of enzyme phenylalanine hydroxylase, located on chromosome #12. *Inheritance:* AR. *Incidence:* 1/15,000; recurrence risk to patient's siblings, 25%. *Prenatal diagnosis:* Possible using cDNA probes and assessment of restriction fragment length polymorphisms (RFLPs) if family is informative. Newborn screening usually identifies affected individuals if they have received protein in their diet. *Treatment:* Dietary restriction of phenylalanine. (Note: women with PKU who are not on phenylalanine-restricted diets are at risk for having children with mental retardation and other abnormalities.) (*See* Chapter 10, p. 162–163.) *Associated complications:* Microcephaly, hand posturing, seizures. *Developmental abnormalities:* Mental retardation; however, with a low phenylalanine diet beginning in infancy, intelligence is normal.
References: Hanley, W.B., Clarke, J.T., & Schoonheyt, W. (1987). Maternal phenylketonuria—A review. *Clinical Biochemistry, 20,* 149–156.
Scriver, C.R., Kaufman, S., & Woo, S.L.C. (1989). The hyperphenylalaninemias. In C.R. Scriver, A.L. Beaudet, W.S. Sly, & D. Valle (Eds.), *The metabolic basis of inherited disease* (6th ed.) (pp. 495–546). New York: McGraw-Hill.
Waisbren, S.E., Mahon, B.E., Schnell, R.R., et al. (1987). Predictors of intelligence quotient and intelligence quotient change in persons treated for phenylketonuria early in life. *Pediatrics, 79,* 351–355.

Prader-Willi syndrome   Severe obesity, mental retardation, small hands and feet, small genitalia. In infancy, problems with poor tone, feeding, and body temperature control. With time, tone improves, but obesity follows. Short stature, behavioral abnormalities. *Cause:* Over 50% have a deletion of chromosome #15. *Inheritance:* Usually SP, but rare AR forms. *Incidence:* 1/15,000; recurrence risk, 0.1%. *Prenatal diagnosis:* Genetic counseling. *Associated complications:* Feeding problems in infancy, scoliosis, diabetes mellitus in second decade. *Developmental abnormalities:* Mental retardation, behavior problems.

References: Butler, M.G. (1990). Prader-Willi syndrome: Current understanding of cause and diagnosis. *American Journal of Medical Genetics, 35,* 319–332.

Casamassima, A.C., Shapiro, L.R., Wilmot, P.L., et al. (1991). Prader-Willi syndrome and Robertsonian translocations involving chromosome 15. *Clinical Genetics, 39,* 294–297.

Knoll, J.H., Nicholls, R.D., Magenis, R.E., et al. (1989). Angelman and Prader-Willi syndromes share a common chromosome 15 deletion but differ in parental origin of the deletion. *American Journal of Medical Genetics, 32,* 285–290.

Propionic acidemia Inborn error of organic acid metabolism. Recurrent episodes of vomiting, lethargy, and coma. Intelligence is often impaired. *Cause:* Deficiency of enzyme propionyl CoA carboxylase. *Inheritance:* AR. *Incidence:* Unknown, but rare; recurrence risk to patient's siblings, 25%. *Prenatal diagnosis:* Amniocentesis or chorionic villus sampling and enzyme analysis. *Treatment:* Special dietary protein restriction. Some patients respond to biotin supplementation. *Associated complications:* Recurrent episodes of metabolic coma. *Developmental abnormalities:* For those that survive, developmental delays usual.

References: Nyhan, W.L. (1987). Propionic acidemia. In W.L. Nyhan (Ed.), *Diagnostic recognition of genetic disease* (pp. 36–41). Philadelphia: Lea & Febiger.

Wolf, B., Hsia, Y.E., Sweetman, L., et al. (1981). Propionic acidemia: A clinical update. *Journal of Pediatrics, 99,* 835–846.

Respiratory distress syndrome (RDS) Respiratory failure resulting from inadequate surfactant production in preterm infants; leads to lack of expansion of alveoli and poor gas exchange. Mechanical ventilation is often needed. *Cause: See* Chapter 7. *Inheritance:* SP. *Incidence:* 20% of premature infants; recurrence risk, greater than normal of having a second premature infant. *Prenatal diagnosis:* Amniocentesis can reveal lung maturity. *Associated complications:* Bronchopulmonary dysplasia. *Developmental abnormalities:* Same as prematurity.

Reference: Piekkala, P., Kero, P., Sillanpaa, M., et al. (1987). Growth and development of infants surviving respiratory distress syndrome: A two-year follow up. *Pediatrics, 79,* 529–537.

Retinitis pigmentosa A group of diseases associated with retinal degeneration and progressive blindness; starts with night blindness in adolescence or adult life. *Cause:* Unknown. *Inheritance:* AR in 30%–40% of cases; AD and XLR also seen. *Incidence:* 1/2,000–1/7,000; recurrence risk, depends upon cause. *Prenatal diagnosis:* Unavailable. *Associated complications:* Myopia, cataracts, hearing loss. *Developmental abnormalities:* Impairment of visual fields and abnormal night vision, progressing to blindness.

Reference: Pagon, R.A. (1988). Retinitis pigmentosa. *Survey of Ophthalmology, 33,* 137–177.

Reye syndrome Acute **encephalopathy** following viral illness. Fatality rate: 40%. Reversible liver abnormalities and blood clotting disturbance, brain swelling. *Cause:* Virus and toxin; aspirin implicated. *Incidence:* Less than 1/100,000; recurrence risk, low. *Associated complications:* In severe cases, neurological abnormalities. *Developmental abnormalities:* Depends upon severity of illness.

Reference: Glasgow, J.F. (1984). Clinical features and prognosis of Reye's syndrome. *Archives of Disease in Childhood, 59,* 230–235.

(Congenital) Rubella syndrome Intrauterine growth retardation, mental retardation, microcephaly, cataracts, sensorineural hearing loss, chorioretinitis, congenital heart disease. *Cause:* Maternal infection with rubella prior to 17th week of gestation. *Inheritance:* Not inherited. *Incidence:* 1/10,000 in areas where vaccination is widely administered; higher in unvaccinated populations. *Prenatal diagnosis:* Amniocentesis has been used but has not always been successful in distinguishing infected and uninfected fetuses at risk. (*See* Chapter 4, p. 45–46.) *Associated complications:* Glaucoma, cataracts, hematological problems. Mortality is high if patient has thrombocytopenic purpura in newborn period; diabetes mellitus. *Developmental abnormalities:* Mental retardation, cerebral palsy.

Reference: Miller, E., Cradock-Watson, J.E., & Pollock, T.M. (1982). Consequences of confirmed maternal rubella at successive stages of pregnancy. *Lancet, II,* 781–784.

Rubinstein-Taybi syndrome Short stature, downwardly slanting eyes, large beaked nose, very broad thumbs, large toes, mental retardation, microcephaly. *Cause:* Unknown. *Inheritance:* SP. *Incidence:* 1/33,000; recurrence risk to patient's siblings, 1%. *Prenatal diagnosis:* Unavailable. *Associated complications:* Abnormal glucose tolerance, foot abnormalities, coloboma of eyes, large tongue. *Devel-*

opmental abnormalities: Motor and language delays; 80% have moderate-to-severe mental retardation. *Reference:* Berry, A.C. (1987). Rubinstein-Taybi syndrome. *Journal of Medical Genetics, 24,* 562–566.

Sotos syndrome (Cerebral gigantism)   Prenatal onset of excessive size, large head with prominent forehead, widely spaced eyes, prominent, narrow jaw, coarse facial appearance, bone age appropriate for height age, enlarged ventricles. *Cause:* Unknown. *Inheritance:* SP or AD. *Incidence:* Rare; recurrence risk to patient's siblings, usually low; however, rare AD forms carry additional risk. *Prenatal diagnosis:* Unavailable. *Associated complications:* Thyroid abnormalities, EEG abnormalities. *Developmental abnormalities:* Poor fine motor coordination, moderate-to-severe mental retardation. *Reference:* Cole, T.R., & Hughes, H.E. (1990). Sotos syndrome. *Journal of Medical Genetics, 27,* 571–576.

Spina bifida (Myelomeningocele)   Incomplete closure of the embryonic neural tube that results in a defect of the spine and paralysis below the level of the lesion. Hydrocephalus. *Cause:* Unknown, however vitamin supplementation in early pregnancy has reduced prevalence. *Inheritance:* MF. *Incidence:* 1/500–1/2,000 live births; recurrence risk to patient's siblings, 2%–5%. *Prenatal diagnosis:* Ultrasound, amniocentesis, and measurement of alpha-fetoprotein in the amniotic fluid. (*See* Chapter 25, p. 473–474.) *Associated complications:* Depending upon the level of the lesion: neurogenic bladder; cranial nerve abnormalities; orthopedic abnormalities, including scoliosis. *Developmental abnormalities:* Mental retardation or learning disabilities common.

References: Charney, E.B., Weller, S.C., Sutton, L.N., et al. (1985). Management of the newborn with myelomeningocele: Time for a decision-making process. *Pediatrics, 75,* 58–64.

Milunsky, A., Jick, H., Jick, S.S., et al. (1989). Multivitamin/folic acid supplementation in early pregnancy reduces the prevalence of neural tube defects. *Journal of American Medical Association, 262,* 2847–2852.

Spinal-muscular atrophy (Werdnig-Hoffman syndrome)   Progressive respiratory failure and severe muscle weakness in infancy. Normal intelligence. Survival is unusual past 2 years of age. *Inheritance:* AR. *Incidence:* 4/100,000 in northeast England; recurrence risk to patient's siblings, 25% for AR forms. *Prenatal diagnosis:* Unavailable. *Treatment:* Supportive. *Associated complications:* Contractures, cardiomyopathy, respiratory infections, scoliosis. *Developmental abnormalities:* Infantile forms are incompatible with prolonged survival; however, juvenile forms are compatible with survival but require aggressive physical therapy and orthopedic care. These children usually have normal intelligence.

Reference: Wessel, H.B. (1989). Spinal muscular atrophy. *Pediatric Annals, 18,* 421–427.

Sturge-Weber syndrome   Tumor composed of blood vessels over half of face and in brain, intracranial calcifications, seizures. *Inheritance:* SP. *Incidence:* Unknown, rare; recurrence risk to patient's siblings, unknown. *Prenatal diagnosis:* Unavailable. *Associated complications:* Progressive problems. Hemiplegia on the side opposite the facial "stain." *Developmental abnormalities:* Mental retardation. *Reference:* Enjolras, O., Riche, M.C., & Merland, J.J. (1985). Facial port-wine stains and Sturge-Weber syndrome. *Pediatrics, 76,* 48–51.

Sudden infant death syndrome (SIDS)   Infant is found lifeless in crib after being well when going to sleep. *Cause:* Unknown, although in rare cases, inborn errors of metabolism have been found. *Inheritance:* Not inherited except in cases of inborn errors, which are AR. *Incidence:* 1/1,000–2/1,000; occurs primarily in premature infants during first 6 months of life. *Prenatal diagnosis:* Not available. *Associated complications:* Death, or brain injury resulting from anoxia. *Developmental abnormalities:* Cognitive and motor deficits.

Reference: Goyco, P.G., & Beckerman, R.C. (1990). Sudden infant death syndrome. *Current Problems in Pediatrics, 20,* 297–346.

Tay-Sachs disease   Progressive nervous system disorder, deafness, blindness, seizures. Rapidly fatal, usually by 4 years of age. *Cause:* Deficiency of enzyme hexosaminidase A. *Inheritance:* AR. *Incidence:* 1/3,800 in Ashkenazic Jews; recurrence risk to patient's siblings, 25%. *Prenatal diagnosis:* Carrier blood testing, and measurement of enzyme in fetal cells obtained by chorionic villus sampling or amniocentesis. (*See* Chapter 2, p. 13–16.) *Associated complications:* Feeding abnormalities, aspiration. *Developmental abnormalities:* Progressive neurological deterioration.

References: Myerowitz, R., & Costigan, F.C. (1988). The major defect in Ashkenazi Jews with Tay-Sachs disease is an insertion in the gene for the alpha chain of beta hexosaminidase. *Journal of Biological Chemistry, 263,* 18587–18589.

Neufeld, E.F. (1989). Natural history and inherited disorders of a lysosomal enzyme, beta-hexosaminidase. *Journal of Biological Chemistry, 264,* 10927–10930.

(Fetal) Thalidomide syndrome   Phocomelia (shortened limbs). *Cause:* Maternal ingestion of thalidomide during sensitive period of embryonic development in first trimester of pregnancy. *Inheritance:* Not inherited. *Incidence:* Thalidomide no longer available for use by pregnant women; recurrence risk, related to maternal ingestion. (*See* Chapter 4, Figure 4.5, p. 43.) *Associated complications:* Deafness; blindness; congenital defects of heart, kidneys, gastrointestinal tract, and reproductive organs. *Developmental abnormalities:* Usually normal intelligence.

Reference: Newman, C.G. (1985). Teratogen update: Clinical aspects of thalidomide embryopathy— A continuing preoccupation. *Teratology, 32,* 133–144.

Torsion dystonia (Dystonia musculorum deformans) Progressive involuntary movement disorder, normal intelligence. *Inheritance:* AD or AR. *Incidence:* 1/20,000 in Ashkenazic population; recurrence risk for offspring of patients with AD form, 50%; to siblings of patients with AR form, 25%. *Prenatal diagnosis:* Unavailable. (*See* Chapter 15, p. 256–257.) *Associated complications:* Contractures in affected limbs. *Developmental abnormalities:* Patients have normal intelligence; progressive motor abnormalities.

Reference: Wachtel, R.C., Batshaw, M.L., Eldridge, R., et al. (1982). Torsion dystonia. *Johns Hopkins Medical Journal, 151,* 355–361.

Treacher Collins syndrome (Mandibulofacial dysostosis) Characteristic facial appearance with malformation of external ear, flattened area near cheekbones, absence of lower eyelashes, cleft palate, small mandible, conductive hearing loss. Intelligence is normal in 95% of cases. *Cause:* Mutation. *Inheritance:* AD. *Incidence:* Unknown; recurrence risk to patient's children, 50%. *Prenatal diagnosis:* Unavailable. *Treatment:* Surgical repair of most malformations. *Associated complications:* Choanal atresia, respiratory and feeding problems in infancy, obstructive apnea. *Developmental abnormalities:* Hearing loss.

References: Dixon, M.J., Read, A.P., Donnai, D., et al. (1991). The gene for Treacher Collins syndrome maps to the long arm of chromosome 5. *American Journal of Human Genetics, 49,* 17–22. Poswillo, D. (1988). The aetiology and pathogenesis of craniofacial deformity. *Development, 103* (Suppl), 207–212.

Trisomy 13 Microphthalmia, cleft lip and palate, and polydactyly, dysmorphic appearance (i.e., low-set ears, hypertelorism, scalp defects), microcephaly, brain malformations, congenital heart defects, flexion deformity of fingers, eye abnormalities, kidney and gastrointestinal tract malformations. *Cause:* Nondisjunction resulting in extra #13 chromosome, rarely translocation. *Inheritance:* SP. *Incidence:* 1/8,000 births; recurrence risk, less than 1% except in cases of translocation, which carries a risk of 8%–15%. *Prenatal diagnosis:* Chromosome study of amniotic fluid cells or chorionic villus. *Associated complications:* Multi-organ system involvement. *Developmental abnormalities:* Profound mental retardation, visual impairment, cerebral palsy.

Reference: Rodriguez, J.I., Garcia, M., Morales, C., et al. (1990). Trisomy 13 syndrome and neural tube defects. *American Journal of Medical Genetics, 36,* 513–516.

Trisomy 18 Small for gestational age, low-set ears, clenched hands with overriding fingers, congenital heart defects. Limited survival. *Cause:* Nondisjunction resulting in trisomy for chromosome #18. *Inheritance:* SP. *Incidence:* 1/6,600; recurrence risk to patient's siblings, 1%. *Prenatal diagnosis:* Amniocentesis or chorionic villus sampling and chromosome analysis. *Associated complications:* Feeding problems, aspiration, diaphragmatic hernia. Most do not survive first year of life. *Developmental abnormalities:* Severe mental retardation.

Reference: Van Dyke, D.C., & Allen, M. (1990). Clinical management considerations in long-term survivors with trisomy 18. *Pediatrics, 85,* 753–759.

Trisomy 21 *See* Down syndrome; *See* Chapter 16, pp. 259–290.

Tuberous sclerosis Hypopigmented areas, acne-like facial lesions in young children, infantile spasms, calcium deposits in brain. *Inheritance:* AD. *Incidence:* 1/10,000–1/50,000; recurrence risk for patient's children, 50%. *Prenatal diagnosis:* Unavailable. *Associated complications:* Malignancies, hydrocephalus, tumors of the heart. *Developmental abnormalities:* Mild-to-moderate mental retardation.

References: Cassidy, S.B., Pagon, R.A., Pepin, M., et al. (1983). Family studies in tuberous sclerosis. *Journal of the American Medical Association, 249,* 1302–1304. Pinto, F.J., & Bolognia, J.L. (1991). Disorders of hypopigmentation in children. *Pediatric Clinics of North America, 38,* 991–1017.

Turner syndrome (XO syndrome) Short stature; female; broad chest with widely spaced nipples; short appearing neck with extra skin folds at back of neck; congenital heart disease; ovarian dysgenesis; resulting in infertility; usually normal intelligence. *Cause:* Chromosomal nondisjunction resulting in a single X chromosome. *Incidence:* 1/5,000 live births; recurrence risk, Unknown, but low. *Prenatal diagnosis:* Amniocentesis or chorionic villus sampling and chromosome analysis. (*See* Chapter 1, p. 7–8, and Chapter 2, p. 20.) *Associated complications:* Coarctation of the aorta or other types of

congenital heart disease, thyroid abnormalities, diabetes mellitus, kidney abnormalities. *Developmental abnormalities:* Learning disabilities.
Reference: Bender, B., Puck, M., Salbenblatt, J., et al. (1984). Cognitive development of unselected girls with complete and partial X monosomy. *Pediatrics, 73,* 175–182.

Usher syndrome Sensorineural deafness and retinitis pigmentosa. *Cause:* Inherited. *Inheritance:* AR. *Incidence:* 3/100,000–5/100,000; recurrence risk to siblings, 25%. *Associated complications:* Ataxia, psychosis, cataracts. *Developmental abnormalities:* Congenital deafness, night blindness, mental retardation.
Reference: Samuelson, S., & Zahn, J. (1990). Usher's syndrome. *Ophthalmic Paediatrics and Genetics, 11,* 71–76.

VATER association (Vacterl association) Vertebral defects, Anal atresia, Tracheoesophageal fistula (i.e., connection between trachea and esophagus), Esophageal abnormalities, Radial (arm) abnormalities, and Renal (kidney) anomalies. *Cause:* Unknown. *Inheritance:* Usually SP; rare families with AR. *Incidence:* Not known; recurrence risk, usually low, unless AR. *Prenatal diagnosis:* Unavailable. *Associated complications:* Respiratory, cardiac, and renal abnormalities can be severe. *Developmental abnormalities:* Usually normal intelligence.
References: Khoury, M.J., Cordero, J.F., Greenberg, F., et al. (1983). A population study of the VACTERL association: Evidence for its etiologic heterogeneity. *Pediatrics, 71,* 815–820.
Lubinsky, M. (1986). VATER and other associations: Historical perspectives and modern interpretations. *American Journal of Medical Genetics, 2*(Suppl.), 9–16.

Von Recklinghausen disease *See* Neurofibromatosis.

Waardenburg syndrome Unusual facial appearance, irises of different colors, confluent eyelashes, a white forelock, and a stable sensorineural hearing loss. The organ of Corti may be absent. *Cause:* Inherited. *Inheritance:* AD. *Incidence:* 1/20,000–1/40,000; recurrence risk, 50% in siblings if not a new mutation. *Associated complications:* Impairment of vestibular function, premature graying, vitiligo, occasional glaucoma. *Developmental abnormalities:* Congenital deafness.
Reference: Da Silva, E.O. (1991). Waardenberg I syndrome: A clinical and genetic study of two large Brazilian kindreds and literature review. *American Journal of Medical Genetics, 40,* 65–74.

William syndrome (Hypercalcemia-Elfin Facies syndrome) Short stature; full lips and cheeks; periorbital fullness; star-like pattern to iris; hoarse voice. Cardiac abnormality, often supravalvular aortic stenosis. *Inheritance:* Unknown, rare familial reports. *Incidence:* Approximately 1/10,000; recurrence risk for patient's siblings, low. *Prenatal diagnosis:* Not available. *Associated complications:* Hypercalcemia, stenosis of cardiovascular system, renal abnormalities, hypertension, contractures. Phenotype changes over time. *Developmental abnormalities:* Hyperactivity, temperament abnormalities, mild-to-moderate mental retardation.
References: Morris, C.A., Demsey, S.A., & Leonard, C.O. (1988). Natural history of Williams syndrome: Physical characteristics. *Journal of Pediatrics, 113,* 318–326.
Tomc, S.A., Williamson, N.K., Pauli, R.M., et al. (1990). Temperament in Williams syndrome. *American Journal of Medical Genetics, 36,* 345–352.

XYY syndrome Subtle abnormalities, including tall stature, poor fine motor coordination, aggressive behavior, severe acne. *Cause:* Chromosomal nondisjunction. *Inheritance:* SP. *Incidence:* 1/1,000; recurrence risk to patient's siblings, 1%. *Prenatal diagnosis:* Amniocentesis or chorionic villus sampling and chromosome analysis. (*See* Chapter 2, p. 20.) *Associated complications:* Slow nerve conduction velocities, tall stature, large teeth. *Developmental abnormalities:* IQ is in the same range as siblings; however, learning disabilities, particularly with language, decreased speed of information processing, impaired sensorimotor integration skills, and possible behavior problems.
Reference: Stewart, D.A., Netley, C.T., & Park, E. (1982). Summary of clinical findings of children with 47,XXY, 47,XYY, and 47,XXX karyotypes. *Birth Defects, 18,* 1–5.

Zellweger syndrome Muscle hypotonia, absent deep tendon reflexes, absent psychomotor development, severe feeding problems, seizures, dysmorphic facial appearance (i.e., high bulging and receding forehead, wide fontanels, hypertelorism, epicanthal folds, low set ears, micrognathia), minor limb malformations, glaucoma, cataracts, congenital heart lesions, enlarged liver, elevated very long chain fatty acids, elevated phytanic acid, decreased catalase, high pipecolic acid. Most die in first year of life. *Cause:* Absence of peroxisomes. *Inheritance:* AR. *Incidence:* 1/25,000–1/50,000; recurrence risk in siblings, 25%. *Prenatal diagnosis:* Measuring very long chain fatty acids. *Associated complications:* Multiorgan system involvement. *Developmental abnormalities:* Profound mental retardation.
Reference: Zellweger, H. (1987). The cerebro-hepato-renal Zellweger syndrome and other peroxisomal disorders. *Developmental Medicine and Child Neurology, 29,* 821–829.

GENERAL REFERENCES

Buyse, M.L. (Ed.). (1990). *Birth defects encyclopedia*. Dover, MA: Center for Birth Defects Information Services.

Jones, K.L. (1988). *Smith's recognizable patterns of human malformation* (4th ed.). Philadelphia: W.B. Saunders.

McKusick, V.A. (1990). *Mendelian inheritance in man* (9th ed.). Baltimore: The Johns Hopkins University Press.

Scriver, C.R., Beaudet, A.L., Sly, W.S., & Valle, D. (Eds.). (1989). *The metabolic basis of inherited disease* (6th ed.). New York: McGraw-Hill.

Appendix C

Resources for Children with Disabilities

NATIONAL ORGANIZATIONS

Listed below are a number of national organizations that provide services in the area of developmental disabilities. A brief description of the purpose of the organization follows each listing. This section is a representative sample and is not intended to be all-inclusive. We have tried to make addresses and phone numbers as current as possible. We apologize if readers find any of these have changed.

ACCESSIBILITY

Barrier-Free Design Centre, 2075 Bayview Ave., Toronto, Ontario M4N 3M5, Canada (416-480-6000; FAX: 416-480-6009)

A not-for-profit organization that operates information, referral, and direct services for individuals, organizations, and professionals seeking expert advice on how to make facilities accessible to people at every level of ability.

In Door Sports Club, Inc., 1145 Highland St., Napoleon, OH 43545 (419-592-5756)

Educates the public to promote and support opportunities that provide accessibility for persons with disabilities everywhere; interested in opportunities for rehabilitation and employment for persons with disabilities.

The Research and Training Center for Accessible Housing, North Carolina State University School of Design, Box 8613, Raleigh, NC 27695-8613 (919-515-3082)

Provides publications and information to parents and professionals concerning accessible housing design and financing issues. Referrals are made to local organizations.

AIDS

National AIDS Hotline [1-800-342-AIDS (1-800-342-2437); 1-800-344-SIDA (1-800-344-7232) Spanish access; 1-800-AIDS-TTY (1-800-243-7889) Deaf access]

A 24-hour service, 7 days a week, that provides confidential information, referrals, and educational materials to the public. The hotline offers information on transmission, prevention, testing, and local referrals.

National AIDS Information Clearinghouse, P.O. Box 6003, Rockville, MD 20850 (1-800-458-5231; TTY/TDD: 1-800-243-7012)

A comprehensive information service for health professionals, including public health managers and officials at the state and local level and health care providers. The clearinghouse offers free government publications and information about resources.

Project STAR, 1800 Columbus Ave., Roxbury, MA 02119 (617-442-7442)

Multidisciplinary services and referral for schools and families of HIV positive children.

ALCOHOL AND DRUGS OF ABUSE

Cocaine Babies: Florida's Substance-Exposed Youth
A 119-page compilation on prenatal drug exposure with reprints of research papers, case studies, sources for help, and the Salvin teaching strategies. Available from Florida Department of Education, Prevention Center, Suite 414, FEC, 325 W. Gaines St., Tallahassee, FL 32399.

National Association for Perinatal Addiction Research and Education (NAPARE), 11 E. Hubbard St., Ste. 200, Chicago, IL 60611 (312-329-2512); FAX: (312-329-9131)
A multidisciplinary society for professionals; conducts research and provides educational opportunities, including seminars, and morale and judicial training workshops.

Today's Challenge: Teaching Strategies for Working with Young Children Prenatally Exposed to Drugs/ Alcohol
The Salvin teaching strategies: Available from Valerie Wallace, Division of Special Education, Los Angeles Unified School District, 450 N. Grant Avenue, Room H-120, Los Angeles, CA 90012.

AUTISM

Autism Society of America, 8601 Georgia Ave., Suite 503, Silver Spring, MD 20910 (301-565-0433; FAX: 301-565-0834)
Provides information about autism and about options, approaches, methods, and systems available to parents of children with autism, family members, and the professionals who work with them. Advocates for rights and needs of individuals with autism and their families.

Institute for Child Behavior Research, 4182 Adams Ave., San Diego, CA 92116 (619-281-7165)
Information and referral for parents, teachers, physicians, and students working with children with autism and similar developmental disabilities. Publishes quarterly newsletter, *Autism Research Review International.*

National Autism Hotline/Autism Services Center, Prichard Building, 605 9th St., P.O. Box 507, Huntington, WV 25701-0507 (304-525-8014)
Provides direct-care services (e.g., group homes, supervised apartments, intensively staffed 1:1 settings for clients with challenging behaviors), information, advocacy, training, consultation, and seminars for individuals with autism and other developmental disabilities.

CAREER COUNSELING

ERIC Clearinghouse on Handicapped and Gifted Children, 1920 Association Drive, Reston, VA 22091-1589 (703-264-9474)
Provides educational information on assessment, intervention, and enrichment for gifted children and children with developmental disabilities.

Higher Education and Adult Training for People with Handicaps (HEATH Resource Center), 1 Dupont Circle, Washington, DC 20036-1193 (800-54-HEATH; 202-939-9320)
Operates as a national clearinghouse on postsecondary education for individuals with disabilities. The center serves as an informational exchange about educational services, policies, procedures, adaptations, and opportunities on American campuses, including vocational and technical schools, independent living centers, and post high school transition and training programs.

Job Accommodation Network (JAN), West Virginia University, 809 Allen Hall, P.O. Box 6123, Morgantown, WV 26506 (800-526-7234; In WV: 800-526-4698; In Canada: 800-526-2262)
Information and resources to make workplaces accessible to those with disabilities.

CEREBRAL PALSY

American Academy for Cerebral Palsy and Developmental Medicine, 1910 Byrd Ave., Suite 118, P.O. Box 11086, Richmond, VA 23230-1086 (804)-282-0036)
Multidisciplinary society that fosters professional education, research, and interest in the problems associated with cerebral palsy. Provides information to the public.

United Cerebral Palsy Association, 7 Penn Plaza, Suite 804, New York, NY 10001 (800-USA-1UCP; 212-268-6655)
Direct services to children and adults with cerebral palsy that include medical diagnosis, evaluation and treatment, special education, career development, counseling, social and recreational programs, and adapted housing for persons with disabilities.

CHILDREN'S SPECIALIZED HOSPITALS

While the majority of children with disabilities can receive services on an outpatient basis, short-term inpatient treatment is sometimes necessary. Some of the prominent hospitals offering pediatric rehabilitation facilities with *both* inpatient and outpatient units and programs include the following:

Canada
Hugh MacMillan Rehabilitation Centre, 350 Rumsey Rd., Toronto, Ontario, Canada M4G 1R8 (416-425-6220)

Delaware
Alfred I. duPont Institute, 1600 Rockland Rd., P.O. Box 269, Wilmington, DE 19899 (302-651-4465)

District of Columbia
Hospital for Sick Children, 1731 Bunker Hill Rd., NE, Washington, DC 20017 (202-832-4400)

Illinois
LaRabida Children's Hospital and Research Center, E. 65th Street at Lake Michigan, Chicago, IL 60649 (312-363-6700)

Maryland
Kennedy Krieger Institute, 707 North Broadway, Baltimore, MD 21205 (410-550-9000)

Massachusetts
Franciscan Children's Hospital and Rehabilitation Center, 30 Warren St., Boston, MA 02135 (617-254-3800)

Minnesota
Gillette Children's Hospital, 200 E. University Ave., St. Paul, MN 55101 (612-291-2848)

New Jersey
Children's Specialized Hospital, New Providence Rd., Mountainside, NJ 07091 (908-233-4176)

Ohio
Health Hill Hospital for Children, 2801 Martin Luther King Jr., Dr., Cleveland, OH 44104 (216-721-5400)

Pennsylvania
Children's Seashore House, 3405 Civic Center Blvd., Philadelphia, PA 19104 (215-895-3600)

CHRONIC ILLNESS

The Candlelighters Childhood Cancer Foundation, 1901 Pennsylvania Ave., NW, Ste. 1001, Washington, DC 20006 (202-659-5136)
An international network of groups of parents of children with cancer; provides support and advocacy and publishes newsletters, reports, and other publications.

Families of Children Under Stress (FOCUS), P.O. Box 1058, Conyers, GA 30207 (404-483-9845)
Publishes bimonthly newsletter for families of chronically or terminally ill children.

Parents of Chronically Ill Children, 1527 Maryland St., Springfield, IL 62702 (217-522-6810)
Provides information, resources, and referrals for families with children who have rare disorders, including information about special education and advocacy.

CLEFT LIP AND PALATE

Cleft Palate Foundation, 1218 Grandview Ave., Pittsburgh, PA 15211 (412-481-1376; 800-24-CLEFT)
Multidisciplinary professional organization that educates and assists the public regarding cleft lip and palate and other craniofacial anomalies and encourages research in the field. CLEFTLINE, their 800-toll free service, provides information and referrals. Referrals are made to cleft palate/craniofacial teams and to parent support groups. Distributes brochures and fact sheets and publishes a quarterly newsletter for parents and patients.

COMPUTERS

ComputAbility Corporation, 40000 Grand River, Suite 109, Novi, MI 48375 (313-477-6720)
Manufactures and distributes computer interfaces, alternative keyboards, computer keyguards, and specialized software programs to aid persons with special needs in their use of computers. IBM, Macintosh, and Apple II computers supported. Free catalog available.

Disabled Children's Computer Group (DCCG), 2095 Rose St., 1st Floor East, Berkeley CA 94709 (415-841-3224)

Offers workshops for parents, teachers, and children to provide hands-on experience with computers; maintains a library of catalogs, articles, and books that relate to computers, disability, and special education. Interested in talking to parents or others who want to set up a similar organization in their community.

Trace Research and Development Center, 1500 Highland Ave., S-151, Madison, WI 53705-2280 (608-262-6966; TDD: 608-263-5408)

Conducts research and development in the areas of communication and computer access for individuals with disabilities. Disseminates information and has a reprint service on a variety of topics.

CYSTIC FIBROSIS

Cystic Fibrosis Foundation, 6931 Arlington Rd., Bethesda, MD 20814 (301-951-4422; 800-FIGHT CF or 800-344-4823)

Provides referral for diagnostic services and medical care; offers professional and public information and supports research and professional training.

DENTAL CARE

National Foundation of Dentistry for the Handicapped, 1600 Stout St., Suite 1420, Denver, CO 80202 (303-573-0264)

Maintains preventive dental health programs for persons with developmental disabilities in four states; operates some dental house-call programs that serve individuals with limited mobility; in 10 states, offers free care for indigent elderly people and people with disabilities.

DOWN SYNDROME

Association for Children with Down Syndrome, 2616 Martin Ave., Bellmore, NY 11710 (516-221-4700)

Information and referral services, including free publication list.

National Down Syndrome Congress, 1800 Dempster St., Park Ridge, IL 60068-1146 (800-232-6372; 708-823-7550)

Provides information and referral materials and publishes a newsletter.

National Down Syndrome Society, 666 Broadway, Suite 810, New York, NY 10012 (800-221-4602; 212-460-9330)

Provides information and publishes newsletter.

EDUCATION

Association on Higher Education and Disability (AHEAD), P.O. Box 21192, Columbus, OH 43221 (614-488-4972 [Voice/TDD])

Professional organization committed to full participation in higher education for persons with disabilities.

Council for Exceptional Children, 1920 Association Dr., Reston, VA 22091 (703-620-3660)

Provides information to teachers, administrators, and others concerned with the education of gifted children and children with disabilities. Maintains a library and database on literature in special education; provides information and assistance on legislation.

IN*SOURCE, Indiana Resource Center for Families with Special Needs, 833 Northside Blvd., Bldg. #1—Rear, South Bend, IN 46617 (219-234-7101; Indiana toll free: 800-332-4433)

Coalition of concerned parents, professionals, and persons with disabilities who are dedicated to the right to a free, appropriate public education for all children with disabilities.

National Association of Private Schools for Exceptional Children, 1522 K. St., NW, Suite 1032, Washington, DC 20005 (202-408-3338)

National organization of private schools that promotes communication among these schools and informs the public about schools across the country; publishes a directory of schools that includes the services they offer and for whom.

National Information Center for Educational Media (NICEM), P.O. Box 40130, Albuquerque, NM 87196 (505-265-3591; Toll free: 800-468-3453)

Provides database of educational audiovisual materials, including video, motion pictures, filmstrips, audio tapes, and slides.

TASH: The Association for Persons with Severe Handicaps, 7010 Roosevelt Way, NE, Seattle, WA 98115 (206-523-8446; TDD: 206-524-6198)

Advocates high quality education for persons with disabilities; disseminates research findings and practical applications for education and habilitation; encourages sharing of experience and expertise.

EPILEPSY

Epilepsy Foundation of America, 4351 Garden City Dr., Suite 406, Landover, MD 20785 (301-459-3700; Information and Referral: 800-332-1000)
Provides programs of information and education, advocacy, support of research, and the delivery of needed services to people with epilepsy and their families.

EQUIPMENT

Independent Living Aids, Inc., 27 E. Mall St., Plainview, NY 11803 (516-752-8080)
Provides, at a cost, aids that make daily tasks easier for those with physical disabilities. Also carries clocks, calculators, magnifying lamps, and E-Z-to-see low vision and talking watches for those with visual problems. Will send free catalog.

PAM Assistance Centre, 601 W. Maple St., Lansing, MI 48906 (517-371-5897; 800-274-7426)
Provides free information from up-to-date ABLEDATA database on devices and equipment available for individuals with disabilities.

FEDERAL

Clearinghouse on Disability Information, Office of Special Education and Rehabilitative Services, U.S. Dept. of Education, Room 3132, Switzer Bldg., Washington, DC 20202-2524 (202-732-1241; 202-732-1245; 202-732-1723)
Responds to inquiries and researches and documents information operations serving the field of disabilities on the national, state, and local levels. Specializes in providing information in the areas of federal funding for programs serving people with disabilities, federal legislation affecting individuals with disabilities, and federal programs benefiting people with disabilities.

National Early Childhood Technical Assistance System (NEC*TAS), NEC*TAS Coordinating Office, CB# 8040, Suite 500 NCNB Plaza, University of North Carolina, Chapel Hill, NC 27599-8040 (919-962-2001 [Voice]; 919-966-4041 [TDD]; FAX: 919-966-7463)
Funded through the Office of Special Education Programs, U.S. Department of Education as part of PL 102-119. Assists states in developing services for children with disabilities from birth to 8 years and their families. Supports the U.S. Department of Education's Early Education Program for Children with Disabilities (EEPCD).

National Information Center for Children and Youth with Disabilities (NICHCY), P.O. Box 1492, Washington, DC 20013 (703-893-6061; 800-555-9955; TDD: 703-893-8614)
Federal center established as part of PL 94-142. Provides free information to assist parents, educators, caregivers, advocates, and others in helping children and youth with disabilities become participating members of the community. Services include personal responses to specific questions, referrals to other organizations or sources of help, prepared information packets, and publications on current issues.

President's Committee on Employment of People with Disabilities, 1111 20th St., NW, Ste. 636, Washington, DC, 20036 (202-653-5029)
One of oldest presidential committees in the United States. Promotes acceptance of persons with physical and mental disabilities in the world of work. Involves the public and the private sector. Promotes the elimination of barriers, both physical and attitudinal, to the employment of persons with disabilities.

GENERAL

ACCENT on Information, P.O. Box 700, Bloomington, IL 61702 (309-378-2961)
Computerized retrieval system that has information on a variety of topics, including employment, aids for independent living, laws and legislation, special education, home management, housing and architectural barriers, and special facilities. Publishes *ACCENT on Living Magazine* and *Accent Special Publications*, a series of books with answers, how-to tips, instructions, and ideas on specific topics.

American Academy of Pediatrics, 141 Northwest Point Blvd., P.O. Box 927, Elk Grove Village, IL 60009-0927 (708-228-5005)
Professional membership association for board-certified pediatricians that offers professional continuing education, health education materials, and other programs.

American Association for the Advancement of Science, Project on Science, Technology, and Disability, 1333 H Street, NW, Washington, DC 20005 (202-326-6672 [Voice/TDD])

Seeks to increase the number of people with disabilities entering and advancing in science, math, and engineering fields. Primarily an information center. Links people with disabilities, their families, professors, teachers, and counselors to scientists, mathematicians, and engineers with disabilities who can share coping strategies. Addresses accessibility, technology, and education issues in the sciences.

American Association of University Affiliated Programs for Persons with Developmental Disabilities, 8630 Fenton St., Suite 410, Silver Spring, MD 20910 (301-588-8252; FAX: 301-588-2842)

Represents the professional interests of the national network of 51 University Affiliated Facilities (UAFs) that serve persons with developmental disabilities.

Avenues, P.O. Box 5192, Sonora, CA 95370 (209-928-3688)

Publishes a semiannual newsletter that provides lists of parents, interested doctors, and experienced medical centers that are concerned with persons with disabilities.

Barnes & Noble/B. Dalton Bookseller (see local yellow pages under "bookstores, retail")

Provides a "Children with Special Needs Collection" of useful books for families with children with disabilities in the Family and Child Care section of their stores.

Center on Human Policy, Syracuse University, 200 Huntington Hall, Syracuse, NY 13244-2340 (315-443-3851)

Advocacy and research organization committed to the rights of people with disabilities; holds local, regional, and national workshops on rights; offers advice and backup assistance to individuals and advocacy groups.

Coalition on Sexuality and Disability, Inc., 122 E. 23rd St., New York, NY 10010 (212-242-3900 [Answering service; staff person will return call])

Organization committed to assisting persons with disabilities to achieve full integration into society with confidence in their sexuality. Offers seminars and workshops on sexuality and disability; advocates for persons with disabilities.

Early Recognition Intervention Network (ERIN), 376 Bridge St., Dedham, MA 02026 (617-329-5529)

A program for young children with disabilities. Specific evaluation and curriculum materials are designed to assist disorganized children, such as the cocaine-exposed. Free brochures and price lists available.

Federation of the Handicapped, Inc., 211 W. 14th St., New York, NY 10011 (212-206-4200)

Services include vocational training and job placement for adults with severe disabilities and/or disadvantages.

Gesell Institute of Human Development, 310 Prospect St., New Haven, CT 06511 (203-777-3481)

Multidisciplinary team that provides primary health care and preventive medicine; also offers consultation on ways to influence the course of chronic disease. Services include psychological and developmental evaluations and workshops for educators.

March of Dimes Birth Defects Foundation, 1275 Mamaroneck Ave., White Plains, NY 10605 (914-428-7100)

Awards grants to institutions and organizations for development of genetic services, perinatal care in high-risk pregnancies, prevention of premature delivery, parent support groups, and other community programs. Campaign for Healthier Babies distributes information about birth defects and related newborn health problems. Spanish-language materials are available.

Mobility International, 62 Union St., London SEI Ltd., England, (01-403-5688); In USA: P.O. Box 3551, 1870 Onyx #E, Eugene, OR 97403 (503-343-1284)

International exchange programs for individuals with disabilities and other young people.

National Association of Developmental Disabilities Councils, 1234 Massachusetts Ave., NW, Suite 103, Washington, DC 20005 (202-347-1234)

Organization of councils that exist in each state; these councils provide information on and advocate for resources and services for persons with developmental disabilities and their families.

National Center for Education in Maternal and Child Health, 38th and R Sts., NW, Washington, DC 20057 (202-625-8400)

Dissemination of publications and fact sheets to the public and professionals in the field; develops and maintains database of topics, agencies, and organizations related to maternal and child health.

National Council on Independent Living, Troy Atrium, 4th St. and Broadway, Troy, NY 12180 (518-274-1979)

Provides referral to local centers for independent living that facilitates achievement of maximum independence in the community.

National Easter Seal Society, 70 E. Lake St., Chicago, IL 60601 (312-726-6200; Toll free: 800-221-6827)

Nonprofit, community-based health agency dedicated to increasing the independence of people with disabilities. Offers a range of quality services, research, and programs. Serves more than a million people each year through a nationwide network of 170 affiliates.

National Organization on Disability, 910 16th St., NW, Suite 600, Washington, DC 20006 (202-293-5960; TDD: 293-5960)

Promotes the acceptance and understanding of the needs of citizens with disabilities through a national network of communities and organizations; facilitates exchange of information regarding resources available to persons with disabilities.

National Organization for Rare Disorders, Inc. (NORD), P.O. Box 8923, New Fairfield, CT 06812 (203-746-6518)

Clearinghouse for information about rare disorders; encourages and promotes research; represents people with rare diseases who are not otherwise represented; educates the public and the medical profession about these diseases.

Society for Developmental Pediatrics, P.O. Box 23836, Baltimore, MD 21203 (410-550-9446; 410-550-9420)

Provides list of pediatricians who specialize in evaluation and treatment of children with disabilities.

GENETICS

National Society of Genetic Counselors, 233 Canterbury Dr., Wallingford, PA 19086 (215-872-7608)

Professional organization of genetic counselors. Can provide referral to nearest source for genetic counseling and services. Does not provide or disseminate information about specific genetic disorders.

The National Tay-Sachs and Allied Diseases Association, 2001 Beacon St., Suite 304, Brookline, MA, 02146 (617-277-4463)

Promotes genetic screening programs nationally; has updated listing of Tay-Sachs prevention centers in a number of countries; provides educational literature to general public and professionals; peer group support for parents.

HEARING, SPEECH, AND LANGUAGE

Alexander Graham Bell Association for the Deaf, 3417 Volta Pl., NW, Washington, DC 20007 (202-337-5220 [Voice/TDD])

Umbrella organization for International Organization for the Education of the Hearing Impaired (IOEHI), International Parents' Organization (IPO), and Oral Deaf Adults Section (ODAS). Provides general information and information on resources. Encourages improved communication, better public understanding, and detection of early hearing loss. Works for better educational opportunities; provides scholarships and training for teachers.

American Deafness and Rehabilitation Association, P.O. Box 251554, Little Rock, AR 72225 (501-663-7074 [Voice/TDD])

Serves deaf professionals and persons interested in deafness. Publishes a journal and newsletter by subscription.

American Society for Deaf Children, 814 Thayer Ave., Silver Spring, MD 20910 (301-585-5400; TDD: 301-585-5401)

Provides information and support to parents and families with children who are deaf or who have hearing impairment.

American Speech-Language-Hearing Association, 10801 Rockville Pike, Rockville, MD 20852 (301-897-5700 [Voice/TDD])

Professional and scientific organization; certifying body for professionals providing speech, language, and hearing therapy; conducts research in communication disorders; publishes several journals; provides consumer information and professional referral.

Captioned Films and Videos for the Deaf/Modern Talking Picture Services, 5000 Park St. N, St. Petersburg, FL 33709 (800-237-6213; 813-541-7571)

Government sponsored distribution of open-captioned materials to eligible institutions and families. Application sent upon request.

The Deafness Research Foundation, 9 E. 38th St., New York, NY 10016 (212-684-6556)

Solicits funds for the support of research into the causes, treatment, and prevention of deafness and other hearing disorders.

Deafpride, 1350 Potomac Ave., SE, Washington, DC 20003 (202-675-6700 [Voice/TTY])

Information gathering and distribution and advocacy programs for the rights of deaf people. Also offers community-based services for the deaf involving AIDS awareness, substance abuse issues, maternal and child health issues, and sign language classes.

Hearing Aid Helpline, 20361 Middlebelt Rd., Livonia, MI 48152 (U.S. and Canada: 800-521-5247)

Information on how to proceed when hearing loss is suspected; free consumer kit, facts about hearing aids, and a variety of literature on hearing-related subjects is available.

National Captioning Institute (NCI), Inc., 5203 Leesburg Pike, 15th Floor, Falls Church, VA 22041 (800-533-9673; 800-321-8337 [TDD]; 703-998-2400)

Provides national closed-captioned television service to any household with decoding device.

National Center for Stuttering, Inc., 200 E. 33rd St., New York, NY 10016 (212-532-1460; Toll free: 800-221-2483)

Provides free information for parents of young children just starting to show symptoms of stuttering; runs training programs for speech professionals in current therapeutic approaches; provides treatment for people over 7 years of age who stutter.

National Information Center on Deafness, Gallaudet University, 800 Florida Ave., N.E., Washington, DC 20002 (202-651-5051; TDD: 651-5052; FAX: 651-5054)

Provides information related to deafness; has a multitude of resources and experts available for individuals with hearing impairment, their families, and professionals. Collects information about resources around the country.

Self Help for Hard of Hearing People (SHHH), 7800 Wisconsin Ave., Bethesda, MD 20814 (301-657-2248; 301-657-2249 [TDD])

Educational organization that provides assistance to those who are committed to participating fully in society. Publishes journal and newsletter and provides advocacy and outreach programs.

Signing Exact English (SEE) Center for the Advancement of Deaf Children, P.O. Box 1181, Los Alamitos, CA 90720 (213-430-1467)

Information and referral services for parents of newly diagnosed children.

LEARNING DISABILITIES

C.H.A.D.D. National (Attention Deficit Disorders), 499 NW 70th Ave., Suite 308, Plantation, FL 33317 (305-587-3700)

Support group for parents of children with attention deficit disorders. Provides continuing education for both parents and professionals, serves as a community resource for information, and advocates for appropriate educational programs.

Dyslexia Research Institute, 4745 Centerville Rd., Tallahassee, FL 32308 (904-893-2216)

Provides training, workshops, and seminars for professionals. Literature sent on request.

Learning Disabilities Association of America, 4156 Library Rd., Pittsburgh, PA 15234 (412-341-1515)

Encourages research and the development of early detection programs, disseminates information, serves as an advocate, and works to improve education for individuals with learning disabilities.

National Center for Learning Disabilities (NCLD), 99 Park Ave., New York, NY 10016 (212-687-7211)

Committed to increasing public awareness of learning disabilities; provides computerized information and referral services to interested parents, friends, and professionals on learning disabilities. Publishes *THEIR WORLD*, an annual magazine for parents and professionals.

The Orton Dyslexia Society, 724 York Rd., Baltimore, MD 21204 (410-296-0232)

Devoted to the study and treatment of dyslexia; disseminates information on dyslexia, sponsors conferences, and has two regular publications.

LEGAL

ACLU Children's Rights Project, 132 W. 43rd St., New York, NY 10036 (212-944-9800)

Nationwide test-case litigation program designed to protect and expand the statutory and constitutional rights of children, in particular those in foster care.

American Bar Association Center on Children and the Law, 1800 M St. NW, Suite 300, Washington, DC 20036 (202-331-2250)

Offers information and advocacy to professionals and parents of children and adolescents with disabilities.

Children's Defense Fund, 122 C St., NW, Washington, DC 20001 (202-628-8787)

Provides information about legislation in health care, child welfare, and special education. Publishes a guide for parents and advocates for the rights of P.L. 94-142, The Education for All Handicapped Children Act of 1975.

Disability Rights Education and Defense Fund (DREDF), 2212 6th St., Berkeley, CA 94710 (415-644-2555)

Law and policy center to protect the rights of people with disabilities. Referral and information regarding rights of people with disabilities is offered. This organization educates legislators and policy-makers on issues affecting the rights of people with disabilities and is educating the public about PL 101-336, The Americans with Disabilities Act of 1990.

Mental Health Law Project, 2021 L St., NW, Suite 800, Washington, DC 20036 (202-467-5730)

Legal advocacy program that works to define, establish, and protect the rights of children and adults with mental disabilities, using test-case litigation, federal policy advocacy, and training and technical assistance for legal services lawyers and other advocates nationwide.

National Center for Law and the Deaf, Gallaudet University, 800 Florida Ave., NE, Washington, DC 20002 (202-651-5373 [Voice/TDD])

Provides a variety of legal services to persons with hearing impairment, including representation, counseling, information, and education.

MENTAL RETARDATION

American Association on Mental Retardation, 1719 Kalorama Rd., NW, Washington, DC 20009-2683 (202-387-1968)

Professional organization that promotes cooperation among those involved in services, training, and research in mental retardation. Encourages research, dissemination of information, development of appropriate community-based services, and the promotion of preventive measures designed to further reduce the incidence of mental retardation.

The Arc (formerly Association for Retarded Citizens of the United States), 500 E. Border St., 3rd Fl., Arlington, TX 76010 (817-640-0204)

National advocacy organization working on behalf of individuals with mental retardation and their families; has 1,600 local units across the United States.

The Joseph P. Kennedy, Jr., Foundation, 1350 New York Ave., NW, Suite 500, Washington, D.C. 20005-4709 (202-393-1250)

Promotes public awareness, provides seed grants for scientific research, and provides models of service for persons with mental retardation. Also sponsors the Kennedy Foundation International Awards in Mental Retardation.

National Association of State Mental Retardation Program Directors, 113 Oronoco St., Alexandria, VA 22314 (703-683-4202)

Organization consisting of one representative from each state. Publishes two newsletters; provides information on state and national trends, statistics, and programs in the field of developmental disabilities.

President's Committee on Mental Retardation (PCMR), 330 Independence Ave., Cohen Bldg., Room 5325, Washington, DC 20201 (202-609-0634)

A body to advise the president and Secretary of Health and Human Services on all matters pertaining to mental retardation.

MUSCULAR DYSTROPHY

Muscular Dystrophy Association, 3561 E. Sunrise Dr., Tucson, AZ 85718 (602-529-2000; FAX: 602-529-5300)

Voluntary health care agency that fosters research and direct care for individuals with muscular dystrophy; concerned with conquering muscular dystrophy and other neuromuscular diseases.

OCCUPATIONAL THERAPY

American Occupational Therapy Association, Inc., 1383 Piccard Dr., Rockville, MD 20850 (301-948-9626)

Professional organization of occupational therapists; provides services including accreditation of educational programs, professional publications, public education, and continuing education for practitioners.

PARENTS

Compassionate Friends, P.O. Box 1347, Oak Brook, IL 60522-3696 (708-990-0010)
National and worldwide organization that supports and aids parents in the positive resolution of the grief experienced upon the death of their child; fosters the physical and emotional health of bereaved parents and siblings.

The Exceptional Parent, 1170 Commonwealth Ave., Boston, MA 02134-4645 (617-730-5800)
This magazine, published since 1971, provides straightforward, practical information for families and professionals involved in the care of children and young adults with disabilities; many articles are written by parents.

Federation for Children with Special Needs, 95 Berkeley St., Ste. 104, Boston, MA 02116 (617-482-2915 [Voice/TTY]; toll-free in MA: 800-331-0688 [Voice/TTY]
A coalition of parent groups representing children with a variety of disabilities; projects include Parent Training and Information, Agent Orange Parent Network, Parent Advocacy League (PAL), Massachusetts Assistive Technology Partnership, Technical Assistance for Parent Programs (TAPP), CAPP National Parent Resource Center (NPRC), and National Early Childhood Technical Assistance System (NEC*TAS).

National Parent Network on Disabilities (NPND), 1600 Prince St., Ste. 115, Alexandria, VA 22314 (703-684-6763); FAX: (703-548-6191 [Voice/TDD])
A coalition of parent organizations and parents that works to influence policy issues concerning the needs of people with disabilities and their families.

PACER Center, Inc. (Parent Advocacy Coalition for Educational Rights), 4826 Chicago Ave., S., Minneapolis, MN 55417-1055 (612-827-2966 [Voice/TDD]; FAX: 612-827-3065; toll free in MN: 1-800-53PACER)
Provides education and training to help parents understand the special education laws and to obtain appropriate school programs for their children. Workshops and program topics include early intervention, emotional disabilities, and health/medical services. Also provides: disability awareness puppet program for schools, child abuse prevention program services, newsletters, booklets, extensive written materials, videos. Services and workshops for parents are free of charge.

Parent Educational Advocacy Training Center, 228 S. Pitt St., Suite 300, Alexandria, VA 22314 (703-836-2953)
Professionally staffed organization that helps parents to become effective advocates for their children with school personnel and the educational system.

Project COPE, 9160 Monte Vista Ave., Montclair, CA 91763 (714-985-3116)
Serves as a link between parents who are raising children with disabling conditions and new parents seeking understanding and hope. Professionally trained and supervised parent volunteers contact new parents at their request. No fees are charged.

Team of Advocates for Special Kids (TASK), 100 W. Cerritos Ave., Anaheim CA 92805 (714-533-TASK; FAX: 714-533-2533)
Provides services to enable children with disabilities to reach their maximum potential. Offers training, education, support, information, resources, and community awareness programs to families of children with disabilities and the professionals who serve them. Conducts an advocacy training course; publishes a bimonthly newsletter.

PHYSICAL THERAPY

American Physical Therapy Association, 1111 N. Fairfax St., Alexandria, VA 22314 (Information Services: 800-999-2782, ext. 3210)
Professional membership association of physical therapists, physical therapist assistants, and physical therapy students. Operates clearinghouse for questions on physical therapy and disabilities. Publishes bibliographies on a range of topics.

RECREATION AND SPORTS

American Alliance for Health, Physical Education, Recreation and Dance, 1900 Association Dr., Reston, VA 22091 (703-476-3400)
Association of professionals in physical education, sports and athletics, health and safety education, recreation and leisure, and dance. Supports and disseminates research, promotes better public understanding of these professions, and supports and provides opportunities for professional growth to members.

American Athletic Association of the Deaf, Executive Secretary: Shirley Hortie Platt, 1052 Darling St. Ogden, Utah 84403 (202-224-8637)

Promotes sports competition on a local, national, and international level for deaf persons and those with hearing impairments.

Boy Scouts of America, Scouting for the Handicapped Division, 1325 Walnut Hill La., Irving, TX 75062 (214-659-2127)

Provides educational, recreational, and therapeutic resource programs through the Boy Scouts of America.

Girl Scouts of the U.S.A., 830 Third Ave., New York, NY 10022 (212-940-7500)

Open to all girls ages 5 through 17 (or kindergarten through grade 12). Runs camping programs, sports and recreational activities, and service programs. Mainstreams children with disabilities into regular Girl Scout troop activities.

National Handicapped Sports, National Headquarters, 1145 19th St., Suite 717, Washington, DC 20036 (310-652-7505; FAX: 301-652-0790; TDD: 301-652-0119)

NHS offers summer programs and competitions, youth and women's programs, fitness programs, "fitness is for everyone" videotapes, and winter ski programs. Local chapters offer activities including: camping, hiking, biking, horseback riding, 10 K runs, water skiing, white water rafting, rope courses, mountain climbing, sailing, yachting, canoeing, kayaking, aerobic fitness, and snow skiing. Provides year-round sports and recreational opportunities to persons with orthopedic, spinal cord, neuromuscular, and visual impairments through a national network of local chapters.

National Wheelchair Athletic Association, 3595 E. Fountain Blvd., Suite L1, Colorado Springs, CO 80910 (719-574-1150)

Governing body of various sports of wheelchair athletics including swimming, archery, weightlifting, track and field, table tennis, and air weapons. Publishes a newsletter.

Special Olympics International, 1350 New York Ave., NW, Suite 500, Washington, DC 20005-4709 (202-628-3630)

Largest year-round sports organization for children and adults with mental retardation; sanctioned by the United States Olympic Committee. Local, state, and national games are held throughout the United States and in over 90 other countries.

Special Recreation, Inc., 362 Koser Ave., Iowa City, IA 52246-3038 (319-337-7578; 319-353-6808)

Serves the recreational needs, rights, interests, and aspirations of people with disabilities. Publishes a compendium of 1,500 resources, digests, and other resource guides. Provides employment information, and referral services.

REHABILITATION

Canadian Rehab Council, 45 Sheppard Ave., E., Suite 801, Willowdale, Ontario CANADA M2N 5W9 (416-250-7490)

Sponsors annual professional conference and sells publications.

National Rehabilitation Clearinghouse, 816 W. 6th St., Oklahoma State University, Stillwater, OK 74078 (405-624-7650; FAX: 405-624-0695)

Provides training materials for professionals in rehabilitation and related professions.

National Rehabilitation Information Center (NARIC), 8455 Colesville Rd., Suite 935, Silver Spring, MD 20910 (301-588-9284; 800-346-2742 [Voice/TDD]; FAX: 301-587-1967)

Rehabilitation information service and research library; provides quick-reference and referral, bibliographic searches, and photocopies of documents. Publishes a free quarterly newsletter and several directories.

SCOLIOSIS

National Scoliosis Foundation, Inc., 72 Mt. Auburn St., Watertown, MA 02172 (617-926-0397; FAX: 617-926-0398)

Not-for-profit organization dedicated to informing the public about scoliosis, promoting early detection and treatment of scoliosis. Publishes newsletter called *Spinal Connection*; has state chapters.

Scoliosis Association, Inc., P.O. Box 51353, Raleigh, NC 27609 (919-846-2639)

Nonprofit group committed to educating the public about scoliosis. Provides support groups; publishes newsletter—*Backtalk*.

Scoliosis Research Society, 222 S. Prospect Ave., Suite 127, Park Ridge, IL 60068 (708-698-1627)
Conducts research on the etiology and treatment of scoliosis and spinal disorders.

SIBLINGS

The Sibling Information Network, A.J. Pappanikou Center: A University Affiliated Program, 991 Main
St., East Hartford, CT 06108 (203-282-7050)
Assists individuals and professionals interested in serving the needs of families of individuals with
disabilities; disseminates bibliographic material and directories; places people in touch with each other;
publishes a newsletter written for and by siblings and parents.

SICKLE CELL DISEASE

Howard University Center for Sickle Cell Disease, 2121 Georgia Ave., NW, Washington, DC 20772
(202-636-7916)
Screening and counseling for sickle cell disease; provides services to both adults and children,
including medical treatment and psychosocial intervention.

National Association for Sickle Cell Disease, Inc., 3345 Wilshire Blvd., Suite 1106, Los Angeles, CA
90010 (213-736-5455; toll free: 800-421-8453)
Provides education, screening, genetic counseling, technical assistance, tutorial services, vocational
rehabilitation, and research support in the United States and Canada.

SPINA BIFIDA

Spina Bifida Association of America, 1700 Rockville Pike, Suite 250, Rockville, MD 20852-1654
(301-770-SBAA; 800-621-3141 for information and referral)
Provides information and referral for new parents and literature on spina bifida; supports a public
awareness program; advocates for individuals with spina bifida and their families; supports research;
conducts conferences for parents and professionals.

SYNDROMES

There are many support organizations and networks for children with various syndromes and their families.
A representative sample is listed here.

Arnold-Chiari Family Network, c/o Kevin and Maureen Walsh, 67 Spring St., Weymouth, MA 02188
(617-337-2368)
Informal family support network for those with Chiari I and Chiari II malformations. Literature and
occasional newsletter provided upon request.

Cornelia de Lange Syndrome Foundation, Inc., 60 Dyer Ave., Collinsville, CT 06022 (203-693-0159)
Supports parents and children affected by Cornelia de Lange syndrome, encourages research, and
disseminates information to increase public awareness through a newsletter and informational pamphlet.

The 5p- Society (Cri du chat syndrome), 11609 Oakmont, Overland Park, KS 66210 (913-469-8900)
Family support and information group for parents, grandparents, and guardians. Publishes a newsletter and sponsors an annual meeting.

Guillain-Barré Syndrome Foundation, International, P.O. Box 262, Wynnewood, PA 19096 (215-
667-0131)
Provides emotional support to patients and their families; fosters research, educates the public about
the disorder, develops nationwide support groups, and directs persons with this syndrome to resources,
meetings, newsletters, and symposia.

International Rett Syndrome Association, Inc., 8511 Rose Marie Dr., Ft. Washington, MD 20744
(301-248-7031)
Provides information and referral, support to families, and acts as a liaison with professionals. Also
facilitates research on Rett syndrome.

Little People of America, Inc., P.O. Box 9897, Washington, DC 20016 (800-24-DWARF; 800-
243-9273)
Nationwide, voluntary organization dedicated to helping people of short stature. Provides fellowship,
moral support, and information to "little persons" afflicted with dwarfism. 800 Helpline provides information on organizations, products and services, and doctors nearest to caller.

National Fragile X Foundation, 1441 York St., Suite 215, Denver, CO 80206 (800-688-8765; 303-333-6155)

Promotes education concerning diagnosis, treatment, and research in fragile X syndrome and provides referral to local resource centers. Sponsors a biannual conference.

National Gaucher Foundation, 1424 K St. NW, 4th Flr., Washington, DC 20005 (202-393-2777)

Publishes bimonthly newsletter, operates support groups, provides referrals to organizations for appropriate services, and funds research on Gaucher disease.

The National Neurofibromatosis Foundation, Inc., 141 5th Ave., 7th Fl., Room 75, New York, NY 10010 (212-460-8980)

Supplies information to laypeople and professionals; offers genetic counseling and support groups throughout the United States.

National Tuberous Sclerosis Association, 8000 Corporate Drive, Suite 120, Landover, MD 20785 (800-225-NTSA; 301-459-9888)

Offers general specific information about manifestations of the disease to newly diagnosed persons, their families, and professionals. Referrals are made to support groups located in most states. Funds research through membership fees and donations.

National Urea Cycle Disorders Foundation, 4559 Vauxhall Rd., Richmond, VA 23234 (800-275-2285)

Provides information and support for families. Supports and stimulates medical research and increased awareness by the public and the legislators of issues related to urea cycle disorders.

Osteogenesis Imperfecta Foundation, Inc., P.O. Box 24776 Tampa, FL 33623-4776 (813-855-7077)

Supports research on osteogenesis imperfecta and provides information to those with this disorder, their families, and other interested persons.

Parents of Dwarfed Children, c/o Margaret B. Badner, 11524 Colt Terrace, Silver Spring, MD 20902 (301-649-3275)

Will respond by mail or telephone to parents of newly diagnosed children with questions or concerns of any kind.

Prader-Willi Syndrome Association, 6490 Excelsior Blvd., Suite E–102, St. Louis Park, MN 55426 (612-926-1947)

National organization that serves as a clearinghouse for information on Prader-Willi syndrome; shares information with parents, professionals, and other interested persons.

Support Organization for Trisomy 18, 13, and Related Disorders, c/o Barb Van Herreweghe, 2982 S. Union St., Rochester, NY 14624 (716-594-4621)

Provides support and family packages with a newsletter and appropriate literature underscoring the common problems for children with trisomy 13 and trisomy 18. There are chapters in most states. A conference is held yearly for families and professionals.

Tourette Syndrome Association, 42-40 Bell Blvd., Bayside, NY 11361 (212-224-2999)

Offers information, referral, advocacy, education, research, and self-help groups to those affected by this syndrome.

Treacher Collins Foundation, c/o Hope Charkins-Drazin and David Drazin, P.O. Box 683, Norwich, VT 05055 (802-649-3020)

Resource and referral for families, individuals and professionals who are interested in developing and sharing knowledge and experience about Treacher Collins syndrome and related disorders. Newsletter, booklet, bibliography, and lending library are available.

TRAUMATIC BRAIN INJURY

National Head Injury Foundation, Inc., 1140 Connecticut Ave., NW, Suite 812, Washington, DC 20036-4002 (800-444-6443; 202-296-6443)

Provides information to educate the public, politicians, businesses, and schools about head injury: its effects, causes, and prevention.

VISION

American Foundation for the Blind, Inc., 15 W. 16th St., New York, NY 10011 (212-620-2020)

Works in cooperation with other agencies, organizations, and schools to offer services to blind persons and those with visual impairments; provides consultation, public education, referrals, information, talking books, and adaptation of equipment for persons with visual impairments.

American Printing House for the Blind (APH), P.O. Box 6085, Louisville, KY 40206-0085 (Phone & FAX: 502-895-2405)

Not-for-profit publishing house for persons with visual impairments; books in braille, large type, and recordings are available. A range of aids, tools, and supplies for education and daily living is also available.

Associated Services for the Blind, 919 Walnut St., Philadelphia, PA 19107 (215-627-3501)

Provides custom transcription of print materials in large print, audio tape, or braille; operates retail store for aids and materials for blind persons; provides social services counseling and support groups for blind persons and their families.

Association for Education and Rehabilitation of the Blind and Visually Impaired, 206 N. Washington St., Alexandria, VA 22314 (703-548-1884)

Inservice training primarily through conferences and publications for educators and those involved in rehabilitation of blind and low-vision persons.

Blind Children's Fund, 230 Central St., Auburndale, MA 02166 (617-332-4014)

Information clearinghouse for parents and teachers of blind infants and preschool children and children with visual impairment. Publishes quarterly parent newsletter.

National Association for Visually Handicapped, 22 W. 21st St., New York, NY 10010 (212-889-3141)

Provides informational literature, guidance and counseling, and referral services for parents of partially sighted children and those who work with them. Publishes free large-print newsletter.

National Braille Association, Inc., 1290 University Ave., Rochester, NY 14607 (716-473-0900)

Produces and distributes braille reading materials for persons with visual impairment. Collection consists of college-level textbooks, technical materials, and some materials of general interest.

National Federation of the Blind, 1800 Johnson St., Baltimore, MD 21230 (410-659-9314; FAX: 410-685-5653)

Goal is the complete integration of blind persons into society on a basis of equality. Offers advocacy services for the blind in such areas as discrimination in housing and insurance. Operates a job referral and listing system to help blind individuals find competitive employment. Runs an aids and appliances department to assist blind persons in independent living. Has a scholarship program for blind college students and a loan program for blind persons who are going into business for themselves. Publishes monthly and quarterly publications.

National Library Service for the Blind and Physically Handicapped, Library of Congress, 1291 Taylor St., NW, Washington, DC 20542 (202-707-5100)

Administers a free library program of braille and recorded books for eligible readers with visual impairments and physical disabilities throughout the United States and for American citizens living abroad.

National Society to Prevent Blindness, 500 E. Remington Rd., Schaumburg, IL 60173 (708-843-2020; 800-221-3004)

Voluntary health agency committed to the reduction of cases of blindness.

PROTECTION AND ADVOCACY AGENCIES

Listed below are the protection and advocacy agencies mandated by law to serve and protect the rights of persons with disabilities.

Alabama

Alabama Developmental Disabilities Advocacy Program, The University of Alabama, P.O. Drawer 870395, Tuscaloosa, AL 35487-0395 (205-348-4928)

Alaska

Advocacy Services of Alaska, 615 E. 82nd Ave., Suite 101, Anchorage, AK 99518 (907-344-2002)

American Samoa

Client Assistance and P and A Program, P.O. Box 3937, Pago Pago, AS 96799 (684-633-2441)

Arizona

Arizona Center for Law in the Public Interest, 363 N. First Ave., Suite 100, Phoenix, AZ 85003 (602-252-4904)

Arkansas

Advocacy Services, Inc., 1120 Marshall St., Suite 311, Little Rock, AR 72202 (501-371-2171)

California

Protection and Advocacy, Inc., 100 Howe St., Suite 185N, Sacramento, CA 95825 (916-488-9950; toll free: 800-952-5746)

Colorado

The Legal Center, 455 Sherman St., Suite 130, Denver, CO 80203 (303-722-0300)

Connecticut

Office of Protection and Advocacy for Handicapped and Developmentally Disabled Persons, 60 Weston St., Hartford, CT 06120-1551 (203-297-4300; 203-566-2102; statewide toll free: 800-842-7303)

Delaware

Disabilities Law Program, 144 E. Market St., Georgetown, DE 19947 (302-856-0038)

District of Columbia

I.P.A.C.H.I., 300 I St., NE, Suite 202, Washington, DC 20002 (202-547-8081)

Florida

Advocacy for Persons with Disabilities, 2671 Executive Center, Circle W, Suite 100, Tallahassee, FL 32301-5024 (904-488-9071; statewide toll free: 800-342-0823; 800-346-4127)

Georgia

Georgia Advocacy Office, Inc., 1708 Peachtree St., NW, Suite 505, Atlanta, GA 30309 (404-885-1234; toll free: 800-537-2329)

Guam

The Advocacy Office, P.O. Box 8830, Tamuning, Guam 96911 (671-646-9026)

Hawaii

Protection and Advocacy Agency of Hawaii, 1580 Makaloa St., Suite 1060, Honolulu, HI 96814 (808-949-2922)

Idaho

Co-Ad, Inc., 1409 W. Washington, Boise, ID 83702 (208-336-5353)

Illinois

P & A, Inc., 11 East Adams, Suite 1200, Chicago, IL 60604 (312-341-0022)

Indiana

Indiana Advocacy Services, 850 N. Meridian St., Suite 2-C, Indianapolis, IN 46204 (317-232-1150; toll free: 800-622-4845)

Iowa

Iowa P and A Service, Inc., 3015 Merle Hay Road, Suite 6, Des Moines, IA 50310 (515-278-2502)

Kansas

Kansas Advocacy and Protection Services, 513 Leavenworth, Suite 2, Manhattan, KS 66502 (913-776-1541; toll free: 800-432-8276)

Kentucky

Office of Public Advocacy, Division for Protection and Advocacy, Perimeter Park West, 1264 Louisville Rd., Frankfort, KY 40601 (502-564-2967; toll free: 800-372-2988)

Louisiana

Advocacy Center for the Elderly and Disabled, 210 O'Keefe, Suite 700, New Orleans, LA 70112 (504-522-2337; toll free: 800-662-7705)

Maine

Maine Advocacy Services, One Grandview Place, Suite 1, P.O. Box 445, Winthrop, ME 04364 [207-377-6202; toll free: 800-452-1948; 207-289-2394 (Augusta area)]

Maryland

Maryland Disability Law Center, 2510 St. Paul St., Baltimore, MD 21218 (410-333-7600)

Massachusetts

Disability Law Center, Inc., 11 Beacon St., Suite 925, Boston, MA 02108 (617-723-8455)

Michigan

Michigan Protection and Advocacy Service, 109 W. Michigan, Suite 900, Lansing, MI 48933 (517-487-1755)

Minnesota

Minnesota Disability Law Center, 222 Grain Exchange Bldg., 323 Fourth Ave., S., Minneapolis, MN 55415 (612-332-7301)

Mississippi

Mississippi Protection and Advocacy System for Developmental Disabilities, Inc., 4793 B. McWillie Drive, Jackson, MS 39206 (601-981-8207)

Missouri

Missouri Protection and Advocacy Services, Inc., 925 S. Country Club Drive, Unit B-1, Jefferson City, MO 65109 (314-893-3333)

Montana

Montana Advocacy Program, Inc., 1410 8th Ave., Helena, MT 59601 (406-444-3889)

Nebraska

Nebraska Advocacy Services, 522 Lincoln Center Bldg., 215 Centennial Mall So., Lincoln, NE 68508 (402-474-3183)

Nevada

Office of Protection and Advocacy, 205 Capuroo Way, Suite B, Sparks, NV 89431 (702-789-0233; state-wide toll free: 800-992-5715; FTS: 4705911)

New Hampshire

Disabilities Rights Center, Inc., P.O. Box 19, Concord, NH 03302-0019 (603-228-0432)

New Jersey

Office of Advocacy for the Developmentally Disabled, Hughes Justice Complex CN 850, Trenton, NJ 08625 (609-292-9742; toll free: 800-792-8600)

New Mexico

Protection and Advocacy System, Inc., 1720 Louisiana Blvd., NE, Suite 204, Albuquerque, NM 87110 (505-256-3100; toll free: 800-432-4682)

New York

New York State Commission on Quality of Care for the Mentally Disabled, 99 Washington Ave., Albany, NY 12210 (518-473-4057)

North Carolina

Governor's Advocacy Council for Persons with Disabilities, 1318 Dale St., Suite 100, Raleigh, NC 27605 (919-733-9250)

North Dakota

Protection and Advocacy Project, 400 East Broadway, Suite 515, Bismarck, ND 58501 (701-224-2972; toll free: 800-472-2670)

North Mariana Islands

Catholic Social Services, Box 745, Saipan, CM 96950 (670-234-6981)

Ohio

Ohio Legal Rights Service, 8 E. Long St., 6th Floor, Columbus, OH 43215 (614-466-7264; toll free: 800-282-9181)

Oklahoma

Protection and Advocacy Agency for DD, 9726 E. 42nd St., Osage Bldg, Rm. 133, Tulsa, OK 74145 (918-664-5883)

Oregon

Oregon Advocacy Center, 310 Southwest 4th Ave., 625 Board of Trade Bldg., Portland, OR 97204-2309 (503-243-2081)

Pennsylvania

Pennsylvania Protection and Advocacy, Inc., 116 Pine St., Harrisburg, PA 17101 (717-236-8110; toll free: 800-692-7443)

Puerto Rico

Protection and Advocacy, Governor's Office, P.O. Box 5163, Hato Rey, PR 00918-5163 (809-766-2388 or 809-766-2333)

Rhode Island

Rhode Island Protection and Advocacy System (RIPAS), Inc., 55 Bradford Street, 2nd Floor, Providence, RI 02903 (401-831-3150)

South Carolina

South Carolina P and A System for the Handicapped, Inc., 3710 Landmark Drive, Suite 204, Columbia, SC 29204 (803-282-0639; 800-922-5225)

South Dakota

South Dakota Advocacy Project, Inc., 221 South Central Ave., Pierre, SD 57501 (605-224-8294; statewide toll free: 800-742-8108)

Tennessee

E.A.C.H., Inc., P.O. Box 121257, Nashville, TN 37212 (615-298-1080; statewide toll free: 800-342-1660)

Texas

Advocacy, Inc., 7800 Shoal Creek Blvd., Suite 171-E, Austin, TX 78757 [512-454-4816; statewide toll free: 800-252-9108 (Voice/TTY)]

Utah

Legal Center for the Handicapped, 455 E. 400 South, Suite 201, Salt Lake City, UT 84111 (801-363-1347; toll free: 800-662-9080)

Vermont

Vermont DD Law Project, 12 North St., Burlington, VT 05401 (802-863-2881)

Virgin Islands

Committee on Advocacy for the Developmentally Disabled, Inc., 31A New St., Apt. No. 2, St. Croix, VI 00840 (809-772-1200)

Virginia

Department of Rights for the Disabled, James Monroe Bldg., 101 North 14th St., 17th Floor, Richmond, VA 23219 (804-225-2042; toll free: 800-552-3962)

Washington

Washington P and A System, 1401 E. Jefferson, #506, Seattle, WA 98122 (206-324-1521)

West Virginia

West Virginia Advocates, 1524 Kanawha Blvd., East, Charleston, WV 25311 (304-346-0847; statewide toll free: 800-950-5250)

Wisconsin

Wisconsin Coalition for Advocacy, Inc., 16 N. Carroll Street, Suite 400, Madison, WI 53703 (608-267-0214)

Wyoming

Wyoming Protection and Advocacy System, Inc., 2424 Pioneer Ave., #101, Cheyenne, WY 82001 (307-638-7668; toll free: 800-624-7648)

UNIVERSITY AFFILIATED PROGRAMS

Listed below are the university affiliated programs that provide diagnostic and treatment services to children with disabilities and their families.

Alabama

Center for Developmental and Learning Disorders (CDLD), University of Alabama-Birmingham, 1720 Seventh Ave., S., Birmingham, AL 35233 (205-934-5471)

Arkansas

University Affiliated Program for Developmental Disabilities, University of Arkansas, South Campus Bldg., 1120 Marshall Street, Suite 306, Little Rock, AR 72202 (501-371-1019)

California

Mental Retardation and Developmental Disabilities Program, University of California-Los Angeles, 300 Medical Plaza, Los Angeles, CA 90024 (213-825-0147)
Center for Child Development and Developmental Disorders, Children's Hospital of Los Angeles, 4650 Sunset Blvd., Los Angeles, CA 90027 (213-669-2151)

Colorado

John F. Kennedy Center for Developmental Disabilities, University of Colorado Health Sciences Center, Campus Box C234, 4200 E. Ninth Ave., Denver, CO 80262 (303-270-7724)

Connecticut

Connecticut's University Affiliated Program on Developmental Disabilities, 991 Main St., East Hartford, CT 06108 (203-282-7050)

District of Columbia

Georgetown University Child Development Center, CG-52 Bles Bldg., 3800 Reservoir Rd., NW, Washington, DC 20007 (202-687-8635)

Florida

Mailman Center for Child Development, University of Miami School of Medicine, P.O. Box 016820—D-820, Miami, FL 33101 (305-547-6635)

Georgia

University Affiliated Program for Persons with Developmental Disabilities, The University of Georgia, Dawson Hall, Athens, GA 30602 (404-542-4827)

Hawaii

Hawaii University Affiliated Program for Developmental Disabilities, University of Hawaii at Manoa, 1776 University Ave., Wist 211, Honolulu, HI 96822 (808-948-5009)

Idaho

Idaho Center on Developmental Disabilities (ICDD), College of Education, University of Idaho, Moscow, ID 83843 (208-885-6849)

Illinois

University Affiliated Program in Developmental Disabilities, The University of Illinois at Chicago, 1640 W. Roosevelt Rd., Chicago, IL 60608 (312-413-1647)

Indiana

Institute for Study of Developmental Disabilities, Indiana University, 2853 E. Tenth St., Bloomington, IN 47405 (812-855-6508)

Riley Child Development Center, James Witcomb Riley Hospital for Children, Indiana University Medical Center, 702 Barnhill Dr., Indianapolis, IN 46202 (317-274-8167)

Iowa

Iowa University Affiliated Program, Division of Developmental Disabilities, University Hospital School, The University of Iowa, Iowa City, IA 52242 (319-353-6390)

Kansas

Kansas University Affiliated Facility-Central Office, Bureau of Child Research, 1052 Robert Dole Human Development Center, University of Kansas, Lawrence, KS 66045 (913-864-4295)

Kansas University Affiliated Facility-Kansas City, Children's Rehabilitation Unit, Kansas University Medical Center, 39th & Rainbow Blvd., Kansas City, KS 66103 (913-588-5900)

Kansas University Affiliated Facility-Lawrence, 1052 Robert Dole Human Development Center, University of Kansas, Lawrence, KS 66045 (913-864-4295)

Kansas University Affiliated Facility-Parsons, 2601 Gabriel, Parsons, KS 67357 (316-421-6550)

Kentucky

Interdisciplinary Human Development Institute, University of Kentucky, 114 Mineral Industries, Lexington, KY 40506-0051 (606-257-1714)

Louisiana

Human Development Center, Louisiana State University Medical Center, Building #138, 1100 Florida Avenue, New Orleans, LA 70119 (504-942-8200)

Maine

University Affiliated Handicapped Children's Program, Eastern Maine Medical Center, 417 State St., Bangor, ME 04401 (207-945-7572)

Maryland

Kennedy Krieger Institute, 707 N. Broadway, Baltimore, MD 21205 (410-550-9000)

Massachusetts

Developmental Evaluation Center, Children's Hospital Medical Center, 300 Longwood Ave., Boston, MA 02115 (617-735-6501)

Shriver Center University Affiliated Facility, 200 Trapelo Rd., Waltham, MA 02254 (617-642-0001)

Michigan

Developmental Disabilities Institute, Wayne State University, 285 Justice Bldg., 6001 Cass Ave., Detroit, MI 48202 (313-577-2654)

Minnesota

Minnesota University Affiliated Program on Developmental Disabilities, University of Minnesota, 6 Pattee Hall, Minneapolis, MN 55455 (612-624-4848)

Mississippi

Mississippi University Affiliated Program, University of Southern Mississippi, Southern Station, Box 5163, Hattiesburg, MS 39406-5163 (601-266-5163)

Missouri

University Affiliated Program for Developmental Disabilities, University of Missouri-Kansas City, Institute for Human Development, 2220 Holmes St., Kansas City, MO 64108 (816-276-1770)

Montana

Montana University Affiliated Program, 52 Corbin Hall, University of Montana, Missoula, MT 59812 (406-243-5467)

Nebraska

Meyer Rehabilitation Institute, University of Nebraska Medical Center, 600 South T St., Omaha, NE 68131-5450 (402-559-6430)

New Hampshire

New Hampshire University Affiliated Program Organization, Institute on Disability, Morrill Hall, University of New Hampshire, Durham, NH 03824 (603-862-4320)

New Jersey

The Center for Developmental Disabilities, University Affiliated Program of New Jersey, University of Medicine and Dentistry of New Jersey, 675 Hoes Lane, Piscataway, NJ 08854-5635 (201-643-4447)

New York

Developmental Disabilities Center, St. Lukes—Roosevelt Hospital Center, 428 W. 59th St., New York, NY 10019 (212-523-6230)

Mental Retardation Institute, Westchester County Medical Center, Valhalla, NY 10595 (914-285-8204)

Rose F. Kennedy Center, Albert Einstein College of Medicine, Yeshiva University, 1410 Pelham Pkwy. S., Bronx, NY 10461 (212-430-2325)

University Affiliated Program for Developmental Disabilities, University of Rochester Medical Center, Box 671, 601 Elmwood Ave., Rochester, NY 14642 (716-275-2986)

North Carolina

Clinical Center for the Study of Development and Learning, Biological Sciences Research Center 220H, University of North Carolina-Chapel Hill, CB# 7255, BSRC, Chapel Hill, NC 27599-7255 (919-966-5171)

Ohio

University Affiliated Cincinnati Center for Developmental Disorders, Pavilion Bldg., Elland and Bethesda Aves., Cincinnati, OH 45229 (513-559-4621)

The Nisonger Center, The Ohio State University, McCampbell Hall, 1581 Dodd Drive, Columbus, OH 43210-1296 (614-292-8365)

Oregon

Center on Human Development, University of Oregon—Eugene, College of Education, Clinical Services Bldg., Eugene, OR 97403-1211 (503-346-3591)

Child Development and Rehabilitation Center, Oregon Health Sciences University, P.O. Box 574, Portland, OR 97207 (503-494-8364)

Pennsylvania

Developmental Disabilities Program, Temple University, 9th Floor, Ritter Annex, 13th St. and Cecil B. Moore Ave., Philadelphia, PA 19122 (215-787-1356)

Rhode Island

Child Development Center, Rhode Island Hospital, 593 Eddy St., Providence, RI 02902 (401-277-5681)

South Carolina

UAF Program of South Carolina—USC, Human Development Center, Winthrop College, University of South Carolina, Rock Hill, SC 29208 (803-777-4839)

South Dakota

Center for Developmental Disabilities, School of Medicine, University of South Dakota, Vermillion, SD 57069 (605-677-5311)

Tennessee

Boling Center for Developmental Disabilities, University of Tennessee, Memphis, 711 Jefferson Ave., Memphis, TN 38105 (901-528-6511)

Texas

Texas Consortium for Developmental Disabilities, University of Texas at Austin, Department of Special Education, EDB 306, Austin, TX 78712 (214-471-7621)
University Affiliated Center, 200 Treadway Plaza, Exchange Park, Dallas, TX 75235 (214-688-7117)

Utah

Developmental Center for Handicapped Persons, Utah State University, Logan, UT 84322-6800 (801-750-1981)

Vermont

Center for Developmental Disabilities, 499C Waterman Building, University of Vermont, Burlington, VT 05405 (802-656-4031)

Virginia

Virginia Institute for Developmental Disabilities Administration, Virginia Commonwealth University, 301 W. Franklin St., Room 1620, Richmond, VA 23284-3020 (804-225-3876)

Washington

Child Development and Mental Retardation Center, University of Washington, Seattle, WA 98195 (206-543-2832)

West Virginia

University Affiliated Center for Developmental Disabilities (UIACCD), West Virginia University, 918 Chestnut Ridge Rd, Suite 2, Morgantown, WV 26506 (304-293-4692)

Wisconsin

Waisman Center UAP, University of Wisconsin, 1500 Highland Ave., Madison, WI 53705-2280 (608-263-5940)

REFERENCE

Annual Directory of National Organizations 1991–1992. (1991). *Exceptional Parent, 21,* D1–D40.

Index

Page numbers followed by "f" indicate figures; those followed by "t" indicate tables.